EDUCATION AND THE SOCIAL ORDER 1940–1990

By the same author
A Student's View of the Universities (1943)
Intelligence Testing and the Comprehensive School (1953)
The Common Secondary School (1954)
Psychology in the Soviet Union (1957) (editor)
New Trends in English Education (1957) (editor)
Educational Psychology in the USSR (1963) (editor, with Joan Simon)
Non-Streaming in the Junior School (1964) (editor)
Education in Leicestershire, 1540-1940 (1968) (editor)
Half-way there: Report on the British Comprehensive School Reform (1970, 2nd edn. 1972) (with Caroline Benn)
Intelligence, Psychology and Education: A Marxist Critique (1971, 2nd edn. 1978)
The Radical Tradition in Education in Britain (1972) (editor)
The Evolution of the Comprehensive School, 1926-1972 (1969, 2nd edn. 1973) (with David Rubinstein)
The Victorian Public School (1975) (editor, with Ian Bradley)
Inside the Primary Classroom (1980) (with Maurice Galton and Paul Croll)
Progress and Performance in the Primary Classroom (1980) (editor, with Maurice Galton)
Education in the Sixties (1980) (editor with Edward Fearn)
Research and Practice in the Primary Classroom (1981) (editor, with John Willcocks)
Education in the Eighties (1981) (editor, with William Taylor)
Does Education Matter? (1985, 2nd edn. 1988)
The Rise of the Modern Educational System: Social Change and Cultural Reproduction, 1870-1920 (1987) (editor, with Detlef Müller and Fritz Ringer)
Bending the Rules: The Baker 'Reform' of Education (1988, 3rd revised edn. 1988)
The Search for Enlightenment: The Working Class and Adult Education in the Twentieth Century (1990) (editor)

Studies in the History of Education
Studies in the History of Education, 1780-1870 (1960) – retitled (1974) The Two Nations and the Educational Structure, 1780-1870
Education and the Labour Movement, 1870-1920 (1965)
The Politics of Educational Reform, 1920-1940 (1974)

Education and the Social Order 1940-1990

by
Brian Simon

Lawrence & Wishart, London

First published in hardback 1991
First published in paperback 1999
Reprinted 2010

The author has asserted his rights under the
Copyright, Design and Patents Act, 1998
to be identified as the author of this work.

British Library Cataloguing in Publication Data.
A catalogue record for this book is available from the British Library

ISBN 9780853158837

Printed and bound by MPG-Biddles, King's Lynn

Published by
Lawrence and Wishart Limited
99a Wallis Road
London
E9 5LN
www.lwbooks.co.uk

Contents

Part II

Part III

List of Tables

Abbreviations

ABCA	Army Bureau of Current Affairs
ABRC	Advisory Board for the Research Councils
ACC	Association of County Councils
ACE	Advisory Centre for Education
ACSET	Advisory Committee on the Supply and Education of Teachers
AEC	Association of Education Committees
AMA	Assistant Masters Association
AMA	Association of Metropolitan Authorities
APS	Assisted Places Scheme
APU	Assessment of Performance Unit
ASE	Association for Science Education
ATTI	Association of Teachers in Technical Institutions
AUT	Association of University Teachers
CAC	Central Advisory Council – England, Wales and Scotland
CAT	College of Advanced Technology
CASE	Campaign for the Advancement of State Education
CCA	County Councils Association
CEA	Council for Educational Advance
CEE	Certificate of Extended Education
CEO	Chief Education Officer
CDRE	Conference for the Democratic Reconstruction of Education
CLEA	Council of Local Education Authorities
CM	Cabinet Minutes
CNAA	Council for National Academic Awards
CP	Cabinet Papers
CSE	Certificate of Secondary Education
CSC	Comprehensive Schools Committee

DES	Department of Education and Science
EPA	Education Priority Area
ESN	Educationally Subnormal
GCE	General Certificate of Education
GCSE	General Certificate of Secondary Education
GDP	Gross Domestic Product
GNP	Gross National Product
GRE	Grant Related Expenditure
GRIST	Grant Related In-Service Training
HCP	Humanities Curriculum Project
HMC	Headmasters' Conference
IEA	Institute of Economic Affairs
ILEA	Inner London Education Authority
LAPP	Lower Achieving Pupils Project
LEA	Local Education Authority
LCC	London County Council
MSC	Manpower Services Commission
NAFE	Non-Advanced Further Education
NALT	National Association of Labour Teachers
NEA	National Education Association
NFER	National Foundation for Educational Research in England and Wales
NUS	National Union of Students
NUT	National Union of Teachers
PCFC	Polytechnics and Colleges Funding Council
PRO	Public Records Office
ROSLA	Raising of the School Leaving Age
SSEC	Secondary Schools Examinations Council
SSRC	Social Science Research Council; now ESRC, Economic and Social Research Council
TES	*Times Educational Supplement*
THES	*Times Higher Educational Supplement*
TRIST	TVEI – Related In-Service Training
TUC	Trades Union Congress
TVEI	Technical and Vocational Educational Initiative
UFC	Universities Funding Council
UGC	University Grants Committee
WEA	Workers' Educational Association
YOP	Youth Opportunities Programme
YTS	Youth Training Scheme

Acknowledgements

The author and publishers gratefully acknowledge the following permissions to quote from copyright material: the Institute of Community Studies for Table 7.1, from Brian Jackson, *Streaming: An Education System in Miniature* (1964), p.21; Macmillan Press for Appendix I, General Election Results, 1935-1983, from David Butler and Gareth Butler, *British Political Facts, 1900-1985*, sixth edition, 1986, pp.226-8.

FOR
JOAN SIMON
Fellow educational historian.
In celebration of a
fifty-year partnership.

Introduction

This is the fourth, and surely the final volume of my Studies in the History of Education. The first, published 30 years ago (1960), later retitled *The Two Nations and the Educational Structure, 1780-1870*, was concerned with the tumultuous period which finally saw the emergence of an organised educational system (or set of sub-systems) designed to reflect, and perpetuate, existing social differences. These foundations were then firmly laid and, to all intents and purposes, still exist today. However intentions, even if clearly defined, have unexpected outcomes; it is hardly possible to legislate for the unknown. Towards the close of the century economic and social changes unleashed new social forces, leading to instability – or dissonance.

It is with the new situation, thus created, that the second volume, *Education and the Labour Movement, 1870 – 1920* was concerned. This followed five years after the first – in 1965, and charted the emergence of the organised labour movement onto the scene in a new way. It dealt also with the crisis developing within the new system and the need for its resolution. Its central focus related, then, to the dramatic events that took place before, during and after the passage of the Education Act of 1902. This Act was carried through Parliament by the Conservative government of that time in the teeth of enormous opposition both inside and, more particularly, outside Parliament. This concerned the religious issue – putting the 'voluntary' schools on the rates – which offended the Nonconformist conscience. But the Act also deliberately put a stop to advanced, democratic developments in education emerging in the great industrial cities of the country – particularly in the north. The School Boards responsible for these new measures were abolished.

Here, then was a new restructuring, aiming to produce a new equilibrium. But in spite of defeat through the passage of the Act, from this point pressure for access to a broad, general education for all, on the part of the labour movement, now took shape and began even to win victories. These were codified in the Education Act of 1918 – a consensus measure preceded by much discussion and agitation and, like the 1944 Act, carried through actually during a war.

There followed the depressing inter-war period of the 1920s and 30s, when everything seemed to grind to a halt. The third volume, *The Politics of Educational Reform, 1920 – 1940*, published in 1974, is in fact an extended case study of these two decades – of the interrelation between economic and social, and educational stagnation. The provisions of the 1918 Act were largely emasculated in succeeding economy drives as the mainly Conservative governments of the period attempted ineffectively to deal with mounting economic and fiscal problems (the two short-lived Labour governments fared little better). It was only towards the close of this period that new perspectives emerged and began to gain popular support, but the deep-rooted fear of social change together with growing international crisis put paid to any prospects of advance. By the outbreak of the Second World War, in September 1939, the continuous frustration of any serious hopes for advance had led to a determination to insist on fundamental educational (and social) change at the earliest opportunity.

This volume starts at that point, when tensions within education were already sharpening within the new circumstances created by the war. It aims to cover the entire half century from 1940 to 1990, but of course it does so selectively, and the criteria for that selection must be partially at least subjective. And here, perhaps, a personal word may be acceptable if only to cast some light on the nature of the selection.

My own direct involvement in education (other than as pupil and student) began in 1937-38 when I trained to teach at the Institute of Education of London University. Here, partly by chance, I became closely involved with the National Union of Students of which I was elected President for 1939-40. The NUS in those days (as now) was much concerned with the public system of education, so that engagement with these issues started early. My wife, Joan Peel (we were married in

February 1941) was, late in 1940, invited by Harold Dent, newly appointed editor of the *Times Educational Supplement*, to assist him in his task, as one of only two young female assistants (with the editor) comprising the entire staff – so coming fresh to education from another world. This was the period when this journal, under Dent's leadership, began to play a crucial role in expressing and mobilising educational opinion in preparation for fundamental legislative change, Dent having firm support from the then editor of the *Times*, Barrington-Ward. From this time my wife and I (though I was otherwise engaged during the war), kept quantities of cuttings from both the national and educational press concerning those aspects of educational discussion and action that appeared to us important – my own involvement being first, as a teacher in the Manchester and Salford area, and, from 1950, as a member of staff of the Education Department of Leicester University. These cuttings, filed and reorganised with much labour, have provided the spine, or to use the modern idiom, the 'data-base' for this book. In other words, the topics selected for discussion, analysis and interpretation are those which have appeared, over these 50 years, as of major importance to participants concerned primarily with the schools at all levels.

Some big issues have, therefore, inevitably been left aside. The main focus of the book is on policy making, both on a national and a local level, on the battles, or differences of view, surrounding these – indeed more generally on the politics of education. Policy making in education relates closely to differing conceptions of the social order, with its preservation or its change – since education mediates social structures. This is an issue, as made clear in the first chapter, on which Harold Dent felt strongly during the war, and in the run-up to the 1944 Act. In various ways this connection emerges very clearly at other times throughout the period studied. Hence the title of the book. I should perhaps make it clear here that the focus is on England and Wales. Developments in Scotland follow a different political (and educational) tradition, and require separate treatment; this is provided in Andrew McPherson and Charles Raab, *Governing Education: A Sociology of Policy Since 1945*, Edinburgh University Press, 1988.

In a recent review of a worthy book on education, Roderick Floud remarked that the book itself is 'remarkably dull'. Education is a subject 'about which most people feel strongly if not passionately, but its historians too often fail to reflect that passion, obsessed as they are with chronicling administrative history rather than seeing education as a reflection of the society within which policy is formed'. This is an acute criticism. Policy is formed within a society which inevitably comprises elements with different, even opposite objectives. It is, therefore, formed in a process of struggle. Passions are aroused, particularly because education is something which closely affects the life opportunities of everyone, whatever their social position. Such struggles are sharp and sometimes bitter. They take place both locally and nationally, as we see very clearly today. In this book I have tried to reflect these passions, however inadequately. To grasp their content and character is essential for understanding.

I have not tried to hide my own position and my own interpretation of these developments. One of the obvious problems about writing what is essentially contemporary (or very recent) history is the historian's own involvement with the events he or she sets out to analyse. In my case this has been rather close on a number of highly contentious issues. But there is no reason in principle why the committed historian should not be able to achieve an objective interpretation. This I have attempted, with what success the reader can judge. Others will see the developments differently, and certainly many alternative interpretations are possible (and will, I hope, be attempted). This volume should be seen only as a contribution to understanding.

To look back on these last 50 years, even in the crudest way, is to see how greatly things have changed. When teaching in an 'all age' school in the centre of Manchester immediately after the war (1946) I remember well visiting a friend – the head of a voluntary (Catholic) school nearby. The school hall housed four classes, each of at least 40, separated only by curtains – the school must have been built before the 'class' system developed. One reached the school down Paradise Lane. Beside it flowed (if that is the right word) the river Irk – bright green in the mornings, yellow in the afternoons. In my own school up the road children aged eight, nine and ten lined up outside the head's study awaiting corporal punishment. Yet, even in those conditions, there was humanity. What impressed me most was the extraordinary professionalism of the ordinary class teachers. No one, from that all-age school, ever passed the 11-plus, or was expected to. These were the remnants of the old 'elementary' system – now long superseded.

This volume traces the attempts to transform that entire system into something better. It adopts, in general, a chronological approach which, if old-fashioned, at least has the advantage that the sequence of development can be followed, and, I hope, understood. The book's pattern also seemed to fall naturally into decades. This is partly because overall political changes roughly took that form and also because in practice succeeding decades do seem to have acquired meaning. The division into three Parts does, however, perhaps obscure the main tendencies over these 50 years, since the great period of educational advance should probably be dated from 1956-57 to 1972-73. This, I hope, is made clear in the text.

Part I, then, covers the war period and through to the end of the 1950s. This focuses, first, on the struggles around education during the war, and the final passage of the Education Act 1944, which laid the statutory basis for all post-war development up to, and including, the present time. There follow chapters on the Labour governments following the war, and the Conservative governments from 1951. It was only, as already mentioned, around 1956 or 1957 that the prospect of new advances in education opened up, so laying the basis for the surge of the 1960s.

Part II, comprising four chapters, concentrates entirely on the 1960s. This pattern is, of course, deliberate. Whatever criticisms may be made of this decade ('the soggy sixties', etc), there can be no doubt that, on any objective evaluation, this period saw a profound sweep forward, and one that affected every level of education from primary school to the university. It was in this decade also, of course, that the swing to comprehensive secondary education got off the ground. Part II is, then, central to the thesis, and structure, of this book.

The 1960s surge pushed into the 1970s, as we also saw earlier. But it was not long before the bitter winds of economic and fiscal crisis swept the country, presaging the end of the great period of expansion and the start of contraction – again right across the board. All this, of course, found its political expression while the matter now began to be complicated by a certain disenchantment with the outcomes of education itself. This forms the subject matter of Part III, starting with a full chapter on the 1970s and so moving to the 1980s, culminating in the passage of the 1988 Education Act which, like that of 1902, was carried by the government in the teeth of opposition from all other political parties represented in Parliament. This Act, it is claimed, has set a new agenda. It is, of course, far too early to make any realistic evaluation of likely outcomes.

It is impossible for me to thank properly all the many people who have helped in carrying through this project. But first, of course, Joan Simon, whose partnership over more than half a century has been consistently stimulating and supportive – a good index of daily joint endeavours is the large number of 'data-base' cuttings bearing her dating, starting during the war period, as well as her many articles cited in the volume on contemporary affairs (though the main focus of her historical studies lies in the sixteenth to eighteenth centuries). Then, if retrospectively, both my parents, who individually played their own different parts in this saga and with whom, of course, many of the issues here dealt with were discussed, frequently and at length. A particular debt is due to those who were kind enough to read the various chapters as these reached completion – Caroline Benn, with whom I worked closely on an earlier project; Clyde Chitty, who has made his own contribution to the issues under discussion, especially those concerning the curriculum and schooling in recent times; Dennis Dean, a painstaking and accurate co-worker in this field; Len Cantor and Jim Hough, whose advice on higher education has been invaluable. But in addition I owe a debt to Norman Morris, educational historian and practical politician and educationist, for assistance on various matters including the interpretation of Labour party policy in the early period; to Peter Gosden, whose contribution to understanding this period in his many writings has been outstanding; to David Allsobrooke, who kindly produced the Welsh statistical tables in the appendix; to Andrew Green for assistance with Appendix Tables 12a and 12b; to the Scottish Education Department for assistance with statistics required for Appendix Table 14a; and very specifically to Philip Cottrell, of the Economic and Social History Department of Leicester University, for unravelling the Byzantine complexities of educational finance in the construction of the three financial Tables (Appendix Tables 15 to 17). Alan Simon nobly read the entire manuscript in draft, saving me from various errors. An author can count himself fortunate to have so much expertise made so willingly available. When all is said and done, however, I clearly must take final responsibility for all that is written here.

My thanks are also due to the officials at the Public Record Office for their consistent helpfulness (and efficiency) when researching in those commodious surroundings. Under the thirty year rule, Cabinet and relevant Department of Education and Science papers have been examined up to and including those released on 1 January 1958. But I should thank also the librarians at the Department of Education and Science where researchers are always welcome; those at the Trades Union Congress and at the Conservative Party's central office; and especially Roy Kirk and Barbara Barr at the well-stocked library at the School of Education, University of Leicester. Their help, and that of their staff, has been continuous, imaginative, consistently reliable and always cheerfully offered and carried through– this library has provided a firm base of operations over very many years (forty, to be precise). Lesley Yorke typed succeeding versions of different chapters with unfailing accuracy and skill – to her also, my warmest thanks.

Brian Simon
1st January 1990

Part I

1 The Second World War and Education

1 The Educational Situation at the Outbreak of War

It may be as well, first, to attempt to reconstruct the educational situation as it was at the outbreak of the Second World War. But this needs setting in context. What existed at that time was itself the outcome of a long period of historical development.

The nineteenth century saw, in Britain as in other advanced industrial countries, the transition from a relatively inchoate educational provision at the start of the century to a highly structured 'system' comprising an articulated set of sub-systems, arranged in a strict hierarchy relating to social class differences towards the close. What I have described elsewhere as the crucial 'moment of change' in this transition took place during the twenty years 1850-1870, when the state intervened in this restructuring in no uncertain manner.[1] In these twenty years no less than five Royal Commissions were established to examine and report on all levels of education, from the ancient universities (Oxford and Cambridge) to the elementary schools for the masses. Each of these commissions was followed by public and parliamentary discussion and eventually by Acts of Parliament which laid the statutory basis for a modernised system (as perceived by the leading social forces at the time).

The result was the firm establishment, in the latter decades of the century, of an hierarchical structure comprising, in theory at least, five distinct levels. These ranged from the newly developed system of the so-called 'public schools' on the one hand, through sets of schools designed to meet the needs of three levels among the middle class (upper-middle, middle-middle, lower-middle in the words of the Schools Inquiry Commission), to the mass of 'elementary' schools for the working class, finally established universally through the 1870 Education Act and later measures. At this period education was clearly and frankly seen and described as relating closely to social class. As the Schools Inquiry Commission put it, each class required its own, differentiated education – 'education has become more varied and complex', they wrote '... the different classes of society, the different occupations of life, require different teaching'.[2] Or, as Geoffrey Best has put it; education had become 'the trump card' in 'the great class competition'.[3]

Such was the set of institutions, and traditions, inherited by twentieth century Britain. It can be argued that this reconstruction, carried through in Victorian times, still determines the basic characteristics of the educational structure as it exists today – roughly 100 years later. But of course there have been modifications – adaptations to meet changing circumstances, both economic and political.

The Education Act of 1870 certainly foreshadowed a considerable, and energetic thrust forward in educational provision, if for a specific class. The decision had at long last been taken that the children should be schooled, and they were. The great buildings of the new school boards were now erected on a mass scale, particularly in the urban areas, and, through successive legislation, new age groups of children were brought compulsorily within their walls. By the turn of the century the mass of working-class children between the ages of five and twelve or thirteen were in these schools.

The first two decades of this century saw another thrust forward, one which took some by surprise. This arose from the use made by certain advanced local authorities, following the Education Act of 1902, of their powers (although only 'permissive') to finance secondary education out of the rates. The result was an unexpectedly rapid development in this field, the establishment of many new schools under local authority control, and so of a modernised 'system' of secondary education, charging fees, but also offering a proportion of 'free places' to scholars from the elementary schools (about 25 per cent). Alongside these there persisted the ancient endowed grammar schools, modernised to some extent in the late nineteenth century, but catering generally for a higher social class, while the so-called 'public' schools straddled the system as a whole.

The two latter sets of schools (the old endowed schools and the 'public' schools) lay, generally speaking, outside the domain of public (or local authority) control. Those within that control, known as 'maintained' or 'grant-aided' schools in England and Wales, comprised by the First World War what were basically two sub-systems, the elementary and the secondary. Between them, these two sets of schools catered, in 1937-38, for some 93 per cent of the nation's children; the other 7 per cent attended the more privileged schools mentioned earlier, as well as the subfusc system of private schools which proliferated in the suburbs.[4] These two parallel sets of schools within the 'maintained' system were, then, already established before the First World War. One of these (the elementary schools) catered for the mass of working-class children, as was originally intended; the other (the secondary schools) generally speaking catered for the lower middle class. It was this latter set of schools, however, that (within the maintained sector) monopolised the route to the professions and to higher education.

This basis structure was maintained, relatively unchanged, throughout the inter-war period – from 1918 to 1939. This, generally speaking, was a period of stagnation, both economically and educationally. The Education Act of 1918, regarded as a great breakthrough at the time, encapsulating, as it did, the hopes of a war weary population, certainly led to limited advances, but generally fell victim to the recurring calls for economy by succeeding, mainly Conservative governments. There was some development within the system of elementary schools which, however, remained essentially a closed system catering for the mass of working class youth throughout the period. The school leaving age was raised to fourteen in 1922 so putting an end to the half-time system which predominated for children over the age of twelve earlier.

This period is often said to have seen a great development of the grammar schools – that is, of the new publicly maintained system of secondary education. But in practice the advances of the pre-war period were now strictly controlled and were not repeated. These schools recruited 96,000 pupils in 1920 and just under 99,000 in 1938, an increase of 3,000 which took place only at the very end of the 1930's. It is true that the total number of pupils in secondary schools in England and Wales rose by about 160,000 – from 308,000 in 1920 to 470,000 in 1938 – but this is accounted for by the fact that these pupils, on average, now stayed one year longer than they did before the war. Fees continued to be charged in secondary schools which were still perceived as providing an appropriate education for the lower middle class, rather than for the working class who were clearly excluded by the cost. The proportion of free places (or scholarships) available in the secondary schools increased slightly (from 30 per cent to 46 per cent), due largely to the efforts of the two minority Labour governments which held power for relatively brief periods in the inter-war years. There was, therefore, a marginal increase in educational opportunity; but the fundamental characteristics of the structure remained as before. In particular, the two levels of schooling above the maintained system retained their hegemony – the direct grant schools (as a large group of the old endowed schools were now called) and the 'public' schools. The former received a grant direct from the Board of Education (the government office) in return for offering a certain proportion of their places free to local children from elementary schools, but their control was not in the hands of the local authorities; these therefore retained their 'independence'.[5] Similarly, as was the case in the pre-war years, the system of 'public' schools, established (as a 'system') in the period 1860-1900, retained its leading position and total independence from both the state and local authorities.[6]

More detailed examination of the system, as it had developed by 1938 (the last pre-war year of official statistics), gives the following picture. The vast majority of the nation's children were catered for in the elementary schools within the maintained system – 88 per cent in 1938. The great bulk of these left at the age of fourteen to enter the labour market. Only a tiny proportion stayed on above this age; a few, who were in differentiated forms of schooling within the elementary system – those in selective central schools, commercial schools and some forms of trade schools, and those in junior technical schools – stayed on in full-time schooling to fifteen and sometimes to sixteen. But the great majority left school at fourteen without any qualifications whatsoever, and certainly without any examination successes (or failures) to their credit. Basically the elementary system at that time retained its original characteristics. The primary concerns were to ease the process of social assimilation and to inculcate an elementary level of literacy and numeracy. Since the turn of the century, however, these schools had gained another function – that of winnowing out a small group, or 'elite', from among their pupils considered capable of profiting from secondary education – and transferring them, through the scholarship or free place system, to the secondary (grammar) schools at the age of eleven – the first step on the ladder of social mobility.

Originally most elementary schools were what were later called 'all-age' schools – that is, they catered for pupils (of both sexes) from the compulsory starting age of five (or earlier) to the leaving age of fourteen (after 1922). Normally the large board school buildings were originally designed to include two or more 'departments'; an infant department for pupils aged five to seven (or eight or even nine sometimes), and two senior departments catering for boys and girls separately (even if, as was usual, within the same building). Problems of organisation and structure developed as the leaving age was twice raised in the 1890s (to eleven and then to twelve), and some authorities began the practice of dividing the school after the infant stage into two further stages, junior and senior, with a break around the age of ten or eleven.

This process became official government policy following its recommendation by the Consultative Committee to the Board of Education in its well known 'Hadow' report of 1926 entitled *The Education of the Adolescent*. This report proposed that all education over eleven within the elementary system should be reorganised to provide three stages: infant (five to seven) junior (seven to eleven) and senior (eleven to fourteen). This is what came to be known as 'Hadow reorganisation'.

This restructuring, though within the elementary system only, was seen as a progressive measure at the time since it made specialist teaching possible for pupils over eleven for the first time; and also because it permitted differentiation in the form of streaming within both junior and senior schools – then regarded as a rational and desirable step. Thus in the inter-war period, 'reorganisation' became the focus of a developing thrust, having wide support. This entailed new buildings – especially for the new senior schools – and so the earnest of some advance. Progress was slow, however, and by 1938, just under half the children below the age of eleven were in separately organised junior schools (or departments), while exactly the same proportion (just under half) of the children aged eleven to fourteen were in separately organised senior departments. Over half of elementary school pupils (to put it in another way) were still in the old, un-reorganised, all-age schools inherited from the past at the time war broke out.[7] This is an important point to bear in mind.

In 1936 the 'National' government finally introduced a Bill as a result of much pressure over many years, raising the leaving age to fifteen but with exemptions for 'beneficial employment'. Critics of the Bill, who were widespread (the movement was lead by R.H. Tawney) held that this clause vitiated the whole measure, since the demand for cheap juvenile labour was at that time widespread. The Bill, eventually an Act, was widely regarded, then, as a con. In practice it never came into operation, since September 1939, the date which it was to be brought in, also saw the outbreak of war, resulting in its cancellation.[8] 'Reorganisation', then, together with a leaving age of fourteen were the only developments of significance in the inter-war period within the elementary system which was then run under its own, separate code of regulations. This defined the conditions within which elementary education operated, at a level very considerably below that of the secondary schools, which had their own, more generous code of regulations, involving better buildings, equipment, and higher salaries for the teachers. These were, in fact, two separate 'systems' of education within the maintained sector, while outside both the direct grant and the 'public' schools remained inviolate.

We may turn now to the secondary system, built up following the 1902 Education Act, though comprising some schools existing before that date. This comprised, in 1938, a total of 470,003 children of whom over half (54.2 per cent) were fee payers, the rest (45.8 per cent) having won a 'free place' (called after 1932, a 'special place' since the National government then abolished 'free' secondary education). The average age of leaving secondary school was sixteen years and seven months indicating that a substantial proportion left at fifteen or sixteen, a minority only staying the full course to eighteen. The numbers at each level are given in Table 1.1.[9]

Table 1.1

Full-time Pupils in Secondary Schools in England and Wales, 1938

Age	Number of Pupils
13 – 14	84,978
14 – 15	81,053
15 – 16	71,290
16 – 17	44,686
17 – 18	19,001

The majority of secondary school pupils who left school in 1938 (58 per cent) entered directly into the labour market, particularly into such occupations as clerical work, banking, insurance, commerce, the civil service, police or nursing. This proportion can be compared with that of 5.2 per cent – the proportion of pupils from the maintained secondary schools who proceeded to universities – or frequently to the teaching training departments at universities where they received a subsidy in return for a promise to teach, a form of indentured labour used as the means of recruitment to the teaching profession[10] Why did such a small proportion of secondary school pupils proceed to universities? The reasons are clear.

First, what might be called the 'opportunity ratio' remained very low throughout the inter-war period, though rising slightly towards the end. Thus the percentage of public elementary school pupils aged ten to eleven admitted to secondary schools in England and Wales rose from 9.5 in 1920 to 14.34 in 1938 – an improvement of nearly 5 per cent but still a low overall proportion (these figures mask the more advanced position in Wales where nearly 26 per cent moved to secondary schools in 1938).[11] Of the total entering secondary schools, as we have seen, only 5.2 per cent gained a place at a university. Entrance to Oxford and Cambridge was dominated by the 'public' schools at this period (as it has been ever since). In 1937-38 only 24.2 per cent of the Oxford intake began their education in elementary schools. It is probable that roughly the same proportion held for Cambridge as well. In these two universities at the apex of the system, then, over 75 per cent of the students almost certainly were educated at schools other than elementary that is, at secondary schools (which often had preparatory departments at that time), direct grant schools and especially at 'public' schools, with some privately educated as well. As regards the universities as a whole, nearly 53 per cent of the students has begun their education in elementary schools. Overall it was calculated that one in 150 of the children in elementary schools reached university. The figure for secondary schools was one in twenty and for public schools one in eight.[12]

University education was also seriously underdeveloped compared with other advanced industrial countries. In the inter-war period there had been some expansion – from roughly 30,000 students just before the First World War to just under 50,000 in 1937-38. Most of this expansion had taken place immediately after the war. The system was dominated by Oxford and Cambridge, which, as we have seen, drew the bulk of their students from the 'public' schools which had very close connections with the colleges at both universities. The extent to which England, in particular, lagged behind comparable countries is well brought out in Table 1.2. which gives the average number of inhabitants of each country per university student. These figures, which define the situation in 1934, were published by the University Grants Committee and are generally accepted as accurate.[13]

Table 1.2
Number of Inhabitants per University Student

Italy	808	England	1,013
Germany	604	Scotland	473
Holland	579	Wales	741
Sweden	543	Great Britain	885
France	480		
Switzerland	387		
USA	125		

Table 1.2 indicates that England in particular (in sharp contrast to Scotland) lagged well behind comparable continental countries. The degree of development in the United States in already very striking by this time.

A few words should be said about the 'alternative system' as it came to be called – that is, the world of 'further education', including technical colleges. There had, of course, been some development here, starting reasonably energetically in the late nineteenth century; but generally this was extremely limited. Most of this work, including even at higher levels, was carried on part-time – largely in the evenings after work. A system of awards, Ordinary National Certificate and Higher National Certificate, had been developed in the inter-war period, and some attention given to technical education by certain local authorities, responsible for developing their own systems. However there was no statutory requirement here, all such developments being the result of voluntary efforts by the authorities concerned. There had then been no major push in this direction and little interest taken. A half-hearted attempt to develop a drive in this area by the National Government following the 1936 Act ground to a halt with little achieved by the time war broke out.[14] The failure to implement the continuation schools sections of the 1918 Act (for all young people between fifteen and eighteen) was symptomatic, both of the attitude of industry and of the state bureaucracy which continued to undervalue technical education, both at school and higher levels. For elementary school leavers, however, opportunities for part-time study were available in the technical colleges – but, of the three million aged fourteen to eighteen who left school at fourteen only one in 25 attended such part-time courses, and only one in 123 attended one of the few voluntary day continuation schools established after the First World War.[15]

Such was the situation in the years immediately preceding the Second World War. However, by the late 1930s a growing disenchantment with the narrow, class-divided and restrictive nature of the system was leading to widespread criticism. This expressed itself with increasing force in a number of ways.

First, there was a growing criticism of the public schools – mainly by those with experience of them. Indeed such criticism had become endemic with the publication of Alec Waugh's immensely influential *Loom of Youth* during the First World War. This was followed by Robert Graves' *Goodbye to All That* (1930), Graham Greene's symposium *The Old School* (1934) and several others. This criticism came from intellectuals within the system and reflected a growing disenchantment with the ethos, mores and procedures of the public schools, perceived as embodying obsolete values, both socially and politically.

Such criticism was external, in the sense that it did not lead to, nor propose, any specific action about these schools – nor would such an approach have received any serious degree of support at that time. However another factor emerged somewhat suddenly towards the end of the 1930s. This was a serious financial crisis among several of these schools, combined with (or perhaps the result of) a decline in the demand for this type of education.

The effect of all this was a sudden scurry of activity among public school heads and governing bodies, who turned immediately (through Cyril Norwood, ex-head of Harrow) to the Board of Education for support – somewhat ironically, since above all these schools prided themselves on their total independence from the state. Leading officials of the Board (of course themselves alumni of these schools) leapt to their assistance, and a series of meetings were held and activities undertaken to try to restore the position. The whole matter was kept confidential through 1938 and 1939, but then became public knowledge. For the first time in their history, then, at the outbreak of war these schools were experiencing sharp and sustained criticism from outside their confines, and also a severe economic crisis which seemed to threaten their future and general viability as a 'system'[16]

Second, there was equally mounting criticism of the restrictive and hierarchical nature of the publicly maintained (or state) system. This had developed slowly but consistently throughout the inter-war period, and focused especially on two main issues. First, there was consistent pressure to raise the school leaving age to fifteen and even to sixteen (a target many had already espoused, for instance the trade union leader, Ernest Bevin, in the early 1920s). We have seen that this forced the presentation of the basically unsatisfactory 1936 Bill and later Act. But, of equal importance was the growing pressure throughout the 1920s and 30s to abolish the distinction between elementary and secondary education, and to bring all schooling for pupils over the age of eleven under a single code of regulations – the secondary code.

This proposal had been presented, if in a modified and restricted form, as early as 1926, in the report of the Consultative Committee to the Board of Education of that year. All education for those over eleven, the committee argued, should be regarded as 'post-primary', or fundamentally as 'secondary'. The actual recommendation that all 'post-primary' education should be brought within the secondary code of regulations was, however, made specifically and deliberately, in a later report of the Consultative

Committee published at the close of 1938 and titled 'Secondary Education'.[17] In Chapter 9 of that report the local authority representatives on the committee (with the full committee's support) outlined this basic change in provision as essential. The committee proposed, in effect, that there should in future be three types of secondary school, catering for all over eleven – the grammar school (the previous 'secondary' school), the 'modern secondary' school, and the technical high school (to be developed from the existing junior technical schools). This committee also proposed abolition of all fees in maintained schools, and so the provision of free secondary education for all.

This, at that stage, was a radical proposal, although expected. It was in line with the Labour Party's famous 1922 manifesto, drafted by R.H. Tawney, entitled *Secondary Education for All*. By the time of the publication of the Spens Report (as it was named after its Chairman), support for a progressive move forward along these lines was widespread, particularly among teachers' organisations, administrators, and the main labour movement organisations including the Trades Union Congress

The Consultative Committee was a group of independent educationists, though appointed by the President of the Board of Education. It was established originally in 1899 at the same time as the Board of Education itself was brought into being. Its object was to provide expert 'educational' advice to the Board, which consisted, of course, of civil servants with no special expertise in education. As a body, by this time it had considerable prestige. However this did not prevent the government of the day (still the 'National' government) from turning down the recommendations of the Spens Report out of hand, under the advice of Board of Education officials who described these propositions as 'unacceptable', 'premature', generally 'utopian', and totally unnecessary.[18]

This government response was announced in February 1939 several months after the Munich Agreement of the previous summer had marked the climax of the appeasement policy carried through by the Chamberlain government, and represented in the House of Commons by the adept Foreign Office spokesman, the young R.A. Butler.

By the outbreak of war, some seven months later, then, official policy was as obstructionist as it ever had been throughout the inter-war period. The system as a whole, with its sharp divisions, had been maintained basically unchanged throughout the inter-war period. Britain entered the war with a low level education for the great mass of the people, who left school and all educational contact at the age of fourteen. Alongside these a small elitist group continued, on average for five years only, within the secondary (grammar) schools. The country, however, was still, to all intents and purposes, being run by the products of schools quite outside the two parallel systems – the 'public' schools. These dominated parliament (both Houses) and Cabinet, the armed forces, the judiciary, civil service and the church. It was they who were now to be put to the test

2   New Thinking in Education

It is a striking fact that each of the three main Education Acts of this century (apart from the 1988 Act) were all carried through as the immediate result of war. That of 1902 was conceived during the Boer War and the crucial debates opened the day peace was concluded (2 June 1902). 'It is in the classrooms ... that the future battles of the Empire for commercial prosperity are already being lost' wrote Sidney Webb, the Fabian leader and a strong proponent of the Bill.[19] It was the same story in 1918 when an Education Act, introduced during the height of the trench warfare one year earlier was finally passed three months before the armistice was signed. In the Second World War the most recent of these Acts became law eight months before the end of the war with Germany. In each case, however they may be evaluated, these Acts marked a new phase of development, enacting demands or proposals that had been strongly pressed over previous decades. Up till recently, then, it seemed that, in Britain, it took a war to get things moving – at least as far as education is concerned. This option hardly extends into the future.

The Second World War, seen as a whole, certainly operated to promote new feelings and aspirations. As in the case of the First World War, scientific and technological deficiences soon became apparent and there developed a determination to remedy these in the future. Typical of the flood of committees set up towards the close, to plan for the future, was that on Scientific Manpower (the Barlow Committee) which recommended as an immediate aim doubling the output of graduates in science and technology. Other reports recommended greatly increasing the number of graduate engineers (the Percy Report 1945), reorganising the system of teacher training (the McNair Report, 1944), making proper provision for higher agricultural education (the Loveday Report, 1946), modernising and expanding the system of medical education (the Goodenough Report, 1944).

If war promoted technological demands, which in turn underlined educational deficiences, it also brought to the fore human aspects too readily disregarded in peace time. When men (and women) are required to die for their country, the thought necessarily arises that a country worth dying for must also be worth living in – not merely for the fortunate few but for all citizens. In death the sacrifice is equal, so also should be the opportunities for life, in particular for the future generation, the children. New aspirations now rise to the surface and few feel in a position to draw distinctive lines between those who deserve a good education and those who are not worth bothering about by comparison. So education emerges onto the agenda, now with greatly increased popular concern.

The conditions of war, of emergency measures, revealed new, unexpected potentialities among, for instance, the previously rejected. Primary school teachers, thrown back on their own resources in the chaos of evacuation, learnt how much young children could gain from work with improvised apparatus, pioneering group and informal methods of working, and forays into the countryside. Many of the more advanced techniques in our primary schools were worked out at this time.

An insistent demand for new skills developed, and led to new methods of educating 'ex-elementary' pupils who had marked time in school to fourteen. And the successes achieved threw new light on the educability of the 'average' child. Technical colleges, under heavy pressure, turned out skilled engineers, radio mechanics and electronic experts from among students whom pre-war teachers might have written off as incapable: the need was there and had to be met.[20]

As the war proceeded a widespread realisation took root – that it was impossible, if Britain was victorious, to go back to the stagnant, class-ridden depressing society of the 1930s. This

was recognised even in leading, official circles.[21] One striking
development early in the war was the way in which that
establishment organ the *Times,* which had fully supported
Chamberlain's appeasement policy, now emerged as a front
runner in radical politics, especially relating to the future. The
editor, Barrington-Ward, referring to a talk with E.H. Carr
(shortly to join the staff) about six weeks after Britain's defeat
at Dunkirk, noted in his diary:

> The *Times* almost alone in the Press and certainly first is trying to get
> the right 'answer to Hitler' in a statement on our plans for war and
> peace to show that we are fighting for a new Europe not the old – a new
> Britain and not the old. I wholly agree with Carr: planned
> consumption, abolition of unemployment and poverty, drastic
> educational reform, family allowances, economic organisation of the
> Continent, etc. But all this needs the right presentation.[22]

It is, perhaps, significant that Barrington-Ward singled out
'drastic educational reform' as a major issue, and that he gave
his personal, and full support to the recently appointed editor
of the *Times Educational Supplement,* Harold Dent, who
played a crucial role as a leader of professional opinion during
the war.[23] In a series of four striking leaders in June and July
1941 Dent defined what he saw as the totally new approach to
education demanded by current circumstances. The principle
of equality of opportunity, now being widely enunciated,
'demands total reform based on a new conception of the place,
status and function of education in a democratic State, not a
patching and padding of the present system'. If we failed now
to rise to that conception and to act upon it, 'we miss an
opportunity which may not recur for centuries – if ever.' Such a
reform, based on new principles, will not be desired by many
people, Dent correctly stated. The educational system we have
built up 'has been a most effective safeguard of the social
stratification we all in our heart of hearts bow down to and
worship'; so educational advance, based on equality of
opportunity, will be fought 'openly, subtly, or most dangerous
of all, unconsciously'. Hence the supreme importance that
'every one of us makes absolutely certain that he or she realises
to the full and precisely the implications of this most
revolutionary principle'. Only so can everyone be given 'the
fullest opportunity to develop every innate power. Only thus
can we hope to produce a noble race'.[24]

Dent sharply rejected the proposals now emanating from an

informal committee of officials and although not yet published, known to an inner circle. These proposals, wrote Dent, 'do not alter in the least the relation of the educational system to the social order as a whole, and by their nature they presuppose a social order after the war substantially the same as that of today – or yesterday'. In the last of the four leaders, Dent again insists that 'the full working out of the principle of equality of opportunity will involve changes in the social order extending far outside the field of education', that is in the structure of society itself.[25]

That such language should appear in the hallowed columns of the *Times* (if in a supplement) may seem remarkable.[26] Nevertheless the outlook and even the rhetoric was appropriate to the circumstances, to the new thinking and determination of the period. In the series of powerful leaders, just mentioned, Dent spelt out the nature of the transformation required. This was at the early stage of new thinking about educational change, more than two years before the presentation of an Education Bill in parliament. The leaders called for the emergence of

> a united and informed body of opinion ... strong enough to ensure that its demands shall be heeded, ... resolute enough – ruthless if need be – to press them without faltering in the face of the strongest and bitterest opposition, and sufficiently well armed to secure the victory.[27]

The military analogy and language again appeared as appropriate. The war had given the opportunity. The determination was to seize it, and use the time to transform circumstances; to build a new Britain (in Barrington-Ward's words) and not the old.

The demand for fundamental change was widespread – in education and elsewhere; indeed as the war proceeded this outlook was strengthened. In the field of education, widespread discussion among a great variety of organisations – covering the labour movement, teachers, administrators as well as others of a political and social character – resulted, by the autumn of 1942 in a massive number of pamphlets, leaflets, statements of policy, submitted both for public discussion and for consideration by the Board of Education in determining policy. Some of these will be considered in more detail later. The result was a developing consensus around a radically progressive policy for educational change having very considerable social implications. The basis for this consensus its content and character, forms the subject matter of this section.

The Public Schools
Already before the war, as we have seen, deep concern was beginning to be expressed, by public school headmasters and the like, about the growing financial and recruitment difficulties of these, historically and traditionally the leading schools of the country. During the summer of 1939 the *Journal of Education* reported that the governors of Harrow had decided to close one boarding house, and reduce the school's overall size from 600 to 500. Other schools with less than 500 pupils were likely to follow this lead, the journal predicted; some recent foundations of the boom which followed the First World War 'may find it difficult to survive'. All this was due 'to the general state of insecurity, financial difficulties and losses' as well as to the 'improvement in the quality of instruction at ordinary secondary schools'.[28] Three months later, reporting the proposal to close by St Bees (though the school was eventually saved by old boys and 'other interests'), the journal showed its hand by arguing that the government was entitled to intervene 'if these important national institutions are threatened with extinction'. The best plan would be 'a form of scholarship system promoted by the Board of Education'.[29] This would have the advantage that the schools would receive state support without loss of 'independence'.

   In the summer of 1939 the *Journal of Education* carried a severely critical article by Charles Douie, a Rugby alumnus and formerly Assistant Principal and Secretary of University College, London. Douie launched a sharp attack on the claim of 'special fitness to rule'. Coming from a public school family all of whom found employment in the upper reaches of the civil service and elsewhere, he reported 'a sense of shame' since in all professions special consideration is given to the public school boy. 'It is not only in war that the class division created by the public school system arouses resentment and disunity', he wrote. This is compounded by the fact that, throughout his life, the public schoolboy continues to remind all others of his exclusiveness. Douie's solution was that the public schools 'should be freely open to the sons of workers in office and factory as Oxford and Cambridge are today'. To achieve this, government and local authorities must play their part. All this would create goodwill and, Douie clearly believed, overcome existing inequalities. 'I cannot believe that the England of tomorrow will tolerate privilege in education', he concluded. It was, indeed, 'intolerable' that only the sons of the well-to-do should have access.[30]

Already before the war, then, it appeared that the crisis was coming to a head, with the ground being laid for financial support from the state legitimised through a democratic rhetoric. This was to remain the theme, on the part of public school supporters, throughout the period of 'discussion' leading to the appointment of an official committee of enquiry, the Fleming Committee, in July 1942. It was, for instance, strongly pressed by public school masters in a series of articles shortly after the war had started in the (conservative) weekly, the *Spectator*, while a leader proclaimed that the financial crisis now facing these schools was 'complicated' by the tendency in a democratic society to ask 'by what right' the 'splendid privileges' of the public schools should be reserved for those who are rich enough to pay. The state, it is argued, should give a grant to be used for scholarships. The public schools, wrote Cyril Norwood in two long articles on 'The Crisis in Education', are encountering 'growing hostility' – since access is confined to those with money. 'It is hard to resist the argument', Norwood continues,

> that a State which draws its leaders in overwhelming proportions from a class so limited as this is not a democracy, but a pluto-democracy and it is impossible to hope that the classes of this country will ever be united in spirit unless their members cease to be educated in two separate systems of schools, one of which is counted as definitely inferior to the other

The nation, however, cannot afford to lose the public schools (Norwood argued that 'they have shown that they can produce leaders, and for this reason they are one of the few features of our country's life which Hitler has attempted to copy'). They must, then, be brought into 'the national system'; this could be done by changing the age of recruitment together with financial support from 'Whitehall' (not the local authorities) so ensuring that 'not less than 10 per cent' of their intake come from elementary schools.[31] The modest nature of this proposal from the standpoint of the public schools contrasts rather sharply with the preceding democratic rhetoric - this was to be a main feature of the whole extended discussion by those seeking to ensure the continued existence of the system.

It was just at this point – early 1940 – that the public schools figure as a major issue in a seminal little book, *Education and Social Change,* by Fred Clarke, recently appointed Principal of the University of London Institute of Education. Clarke was, at this time, emerging as an educational statesman on the grand scale, most of whose experience, however, had been in the British dominions. He was therefore able to approach British problems with a fresh eye. Clarke was, in fact, one of the first educationists to bring a sociological dimension into his analysis, being now greatly influenced by Karl Mannheim, a leading Continental sociologist now in England.[32] In his book, Clarke argues that, in English educational discussion, too many issues are 'taken for granted', citing as a striking example, the Spens Report on Secondary Education (1938). Though the report is directly concerned with secondary education throughout its whole range, he wrote,

> the leading secondary schools in the country – those which claim to be in a special and peculiar sense representatively *national* – are nowhere discussed within its pages and no attempt is made to relate them organically to the system of schools, largely state-provided but somehow less 'national', in which the mass of the population is educated.

These 'leading' schools are 'intensely jealous of their private and independent status'; they are 'the tied prisoners of their own history'. 'We can hardly continue to contemplate an England where the mass of the people coming on by one educational path are to be governed for the most part by a minority advancing along a quite separate and more favoured path'. This, he added would be 'hardly intelligible' in 'any British dominion or the United States'; its continuance is 'probably doing more harm to English social unity and to English relations with the world than many other more noticed and openly criticised influences'. In a section entitled 'Unification of the system over the whole range', Clarke argues that

> there is no honest defence, no democratic defence, indeed no genuine *aristocratic* defence for the continuance of their present position. To continue it against all the forces that are coming into play will both

intensify social conflict and weaken the power of Britain to co-operate with the other free peoples of the world, even within the British Commonwealth itself.[33]

Falling demand, financial crises, increasingly outspoken public criticism together with a sense of unease on the part of public school heads and defenders – all these were evident from the early months of the war, or even earlier.[34] But it was the events of May 1940 – the defeat in France and Belgium followed by the Dunkirk saga – that really set things alight.

Barbarians and Philistines, a powerful attack on the public schools from within by T.C. Worsley, a schoolmaster at Wellington, reflects the anger and indignation widely felt at that time about those who controlled things generally and who had formed the governments in the inter-war years which had lead to the present debacle. This is an outspoken and very sharp attack, published at a black moment early in the war, on everything the public schools stood for, by one who had considerable experience of them, both as student and teacher.[35] 'We are where we are,' wrote Worsley, 'and shall be where we shall be, owing, largely, if not wholly, to the privileged education which the ruling classes have received in the last forty years.' 'If the public schools,' he continues, 'are national assets because of their leadership training qualities, what are we to think of those qualities when we survey the mess into which their leadership has brought us?' Worsley concludes with a cry for a common education for all; 'to achieve a common elementary education for *all* would be itself a great advance. For the main problem which faces democracy may be expressed as the problem of achieving social cohesion' (Clarke's point also, incidentally). This could only be achieved *democratically* by a reorganisation of the educational system.[36]

Again, in 1941, in another book entitled *The End of the 'Old School Tie'* (in a series edited by George Orwell) Worsley argued the need to unify the whole system. 'This must be done *now* (yes, when the bombs are falling) – the war has presented us with another chance for the future.' This 'discussion' book (the preface is dated May 1941) again starts with a massive attack on the public schools whose products are held responsible for Britain's predicament.[37] And, to complete this analysis, here is a closely relevant quotation from a sympathetic foreign observer and scholar, E.C. Mack, the second of whose massive, two volume and highly scholarly studies of the public schools was published in 1942. After concluding that over the last 25 years the 'public school man', whatever his virtues, cannot be called a success, he finishes his study with these words, written in April 1941:

> In 1919 the world was crying for a new order of things, but the public schools, clinging to a tradition which socialist–liberalism tried futilely to undermine, not only failed to provide the leaders necessary to make that new order, but stood squarely in the way of its realisation. Though many others must share the responsibility for social and political failure, the conclusion is irresistible that, had the public schools actually produced real social sympathy among their graduates there would have more unity in the nation and fewer men in high places willing to sacrifice Spain, Czeckosolakia, and possibly the Empire, rather than face the possibility of real progress at home ... Certainly one has the impression of disastrous bungling, inefficiency, and lack of vision in high places, and for these sins the public schools can hardly be completely freed from blame ... In short, they did little to make England ready for 1939 ... The upper classes and the public schools, having failed to create a better world, seem also to have lost the power or the will to save this one.

The public school system, he goes on, 'is in a very precarious situation':

> Even should British win the war, it is hard to believe that her economic, political and social systems will not experience revolutionary changes. It seems, indeed, to a casual observer in this year of 1941 that the long development in terms of original structure, which England's institutions have undergone, is on the verge of being rudely shattered.

Enough has been said, perhaps, to make the main point. The public schools were very definitely under fire, particularly from the spring of 1940. In that year there was also a wide popular, or populist, move against these schools and their hold on access to positions of power and responsibility, the fuse being recruitment to officer rank in the armed forces (and the sudden dismissal or 'resignation' of Hore-Belisha as Secretary of State for War in January 1940).[39] Even Winston Churchill, the Prime Minister, entered the fray, being reported in the *Sunday Dispatch* early in 1941 as arguing that the public schools should revert to their original purpose of providing education for poor scholars – the Prime Minister's protest, commented the *Journal of Education,* 'was presumably against the use of pious endowments to perpetuate class distinctions'.[40]

Throughout this period these schools themselves were working out a consensus in their defence. The *Journal of Education* acted as a kind of house journal for public school heads and others in publishing an endless series of articles and letters from all the leading headmasters (the girls' schools took no part). Almost without exception these proclaimed the lasting value of the public schools, the need to preserve them but to open them up to democratic needs through variations in the Douie-Norwood proposals for state subsidies through scholarships – or some similar solution. The schools should be 'thrown open' to those best qualified in intelligence and character, proclaimed an editorial comment, they must become 'an integral part of our national system of education' – they should stand 'at the apex of our secondary school system', a 'substantial proportion' of their pupils through a 'generous provision of scholarships' should come eventually from the elementary and the secondary schools aided or maintained by local authorities. They must be 'democratised', but they must survive wrote a typical headmaster (Skinner). 'All classes must benefit', wrote another; the public schools should be 'stepping stones' between the state schools and the universities (Wolfenden of Uppingham).[41]

But the heads and others wishing to preserve the schools did not have things all their own way, even in this august journal. The discussion so far, wrote Fred Clarke in the first of two major articles entitled *The Public Schools and the Nation* (March 1941), has shown an 'amateurish and unprofessional' approach, as well as a 'quite inadequate appreciation of the grim facts of the actual contemporary situation'. Clarke specifically condemned 'the serious social mischief now being caused by claims on behalf of the public schools'. He drew attention to what he defined as 'the rising spirit of resentment' against these schools, and of the need to appreciate 'the real extent' of the change of heart and outlook that must take place.[42]

By early 1942 a large number of public organisations had published their proposals for educational reconstruction – an aspect of the popular surge for a transformation of the system which resulted, finally, in the passage of the Education Act of 1944.[43] Proposals that the public schools should be brought into the popular system were now advanced across a wide front not only by organisations of the labour movement (and these were unanimous) but also by teacher organisations and those of local authorities.

Among the statements most strongly critical of the position of the public schools was that issued by the Association of Directors and Secretaries of Education – that is, the body uniting the chief local authority officials in the country. In *A Plan for the Future* (1942) this was one of the first bodies to define and publish a comprehensive programme of reform. In this sense, and because it represented the views of a group of highly respected professionals, it took on considerable significance, and what is striking about it is that from the start the public school issue is given the major emphasis.

The war, the pamphlet states, has 'quickened the public conscience and presented an opportunity which should not be missed of enquiring into past shortcomings and neglect'. In view of the demands now being made on ordinary people, and the qualities now being revealed 'qualities and capabilities of a high order', the clear need is for 'much wider provision' than in the past. The education system cannot 'rightly be described as national', they claim. On the contrary, there now exist two systems, side by side. These are 'strongly differentiated by their method of recruitment'. The public and private preparatory schools 'are available almost exclusively to those who can afford to contract out of the educational provision made from the public purse'. On the other hand 'there is the public system of education'.[44]

Even within the public system there is 'a differentiation by caste which has no educational justification'. But what is fundamentally necessary 'to the development of a truly national system of education' is that the 'public' schools and those financed wholly or in part from the public purse (including direct grant schools) 'should be merged into one system'. It is urgently necessary, they conclude, 'that all the schools should be brought into one coherent whole which will provide in successive stages equality of opportunity for all children'. So there should be established 'a common system of education national in scope ... free, compulsory and universal'.[45]

Other organisations took a similar view. In the *The Post War Reconstruction of Education*, for instance, the National Association of Schoolmasters demanded, in effect, the elimination of the public schools on the grounds that schools which cater for 'one caste' only cannot be included in a national system. Public schools being 'the most exclusive employment agency in the world' have no place in a reconstituted system. Further, the 'virtues' of these schools (leadership training) are incompatible with democracy.[46]

Both the National Union of Teachers and the grammar school associations pressed for the assimilation of the public schools into the national system.[47] Symptomatic of this trend was the powerfully expressed view of the 'Conference for the Democratic Reconstruction of Education' (CDRE). founded (in 1942) by a group of very respectable but also radical grammar school headmasters (including Raymond King). These issued strongly worded statements and conducted a countrywide campaign in 1942 and 1943 demanding the 'absorption' of the public schools into local systems of education (or the use of their buildings for other educational purposes).[48]

Finally, the main organisations of the labour movement, in their statements during the early phase of the war, already made clear their hostility to the existence of the public schools as a separate 'system'. The TUC, especially influential as the Labour Party was now a partner in a coalition government, issued a *Memorandum on Education After the War* in 1942. Although a moderate document, a full-blooded statement demanding the assimilation of these schools within a national system was later sent as evidence to the Fleming Committee.[49] But, traditionally, the Workers' Educational Association (WEA) had expressed a wider consensus as to labour movement attitudes and, during the war, this organisation maintained a consistent opposition to the public schools. In *A Plan for Education*, again published in 1942, the WEA stressed the growing sense of urgency relating to educational change. Large numbers of well attended meetings and discussions were taking place all over the country 'showing grave discontent with the present position'. A plan for reconstruction, drafted by a special committee, was approved at a special conference held in July. This was 'the largest and one of the most enthusiastic conferences the association has ever held'. Among the measures proposed was that couched in the memorable phrase 'Democracy must itself take possession of the public schools'.

Other Reform Proposals

The single code of regulations. It was around the public schools issue that the most radical proposals were made for educational change – or, at least, proposals having the most radical implications, as was clearly understood at the time. The abolition, or even 'assimilation' of the public schools within democratically controlled local systems involved a clear challenge to one of the most effective, and deep-rooted bastions of the existing social order. It was here that educational politics abutted most closely onto major political and social issues.

But, of course, within the field of education there were other important areas which also had implications for the social order of the future. Chief among these were those features of the existing structure of publicly provided education which corralled the working class – that is, the great mass of the population – within its own separate system of 'elementary' education. Proposals to transform the system before the war, as we have already seen, were rejected with contumely as recently as February 1939. Now was the time when a breakthrough might be made.

The crucial issue here was the fight for a single, or common code of regulations for all schools catering for children over the age of eleven. It is, perhaps, difficult to recognise the significance of this demand today since it is now, after nearly fifty years, so much taken for granted. But it was then seen as the key issue so far as the publicly provided system of education was concerned. Its acceptance would mean (or so it appeared at the time) a clear thrust forward as compared with the existing parallel but unequal systems of elementary and secondary education which had been inherited from the past – in England and Wales at least, if not in Scotland. This reform would bring elementary education, until now hived off separately, into the mainstream of a restructured system. It would, it was thought, make a reality of the great inter-war slogan and demand, 'Secondary Education for All'.

A striking feature of all the early reform pamphlets, publications and programmes, is the priority given to this issue – its constant reiteration underlines both a lack of trust in the *intentions* of the authorities, and the strength of feeling and indeed the unanimity that had by now developed. The consciousness that the existing system operated as a major factor perpetuating class differences comes through clearly in the many statements published. All differences between 'types' of school (elementary and secondary) 'must be entirely eradicated as being relics of a system based upon class or social cleavage', maintained the Association of Directors and Secretaries; what is needed is 'a unified system' with all schools ('of varying type or purpose') under a common code. All secondary education should be free, including the direct grant schools which, like other secondary schools, should be funded through local education authorities.[50] The Association of Education Committees, at that time a prestigious and powerful organisation, the Association of Municipal Corporations and other local government associations strongly supported this move, as well as teachers' organisations.[51] But it was particularly the labour movement which gave this demand overall priority – the Trades Union Congress, the Co-operative Union and the WEA.[52] Indeed when these three organisations, together with the National Union of Teachers, formed the Council for Educational Advance late in 1942 to launch a wide public campaign for an effective Education Bill, the provision of 'free education under a single secondary code for all children after the primary stage', together with common standards of staffing, equipment and amenities in all schools formed the central priority issue around which this organisation's very effective campaign was organised.[53]

Closely related to this was the question of the actual structure of the new secondary system, and in particular the concept of the multilateral, multi-bias, or (later) comprehensive school (sometimes called the common school). This had considerable support even before the war, in particular among teacher organisations and those of the labour movement. This is clearly exemplified in the evidence given to the Spens Committee (the Consultative Committee) in the late 1930s.[54] In 1935 the London County Council, now under Labour control, declared against segregated secondary education and determined to move towards the single secondary school as soon as it was legally possible. During the war, support for this solution grew rapidly; a strong advocate, for instance, was H.C. Dent, editor of the *Times Educational Supplement,* while the Labour Party, at its conference in 1942, came out in its favour.[55] On the whole it was the left which now made the running, though there was some support among individual members of the Conservative Party.[56]

Within the Labour Party the National Association of Labour

Teachers (NALT), which operated as a particularly effective internal pressure group, fought strongly for official party support for this proposal throughout the war. In *The Post-War Reconstruction of Education* published late in 1941, NALT argued for the single multilateral secondary school, giving a general education for all to the age of thirteen, followed by differentiated courses but within the single school. Similarly the Communist Party, now (1942-44) in a period of rapid expansion and growing influence, in a memorandum issued early in 1943 claimed that the TUC, Labour Party, Co-operative Union and the WEA all aimed 'to remove inequalities by proposing the abolition of fees and the establishment of multilateral or many-sided schools for children over 11'. This would be 'a step in the advance towards a democratic system', but the party argued for a general education for all to the age of fifteen at least, avoiding any specialised or vocational education until after the age of sixteen. This memorandum spelt out in some detail the content of such an education.[57]

But the movement gained support well beyond the left among educationists generally. Among those to argue very forcefully for the single secondary school for all were the four grammar school heads mentioned earlier (and now known at the headquarters of the Secondary Associations as 'The four horsemen of the Apocalypse'). CDRE, which they had founded in 1942, came out as a very strong proponent and active propagandist for the single secondary school, issuing a detailed curriculum and organisational plan – probably the first blueprint for the future comprehensive school to be published in this country.[58]

Some indication of the extent of support among teachers, administrators and university and college lecturers comes from an unexpected source. In April 1942 the then distinguished psychologist, Cyril Burt, sent the Ministry of Information the results of an extended enquiry he had conducted among professional educationists covering an enormous range of issues. A question on multilateral (as opposed to separate specialised) schools found that 72 per cent of those responding favoured multilateral schools, only 23 per cent specialised schools. Further, 84 per cent held that 'even in areas where a general scheme of multilateral schools is at present impracticable' whatever scheme is actually established 'should be permeated as fully as possible by the multilateral principle'.[59]

Support for this principle continued to escalate through 1943 and 1944. Fred Clarke, who may be taken as representative of enlightened liberalism, in an article paying tribute to Burt's criticisms of the Norwood Report (see below), stressed the necessity of reconsidering the 'cultural-vocational distinction' sharply posed by this document. 'Some of us may feel' he wrote, 'that the case of the multilateral school gains in strength as we penetrate deeper into the implications of secondary education for all.[60].

There were those who supported this move in high places – though apparently mainly influenced by social engineering rather than strictly educational considerations. Here the major proponent, if behind the scenes, was Graham Savage, since July 1940 London's Chief Education Officer, but before that Senior Chief Inspector at the Board of Education and therefore still carrying influence there. On 1 May 1942 the Permanent Secretary of the Board of Education, Maurice Holmes, arranged a meeting of top officials and Inspectors (HMIs) to discuss the whole issue among themselves. A briefing memorandum was a closely argued four page document by Savage, whose Education Committee had already decided to go comprehensive as soon as possible.[61]

Savage detailed the tripartite system and indicated the critique. This system implied three types of school in descending order of status. If formal equality is conceded the schools will still be differentiated in the minds of the public (this, according to Savage, is what had happened in Denmark).

> For these reasons the multilateral school has been and is being advocated. The view is that we ought to make progress in the direction of the evolution of a classless society. If we do not reformers will, sooner or later, try to force such a form of society by revolution, with the inevitable result that a new arrangement of classes separated by hatreds may emerge. Whilst it is true in some degree that our system of education must be a reflection of the order of society in which it is set, it is wise in planning reforms to look ahead and to plan education a little in advance of the existing state of society, and our ideas on education should be informed by sociological ideals.

Savage apparently saw, or thought it politic to sell, the comprehensive school as a counter-revolutionary policy. His approach has clear similarities to that of Anthony Crosland fourteen years later (*The Future of Socialism, 1956*). Although pupils in multilateral schools should be 'sorted out' at the age of twelve into 'appropriate lines of study' all are part of one school 'partaking in the same corporate life'. 'One of the most important, perhaps the most important, function of education … is to teach people of all kinds, rich and poor, dull and bright, male and female, to live together helpfully and happily'. For these reasons, he concludes, children should not be segregated from each other at the age of eleven.

Clearly the motivation here differed from that of NALT, CDRE, or the labour movement generally, which saw the establishment of the single school as an essential means of opening up educational opportunity, and as a blow against the early determination of educational and career chances at the age of eleven. And it was basically for this reason that the mass organisations of the labour movement expressed their continuing support for this solution. 'Really substantial experiments', said the TUC, 'are needed in multilateral schools. So long as the three types of school are separately housed, the old prejudices will die hard and equality in fact will not be achieved.'[62]

The single code for secondary education, then, had mass support but this policy alone involved acceptance of the existence of different types of school within the new secondary system. Within the labour movement and among the more radical teachers the demand was a logical one – that the single code required the single school. This key issue was now placed firmly on the agenda for the future.

Raising the school leaving age. The other measure around which a broad consensus was quickly established was the need to raise the school leaving age from fourteen to sixteen. As we have already seen, the demand to raise the age, first to fifteen and then to sixteen had been a major aim of the labour movement and others since the end of the First World War. Ernest Bevin had already forcefully argued for fifteen.[63] In the mid-1930s the School Age Council had campaigned on this issue and in 1936 the abortive Act of that year had in fact raised the age to fifteen, though with exemptions for 'beneficial employment'.[64] The strength of feeling on this issue was immense, shared by teachers, administrators, the wider labour movement, the Liberal, Labour and Communist Parties.

Indeed this measure was seen as having absolute priority, though most organisations were prepared to recognise that the age of fifteen should be the first step, to be followed shortly after by a further measure – to sixteen; this to be specifically written into any Bill now being prepared.

The Association of Directors and Secretaries demanded, in 1942, that statutory provision should be made immediately for a leaving age of sixteen; the Association of Education Committees in the same year demanded full time schooling for all to sixteen 'at the earliest possible moment'; the Association of Municipal Corporations followed suit as did the NUT and other teacher organisations. As far as the labour movement was concerned, these organisations were again unanimous. The Co-operative Union in 1942 and the TUC in its 1942 memorandum *Education after the War* both insisted on a statutory leaving age of sixteen (fifteen immediately after the war, then sixteen at a definite date) as did the WEA. This, according to the TUC, was *the* main issue.

Raising the age to sixteen became a major campaigning issue for the Council of Educational Advance (CEA) from its foundation in September 1942. The first point a new Education Bill should contain, the CEA argued, was a clause raising the leaving age to fifteen without exemptions by the end of the war, and to sixteen not less than three years after. Later the CEA issued a short, punchy campaigning leaflet (Education Leaflet No.3.) strongly arguing the case for a leaving age of sixteen – *The School Leaving Age and Educational Opportunity*.

Here, then, was a widespread and common determination to insist on a rapid and major thrust forward – in effect the raising of the age by two years within a short period following the close of hostilities. This measure, which would bring two complete age cohorts into the schools, was seen by its supporters as guaranteeing a necessary and serious content to the concept of 'secondary education for all'.

The dual system. Finally, there was the vexed question of what was then known as the 'dual system' – the co-existence of the 'voluntary' (Church) schools and the publicly provided system. This, of course, was the product of the long (historical) bid of the Anglican Church to control the education of the people in the face of the secular movement which gathered pace from the

1850s, a struggle which culminated in the 1870 Act establishing a national system through the locally elected school boards, largely (originally) funded out of the rates. From 1870 to 1902 there were, then, two main groups of 'elementary' schools, the Board schools which received rate aid, and the church (voluntary) schools maintained by subscription from supporters, many of which had been brought into being earlier in the nineteenth century and before. Both sets of schools received grant aid from the state – the Department of Education. The 'dual system', as it existed before and during the First World War was, however, the immediate product of the 1902 Education Act whereby the financing of the voluntary (church) schools was also brought onto the rates. This measure, very strongly contested at the time by the then powerful Nonconformist and the nascent Labour movements, gave a new lease of life to the 'dual system' leaving control of well over half the elementary schools in the country in the hands of the churches (both Anglican and Catholic – the former largely predominating).

However, in the inter-war period and particularly during the late 1930s the failure of the Churches to cope at all effectively with their schools had become strikingly apparent. This had been especially highlighted by their inability to carry through the 'reorganisation' required as government policy, following official acceptance, in 1928, by a Tory government of the Hadow committee's recommendations. By 1938 only 16 per cent of Church schools had been reorganised compared with 62 per cent of Council schools. [65] This meant that, at this date, several million children still experienced their entire schooling within a single, old-type, unreorganised, 'all-age' school taking children often from five to fourteen and normally unable to offer any specialised teaching whatsoever. Further these Church schools were generally decrepit and in a state of chronic disrepair. Of the near 3,000 'black listed' schools condemned by the Board of Education in the inter-war period (1925) as 'unfit for further use', the great bulk were Church schools. Local authorities, and others, were in despair about the situation.

There is little wonder, then, that, when educational reconstruction came under consideration, a strong groundswell of opinion, particularly among teachers and administrators, manifested itself on this issue. Here, it seemed to many, was an opportunity to clear up this question once and for all, to establish a rational system of administration, and to bring all publicly provided schooling under local democratic control. Indeed to many this now seemed inevitable. The churches had clearly shown that they were in no position to modernise their schooling.

Here, as mentioned above, it was primarily those concerned with the administration of the system who took the lead. In their evaluation of the existing position the Directors and Secretaries launched a very strong attack on the dual system. The Church schools are generally a disgrace, they wrote. The Churches are incapable even of maintaining the fabric of their schools. In a chapter devoted to this issue, the authors make no bones about their outlook. The dual system must be abolished. It is administratively hopeless. A set of specific proposals follow as to how this can be achieved.[66]

The same note was struck by the influential Association of Education Committees, which then united local authority education committees throughout the country. Indeed, in their view, this was the main issue requiring reform. The voluntary schools would be quite unable to cope with the demands that must be made on them. Detailed proposals were made as to how the system could be changed. [67]

The labour movement was also united on this issue. The Co-operative Union insisted that the dual system 'should cease forthwith'. The TUC wanted an end to state support for church schools – these should be placed on the same basis as private schools and bear the whole cost. The WEA took a similar line as, in general, did the National Union of Teachers and many other organisations. Indeed by the close of 1942 a wide measure of agreement had been reached on what was seen as perhaps the most crucial issue requiring settlement if the way was to be cleared for educational advance.[68]

So there emerged, from an early stage in the war, a clear, radical policy on educational change and especially after the first turns in favour of the allies in the late autumn of 1942. Briefly summarised this is the programme;

1. Abolition, or at least effective assimilation, of the public schools as a step towards the creation of a single, *national* system of education.

2. Secondary education for all over the age of eleven. Abolition of fees in all maintained secondary schools

(including direct grant grammar schools). A common code of regulations for all secondary schools (and, in a more advanced form, the establishment of the single, common or multilateral secondary school).

3. Raising of the school leaving age to the age of sixteen.

4. Abolition of the dual system. All schools to be equally under public control.

Such a policy posed a real and serious challenge, implying a new order in English education and definitely involving social change.

3 The Mounting Pressure

Perhaps the best way to give an indication of the mounting pressure for reform is to quote from a short book, written by Harold Dent and published in October 1942. As already indicated, Dent acted as a tribune for reformers – and was then widely accepted as such. Hence his importance, and the space accorded to him at this point.

It was an advanced educational policy of the kind outlined at the end of the last section that Dent presented in his powerful polemical booklet, which rapidly obtained a mass sale. *A New Order in English Education* drew on Dent's experiences and contacts over the last two years, and particularly on the series of four major leaders on educational reform published in the *Times Educational Supplement* June and July 1941, which have already been referred to – leaders which set the tone in educational discussion. The rhetoric Dent uses is very characteristic of the spirit of the time.

'I believe that the overwhelming majority of people in this country desire radical changes in its social order,' he wrote, 'changes that shall lead to a planned society based on democratic principles, infused with a genuinely democratic spirit, and ordered in fully democratic lines'. If the opportunity is not taken now it will be 'lost for ever' – the result will be 'national disintegration and deterioration'. Of all the reforms which must be made 'drastic reconstruction of our educational system stands first and foremost'. Without it the undemocratic elements in our society will be perpetuated and strengthened. 'We can look for no permanent new order in society unless we have a new order in education.' Our educational system, he goes on, 'represents the very essence of inequality of opportunity'. It is 'socially stratified to a degree that would be ludicrous were it not so tragic'. In essence it represents the values of an acquisitive and hierarchic society.[69]

This, he claims, is widely accepted. 'The necessity for radical reform of the entire educational order in England is scarcely contested. The desire for it is virtually universal'. In a chapter on 'Defects of the Existing Order' Dent launches a sharp polemic about the existing situation – the 'abominable' conditions in which the elementary schools have to work 'condoned and perpetuated by the very institution in society – organised religion – which properly ought to be most concerned to improve them', the clear class divisions and the failure to provide a meaningful education. The dual system is highly culpable – dual control 'has caused consistent trouble ever since the State began to assume responsibility for public education'. But the real reason why these buildings are such a disgrace is that the public elementary school is provided by 'the upper orders' for the children of 'the lower orders'.

> As for the churches, it is easy to appreciate their concern that children shall be instructed in the Christian faith according to their particular tenets, but it is difficult for the impartial observer to reconcile the tender care they manifest for the children's souls with the disregard they exhibit for their bodies.[70]

Dent specifically places the main responsibility for the sorry state of education squarely on the public schools. From the late nineteenth century these have grown 'more aloof and exclusive' – and so steadily widened the gulf between the 'two nations' of 'rulers and ruled, privileged and unprivileged'. Selection is now based solely on 'social standing and the ability to pay heavy fees'. Their social function is now to act as 'an instrument to maintain an indefensible system of wholesale nepotism'. The public schools have 'bred ... an exclusive social caste ... which ... has seized and holds fast the keys to political, diplomatic, religious, social and economic power', and which has used and uses this power 'for its own benefit rather than for the common good'. It is this caste, Dent avers, which has always checked and balked the development of the public system of education. Allied with industry, which wants cheap labour and which 'has always opposed bitterly any extension of educational opportunity', the public schools have feathered their own nests at the expense of the well-being of the mass of the people.[71]

Dent argues, from this premise, that the first priority is to overcome the two systems now existing. Instead there must be a single unified system of education for the nation as a whole. There is overwhelming evidence, he concludes, that to perpetuate the existing, divisive system 'in any shape or form' would be 'disastrous' for the future of Britain.[72]

Dent is equally radical when he considers the future of secondary education as a whole. Here also he comes out uncompromisingly for the single secondary school. However much children may differ in character, temperament, ability and aptitude, he writes, 'I am utterly opposed to the idea of segregating adolescents in different types of school'. Or, for that matter, he goes on, 'of segregating them on the score of ability in different classes in the same school'. Instead, 'All should be members of one school, which should provide adequately for diversity of individual aptitudes and interest, yet unite all as members of a single community.' While most current plans advocate a variety of secondary schools, he adds, 'There is at least a strong minority opinion (latterly growing increasingly in strength) among educationists in favour of the ... "multilateral school", i.e. the single school with a wide enough range of activities to meet the needs of all pupils.' Here Dent refers to the Labour Party Conference resolution of 1942, the WEA programme entitled 'Educational Reconstruction', the TUC memorandum *Education After the War* (1942) and also the views of the London County Council. [73]

Dent goes on to outline further reform proposals – for instance that, after the compulsory leaving age of sixteen all should go on to a further two years combination of education and training (a proposal more than 40 years in advance of its time). He deals with university, adult and leisure education and demands a serious radical measure of educational change covering the whole field. Further, he stresses its urgency. If we plan now, he claims, the overall scheme he proposes could come into being 'immediately after the war'. At all costs a gradualist approach should be avoided. This would be the path to certain failure. 'The reactionary interests are already

concentrating their forces and marshalling their munitions'.[74]
Events were to prove the truth of the assessment.

Dent's polemic and programme has been stressed because,
as already mentioned, he had by now developed a unique
position as spokesman for the whole movement for educational
change – a movement which may be said to have reached its
peak in the late autumn of 1942. By this time most of the
organisations concerned had hammered out their proposals –
these had been published during this crucial year. Just at the
point when Dent's book appeared the Council for Education
Advance was formed, uniting the TUC, NUT, WEA and the
Co-operative Union in a joint campaign for an agreed
programme of educational advance. The pressure was on – and
to some it may have seemed that matters were getting out of
hand. We may now turn to official responses to what was now
becoming a broad, popular movement for educational and
social change.

4 Manipulation and Control

While organisations representing the labour movement, the
teachers, administrators and local authorities were formulating
their proposals for educational change, those formally
responsible for the system – the Board of Education officials
and government ministers – had not been idle. Indeed already
by November 1940 a planning group of senior officials had
been set up by the Permanent Secretary, Sir Maurice Holmes.
'It is clear from references in the press,' minuted Holmes, 'that
other persons and bodies have ideas on post-war educational
reconstruction and I think this is a matter in which the Board
should lead rather than follow.' At the start of his minute
Holmes refers to 'problems' which are likely to ('will') arise
'when the war is over'.

In his comprehensive study of ministerial and Board of
Education activities during the war (*Education in the Second
World War*, 1976), P.H.J.H. Gosden has extensively chronicled
the actions taken by top Board officials to pre-empt reform
planning early in the war. As a result a great deal is known
about the planning group, based at Bournemouth, where the
main offices of the Board were evacuated for the duration. As
Holmes suggests in his minute, this was established when it
became clear that the question of post-war reconstruction could

not be avoided. Already in late 1939 and certainly during the early months of 1940 discussions on educational reconstruction were widespread – partly spurred by the very serious disruption of the schools as a result of evacuation – a saga in itself.[76] At this time the President of the Board, Herwald Ramsbotham, who had succeeded Earl De La Warr early in April 1940, began to espouse the cause of educational reform, in particular with the issue of the plans concocted at Bournemouth in the famous (or notorious) 'Green Book' circulated 'confidentially' as early as June 1941, and entitled *Education after the War*. It was the more positive points embodied in this document that Ramsbotham began to propagate in a series of speeches in the summer of 1941. Ramsbotham, however, was not a Churchillian and, perhaps partly as a result of this activity, but more probably of wider political considerations, was replaced by R.A. Butler shortly after the issue of the Green Book late in July 1941.[77]

The pre-emptive planning, resulting in the Green Book, was clearly an attempt on the part of Board officials to take the high ground, as it were, and to go through the then necessary exercise of discussion with the Board's main 'partners' (teachers' organisations, local authorities, the voluntary bodies – the Churches) without, however, encouraging widespread popular debate. This is why the Green Book was originally circulated only to named representatives under the bond of secrecy. If such was the intention, as seems likely, the attempt proved an abysmal failure – though causing considerable inconvenience to many influentially placed people who had considerable difficulty in acquiring a copy (among them R.A. Butler, who apparently never forgave the Board's officials for leaving him off the list).[78] However this experience only alerted others to the need to promote discussion of the main issues widely among all those involved and interested. It was partly as a direct result that organisations and groups concerned now began precisely to formulate their objectives.

In some respects the Green Book embodied what were now becoming widely popular demands. It included the proposal, for instance, that there should be a common code of regulations for all schools catering for children above the age of eleven – that is, it accepted, if in a formal sense, the need for 'secondary education for all', though insisting that this should be made available in different types of school among which the selective grammar and technical schools should remain pre-eminent. It also accepted the need to plan for the raising of the leaving age to fifteen (though not sixteen) to be followed by part-time attendance at continuation schools for the equivalent of one day a week. It has, indeed, been argued that, with the exception of the solution finally found on the religious issue, and on certain aspects of administration (Part 3 authorities, etc.) the proposals in the Green Book, concocted by civil servants, in fact appeared generally unchanged in the Education Bill, first presented to parliament in December 1943.[79]

There is, here, one issue of great interest. Why was it that these officials were now prepared, only two years after they had turned down with contumely (even contempt) recommendations from the Spens Committee for a single code of regulations to cover all post-primary schooling, to make precisely this proposal the cornerstone of their programme? Acceptance of this proposal, of course, implied a definite measure of educational advance and appears as a clear concession to rising expectations already made manifest. This interpretation receives support from a minute sent to the officials' planning group by R.S. Wood, the Deputy Secretary of the Board, who, located in London rather than Bournemouth, 'had the advantage' as Gosden puts it 'of being able to keep perhaps more closely in touch with political feeling ... than his colleagues in Bournemouth'. In any case, Wood's note shows remarkable political prescience. The war, he wrote is 'moving us more and more in the direction of Labour's ideas and ideals'; planning should be more to the left than was currently supposed. Under their likely post-war political masters it would be fatal for officials to have formulated their ideas in a spirit of timidity. Gosden goes on to comment that 'the classical reason why civil servants should be ready with appropriately persuasive plans and advice for the next colour of the political spectrum likely to enjoy power is now spelt out.' If planning was mean and meagre it would be disregarded, the views of officials would be discounted and outsiders would be 'asked to design the New Jerusalem'. So Wood sketched out his plan which, to all intents and purposes, was accepted. This included the proposal that all types of secondary schools should be brought under one code of regulations; that secondary education should be free; that the leaving age be raised to fifteen followed by compulsory part-time attendance at continuation schools.[80]

So a set of reforms that might have had to wait years for implementation were, under the pressure of war and its probable political outcome, as well, no doubt, of the developing progressive consensus, now conceded with no argument whatsoever. By this time it was already clear that there were other strongholds to defend now seen as more important. There was, for instance, no mention whatever in the Green Book of the public schools, while the separate existence of the 'system' of fee-paying direct grant grammar schools was strongly defended.[81] Further, the Green Book 'took for granted' that, as Maurice Holmes put it in his foreword, secondary education 'will be conducted in three types of secondary school', modern, grammar and technical.

The Norwood Report

The issue as to the pattern of secondary education was clearly of particular importance in any planning for the future – especially in view of this early concession of 'secondary education for all'. Was differentiation by type, as proposed in the Green Book, to be the main feature of the new system of secondary education, or was there, as Dent, the TUC, the Labour Party and others were now arguing, to be a single 'multilateral' or common secondary school? By the autumn of 1942, as we have seen, a strong movement was developing in favour of the single school, and indeed this had already gained considerable support before the war.

Throughout the inter-war period the Board's policy had been clear. At all costs the (selective) grammar schools, then the only form of 'secondary' school, must be preserved as independent entities for an elite. But in the new dispensation, this had to be argued – the continued existence of a highly selective school type legitimised. It is here that one action, initiated by the Bournemouth group of officials, can now be seen as a master stroke: the appointment of a Committee on Curriculum and Examinations in Secondary Schools, chaired by Cyril Norwood, now doyen of the educational establishment outside the Board (and recently the leading spirit in the attempt to rescue the public schools from disaster).

The politics of this committee are particularly devious; even its origin is shrouded in a certain amount of mystery, though

Gosden has unravelled some of this.[82] Apparently, shortly after the Board's officials had 'turned their attention to reconstruction' in the autumn of 1940 the decision was taken that they needed an 'independent' committee to 'advise' on the whole structure of secondary education (even the public schools at first) as well as on examinations (even though the Spens Committee had already reported on examinations late in 1938). They then persuaded the Secondary Schools Examination Council (SSEC), whose Chairman was Cyril Norwood, to get 'the sanction of the Board' (i.e. themselves) to the setting up of 'a small committee to review the existing system of school examinations and to submit a report to the Board through the council.'[83] Yet, in fact, the actual establishment of this key committee (which was accordingly appointed) was kept a secret and it hardly met for several months. Finally, but not until October 1941 (10 months later) its appointment and terms of reference were announced by Butler in the House of Commons.

The committee, as is well known, gave itself a wider brief than its title (or terms of reference) and in effect produced the essential ideological underpinning for what became known as the 'tripartite' system; its conclusions were later regarded, by one critic at least, as having been taken as 'The Tables of the Law' by the Ministry of Education (as the Board became) in the post-war situation – a quite accurate assessment.[84] The main set of arguments offered grounded the proposed restructuring of secondary education – into grammar, technical and modern schools – in the nature of the child. Some (a few) were capable of abstract thought and interested in ideas, in 'learning for its own sake' – for these grammar schools should be provided. Others (also a few) were more interested and adept at the application of ideas in technology – for these there should be (selective) technical schools. The great majority, however, were more concerned with practical activities and the immediate environment – for these the new type of secondary 'modern' schools should be designed. The Norwood Committee claimed that they based this proposal on 'child-centred' ideas. Each of the three types of school were needed to 'match' the nature of the child.[85]

The Norwood Committee reported at the end of July 1943; that is, just *after* the publication of the government's White Paper on Education presaging the Education Bill – one of a series of measures which will be dealt with in the next section. The White Paper had also 'taken for granted' a tripartite division within secondary education.[86] Coming precisely at this time, and clearly bearing official sanction, the Norwood Report was seen as an aspect of the educational reconstruction of that crucial time. 'This well written report', noted Butler at the time, 'will serve our book very well – *particularly its layout of the secondary world'* (my emphasis, B.S.).[87]

The report generally received a warm welcome from the press, even, perhaps surprisingly, from H.C. Dent who wrote that it was full of 'enlightening proposals'. The committee, he added, had rendered 'a great service', especially as their concept of the future of education was 'derived from a reasoned philosophy of education.'[88] But the report, quite apart from the service it rendered in 'taking for granted' that the future secondary school system should be cast in the tripartite mould, and in providing a 'philosophical' rationale for this proposal, made no attempt whatsoever to deal with the secondary curriculum as a whole, even though by that time it was generally agreed that the rubric 'secondary education' should cover all post-primary schooling. On the contrary, only two short sections (pp.20-21) are devoted to the future secondary modern and technical schools. The great bulk of the text is confined to the secondary grammar school curriculum, which is discussed in some detail, together, of course, with proposals about the reform of the secondary school examination, the School Certificate. The committee generally favoured the actual abolition of this examination, or its replacement by internal assessment at sixteen though it favoured the retention (with modifications) of the Higher School Certificate relating to university entry. Here we find the first formulation of the concept that grammar schools should be reserved only to those who will stay the full course to eighteen as well as the further suggestion that the proportion of any age group proceeding to these schools should be reduced (there were many, they argued, who would be better off outside – or elsewhere).

The appointment of this committee can be judged as a master-stroke because of the way in which its report appeared to lay down a clear pattern (and rationale) for a divided system of secondary education following whatever reforms were to be brought about by legislation. The way this report was actually dealt with raises a number of issues. First, Norwood, as Chairman of the SSEC, was appointed Chairman of the Committee with the right to *nominate* its members (in consultation with G.G. Williams, a traditionalist *par excellence* at the Board). Second, the committee, in the outcome, reported *direct* to the President (Butler) without reference to the SSEC, of which it was officially a sub-committee. Then, but only *after* the report was published, the SSEC was called together and simply presented with it. When objections were raised, according to one member (J.A. Petch), the SSEC was 'unceremoniously dismissed'.[89] If there was ever a case of devious practice, this is it. Clearly the Board and its officials were determined that the policy they favoured should be thrust to the forefront – almost by whatever means.

In the event, after the early press encomiums, the Norwood Report generally had a highly critical reception. A few weeks after publication, Julian Huxley published a penetrating critique both of the report's reliance on the outmoded doctrine of 'knowledge for its own sake' and of 'absolute values', and its neglect – even contempt for – science and scientific procedures, in a long article in the *Times Educational Supplement*.[90] A few months later Cyril Burt, then the doyen of educational psychologists, who had been personally affronted that no attempt was made to gain his advice and evidence, launched a sharp attack on the theory of three types of mind, claiming that this theory could not be upheld on the basis of psychological data.[91] Among those adopting a critical stance, following Burt, was Fred Clarke and the historian, S.J. Curtis, who wrote later in the strongest terms:

> Seldom has a more unscientific or more unscholarly attitude disgraced the report of a public committee ... The suggestion of the committee seems to be that the Almighty has benevolently created three types of child in just those proportions which would gratify educational administrators.[92]

This report, then, was clearly intended to settle the question of the organisation of secondary education following the concession of the single code and 'secondary education for all'. The multilateral school had been given its quietus; selection and an elitist structure was not only to be maintained, but strengthened. In particular, the grammar school would remain inviolate, catering for a *reduced* proportion of the child population. This is the importance of the Norwood report, and the real significance of the manipulations around its formation.

The Fleming Committee

Concern for the preservation of the existing social order was again manifested on the issue of the public schools, now, as made clear earlier, under very sharp attack from a wide spectrum of public opinion extending far beyond the labour movement itself. We need to look again at this from the standpoint of how the issue was dealt with by those in authority. Was the public school question to be tackled seriously? Was there, or was there not to be a fundamental reform of the system as a whole? As the war proceeded through 1942 and 1943, with the tide now turning in favour of the Allies and with public concern with social (and educational) issues increasing, this question came very much to the fore. The early disenchantment had been, if anything, reinforced by such massive popular pampleteering as the publication of *Tory MP* by Simon Haxey (late 1939), *Guilty Men* by Michael Foot *et al.* (immediately after Dunkirk) and *Your MP* by Tom Wintringham (1944). The criticism, far from dying down, was even exacerbated at this time.

Butler was able to deal with this with his usual skill, and indeed he is astonishingly frank about it in his autobiography, *The Art of the Possible*, published in 1971. As is well known, he adopted the time-honoured procedure of setting up a committee of enquiry at a point when criticism maximised (summer 1942) with the brief of reporting on possible lines of action, or rather 'to consider means whereby the association between the public schools ... and the general educational system of the country could be developed and extended'. As Gosden notes, this was generally taken to mean that action was imminent to 'democratise' the public schools in some way; indeed several newspapers took it as a foregone conclusion that the appointment of this committee meant, as the *Daily Express* put it, that a 'public school revolution' was under way.[93]

But this meant that, when the Education Bill was finally published, in December 1943, the Fleming Committee (as it is known, after its Chairman) was still sitting; it had issued an inconclusive interim report confidentially to Butler on fees in grant-aided secondary schools (direct grant schools) in

February 1943. [94] So this committee, under its Scottish law lord was taking its time. Nothing of any significance appeared on the independent schools in the original Bill (except a set of clauses relating to compulsory registration). And this could then be justified on the grounds that the matter was still under investigation. Indeed the Fleming Committee did not report finally until 26 July 1944, that is over two months *after* the Education Bill had been given its third reading, and literally only a week or so before the Act received Royal Assent (3 August 1944). As Butler stated afterwards in self-congratulation, 'the first class carriage had been shunted onto an immense siding'.[95]

This puts the matter very precisely. Butler himself was very concerned (as D.W. Dean has shown) to dissuade his own party's education sub-committee from issuing a strong defence of the public schools in 1943 – fearing trade union and labour movement reaction.[96] He even persuaded Churchill, when preparing his key speech on social issues in March 1943, to exclude statements to the effect that the day of the 'old school tie' were over. And, of course, when the Fleming Committee did finally produce what Butler later characterised as its 'sensationally ingenuous report'[97] – with the proposal that those independent schools that wished should offer 25 per cent of their places to 'qualified' pupils from primary schools who would be granted a bursary by the Board of Education or local authority – no one was particularly interested. The time for radical change had passed.

5 The Run-up to the Act

We may now turn to the Act itself, focusing only on the major issues. The manipulative politics resorted to on questions perceived as central to the social order – the public schools and the future structure of secondary education – should not blind us to the positive features of this measure. As things turned out, the formulation in the Act concerning the latter question in fact left things open, in statutory terms, for a future government to transform the situation without resource to legislation – had it the necessary will and force of conviction. A balanced assessment requires attention to what the Act in fact achieved – or embodied – across the whole field of education generally. That this measure remained virtually unmodified for over forty years as the chief statutory instrument covering the field is perhaps a strong argument in its favour; though more recently many came to feel that its lacunae urgently required attention.[98]

The fact that the Act, as finally passed, conceded very many of the demands made by democratic organisations and opinion explains, in part, how it was possible for those in authority to 'get away with' avoiding confrontation on major issues by the use of the manipulative politics discussed earlier. The early concession (in the Green Book and later the 1943 White Paper) of the virtually unanimous demand for a single code covering all post-primary education did not so much steal the thunder of the reform movement as give it added confidence in its power to insist on important changes. And here it must be said that there was, of course, no guarantee in the early years of the war that the battle for legislation would, in fact, be successful. The coalition government was dominated by (or at least relied on) the serried ranks of Conservative MPs largely of the old fashioned traditional Tory type. Their attitude to education, at least as publicly expressed in two extraordinary reports published in 1942, seemed to many more akin to fascist ideology than to democratic reform.[99]. Even Butler, as we have seen, regarded them as an embarrassment. How could a progressive educational measure, then, possibly gain acceptance from a parliament with such a composition? What was needed was a massive popular campaign to make quite certain of its presentation, and passage through parliament.

The main pressure now came directly from the labour movement. In May 1942 a strong resolution was passed at the Labour Party Conference demanding an Education Bill now. In moving this, Harold Clay (NEC) stressed the need for fundamental and far-reaching changes in education. The Bill was wanted *now* 'when the minds of men and women are attuned to change, when they are receptive to new ideas, when industry is in a plastic state, when the whole of our social make-up is in the melting pot'. This, he said, was the right time to demand, as the basis of a new order 'a sound and comprehensive education system'. It is time, he added, that 'the double status' in education 'was completely wiped out, and that the idea of the two nations was eradicated from our educational system'.[100]

The Labour Party was, of course, a major partner in the

coalition – James Chuter Ede its representative as Butler's junior minister – so that this unanimous expression carried weight. It was with this in mind that, late in 1942 as we have seen, organisations representing the labour movement and teachers joined together to set up the Council for Educational Advance, uniting the TUC, WEA, the Co-operative Union and the NUT – then by far the largest and most representative of the teacher organisations.[101] All these, of course, comprised local as well as national associations, and the united organisation was, therefore, well placed to organise meetings in the localities as well as nationally. A very large number of such meetings were held, particularly in 1943, when the pressure for legislation was maximised (the TUC claimed that a total of 200 meetings and conferences were organised by the CEA in the year following its formation in September 1942 in an 'extensive campaign in support of educational reform').[102]

In a series of short, sharp and punchy leaflets the CEA sought to arouse mass opinion for action. 'Immediate legislation to provide equality of educational opportunity for all children, irrespective of their social or economic condition' was stated as their aim in the first of these, which also outlined a minimum programme accepted by all the four organisations participating. Shortly after another popular pamphlet spelt out the programme in more detail (Education Leaflets No.2), to be following by another arguing the urgency for a leaving age of sixteen (No.3) and another on the need for free secondary education for all (No.4). The fifth leaflet, 'A New Start in Education' was published immediately after the White Paper on educational reconstruction, announcing legislation, was issued. But this was seen, perhaps correctly, as a delaying tactic. Striking a note of urgency the CEA argued that a new Education Bill should be introduced without delay. The White Paper is full of good intentions, but 'the time has come for action'. Other issues may arise 'to give an excuse to those who wish to shelve educational reform'. 'Delay is dangerous'. Criticisms are made of the proposals in the White Paper which will be considered later. The leaflet ends with these words.

> The war has shown that measures required for the safety of the country can be put through at high speed. On any but the shortest view educational reforms necessary to the welfare of the rising generation are among such measures. They ought not to be jeopardised or retarded by needless procrastination.

Butler had issued his White Paper. *Educational Reconstruction* which implied the probability of legislation though promising nothing, in July 1943. At this stage his Bill was not yet ready;[103] the White Paper was designed to fill this lacuna – and give an earnest that the government was serious about educational reconstruction. The Paper in fact met the needs of the moment, but is a curious document in retrospect. Headed by the motto 'Upon the education of the people of this country the fate of this country depends' (the words are Disraeli's), the document opens with unexceptionable rhetoric:

> The Government's purpose ... is to ensure for children a happier childhood and a better start in life; to ensure a fuller measure of education and opportunity for young people and to provide means for all of developing the various talents with which they are endowed and so enriching the inheritance of the country whose citizens they are.

However a note of warning here immediately enters. The 'new educational opportunities' it is stated, 'must not ... be of a single pattern'. More precisely, to achieve 'diversity' is just as important 'as it is to ensure equality of opportunity'. However (another qualification now of opposite tendency) 'such diversity must not impair the social unity within the educational system which will open the way to a more closely knit society and give us strength to face the tasks ahead'.[104]

The democratic movement pressuring for change took encouragement from the opening words of the section entitled 'The Present System'. These appeared as a forthright rejection of the selective character of post-primary schooling and as a guarantee of fundamental change. 'There is nothing to be said,' declared the government in what became a famous phrase, 'in favour of a system which subjects children at the age of 11 to the strain of a competitive examination on which, not only their future schooling, but their future careers may depend.' However the authors of the White Paper in fact hedged their bets on the by now sensitive issue of the organisation of secondary education. In the introduction it had already been clearly stated that the government intended 'to recast' the national educational service as a series of stages (in place of the elementary/secondary divide), but this is followed immediately by the statement that 'after 11 secondary education, of diversified type but on equal standing, will be provided for all children'. Later the White Paper spells out very precisely these diversified types. 'Such, then, will be the three main types of secondary schools to be known as grammar, technical and modern schools.' But here again, a seeming concession is inserted:

> It would be wrong to suppose that they [the three types, B.S.] will necessarily remain separate and apart. Different types may be combined in one building or on one site as considerations of convenience and efficiency may suggest.[105]

The White Paper spelt out in some detail many of the proposals which had already appeared in the Green Book and were to reappear as clauses of the Education Bill. One area of difference, however, concerned the precise form of the religious settlement and it was here that Butler, as president, had concentrated his efforts, finally arriving at an agreed solution (though the Catholics remained recalcitrant). This was certainly a necessary condition for any serious approach to educational advance.[106] The White Paper also made reference to both the Norwood and the Fleming Committees' work – neither had by this time reported. While structural reform is important, it is stated, there is also need to improve the content of education itself – this is what the Norwood Committee is considering (a half truth as it turned out). As regards what the White Paper refers to as 'the one important' link remaining to be forged – that between 'the Public Schools and other analagous schools and the general system', this is what the Fleming Committee is charged to investigate. 'It is the government's intention to devise ways and means by which these schools can be more closely associated with the national system,' a clear reassurance to these schools, and their supporters in the Tory Party and elsewhere that there would be no radical change in their position – though this seems not to have been clearly recognised at the time.[107]

An appendix set out the financial implications of the proposals together with an outline timetable for implementation. It was this that aroused the suspicion, and indeed opposition, of the CEA and many others. The approach appeared both dilatory, and ineffective in terms of resources. *No* reforms were to be introduced before the end of the war. The school leaving age could be raised to fifteen in the first year thereafter, but the cost of a further rise to sixteen, though estimated (£8.95 million), is not included in the estimate of the total cost of implementing the programme. Reform of the dual system would not involve any extra expenditure until three years after the war – when local authorities had worked out the restructuring that would be necessary. Fees in secondary schools would not be abolished until three years after the war. The proposal for 'young peoples' colleges' (part-time compulsory attendance for ages fifteen to eighteen) would not involve substantial expenditure until four years after the war. The total ultimate estimated additional expenditure due to the reforms amounted to £67.4 million – that is, a rise of about 50 per cent on total expenditure from public funds in England and Wales (derived from both rates and taxes). But it would be well over seven years before this full extra cost fell due. Incidentally it was estimated that the revision of the grant system proposed to assist local authorities would involve a rise in the Exchequer contribution from 52 per cent of the full cost in the first year after the war to 55 per cent in the fourth. Before the war the Exchequer contribution was 45 per cent.[108]

This dilatory timetable, and the paucity of expenditure envisaged for the immediate post-war years, scarcely accorded with the wishes of the popular organisations united in the CEA, as we have seen, and these immediately launched a powerful public campaign both critical of the general tenor of the Paper and demanding immediate legislation. The government has adopted a 'far too leisurely approach' to the whole question of reform, declared the TUC in September. 'This ill fits the necessities and the temper of the times, and lags a long way behind the large body of public opinion which is eager that the opportunity of reconstructing our educational system should be grasped now.'[109] At this point, in the early autumn of 1943, the pressure was clearly on. But there is another aspect to developments in this period which throws considerable light on the tortuous politics of education, the White Paper and of the Act itself.

As things turned out, the Education Act of 1944 was certainly the main measure of social advance carried through actually *during* the war (as, indeed, the 1918 Act had been in its time). How did it come about that education was to have this honour? Admittedly, as we have seen, a broad popular movement insisting on radical changes had built up rapidly almost from the start of the war. But this could be no guarantee in itself of success, particularly when we recall the composition of the House of Commons (not to speak of the Lords – at that time an entirely hereditary body).

The coalition (war-time) government was based, as already mentioned, on a House of Commons consisting of an overwhelming number of Tory MPs elected at the 1935 election (432). Labour had increased its representation at that election, but was still very much in a minority (with 154 MPs), while the Liberal Party and various fission groups counted for very little. These Tory MPs were mostly of the old fashioned sort, and were certainly not proponents of social change, let alone advance (two were the author's uncles). By this time, however, there was a group of about forty 'progressive Tories', now much concerned with the image of the Tory Party, who included, for instance, Lord Hinchingbrooke, Quintin Hogg, Lady Astor and Thelma Cazalet-Keir. These began to have some influence, especially as public opinion in the country began to swing towards concern with progressive social reconstruction policies after 1942 – a movement reflected in the formation of the Army Bureau of Current Affairs (ABCA) and the clear swing of interest and concern among the forces about these issues at this time (Butler later accused what he called 'the left-wing influence of the Army Bureau of Current Affairs' of virtually winning the whole of the forces vote in the 1945 election for the left).[110]

Within the government reconstruction was largely in the hands of the Labour leaders under the chairmanship of Greenwood. The Cabinet's reconstruction committee included Morrison and Bevin, as well as Attlee, Butler being 'the only seasoned politician' (among them) in home affairs from the Conservatives. The Labour ministers now began to apply some pressure for action on social issues, a pressure clearly reflecting popular concern, and distrust, about plans for the future and their implementation.

The catalyst was the Beveridge Report, covering the whole field of social security. This made a series of radical proposals. Beveridge's introduction set the tone: 'A revolutionary moment in the world's history is a time for revolutions, not for patching'. The preparation and finalisation of this report coincided with the Allies' first really successful operation in North Africa (in November 1942). Beveridge (in Addison's words) had the 'good fortune that his report was timed to catch the high tide of euphoria'.[111] The Cabinet was much concerned

– especially Churchill. Various actions were taken to mute Beveridge's public exposition of the report himself. However, the line was then changed, and on 1 December 1942 the report was given the full treatment on the BBC in 22 languages. The reception of this report in Britain was extraordinary. A queue a mile long formed down the road from the Kingsway HMSO Centre for copies – a total of 635,000 were sold. As far as the armed forces were concerned, an ABCA bulletin summarising the report was vetoed by the Secretary of State for War and it was not until the summer (six months later) that the veto was finally withdrawn and the summary issued, in over 100,000 copies. Home Office enquiries revealed that there was an extraordinary anxiety among the public at large that somehow the report would be 'watered down or shelved'. The report was 'a powder keg'. There was at this point a clear danger of a break in the government consensus.[112]

Tory backbenchers put up a struggle against action. But in a series of six by-elections, seen as a minature general election, held in the month of the parliamentary debate on Beveridge (February 1943), in which the report proved to be the principal issue, the Tories did badly. Churchill eventually committed himself to action for social reform, but only 'when hostilities end', in his famous broadcast of 21 March 1943. But Gallup polls now showed a rising Labour lead.[113] Other polls conducted by Mass Observation reflected 'a profound sense of disillusion' with the government. Whereas over 50 per cent of respondents had previously expressed themselves satisfied with the way the House of Commons represented general opinion, this figure had now dropped to under 25 per cent. Something had to be done. Churchill's March broadcast on social policy was an endeavour to rally opinion behind the government; but he made no firm commitment. It was just at this moment, when things were boiling up, that Butler had (or got) his Bill ready, from which (as Addison puts it), he had 'skilfully defused the politically controversial aspects'.[114] Butler himself says, in his autobiography, that no other legislative measure was ready.[115]

So, Addison argues, the White Paper on Education (July 1943) 'provided a diversion from the Beveridge Report'.[116] By commissioning a public opinion survey after it was published, Butler was able to assure the Cabinet both of public interest and a general consensus as regards raising the school leaving age and the abolition of fees in secondary schools. He also indicated that the Act would be cheap – at least in the immediate post-war years. Finally, Addison argues, there was a 'direct party motive in promoting education: the eclipse of Beveridge by a Tory project'.[117] When the Bill was published in December 1943 'it was welcomed by the (Tory) Chief Whip, James Stuart, as a means of keeping MP's occupied without provoking party strife' – a point later confirmed by Butler.[118]

6 The 1944 Education Act

Butler published 'his' Bill in December 1943. As predicted, it took a lot of parliamentary time, though with one exception – equal pay – there was no serious opposition to any of its clauses.[119] The third reading was completed on 12 May and the Bill received the Royal Assent on 3 August. The long saga was over.

Was this Act, as many now maintain, a characteristically 'Tory' measure? An examination of its main features will assist in a balanced assessment.

First, then, the Bill (and Act) contained nothing of any significance about the public schools. As mentioned earlier, any attempt to raise this issue was met by the bland statement that the government was awaiting the recommendations of the Fleming Committee. This would then determine (or influence) action. As we have seen, this committee reported only one week before the Act received Royal Assent, so its proposals were far too late for parliamentary discussion on the Bill. To all intents and purposes, then, the public schools were saved, and indeed are still with us nearly half a century later. Can one doubt that this was a major Tory objective, especially in view of the mounting radical critique in the early stages of the war?[120]

Second, while the relevant section (8) in the Act defined 'secondary' education in such a way that the multilateral (or comprehensive) school now for the first time became a statutory, or legal possibility, the precise wording of the section, with its emphasis on the provision of secondary education according to the pupils' 'ages, abilities and aptitudes', was based ideologically on the thinking of the 1930s, reiterated and extended first in the relevant formulations in the Green Book (1941) then in the White Paper (July 1943), and finally celebrated in the Norwood Report (also published in July 1943). Implicitly, then, the Act appeared to legitimise a tripartite structure of secondary schools, and to reject the multilateral idea.[121]

Thirdly, while a leaving age of fifteen was specifically written into the Act (Section 35), the pressure to achieve the same sharpness of definition for the further rise to sixteen was not successful. Thus, although sixteen as the desirable leaving age was, in fact, written into the Act, indefinite postponement was possible without asking parliament for legislation.[122] As we now know, this further reform was only finally carried through a whole generation (28 years) after the passage of the Act.

Finally, the dual system was not abolished, as the directors of education and sections of the labour movement (and others) had demanded. It was modified by Butler's religious settlement by which extra public funds were made available in return for increased democratic, or local, control – so defusing the issue. In effect, as Murphy puts it, 'a Conservative minister had once again intervened to ensure the continuance of the dual system'.[123]

It is evident, then, that the 'democratic programme' defined on pp. 53 and 54 was, in fact, very largely beaten back. This movement was defeated on the public schools – a major issue carrying important social implications. Although successful in achieving the single code of regulations for secondary education, it was, generally speaking, defeated on the concept of the single secondary school. Although also successful in terms of raising the leaving age to fifteen, it was clearly defeated in practice on the crucial demand – that sixteen be the leaving age. On the dual system again it was in fact defeated since, although admittedly modified, this system, as a system survived.

In effect, after all the discussion and legislation, the country emerged with an hierarchical educational structure almost precisely as planned and developed in the mid-late nineteenth century, and referred to at the start of this chapter. This still comprised five (or even six) grades or levels, serving differentiated social strata. First, the established 'system' of public schools at the top; second, the direct grant schools, having won the right to continue to charge fees, survived unscathed; [124] third, the grammar schools – the elite group within the maintained (or 'grant-aided') sector; fourth, technical, some 'central' and other types of 'trade' schools; and

fifth (for the masses) the pre-war senior elementary sch
now to be known as 'secondary modern'. For a considera
period there was also to be the remnant of a sixth level – ...c
old, unreorganised 'all-age' elementary schools which,
however, had received their death sentence in the Act. (These
took another twenty years to extirpate.) Clearly, then, no
restructuring of a fundamental character was achieved. Nor
was there any serious threat to the 'social order'.

On the other hand, important gains were recorded for the
reform movement. Secondary education for all was now finally
conceded, if in a formal sense; its form and structure, within
the maintained sector, and therefore its essential content, were
left for future battles. The single code for secondary schools
meant that it was no longer possible to make a sharp and overt
discrimination between the financing of the elite schools (now
known as 'grammar' schools) and the rest. This implied
improved conditions for the new secondary modern schools (as
compared with the pre-war senior elementary schools) when
new schools came to be erected, as also a single salary structure
(though means were found to erode this through Burnham
agreements later). The Act included positive Sections
concerning the provision for nursery schools or classes (Section
8), for pupils requiring 'special educational treatment'
(Sections 33 and 34), for the development of further education,
including 'leisure-time occupations' (Sections 41 and 42);
medical inspection and treatment (48), the provision of free
milk and school meals (49), social and physical education (53)
and for the registration and inspection of independent schools
(70) – the target here was modern versions of Dotheboys Hall,
as set out in the White Paper. It dealt also with negotiating
procedures for teachers' salaries (89), the system of grants in
aid to local authorities, as well as with the system of local
administration (Section 6 and First Schedule – these abolished
the 'Part III authorities' and established divisional executives
in their place). The Act also provided for a compulsory act of
daily worship, and made religious instruction compulsory,
though retaining the right of withdrawal (Section 25). Finally
the 'Board of Education' became a Ministry, the President
being now the Minister – a section added as an amendment
during the passage of the Bill: it also allotted greater powers to
the Minister whose duty was defined as 'to promote the
education of the people of England and Wales and the

progressive development of institutions devoted to that purpose' and 'to secure the effective execution by local authorities, under his control and direction, of the national policy for providing a varied and comprehensive service in every area' (Section 1). The greater powers now allotted to the Minister included powers 'to prevent unreasonable exercise of functions' by local education authorities or school governors (Section 68), to determine the scale of remuneration for teachers (having received the advice of committees appointed by him or her, Section 89), and to act in the case of default by local authorities or managers or governors (Section 99). The Act also established Central Advisory Councils for England and Wales respectively, these having the duty of advising the Minister 'upon such matters connected with educational theory and practice as they think fit, and upon any questions referred to them by him' (Section 4); these were to take the place of the single Consultative Committee first established in 1899.

Finally, the Act included also, of course, a set of Sections (43–47) theoretically establishing young peoples' or 'county colleges', in which compulsory part-time education (one day a week) for all between the ages of fifteen and eighteen would be provided – but here no precise definition was actually written into the Act as to the starting date which, if it had been, would have required specific legislation for its abrogation.[125] In the outcome, of course, these sections were never implemented, but this is another story. Perhaps that section of the Act which embodied most hope for the future was that laying down that local authorities must, within a year, produce Development Plans covering primary and secondary education and giving effect to the Act's conditions (section 11). This was to be the basis for post-war planning for the future.[126]

This is not a complete summary of the Act, which also, of course, gave effect to Butler's general religious settlement (bringing in the voluntary-aided and voluntary-controlled categories). The Act also dealt with a number of other important, but for our purposes, peripheral issues.

In the circumstances the reader is surely best placed to judge for him or herself whether the 1944 Act is best evaluated as 'a Tory measure'[127] It was certainly seen at the time, even by those on the left, as a triumph – for all its weaknesses. G.C.T. Giles, President of the NUT in the fateful year of 1943–44, and well known as a leading member of the Communist Party, hailed its passage as a victory for democracy. For Harold Dent, its chief protagonist and celebrator, it was 'the greatest measure of educational advance since 1870, and probably the greatest ever known', as he wrote at the time.[128] The important issue now was implementation. After the dreary decades of the 1920s and 30s, the disruption of the war and the long battle against the Tories and the men of Munich, here was a measure which gave hope for the future, in terms of the life experiences of the mass of ordinary people. If this view was tinged with a certain euphoria, in the circumstances this was understandable. Something of real significance had, it seemed, at long last been achieved.

7 Conclusion

The Education Act received Royal Assent in August 1944. In May 1945 the war with Germany was brought to a close, after five and a half years of bitter struggle. As the lights went up in London and throughout the country the coalition Government also expired, Labour refusing to accept Churchill's invitation to continue until the war in the East was over. For a short time (25 May to 26 July) the Conservative Party ruled alone, Butler moving to the Ministry of Labour and National Service, a little known Tory, Richard Law, taking over what had now become the Ministry of Education. But clearly a general election had to be called, and this was arranged for early July. The campaign was on.

The result, as is well known, represented the greatest electoral turnabout since the famous Liberal landslide of 1906 – partly, in that case, due to very widespread opposition to the previous Tory government's educational policy, specifically the Act of 1902. If the 1944 Act was a 'Tory' measure it did little to rescue the party from the very severe defeat now inflicted by the electorate. Though the election took place in early July the votes were not counted until near the end of the month, to allow time for collection of the armed forces vote scattered throughout the world. The results, first declared in the early morning of the 26 July, were totally unexpected by the great majority of the people – including all, or most, leading politicians themselves.[129]

The Labour Party had won a massive victory. It obtained a total of 393 seats to 213 for the Tories and 12 for the Liberals. Two Communists and some others were elected. In fact 47.8

per cent of the total vote went to Labour, just under 40 per cent (39.8) to the Tories and 9 per cent to the Liberals. [130]

As regards the forces vote, matters were not as simple as they later seemed to some (e.g. R.A. Butler). A special Service Register was drawn up in November 1944 but only 64 per cent of those eligible in fact registered. Only just over half of those registered in fact cast their vote – a total of 1,700,653 (of a total of more than 4 million in the armed services). [131] 'As the Service votes were taken from separate boxes to be counted', writes Addison, 'it was an open secret that they were predominantly Labour'.[132] Another very specific retrospective study concluded that, of the one-fifth of the electorate (21 per cent) who were voting for the first time (and therefore largely below the age of 30 at the time of the 1945 Election), 61 per cent voted Labour. The preponderance among this age group alone, it has been calculated, would have been nearly enough to account for Labour's margin of victory (nearly 2 million).[133] It is clear, then, that the services vote could not in any way have determined the final election result. The conclusion that their vote confirmed through it did not cause, the swing to Labour in the constituencies seems a just one, even if the services vote was preponderantly Labour. In fact, the election results showed a clear overall swing to Labour, which increased its vote (from 1935) by more than 3.5 million – or nearly 50 per cent.

It cannot be a function of this book to attempt an explanation of the profound movement of opinion that finally found expression in the election results announced to an astonished world on 26 July. This relates to the growing disenchantment, particularly through the 1930s, with government actions both in the field of foreign policy (Chamberlain's appeasement policies), and in that of domestic reform. Though economic conditions improved marginally in the late 1930s, what might be called a democratic consensus, demanding radical changes, emerged during the war, to climax in the years 1942 to 1944. The trend of events in education, outlined in this chapter, was symptomatic. It was this trend that found expression in the July election. But in addition there had been during the war, an explosion of discussion and debate on social, cultural and political issues. This had developed both spontaneously and in an organised way throughout the war both in the armed forces and among the civilian population. It is arguable that it was partly activities of this sort, which remain to be effectively chronicled and analysed, [134] which lead to what was, in an important sense, a change in consciousness among the British people.

The election result, crystallising these trends, approved at the time to herald a major break with the past. The possibility now existed, it seemed to many to reconstruct society along new, more democratic and more equitable lines. The Conservative Party, which had held the line for so long, was reduced almost to a rump, lacking prestige and support, out of touch with the times. Among other wartime legislation, the Education Act was on the statute book. Its implementation was to become a major issue over the years to come.

Notes and References

1. Brian Simon, *The Two Nations and the Educational Structure. 1780-1870* (first published as *Studies in the History of Education, 1780-1870*), London 1960, Chapter 6. Equivalent restructuring in France and Germany is analysed in D.K. Müller, Fritz Ringer and Brian Simon (eds.), *The Rise of the Modern Educational System*, Cambridge 1987, especially Chapters 1 and 2.

2. Schools Inquiry Commission *Report*, Vol. 1 (1868), p.93.

3. Geoffrey Best, *Mid-Victorian Britain, 1851-1875*, London 1973, p.170.

4. In 1937-38, of the total (estimated) population aged 5 to 14 of 5,396,000, 4,755,105 were in elementary schools, 243,390 in secondary schools (grant-aided), and 6,561 in junior technical schools, giving a total in these three types (aged five to fourteen) of 5,005,056. The remaining 390,944 children presumably attended independent ('public' and private) schools. (Most elementary school children left at fourteen, but in secondary schools 226,385 stayed on, giving an overall total of 470,003 in these schools). *Education in 1938*, HMSO 1939, Table 2, p.91.

5. For the origins of the direct grant system, see *The Public Schools and the General Education System* (the Fleming Report), HMSO 1944, pp.32-3, and the Public School Commission, *Second Report*, Vol. 1. *Report on Independent Day Schools and Direct Grant Grammar Schools* (the Donnison Report), HMSO 1970, pp.47ff. In 1942 there were 232 such schools.

6. For a study of the inter-war period, Brian Simon, *The Politics of Educational Reform, 1920-1940*, London 1974. The figures quoted in this paragraph are taken from Tables 1, 2 and 3, pp.363-5 in this book.

7. Simon, *The Politics...*, Table 8, p.370.

8. See 'Negation by Legislation: the 1936 Act', in ibid., Chapter 5.

9. *Education in 1938*, Table 43 p.138.

10. In addition, 4.6 per cent entered teacher training colleges, another 11.7 per cent are listed as entering 'other educational institutions' (further education). Ibid., Table 46, p.143

11. Simon, *The Politics...*, Table 4, p.366

12. See Brian Simon, *A Student's View of the Universities*, London 1943, pp.39-40.

13. University Grants Committee *Report for the period 1929-30 to 1934-35*, HMSO 1936, pp.28-29.

14. See Bill Bailey, 'The Development of Technical Education, 1934-39', *History of Education*, Vol.16, No.1, March 1987.

15. Correlli Barnett, *The Audit of War*, London 1986, p.201. Barnett develops a comprehensive indictment of educational policy between the wars.
16. See Simon, *The Politics...*, pp.270-83 (section entitled 'The preserve and preservation of the public schools'). For the nature of the criticism of the public schools at this time, E.C. Mack, *Public Schools and British Opinion Since 1860*, New York 1941, pp.405ff.
17. *Secondary Education with Special Reference to Grammar Schools and Technical High Schools*, Report of the Consultative Committee to the Board of Education, HMSO 1938.
18. See Simon, *The Politics...*, pp.264-70.
19. Quoted in B. Semmel, *Imperialism and Social Reform*, London 1960, p.73.
20. H.M.D. Parker, *A Study of Wartime Policy and Administration*, London 1957, pp.326-30. I owe this reference to C. Barnett, op. cit., p.287.
21. In August 1940 the war cabinet created its own war aims committee, at the instigation of Lord Halifax, to prevent the topic getting into the hands of 'professors and propagandists', as he put it. In the papers produced for this committee, by Harold Nicolson and Arnold Toynbee, educational reconstruction was seen as crucial. However the cabinet decided, in January 1941, to publish no such statements. Barnett, op. cit., pp.20-1.
22. Donald McLachlan, *In the Chair. Barrington Ward of The Times, 1927-1948*, London 1971, p.215. Entry made 31 July 1940.
23. Harold Dent had previously been a schoolmaster in Leicester and elsewhere. 'Those war-torn years when H.C. Dent drove himself on all cylinders to take a lead in policy-making using a reinvigorated educational supplement as his vehicle, must rank as the most exhilarating, demanding and influential in the paper's history', writes Patricia Rowan in 'Out of the Shade', 75th anniversary supplement to the *Times Educational Supplement*, September 1985, p.5. 'The *TES* became not just a forum for discussion of the nascent 1944 Act but a new kind of educational journal campaigning for a reform thorough enough to last beyond post-war euphoria.' For a study of the role of the *TES* at that time, by a participant, see Joan Simon, 'Promoting Educational Reform on the Home Front: *The TES* and the *Times*, 1940-44', *History of Education*, Vol.18, No.3, September 1989.
24 *Times Educational Supplement*, 28 June 1941.
25. Ibid., 5 July 1941, 19 July 1941.
26. The previous editor of the *Times Educational Supplement*. Donald McLachlan (who later became editor of the *Daily Telegraph*) thoroughly objected to Dent's policy. Writing to Barrington-Ward in 1942 he argued that these policies were 'not such as would be advocated in the *Times*.' Hopes were held out for 'a new order' in education which was quite clearly impracticable. The supplement was too controversial and unstable at a time when it and the *Times* should be giving a strong lead. Barrington-Ward, supporting Dent in reply, adduced a 'great volume of appreciation for the contents of the Supplement'. Dent was an enthusiast 'and impatience and impulsiveness are apt to be the by-products of enthusiasm'. It was no bad thing that the Supplement should be a pace-maker in the formation of policy. He worked closely with Dent, and knew first hand that he had R.A. Butler's respect. From Rowan, op. cit.
27. *Times Educational Supplement*, 5 July 1941.
28. *Journal of Education*, May 1939. This journal, which ceased publication in the late 1950s, acted as the main forum for the discussion of the problems facing the public schools throughout this period.
29. Ibid., August 1939.
30. Ibid., July 1939.
31. *Spectator*, 17 November 1939, 9 February 1940, 16 February 1940.
32. Clarke's book was written before the war – on a boat to Canada in the summer of 1939, though the preface is dated 1 January 1940. Clarke later became the first Chairman of the Central Advisory Council for Education (England): for a biographical study, see F.W. Mitchell *Sir Fred Clarke, Master-Teacher 1880-1952*, London 1967. For

Mannheim, see Colin Loader, *The Intellectural Development of Karl Mannheim*, Cambridge 1985, especially Chapter 6, 'The Synthesis of Democratic Planning'; David Kettler, Volker Meja and Nico Stehr, *Karl Mannheim*, London 1984; and Jean Floud, 'Karl Mannheim' in Timothy Raison (ed.), *The Founding Fathers of Social Science*, Harmondsworth 1969.

33. Fred Clarke, *Education and Social Change*, London 1940, pp.9-10, 37-38, 44, 57.

34. Hugh Lyon, Head of Rugby, wrote that heads have 'uneasy consciences'; they were disturbed by the criticism that 'they thrive upon, and tend to perpetuate, a class system which is undemocratic and unjust.' *Spectator*, 24 January 1941. Of some interest, historically, is a radical article by E.G.R. Heath, 'A Secondary Schoolboy's View', ibid., 19 April 1940. This strong attack on the public schools' preferred solution (bursaries) concludes that at least all are agreed on the ultimate aim – 'to establish equality of opportunity ... by abolishing inequality in education'.

35. Worsley's teaching experiences at Wellington in the 1920s and 1930s are ironically described in *Flannelled Fools*, London 1967.

36. T.C. Worsley, *Barbarians and Philistines; Democracy and the Public Schools*, London, n.d. (1940), pp.274, 281.

37. T.C. Worsley, *The End of the 'Old School Tie'*, London 1941, pp.9-16.

38. E.C. Mack, *The Public Schools and British Opinion Since 1860*, New York 1941, pp.460-2, 458.

39. Hore-Belisha's resignation was greeted with incomprehension by the press and public since the true reasons were not divulged. Press headlines were, however, closely accurate. 'Brass Hats Have Won'; 'Generals Get Their Own Way'; 'Generals Resented his Drastic Reforms'; 'Pushed Out by the Old Gang', etc. 'It did not occur to me to consider that we were making the army too democratic to fight for democracy', said Belisha (an ex-Liberal) in his resignation speech. R.J. Minney, *The Private Papers of Hore-Belisha*, London 1960, pp. 226-86.

40. *Journal of Education*, February 1941, p.38. In a speech to Harrow boys in December 1940, Churchill said that 'When the war is won ... it must be one of our aims to work to establish a state of society where the advantage and privileges which hitherto have been enjoyed only by the few should be more widely shared by the many and the youth of the nation as a whole'. Martin Gilbert, *Winston S. Churchill*, Vol.VI, *Finest Hour, 1939-1941*, London 1983, pp. 949-50. For Churchill's later views on legislation relating to the public schools, see Anthony Howard, *RAB, The Life of R.A. Butler*, London 1987, pp. 115, 119.

41. *Journal of Education*, September to December 1940; articles (and letters) by J.W. Skinner (Culford School), W.F. Bushell (Birkenhead), J.F. Wolfenden (Uppingham), G. Turbeville (Eltham), J.K. Derry (Mill Hill), F.C. Happold (Bishop Wordsworth), Frank Fletcher (Charterhouse) and others.

42. Ibid., March 1941.

43. Some of these were triggered as responses to the Board of Education's reconstruction plans circulated (initially confidentially) in June 1941, see pp. 57-60.

44. Association of Directors and Secretaries of Education, *A Plan for the Future*, 1942, pp.4-5

45. Ibid., p.14

46. National Association of Schoolmasters, 'The Postwar Reconstruction of Education', n.d., (1942). Mimeograph (date-stamped 1942 on the Department of Education and Science library copy).

47. See, for instance, Incorporated Association of Assistant Masters (IAAM), 'Memorandum on the Education Bill' n.d. (1943?).

48. For CDRE, see Raymond King Memorial Lecture in Brian Simon, *Does Education Matter?*, London 1985, pp. 152ff.

49. P.H.J.H. Gosden, *Education in the Second World War*, London 1976, p.349. For the Fleming Committee, see pp.346-55.

50. Association of Directors and Secretaries, *A Plan for the Future*, 1942, pp.12-3.

51. Report of the Association of Education Committees (4 May 1942) and of the

Association of Municipal Corporations (23 July 1942) are among the many pamphlets, documents, etc. concerning educational reconstruction at this time collected in two large folders in the library of the Department of Education and Science, Elizabeth House, London.

52. See the Trade Union Congress's *Memorandum on Education after the War* (1942), The Co-operative Union's war-time Booklets 1, 'Plans for an Educated Democracy' (1942) by John Thomas, and the Workers' Educational Association's *Plan for Education* (1942).

53. Council for Education Advance, Education Leaflet No.1. n.d. (1943). (This series of leaflets are in the DES library.)

54. Simon, *The Politics...*, pp.258ff.

55. The relevant resolution called on the Board of Education 'to encourage, as a general policy, the development of a new type of multilateral school'. *Labour Party Conference Report 1942*, p.140.

56. For pressure by the (well-organised) educational left in the Labour Party on this issue during the war, see R.G. Wallace, 'Labour, the Board of Education and the Preparation of the 1944 Act', unpublished University of London Ph.D thesis, 1980. Wallace sees the Act as a 'defeat for Labour'.

57. National Association of Labour Teachers, *The Post-War Reconstruction of Education (1941)*. In *Britain's Schools*, a memorandum issued by the Communist Party of Great Britain, n.d. (February 1943), the object was stated to be to 'incorporate into one school ... the technical, commercial, scientific and academic education now provided in separate schools.'

58. This 15,000 word pamphlet, entitled *A Democratic Reconstruction of Education* (1942), covered all areas of education. Its strongest criticisms were reserved for the public schools.

59. Cyril Burt, 'Problems of Post-War Reconstruction', preliminary report (mimeograph); copy sent to Julian Huxley, now in the possession of Joan Simon. This report was written up for *Occupational Psychology*, as 'An Enquiry into Public Opinion Regarding Educational Reform', Parts 1 and 2, Vols 17 and 18, 1943 and 1944.

60. Fred Clarke, 'Educational Research in the New Setting', *British Journal of Educational Psychology*, Vol. XIV, Part 1, February 1944.

61. PRO ED136/300 for Savage's document and related materials including a full record of this discussion. See Simon, *The Politics ...*, pp. 324-28; Gosden, op.cit., pp. 302-3.

62. TUC *Memorandum on Education After the War* (1942), p.4.

63. Sir Alan Bullock, *The Life and Times of Ernest Bevin*, Vol.1, *Trade Union Leader*, London 1960, pp.84-85. For Bevin's powerful support for the 1944 Act, see Vol.II (1967), pp.237-38. See also R,G. Wallace, 'The Man Behind Butler', *Times Educational Supplement*, 27 March 1981, and, in particular, the Chuter Ede diaries (12 vols.), British Library Add. MSS., 59690 – 59702; for instance, entry for 7 December 1943.

64. For the School Age Council, Simon, *The Politics ...*, pp.199-202.

65. Nigel Middleton and Sophia Weitzman, *A Place for Everyone*, London 1976, p.225.

66. Association of Directors and Secretaries, *A Plan for the Future*, Chapter 4.

67. Association of Education Committees report op. cit., (May 1942).

68. For a useful summary of these views, Middleton and Weitzman, op. cit., pp.251-5.

69. H.C. Dent, *A New Order in English Education*, London 1942, pp. 5-7, 14.

70. Ibid., pp.13, 22-25.

71. Ibid., pp.31-36.

72. Ibid., p.41.

73. Ibid., pp.58-9. The LCC's support for the multilateral school was very clearly expressed in their evidence to the Norwood Committee of July 1942. For this committee, see pp. 60-4 above. At about this time Chuter Ede, after lunching with

'various education people' (including a University Vice Chancellor) noted in his diary (op. cit., 10 July 1942), 'It was surprising that we were all agreed that multilateral schools were the right solution to the secondary problem.'

74. Ibid., p.81.

75. Quoted from Gosden, op. cit., p. 238. Holmes was already clearly concerned about the activities of bodies like the WEA.

76. For a contemporary evaluation of the effect of evacuation, H.C. Dent, *Education in Transition*, London 1944, Chapters 1 and 2. See also Gosden, op. cit., pp.12ff and Richard Titmuss, *Problems of Social Policy*, HMSO 1950 (the official history), chapters 7-10, 18 and 21. Specialist studies include John MacNicol. 'The Effect of the Evacuation of Schoolchildren on Official Attitudes to State Intervention' in Harold L. Smith (ed.), *War and Social Change*, Manchester 1986; Travis L. Crosby, *The Impact of Civilian Education in the Second World War*, London 1986; Ruth Inglis, *The Children's War*, London 1989.

77. The so-called 'Green Book', a lengthy, detailed document, is reprinted in full as an appendix in Nigel Middleton and Sophia Weitzman, op. cit. For a fair assessment of Ramsbotham's role as President of the Board ('he sowed a harvest which his successor, Richard Butler, was to gather in'), see ibid., pp.217-34; see also Chuter Ede diaries, op. cit., entries for 20 and 21 July 1941. Ramsbotham 'has grieved at going ... he wanted to get his scheme for education through'.

78. Neville Heaton. 'Forty Years On', *Times Educational Supplement*, 20 January 1984.

79. R.G. Wallace, 'The origins and authorship of the 1944 Education Act', *History of Education*, Vol. 10, Number 4 December 1981, pp. 283-90. In 'R.A. Butler, the Board of Education and the 1944 Education Act', *History*, 69 (227), October 1984, Kevin Jefferys challenges Wallace's interpretation, emphasising the importance of Butler's personal contribution to both Bill and Act.

80. Gosden, op. cit., pp.248-9.

81. 'The variety of tradition which ... relative financial autonomy has enabled them to preserve is an element of great and characteristic value in English education'. *Green Book*, Middleton and Weitzman, op. cit., p. 458.

82. Gosden, op. cit., pp.367ff.

83. Ibid., p.368.

84. J.A. Petch, *Fifty Years of Examining*, London 1953, p. 166. Petch's analysis of these events is of considerable interest, and relevance. He was Secretary of the Northern Universities Joint Matriculation Board and a member of the SSEC.

85. *Curriculum and Examinations in Secondary Schools* (The Norwood Report), HMSO 1943, pp.1-4.

86. After describing grammar, 'senior' (modern) and technical schools, the paper states. 'Such, then, *will be* the three main types of secondary schools to be known as grammar, modern and technical schools' (my emphasis, B.S.).

87. PRO ED136/681 (Butler to Holmes and Williams, 6 June 1943).

88. H.C. Dent, *Education in Transition*, London 1944, pp.230-1.

89. Gosden, op. cit., pp.368, 384; Petch, op. cit., p.165. Petch describes this procedure as 'official chicanery'.

90. Julian Huxley. 'Philosophy of the Norwood Report', *Times Educational Supplement*, 28 August 1943. For the first penetrating criticism of Norwood's 'philosophy', see letter headed 'Learning for its own sake', from Joan Simon, *TES* 31 July 1943. The Huxley article was commissioned at her suggestion.

91. 'The Psychological Implications of the Norwood Report'. *British Journal of Educational Psychology*, Vol. 13 Part 3, November 1943, pp. 126-40. Hearnshaw, Burt's biographer, comments as follows: 'It is hard not to feel that some of (Burt's criticism) were actuated by pique against the neglect of psychological evidence, including his own, and that they mask a basic agreement with the recommendations, which in principle did not differ so much from those of the Spens Committee which he had earlier approved'. L.S. Hearnshaw, *Cyril Burt, Psychologist*, London 1979, pp. 117-8.

92. Fred Clarke, 'Educational Research in the New Setting', *British Journal of Educational Psychology*, Vol. XIV, Part 1, February 1944. S.J. Curtis, *Education in Britain Since 1900*, London 1952, pp.114-5.

93. Gosden, op. cit., p. 345. For Butler's 'failure of nerve' on the public school issue, see Anthony Howard, op. cit., pp. 118-23. It is Howard's assessment that Butler's handling of the public school question 'represented the one real failure in his general strategy for educational reconstruction', adding that 'The time was ripe, the public mood was propitious, the opportunity was there' (p.122).

94. An episode effectively dealt with by Gosden, op. cit., pp.351-3.

95. Lord Butler, *The Art of the Possible*, London 1971, p.120.

96. D.W. Dean, 'Problems of the Conservative Sub-Committee on Education, 1941-45', *Journal of Educational Administration and History*, Vol. III No. 1 (December 1970), pp. 266-7.

97. Butler, op. cit., p. 119.

98. The reference here is not to the Baker legislation (1988 Act) but to Sir William Alexander, *Towards a New Education Act*, London 1969; Richard Aldridge and Margaret Leighton's *Education: Time for a New Act?* (Bedford Way Papers 23, 1985) and similar publications.

99. In 'Looking Ahead', the first interim report of the Conservative party's Sub-Committee on Education (September 1942) the committee state that 'It must be a primary duty of national education to develop a strong sense of national obligation in the individual citizen, to encourage in him an ardent understanding of the State's needs, and to render him capable of serving those needs'. Our children 'must be taught to be proud of their ancestors and their inheritance, and to accept the consequent responsibilities of a colonising and missionary world-power'. What was needed was 'a thorough-going overhaul of the whole educational system'. The second interim report, entitled 'A Plan for Youth', stressed the need for the enrolment of all young people aged fourteen to eighteen in organisations giving them opportunities for 'service to the State', and ensuring that all have opportunities 'for individual training of body, mind and character as well as for collective discipline'. After the furore occasioned by these two publications, the sub-committee was quiescent until, in January 1944, it published its third 'interim report', on 'The Statutory Education System'. This final report, under Butler's influence, adopted a more constructive approach than the earlier ones. The chairman of this sub-committee was G.S. Faber, a publisher and not an MP. For the work (and politics) of this committee, D.W. Dean, op. cit.; see also Jose Harris, 'Political Ideas and Social Change' in Harold L. Smith (ed.), *War and Social Change*, Manchester 1986, pp.239-46.

100. *Labour Party Conference Report, 1942*, p.141. Butler himself remarked that at this time 'much of the drive' towards educational reform 'comes from Labour'. Howard, op. cit., pp.116-7.

101. The Chairman of the Council for Educational Advance was R.H. Tawney. Ernest Green and Harold Shearman were Hon. Treasurer and Hon. Secretary respectively. All three were leading members of the Workers' Educational Association. In addition there were 15 others, including Ronald Gould and A.E. Henshall from the National Union of Teachers.

102. *TUC Report*, 1942 p.60.

103. Butler had received Cabinet approval for his proposal to draft a Bill on 18 December 1942. But negotiations with the churches still held things up. Middleton and Weitzman, op. cit., p.263.

104. *Educational Reconstruction*, Cmd 6458, HMSO 1943, p. 3. The emphasis on 'variety' was frequently stressed by Butler. 'The strength of our institutions, as Disraeli said, lies in their vigour and variety. In every speech I have made on education I have applauded the variegated structure of our system ... we should attempt to keep in our educational system openings and opportunities for different types and aptitudes'. *Times Educational Supplement*, 1 October 1942.

105. *Educational Reconstruction*, pp. 6, 3, 10.

106. This settlement, which in fact saved the dual system, was, of course, Butler's main contribution to the Act, as he himself stressed later. In *The Art of Memory*, 1982, Butler wrote, 'As I have already pointed out, much of my time had been spent negotiating a diplomatic solution to the problem of the relationship of state and church schools'. For differing interpretations of the significance of Butler's role, see R.G. Wallace, op. cit., and K. Jefferys, op. cit. See also Marjorie Cruickshank, *Church and State in English Education*, London 1963; James Murphy, *Church, State and Schools in Britain, 1800-1970*, London 1971; and Anthony Howard, *RAB, The Life of R.A. Butler*.

107. *Educational Reconstruction*, pp. 4, 11.

108. Ibid., Appendix 'The financial implications of the proposals', pp. 34-36.

109. *TUC Report*, 1943, pp. 64-5.

110. Lord Butler, *The Art of the Possible*, p.129.

111. Paul Addison, *The Road to 1945*, London 1975, pp. 216-17. See Chapter 8, 'The People's William', for a precise analysis of this episode.

112. Ibid., Hartmut Kopsch in 'The Approach of the Conservative Party to Social Policy during World War Two', unpublished University of London PhD thesis (1970), pp. 52ff., includes a detailed account of the deep concern, among Conservative members of the government, at the implications of the Beveridge report.

113. Addison, op. cit., pp.224ff.

114. Ibid., p.237.

115. Butler, *The Art of the Possible*, p.117. This is clearly confirmed by Chuter Ede, op. cit., entry for 1 November 1943.

116. Addison, op. cit., p.237.

117. Ibid., p. 238.

118. Ibid., 238; Butler, *The Art of the Possible*, p.117.

119. The Bill was (unusually) discussed in committee of the whole House (of Commons) – a means of keeping MP's occupied. Two clauses were in fact threatened, due to the coincidence of discontent on the Labour backbenches with a decision by the Tory Reform Committee to challenge the government. Thelma Cazalet-Keir, a member of this group, moved two amendments in March 1944. The first called for a leaving age of 16 by 1951 to be written into the Bill, the second demanding equal pay for women teachers. On the latter issue the government was defeated by one vote (117 to 116) – according to Addison 'the only significant point on which the Coalition was beaten in a division' (there were 150 abstentions). The next day Churchill demanded a reversal of the vote, treating it as a vote of confidence, and winning by a large majority. Addison, op. cit., pp. 238-9; this incident is fully treated in the Chuter Ede diaries, op. cit., entries for 28 March to 4 April 1944. This action had the effect of muting any further attempts at securing amendments to the Bill.

120. For actions taken after the Fleming Committee reports, see Gosden op. cit., pp.355ff. By 1944 the public schools had weathered the financial storms of 1939-41 and were no longer seriously interested even in a slightly closer relation with the maintained system, as Fleming had proposed.

121. The relevant paragraph of the famous secondary education section reads as follows: 'The schools available for an area shall not be deemed to be sufficient unless they are sufficient in number, character and equipment to afford for all pupils opportunities for education offering such variety of instruction and training as may be desirable in view of their different ages, abilities and aptitudes, and of the different period for which they may be expected to remain at school, including practical instruction and training appropriate to their respective needs'.

In connection with this formulation, Edward Boyle's description of how Butler's chief parliamentary draughtsman, Sir Granville Ram, assured him 'that the Act could meet the needs of at least a generation provided it does not seek to exclude experiments with multilateral schools' is worth recalling, as an example of the care then taken. Philip H. James, *The Reorganisation of Secondary Education*, Slough 1980, p.72.

122. After stating that 'compulsory school age means any age between 5 and 15 years', section 35 continues 'provided that, as soon as the Minister is satisfied that it has become practicable to raise to 16 the upper limit of the compulsory school age', he shall lay a draft Order before Parliament giving effect to this decision.

123. James Murphy, *Church, State and School in Britain, 1800-1870*, London 1971, p. 114. Murphy deals effectively in this book with developments in this area through the 1950s and 1960s.

124. The Fleming Committee was asked, on 7 November 1942, to report on the abolition of fees in grant-aided secondary schools. The majority (eleven) favoured abolition, with a minority (of seven) opposed abolition (*Abolition of Tuition Fees in Grant-Aided Secondary Schools*, HMSO 1943). In a *Guardian* leader later, R.H. Tawney defined Butler's refusal to implement this advice as 'capitulation'. 'Hard pressed by the diehards of his party, to whom the suggestion that 'capacity and promise' should count for more than money smelt alarmingly of Bolshevism, he surrendered to an arrangement condemned in advance by the words of his own White Paper'. *Manchester Guardian*, 7 May 1945.

125. The relevant section (43) states that 'As soon after the date of the commencement of this Part of the Act (1 April 1945, Section 119) as the Minister considers it practicable to do so, he shall direct every local education authority to estimate the immediate and prospective needs of their area with respect to county colleges having regard to the provisions of this Act ...'. In practice, succeeding Ministers never considered it 'practical to do so'. This, and related, sections were (ironically) repealed by the 1988 Education 'Reform' Act (Section 120(5)).

126. The relevant part of Section 11 reads as follows: 'As soon as may be after the date of the commencement of this Part of this Act every local education authority shall estimate the immediate and prospective needs of their area having regard to the provisions of this Act and of any regulations made thereunder and to the functions relating to primary and secondary education thereby confirmed on them, and shall, within one year after that date or within such extended period as the Minister may in any particular case allow, prepare and submit to the Minister a plan (in this Act referred to as a 'development plan') in such form as the Minister may direct for securing that there shall be sufficient primary and secondary schools available for their area and the successive measures by which it is proposed to accomplish that purpose'. Similar provision was made for schemes of further education (Section 42). The Act made the provision of 'adequate facilities for further education' a 'duty' of local authorities, rather than a permissive power, as previously (Section 41).

127. Paul Addison regards the Act as a cautious, typically conservative measure (or 'Tory project'), quoting approvingly Hartmut Kopsch's evaluation:
   'Conservative MPs did not perfunctorily acquiesce in Butler's proposals for educational reform; they applauded the White Paper on educational reconstruction and the Education Bill, since these measures incorporated many key Conservative beliefs, notably the belief in the relevance of traditional religious values, the belief in variety and quality rather than "gross volume", the belief in the desirability of preserving educational privileges and the belief in hierarchy.' Addison, op. cit., pp.237-8; the quotation is from Kopsch, op. cit., pp.385-6.

128. G.C.T. Giles, *The New School Tie*, London 1946, p.25; H.C. Dent, *The New Education Bill, what it contains, what it means, and why it should be supported*, London 1944.

129. In spite of a clear warning from successive opinion polls over the last few months, Addison, op. cit., pp.248-49. One to be greatly surprised was James Chuter Ede. On the day before the election result was announced (25 July) he noted in his diary that he was told that G.R. Strauss had foretold an absolute majority for Labour, 'but I know no one else who takes so optimistic a view'.

130. David Butler and Gareth Butler, *British Political Facts 1900-1985*. 6th ed., London 1986, p.226. Total votes for the main parties in 1935 and 1945 were as follows: Conservative 11,810,158 in 1935, 9,988,306 in 1945. Labour 8,325,491 in 1935,

11,995,152 in 1945. Liberal 1,422,116 in 1935, 2,248,226 in 1945. Labour therefore increased their vote from 8 million to nearly 12 million – an increase of more than 3.5 million. The Conservative vote was reduced by some 2 million. The Liberals gained nearly a million more votes in 1945. The main feature is clearly the big extension of the Labour vote (the total vote in 1945 was up by 3 million over 1935). See Appendix I, p.563.

131. Addison argues that nearly 3 million in the services were entitled to vote, i.e. those 'whose officers managed to arrange for their names to be placed on the service register', Addison, op. cit., p.267. For the different way commanding officers carried out this duty, see Angus Calder, *The People's War, Britain 1939-45*, London 1969, pp.581-2; also R.B. McCallum and A. Readman, *The British General Election of 1945*, London 1947, p.43.

132. Addison, op. cit., 'Those with memories of the separate count made of the servicemen's ballot papers recall that it was overwhelmingly Left Wing, e.g. 90% Labour in the case of Reading, where Ian Mikardo was candidate', Penelope Summerfield, 'Education and Politics in the British Armed Forces in the Second World War', *International Review of Social History*, XXVI (1981) Part 2, p. 133. This article contains an acute analysis of the role and development of army education in World War II.

133. Addison, op. cit., pp.267-8.

134. A start has been made, as regards army education, by Penny Summerfield (note 132), and by Neil Grant, 'Citizen Soldiers: Army Education in World War II' in Formation Editorial Collective, *Formation of Nation and People*, London 1984. See also N. Scarlyn Wilson, *Education in the Forces, 1936-46, The Civilian Contribution*, London, n.d. (1948-9?).

2 The Labour Government in Control, 1945-51

1 Excitement and New Hopes

Assessing the Labour victory of 1945, Kenneth Morgan concludes that, 'Labour was uniquely identified with a sweeping change of mood during the war years, and with the new social agenda that emerged.'[1] A variety of factors, he continues, 'enabled Labour to exploit the vogue for planning and egalitarianism during the war, and to turn them to electoral advantage in a way impossible for the Conservative members of the late Coalition'. In face of the long-term Liberal decline, 'Labour alone seemed to understand and project the new mood'. It reinforced it 'by bringing its own traditional supporters out to vote in unprecedented numbers', and by breaking down old parochial and ethnic barriers in the major industrial cities 'which had long held back the Labour cause'. The massive victory 'left its leading figures stunned and for a moment almost overwhelmed'.[2] The House of Commons, when it first reassembled after the election, reverberated to the enthusiastic singing by the massed ranks of Labour of the traditional socialist song, The Red Flag. A new era, it seemed, had opened. Many felt that the old order could never again be re-imposed.

The Labour electoral programme had been finalised, not without opposition, in April 1945 (three months before the election). This included a series of radical measures involving the nationalisation of the coal industry, of gas, electricity, transport, of the Bank of England, and, more controversially, of iron and steel – a measure originally opposed by Greenwood and Morrison. 'No clearer indication could be found of the grass roots vitality within the party surging up during the war years', writes Morgan, 'than this decision on steel nationalisation'. These measures, largely relating to industry, formed one prong of the Labour government's programme. The other, of at least equal importance, concerned the creation of the welfare state, including the maintenance of full employment. Here Labour reaffirmed their determination to implement the 'key sections' of the Beveridge Report concerning social security, to establish a National Health Service, and to carry through a major drive on housing (an important issue in the election).[3] There were, of course, other areas where action was promised, including, for instance, town and country planning. Among these was education, where the Act providing the framework for development was already on the statute book, having received Royal Assent almost a full year before the election results of 1945 were declared.

Education: The Changed Atmosphere

The Act, as we have noted, placed many new duties on local authorities who, among other things, now had to produce development plans for both primary and secondary education within their areas, as well as working out plans covering the whole field of further education. A sense of the movement – even excitement – of the period has been well caught by Martin Wilson, Shropshire's Chief Education Officer from 1936 to 1965. Looking back on this period after retirement, Wilson remembers it as one of massive, even frenetic, activity. He writes that:

> There was, of course, too much of everything to be done at once, and thus high pressure, much tension and turbulence, feverish endeavour liable to be thwarted by events. Piles of paperasserie. A multitude of meetings. A clangour of consultations and claims. No hours enough in the seven days (but, he adds) tremendously invigorating, taut, demanding, challenging, speculative, open.

This was 'the epoch ... that one had been waiting for', and, in local administration, 'one was at the grass roots of growth'. Perhaps, he adds, this was 'the last grand flourish and fanfare of local government'.[4]

The formulation of the development plan for Shropshire

> was a tough and infinitely complex administrative exercise. Every school had to be surveyed, the state of its building, the disposition of its children and probable population and housing trends; and a decision

made about its future. [Then] a new pattern of secondary education
had to be worked out, for all children, to a higher age.

All this had to be turned into 'a costed programme, phased
into priorities year by year'. No sooner was this done 'than the
whirl of planning was to be plunged into all over again – to plot
the future needs of all beyond school age'. So, concludes
Martin Wilson, 'the addition of the Scheme for Further
Education to the development plan for primary and secondary
education presented for the first time an all-embracing
educational programme from the cradle to the grave'.[5]

Such perspectives, and indeed activity, if necessarily in
forward planning, was something quite new in the experience of
most local education authorities and their officers. These had
survived the depressing period of retrenchment, characterised
by succeeding economic cuts, between the wars. Now,
suddenly, it seemed, the brakes were off. Planning for the
future was a new experience, but now such planning, in all
spheres, very much met the ethos of the time. Seen from this
angle, the new ministry suddenly appeared as a highly activist
department of government, in sharp contrast to its image
before the war. From 1 April 1945 – the 'appointed day' for
the Education Act of 1944 – 'a regular spate of circulars,
memoranda, and regulations proceeded without pause from
the ministry', wrote F.F. Potter, Cheshire's Chief Education
Officer since 1922, and now approaching retirement. 'Local
chief officers and their staffs made brave efforts to deal with
this flood of 'paper', and every department of the office
worked at full pressure'.[6] The New Act 'imposed upon
authorities an immense volume of new work' whilst national
(and possibly political) considerations required that 'much
should be accomplished in a limited time'. By 1947, Potter
concluded, the 1944 Education Act 'had at least *trebled* the
volume of work in an ordinary county education department'.
Somewhat ruefully, Potter (very much a traditionalist)
concluded that it had been his fate, at the end of his career, to
see the fabric of public education in Cheshire 'so patiently
fashioned in the years from 1922 – 1939, somewhat ruthlessly
overhauled and drastically reconditioned by post-war needs
and requirements'.[7]

Neither Cheshire, nor for that matter Shropshire, can be
said to have been in the van of educational progress, either

before the war or after. Both were, perhaps, rather typical of the 'shire county' educational organisation and ethos that was brought to a sudden end by local government reorganisation in 1972. Nevertheless few local education administrators have left their memoirs, or written of their personal experiences in this period. The witness of Wilson and Potter therefore has value; the pressure on the large urban authorities, where the mass of population are educated, was probably even greater than appears from these two accounts. 'It is difficult to write about the elan and zest of those early post-war years,' wrote Alec Clegg, appointed Director for the West Riding, a highly populous area, in 1945. 'We had been held back for eight years and all of us, central government, local committees and officials, were eager to forge ahead.' This well encapsulates the feeling at that time.[8]

New Plans in Higher Education

But it was not only in the fields of primary and secondary education that plans were now being made for the future. Already towards the close of the war attention had turned towards the whole, relatively backward area of university and higher technological education. The Education Act of 1944 left these important areas totally untouched – but war experience and discussions underlined the need for change.[9] As a direct result of growing criticism from industrialists, technical college principals and others about the lack of concern for technical education as well as the minimal funding proposed in the 1943 White Paper for post-war development, the wartime Coalition government appointed a committee on Higher Technological Education, chaired by Lord Eustace Percy, on 5 April 1944. This reported in the summer of 1945, setting out a comprehensive and, to some extent, a radical policy aimed at rapidly expanding, and raising the status, prestige and level of 'a limited number' of local technical colleges which should develop courses comparable to university degree courses. The perspective was that, by this means, an alternative structure should be developed alongside the universities.[10]

Again, in April 1944, replying to a debate in the House of Commons on research and scientific knowledge, Attlee, as Deputy Prime Minister, gave a number of assurances as to future action. A motion, moved by the Tory Sir Granville Gibson, urged 'the declaration of a bold and generous government policy of financial assistance directed to the expansion of teaching and research facilities in our universities and technical colleges'. 'This', said Attlee, 'we shall give'; he added that the government (fully) recognised that there would have to be 'much greater expenditure both on fundamental research and on teaching at the universities'. It is 'quite obvious', he concluded, 'that it would be rather a futile thing to be passing a great education bill through the house and to neglect the universities at the top'.[11]

It was not, however, until December 1945, five months after the election, that the main committee concerned with university expansion and development was appointed. The Barlow Committee (chaired by Sir Alan Barlow, Second Secretary to the Treasury) was set up specifically to propose policies relating to scientific manpower over the next ten years – hence the title of its report 'Scientific Manpower' (The Barlow Report) which it was asked to produce 'at an early date'. In fact this committee of leading scientists (it included Sir Edward Appleton, Professor Blackett, Professor Zuckermann, with C.P. Snow as 'Scientific Assessor') worked quickly, the report being published within five months (in May 1946).[12] 'Never before has the importance of science been so widely recognised or so many hopes of future progress and welfare founded upon the scientist,' wrote the committee setting the tone for their proposals. Calculating the total number of scientists as 35,000, and that on existing plans this would rise to 64,000 by 1955, they estimated actual demand in that year at 90,000. Output must, therefore, be raised 'very much above the level of present university proposals'. The immediate aim 'should be to double the present output, giving us roughly 5,000 newly qualified scientists per annum at the earliest possible moment'.[13]

The report reflects the contemporary sense of urgency. The committee were well aware of the opposition from traditionalists to radical university expansion. Where was the expanded output of science graduates to come from? Here the committee, interestingly (in retrospect) relied on the evidence (or opinions) of psychologists – specifically from Professor Godfrey Thomson and Dr Leybourne White who tested samples of students from Scottish universities and Manchester University respectively. This indicated that 5 per cent of the population had intelligence as great as the upper half of the students, who amounted to only 1 per cent of their age cohort. It followed that only one in five, with intelligence on a level with this top half of the students, actually reached university. From this the committee concluded that 'there is already an ample reserve of intelligence in the country to allow both a doubling of the university numbers and at the same time a raising of standards'.[14]

The universities had already been asked to prepare plans for expansion by the University Grants Committee. According to the Barlow Committee, the response of both Oxford and Cambridge to this request had been a refusal to countenance any expansion whatever over the 1938-39 position, when both universities together contained 11,000 students. The civic universities (Leeds, Manchester, Bristol, Birmingham, etc.), on the other hand, had themselves proposed an expansion of 86 per cent, the University of Wales 50 per cent, the Scottish universities 32 per cent and London University 53 per cent, giving an overall proposed expansion of 45 per cent. But this, the committee held, would be inadequate, and in fact it proposed a full doubling of the output of scientists. Arguing that there was likely also to be a big increase in the demand for 'trained ability' generally and that 'all branches of learning' should 'flourish in harmony', the committee also gave their support to 'a substantial expansion' in the number of students studying the humanities – these 'should not be sacrificed to the need for an increased output of scientists and technologists'.[15]

A number of recommendations were made concerning buildings, teachers and equipment, while the need for a greatly enhanced exchequer grant to the University Grants Committee (UGC) was underlined. The Barlow Committee also strongly supported the foundation of 'at least one new university', as well as the proposal that the five (then small) existing university colleges (Nottingham, Southampton, Exeter, Hull and Leicester) should become fully fledged universities 'at the earliest possible date'.[16] The UGC itself, from operating as a 'passive body' must 'concern itself with positive university policy' – its terms of reference might be strengthened. Among its recommendations the committee supported the recent Percy Committee's proposals relating to the establishment of full-time university type courses at 'a selected and limited number of technical colleges' and for the setting up of a few Institutes of Technology 'preferably in the university cities'. They added 'the parallel needs of the special technical colleges must be met and a regional and national system developed for knitting together the schools, the technical colleges, the higher technical institutes, the universities and industry'. 'When all possible measures are taken,' the committee concluded, 'the nation will certainly be seriously short of scientists in 1950 and is unlikely to have an adequate supply by 1955'.[17]

The concerns of the Barlow Committee were underlined seven months later (December 1946) by a report on 'universities and the increase of scientific manpower' by the Parliamentary and Scientific Committee – an unofficial body comprising 200 MP's and peers, together with representatives from 70 scientific and technical institutes. This was an important pressure group taking a very positive line. The committee welcomed the Barlow Report's recommendation that at least 90,000 scientists would be needed by 1955. This, it added, needs 'an urgent and determined attack on the problems involved'. 'A bold policy by the universities backed by firm assurances from the government of adequate financial support and an adequate influx of students, are essential'. The committee estimated that the capital cost of university expansion over the next decade would amount to £100 million, and that annual expenditure would have to rise to about £30 million. 'As far as possible,' it insisted, pre-figuring the 'Robbins principle', 'no young person of requisite ability should be prevented by financial considerations from participating in these increased facilities for university education.' The need for a parallel expansion of secondary education was also stressed. The committee's main conclusion is printed in capitals. Government help must be forthcoming without delay. But financial assistance alone is inadequate. The highest priority must be given to provision of the manpower and materials needed for the increased accommodation required at the universities. Without such priority it would not be possible to 'secure that rapid and sustained increase in scientific manpower which is so vital to the well being and prosperity of the British Commonwealth in the years that lie ahead'.[18]

The Parliamentary and Scientific Committee proposed expansion of the total number of students over the next five years to 108,000, estimated the cost of expansion, and proposed an all-embracing Council of Higher Education, including students, as a forum for effective discussion of the whole field, as in fact this body had already proposed in an earlier report (1943).[19]

There was, then, engendered in the early post-war phase an atmosphere of urgency in the area of planning expansion in university and higher technological education generally, just as there was in the schools and so among local authorities. It is clear that the big issue in higher education was seen to be a radical expansion in science and to a lesser extent in technology, to meet the needs of the economy – and particularly development of the export trade. Neither of these two reports argues for the expansion of education as a 'good' in itself, though the Barlow Report, as already mentioned, finishes with an encomium on this, deliberately rebutting the charge that their approach is purely materialist. The report of the Parliamentary and Scientific Committee also refers briefly to the need for balance in university studies, and accepts that non-scientific studies should expand *pari passu* (though no clear argument is presented for this). It was in this climate of expansion, and recognition of the national responsibilities of universities, that Hugh Dalton, as Chancellor of the Exchequer, committed government and universities to a new relationship in his announcement of July 1946. This concerned the extended role of the UGC, emphasising that in future this body should assist 'the preparation and execution of such plans for the development of the universities' as may be required 'to ensure that they are fully adequate to national needs'.[20]

The Perspective of the Act: A View From 1945

There were, then, plans for educational advance right across the board, and high hopes for the future. The tone and feeling of the time is well caught in G.C.T. Giles' book *The New School Tie*, published early in 1946. Giles had been President of the National Union of Teachers – then by far the largest and most prestigious teacher organisation – during 1944, the year of the Act, and had been involved in negotiations relating to its passage, as well as speaking at more than 200 meetings on both Bill and Act in a single year. For many years headmaster of Acton Grammar School, an old Etonian and yet a long-standing and staunch member of the Communist Party, Giles was widely respected and a strong supporter of the Act and its potential, while also clearly aware of its major weaknesses. In his book, written in 1945, he was concerned to stress the positive aspects of the Act, its potential for inaugurating fundamental changes in the structure and ethos of education, while stressing also 'the magnitude of the task' and the obstacles that lay ahead. Strongly critical of the tripartite system, Giles devoted a full chapter to 'The Secondary School of the Future' which argued that the only appropriate educational form meeting the needs of mid-century must be the single comprehensive, or multilateral school embodying a common curriculum, or core, for all between eleven and thirteen. He also placed great emphasis on the establishment of county colleges – 'with a real drive to speed up the emergency training scheme, and a well-organised building plan, it should be possible', he claimed 'to staff and accommodate the county colleges in 1948'. This is in connection with the ministry's recent announcement that the county colleges would be established in 1950. In a final chapter entitled 'It's Up to Us' Giles reiterates his view that 'in spite of certain weaknesses', the Act is progressive and democratic, adding that it provides 'a practicable working drawing for a new system'. Already, he says, 'the champions of the old school tie have plucked up their courage, and are fighting to retain their privileges'. Others are exploiting to the full 'the delaying tactics of a defeated and retreating army'. However, 'a new democratic consciousness is arising'. Already it has found practical expression 'in the surge of feeling which swept Labour to power in the General Election ... It is sweeping away the political obstacles in the path of social including educational advance'. Giles finishes his book on a note of welcome to Ellen Wilkinson 'the first Labour Minister of Education'. Coming up through the hard way herself, 'she has shown already that she realised that there can be no real and lasting democracy without a democratic educational system'. We, the common people of Britain, 'share with her a tremendous task and a grand opportunity' Giles concludes. It is up to us. 'The old is dead. We shall die with it unless we can give birth to the new.'[21]

2 New Developments in Education

Many of the provisions of the Education Act of 1944 came into force, as we have seen, on 1 April 1945. An indication of what this meant in practice is that, after a series of tough negotiations ('prolonged and difficult' according to Giles), on this date agreement was reached in the Burnham Committee on a new salary structure for teachers, so wiping out discrimination against teachers in the old elementary schools and laying down basic national scales for all qualified teachers (though retaining discrimination against women teachers). Draft regulations published in March 1945, covering primary and secondary schools, as well as draft building regulations published earlier (November 1944), embodied the principles of unification and levelling up as defined in the Act. All such measures followed directly on the legislation of 1944.[22]

Raising the Leaving Age

A major immediate issue was, of course, that of raising the school leaving age to fifteen – still generally seen as the initial step in a rise to sixteen. The Ministry of Education estimated that 200,000 additional school places would be required as well as 13,000 teachers over and above those required to meet natural wastage. Since this is the only (serious) matter that Ellen Wilkinson brought to the Cabinet for decision, and since recent defences of Ellen Wilkinson's actions as minister have placed great stress on her role here, it is worth devoting some attention to this issue.

There is no doubt that there was a battle within the Labour government on this question, though hardly reaching the epic proportions that have been suggested. This was fought out in Cabinet committees, and finally successfully in full Cabinet. The date for implementing this section of the Act had already been postponed by Butler as early as 17 August 1944 (that is, just two weeks after the Act had received Royal Assent).[23] By the Order then made the raising of the age was postponed 'to a date not later than 1st April 1947'. The issue was, should this date be adhered to or should this measure be further postponed?

The matter was first raised in Cabinet in August 1945. A memorandum by Ellen Wilkinson set out the position as regards teachers and accommodation and stated clearly that she was satisfied that, while there was no possibility of raising the age earlier, 'it can be done by that date'. 'I regard it as of importance that the government's decision ... should be announced without delay', she continued, so that local authorities realise that the government is in earnest. 'We must make it clear also that we intend to stick to this date'. Since the issue had labour resource implications she 'needs a decision of the cabinet [on the] urgency of the matter'.[24]

At the Cabinet meeting itself, Ellen Wilkinson pointed out that this measure could not be postponed beyond 1 April 1947 without legislation. She added that local authorities would not press on with effective preparations unless the government made its decision clear, saying also that the measure was 'politically necessary'. The Cabinet minutes record general agreement that, from the political point of view, it would be a great embarrassment to the present government to legislate for postponement (a clear reference to the strength of popular expectations). Chuter Ede, now Home Secretary, revealed that he and Butler had intended to raise the age on 30 September 1946, but he now thought April the better month and strongly supported Ellen Wilkinson. Aneurin Bevan expressed concern about its effect on the housing programme, local authorities had been urged to give this 'immediate attention'. The outcome was referral to an ad-hoc committee chaired by Herbert Morrison (Lord President) to report back as soon as possible.[25]

The committee reported in the following month. Holding that the raising of the school age would be 'generally regarded as a test of the government's sincerity' and that 'for political reasons we must stick to the date provided for it in the Education Act 1944 if it is humanly possible to do so', the committee finally decided, after a long discussion on accommodation and teacher supply problems, that it was possible. It would be necessary for a time to accept very imperfect conditions, with temporary and makeshift accommodation and over-large classes, but, the committee agreed, the step can and should be taken. This recommendation was endorsed by the Cabinet after a short discussion on 4 September 1945.[26]

External pressure to implement this section of the Act, and indeed, to ensure effective preparation to raise the leaving age to sixteen was now maintained. In May 1946 a deputation from the TUC pressed this specific issue on the Minister, an action that was supported by a powerful first leader in the *Manchester Guardian* from the pen of R.H. Tawney. County Colleges, he argued, should provide for those aged sixteen to eighteen. Under the Act, whatever the type of school, 'the minimum leaving age should be the same for all'. The government should announce *now* the future date by which 'if all goes well, the minimum school-leaving age will become sixteen'.[27]

As far as the more modest intention to raise the age to fifteen is concerned, following the Cabinet's decision all might have been plain sailing and, as we shall see shortly, emergency measures were put into operation to ensure success. This was not, however, the end of the affair. Early in January 1947 the Ministerial Committee on Economic Planning, chaired by Hugh Dalton, reporting to the Cabinet on the economic survey for 1947, stressed that raising the school age on 1 April would mean 'a direct loss to the national labour force which will reach 370,000 by September, 1948'. This would mean a serious diminution of resources 'at a time when the whole economy of the country is badly overstrained'. The committee proposed that the measure should be postponed for five months – until 1 September 1947. Such a postponement would have the added advantage that preparations 'will be much more complete'.[28]

Clearly Ellen Wilkinson, not a member of this committee, felt that this proposal had to be scotched in Cabinet. No educational grounds, she argued, when the matter came up for discussion, could justify this proposition.

> It would deprive 150,000 children of a whole year's education, and the children to suffer would be precisely those whose education had been most seriously interrupted by the war. They would all be children of working class parents; and parents in better circumstances would remain free to keep their children at school.

The minister went on to make a powerful, indeed impassioned case for no further postponement of this measure.[29]

In the discussion which followed it was argued that postponement would result in great social and educational hardship for very little economic advantage; it was also shortsighted – the country needed higher levels of skills and therefore a longer education was a necessity. Further postponement would bring the political disadvantage associated with breaking a clear pledge. As the minutes recorded it, the discussion seemed virtually unanimous. Hugh Dalton, Chancellor and chairman of the committee is recorded as saying that, in view of the Cabinet's attitude, 'he did not desire to press this particular recommendation'.[30]

There can be no doubt that defeat on this issue would have

had a most serious effect not only on the credibility of the minister herself but also, more importantly, on the whole status of education and the priority to be given to it – in particular in implementing the Act. This was clearly seen by top officials at the Ministry. John Maud, who had recently been appointed Permanent Secretary, put the issue clearly in his memoirs:

> Ellen realised that this was a fight she must win. If she won it the Cabinet would have to find her the precious resources which otherwise would go elsewhere.[31]

This was Ellen Wilkinson's last important action as minister. Early in February 1947 she died suddenly and unexpectedly, to be succeeded by George Tomlinson. 'It was singularly fitting', wrote W.P. Alexander in a memorial notice, 'that in the last weeks of her life she should have to fight for the first of the major educational reforms to which she was dedicated'.[32]

Teachers and Accommodation

The decision, originally taken in 1945 as we have seen, to raise the school age of 1 April 1947, meant that emergency measures would have to be taken to provide the teachers and accommodation minimally necessary. Although there was a great deal of criticism – from local authorities and others – of the Ministry's tardiness and ineffectiveness on both counts, these minimal targets were in fact achieved within the allotted time span, and in practice the measure for raising the age went through relatively smoothly. An Emergency Training Scheme, whereby temporary colleges were established providing a shortened one-year course (mainly for ex-service personnel) was inaugurated, but this only seriously got underway in 1947 – in May 1946, less than a year before zero hour, only seventeen colleges with 3,250 students had been opened, though a total admission of 12,600 was hoped for by the end of December 1946.[33] This, then, was one major prong of the attack on the issue for which the ministry – and the minister – was responsible.

The other was accommodation. The Ministry of Education made it clear from the start that the only way to achieve the target was to concentrate entirely on prefabricated huts 'which can be quickly erected and with the minimum expenditure of skilled labour'.[34] Arrangements were made with the Ministry of

Works to supply and erect the estimated requirement of 6,000 classrooms and practical rooms. Progress, however, was slow – by March 1946, for instance, such huts had only been erected 'at about 100 schools'.[35] In the event, sufficient were erected to make the transition to a leaving age of fifteen practicable – if severely uncomfortable for many children and teachers. Building projects related to this measure continued to be necessary through 1947 and 1948 – the £24 million operational building programme announced by George Tomlinson, late in October 1947 still included 200 projects required for raising the age (costing £11 million).[36]

These prefabricated huts were urgently required, but as the *Times* commented, it would be

> foolish in the extreme to imagine that their erection will constitute a major contribution towards the raising of the standard of accommodation and amenities that is as necessary for the full application of the Education Act as the expansion of the teaching force.[37]

The building restrictions still in force then (May 1946) made it impossible even to begin reconstructing existing schools so that they complied with the standard prescribed by the ministry under Section 10 of the Act.

Already by the summer of 1946 hopes for the full implementation of the Act were turning sour. A main issue was the supply of teachers – only if this could be greatly expanded was there any chance of reducing the size of classes to a maximum of 30, as spelt out in the Act as the objective, as well as establishing county colleges as promised. The further raising of the age to sixteen would require another large increase. Government plans reached nowhere near these targets. In a series of Parliamentary statements at this time the minister (then Ellen Wilkinson) announced that, by September 1948, two aims would have been achieved – the raising of the age to fifteen and the provision of a comprehensive free milk and meals service, while some progress would have been made in reducing class size. For the period beyond 1948 three 'main tasks' were set; better buildings, county colleges, and some major colleges of further education. However, as G.C.T. Giles pointed out, in a powerful letter to the *Times Educational Supplement*, the Parliamentary Secretary (David Hardman), in winding up a debate in the Commons, 'went out of his way to correct a "widespread belief that county colleges are due to open on 1st April, 1950".' It would be 'irresponsible', he said 'to fix the date on which further education to the age of 18 would be compulsory'. During this debate Ellen Wilkinson herself remarked that the implementation of the Act was a job for a generation. Giles concluded with a strong plea for more urgency, and the allocation of effective resources – the local authorities especially needed 'more generous assistance from the national exchequer'. It is already two years since the Act was passed, concluded Giles. 'It had and still has the enthusiastic support of public opinion and particularly of parents and teachers'. A resolute effort was required – 'as a nation we simply cannot hold our own in a scientific world without a higher standard of general education'. Present targets were 'too low' and the present pace 'too slow'.[38] Earlier that year, the *Times Educational Supplement* had carried a leader (by H.C. Dent, presumably) supporting earlier comments by Giles on teacher supply, commenting only that he 'erred on the side of caution'. A total teaching force of 300,000 was required, involving a rapid and substantial increase in recruitment. Everything depended on 'how quickly the Minister of Education and her advisers can free themselves from the apathy and complacency' that seemed to characterise their approach to teacher recruitment.[39]

3 New Forms of Control

The Imposition of Tripartitism

A crucial issue arising from the Act, as we saw in Chapter 1, was that of the organisation, or actual structure, of the new system of 'secondary education for all'. Was this to be based on the pre-war position, as recommended by the Spens Committee, involving three types of school in parallel (grammar, technical and 'modern'), or was there to be a basic transformation of the situation with the development of the single, multilateral, or comprehensive school?

As we have seen, the Act itself kept the question of structure open. On the other hand, official thinking on this issue had been made abundantly clear, both the White Paper of 1943 (based on the 'Green Book') and the Norwood Report coming down very clearly and definitely in favour of the tripartite system.[40]

However the situation was now radically altered. A Labour government was in power, based on a large majority in the House of Commons. The Labour Party was in fact committed, by unanimous conference resolutions in 1942 and 1943 to support widespread experiment with multilateral schools. At the party's conference held towards the end of May 1945 – a few weeks only before the General Election – Alice Bacon gave a firm assurance on this specific issue. 'We say that as far as secondary education is concerned, we favour multilateral schools where all children are educated in one building,' (finishing with the words) 'We promise that if we get power we will have a free democratic educational system on which we can build up a free and democratic country.[41]

The single (comprehensive) school was, of course, also the clear and deliberate policy of the largest and most prestigious local authority in the country – the London County Council (as it then was) – and indeed had been its policy (as a perspective) since 1935.[42] It had gained widespread and increasing support among teachers and educationists generally during the war as we have seen – especially during 1943-44. This does not, of course, mean that the Labour Party as a whole was won over to this policy – this was not finally to be achieved until much later (in the mid-1960s). But it does mean that a Labour government had carte blanche to encourage the implementation of such a policy, had it the will and means.

This issue is often discussed in relation to the personality, and outlook, of Ellen Wilkinson, who was, after all, the minister directly responsible for policy during her term of office (3 August 1945 to 5 February 1947). But in practice it should be recalled that several of the crucial decisions were taken *before* Labour's victory of July 1945. What we have to note, then and thereafter, is the highly systematic and determined approach by ministry officials, through three different governments (the wartime coalition, the Tory caretaking government which succeeded it and the Labour government) having the objective of ensuring that local authorities should, generally, frame their development plans in terms of the tripartite structure, and *not* in terms of comprehensive schooling. It may be as well, first, to trace key developments from the moment when the Act received Royal Assent, on 3 August 1944, even if its main provisions only became effective from 1 April 1945.

Under Section 11 of the Act all local authorities, as we have seen, had to prepare development plans covering primary and secondary education, indicating how the Act would be implemented locally, for submission to and approval (or otherwise) by the minister.

The historical record shows a heavy weight of 'advice' and 'guidance' from the centre to the periphery – the local authorities – from a very early date. Indeed the very first Circular issued by the new ministry only a week after the bill had received Royal Assent dealt with this issue (Circular 1, 'Education Act 1944', 15 August 1944). Notifying authorities that, from 1 April 1945, they must begin preparation of their development plans, the Circular continues:

> The preparation of these plans will raise many educational issues and for the assistance of authorities the Minister proposes to issue a memorandum of guidance on the aims and organisation of the various types of schools in the primary and secondary fields ... These plans should be framed, as far as practicable, on uniform lines...

Immediately after local authorities had begun their planning – that is, early in May 1945 – a further Circular, while asking that plans be submitted by 1 April 1946, specifically drew the attention of local authorities 'to the general principles set out in the Ministry of Education pamphlet entitled 'The Nation's Schools', which is being issued at the same time as this Circular'.[43]

We should note that this highly controversial, indeed notorious pamphlet, the first in the ministry's new series (which took the place of the memorandum promised earlier), was published when the wartime Coalition government was still in office, with R.A. Butler and James Chuter Ede as the responsible ministers. The pamphlet was in fact published one day after the war with Germany was brought to a close (7 May) and most people had other things to think about just then. The pamphlet was, of course, drafted earlier – there is evidence that Chuter Ede saw it in draft and 'suggested certain corrections' which would, of course, be normal practice. When the pamphlet was first criticised in the House of Commons the new minister, Richard Law (Minister of Education in the Caretaker government) claimed that Ede had in fact accepted it.[44]

The Nation's Schools certainly argued heavily against the comprehensive school, called for a reduction in the number of grammar school places and stated frankly that the new secondary schools should be conceived as schools for working-class children 'whose future employment will not demand any measure of technical skill or knowledge'. Turning to the structure of the new secondary system, the pamphlet asserted that 'The first problem will ... be to decide what provision should be made for each of these three broad types' (grammar, technical and modern, which had been described in the previous paragraph). Secondary education in an area, the pamphlet continued, 'should be envisaged as a whole consisting of different types'. The pamphlet then castigated the multilateral school on four counts: such schools must be very large and this is undesirable; selection must anyway continue within them; schools work best when they have one specific aim or function; planning must, in any case, derive from existing plans. 'It would be a mistake', the pamphlet continues, 'to plunge too hastily on a large scale into a revolutionary change ... Innovation is not necessarily reform'.[45]

The Nation's Schools was powerfully attacked almost immediately in a major article by G.C.T. Giles. There is nothing in the proposals, he wrote, 'to meet the challenge of the 'changes and advances now to be made', nothing of the progressive democratic spirit of the White Paper and the Act. It is back to 1939 and all that. The pamphlet, he concluded, does not attempt to meet the present challenge. 'It stands condemned by its complacent acceptance of the *status quo ante* Butler.'[46] Two months later this view was reinforced by Harold Dent in a leading article in the *Times Educational Supplement*. 'No greater mishap could overcome the new order in English education', he wrote, 'than that there should be established in it three different grades of secondary school.'[47]

The pamphlet set out very clearly the ministry's view as to the future pattern of secondary education *before the Labour Party won power*. It is well known that it led to an explosion of anger a year later at the Labour Party conference in June 1946, when a striking speech by W.G. Cove was successful in winning unanimous support for a resolution demanding its withdrawal, against the very confused protests of Ellen Wilkinson.[48] In practice the pamphlet was not withdrawn, though the Minister stated that certain parts of it no longer represented government policy. The pamphlet was not, however, re-issued.

The Nation's Schools was published in May 1945. A few months later the heavy guns were really brought out – in

December of that year, when the Labour Government had been in office nearly six months with Ellen Wilkinson as Minister and David Hardman (now) as Parliamentary Secretary. And it is perhaps worth remembering that the Ministry now also had a new Permanent Secretary, the extreme traditionalist, Sir Maurice Holmes, retiring in autumn, to be succeeded by John Maud (later Lord Redcliffe-Maud), who came new to the Board from the Ministry of Reconstruction. So now there was a new Minister and a new Permanent Secretary. The policy, however, perhaps unsurprisingly, remained the same; this was made abundantly clear with the issue, on 12 December 1945, of Circular 73, entitled 'The Organisation of Secondary Education'.

Queries are coming in, the Ministry reports, relating to development plans, so 'guidance' is required. *The Nation's Schools* is again recommended at the start (the Labour Party Conference, where the pamphlet was to be rejected *in toto*, had not yet taken place). This pamphlet, states the Circular, 'contains a full statement and discussion which should be borne in mind when ... planning'. This new Circular, however, aims to 'guide administration in more detail'.

As a general rule, the Circular goes on, 70 to 75 per cent of places 'should be of the modern type', the remaining 25 to 30 per cent being allocated to grammar and technical schools 'in suitable proportions'. There follow the crunch lines:

> *it is inevitable* for the immediate purposes of planning and in the light of the existing layout of schools, for local education authorities at the outset to think in terms of the three types, and to *include information of the amount of accommodation allocated to each type in the development plan* (my emphasis, B.S.).

That clear instruction is only slightly modified by the succeeding section which suggests that 'this separate classification of schools' may not be irrevocable. The main message of the Circular is, however, quite clear. Plans must provide for places as prescribed precisely for each of the three types.

This document, published just at the time when local authorities were working out their development plans, seems best interpreted as a clear attempt at closure. The advice is a developed version of *The Nation's Schools* published *before* the Labour government took office. This is surely evidence of a clear ministry line. John Maud, now Permanent Secretary, confirms this analysis in his autobiography. The Act, he writes, made

> the local authorities, not the minister, responsible for providing schools, but local authorities were to act 'under the direction and control' of the minister; in particular, they were to draw up 'development plans' (requiring the minister's approval) showing how they intended to provide primary and secondary education.

So, Maud goes on, 'before local authorities could get to work on either long-term or immediate programmes, the minister must declare her hand'. She did – and approved the Circular drafted by the Inspectorate (a point worth noting). 'Local authorities could propose what they liked' concludes Maud, *'but they were given a broad hint of what would and what would not get her approval'* (my emphasis, B.S.).[49]

Local authorities took a great deal longer to prepare their plans than was envisaged in the 1944 Act; further it seems likely that the ministry was growing increasingly concerned at the evident move, on the part of several authorities, to prepare fully comprehensive systems – or partially so – in spite of the 'guidance' received. Reading, Oldham, Coventry, Southend as well as London were among the former. An analysis of 54 plans (one-third of local authorities) submitted by early 1947, published by the Fabian Society in April that year, indicates that fourteen of them (a little less than a quarter) were in fact proposing to provide one or more multilateral schools while another twenty proposed bilateral schools (either technical-modern or grammar-modern) – well over half of the authorities analysed, then, wanted more flexible structures than under the strict tripartite mode.[50]

Possibly because of a continuing groundswell in favour of comprehensive (or multilateral) schools, the ministry returned to this issue yet again, publishing Circular 144 eighteen months later in June 1947 – and at the same time publishing yet another pamphlet, *The New Secondary Education*, an updated (and more tactfully worded) version of *The Nation's Schools*, Circular 144, entitled 'The Organisation of Secondary Education', once again 'offered guidance on the educational principles which underlie the planning of secondary education'. George Tomlinson was now the responsible Minister, Ellen Wilkinson having died early in the year.

This lengthy and heady-handed Circular was specifically concerned with pressing the ministry's view of the nature, size and organisation of multilateral and bilateral schools. It starts by announcing that:

> It is not possible to deal intelligibly with the organisation of secondary education without reference to the three broad types – modern, technical and grammar – in terms of which its varieties are generally known and described.

It then argues that the normal minimum size of a multilateral school should be a ten or eleven form entry school with 1,500 to 1,700 places, also pointing to the problems that would arise with schools of this size. In rural areas a school of 900, it concedes, 'would not be entirely unreasonable'. The pamphlet issued concurrently, *The New Secondary Education*, written for the general public, in fact devotes only one or two dismissive paragraphs to the single school (on p.24), focusing instead at length on each of the three received 'types' of secondary education. Certainly neither this Circular, nor the new pamphlet, offered one iota of encouragement to authorities planning comprehensive schools.

This Circular and pamphlet completes the barrage of official advice and 'guidance' – at least in the sense of that offered openly (and at a particularly sensitive time) from the ministry.

When George Tomlinson took over in February 1947 he inherited some of the animus against his predecessor from those espousing the cause of the single secondary school. Reference has already been made to the explosion of anger at the 1946 Labour Party Conference relating to *The Nation's Schools*. But it was a year later, in 1947, that indignation at the negative policies pursued by succeeding ministers boiled over. At the Labour Party Conference that year a resolution moved by the Bristol Labour Party gained unanimous support. This protested against the fact that previous conference resolutions on multilateral schools had been ignored and urged the minister:

> To take great care that he does not perpetuate under the new Education Act the undemocratic traditions of English secondary education.

This conference, the resolution went on,

> draws attention to the fact that on four occasions during the last five years it has passed resolutions emphasising the need for the rapid development of a ... common secondary school ... It calls upon the minister to review the educational system in order to give real equality of opportunity to all the nation's children.[51]

The real test, of course, was how the more radical development plans submitted were dealt with. The key issue here was the plan finally submitted by Middlesex County Council in 1948. Already in 1946, with a Labour majority, the County Council proposed, through using and adapting existing buildings (and building new comprehensives on new estates) to transform the system relatively quickly by organising schools of between 570 and 850 pupils, offering a common curriculum for all to the age of thirteen or fourteen. The aim was to give 'some earnest ... to parents of the determination of the County Council to provide a real secondary education for all pupils of secondary age'.[52] In May 1948 the Council proposed the immediate transformation of six schools into comprehensives and sought the minister's approval. The minister 'welcomed the initiative', but approved only two such schools, later (under protest) extended to three.[53]

Finally, later that year (1948) the Council submitted its full development plan for a comprehensive system. This aroused great interest at the time, as the plan embodied the ideas of advanced sections of the labour movement both on the common curriculum in place of separate courses for different 'types of child', and also on an approach which would have made possible a *rapid* transition (instead of waiting for the building of huge eleven to eighteen schools). In January 1949, apparently impervious to the Labour Party conference resolution mentioned earlier, the minister returned the plan asking for a complete review on two well-worn, or at least well-prepared grounds. First, the proposed schools were 'too small'; second, what were needed were different schools for different types of child.[54] Nor was Middlesex the only authority whose plans were rejected on these grounds. In 1948 the minister also rejected a proposal of five schools in the North Riding, as 'too small'.[55]

There was, however, some movement. Multilateral schools, as we have seen, were officially acceptable in rural areas. Presumably under this category Anglesey, which had decided already before the war to go comprehensive when possible, made its move which was accepted. The West Riding, which strongly criticised official thinking in the introduction to its development plan, issued in 1948, also proposed to develop some comprehensives in rural areas, and the plan was accepted. There is also the case of the Isle of Man to which the 1944 Act did not apply, but under the Manx Education Act which followed it, that authority was one of the first to move effectively to establish a complete system of comprehensive schools covering the island. In Westmorland, the grammar school at Windermere was reorganised as a comprehensive as early as 1945 (with only 220 pupils incidentally) – this seems to have been acceptable.

And finally, of course, there was the case of London which published its massive, and path-breaking, London School Plan as early as 1947 (though it was not finalised for submission until two years later). This and related developments, however, will be considered later.

It seems clear that the policy determined on by the ministry officials prior to Labour's victory was in fact that accepted and carried through by Labour ministers and government. The crucial moment for action, if Labour were to follow conference resolutions and set out to transform the system of secondary education, was clearly in the early months immediately after taking power, when 'advice' and 'guidance' to this effect could have been sent to local authorities.[56] But in fact the opposite policy was pursued and apparently quite deliberately. Labour's political leaders – Ellen Wilkinson in particular – must, of course, take responsibility for the Circulars and pamphlets issued under their name from July 1945, as well as for the actual decisions made on development plans submitted during their period of office. It is well known that Ellen Wilkinson personally made various statements on a number of occasions fully supporting the tripartite system. In Kenneth Morgan's view, she was 'deeply committed' to the 1944 Act and 'embodied Labour's instinctive faith in the grammar schools'. She had also 'moved to a distinctly more centrist position in the party during the war years'.[57] Betty Vernon makes a similar assessment of her outlook in her sympathetic, but not uncritical, biography. [58] It seems clear enough that she personally had no quarrel with ministry policy as she found it on first taking office and, as her close friend Leah Manning has put it, was very ready to rely heavily on advice from her officials.[59] However the policy pursued by the government cannot be explained solely in terms of the minister's personality. There was, in fact, a lack of clarity and purpose on this issue in the key power centres of the Labour Party, as Caroline Benn has shown.[60] As a direct result, a clear opportunity to bring about a decisive change, and at a favourable moment, was lost.

Examinations Policy

There was another challenge, by which the Labour government's educational policy can be tested – as to whether this was, in effect, one of containment rather than the radical advance that had been hoped for after Labour's electoral victory. This arose from the lengthening of school life due to the raising of the leaving age at fifteen with the likelihood, then, of a further rise to sixteen not long after. This posed the possibility that, even within the strict tripartite system officially favoured, increasing numbers would qualify for the universities and professions, leading to disequilibrium in the labour market, disappointed expectations and, as a result, to social instability. What actions did the new government take in this situation?

Here there are two inter-related policy areas. First, ministry policy relating to grammar schools, developed towards the close of the war, where the intention, clearly established and stated from time to time, was to *reduce* the intake in order to transform these into elite schools holding pupils through the full course from eleven to eighteen. The second policy area related to the opportunities offered in secondary modern schools to which the bulk of the child population aged eleven upwards would eventually go.[61]

The grammar school issue will be tackled later. As regards secondary modern schools (as the pre-war senior elementary schools were renamed – or recategorised – on 1 April 1945) the issue seems to have been how to prevent a surge relating to the School Certificate examination resulting from the raising of the school leaving age. This whole issue appears to have reached a sudden crisis in the early summer of 1946. It was, of course, accepted at that time that the school leaving age would be raised to fifteen on 1 April 1947 (as in fact it was). Several secondary modern schools had by now begun actively to consider entering pupils for School Certificate, then the main grammar school external examination. In most cases this would have meant pupils staying on for an extra year (to sixteen) and, of course, arranging special courses of tuition for them; but in some areas this was entirely possible. Realisation that early action was necessary if this was to be prevented seems to have hit the ministry early in 1946 when requests to enter pupils for School Certificate by secondary modern schools suddenly, and clearly unexpectedly, reached the ministry.[62]

In May Circular 103 entitled 'Examinations in Secondary

Schools', was issued. This has an air almost of panic. Something must be done, the Circular argues, about the School Certificate. There follows a passionate argument for the complete abolition of any external examination at fifteen or sixteen 'as soon as circumstances permit'. The rationale for this proposal came from the Norwood Report, with which, the Circular states, the minister (Ellen Wilkinson) is in agreement. Far better, it is suggested, that 'objective Intelligence Tests' should be developed to take the place of the first examination. The Circular concludes by conceding that some believe the School Certificate should continue if it is radically reformed – for instance, through using internal assessment – together with the statement that the minister proposes to seek the advice of the Secondary Schools Examinations Council. (SSEC) as to what action should now be taken. A section on interim arrangements reiterates that grammar school pupils should in any case stay at school to seventeen or eighteen, so a first examination should be unnecessary.[63]

The real crunch, however, comes at the end of the Circular. This announces the publication of regulations preventing schools *other than* grammar schools from entering *any* pupils for *any* external examination under the age of seventeen. In other words, the secondary modern schools were quite simply debarred from entering pupils for School Certificate unless they could persuade them to stay *two* years beyond the new statutory leaving age (and even then they would require special permission from the ministry). Schools actively planning to enter pupils had, quite simply, been forestalled.

A few weeks later (26 June 1946) Circular 113 ('Secondary School Examination Council') made the important announcement that the minister was assuming full responsibility 'for the direction of policy and general arrangements in regard to school examinations'. The statutory basis for this initiative, which upset many people, lay in the Education Act.[64] A total reconstitution of the SSEC was announced, and the new council asked to make proposals for a new examination. The previous council had *no* ministry representatives, consisting of ten from the Examining Boards (mostly from universities), ten from local authorities, and a further ten teachers. The new constitution included *five nominees* from the ministry itself, eight from local authorities (CCA, AMA, AEC, etc.), eleven from teachers organisations (Joint Four, NUT, etc., including HMC), six from universities and one from Wales – a total of 31. Ministry control was epitomised by the appointment of the recently retired but by now highly prestigious Permanent Secretary, Sir Maurice Holmes, as Chairman, and of HMI R.H. Barrow (who wrote much of the Norwood Report) as Secretary. But for the purpose of the reconstituted council's immediate task – reporting on the new examination – four further high ministry officials were included, plus two ministerial secretaries.

In April 1947, after the 'battle' in the cabinet, discussed earlier, the leaving age was finally raised to fifteen. In September that year the report of the reconstituted SSEC 'Examinations in Secondary Schools', was published. This turned out to be a curt and extremely unrevealing document, defining the character of the proposed new examination – the General Certificate of Education (GCE). In general the report obediently followed the ministry's directions as set out in Circular 103, though in detail there were differences. In particular the council did not, in fact, propose the complete abolition of an external examination at sixteen though the way was paved for its abolition. The council recommended that the minimum age limit for taking GCE be fixed at sixteen (on 1 September), but that it should subsequently be raised further. There is reason to believe that the actual abolition of an external examination at sixteen was strongly opposed by some members of the reconstituted council. It is also well known that on the whole issue of the age limit the council was deadlocked. Outward unanimity was only finally achieved in order to prevent a complete breakdown.

The report was accepted in principle by the Minister (Circular 168, 23 April 1948) and the new examination, which differed from the School Certificate in that it was a subject examination and that subjects were not grouped as they had been, was first introduced in 1951. In a sense it might seem that the carefully laid plans of the ministry had been thwarted. For the external examination at sixteen remained, and with it the danger of the modern schools achieving a new status. But it seems that a bargain had been struck to achieve the official ends by different means. If the *standard* of a pass in the examination was raised, this would have the effect both of excluding secondary modern children (a miscalculation, as it transpired) and of preparing the way for excluding a considerable number of pupils from grammar schools, since many would not now pass (a correct prediction). This was the significance of the council's recommendation that to *pass* in the new GCE, pupils must reach the same standard as the 'credit level' in the old School Certificate (i.e. a standard well above the old pass level), a recommendation later accepted by the minister (Tomlinson) with the rest.[65]

This was a step of major importance in educational policy, ultimately affecting the work of every grammar school in the country. Yet the crucial suggestion that the pass standard be raised is accorded precisely two short paragraphs in the report. No reasons whatsoever are given for the change, apart from the naive and question-begging statement that the effect on standards would be 'beneficial and stimulating', and that a 'pass should have real significance'.

As for the crucial age limit of sixteen this was widely seen at the time as essentially a means of excluding pupils from secondary modern schools, though there was also an argument about reducing the dangers of early specialisation. 'It has been widely maintained that the minimum age was fixed at sixteen in order to prevent the new secondary modern schools from taking the examination,' claimed a writer in the *Times Educational Supplement* in July 1948. 'This is a political and not an educational argument and a firm denial would prevent the clouding of debate. What is needed is a thorough revision of the reform on educational grounds'.[66] George Tomlinson was unable to deny the charge; in his reply to this and similar assertions he claimed that the age-limit was not imposed '*solely* in order to protect the modern schools' (my emphasis, B.S.).[67] In the words of J.A. Petch, secretary to the Joint Northern Matriculation Board, the ministry had by now exemplified 'its domination by imposing a new examination and endeavouring to control the details of its working'. If the ministry contributed nothing else to the council's scheme for the General Certificate of Education, 'it inspired the imposition of an age limit'. When the scheme was being drafted

it was ministerial policy that the new secondary schools which were not grammar schools should not become interested in the existing examination system or derivations from it; an age limit of sixteen on entry to the GCE would involve pupils from these schools in staying for one year beyond the statutory leaving age and thereby discourage all but a few of them from the attempt.[68]

Whatever the intention – and no serious educational argument was put forward in support of this measure – its objective significance was clear enough. By this step a strong barrier had been placed between grammar and modern schools which were supposed, following the Act, to be of equal status. By erecting this barrier in this manner, and at this particular point in time, the government perpetuated in a new form the old separation between elementary and secondary schools. The divided structure of the pre-1944 Act situation was now to persist, if in a new form.

By 1947-48, then, the government (and the ministry) had shown its hand quite clearly on two key issues following the Act. First, a determination to impose a tripartite solution on the nation's secondary schools, and second, an equal (but less visible) determination to ensure that the new dispensation did not radically open up new opportunities for the hitherto disadvantaged – that is, to the working class as a whole.

Thus, in spite of the hopes of the immediate post-war years, the early surge, the enthusiasm and the planning, behind the scenes new strong-points were being erected against the forward, democratic movement which sought to realise the full potentialities promised by, or embodied in, the Education Act. Even under a Labour government, elected with a massive majority, the mediation of existing class relations was still seen as the major function of the education system – or, if this was not overtly realised at the time, measures were permitted to be taken, and carried through, which objectively reinforced the traditional purposes of the existing educational structure. Steps such as those discussed certainly did not provide the means for any serious challenge to the social order, through any basic or challenging restructuring of the educational system, as was entirely possible even within the limits set by the Education Act of 1944.

4 Economic and Political Difficulties and Education, 1947-48 to 1951

In his autobiography, F.F. Potter, Cheshire's Director of Education, after describing the economy wave that hit the country after the First World War, adds that this was not to be his only such experience. His tenure of office, from 1922 to 1947 was, he says, 'marked by a succession of these financial and other crises'; these were indeed 'troubled years' and it was very clear 'that progress for an officer with any hopes or ideals in education, was hindered by a series of setbacks ending, after the Second World War, in a feeling of complete frustration'.[69] Potter's retirement, in 1947, coincided with what Morgan describes as 'a year of almost unrelieved disaster', and what Dalton, then Chancellor, stigmatised as 'annus horrendus'. Starting with a calamitous crisis in coal production through an exceptionally freezing winter, followed by a fierce internal battle within the Labour Party on defence expenditure (there were substantially more than 1 million men and women still in the armed forces) the year climaxed with a serious financial crisis over convertibility of sterling in August, when the country faced bankruptcy. The American postwar loan of nearly $4 billion intended to help put the country on its feet and to last until 1951, suddenly all but disappeared. Unprecedented criticism of the government broke out together with internal battles for the leadership.[70] However it was not only economic problems that were important. Already as early as March 1946 Winston Churchill had made his Fulton speech, heralding the unleashing of the Cold War – to culminate, in 1950, with the outbreak of the Korean War.

The result was that official attitudes now began to reflect the sharp, worldwide, political struggle between the Soviet Union and the United States. In 1948 the United States intervened very directly in the Italian General Election in a successful attempt to beat back the growing strength of the Communist – Socialist alliance. Earlier in Greece, Britain had been directly involved in the forcible repression of the revolutionary forces lead by EAM (and the Communist Party). In June 1948 matters reached a crisis with the Berlin blockade which lasted a full year. In April 1949 the foundation of NATO crystallised international divisions. In Britain itself towards the end of the decade a growing strike movement in favour of improved wages and conditions now hit the London docks, printers and other sections of workers – the immediate post-war consensus on the need for sacrifice to enhance productivity was now at an end. In these years (1949 and 1950 especially) the Cabinet seemed obsessed with the 'Communist threat' both at home and abroad. The issue arose at meeting after meeting at Cabinet level. Now also, a policy of massive rearmament, strongly encouraged (or demanded) by the United States, strained the already overburdened economy to the uttermost – resulting in yet further shortages of steel, building materials and labour. [71] The new initiatives required under the Act – and even the maintenance of the system in a period of rising school population – were again at risk.

The result was a changed political atmosphere. Morgan refers to 'the rightwards tendencies in social change, cultural movements and the public psychology' which surfaced at this period. The hopes of the early days now began to evaporate. In various forms those who wished to hold back the rate of advance – in education as well as elsewhere – now began to raise their voices and press their arguments with a new confidence. For the post-war Labour governments, the years 1947-48 marked a watershed. For them and their supporters, as Morgan puts it, it would never be 'glad, confident morning again'. 'The strength and vitality of the Labour Government fled, never really to return.'[72]

The government, however, weathered the storm, though emerging from the 1947 crisis battered and bruised. Owing to Dalton's budget indiscretion, his place as Chancellor was taken by Stafford Cripps who, through austerity measures, assisted in nurturing a degree of internal economic revival. Cripps was generally successful in protecting social services expenditure at and around the level then reached. However, with the outbreak of the Cold War, at the end of the decade, involving sudden and immense expenditure on rearmament, this situation was to change.

Financial Cuts

It may be as well to take stock of the position in education as it had developed by 1949, five years after the passage of the Act, through the eyes of a percipient and closely involved observer. In a letter to the press in April 1949, Shena D. Simon, of the Manchester Education Committee, Chairman of the WEA's education advisory committee (and ex-member of the Spens Committee in the late 1930s) summed up the progress made at this date. [73] By this time, she argued, very little of the Act had in fact been implemented and only a few had benefited. Those whose children gained places in grammar schools no longer had fees to pay; the much smaller number winning scholarships to university had more generous maintenance allowances. Those, again a minority, who had moved to one of the new housing estates with children over five were, very slowly, getting new schools. But no nursery schools were being built. The older children now had an extra year of school life, but a substantial proportion of these were spending this either in the top class of an old, unreorganised all-age school (where specialist teaching could not normally be provided), or in a prefabricated classroom added to an old school.

The section of the Act which laid it down that primary and secondary education was to take place in separate schools was in abeyance, as 'Hadow reorganisation', except in new secondary schools on new housing estates, was not being carried out (the letter went on). Parity between secondary schools – a main provision of the Act – was only applied in the case of *new* schools (a very important point that needs to be understood). Reconstruction of existing secondary modern schools (the pre-war 'senior elementary') remained a dead letter, while competition to enter grammar schools (in spite of the famous White Paper promise – see p. 68) was now, in fact, more intensive than ever. As for the junior and infant schools, nothing had been done except, at best, the addition of further prefabricated classrooms to meet the urgent need of the post-war birth rate bulge. 'Classes of 50 and 60 in buildings many of which had been on the official blacklist since before the war, and others which ought to be on it now, are common.'

Such was the situation, as summarised by an experienced observer and education committee member at that time. In the immediate post-war years new, and perhaps unforeseen, problems had arisen which added substantially to the magnitude of the task in hand.

The first of these was the rapid (and unexpected) increase in the birth rate. After a long period of secular decline from the turn of the century (births had reached a peak of 948,000 in 1903, and fell to 579,000 in 1941), the birth rate began its upward trend relatively early in the war (1941-42) reaching a new peak of 881,000 in 1947 after which there was a further decline.[74] This annual increase – to 1947 – hit the schools five years later (not to speak of the increased demand for pre-school facilities), so that the years 1947 to 1952 saw it maximised, with a growth of between 60,000 and 140,000 children aged five in five of the six years. Here, then, was one problem that *had* to be solved, if the law was to be complied with.

The other was the needs of the population in the new housing estates – a policy given priority by the government in its housing drive. Here, new schools were (in most cases) an absolute necessity; and indeed the bulk of the modest new building that was achieved was sited on these new estates, leaving the vast majority of existing schools (which included over 500 'blacklisted') untouched.

Clearly, if there was to be a serious attempt to implement the Act, there had to be a fundamental shift in national priorities. This was necessary to provide the resources required to realise what was certainly the greatest measure of social advance to reach the statute book actually during the war – one widely supported by all parties and, indeed, by the population as a whole. But such was the policy of the government, and its entanglement with the developing Cold War, that this was never achieved. In fact developments took an opposite direction. An immense and growing investment in rearmament, over and above an already swollen defence expenditure start line, ensured that over the last two years of Labour's administration, resources for education were increasingly squeezed.

Table 2.1

Budgetary Expenditure on Education, 1939-40 to 1951-52

Year	Ministry of Education Vote	Increase on previous year
1939-40	£51,000,000	
1947-48	£138,000,000	
1948-49	£162,000,000	£24,500,000
1949-50	£182,000,000	£19,500,000
1950-51	£192,000,000	£10,500,000
1951-52	£200,000,000	£7,500,000

Source: Ministry of Education annual reports

Total expenditure on education was at this time derived largely from two main sources – from taxes and the rates. At this period a specific grant formula determined the extent of government grants to assist the latter (rates) – a system revised in 1948. Such government grants were payable only on 'net recognisable expenditure', so that central government in fact determined overall expenditure (local authorities' estimated costs were often very severely pruned by the Ministry of Education).[75] The best indicator of trends in government support for education, therefore, lies in the Ministry of Education's vote as providing budgetary expenditure each year. The table above gives the relevant date for the Labour administrations, as far as they are available.

These figures need to be treated with care. Although showing an annual increase the crucial issue is the consistent *reduction* in the rate of increase in post-war budgetary expenditure from 1948-49. Increases in expenditure were in any case inevitable. These were due to two main causes: first, to meet the secular rise in costs of goods and services, i.e. inflationary pressures, and second, to meet increased costs due to the rise in the number of teachers (both for raising the leaving age and to meet the increase in the number of pupils as a result of the increased birth rate). Just keeping the machine ticking over, then, inevitably meant an annual increase in expenditure, quite apart from the cost of implementing the Act in more general ways.

The rate of decline of this annual increase is, therefore, a true indicator of the increasing squeeze on education in the last years of the Labour governments. Table 2.1 shows that the rate of increase declined consistently – from £24.5 million in 1948-49 to £19.5 million in the following year (1949-50), to only some £10 million in 1950-51 and further down to £7.5 million in 1951-52. This sudden reduction was the direct result of a new economic (or financial) crisis in the summer of 1949, when the country again faced bankruptcy. The immediate problems were solved by the massive devaluation of the pound in September – to an exchange value of $2.40 from $4.03. Cuts in public expenditure followed in October when, as the ministry report for that year indicates, the minister drew the attention of local education authorities to 'the need to exercise the strictest economy'. Reductions were requested in local authority administrative staff, a penny was put on the price of school dinners (up to 6d). Fees for students in further education were increased, economies demanded on school transport, and other measures taken to reduce expenditure, though Tomlinson claimed (after a private battle with Attlee) that there would be no going back on reforms relating to the Act, nor on the plans to increase the output of teachers, nor would cuts be made in the building programme (already approved).[76] Two economy Circulars were issued, Circular 209 which dealt with capital expenditure, and Circular 210 with recurrent expenditure, both on 28 October 1949. The first imposed a 12.5 per cent reduction on average cost per place for new primary and secondary schools (to £170 and £290 respectively), the second outlined the economy measures just cited.

The government's decision at this time to cut a total of £250 million in expenditure involved an education cut (in the estimates) of £5 million. These measures were greeted with great disappointment by the educational world. 'The realisation of some of the fondest hopes of teachers must recede yet further into the future than before,' commented the *Times Educational Supplement*.[77] Five years after the passing of the Act, wrote Giles to this journal, detailing the failure to progress across a broad field, 'the undemocratic structure of education remains substantially unchanged. There are still two systems of education in Britain, one for the privileged few and one for the unprivileged many'. According to official statements, Giles continued, only 38 new primary schools and thirteen new secondary schools had been completed between 31 December 1945 and 4 April 1949, yet Tomlinson himself had estimated that some 3,000 would be needed simply to provide accommodation for the additional school population by 1952. But the minister himself now announced that 'there will be some slowing down of our advance'. Where would we be in 1952?[78] In the following year (1950) maximum costs per place of new buildings were again reduced – this time to £140 for primary schools and £240 for secondary schools (Circulars 215 and 219). The squeeze was by now harshly applied; prospects for the future looked bleak indeed.

The Witch Hunt

The Cold War, which led directly to the sudden decision for a massive drive on rearmament, resulting in the imposition of stringent economy measures in the social services, broke out into a shooting war in Korea in the summer of 1950. In the United States, McCarthyite witch-hunting now reached its height, with the imposition of loyalty oaths among university teachers and a number of court hearings which received maximum publicity. In Britain also, the summer of 1950 saw similar moves, if on a lesser scale. These culminated in the 'Middlesex Ban', against Communist and Fascist teachers.

The issue was first raised in a widely publicised debate in the House of Lords on 29 March 1950. Lord Vansittart, before the war Permanent Secretary of the Foreign Office, in a wide-ranging speech, called attention 'to the extent of Communist infiltration into the public service and other important branches of public life ... and to move to resolve that continuous and resolute precautions are necessary for public security'. *Hansard* continues: 'the noble Lord said ... there are ninety and six ways ... of enabling Communists to earn a living, but I do not think that teaching and broadcasting should be among them'. Vansittart made a very specific attack on the Extra-Mural department at Birmingham University (or on one of its lecturers – actually a non-Communist clergyman, characterised by Vansittart as 'a particularly murderous priest').[79]

This unprecedented attack reflected the growing polarisation of the world into opposing military blocks and, as one commentator has put it 'when Lord Vansittart rose to make his sustained McCarthyite attack on Communists and 'fellow-travellers' ... he was doing no more than giving public expression to views which had become commonplace over the previous two years'. The high hopes 'for a new socialist society built on liberal foundations, which seemed so promising in 1945' were 'shattered by the freezing atmosphere of the Cold War only three years later'.[80]

It was not until 1950, however, that the issue was so raised in parliament and became a national concern. Vansittart's attack was followed, in the summer and late autumn, by three separate debates in the House of Commons, and, in October, by the Middlesex action. The running was made in the Commons by a young right-wing Tory MP, Major Tufton Beamish (later Lord Chelwood).[81] In a series of intemperate speeches and interventions, in July, and again in October and November, Beamish returned to the fray demanding an investigation into 'subversive influences in the teaching profession' where, he claimed, Communists were engaged in a 'softening up process'.[82]

Beamish did not confine his attack to teachers; he warned against the activities of what he called 'the Woodland folk' (actually Woodcraft, a Co-operative youth organisation), sharply criticised the official Army Bureau of Current Affairs, which still continued (revealing that he 'did not allow anybody in my company to read ABCA') and made further charges. He did not call for the banning of the Communist Party at this stage, he added, because 'I do not know where the dividing line is' – looking meaningfully at the Labour MPs opposite him. Beamish's demand was supported by Henry Brooke, Tory MP and at that time leader of the Conservatives on the London County Council, who wanted action against Communist lecturers in teacher training colleges.[83]

The same sort of charges were made in each of these debates, though when challenged by Tomlinson and Hardman, who deplored them, not one shred of evidence could be produced. That, however, was hardly the point ... rather the purpose was to sharpen polarisation and isolate radicals, Communists in particular. It was an insult to the Communist teachers, Beamish claimed, 'to suggest they lost any opportunity of teaching their creed of bloody revolution, class hatred and atheism'.[84] A particular attack was made on the teachers at Acton Grammar School (in Middlesex) where G.C.T. Giles was headmaster, as on Giles himself who had claimed, perhaps provocatively, at the NUT Conference in May that there were 2,000 members of the Communist Party in the teaching profession.

It would be wrong to think that this was merely a maverick attack by an extreme right-wing politician. Beamish received support from other Tory MPs and, indeed, at his first intervention, from the Labour benches (in the form of George Thomas, a teacher and later Speaker of the House of Commons). Thomas said that he 'hoped the minister would enquire into Mr Brooke's serious allegations that training colleges were turning out teachers who had come under the influence of Communists'.[85]

In October, as mentioned earlier, the Middlesex Education Committee, where Labour had lost control at the 1948 elections, recommended to the county council 'that persons who are known to be members of the Communist or Fascist parties or to be associated with either of them in such a way as to raise doubt ... about their reliability, be debarred from certain teaching posts' (including school headships). The matter was raised in connection with a particular teacher recommended for the headship of a primary school where the education committee now proposed that another name be submitted. [86] This recommendation was upheld by the county council shortly after by a vote of 54 to 29.[87]

The Middlesex ban continued in force for several years – until

1956, when Labour once again won control. It was opposed, somewhat ineffectively, by the National Union of Teachers, which saw it as an affront to the freedom of teachers and a slur on their professionalism.[88] No other local authorities followed suit and, generally, this initiative was deplored in educational circles. On the other hand the Middlesex ban crystallised the increasing polarisation arising out of the Cold War – while it was in force the threat of its extension was always there. On this matter, the *Times Educational Supplement* later made the point that

> the ban is now of several years standing. The only odd thing about it is that the Middlesex Authority voted it by formal resolution. Almost all other authorities observe the ban, but they have, perhaps wisely, been less frank and not made it a printed rule.[89]

The singling out of Communists as a threat also acted to downgrade educational issues with which they were particularly concerned and committed. Chief among these was the comprehensive school – it was Middlesex, when under Labour leadership, which had produced the most radical development plan, in the drawing up of which Communist teachers, especially G.C.T. Giles and Max Morris, had played a significant part. Others, for instance Margaret Clarke (NUT executive committee member and a highly respected headteacher), played a leading part in the establishment of London's early ('interim') comprehensive schools.

The Cold War also penetrated the universities where known Communists now found it difficult to gain appointment but its effects were most striking in university extra-mural departments – a sensitive area since these were responsible for wide-ranging educational activities among the working class (and trade unions) and even in the colonies. In *Adult Education and the Cold War*, subtitled 'Liberal Values under Siege, 1946-51', Roger Fieldhouse has made a detailed and scholarly study of this phenomenon. In the event, several tutors were relieved of their posts, while a covert policy of discrimination in appointments was brought into action very widely. Fieldhouse concludes that in the late 1940's, 'the liberal tradition of adult education' was 'besieged by Cold War anti-Communism in the extra-mural world, in the Workers' Educational Association, in the adult education exported to the colonies and in the civilian adult education provided for H.M. Forces'. There was a real danger, he adds,

> that the perceived need to preserve western, 'free, democratic' society would eliminate the liberal approach ... which aimed to give students access to a whole range of arguments and to develop their critical faculties so that they could question all assumptions, formulate alternative interpretations, and come to their own conclusions about the important issues of the day.[90]

The fear that this liberal tradition would be subverted, concludes Fieldhouse, was sometimes justified. 'McCarthyite proscription of tutors and ideas revealed some very 'illiberal tendencies' within those responsible for adult education ('Responsible bodies') 'and their paymasters'. State aided education, he concludes, cannot 'remain immune from the ideological forces predominating in society at large.' But unless the educational system is reduced to a mere propaganda machine, the dialectical process of education 'must always leave room for alternative perspectives to survive – and eventually to prosper'. The democratic, open and socially purposive characteristics of the liberal tradition 'were not completely destroyed by the Cold War siege', Fieldhouse concludes. 'They survived, to reappear in the 1960's and 70s', though they were to come under threat once again in the 1980s.[91]

If, as Fieldhouse suggests, no irremediable damage was done in the field of adult education, and if the Middlesex ban was finally withdrawn, some careers had been displaced, a threatening warning given not to step out of line and a general atmosphere developed hostile to critical thinking and intelligence as well as to radical innovation in education. All this needs taking into account in interpreting the swing to the right which was the main characteristic feature of the early 1950s.

The Revival of Elitist Ideology

In the complex web of educational politics another feature surfaced at about this time having a close bearing on the structure, ethos and nature of the now evolving system. This concerned the fight for the primacy of the grammar schools within the maintained system and involved the formulation and propagation of an unashamedly elitist ideology. This movement also had as an objective the denigration of the idea of the common secondary, or comprehensive, school, which, as we have seen, gained substantial support during and after the war.

The grammar schools – or rather some of their teachers and organisations – felt themselves under attack, or at risk, as a result of the Act. This view was strongly expressed, for instance by John Garrett, head of Bristol Grammar School (a direct grant school), in a series of articles early in 1947. These schools, he claimed, 'came off badly' from the wartime reform and 'ever since they have battled against increasingly heavy odds'. The Burnham salary award of 1945 was 'a miserly recognition of a university degree', holidays were reduced 'to achieve closer parity with primary schools', clerical duties 'piled on the staff' and there is 'a suffocating plethora of forms'.[92]

In so far as there was any reality behind these charges, this arose from the Act's provision of secondary education for all and parity of conditions. But Garrett went much further in his charges, speaking of a 'campaign of vilification' and claiming that the techniques used were similar to those of the fascists 'when they set about undermining intellectual values'. Hardman, the very moderate Parliamentary Secretary to the Ministry of Education, was accused of making 'belittling references' to the grammar schools while 'his vague and ill-defined espousal of a new order in education which shall have closer connection with something called "real life", are doing more to denude grammar schools than any consideration of gain', (Garrett had claimed an exodus of 1,392 masters (sic) between April 1945 and December 1946). Finally Garrett assaulted alternative perspectives: 'To produce a classless society, clamorous demand is made for the common school for the common man, whose century it is.' That way lay disaster.[93]

It was this whole issue that was taken up, the invective being moved to a higher plane, by Dr Eric James, appointed headmaster ('high master' according to historical tradition) of Manchester Grammar School in 1945 at the youthful age of 36. Manchester Grammar School, probably the leading grammar school in the country, was again not under local control. As a direct grant school it provided an effective base for James's subsequent activities as the leading proponent of an elitist concept of education. In 1949 he published his well known short work, *An Essay on the Content of Education*, which set out his rationale in some detail, and was highly influential.

But already earlier than this James had been on the warpath. In a series of articles and speeches he set out to defend the grammar school and its approach as an education appropriate to a meritocratic elite. In a full page article in the *Times Educational Supplement* early in 1947 entitled 'The Challenge to the Grammar School' and subtitled 'Attack upon Standards and Values', James claimed that the 'feeling of despondency' among those teaching in grammar schools had deep roots based in 'certain contemporary tendencies'. The 'educational world' he claimed 'does not recognise sufficiently the value of their work' or their true purpose, which is to provide 'an education of the fullest kind for the academically most gifted section of the population'.[94]

This concept was central to James's thinking. In every field of social advance, he wrote, 'we have to make the fullest use of the intellectual capacity of our people, above all of the most intelligent'. To fail here would be 'a national disaster'. It is a dangerous delusion, he continued, 'to believe that our problems can be solved by any except those capable of dealing with principles, abstractions, and general relationships – that is to say, by any but the academically most gifted'.[95]

This, he said, is what the grammar schools know how to do – after 45 years experience (a reference to the 1902 Education Act). Yet they see 'this great achievement' in danger of replacement by 'new types of school'. James develops a series of arguments here against the concept of the common, or comprehensive school, which, he claims, 'inevitably leads to grave social, educational and cultural evils'. Such a school cannot adapt its teaching to the needs of the wide range of individuals who would attend, could not provide teaching in some of the subjects grammar schools provide (e.g. Greek) and, above all, would involve 'a retardation in the progress of the most gifted children' which would be both a denial of equality of opportunity and 'a national disaster'.[96]

It is clear that battle lines were now being drawn on the whole issue of the structure of secondary education, its ethos and direction. James's outlook received support from prestigious sources. Again, early in January 1947, Sir Richard Livingstone, ex-Vice Chancellor of Oxford University and an educationist in the classical/humanist tradition, delivered a presidential address to the Conference of Educational Associations entitled 'Equality in Education: its Dangers and

Difficulties'. Livingstone also claimed that secondary school salary equalisation (arising from the Act) would 'deal higher secondary education a blow which will be disastrous to it and to the nation.'[97] Those teaching pupils of higher intellectual ability must be paid more than the others – 'otherwise the quality of the higher stages of secondary education will fail'. Livingstone also poured scorn on the concept of the single school, relying largely as did James, on writings from the United States (which, incidentally, while often critical, never proposed an alternative system). Such schools would be 'of excessive size'; would turn their backs on 'rigid selection' and so may be described as 'sentimentally inclusive'. Democracy at the average level of a people's taste was democracy at a low level. Unless we were careful, this would happen here. The function of education was to foster aristocracy, 'a national elite based on true merit'. The implications were clear.[98]

Prestigious support for the crucial argument – that a minority elite of the 'highly intelligent' required a special segregated education – came at this time from the poet and sage, T.S. Eliot. In his *Notes Towards a Definition of Culture* (1949), Eliot developed Mannheim's 'elite' theories, if in a surprisingly old-fashioned or traditional way. A classless society, he argued, cannot work because it provides no satisfactory mechanism for selecting and preserving elites, and so preserving the stability of society.

Eliot's own solution rested, in large part, on his mystical conception of the family 'persisting from generation to generation, each in the same way of life'. Society must remain static, arranged in 'a continuous gradation of culture levels'. These will also be levels of power; but the culture-class system would be leavened by the infiltration of gifted individuals from below. The governing elite, of the nation as a whole, would consist of those whose responsibility was inherited with their affluence and position, and whose forces were constantly increased and often led, by individuals of exceptional talent. The selection and shaping of this elite should be in the hands of the hereditary aristocracy, based on birth and wealth, and recognising divine authority. In such a society the limitation of education appears as a cultural necessity. 'To aim to make everyone share in the appreciation of the fruits of the more conscious part of culture', concluded Eliot, 'is to adulterate and cheapen what you give. For it is an essential condition of the preservation of the quality of the culture of the minority, that it should continue to be a minority culture'.[99]

Such arguments were now pressed at various levels. At the annual meeting of the prestigious North of England Education Conference, Professor Kandel (an Englishman who had been Professor of Education at the University of Columbia in New York) drove home a similar point on a different level. The comprehensive school was not the answer, as, he claimed, American experience had proved. What was needed was a differentiated system.[100]

> Everything that it known about individual differences in ability; everything that is known about the varying needs of boys and girls; everything that is known about the needs of modern life seems to point in the direction of schools functionally organised so that each can carry out its specific aims and purposes; all of them by different methods and adaptation of content contributing to the same common end – the preparation of every boy and girl for their tasks as citizens, workers and human beings.

English education, commented W.P. Alexander, Secretary to the Association of Education Committees, owes a debt to Professor Kandel 'for having placed forty years of experience in the American educational world so clearly before us'. 'All engaged in educational administration will weigh his words carefully.' It is comforting, he added, that 75 per cent of development plans 'adopt the policy of functional organisation of schools'.[101]

This, of course, was the main issue at stake. What, in fact, was now happening on the ground, in terms of planning for the future?

Constructing a Divided System

Alexander's claim that 75 per cent of development plans adopted 'the functional organisation of schools' (by which he meant the tripartite system) was derived from the Fabian survey referred to earlier, published in April 1947.[102] This, in fact, analysed only 54 local authority development plans already submitted to the minister (of the total of 146 local education authorities, only about a third had, in fact, submitted plans by that date). The survey brought to light a variegated picture. Of the eighteen county boroughs surveyed, four had, in fact, opted for 'multilateral' schools for all their pupils (Southend, a Tory authority) or for most of them

(Reading, Oldham and Coventry). Of the county councils, one (Westmorland) had opted for multilateral schools in some places. The London County Council, of course, was planning for 67 such schools to take 91 per cent of London's secondary pupils. In addition, many authorities (thirteen county boroughs and eleven county councils) were planning to establish bilateral schools (largely grammar-modern).

On the other hand, a strict count of schools and of the numbers of pupils planned for each type did indeed show that 74 per cent of schools were planned in the tripartite mode (comprising 59 per cent of pupils) while 24 per cent were planned either as 'multilateral' or 'bilateral' comprising 40 per cent of pupils – the fact that the LCC is included in this calculation, with large schools planned, must be taken into account. The general picture, concludes the author, is of the 'overwhelming preponderance of the modern school' (comprising 50 per cent of schools, 41 per cent of pupils), and 'acceptance of the policy of segregating secondary pupils into grammar, modern and technical schools'.[103]

Whether these submissions were all accepted, of course, is another question; nor has a full analysis yet been made of development plans as a whole. Further, whether local plans, even if accepted, were actually implemented, is yet another question. Nevertheless the survey is of value in crystallising the outcome of the planning process at this precise moment in time. It is also a fair indication that the 'advice' and 'guidance' so profusely tendered by the ministry had had its effect. In practice the wave of support for the single school had been beaten back – or at least very effectively contained. The system that was to be developed nationally was, generally speaking, the tripartite system. It was, therefore, on this basis that new schools were to be designed and planned – a matter which later, of course, was to lead to endless difficulties.[104]

Comprehensive plans for a few, determined, authorities were, however, finally approved by the Labour minister. These included Anglesey (which established its first school, Holyhead, in 1949), Coventry (where the existing schools were largely destroyed by wartime bombing), the West Riding (a proportion of its secondary schools, though its development plan argued strongly against the selective system), and, of course, the London County Council – by far the biggest authority in the country which, as we have seen, began planning for this transition as early as 1935.

The case of London is interesting. The ambitious London School Plan first published in 1947, finally received ministerial approval (in principle) on 17 February 1950, with the important proviso that proposals relating to individual schools would be 'subject to further consideration' when submitted for approval.[105] The London County Council was, of course, determined to introduce their comprehensive plan; had important links with the Labour Party leadership; had prepared their plan with a high degree of professionalism; while London schools had, of course, suffered greatly from destructive bombing during the war. An additional factor (according to Margaret Cole) was that at this time the opposition (Tory) Councillors at County Hall 'while not subscribing to the comprehensive idea in general, were willing to see it tried out'.[106] Further London's Chief Education Officer, Graham Savage, was, as we have seen, 'one of us' – in terms of ministry officials – and the records show the key role he played in easing the plan through a series of discussions at the ministry.[107] Given the situation, it would hardly have been practical politics for a Labour minister to have rejected the London Plan. The rejection of the original Middlesex plan which would have allowed a rapid transition using existing buildings and relatively small schools, had put paid to any further such proposals. The London schools were to be large, and so would theoretically allow a 'multilateral' form of internal organisation, so meeting the requirement of Circular 144. [108] Further, most of these would require new buildings. The perspective of a complete transition to comprehensive education was, therefore, comfortably remote.

So, generally speaking, although there were some new developments reflected in a minority of development plans, the strict tripartite system was now effectively imposed on England's schools – although we should note that, in 1948, the Scottish Advisory Council on Education came out very strongly for the 'omnibus' (or comprehensive) school as the most appropriate solution for Scotland, while the Welsh Advisory Council in its 1949 report, favoured either multilateral or bilateral schools.[109] On 1 April 1945 the pre-Act senior elementary schools were renamed 'secondary modern', and this new type of school, with a leaving age (from April 1947) of fifteen now came into being – as it were, by a stroke of the pen. As we have seen, it was schools of this type, planned to cater for some 70-75 per cent of the nation's children, that largely predominated in the early development plans analysed by Thompson.

'Free from the pressure of any external examination, these schools can work out the best and liveliest forms of secondary education suited to their pupils,' pronounced *The Nation's Schools* early in 1945. 'It is essential that they should retain this invaluable freedom which the best of their predecessors have used to such advantage, and should be enabled to advance along the lines they themselves feel to be right.' So the problem of the content of education, or of their pupils' activity, was now left to the teachers, who were encouraged to find their own solutions to the problems they faced – it will be remembered that the Norwood Committee, asked to report on 'Curriculum and Examinations in Secondary Schools.' devoted literally half a page to these schools, compared to nearly 100 to the grammar schools (in fourteen chapters, the first entitled 'The Curriculum in General'). To consider the curriculum of the secondary modern school, they argued, 'is outside our scope' but, they added, 'in our view' it would fulfil its role 'if it provided curricula closely related to the immediate interests and environment of its pupils and adopted a method of approach which was practical and concrete'. We look forward, they concluded, 'to much fruitful growth and many experiments in this field of education.'[110]

As we have seen, decisive steps were taken already by 1947 to ensure that pupils from these schools could not enter for the then grammar school examination; nor, in terms of planning at that time, for the new General Certificate of Education (1951). In the pamphlet which succeeded *The Nation's Schools*, after the 1946 Labour Party conference attack, this point is reiterated. *The New Secondary Education* (1947) states definitively that:

> In schools that have to cope with the wide ranges of ability and aptitude that are found in all modern schools, it is impracticable to combine a system of external examinations, which presupposes a measure of conformity, with the fundamental conception of modern school education, which insists on variety.[111]

So the secondary modern school, cut off from any organic links with full-time higher education, was launched on its career.

This is where the mass of the children were in fact to be educated. These schools now began their quest for parity of esteem and of status, which, according to the Norwood Report – that architect of tripartitism – could 'only be won by the school itself'. In a sense it was here that, perhaps inadvertently, the country was launched on a new and huge educational experiment.[112]

The other main leg of the system (if we postpone consideration of technical schools for the moment) was, of course, the grammar school. Here the plans (and thinking) of the ministry were a great deal more precise; and had indeed clearly been thought out during the war, as many indications show.

The main thrust of this policy, as we have already seen, was actually to reduce the intake into these schools and to work towards a situation where all pupils stayed the full course (in 1938 about 50 per cent left at sixteen or before). The White Paper of 1943 had already argued that a grammar school course was not appropriate for a substantial proportion of its pupils, who should, therefore, be reduced in number. The Norwood Report, holding similarly that the grammar school curriculum is not 'suitable' for many of its pupils, also proposed a reduction in intake. This thinking surfaced as policy in Circular 73 – the first to give guidance on development plans. This indicated that where existing grammar school accommodation is 'disproportionately large' some of this could be adapted to 'courses of a technical character'. Local authorities were further warned not to increase 'the present intake' into existing grammar schools – this would be 'likely to hinder rather than help the proper development of secondary education' – the additional pupils may find the curricula 'not best suited to them', and so 'jeopardise the standard and the objectives which are and must be peculiar to the grammar school type of education'. Here the ministry's cherished plan to work towards all grammar school pupils staying the full course of education up to eighteen is again stressed.

Towards the end of Labour's administration this policy culminated in the publication of a weighty pamphlet, *The Road to the Sixth Form*. This was specifically concerned to outline 'the special distinguishing character of education of the grammar school type' – that is, for 'the more intellectually gifted of the nation's children' – or 'The gifted minority'. Scattered with quotations from Horace, Juvenal and Virgil – not to speak of Milton, Shakespeare and Defoe – this pamphlet reflected the elitist ideology discussed in the last section in its constant reiteration of the special quality and needs of 'gifted children' (who are, however, nowhere defined). Referring at the close to the 'feeling of unease, amounting at times to something like despondency', about the difficulty of 'maintaining intellectual and other standards' in today's changing society, this pamphlet set out specifically to stress the value of grammar school education, to promote some rethinking, and to establish the schools in their new meritocratic form as providing a complete course to eighteen for the great bulk of their pupils, girls as well as boys. The pamphlet, however, aroused massive opposition among grammar school teachers for its proposal that, with the new General Certificate of Education, pupils should jump the O level stage at sixteen, and sit all examinations (O and A levels) together at eighteen; also that, where there was a conflict, the interests of those who left at sixteen (after O level examinations only) should be sacrificed.[113]

The third leg of the tripod was, of course, the secondary technical school, selective in character, and recruiting at the age of eleven instead of at thirteen plus (as before the Act). Great emphasis had been put on the necessity of developing schools of this type by the Spens Committee, in its report entitled (it is worth recalling) 'Secondary Education with Special Reference to Grammar and Technical High Schools' (1938). The general intention, as outlined in the White Paper as well as the Norwood report, was that schools of this type should take about half the selective intake – 15 per cent, though this was never precisely laid down. However, as we have seen, local authorities were guided to provide such schools in their Development Plans.

In the immediate post-war period there were in existence 317 such schools or departments attended by some 66,000 pupils; they represented, therefore, only a tiny proportion of all secondary school pupils (about 3 per cent). [114] Joan Thompson's analysis of about a third of Development Plans, previously discussed, gives the position based on plans available in 1947. This indicates that this sample of authorities had planned that 7 per cent of their schools should be technical schools, catering for only 6 per cent of pupils (although several authorities were planning bilateral modern-technical schools, catering for another 10 per cent of pupils).[115] There is no contemporary indication that the Ministry, in approving local authority plans, insisted on a higher proportion of technical school provision, though this is a matter that requires further research.

The test, however, must lie in the outcomes of this planning. This is a matter which is referred to again later, but in terms of the period covered by this chapter, only modest progress had been made by the end of the Labour government's administration. In January 1952 official statistics show that the number of schools or departments classified as 'Technical' had actually declined (from 317 in 1947 to 291), but this may have been the effect of re-categorisation. The number of pupils so categorised had, on the other hand, risen, if slightly (by about 8,000 to a total of 74,927 see Appendix Table 5a, p.583). There were by this time a few thousand pupils in bilateral (technical-modern and grammar-technical), but no attempt is made to identify those following a specifically technical curriculum in these schools (the total number of pupils in these bilateral schools was about 11,600).[116]

From this it is clear that, in spite of a good deal of pressure and talk about the need to develop secondary technical education, very little was achieved, either on the ground or in terms of planning in the immediate post-war period. Technical schools continued to cater for only about 3 per cent of the child population (mainly boys). There was, in fact, no *serious* attempt to establish a strictly *tripartite* system in spite of the rhetoric (not even in England – Wales and Scotland, as we have seen, rejected the concept). What was in fact established was, to all intents and purposes, a bipartite system of grammar/modern schools, with a few frills around the edges. This was the actual, concrete outcome both of the Act itself, and of developments on the ground in the years that followed. It was to be several years before a serious attempt began to be made to rectify this anomaly but then only as a counter to the growing popular demand to overcome the divisive system now being so ruthlessly imposed; but these events belong to the next chapter.

The Public Schools

In the immediate post-war years the public schools kept a low profile. During the war their very existence, as we saw in

Chapter 1, was called into question – their survival as independent and autonomous entities was due largely to the political skill of the then President of the Board, R.A. Butler. The ethos and mood of the country following Labour's 1945 victory was still by no means sympathetic to these schools, which certainly still felt themselves at risk. In this situation they did as little as they could to draw attention to themselves.

Their financial crisis – the immediate cause of their initial pre-war panic and of their new found concern to relate themselves in some way with the school system as a whole – was now, however, at an end. With increased affluence among the upper and middle classes, these schools were, in fact, now finding little difficulty in recruitment. Probably as a direct result, they rejected (if informally) the proposition in Scheme B of the Fleming Report – that those schools that wished to should offer 25 per cent of their places to pupils from the state system, whose fees would be covered directly from the Ministry of Education under a national scheme for bursaries.[117]

Some were, however, anxious to make a relationship with the state system, however tenuous, while also wishing, if possible, to gain financial support from public funds without conceding control – as had always been the perspective of those involved during the war. This they in fact achieved with the active assistance of the two Labour ministers. Early in 1946 the ministry issued two Circulars (83 and 90) and later another (120) dealing with boarding school education (among other things). In effect, these circulars actively encouraged local authorities to enter into arrangements with individual boarding (i.e. largely independent or 'public') schools and to offer to pay the full fees, not only for children with special needs but also for 'normal' children, where the parents desired this and provided the authority agreed the request as 'reasonable'.[118] As a direct result, a number of such arrangements, with schools like Eton, Harrow, Mill Hill and, for girls, Westonbirt and Wycombe Abbey, were agreed to by certain authorities (for instance, Dorset, Middlesex and others). These circulars aroused sharp criticism from the Workers' Educational Association, which kept a close eye on all such developments. Early in 1947 a memorandum was published criticising these arrangements. This was followed a year later (March 1948) by a deputation by the leading officials of both the WEA and the

NUT to the Minister (Tomlinson). Nothing of substance was, however, achieved at the subsequent exchange of views.[119]

The Labour government, as the WEA pointed out, had made no statement whatever about the Fleming proposals since taking office; yet here was active encouragement for an 'association' which had not been agreed or announced. The history behind these measures is of some interest. It is clear that Head Masters' Conference (HMC) – the powerful organisation which united the public schools – in its initial reaction to the Fleming Committee's proposal, refused to agree to the 25 per cent minimum 'bursary' places. So a committee under Sir Maurice Holmes was set up in secrecy, probably because it was hoped that it might make another proposal more acceptable to the HMC. Whatever these proposals may have been, the HMC (the Chairman was Wolfenden, then head of Uppingham) and ministry officials apparently decided after the 1945 General Election that they would not be acceptable to Ellen Wilkinson, so nothing more was heard of them. No decision of any kind about the original Fleming proposals was announced or apparently made by Ellen Wilkinson. But clearly the suggestion was made, perhaps by an official to the minister, that individual schools might be advised (privately) to approach specific local authorities, if they wished to, to make whatever arrangement (about bursaries) they required.[120]

This required some alteration of administrative procedures. Local authorities already had the power to finance attendance at boarding schools for specific categories of pupils – but not for 'normal' pupils. Hence the issue of Circular 90 (which conceded these powers) and of Circular 120, which reinforced them.

At this time (early 1947) the Minister, George Tomlinson, in a letter to the WEA, defended the ministry's action by referring to the 'pressing needs' for boarding school education. But, as Shena Simon pointed out, it was reasonable to ask why this need (no greater, presumably, than it had been earlier) had suddenly become more 'pressing' – than, for instance, the provision of nursery schools. While Wolfenden, as Chairman of the Head Masters' Conference, protested loudly that there had been no 'surreptitious and backdoor negotiations' between the ministry and the schools, it was quite evident to those with access to the necessary information that a good deal of discussion and negotiation had in fact been going on precisely between the ministry and the schools (as it had done, of course, earlier in 1939-40).[121]

The WEA, in its memo on this issue, reiterated its attitude to these schools. In its view, 'the continued existence of a highly privileged system of schools occupying the key positions which are at present held by the public schools, will militate seriously against the development of a democratic educational system'. Any subsidisation of these schools at public expense should be rejected. It concluded that no arrangements should be permitted between Local Education Authorities (LEAs) and independent schools 'until the minister has reached a decision on the recommendations of the Fleming Committee and made a statement thereon'.

In the outcome, no such statement was ever made. Further, local authority arrangements with individual schools never reached significant proportions and the whole movement gradually died away. As the public schools rehabilitated themselves over the next few years, their enthusiasm, such as it was, evaporated. They no longer had any need to seek funding from public moneys. The rhetoric so many of the heads had generated early in the war, as to the need to overcome the undemocratic and divisive nature of this system of schooling, was now forgotten.[123]

Finally, but not until 1948, the public schools at last began to assume a higher profile. In that year King George VI and Queen Elizabeth paid an official visit to Marlborough College – an event attended with much publicity and fanfare of trumpets. The public schools were back. It may be worth noting, however, that Queen Elizabeth (who shortly succeeded to the throne) and her husband, the Duke of Edinburgh, later rejected the established (traditional) public schools for their own (male) offspring – sending them instead to the innovative new school, Gordonstoun, established by the German educationalist Kurt Hahn, in the mid-1930s.

George Tomlinson, as minister, went out of his way to reassure the independent schools as to their security under a Labour government. The circulars, easing new relations with local authorities, were part of the process. Towards the close of his period as minister, Tomlinson assured the IAPS (Incorporated Association of Preparatory Schools) that the Education Act recognised a place for independent schools and that 'the latest government statement of educational policy made no suggestion of absorbing them into the state system'. Asking the assembled heads of these schools to 'experiment boldly' the report concludes that he sat down to the 'weekend's most rousing applause'.[124] His greatest success in this direction, however, was gained during a visit to Eton.[125]

It was not only the public schools, however, which no longer faced a challenge. We saw in Chapter 1 that the direct grant grammar schools, in spite of the proposal in the first (interim) report of the Fleming committee that fee-paying in these schools should be abolished, in fact survived in the same condition as they were before the war. On this issue, as R.H. Tawney put it in a *Manchester Guardian* leader, Butler 'capitulated', after pressure by the 'die-hards of his party'. This meant that, in spite of the promise of 'secondary education for all', in one sector of schools supported out of public funds, fees were to continue to be charged.[126]

This was not acceptable to many in the labour movement. Shortly after taking office, Ellen Wilkinson announced her intention to continue the direct grant schools as a separate category, but indicated that fees were to be abolished.[127] But in fact they were not. The income level (means test for payment) was raised which might be regarded as a step towards free education, but the final step was never taken. Fees continued to be charged, in spite of protests. One further step was to reduce the number of schools on the direct grant list – excluding those which in fact operated like local grammar schools. As a direct result, a few of these went independent, the rest were simply transferred to local authority control and finance. By this means the number of direct grant schools was reduced from 232 to 164 by June 1946. Nevertheless the direct grant schools, as a specific category of schools funded directly by the Ministry of Education and charging fees, survived largely intact both during the war, and, more particularly, during the period of the Labour government's terms of office in the post-war period. This 'system' then, if somewhat reduced, continued to function as an outpost of the public schools – their defence, as we saw in Chapter 1, being regarded as a major objective by high ministry officials during the war itself and of course thereafter.

Labour's Achievement
In February 1950 the Labour government called a new

election, having nearly run its full course from July 1945. The government was returned with an increased vote (the turnout was up to 84 per cent from 73 per cent in 1945) but with a very small overall majority – of eight (see Appendix I, p. 564) The new administration, beset by many difficulties, weary, and now very clearly running out of steam, lasted about twenty months. Its most critical moment was, of course, occasioned by the resignation of Aneurin Bevan, architect of the National Health Service, in April 1951. This was a direct result of economic difficulties arising from American pressure for a huge rearmament programme (costing £6,000 million) in December 1950 – a measure related to the outbreak of the Korean War in June. The rearmament programme was scaled down (to £4,700 million), but remained massive. Bevan's actual resignation was sparked by Hugh Gaitskell's insistence, as Chancellor, on a fee charge for dentures and optical services.

Although attempts were made to regain normalcy, it soon became evident that the government was doomed, although retaining wide support in the country. At the general election which followed dissolution, held on 25 October 1951, Labour in fact polled its highest ever vote – of just under 14 million from a turn-out of 82.5 per cent. The Tories, however, with over 200,000 fewer votes, gained more MPs and now had an overall majority of twenty (or seventeen if 'others' – three – are included as opposition). Winston Churchill now returned and formed his new administration, so ushering in thirteen consecutive years of Tory rule. The Utopian perspectives of 1945 now receded into the distant past.

In his magisterial, and, generally speaking, sympathetic assessment of the record of the two Labour governments, Kenneth Morgan highlights education as a specific area of failure, or at best of negative achievement. No new initiatives, or new thinking, of any significance, he says, were provided by Labour. While giving Ellen Wilkinson due credit for fighting through the leaving age (in 1947) against opposition from some Cabinet colleagues, Morgan regards both Ellen Wilkinson and George Tomlinson's failure to support a move to comprehensive secondary education as reprehensible. He is also severely critical of the Labour government's failure to tackle the issue of the public or independent schools. With such 'docile' ministers, Morgan concludes, these schools could rest in peace.

This criticism is all the more striking in that, generally, Morgan celebrates what he assesses as the many positive achievements of the Attlee governments.[128]

In fact it is the case that, by the close of Labour's period of office, very few schools that could conceivably be defined as comprehensive had been brought into being. In a House of Commons debate in August 1950, Hardman (Parliamentary Secretary) claimed 'a comprehensive school in Walsall, three in Middlesex, and on an experimental basis, four in London' (these were the pioneering 'interim' schools).[129] Local authorities throughout this period were, on the other hand, actively dissuaded from planning for them; the most advanced, where this was done, were (except in the case of London) actively rebuffed. The 1951 ministry report reflects this tiny embryonic movement to comprehensive education. 11,830 pupils were credited to this new category, comprising 0.7 per cent of all secondary school pupils in the maintained sector in England and Wales (see Appendix Table 5a p.583)[130] This was the sum of Labour's achievement in this area. The *Times Educational Supplement* was surely correct in its summing up of Labour government policy. Now under new editorship, it commented approvingly that it was 'extremely doubtful' whether Mr Tomlinson ever once lifted a hand to increase the number of comprehensive schools.[131]

The policy pursued by the Labour government in education was basically one of consensus. It had the complete approval of the Tory Party – at least up to July 1951 when Florence Horsbrugh and others began to make capital – oddly enough (in view of the government's policy), on the comprehensive issue.[132] The one major success, a political necessity, was the raising of the leaving age, involving priority for the provision of accommodation and the training of teachers under the emergency scheme, celebrated by the ministry in its extended pamphlet *Challenge and Response*. There was also the provision of school meals and free milk which certainly represented an important advance. On the other hand, no progress whatever was made with the establishment of county colleges, while the promise of the youth service, established early in the war, also gradually waned. Nor, as Morgan points out, was any action taken about the public or independent schools. At the level of higher and technical education, the post-war surge in university numbers was followed by a period of 'consolidation' – only one new university successfully broke into the charmed circle (Keele), though this admittedly embodied new approaches.[133] It is on her achievements relating to the leaving age that H.D. Hughes, Ellen Wilkinson's Parliamentary Private Secretary, mounted her defence in the pages of *History Workshop Journal* (against a severe critique by David Rubinstein) in 1979.[134]

How far did the Labour government open up opportunity, in the sense of extending provision for a selective education in these years? The key figure here is the proportion of thirteen year-olds within the maintained system obtaining a selective education. In 1947 the first post-war year for which statistics are available, the figure was 22.3 per cent. In 1951, four years later, the figure is much the same at 22.6 per cent (embodying a slight reduction in the proportion going to grammar schools and a slightly larger increase in that going to technical schools, now at 3.6 per cent).[135] In other words, given *support* for the tripartite system, what may be called the opportunity ratio hardly increased at all under Labour, although since places in grammar schools were now free, some increase may have taken place in working-class representation. However, the Floud, Halsey and Martin (1956) investigation in Middlesbrough and Hertfordshire showed that in these two areas the effect was marginal.[136] This failure to open up the grammar schools stands in sharp contrast with the objectives (and actions) of the two inter-war minority Labour governments.[137] The abolition of fees through the 1944 Act seems to have been accepted as the consummation of policy.

Was the policy pursued during this period one of advance, or of containment? And if so, whose policies were these? Certainly the hierarchical structure, established during the last century, emerged unscathed, if modified in detail. A closely knit 'system' of public schools, if briefly threatened, now again retained primacy. The two levels of 'grammar' schools, direct grant and maintained, existing before the war with roots further back, still catered for different elements among the middle classes (in the phrase of the Schools Enquiry Commission, the 'middle-middle' and 'lower-middle'). The senior elementary schools, now 'secondary modern', were overwhelmingly attended by the working class, among whom manual workers still preponderated. Gender discrimination characteristic of pre-war schooling was also now reproduced anew. Any developments which might have lead to disequilibrium in the labour market and, as a result, to social instability, were kept under close control (as we have seen, for instance, in relation to examinations). In fact, no serious challenge; indeed, no challenge of any kind, had been launched at the citadels of power in the world of education. And this at a time when the labour movement experienced an outstanding and perhaps unrepeatable electoral success. The explanation, perhaps, lies at a deeper level than covered in this analysis – in terms of the historical role of education in the assimilation, in a Gramscian sense, of subaltern (or subordinate) classes within the social complex. The experience of the Labour government once again highlighted the role of education in the mediation of class relationships within a capitalist society.

Notes and References

1. Kenneth Morgan, *Labour in Power 1945-51*, Oxford 1984, p.44.
2. Ibid.
3. Ibid., pp.33, 142-3.
4. Martin Wilson, *Epoch in English Education, Administrator's Challenge*, Sheffield City Polytechnic, Papers in Education Management No.39, 1984, p.24
5. Ibid., p.25.
6. F.F. Potter, *Educational Journey, Memories of Fifty Years in Public Education*, London 1949, p.133.
7. Ibid., pp.138-9.
8. Sir Alec Clegg, 'Teamwork and Beauty' (the first of four autobiographical articles), *Times Educational Supplement*, 20 September 1974.
9. See Correlli Barnett. *The Audit of War*, London 1986, pp.288ff., for a summary of widespread criticism in this area.
10. *Higher Technological Education* (the Percy Report), HMSO 1945.
11. *Hansard*, House of Commons, 19 April 1944, Cols. 305, 311.
12. The Barlow Committee was appointed on 9 December 1945. It reported to the Lord President of the Council (Morrison).
13. *Scientific Manpower* (the Barlow Report), p.8.
14. The arguments of the Barlow Committee on this issue interestingly parallel those later used by the Robbins Committee on higher education (1963) when making the case for a radical expansion some 20 years later. See pp.232-41.
15. *Barlow Report*, pp. 11, 23.
16. Ibid., pp.16-7.
17. Ibid., pp.11, 20, 25.
18. Parliamentary and Scientific Committee, *Universities and the Increase of Scientific Manpower*, December 1946, pp.2-3.
19. Ibid., pp, 17, 23. The Parliamentary and Scientific Committee opposed the establishment of a new university 'as proposed by Barlow'. Establishment of a new university was also opposed by the Committee of University Vice Chancellors. In *A Note on University Policy and Finance, 1947-56*, of July 1946, the Vice Chancellors cautiously accept what they perceive to be contemporary trends and demands – though

the tenor of the document is querulous. They argue for 'balance' at each university – if science is to be doubled, then the universities as a whole must be doubled. Standards, they argue, if lowered (by expansion) will never be retrievable. While willing to accept more government guidance, universities must remain autonomous.

20. *University Development from 1935 to 1947*, Report of the University Grants Committee, 1948, p.7.

21. G.C.T. Giles, *The New School Tie*, London 1946, pp.111-2.

22. Ibid., pp.24-5

23. Under Sections 35 and 108(3) of the Act, the school leaving age was to be raised to fifteen as from 1 August 1945, but if the minister was satisfied that the supply of teachers or of school accommodation was insufficient, he was empowered to defer the order 'to a date not later than 1 April 1947'.

24. CP (45) 117, Memorandum of 16 August 1945 (CP = Cabinet Papers).

25. CM (45) 25, Cabinet meeting of 23 August 1945 (CM = Cabinet Minutes).

26. CP (45) 140, 1 September 1945, Memorandum by Lord President of the Council, 'Raising the School Leaving Age'. CM (45) 28, Cabinet meeting of 4 September 1945.

27. *Manchester Guardian*, 15 May 1946.

28. CP (47) 25, 10 January 1947, Economic Survey for 1947: Report from the Ministerial Committee on Economic Planning.

29. CM (47) 8, Cabinet meeting of 16 January 1947.

30. Ibid.,'In a diary note written later Dalton accepted his defeat on this matter without rancour, observing "I had not minded much that the cabinet had declined to postpone the school leaving age by five months. I had never been keen on this." ' H. Dalton, *Diaries*, 27 January 1947, quoted by D.W. Dean, 'Planning for a Postwar Generation: Ellen Wilkinson and George Tomlinson at the Ministry of Education, 1945-51', *History of Education*, 1986, Vol. 15, No. 2, p.104.

31. Lord Redcliffe-Maud, *Experiences of an Optimist, the Memoirs of John Redcliffe-Maud*, London 1981, p.53.

32. *Education*, 14 February 1947.

33. *Times Educational Supplement*, 25 May 1946. For the Emergency Training Scheme, see *Challenge and Response*, Ministry of Education Pamphlet No. 17, HMSO 1950. In 1946 'applications had surpassed all expectations both in quality and in quantity' – especially from service men and women. But lack of space and planning meant candidates had to wait anything up to two years. Ibid., p.12.

34. Circular 106, 22 May 1946, on the Emergency Training Scheme. For a detailed assessment of the teacher supply and buildings situation at this point, see 'Advance in Education', *Times*, 22 May 1946.

35. Minister of Education, House of Commons, 15 March 1946, *Times*, 22 May 1946.

36. *Education*, 31 October 1947. This programme also included another 235 projects required to meet new housing developments in 1947.

37. *Times*, 22 May 1946.

38. See letter from G.C.T. Giles, *Times Educational Supplement*, 10 August 1946.

39. *Times Educational Supplement*, 25 May 1946. One problem the government faced was the need to provide in the building programme for developments (as Tomlinson put it) outside the sphere of education: (i) the rise in the birth rate (births were up from 579,000 in 1941 to 881,000 in 1947), (ii) new housing developments, (iii) further education – 'pressing demands from employers and trade unions'. *Education*, 31 October 1947.

40. Although it is often forgotten that the Norwood Report recommended 'a roughly common curriculum' for pupils aged eleven to thirteen in all three types of secondary school.*Curriculum and Examinations in Secondary Schools*, HMSO 1943, p.70.

41. *Labour Party Conference Report*, May 1945, p.126.

42. For the origins of this policy, Brian Simon, *The Politics of Educational Reform*, London 1974, pp.192-5; see also Stuart Maclure, *One Hundred Years of London Education, 1870-1970*, London 1970, pp.111, 124-27. For a full analysis of Labour

Party policy in London from 1918 to 1950, M.D. Richardson, 'The Politics of Educational Reform: A Study of the London Labour Party and the Reform of Secondary Schooling, 1918-1950', unpublished PhD thesis, University of London 1989.
43. Circular 28, 'Preparation of Development Plans', 8 May 1945.
44. R.G. Wallace, 'Labour, the Board of Education and the Preparation of the 1944 Act', unpublished PhD thesis, University of London 1980, p.277. Light is thrown on this in the Chuter Ede diaries. On 11 December 1944 Ede noted: 'Holmes has sent me the draft of a long document to be issued as a circular on "The Nation's Schools" (Circular 28, presumably). Later entries imply that Ede had read the draft of the pamphlet itself. On 12 December 1944 he noted: 'I have read the Paper on 'The Nation's Schools'. I greatly dislike its references to the multilateral school.' On 18 December be recorded a discussion with Butler: 'He said he was not satisfied with the notes for 'The Nation's Schools' and had written a sharp criticism. I said I did not like the dismissal of the multilateral school with a sneer. He said he was more in favour of the multilateral school than any of us.' However that may be (and there are no further relevant entries), while modifications may have been made to the draft document(s), in practice the ministry's line clearly finally prevailed on this crucial issue.
45. *The Nation's Schools*, HMSO 1945, pp.13, 21-4.
46. G.C.T. Giles, 'Secondary Education for All', *Times Educational Supplement*, 26 May 1945.
47. *Times Educational Supplement*, 15 July 1945.
48. *Labour Party Conference Report*, 1946, pp.189-95. W.G. Cove was a Member of Parliament and ex-President of the NUT.
49. Lord Redcliffe-Maud, op. cit., p.56.
50. Joan Thompson, *Secondary Education for All*, Fabian Research Series No. 118, April 1947. H.C. Dent, in a book also entitled *Secondary Education for All*, London 1949, states that 'hardly any of the local education authorities were planning on strictly tripartite lines' (p.144), though I believe this to be an exaggeration.
51. *Labour Party Conference Report*, 1947, pp.198-204.
52. *Education*, 26 August 1946.
53. Ibid., 9 July 1948.
54. Ibid., 25 February 1949.
55. On the Middlesex developments, see I.G.K. Fenwick, *The Comprehensive School 1944-1970*, London 1976, pp.45-8, and Rene Saran's specialist study, *Policy Making in Secondary Education: A Case Study*, Oxford 1973. Several files at the Public Record Office cover the Middlesex story: ED132/110-114. It must be admitted that the original North Riding Development Plan appears somewhat confused, see PRO ED132/189-191.
56. As, of course, was to be done in 1965, after another successful election.
57. Morgan, op. cit., p.174.
58. Betty D. Vernon, *Ellen Wilkinson*, London 1982.
59. Caroline Benn, 'Comprehensive School Reform and the 1945 Labour Government', *History Workshop Journal*, 10, Autumn 1980, pp.197-204.
60. Ibid.
61. In January 1946 there were 763,719 pupils in secondary modern schools and 472,390 pupils aged eleven and over in all-age schools. These latter were now categorised by the Ministry of Education as 'primary' schools. Tables 3 and 5, *Education in 1947*, Ministry of Education Report, 1948, pp.100-1, 104-5 (see Table 2a, p. 576).
62. Peter Fisher, *External Examinations in Secondary Schools in England and Wales, 1944-1964*, Educational Administration and History Monograph No. 11, University of Leeds, 1982, p.31. Fisher states that 'it was the demand from a few of the new secondary schools which prompted Williams [the civil servant involved, B.S.] to set in motion the train of events which led to Circular 103'.
63. Ministry policy originally stated in the 1943 White Paper and reiterated in the Norwood Report, was that grammar school pupils, who should be reduced in number

should normally stay the full course to seventeen or eighteen. This policy was finally clearly articulated in Ministry of Education pamphlet No. 19 *The Road to the Sixth Form*, 1951.

64. This is simply asserted in the Circular in the following terms: 'Having regard to the new statutory duties imposed on her under the Education Act, 1944, the Minister is no longer justified in limiting her functions to those of a Co-ordinating Authority'. This latter position had been announced by Circular 996 (25 May 1917) when the Board of Education first established the Secondary Schools Examinations Council, devolving its responsibilities on to the Council, to be conducted 'on behalf of the Board'.

65. The Minister announced his acceptance ('in principle') of the main recommendations of the SSEC Report in Circular 168, 'Examinations in Secondary Schools: Report of the Secondary Schools Examinations Council'. 23 April 1948.

66. Russell Meiggs, 'New School Examination', *Times Educational Supplement*, 3 July 1948. The author was a fellow of Balliol College, Oxford.

67. Ibid., 8 January 1949.

68. J.A. Petch, *Fifty Years of Examining: The Joint Matriculation Board, 1903-1953*, London 1953, pp.164, 170. This interpretation was later officially confirmed by the Beloe Committee, which, in 1960, proposed the examination which became known as the Certificate of Secondary Education (CSE). The SSEC, they say, 'hoped that by fixing a minimum age of sixteen (with the intention of raising the minimum to a still higher age at a later date) and by proposing a pass standard equivalent to the old School Certificate Credit, they had devised an examination which would in practice be beyond the reach of any but those in selective courses'. *Secondary School Examinations other than GCE* (the Beloe Report), HMSO 1960, p.7.

69. Potter, op. cit., p.101.

70. Morgan, op. cit., pp.330ff.

71. Ibid., pp.424ff.

72. Morgan, op. cit., 329, 334.

73. *Times Educational Supplement*, 3 April 1949.

74. Annual births, England and Wales, 1940-47 (See Appendix Table 1, p.575).

1940	590,000
1941	579,000
1942	652,000
1943	684,000
1944	751,000
1945	680,000
1946	821,000
1947	881,000
1948	775,000

75. For the grant formula, Ministry of Education Report, *Education in 1947*, pp.6-7.

76. Ministry of Education Report, *Education in 1949*, p.4. For Tomlinson's protests to Attlee at more radical plans for cuts, PRO ED136/891.

77. *Times Educational Supplement*, 4 November 1949.

78. Ibid., 11 November 1949.

79. For this and similar episodes, see Roger T. Fieldhouse, *Adult Education and the Cold War*, Leeds 1985, p.20 (and *passim*): for the Lords debate, *Hansard* (Lords), Vol. 166 (1950), Cols. 607-661.

80. Fieldhouse, op. cit., p.6.

81. Oddly enough, one of the author's first cousins.

82. *Times Educational Supplement*, 17 November 1950, Parliamentary report.

83. *Daily Worker*, 9 October 1950, Parliamentary report.

84. There is a full report of this debate in *The Schoolmaster*, 16 November 1950.

85. *Education*, 28 July 1950.

86. *Times Educational Supplement*, 6 October 1950.

87. Ibid., 3 November 1950.

88. The NUT showed its power in the closed shop issue enforced by the Labour-controlled Durham County Council at precisely the same time – withdrawing labour and forcing the council to backtrack. Similar action was not taken in the case of Middlesex, although Middlesex schools were blacklisted.

89. *Times Educational Supplement* 9 September 1955. This journal was now under a new editor, Walter James.

90. Fieldhouse, op. cit., p.92.

91. Ibid., pp.92-3.

92. John Garrett, 'Politics and the Grammar Schools', *Sunday Times*, 13 April 1947.

93. Ibid. The Incorporated Association of Head Masters (IAHM) published a memorandum as early as September 1946 entitled 'The Threat to the Grammar Schools'. In a dignified critique, W.P. (later Lord) Alexander (Secretary of the Association of Education Committees) claimed that the pamphlet was not concerned with standards of education of grammar school pupils. 'It is concerned with the dignity and privileges of the head masters of such schools. That dignity would have remained in higher esteem had this pamphlet not been published.'. *Education*, 20 September 1946.

94. *Times Educational Supplement*, 1 February 1947.

95. Ibid.

96. Ibid., James's article was countered in a main leader, 'Learning and Liberty', by Harold Dent, who again declared his allegiance to the 'real and substantial advantages' which would flow from the 'common secondary school'. Ibid.

97. *Education*, 3 January 1947. Livingstone had published two short books on education during the war: *The Future in Education*, Cambridge 1941, and *Education for a World Adrift*, Cambridge 1943.

98. Ibid.; see also *Times Educational Supplement*, 4 January 1947.

99. T.S. Eliot, *Notes Towards a Definition of Culture*, London 1949, pp.48, 106-7.

100. *Education*, 9 January 1948.

101. Ibid., 16 January 1948.

102. Joan Thompson, *Secondary Education for All*, Fabian Research Series No. 118, 1947.

103. Ibid., p.9.

104. Even comprehensive schools had to be designed in this way. 'Though LEAs have freedom to experiment, yet the Minister seems to consider large multilateral schools with some dubiety, as they have to be built so that they can be subdivided to separate schools if they do not prove a success.' Thompson, op. cit., p.7.

105. The official letter of approval (17 February 1950) reads: 'This approach is without prejudice to any decision that the Minister may be required to give as a result of the publication of Notices under Section 13 of the Education Act of 1944, in respect of individual proposals included in the Development Plan as falling within the provisions of that Section, and so subject to further consideration of the details of individual proposals as and when submitted to the Minister for approval.' PRO ED152/107 (London 1947-52).

106. Margaret Cole, *What is a Comprehensive School? The London School Plan in Practice*, n.d. (1953?), p.3.

107. For ministry discussions, memoranda, minutes, etc., on the London County Council's Development Plan, PRO ED152/105 and 152/107. In the course of the negotiations, the ministry expressed the view that only a few comprehensive schools should originally be established, and that these should be regarded as experimental, and so capable of reverting to the separate tripartite organisation if it was so determined. Savage replied that 'it was unreal to think in terms of experiment with a very limited number of such schools', going on to say that 'when "the Dreadnought" was projected it was not designed so that it could be converted into three cruisers'. There must, he added, 'be an act of faith in the provision of multilateral schools'. (Interview memorandum, 24 April 1947).

108. Circular 144. 16 June 1947, argued that a 'multilateral' school should have a 10 or

11 form entry. This would allow two 'grammar' and two 'technical' streams, plus six or seven 'modern' streams. The *minimum* size acceptable on these criteria was about 1,600 pupils.

109. In its Report, *Secondary Education*, (1948), the Scottish Advisory Council on Education totally rejected the tripartite system 'proposed for England' as suitable for Scotland, especially the theory behind it 'that children sort themselves out neatly into three categories to which [the] three types of school correspond'. This is an assumption, they state, 'which teacher and psychologist alike must challenge'. The Council came out strongly in favour of the single ('omnibus') school with an average of about 800 pupils in the age range twelve to sixteen. See Chapter 7, 'The Organisation of Secondary Education'. In *The Future of Secondary Education in Wales* (1949) the Welsh Advisory Council covered a similar remit, recommending (a) multilateral schools, or (b) a dual system consisting of grammar-technical and modern-technical schools. Neither Scotland nor Wales proposed a tripartite system. It is worth noting that no such enquiry was carried through by the Advisory Council for England at that time (nor later).

110. *Curriculum and Examinations in Secondary Schools* (the Norwood Report), p.21.

111. *The New Secondary Education*, p.46.

112. The best evaluation of this whole enterprise is William Taylor. *The Secondary Modern School*, London 1963, described (in a 'critical bibliography') as 'the book to end all books on this subject'. W. Kenneth Richmond, *The Literature of Education*, London 1972.

113. *The Road to the Sixth Form*, Ministry of Education Pamphlet No. 19, HMSO 1951, pp. 1, 13, 17, 53, 58.

114. *Education in 1947*, 1948, Table 2, p.99.

115. Jane Thompson, op. cit., p. 8; see also Appendices.

116. *Education in 1952*, 1953, Table 1, p.67.

117. The tortuous negotiations that took place in the year following the publication of the Fleming Report are recounted in detail in Gosden, op. cit., pp.355-66. Nothing of any significance was achieved.

118. Circular 83, 'Choice of School', 14 January 1946; Circular 90, 'Development Plans', 8 March 1946; Circular 120, 'Boarding Education', 19 August 1946.

119. 'Boarding School Education', A Memorandum prepared by the Education Advisory Committee of the Workers' Educational Association, n.d. (1947?); 'Report of Deputation to the Minister of Education, 16 March 1948', WEA and NUT (in the author's possession).

120. This, and the next paragraph, is based on a file kept by Lady Simon of Wythenshawe who at that time was chair of the Education Advisory Committee of the WEA, which she passed to the author. Her interpretation, which is given here, finds support from Gosden's official account of developments in 1945-46. Gosden, op. cit., pp.355ff.

121. Letter, George Tomlinson to H. Poole (WEA), 18 February 1947: memorandum entitled 'Comments on the papers circulated by Mr. Poole, March 1947', by Lady Simon of Wythenshawe (both in the author's possession). The speech by Wolfenden referred to was made to the HMC in February 1947. The author's file copy is marked 'Confidential' and dated 19 February 1947.

122. WEA memorandum, cited in note 119.

123. 'If the experiment [of bursaries to public schools, B.S.] ... is today recalled at all, it is probably only because it provided the raw material for a film that helped launch Sir Richard Attenborough on his post-war screen career.' Anthony Howard, *RAB, the Life of R.A. Butler*, p.122. This was *The Guinea Pig*, first produced as a play in London in 1946.

124. *Times Educational Supplement*, 15 September 1950.

125. Fred Blackburn, *George Tomlinson*, London 1954, pp.6-8.

126. *Manchester Guardian*, 7 May 1945.

127. *Times Educational Supplement*, 6 October 1945. Her actual words, as reported,

were that one of her 'guiding aims' was 'to secure that full effect was given to the provisions in the regulations to all grant-aided schools (including direct-grant schools, the status of which she proposed for the present to retain) was made on the basis of merit'.
128. Morgan op. cit., pp.174-9. Henry Pelling, in his study *The Labour Governments 1945-51*, London 1984, seems equally unenthusiastic, though attempting no serious analysis. See pp.113-6.
129. *Education*, 4 August 1950. London's 'interim' comprehensive schools are referred to in Chapter 3 (p.170).
130. *Education in 1951*, 1952, Table 4, pp.86-7.
131. *Times Educational Supplement*, 19 October 1951. Tomlinson believed in a 'variety of approach' to the problems of secondary education. 'The Party are kidding themselves', he wrote in February 1951, 'If they think that the comprehensive idea has any popular appeal.' Quoted in Rodney Barker, *Education and Politics 1900-1951. A study of the Labour Party*, Oxford 1972, p.95.
132. This is argued in Peter Wann, 'The Collapse of Parliamentary Bipartisanship in Education, 1945-53', *Journal of Educational Administration and History*, Vol. III, No. 2, June 1971.
133. On the Labour government's university policy, see D.W. Dean, op. cit., pp.105-107. For the foundation of the University at Keele, Sir James Mountford, *Keele, an Historical Critique*, London 1972; and Roy Lowe, 'Determinants of a University Curriculum', *British Journal of Educational Studies*, Vol. XVII, No.1. February 1969. In September 1951 the government issued a White Paper on 'Higher Technological Education'. This proposed modest development of post-graduate courses in technology, the establishment of a 'College of Technology' with certain limited functions, and rejected action in the foreseeable future on the widely canvassed proposal to establish a technological university with 2,000 to 3,000 students. These proposals, generally regarded as being cautious and highly conservative ('The White Paper, six years later, is still far short of the Percy report', *Times Educational Supplement*, 21 September 1951), fell with the government's demise shortly after their publication.
134. H.D. Hughes, 'In Defence of Ellen Wilkinson', *History Workshop Journal*, 7, Spring 1979, pp.157-60; David Rubinstein, 'Ellen Wilkinson Reconsidered', Ibid., pp.161-69; and Caroline Benn, 'Comprehensive School Reform and the 1945 Labour Government', ibid., 10, Autumn 1980, pp.197-204. See also Betty D. Vernon, op. cit., Chapter 10.
135. These percentages are calculated from the Ministry of Education *Reports* for 1947 (Table 3, pp.100-1) and 1951 (Table 2, pp.82-83).
136. J.E. Floud, A.H. Halsey and F.M. Martin, *Social Class and Educational Opportunity*, London 1956, pp.142-3 (conclusions).
137. Brian Simon, *The Politics of Educational Reform, 1920-1940*, London 1974, pp.78-84, 151ff.

3 The Tory Government and Education, 1951–56

1 The Crystallised Structure

By the early 1950s the outlines of the new post-war structure of the educational system were becoming clear. Within the tripartite system of grammar, technical and secondary modern schools now successfully imposed there had been no increase, as we have seen (in Chapter 2), in educational opportunity – measured in terms of access to selective schools and so to higher education and the professions. Expectations, particularly among skilled workers, had risen greatly compared to the pre-war situation. Pressure for access to selective schools was now on the increase.

An investigation into parents' preferences in Hertfordshire in 1952, for instance, revealed that over half of all parents with children aged from ten to eleven preferred the grammar school for their children, a fifth the technical school and only 16 per cent wanted the modern school. The enquiry showed that the more thought parents had given to their child's education, the more marked was their preference for the grammar school, and that the majority of parents who felt this way held their opinions strongly.[1] Summing up the evidence two years later, one authority claimed that it revealed 'all too clearly' that 'parents who care about education and realise its influence on future careers ... are immensely anxious to get their children into grammar schools'. There is, he concluded, 'a great deal of frustrated educational ambition'.[2]

A striking example of the strength of parental aspirations at this time (1954) comes from Nottingham, a fairly typical Midland city, but one with fewer grammar school places in proportion to the population than most other cities. In 1954 over 4,400 children were ready to go on to secondary school, but only 447 grammar places were available. At that time and place the 11-plus exam (for the selective schools) was not compulsory. In practice the primary (junior) school heads decided who should enter. Knowing that 90 per cent of the children could not (by definition) gain a grammar school place, the heads selected for entrance those who were thought to have some chance of passing. 1,321 boys and girls were so picked for the 1954 examination. But parents had the right to ask that their children be given a trial; and, in spite of the length of the odds, and of teachers' recommendations, 1,395 Nottingham parents insisted that their children also enter for the examination. In all, then, 2,716 children competed for the 447 places. Inevitably 2,269 'failed'.[3] What this meant in terms of human frustration to both parents and children is easy to imagine, less easy to express.

What repercussions did this situation have in the schools? It provided the conditions for the rigidly streamed and competitively selective system that now developed throughout the country, the primary schools, of course, being most directly affected. In order to maximise the chances of winning places in the grammar schools, those schools which were large enough picked out possible winners from the age of seven or even earlier and brought them together into an 'A' stream, the rest being grouped into 'B', 'C' and even 'D' and 'E' streams in the case of a large school. This form of organisation had, in fact, been strongly recommended from 1931, at the very inception of the 'Hadow' policy of reorganisation of the then 'elementary' schools into two stages – primary and 'post-primary' (later 'secondary'), a recommendation based on full acceptance of the advice of psychologists (specifically Cyril Burt), who at that time held that 'intelligence' (and therefore learning capacity) was both fixed and innate. This theory provided an ideological (psychological) justification for the stratification of school children through streaming. Ideas, and practices, of this kind were, then, already endemic before the passage of the 1944 Act.[4] Increasing aspirations, and therefore competition, in the post-war period merely enhanced a tendency – a structure of school organisation – already apparent.

The result was a divided internal organisation within the

junior school, whose structure now increasingly resembled a series of conveyor belts. This may be represented graphically as in Figure 3.1 taken from a book published in 1953 dealing with the situation as it then appeared.[5] The point was there made that, 'once a child is placed in the "A", "B" or "C" category at the age of six or seven, s/he is almost certain to remain in it as s/he grows older' – a judgement later confirmed by research. Grouping all the more 'advanced' children together in one class, and all the more 'backward' in another also provided the conditions whereby the differences between both groups were inevitably exacerbated in the process of schooling – thus transfers between streams were rare. Given that, on average, only about 25 per cent of primary pupils could be successful in the 11-plus exam, it is clear that, in a three stream school, only those in the 'A' stream could expect to gain a place at a selective school, while those in lower streams had little or no such opportunity. Hence the extreme external pressures favouring streaming as the solution.

This form of organisation had a natural, but profound effect on the nature of the education within the primary school. This

Figure 3.1 *The Streamed Primary School*

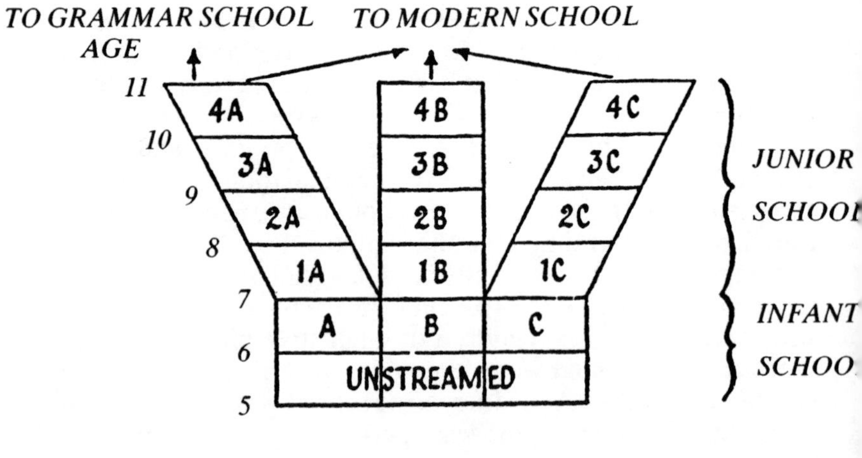

became dominated by the requirements of the selection examination which, in most areas, by this time took the form of so-called 'objective' tests in 'intelligence', English and arithmetic.[6] Much coaching went on in the junior schools in these subjects, particularly, of course, in the 'A' stream. A growing concern about the resulting narrowness of junior school education began now to be widely expressed. Typical of this was a comment by Ralph Morley, an experienced (and distinguished) teacher and now Member of Parliament, in a Commons debate in 1953:

> Some headmasters [*sic*] have moulded the whole of their curriculum around the grammar school entrance examination. From the time the child comes into the primary school at the age of seven, his attention is directed towards (this) examination. The whole of the primary school curriculum is distorted and warped ... and this warping ... is a very evil thing.[7]

A very similar point was made at this time by Alec Clegg, Chief Education Officer for the West Riding (Yorkshire):

> If the [Education] Committee were to decide that henceforth they would select for grammar schools solely on the children's ability to do long division, this form of calculation would be the main and most serious occupation of certain junior schools for the whole of their four-year course, to the detriment of many other activities which ought to be occupying these years.[8]

Relevant research at this time underlined the extent to which children suffered from parental pressures. One teacher, noticing symptoms of anxiety and worry in her class a year before the examination, did a careful investigation, reaching the conclusion that the examination was 'a positive danger to the mental and physical well-being of many children' in her class. Several showed signs of nervous instability, many complained of disturbed nights, especially on the eve of the examination. 'I had a smashing night's sleep – I took four aspirins.' Their dreams were significant. 'I had passed it, and got a bicycle but it was in pieces'; 'I had a nightmare and went in to Mummy'; 'I dreamed of fainting half-way through'; 'I went to sleep and woke up crying'. The prizes offered by parents to this one class included: sixteen new bicycles, three watches, three puppies, a bedroom clock, a portable radio, a tennis racket, a perm, a pair of roller skates, and so on. 'All,' the teacher reported, 'built up the tension, and sharpened the children's perceptions of their parents' fear'.[9]

By the early 1950s, then, the 11-plus was becoming the flash-point of educational criticism. In spite of valiant efforts on the part of the teachers in the new and rapidly expanding secondary modern schools, these were not achieving that 'parity of esteem' that apologists for the tripartite system (above all, the Ministry of Education) held out as their objective, in spite of serious attempts in some areas to develop a specific content and pedagogy then deemed as relevant to their pupils. A good example of this was the work done in Chesterfield and reported in *Theory and Practice in the New Secondary Schools* by A. Greenough, Borough Education Officer and F.A. Crofts, head of a local school. This book, published in 1949, focused on experimental work in a single school based on new curricular developments and relying heavily on a wide range of psychological testing to evaluate results and provide data for new forms of grouping and re-grouping of pupils.

The authors argued that:

> When we have faith in our competence to assess age, ability and aptitude equal to the faith we now have in our competence to measure degree of intelligence using verbal intelligence tests, we may expect to find in our secondary school children representatives of the whole range of intelligence for whom a practical approach to their general education at the secondary stage is appropriate.

These were the children whose intelligence was rated as 'from average plus downwards.' This, the authors argued, was a 'forward-looking' approach. 'Parity of esteem', wrote the distinguished educationist Sir Fred Clarke (now Chair of the Central Advisory Council for England) in his foreword, 'is still only a hope and a prospect, not yet an achievement'. But if the 'modern' school sets itself to the task, 'with the skill and insight that are revealed in this book ... 'esteem' may yet undergo some striking reversals'. Merited prestige, Clarke wrote, will not come by imitating older institutions, 'it can only come by the resolute and clear-sighted solution by the school of its own problems in its own way'.[10] But already by the early 1950s it was becoming apparent that secondary modern schools had been put in an impossible position.

While the schools for the mass of the children, both primary and secondary, were facing new problems, the Ministry of

Education single-mindedly pursued its cherished policy of building up the grammar schools as elite institutions – as *the* avenue to meritocratic achievement. As we have already seen (in Chapter 2), the ministry's 1951 pamphlet entitled *The Road to the Sixth Form* was concerned specifically with the education of 'the gifted minority'. It is precisely at this point that elitist ideas in education which, as we have seen, surfaced strongly in the late 1940s, now received welcome support from an unexpected quarter.

This took the form of a broadside from the Fabian element within the Labour Party, strongly opposing a policy of support for comprehensive education. In an issue of the *Political Quarterly*, edited by Leonard Woolf and William A. Robson,[11] published shortly after the 1951 General Election, the journal editorially took exception to the recently published Labour Party pamphlet *A Policy for Secondary Education*, the report of a committee appointed after the passage of a resolution at the October 1950 Labour Party conference calling on the then Labour government to implement the policy of comprehensive education.[12]

The Fabian element within the Labour Party was, of course, and always had been, determinedly meritocratic. This outlook was originally articulated by Sidney Webb, one of the Society's founders in the late nineteenth century, and given expression in his book *London Education* published in 1904. This was essentially a paean in favour of the London County Council's scholarship system celebrated as a 'capacity-catching' machine of high efficiency. The *Political Quarterly*'s editorial comments, which received widespread press publicity shortly after Labour's electoral defeat, contained a sharp, even vicious polemic against the Labour Party pamphlet, which it characterised as 'a shallow and superficial document', one which would injure the Labour Party. The existing three types of school, the pamphlet argues, 'must be swept away and be replaced by comprehensive schools'. No attempt is made to examine the scholastic implications of such action – as to how to educate together children of all abilities 'who are destined for widely different careers'. The whole issue is argued and decided 'almost entirely on social grounds, in terms of a doctrinaire egalitarianism ...'. The editorial includes a sarcastic summary of the pamphlet's proposal for a two-year general education for all (seen as diagnostic) after which pupils will be allocated to courses according to 'their interests and aptitudes, or catered for by other ill-defined and obscure methods'. Generally, the pamphlet 'stumbles blindly and blandly forward, intent upon one objective only: to obliterate the prestige and/or status which at present attaches to the grammar schools'.

If we want to 'make the most' of the community's intellectual powers, the editorial continues, 'we must accept the idea of an intellectual elite, an aristocracy of brains, based entirely on ability, and without regard to wealth, social standing, or other forms of privilege'. The urgent need is to develop 'the intellectually gifted boy and girl to the highest possible degree'. Indeed this subject, continues the editorial, 'is admirably discussed' in *Education and Leadership*, a short book recently published by Eric James entirely directed to making the case for a special, segregated education for the gifted minority.[13] Here it is argued that 'a system of selective secondary education, so far from creating class barriers is actually the most powerful solvent of those that still exist', a statement approvingly reproduced by this Fabian journal which went on to claim that, by and large, the grammar schools are 'the most excellent components of our educational system'.

Turning their guns on London's School Plan, the *Political Quarterly* expressed the view that, while there was admittedly a case for 'experiment', it was 'scandalously irresponsible for the largest education authority in the country to adopt a whole-hogging [sic] policy in favour of giant comprehensive schools'. Such a policy, in London as elsewhere, by introducing 'sweeping and irrevocable changes' will lead to severe electoral setbacks. An alternative policy should be to speed up improvements in secondary modern and technical schools (the secondary modern school concept, it is argued, 'has much to commend it, especially from a Socialist standpoint')[14], and to carry through 'carefully designed experiment' in 'different types of comprehensive schools'.

This somewhat unexpected outburst was followed by an angry protest from Margaret Cole, member of the LCC Education Committee and a well-known and consistent supporter of comprehensive education; and this in turn was followed by two further articles, by Helen Bentwich (Chairman of the LCC Education Committee) and Mrs C.D. Rackham (Chairman, Cambridge Education Committee), the former supporting the London School Plan, the latter the tripartite system and especially the grammar school. Secondary modern schools, in Mrs Rackham's view, should give an education for the 'great majority' of their pupils of 'a general character with a strong practical bias'. Comprehensive schools might be established 'in scattered neighbourhoods'. From all this the *Political Quarterly* concluded that, since both these Labour Party members held views which 'happen to be diametrically opposed', the comprehensive school should not be made 'a party question,' while opposition to comprehensive education should not be seen as inspired by 'political hostility to socialist ideas in education'.[15]

This discussion has been dealt with at some length in order to indicate the complexity of the situation, and to some extent, of the illusions still persisting among relatively intelligent, if remote, people as to the realities of the situation as opposed to the myths comfortably created, and as comfortably accepted, over the years.

It was at this point that the theory and practice of intelligence testing – or psychometry – exerted its most direct influence over the educational system, both as a means of legitimising the fractured (or divided) structure now coming into being, and as a lubricant ensuring its smooth functioning. Cyril Burt, then the leading and highly prestigious psychologist concerned with education, held that each child was born with a given 'quantum' (amount) of 'innate general cognitive ability'. In a series of popular broadcasts in 1950 he stated that:

> In an ideal community, our aim should be to discover what ration of intelligence nature has given to each individual child at birth, then to provide him with an appropriate education, and finally to guide him into the career for which he seems to have been marked out.[16]

A more or less accurate assessment of this 'innate intelligence', it was believed (or at least generally bruited abroad by leading psychologists, even if many had their own reservations) could be achieved by the relatively simple and cheap method of administering a group intelligence test (together with other tests) – as, of course, was by now done by most local authorities. Thus the educational system was seen to reflect nature, distributing, as it did, all children in the relevant age cohorts across three types of school each graded according to the intelligence level of its pupils; within each primary school and each secondary school of whatever type, the practice of streaming ensured a further internal differentiation, again reflecting the natural order of things (see Figure 3.2). So the actual practice of streaming which exacerbated differences among pupils by grouping each level with their fellows, ensured outcomes reflecting the original differentiation, or stream (or school) placement. The theory legitimising the system was therefore (inevitably) borne out by the practice, the whole appearing as an unbreakable unity. Theory legitimised the practice which in turn confirmed the theory. Herein lay the strength or power of the system.

Figure 3.2 *The Streamed System of Education*

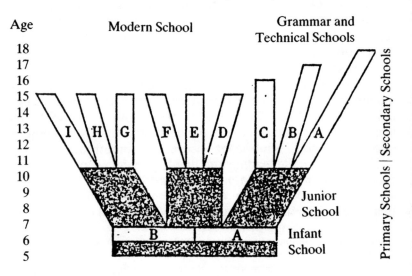

This then, was a period of hegemony of a form of educational fatalism that had its roots, both as regards theory and practice, in the economically and socially stagnant period of the inter-war years. It was, however, only now that it reached its apotheosis. Research in education, carried on at the newly founded National Foundation of Educational Research[17] was now dominated by mental testing, while the foundation itself became a large scale test agency – especially in the production of intelligence (and very similar English and arithmetic) tests required by local authorities for their selection examinations. Analysis of university theses in departments of education shows that in the period 1948-51, nearly 70 per cent fell into the category of 'psychology and experimental education', the bulk of these being psychometric survey research of one kind or another, the other 30 per cent being shared by historical and comparative studies, studies in 'method' (teaching) and in the philosophy and principles of education.[18] The main centres of psychometric (in fact, largely statistical) studies which were now greatly expanded, were first, the two Scottish universities of Edinburgh and Glasgow (where such studies had a long tradition), and secondly London University's Institute of Education (under Professor P.E. Vernon), Birmingham University (under Professor Fred Schonell) and especially Manchester University, where Professor R.A.C. Oliver and two other members of his staff, Stephen Wiseman and Frank Warburton, were all leading psychometrists. This was, indeed, a period when one particular research approach to education achieved an overall hegemony now difficult to appreciate.

The objective effect of this system, with its appropriate ideology, was to engender a new type of educational fatalism. Teachers (of course with exceptions) became convinced that the mass of the children could achieve little, and lowered their sights accordingly. Children themselves assimilated a negative self-image, and this affected their level of aspiration and so their achievement; the theory was inevitably used to convince parents of the innate failings of their own children. A whole ethos of failure developed which profoundly affected attitudes to education, and therefore the process itself. What was being constructed in terms of an educational system was, in fact, a near perfect means of social control – or, in another sense, of buttressing the existing social order. Further, perhaps partly because this system had been formed under a Labour administration, its establishment had the official support of all the main political parties – at least up to 1951. The comprehensive surge, which directly challenged the existing structure, appeared defeated. Under the system of 'partnership' in the administration of education that was then in its heyday – between the state (Ministry of Education), local authorities, teachers' organisations – everything seemed to be settling down; for many the main, and certainly the crucial, battle was on the provision of sufficient teachers and classrooms to keep the system viable – not to change it. In the early 1950s, anti-Communism was still a keynote. No one should rock the boat.

There was, however, a powder-keg underlying this carefully constructed system – as well as its baroque theory. The parents in Nottingham and Hertfordshire were by no means happy about the entire set-up. Frustration was mounting.

2 The Horsbrugh Period, 1951-54

Economic and Social Change

Such was the emerging educational situation when the Tories finally returned to form a new administration under the ageing Winston Churchill in October 1951. There had been no serious differences in education between the Labour and Conservative parties throughout the period of Labour government – indeed Conservative spokesmen went out of their way to express support for the various measures taken, none of which as we have seen, threatened any vital interests of those traditionally supporting the Conservatives; nor threatened any inroads in the balance of power, or advantages, within the general texture of the educational system.[19] However, before focusing on the transformation of the general political scene consequent on the election results, a few words on the economic situation and (underlying) structural change may help in interpreting overall developments in the 1950s.

At the start of the decade, Britain, which had emerged victorious but of course weakened from the Second World War, was still one of the three or four leading industrial countries in the world. Throughout the 1950s full employment was maintained, while a slow but steady rate of economic growth was also sustained, in spite of two cycles of restraint, each followed by a minor slump followed by a boom (in both cases involving the use of monetary controls). The first cycle covered the period 1951-55, the second 1955-60.

In historical terms the growth-rate achieved was in fact out-standing; *never* before had the country experienced anything so steady and consistent. But of course the whole (Western) world was now experiencing extraordinary boom conditions. What people (or, better, the authorities) in Britain failed to realise until the very end of the decade was that most other industrial countries, particularly those in Europe, were achieving a much faster rate of growth than that in Britain; a phenomenon that for those nations was also historically unparalleled.

The German 'economic miracle', under the impact of the

Erhard reforms, took off from roughly 1948-49. Right through the 1950s the German rate of growth was much higher than Britain's. France, Belgium, Denmark – indeed most European countries – had by 1960 first overtaken and then surpassed Britain effectively in productivity and in the rate of growth of the Gross Domestic Product (GDP) per head. Only Italy lagged behind, though even here the rate of growth in the North far exceeded Britain's.[20] In sum, the 1950s was the decade when the seeds of Britain's post-war relative decline, reaching crisis proportions in the 1970s, were sown.[21] This forms the background against which educational initiatives need to be assessed.

The 1950s also saw the continuation of the long-term secular trend towards the decline of the basic industries employing a high proportion of manual labour, and towards enhanced investment in new industries involving the application of modern scientific and technical knowledge. The result was a long-term shift in occupational structure which inevitably had repercussions on education. The number of unskilled workers (social class 5) showed a massive decline (by almost 1 million or 42 per cent) during the decade. At the other end of the social spectrum, those categorised as social class I (professional, etc.) in the census returns of 1951 and 1961 showed a substantial increase. Growth was most rapid among white-collar employees: scientists and engineers, for instance, more than doubled (from 187,000 to 378,000); draughtsmen and laboratory technicians increased by nearly 40 per cent.[22] This striking growth rate reflected the needs of a modern economy and, of course, was certainly a main factor in raising educational aspirations.

This indeed was a main characteristic of the period, resulting in a growing tension between, on the one hand, fairly rapid and insistent economic and industrial change, bringing changes in the occupational structure with new demands on education, and, on the other, consistent and severe restrictions on resources devoted to education, particularly during the first cycle, to about 1955. This conflict expressed itself in various ways. In particular through a developing tension between the imposition of what C.P. Snow (in his famous *Two Cultures* lecture) characterised as 'the rigid and crystallised pattern' of education on the one hand and enhanced aspirations on the other – leading to conflicts about the structure of the school system. It also found expression on the level of ideology – specifically on the whole issue of educability versus the concept of total genetic determination, a conflict which focused specifically around the question of Intelligence Quotients (IQs) and selection. It was these issues that now began to dominate educational discussion, controversy and policies – areas of contention which reached crisis point in the early 1960s.

Before tackling these issues, however, we may turn to the actual position when the Tories came in in October 1951, on a minority vote, but, as we have seen, with a majority of about twenty in the House of Commons. Two inter-related aspects of the situation should be mentioned. First, the new government was committed to a really massive rearmament programme. This it inherited from the Labour government which, as we have seen, had acceded to American pressure on this issue – largely a product of the Korean War, which had broken out in 1950. Second, on taking office, the government faced a drain on the dollar and gold reserves and so on the balance of payments which, according to some (and certainly to the Treasury) required emergency measures. And third (it might be added) the government was clearly committed, through election pledges, to reduce taxation.

Such was the situation. With Churchill as Prime Minister, R.A. Butler was (to his surprise) appointed Chancellor of the Exchequer.[23] As architect of the 1944 Act, some may have hoped for sympathetic treatment for education. However the fact that Florence Horsbrugh, the new minister, was not accorded a seat in the Cabinet seemed to some an ominous move, implying, as it did, a serious demotion of education. It was to be nearly two years before this was rectified – on 3 September 1953.

New Economies in Education

Florence Horsbrugh gained the reputation of a cheese-paring Minister during her term of office, which lasted for three years. In October 1954 she was unceremoniously dropped and replaced by a very different character – David Eccles. The change also marked a change in policy. The severe restraint imposed during Horsbrugh's term of office was first relaxed with Eccles' appointment, while by 1956 the first genuine advances in post-war education (apart from the raising of the school age in 1947) were under way. It may be convenient, then, to deal first with the Horsbrugh phase, as a case study in policy formation in a period of severe restraint.

Education was not to be given any priority by R.A. Butler as Chancellor of the Exchequer. On the contrary, what comes very clearly through the records both of the Cabinet and of the Ministry of Education[24] is the consisent, ruthless and unremitting pressure exerted by Butler on Horsbrugh to cut educational spending to a minimum and, if possible, even more severely.[25] The leading civil servants at the ministry appear to have spent most of their time elaborating one set of arguments after another, year by year, in defence of what they saw as minimal expenditure necessary to keep the machine ticking over. Nothing of any significance is discussed. The same is true for educational discussions at Cabinet level. The main thing that emerges from all this is that Florence Horsbrugh in fact, while presenting a brassy (and often complacent) front to the outside world, was forced to carry through a very tough battle in defence of her patch.

Throughout the whole period but particularly at the start, the possibility of making large savings by drastic measures was under continuous discussion. There was, for instance, a serious threat that the school-leaving age, only raised to fifteen four years earlier, in 1947, would be lowered again to fourteen ('during the period of rearmament' as Butler put it); or alternatively, that the school entry age should be raised to six – a proposal made in 1922 by the Geddes Committee on which the government of the day immediately lost two by-elections by large majorities.[26] Another option proposed by Butler was the introduction of fees, either in *all* maintained schools, or for all staying on beyond the statutory leaving age. Finally, the proposal drastically to reduce the Exchequer grant to local authorities, which had been fixed at 60 per cent was also seriously on the agenda. Each of these measures would have resulted in substantial budgetary savings; all would have required legislation except the grant proposal, which would have involved a breach of agreement (and so of faith) with the local authorities.[27]

In the outcome, none of these was done. But the fact that so much time and energy was spent on these issues indicates the amosphere of the time. In the end the government had to be content with scrimping and saving in all directions, and in allowing no development, apart from the necessary one of providing roofs and teachers for the extra million children who crowded into the schools between 1950 and 1960 as a result of the post-war birth rate increase or baby boom. It was this factor, which seems consistently to have annoyed Butler, which pressed on educational resources, involving an increase in budgetary provision of about £10 million a year simply to cope with it – and of course with the provision of new schools to provide for the fairly massive rehousing in suburban areas where there were none – the result of Harold Macmillan's successful housing drive.

The government does not appear to have had any plans for education apart from keeping things going at a minimal level.[28] This partially, of course, accounts for the crystallisation process described in the last section. Butler's first action as Chancellor was to declare a moratorium of three months on school building (the steel was diverted to armaments) – and this of course set the whole programme back. Emergency measures were also quickly agreed to cut back on the social services. Early in December 1951 Horsbrugh issued the notorious Circular 242, which led to an outcry from the educational world (and beyond) and first gave her her reputation as a skinflint. This called for a 5 per cent reduction in local authority estimates for 1952, by which the government grant could be reduced by £13 million. Its object, as Horsbrugh put it, was to 'cut out the frills' but to maintain 'the essential fabric'. The fact that this circular was issued on the day Parliament rose for the Christmas recess did not endear the minister to the education world; while its publication before the government had effectively made the case for drastic economies did not endear her to Churchill, who rapped the minister over the knuckles for precipitate action.[29] Indeed, Horsbrugh appears at this early stage almost too keen to carry out government policy which perhaps gave the green light to Butler to continue pressure on her long after it had ceased to be productive.

Within two months, in February 1952, another circular (245) was issued, this time on the school-building programme. This also stressed the need for economies and referred to the shortage of steel – all of which necessitated a revision and slowdown of the school-building programme for 1952, with special reductions in further education (covering technical education).[30] So education was singled out for cuts at the very start of the new government's life. But it was only *after* the issue of Circular 242, early in December 1951, that the pressure started on Horsbrugh to make the more drastic cuts mentioned earlier. After a preliminary discussion, the Cabinet agreed with Butler that, on the question of reducing the school-leaving age, he should consult 'further' with Horsbrugh and submit a memo to the Prime Minister.[31] For the time being the proposal was scotched, but not before the educational world, supported by the labour movement (and especially the TUC) had expressed serious concern.[32]

It would be tedious, and in any case there is not space, to go into the detailed history of those battles over the next three years, battles which were particularly fierce when departmental estimates were being prepared for scrutiny in the months before each budget. In the autumn of 1952, for instance, required to take 'drastic action', Horsbrugh counters that no major economies can be found, but promises a 'severe scrutiny' to 'squeeze out every drop of expenditure that can be avoided'.[33] A few months later the school leaving age issue is again pressed, while the Treasury proposes raising the school entry age, the advantages being (in their view) 'fewer children, fewer teachers, less new buildings, less expenditure generally'.[34] In 1953 new meetings take place and all the options are discussed again. 'Dear Florence', writes Butler,

> I need not conceal from you that I am most disturbed about the paucity of the economies we have been able to make in the last two years. We can't get healthy tax remissions, nor a healthy economy without these. There is no time to lose – we must think in terms of major changes in policy as well as constant pruning.[35]

In the next year (1954) Butler had a Cabinet committee appointed (the Swinton Committee) with the specific job of paring £100 million off civil expenditure. By this time the government was desperately trying to claw back money from teachers and local authorities through the Teachers Superannuation Bill, which is a saga in itself. The object was to get £2 million from each of them. This Bill was running into all sorts of difficulties but the assumption was that, in the early summer, it would go through.[36]

But now Horsbrugh resisted all attempts to impose drastic economies of the radical type discussed earlier. She and her officials were really close to the end of their respective tethers. 'There can be no question', wrote the Permanent Secretary (Flemming) in a note to Horsbrugh, 'of cutting back educational expenditure' as proposed by the Swinton Committee. 'The simple fact is', he adds, 'that we have been operating a policy of strict economy in this department for over two years now on top of a number of restrictions which your predecessors had found it necessary to impose.'[37] There was no hope of significant savings, Horsbrugh told the committee. Education had borne the brunt of severe economy measures which had not been applied to other social services. But even now Butler, characteristically, was not satisfied. There should be a general approach to local authorities, demanding further savings. They should be told 'to plan not for future expansion but for a period of consolidation'.[38]

The Response to the Cuts
From the start the government's actions invoked a vigorous response. 'No part of the government's economy drive', commented the *Economist*, 'has incurred so much criticism as the cuts in educational expenditure.'[39] In a backhanded way, Florence Horsbrugh made the same point a few weeks after the issue of circular 242. The extreme interest in this measure, as she put it, lay in the fact that it appeared as the forerunner of the full statement of the government's plans to deal with the country's economic difficulties. 'Never before', she boasted, '... has education had so much publicity.'[40] This, perhaps, was one way of putting things.

Certainly the issue of Circular 242, followed shortly by 245, produced consternation. This was partly because both were published after rumours had already circulated about the more drastic actions mentioned earlier. W.P. Alexander, Secretary of the Association of Education Committees (representing local government) set the scene already in November 1951 in his comments on Butler's declaration of a moratorium on school building – perhaps his first act as Chancellor. If there were to be more cuts following this, warned Alexander, there would either have to be a reduction of school life or massive overcrowding in the schools. Thus additional cuts would 'force a major change in policy', and, were this decided on, 'all educational opinion will be in opposition'. Already the proposal to reduce school life was known publicly, the Association of Education Committees having resolved at a general meeting to resist any such measure. 'There is the need for the utmost vigilance on the part of those concerned with education,' concluded Alexander.[41]

The publication of Circular 242 (on 7 December 1951) seemed to confirm general fears that education was to be singled out for drastic cuts. In a forthright and characteristic leader in the *Manchester Guardian*, R.H. Tawney, still, in his old age, sharply monitoring events on behalf of the children, made his critique. To introduce legislation to lower the school age, wrote Tawney, would be a breach of faith. The present policy of 'economising at the expense of the children' was only to be expected from the present government, he added, referring to the 'preposterous Geddes and May rackets' – the two main inter-war economy campaigns – 'launched with the maximum of ignorance and minimum of circumspection by governments whose indifference to the welfare of common children turned the thing into a ramp'.[42] A strongly worded (and so, uncharacteristic) protest from W.O. Lester Smith, until recently Manchester's distinguished Director of Education (now Professor at the London University Institute of Education) reflects the apprehensions and suspicions of the time. Also recalling the days of the Geddes Axe (1922), Lester Smith told his readers to 'beware of the hard-faced men', now again on the rampage. He also argued strongly against the proposal to lower the leaving age, appropriately recalling a scene at a railway station among working women when the Geddes proposals surfaced. Their language left nothing to the imagination. Education has, however, one asset today that it sorely lacked in the past – a large army of enlightened parents who value secondary education and consitute a powerful element of public opinion.[43]

A strongly influential voice raised against the cuts was that of George Tomlinson, Labour's Minister of Education (who had only a few months to live). Tomlinson had personally conducted a battle with Attlee and got a specific guarantee for the steel required to maintain the school-building programme effectively. If this is diverted elsewhere, he wrote in the then popular Sunday newspaper *Reynolds News*, 'We shall not have enough places for the children.' These vicious economising measures mean 'a return to class differentiation'; the labour and trade union movements must mobilise all their forces to defend the children.[44] The Trades Union Congress weighed in with a measured and serious protest letter in January (21st).

Under the Education Act of 1944 some real progress was being made towards equality of opportunity in education. The economies now proposed, or foreshadowed, together with the threat to reduce the length of the school-life of children, will not merely halt this progress – they will thrust the education service back to the position before 1944 and create once again a large under-privileged class among the nation's children.

Meetings and deputations were organised with local education authorities, and this and other resolutions sent to the Prime Minister and others. Public meetings and delegate conferences were carried through by local trades councils.[45]

As we have seen, it was finally decided not to lower the leaving age. But the strength of feeling in defence of the public system of education had made itself felt, and this perhaps accounts for Butler's continued sense of frustration at his inability to achieve a really radical cut in educational expenditure, as well as his consistent harrying of Horsburgh to achieve minor economies. The crisis situation that had developed around the Korean War and the consequent enhancement of the Cold War was a main rationale for this policy. In defending her economies (particularly the two circulars), Horsburgh made it quite clear that the demands of rearmament had over-riding priority. Savings must be made, especially on capital expenditure. 'We too must take into account the pressure of the essential rearmament programme,' she told the Tory conference at Harrogate at the end of January 1952.[46] Later, at the NUT Conference at Scarborough, defending her policy, she said that, 'at a time of unprecedented economic strain, when we are faced by common consent with the problem of increasing our armaments in order to deter aggression, increasing our exports to pay for our food and raw materials', these cuts were essential.[47] And in fact by 1953-54 estimated arms expenditure had increased to the enormous total of over £1,600 million. This was *seven times* as great as estimated budgetary expenditure on education (£231 million).[48]

Protests against this policy continued throughout the Horsburgh period – reflected in debates at the TUC Congress, in the House of Commons and elsewhere.[49] A Select Committee, with a majority of Tory MPs, revealed 'a most disquieting situation'. 'At every point', they reported, 'they were confronted with overcrowding, lack of schools, heavy transport costs, a shortage of teachers and often deteriorating and even dangerous school buildings.'[50] This report was exceptionally outspoken.

At this point, Kathleen Ollerenhaw, a Conservative councillor in Manchester, launched an extremely well documented campaign, based on a local survey. The old schools, built before 1903, are truly terrible, she reported; it was ridiculous to talk of equality of opportunity when such gross inequalities exist. It is 'a complete negation of the 1944 Act not to make every practicable improvement' – or to 'replace them forthwith whatever the cost'. This applies not to just a few schools in Manchester '*but over a hundred*' – nearly half the maintained schools in the city. It was likely that a similar situation obtained elsewhere.[51] Yet the rate of school construction had deliberately been slowed – in 1953 there were 177 fewer schools under construction than two years earlier. Nine nursery schools had been opened in that year but fourteen closed. Junior and infant classes with over forty pupils had increased substantially (to a total of nearly 5,000) while the same for senior classes had only marginally decreased. It was not only school building that was suffering. In 1953 there were 2,000 *fewer* university students than two years earlier.[52]

The social research organisation Political and Economic Planning (PEP) estimated in 1953, that there had in fact been no increase in the share of resources devoted to education between 1938 and 1951. The proportion of National Income spent on education had increased from 2 per cent in 1938 to 2.2 per cent in 1951; but the number of children in the schools had also increased by one tenth.[53] W.P. Alexander argued that expenditure per child was now actually below that in 1938 (in terms of purchasing power).[54] However this may be, during the Horsburgh period everything seemed to be grinding to a halt.

3 Contradictions and New Aspirations

The Comprehensive Thrust, and the Response, 1951–54

The policy of stringent economy, which obtained throughout the Horsbrugh era, operated to harden the crystallised structure described earlier. But there was one area where, in spite of an increasingly hostile climate, movement was now beginning to take place – in the few embryo comprehensive schools which had by now been permitted to emerge, mostly, at the start of the period, in certain remote rural areas and in Anglesey and the Isle of Man.

But the exception here was, of course, London itself. The London School plan, as we have seen, was finally approved by Tomlinson in 1950. The first new, purpose built comprehensive was to be Kidbrooke, a school for girls only, planned to open its doors in the autumn of 1954. But, as already mentioned, the Education Committee had wished to gain experience of comprehensive organisation, and by 1948 had opened eight so-called 'interim' schools formed by the amalgamation of a 'central' (selective) school with neighbouring secondary moderns.[55]

By the early 1950s these schools, which developed new, more flexible forms of organisation than was then usual, were functioning very effectively. A very fine set of heads and staff were appointed, generally enthusiastic about this new venture. These experimental schools, wrote the LCC later, 'blazed a trail which has become a broad highway, and under conditions of great difficulty and in fact of some hostility they carried out pioneer work of the utmost value.'[56] This work, however, was not made widely known at the time. Nor could any of the schools be called fully comprehensive, since none embodied an existing grammar school. But these schools certainly helped to prepare the way for the implementation of the London Plan as a whole.

In 1953, Margaret Cole, a leading member of the LCC's Education Committee, and, as we have seen, a consistent proponent of London's Comprehensive Plan, wrote of the extreme hostility engendered by the Tories both to the early efforts to implement the plan (to which the Tories on the LCC had agreed), and to halt further developments.

> They stage debate after debate in Committee and in Council; they fill the press with angry cries; they endeavour ... by means of engineered propaganda among teacher, parents and even children ... to ensure that each new school shall start life in an atmosphere of strife and prejudice ... they want them to be failures.[57]

In fact, though the concept of comprehensive education had not been a party political issue during the bulk of the Labour government's administration (since the government clearly did not favour them) rumblings had been heard from about 1948.

But it was during a Parliamentary debate in July 1951 (when the Labour government was still in power) that the heat was really turned on. The comprehensive school, claimed Florence

Horsbrugh for the Conservatives, was being advanced for political, not for educational reasons. 'At the Labour Party Conference', she said, 'it was suggested that the comprehensive school would bring about the right Socialist outlook on the State', persisting in this line despite Labour protests. Charles Hill (the radio doctor, later Chairman of the Board of Governors of the BBC) claimed that 'There are many of us who have tried to approach it with an open mind, but to find that it is being claimed that comprehensive schools will manufacture more and more little Socialists for the community.'[58]

Here political capital was being made based on the ill-considered remarks of a single delegate at a Labour Party Conference – at a time when the clear weakness of Labour across the whole field of policy encouraged a sharpening of political critique.[59] Indeed, the point when positions really began to harden on this issue was 1951, largely around London developments. It was in the next year, 1952 and 1953, that motions totally opposing the concept of comprehensive education received virtually unanimous support at succeeding Tory Party conferences.[60]

The whole issue climaxed in the autumn of 1953 on the issue of Kidbrooke, London's first, purpose-built comprehensive school. This was planned to embody a grammar school (Eltham), two technical and two modern schools and fuse these into a single, all-through girls' comprehensive with up to 2,000 pupils. Tomlinson, when Minister, had already given specific approval to this development in September 1949 – that is, before overall approval was given to the Plan as a whole; presumably to expedite building.[61] The opening of Kidbrooke, planned for September 1954, would have marked the first decisive step towards the unification of secondary education in an urban area.

In June 1953, however, the Minister suddenly and unexpectedly required the LCC to issue public notices of its intention to cease maintaining the five separate schools concerned. Although the action was later sharply criticised by Dr Alexander, Secretary of the Association of Education Committees, as 'unsound procedure', the LCC had to comply.[62] During the succeeding two months it was open to any ten or more local electors to lodge a protest.

It was at this point that the Minister made a directly political intervention. Addressing a London Conservative Women's Conference on 26 October she urged her hearers to strengthen her hand by organising local protests against the closing down of existing schools, and 'declaimed against the LCC's "enormous" comprehensive schools.'[63]

The matter was immediately raised in the House of Commons where the Prime Minister attempted to defend his minister's action against strong criticism from the Labour benches, especially from Herbert Morrison. The Minister, Morrison argued, had to act in the matter 'in a quasi-judicial capacity', and should not, therefore, encourage supporters 'to send her all the objections they could think of in order that her mind might be influenced'.[64]

Local Conservatives, however, took the hint – or followed her lead – and subsequently organised a protest against the closure of the girls' grammar school concerned (Eltham Girls' High School); this, supported by nearly 4,000 signatures, was forwarded to the Ministry. In March 1954 the Minister announced that she was unable to approve the closure of this school.[65]

This decision met with widespread opposition, and many protests. These included a petition from 5,669 signatories from the Kidbrooke area strongly objecting to the Minister's decision and expressing 'wholehearted support' for the LCC's proposal for a fully comprehensive school; a deputation of protest from the LCC was accompanied by representatives from the Association of Education Committees, which thoroughly objected to this destruction of local autonomy in planning secondary education.[66] None of this, however, caused Horsbrugh to shift her approach. Claiming, later, that her decision 'was in no way an attack on the idea of comprehensive schools', she in fact intervened again, four months later, to prevent the LCC from extending the Bec Boys' Grammar School in order to make it fully comprehensive.[67]

During her term of office, Florence Horsbrugh did not approve a single comprehensive school in the London area which involved the absorption of a grammar school. And indeed this is the significance of her action on Kidbrooke. From now on the defence of the grammar school became a major issue of policy for succeeding Tory governments – a policy which was held to firmly throughout the 1950s. It was in this context that the bulk of the early comprehensive schools came into existence.

Nevertheless, within these constraints, a distinct move towards comprehensive education was taking place. Four small grammar schools had been embodied within comprehensive schools in Anglesey and, in fact, a fully comprehensive system established in the island already in 1952. 'From now on', announced Mr A. Ifan-Jones, Chairman of the Education Committee, 'every child of 11-plus in the county will be automatically received into a secondary school.' Here the selection examination at 11-plus was now actually abolished. 'Anglesey is the first authority in the country to be able to do this, and we are proud of our achievement.'[68] In the Isle of Man, similar developments had taken place, again involving grammar schools (in this case, two). Four comprehensive schools (one a new school at Castle Rushen, having only 390 pupils) now provided all the secondary education within the publicly maintained system on the island.[69]

Elsewhere there were only isolated comprehensive schools, though both the Calder High School in the West Riding and the small school at Windermere had been developed from grammar schools. The two schools which survived from the original Middlesex Plan (Mellow Lane and Mount Grace) had no grammar school base, but were organised internally as comprehensive schools. There was, in addition, a school at Walsall.

By early 1954, then, a total of thirteen comprehensive, or near comprehensive schools were in existence in England and Wales (including the Isle of Man), to which London's eight 'interim' comprehensives might be added. By this time also nearly forty bilateral schools, largely grammar-modern, had been established – in Warwickshire, the North Riding, in Wales and elsewhere. By the end of that year (1954), however, three further purpose-built 'comprehensives' had been opened – Kidbrooke in London and two (Caludon Castle and The Woodlands) in Coventry.

Kidbrooke, though without its planned grammar school element, opened to a fanfare of trumpets in September 1954 – London's first purpose-built 'comprehensive'. 'Britain's new palace of educational varieties', reported the *New Chronicle*, 'a blaze of colour – crimson, yellow and blue'. More soberly, the *Manchester Guardian* commented that the school had had 'a more controversial beginning than can have been experienced by any other educational project'.[70] Both educationists and the general public were fascinated by this new school for girls with its six science laboratories, nine housecraft centres, five gymnasia and sixteen and a half acres of playing fields. The headteacher appointed, Miss Green, was an experienced grammar school teacher and head – an appointment perhaps calculated to allay some of the doubts and indeed open hostility which surrounded the school's foundation.

So, in the autumn of 1954, the London School Plan finally got off the ground, if in a distorted form. But now London was joined by a second urban authority which had decided to go comprehensive some years earlier. Coventry schools had suffered severely from the blitz and later bombing during the war and planned to develop comprehensive schools in new buildings on a series of 60-acre sites surrounding the city which had been purchased with educational developments in view. The Coventry Plan did not and could not embrace two well-established direct grant grammar schools (both for boys) which served the area. It was proposed, however, that 'grammar school places' would be provided in the new schools.

Coventry's plans were finally 'provisionally' accepted by Florence Horsbrugh towards the close of 1953, but the Minister then insisted that each school should be so designed that it could be split up into separate schools 'should this course be found desirable'.[71] It will be remembered how Graham Savage reacted to an equivalant proposal for London. However that may be, the opening of Coventry's first purpose-built eleven-to-eighteen comprehensive schools marked a definite stage in the evolution of the comprehensive movement.

Indeed in 1953-54 the pressure mounted at a rate possibly equivalent to the now rapid growth of parental frustration. In 1953 Staffordshire, a Labour authority, which had for some years been planning to provide secondary education throughout the county by means of relatively small comprehensives, obtained the sanction of the Minister. 'We have three comprehensive schools planned,' wrote the Director of Education to a correspondent in November 1953, 'two of them building, one almost ready to build.' Of the plan as a whole, the Director writes, 'personally, I am an advocate for these smaller schools' – a memorandum he drafted 'is to convince the ministry that they can work'. 'They have allowed us three only, as an experiment'.[72] 'Small' rural comprehensives with about 900 pupils (as proposed in Staffordshire) were, it will be remembered, officially regarded as potentially acceptable from the early 1940s.[73] Nevertheless even partial acceptance of the Staffordshire Plan appeared as something of a breakthrough. Now Birmingham, Manchester and other authorities were planning to establish one or more new, purpose-built comprehensives, while London proposed to open as many as five new comprehensives in September 1955.

So, in spite of strict restraints imposed from above, some progress was now being made in the attempt to take what many regarded as a vital step towards the realisation of secondary education for all. Occasionally a note of human indignation at petty restraints and procrastination breaks into official reports. 'We have told the ministry we want a comprehensive school,' reported the chairman of the West Bromwich Education Committee at this time. 'We have waited long enough. In fact we had to wait five months for a reply to the first intimation. As far as I am concerned,' he added, 'they can call the school what they like so long as the comprehensive system is operated in it.'[74]

Selection, Theory and Practice
There is no question that the viability of the tripartite system rested, ideologically, on the assumption that intellectual development was determined largely, if not wholly, by genetic endowment. It was this 'fact' forcefully reiterated by Cyril Burt and other psychologists not only during the inter-war period, but again following the Second World War, that legitimised the system, based on early streaming and selection, that had come into being and was now being reinforced through the policy of Hadow reorganisation.

By 'intelligence', Burt had stated in 1933, in a popular radio series,[75]

> The psychologist understands inborn, all-round intellectual ability. It is inherited, or at least innate, not due to teaching or training; it is intellectual, not emotional or moral, and remains uninfluenced by industry or zeal; it is general, not specific, i.e. it is not limited to any particular kind of work, but enters into all we do or say or think. Of all our mental qualities, it is the most far reaching; fortunately it can be measured with accuracy and ease.

It was this view which underlay, or legitimised, the streamed and selective system that now held sway – a view then accepted almost without question by psychologists, teachers and administrators, though by the early Fifties some doubts were beginning to creep in. In 1952, after a sharp public controversy, Professor P.E. Vernon announced that the supposed fixed and unchangeable Intelligence Quotient could be increased by a limited amount of coaching by an *average* of 14 points, a finding having profound significance in terms of who, precisely, was selected at 11-plus.[76] At this time also a considerable amount of new comparative information came to hand – previously unobtainable. Secondary modern schools from a number of areas began to enter pupils for GCE which started in 1951 – often after quite a struggle, as we have seen. Already by 1953 a number of results came in – from Southampton, Essex, Portsmouth, Bournemouth and elsewhere – indicating that 11-plus failures, rejected from the grammar school through lack of 'intelligence', sometimes achieved remarkably good GCE results five years later – while, of course, many of those actually selected failed. One of the most remarkable examples that became widely known in that year was of a twice-creamed secondary modern girls school situated in a working-class district in London. Here 23 girls who stayed on for a fifth year, motivated by the school and career aspirations, achieved 78 passes in 'O' level, an average of 3.4 per child. Only one failed altogether. One, with an IQ of 85 (and arithmetic and English scores of 90 and 92 respectively – both well below average) gained five O level passes as did another with an IQ of 97. Further, the new comprehensive type schools were also now throwing up many examples of 11-plus failures achieving well in terms of exam successes five years later.[77]

All this quite naturally cast increasing doubt on the viability of selection, and on the validity of intelligence test theory on which it was based. But now this theory itself came under attack. In *Intelligence Testing and the Comprehensive School*, published in 1953, the present author elaborated a wide-ranging critique of the theory and practice of intelligence testing as applied to selection, questioning the validity of the underlying assumptions on which the theory was based and reaching the conlusion that such tests basically reflected social class differences.[78] The stress now, it was argued, should be on the educability of the ordinary child. To ensure the conditions for the realisation of potentialities, the comprehensive school, involving the actual abolition of early selection, was suggested as the solution. Shortly after, Alice Heim, a well-known psychologist working in the field, published the *Appraisal of Intelligence* (1954) – again an extremely critical (if 'internal') assessment of the methodology and the theoretical assumptions underlying testing. These two books, according to L.S. Hearnshaw, Cyril Burt's biographer, constituted the 'first wave' of criticism, and launched Burt on his career of fraud and deception in a desperate attempt to shore up the pure 'classic' theory of which he was by now the major proponent.[79]

There were, of course, other related issues which now came to light. The provision of grammar school places varied greatly throughout the country – from the extremes of 64 per cent in Merionethshire to a mere 8 per cent at Gateshead. Yet each authority, conducting its own selection examination (often with great care), claimed that only those who were successful in the 11-plus had sufficient ability (or intelligence) to profit from a selective education. The cut-off point varied considerably across the normal distribution curve. In a sense, this was a nonsense, and now began to be seen as such. Curiously enough, whatever the proportion of a particular age was allowed to pass, relative success rates in public examinations five years later were broadly similar.

Labour's New Commitment
While these developments took place at grass roots level, as it were, and while the hostility of the government to any overall reorganisation on comprehensive lines was being made increasingly apparent, the Labour Party made a new (conference) commitment to precisely such a change. The remodelled programme, *Challenge to Britain*, modified after debate at the 1953 conference, contained a very clear promise to introduce comprehensive secondary education as a major measure of the next Labour government.[80]

The original educational section of *Challenge to Britain* was the product of the committee established after the 1952 conference which had confirmed comprehensive education as party policy. This committee, partly because of its concern to find a way to a more rapid transition than could be achieved through building large eleven-to-eighteen schools, proposed the imposition of a universal two-tier system with a break at fifteen. It was this aspect which was sharply attacked at the 1953 conference and finally withdrawn in favour of the proposal that local authorities, on being required by the minister to submit a 'reorganisation plan' to eliminate selection at eleven, would themselves propose how they would implement this, and, as Alice Bacon said, 'this can be done in a variety of ways'. In essence, this was to be the approach when, twelve years later, the Labour Secretary of State made precisely such a request.

At this conference the National Association of Labour Teachers made the running, as they had so often before. Their amendment to *Challenge to Britain* involved considerable rewording, and contained a series of very firm statements on the need to develop comprehensive schooling. 'Discrimination at the age of eleven is ... both unfair and educationally unsound,' it was stated. The segregation of children into grammar, technical and modern schools must be ended.

> Labour will abolish the practice of selection at 11-plus for different types of school because it is convinced that all children would benefit if during the whole of their secondary education they shared the facilities both social and educational of one comprehensive secondary school.

The Labour teachers were also concerned with more rapid forms of reorganisation, which, they held, could be achieved by utilising existing buildings as well as new, purpose-built schools. These new schools 'may be organised in a variety of ways depending on local wishes and circumstances'.

This amendment, moved by Norman Morris (representing the National Association of Labour Teachers) and Muriel Forbes (of the London Labour Party) received overwhelming support at the conference (while three other amendments were defeated). The most impassioned speech was made by Jennie Lee, who said that, ideally, she would like to see the party 'put all its enthusiasm and skill into comprehensive schools ... We want everything we have got, everything we believe in, to go into common schools.' Ernest Roberts, left-wing official of the Amalgamated Engineering Union and member of a city education committee, stressed the need to pressure the present minister for a more rapid development – his city (Birmingham) was building three comprehensive schools. 'We need twelve ... we are pressing the minister for twelve, but we have only three.' The Labour teachers' amendment was strongly pressed by Arthur Deakin, right-wing Secretary of the Transport and General Workers' Union and, as indicated earlier, fully accepted by Alice Bacon in her reply to the debate on behalf of the Executive Committee.

The sense of conviction now surfacing at a new level in favour of comprehensive education is evident in this debate. Here was an expression of unanimous conviction as to the necessity for making the change – many of the speeches coming from rank and file members of local parties as well as from leading trade unionists (Roberts and Deakin) and party figures (Jennie Lee, Alice Bacon). If it can be argued that earlier resolutions (from 1942) on this issue, though carried unanimously, never gained the full and passionate support of delegates, this could now no longer be said to be the case. The opposition of the *Political Quarterly* Fabians apparently made no impact on the party as a whole. From 1953 and the acceptance of the new programme, *Challenge to Britain*, the Labour Party nationally was clearly committed to non-selective schooling as a major plank in its platform.[81] The issue was now firmly on the agenda for action by a Labour government.

4 Premonitions of Advance, 1954-56

A First Step

Such was the situation, then, at the close of the Horsbrugh period. Beneath the tight control and restraint exercised by the minister on behalf of the government (and specifically of the Chancellor) a fundamental challenge was now emerging concerning both the structure of secondary education and the ideology by which this structure was legitimised. Indeed a confrontation was now developing, the consequences of which were to dominate the educational scene for another three decades. In this process, new battle lines were being formed.

We are now in the period of the upturn in the first 1950s economic cycle. It will be remembered that, through the Swinton Committee, Butler had already in the early summer increased his consistent pressure on Horsbrugh to make further economies; but these, the minister had resisted. Here things petered out; the extreme pressure was not renewed. Indeed Butler himself now clearly felt that he had achieved his immediate objectives. The economy, he now claimed, was on an even keel, as he reported to the Cabinet, to whom he circulated self-congratulatory press notices to that effect.[82] Second, an election was in prospect. The government (and especially Horsbrugh as the minister responsible) had taken a good deal of criticism on education. Could they not now afford a happier image?

Knowledge that more money might be made available clearly reached Horsburgh early in October (1954). There is an odd, laconic, rather badly scrawled note in the files at the PRO. Dated 15 October 1954 this is from Horsbrugh to the Permanent Secretary at the ministry. It refers to the capital investment programme, now under consideration. Striking a new note, she writes:

> The time has come when we ought to be aiming at an increase in the size of the [building, B.S.] programme, not merely for continuing present policies but to make some changes possible. The aim should be to do something for the rural areas which get nothing under present policy, and to get on more quickly with replacing bad schools. We should also do something for village halls, and to get more rapid progress on technical education.

Please see, she concludes, that alternative programmes are drawn up which take all this into account.[83]

What happened now seems somewhat ruthless. Horsbrugh, who had borne the heat of the fray, was suddenly dropped (together with her Parliamentary Secretary, Kenneth Pickthorn). Her position in the Conservative Party had by now been severely weakened by a number of factors – including mounting opposition among Tory MPs to the teachers' superannuation proposals. In her place, on 18 October – only two or three days after Horsbrugh had penned her note – Sir David Eccles took her place as Minister.[84]

It is clear that Eccles had a brief to refurbish the government's image, and, perhaps more importantly, the promise of some relief from constraint to do it with. In any case he immediately presented a paper to the Cabinet with a modest, but positive, programme. The Superannuation Bill, he said, was doing the government irreparable harm and should be dropped immediately.

> We have only a little space in which to give a new enthusiasm for education. Something like shock tactics are required to transform the atmosphere of depression which my predecessor could not avoid and against which she worked so bravely.

The implementation of the 1944 Act had been very slow due to the unexpected post-war baby boom, the raising of the school-leaving age to fifteen and the new housing which had resulted in thousands of children being swept into new estates where no schools existed. Over-large classes had increased, old slum schools had been left untouched, all-age schools still abounded since there had been no building to cope with reorganisation since 1952. Here politics entered directly into his proposals. 'Our friends in the countryside are being roused by this injustice,' he added, while our opponents 'will be quick to capitalise' on these anxieties. Parliamentary questions indicated that, unless something was done about these things, 'We shall find our inaction used to great effect by our opponents.' If his proposals were approved, he concluded, 'We could bring into education some of the feeling of expansion and success which has been the mark of the housing drive.'[85]

The outcome was a modest programme of advance – the first for some years – lifting the cost limits on minor works to £10,000, a four-to-five year programme of rural reorganisation costing £5 million, and more expenditure on technical education, on village halls and related items costing another £5 million in the next year (1955-56). Athough a moderate programme, partly beamed to gain support in traditional Tory rural areas, this does appear as a definite programme of advance in sharp contrast with the continuous restrictions imposed during the Horsbrugh era.

An appendix deals with economies. Proposals to raise the school entry age and to lower the leaving age are both set out and rejected. As regards the latter, Eccles, who appears as a very political animal, makes a telling comment. 'If we, who mostly send our children to boarding schools, encouraged early leaving from the country's secondary schools we should present the Opposition with a first class election issue.' Tactfully concluding that he will try to find economies, Eccles adds that there is, however,

> no escaping the fact that when the army of school children is expanding from 5 to 6 million, and teachers' salaries have to go up in step with other awards, and the 44 Act is on the Statute Book, 'my vote must rise or the standard of education must fall.'

The Cabinet meeting at which this memo was discussed took place on 29 November 1954, with Churchill in the chair. After a brief statement by Eccles the Chancellor made a statement. Pointing out that government expenditure on education had risen since the war from £224 million to £303 million, he conceded that this increase was mainly due to 'the larger numbers of children of school age'. He now seemed reconciled to further increases in expenditure, agreeing that there was a strong case for proceeding with the improvements recommended by Eccles – though adding (in his old style) that he hoped it would be possible to compensate for this by securing 'other savings in government expenditure on education' – though where he hoped these savings could be made was not indicated.[86]

After what appears as a brief discussion it was finally agreed that no substantial economies could be made by raising the entry age or lowering the leaving age – 'unless the government was willing to face the problems involved in dispensing with the services of a proportion of existing teachers'. It seems probable that this was the last heard of this canard; but that these issues should have continued to be seriously discussed right up to 1955 seems extraordinary. In addition, it was agreed that there were 'serious political objections' to increasing charges for school meals (as proposed by the Swinton Committee). Finally the Cabinet, after stressing that there should be 'no unnecessary extravagance' as regards playgrounds for schools in rural areas (since they were less needed there than in towns), approved the programme for further capital investment (including the relaxation of conditions relating to technical colleges) but concluded by inviting the Minister to secure economies in the administration of school meals and in other aspects of government expenditure on education.[87]

Eccles's memo and plan, and the Cabinet discussions, have been dealt with at some length since they marked the beginnings of a definite turn in government policy. In fact, after an actual drop in 1954-55, budgetary expenditure on education rose sharply in 1955-56 to £300 million. At this stage the leading motivating circumstances were probably the imminence of a General Election (as is very clear from the minister's memo) coinciding with a moderate economic upturn leading to a prospect of increased revenue from taxation (which would also allow promised tax reductions). But by gaining Cabinet approval for his programme, Eccles already made his mark as a competent, and determined Minister, whose antennae were sensitively directed to political advantage.[88]

'No Assassination Intended'

Eccles was to emerge by the end of the following year as a moderniser (especially in relation to technical education), but one determined to retain traditional structures unimpaired – a somewhat contradictory position as we shall see. Already, soon after taking office, he made his position clear on secondary reorganisation – coining new, dramatic slogans. 'Minister's Assurance to Grammar Schools', headlined 'the *Schoolmaster*' (published by the NUT) early in January 1955, 'No assassination intended'. In this speech to grammar-school teachers, Eccles claimed that the choice was 'between justice and equality'. 'My colleagues and I,' he assured his audience, 'will never agree to the assassination of the grammar schools'. Striking the contemporary Cold War, anti-Communist note, Eccles stressed that 'the enemies of personal liberty are well armed with dazzling promise', but that provided 'we too embrace the scientific revolution and navigate its mysterious currents,' we were much better equipped than they were. To face this challenge, the teachers 'must go faster and faster: we must have more scientists and each of them with a much broader mind'.[89]

In this very idiosyncratic speech, Eccles put his faith in the development of the grammar schools and science as the means to national survival, already broadly hinting at the availability of more generous resources for his policy.

Three months later, in an address to the annual NUT Conference, Eccles returned to the fray, but now much more explicitly. Here he announced his new slogan: 'Selection for everybody' (as opposed to 'Selection for nobody' – his description of the comprehensive school). The central core of Eccles' speech was his very sharp attack on the comprehensive school, as an 'untried and very costly experiment'. His critique of these schools in terms of their large size drew applause. Perhaps with an eye on the Labour programme, he inveighed against the establishment of comprehensive schools in existing buildings, arguing the case for the development of secondary modern and technical schools as the alternative. This was also an unusual, racy, down-to-earth oration, tactfully pro-teacher, stressing the value of 'partnership' in education, and earning 'loud applause' – generally, an odd mixture of progressive (modernising) ideas and a reactionary traditionalism. In the course of this speech Eccles outlined the five main policy guidelines he would follow:

1. The provision of 15-25 per cent of places in each local authority area as grammar and technical school places will be the aim.

2. New technical schools will be approved only 'where there is a very strong case'.

3. Modern schools will be encouraged to develop extended courses and to strengthen their links with grammar and technical schools and with further education.

4. Transfer between secondary schools should be made as early as possible (to put right 'glaring mistakes' in the selection); otherwise there should be opportunities for transfer at 15 and 16.

5. Comprehensive schools will be approved 'as an experiment' and when 'all the conditions are favourable, and no damage is done to any existing school' [implying that no grammar or modern school serves the area where the comprehensive school is proposed, B.S.][90]

These were both, of course, pre-election speeches, as was the carefully formulated memorandum on school policy Eccles prepared for the Cabinet at this time. This document, which went through several drafts at the ministry in preparation,[91] was a response to a letter from the (new) Prime Minister, Anthony Eden, who, immediately on taking office on 6 April 1955 wrote to Eccles asking if he had any matters to raise. To this Eccles replied in the negative but, he added, 'RAB and I have plans for helping middle-class parents to pay for their children at school and at the university. It is important that these should come off next week.'[92] 'The most political problem in education', he went on, 'is the 11-plus examination and the Socialist proposal to abolish it by rolling up all secondary schools into comprehensive schools.' He would circulate a paper 'describing the counter-measures I am taking'. No decisions would be required.

This memorandum is of interest precisely for the reason Eccles gives – it highlights his proposed 'counter-measures' to the growing movement to comprehensive secondary education; measures which were to form the thrust of the counter movement to preserve the tripartite system intact, if in a modified form, over the next five or more years. Here the main points, which of course ran parallel to Eccles' NUT speech, may be briefly summarised.[93]

'As the 11-plus is likely to be an election issue', the memo opens, 'my colleagues may like to know how the argument stands.' It was hoped, following the 1944 Act, to get 'parity of esteem' between the three types of school developed, and as a result, 'that the diappointment and jealousy felt by parents when their children failed to qualify for a grammar school would disappear'. But this has not yet happened 'and the resentment appears to be growing'. James Griffiths 'has said that the next Labour government will abolish the exam altogether' by doing away with the three kinds of secondary school 'and substituting comprehensive schools, each of which will take all children from a determined area'.

The case against the large comprehensive (each, Eccles says, 'must contain some 2,000 pupils') is made. Difficulties of organisation 'are too great to be overcome'. 'I have told Local Education Authorities', Eccles goes on, 'that I will approve a comprehensive school only when no existing good school is to be swallowed up in the process' and (reiterating Horsbrugh's line) 'that I will not agree to a complete network of comprehensive schools in any area'.

And now comes the crunch. Although the comprehensive school 'is certainly not the right answer, we cannot leave the 11-plus examination where it is. The anxieties and jealousies are too easy to play on.' Our policy must be 'to construct an alternative route to high qualifications and well paid jobs via secondary modern and technical schools and technical colleges, and to encourage more transfer at 15 or 16 to and from the grammar schools'.

The rest of the memo deals with the opportunity now existing to influence the future pattern through the 750,000 new secondary school places that must now be built – so development can take place 'without disturbing what exists'. He is encouraging local authorities to develop 'special courses with a clear vocational interest' within secondary modern schools. This would ensure 'that each school will be able to offer something special that cannot be had elsewhere in the area', so reducing parental complaints about selection.

To sum up, Eccles concludes, reiterating the NUT speech,

> the feelings aroused by the 11-plus exam, both justified and unjustified, force a move towards selection for nobody or towards selection for everybody. Selection for nobody means comprehensive schools with grammar schools abolished and parents' choice practically ruled out. The Socialists support this policy on the principle of fair shares for all. Selection for everybody means developing in each secondary modern school some special attraction and giving parents the widest possible scope.[94]

Such, then, was to be the new Conservative policy. At the time it was formulated it seemed (politically) viable. The Association of Education Committees had recently pronounced in favour of secondary modern schools and so, in effect, against comprehensives. In the final paragraph of his memo, Eccles claimed that, at the NUT Conference he had just addressed, it appeared that 'a big majority of the teachers' is now 'against comprehensive schools and in favour of helping the secondary moderns'. There seemed, then, some popular support, at least within the educational world, for the modified divided (rather than tripartite) system Eccles now hoped to bring into being as the crucial defence against comprehensive education.

Eccles, then, had made his position abundantly clear. In effect his conditions for approving comprehensives (outlined in his 'five points') restricted development, in theory at least, to new housing estates and perhaps to new towns.[95] The post-war plans of certain authorities, for instance Oldham and Bradford, and several others, could not be implemented in accordance with the conditions laid down in 1955 and reinforced later. These conditions inevitably lead to a 'freezing' of the official system which had ministerial support.

All this was made absolutely clear to local authorities shortly after Eccles took office when a number of clashes took place of which the most important were those with Manchester and Swansea. In Manchester the local authority wished to transform existing school accommodation (involving five schools) at Wythenshawe, its satellite city, as three comprehensives, and to open them to a non-selective entry in September that year (1955). The plan was put to the ministry in

April and all the necessary arrangements made to go ahead. Four days before the beginning of the school term the plan was rejected by the minister on the grounds that the units proposed failed 'to provide the conditions in which the merits of this comparatively untried type of school can be properly tested', and that it involved 'an uneconomic use of expensive resources'. A selection examination had to be hurriedly arranged and the children unscrambled and classified to fit the three types of school available. It might be a long time before Manchester and the ministry saw eye to eye again, commented the *Manchester Guardian*; no doubt there was much to be said on both sides but 'one cannot think that the minister's method of handling the question contributes much to a reasonable settlement'.[96]

Later that year the minister rejected a proposal that the four secondary schools in Swansea should eventually be merged into 'multilateral' schools. He could not agree, he told a deputation from the authority, 'to the extinction of the existing grammar schools, whose traditions were too good and too precious to be endangered'. Two of the proposed schools, however, could be established on new housing estates.[97] It is worth recalling that Swansea had proposed a complete system of multilateral schools in its post-war development plan, and that this had been approved, in principle, by Tomlinson as minister in 1949. The authority wished, now, to implement this plan.

Another urban area that wished to go comprehensive at this time, Carlisle, finally withdrew their proposals after strong pressure by the minister,[98] while Walsall carried on a continuous battle, especially against ministerial procrastination.[99] In his Cabinet memo, Eccles stated that his predecessor had approved ten new comprehensives (an average of 3·3 a year) 'and I have added two'. Since he had then been in office for six months, the rate of increase can be said to have increased – though at this rate, the transition to comprehensive education would have taken approximately a thousand years.

Nevertheless, as earlier, there was in fact some development – mostly arising from earlier ministerial decisions. In London, during 1955, following Kidbrooke, five more comprehensives were opened – three in new buildings. These were Woodberry Down, a mixed school for 1,250, Catford County School (1,200 girls), and the Dick Sheppard School in Tulse Hill (1,000 girls). The other two schools involved extensions to existing buildings, Holloway (1,250 boys) and Mayfield School at Putney (2,000 girls) – to which the redoubtable champion of comprehensive education, Margaret Miles (later Dame Margaret) was appointed head. It will be noticed that only the last of these – a highly successful school – reached the giant size Eccles held to be essential for the viability of comprehensive education.[100]

Elsewhere, Birmingham acquired its first comprehensive – Sheldon Heath, which pioneered new forms of inner social organisation; a comprehensive school also opened at Slough[101]. Future developments were, however, presaged by local authority planning. In particular the Essex Development Plan which proposed 23 bilateral schools, in Dagenham, Barking and at the new town of Harlow began now to be pressed.[102] The pressure for structural change within the field of secondary education now sharply increased.

Eccles Digs In

By the spring of 1955 the Conservative government had held office for nearly four years. Winston Churchill had finally and reluctantly resigned as Prime Minister early in April, being succeeded, at long last, by the heir apparent, Anthony Eden (with whom Eccles was on good terms). With the economy apparently in sound order Butler, as Chancellor, took 6d off income tax in his April budget. All seemed, to the government, relatively plain sailing. A General Election was now called for the end of May. How far the promise of advance in education following the Eccles programme and increased budgetary expenditure announced in April contributed to the result it is, of course, impossible to say, but the fact is that the Tories gained a signal victory, increasing their somewhat tenuous (overall) 1951 majority of less than 20 to nearly 60. Once again the great majority of the votes were split between Conservatives (with 49·7 per cent, over 13 million) and Labour (46·7 per cent, nearly 12½ million). The Liberals, with less than a million votes, won six seats (see Appendix I, p.564).

In the new government, Butler continued as Chancellor (until December) and Eccles as Minister of Education – so the line-up was as before. So also was the predictable pressure of the Chancellor on social service expenditure – normally applied most heavily in the early years of a new government's term, to be relaxed as the next election approached. But this time Butler seems to have met his match.

Already in July Butler raised in the Cabinet the growing cost of the social services. Further growth was now expected – related to pensioners, increasing numbers of children in secondary schools (the 'bulge' moving up), and claims for 'more and better technical education and higher education generally', for hospitals and housing. The Cabinet agreed that the Treasury should survey the situation and report.[103] But Butler was already quickly off the mark. Early in August he wrote to all spending ministers urging a radical reduction in planned expenditure. 'As large a reduction as possible' was required for the 1956-57 Estimates, which should be 'below those for the current year'. Eccles, and the others, were asked not only to make a thorough review, but to refrain from putting forward any proposals whatever for new expenditure. These steps were necessary, according to Butler, as a result of new economic problems now surfacing (marking the first phase of the second 1950s cycle). These problems were the result of 'the excessive claim now made by home demand on our national resources' inflating the volume of imports, hampering efforts to increase exports, and helping to force up prices and wages. The solution was to reduce demand 'by all possible means', and here the government must set an example. Government expenditure must be kept 'to a minimum'.[104]

This missive was accorded a dusty – indeed dismissive – answer by the Minister of Education. In a short letter Eccles stated tersely that it was 'impossible to prevent the Estimates in my department from rising', referring to the increase in the number of children, the expansion at the top of the secondary schools (a new feature) and expenditure on further education, 'which', he stated firmly, 'is government policy'. He would, however, do his best to keep the Estimates as low as possible.[105]

In the meantime, however, Butler was preparing an initiative of his own – a direct appeal to local authorities to curb expenditure right across the field. This took the form of a 'Message' to local authorities from the Chancellor of the Exchequer and the Minister of Housing and Local Government (Duncan Sandys), finally issued on 26 October. This asked local authorities to ensure that total capital expenditure (except on housing) in 1956-57 should not exceed that for 1954-55, and that 'no new works, even those already authorised, are undertaken' – unless 'absolutely necessary'.

Eccles, in discussing earlier drafts of this 'Message' with Butler, clearly saw the danger to his programme, especially as regards rural reorganisation and technical education – both of which were central to his 1954 plans which had been agreed by the government when he came in. This had led to some rewording of the 'Message'. 'I hope you will agree', Butler had written, 'that I have gone a long way to meet your difficulties.'[106]

The 'Message' was issued, as already mentioned, on 26 October. It led to an immediate outcry, while Eccles was inundated (or so he claimed) with queries, calls and protests, in particular from the shire counties. In the House of Commons Eden, defending the government but under strong attack in a censure debate, gave a specific assurance that Circular 283 (dealing with rural reorganisation) 'stands' – this was a main issue with the counties. On the same date, Eccles took the highly unusual course of issuing a press statement.

Headed 'No Cuts in Educational Building', this stated unequivocally that the education programme as announced 'is being maintained'. 'Authorities will, therefore, be expected to carry out *all* the projects in the approved programme for 1955-56 and 1956-57.' As a sweetener to Butler, perhaps, a brief paragraph asks for 'every possible economy to be made'.

Clearly Eccles had dug his heels in, and very hard indeed. This press statement, wrote Butler to Eccles immediately, 'is not in accordance with the Message which I had sent to Local Authorities with your concurrence and that of the other ministers concerned'. He understands that some authorities 'will find it impossible to comply with the terms of the Message if they follow the instructions in your statement'. The intention of the Message was that authorities should be free to defer education projects 'if they saw fit'. Eccles had accepted the wording published. 'The effect of your Press Statement is to instruct educational authorities that *all* the projects in the programme are to proceed, and this is not in line with what I have recalled above.'[107]

To this Eccles replied equally firmly. 'The county councils raised a howl when your message reached them' (Eccles never used the capital M). He pointed out the impossibility of the county councils squaring 'your message' with 'our statement on education'. His press statement was the only way by which they could 'honourably extricate' the government from this difficulty.[108] After this clear confrontation, the issue petered out with a somewhat jesuitical letter from Butler claiming that he supported implementation of the full education programme, but only wanted 'to space it out'; 'spacing out priorities within a programme did not in my view represent a going back on a programme'.[109] With this defensive riposte, it might appear, the initiative rested with Eccles.

He was quick to exploit the situation. When the Treasury survey on Social Services expenditure finally appeared for cabinet discussion in December, Butler argued that, if tax reductions were to be achieved, the projected growth rate must be 'moderated'. But here Eccles intervened and again with effect. The Treasury survey had not taken into account long term plans for technical education, now nearly completed. This issue, he held, should be considered separately, since 'technical education, as one of the main elements in the expansion of production, was of a different character' from the rest of the social services (an interesting premonition of human capital theory). Whereupon, as well as setting up a committee to consider a memo on school meals, the Cabinet invited Eccles 'to circulate' in due course 'proposals for the expansion of technical education'.[110]

'A Concert of Battle-cries'

With an iron Chancellor like Butler, whose mind was constantly focused on tax reduction, and whose stop-go short-term monetary policies militated against any kind of long-term planning, a Minister of Education who wished to get things done clearly had to be equally tough. Eccles was proving himself just such a minister, able to understand and mesh into the now growing public concern for scientific and technological developments. In the autumn of 1955 he was already preparing for a major advance in this field. As we shall see, he knew how to seize his opportunities.

Already in July, shortly after the election, he raised the question in Cabinet. In the Commons debate on the shortage of skilled labour, due in a week, the government, he said, would be pressed on this issue. What had been done on the lines of the Queen's speech?[111] As there was, in fact, little to report, he hoped he could refer to 'a five year programme of expansion'. In the outcome, the terms of his statement was left to a small Cabinet committee to determine.[112]

The July debate in fact gave expression to a growing, even vociferous demand for advance in the field of technical education. In a paper drawn up early in October, Eccles referred to the 'clamorous demands of industry' for more trained and skilled technicians that was expressed in this debate, arguing the need for his five year plan. Five or six technicians were needed for every one technologist produced, but the whole level of technical education was backward. Little had been done in the inter-war period when provision was a power only of local authorities, not a duty. There was, therefore, much leeway to make up. Eccles saw his plan as complementing the developments now under way at Imperial College (of 'towering magnitude, costing £15 million'), Glasgow and elsewhere. A survey by the ministry produced a list of 285 separate projects, costing £72 million. More teachers would also be required.[113]

As planning gets under way a sense of enthusiasm develops, perhaps for the first time since the immediate post-war period – Eccles is working with the grain. The Prime Minister is deeply interested in the expansion of technical education, Eccles writes in a note to the Permanent Secretary early in December. 'He expects to produce a programme which will strike the public imagination as adequate to the demands of the scientific revolution. So great is his enthusiasm for this subject that we can risk unorthodox and drastic measures.' There is much ignorance about what has been done. 'The silence must now give way to a concert of battle-cries.'[114]

With this Wagnerian analogy, with Eccles poised on the brink of decisive new developments, we can close this stage of our study. 1956 marks the opening of a new phase characterised by educational expansion – sometimes dramatic. The period of constriction and restraint, from the end of the war till now, reaches its close. New factors, derived from economic and social developments within Britain as well as abroad, now take precedence. A policy, marked by sharp contradictions, as we have seen, will now be projected into the future. The context has changed, and so also the character of the new measures designed to meet the new demands as perceived by those in authority.

Notes and References

1. F.M. Martin, 'An Enquiry into Parents' Preferences in Secondary Education' in D.V. Glass (ed.), *Social Mobility in Britain*, London 1954, pp.160ff.

2. Professor T.H. Marshall, 'Up and Down the Social Scale', *Times Educational Supplement*, 20 August 1954.

3. *Education*, 27 August 1954.

4. These inter-war psychological and pedagogical developments, which remained profoundly influential after the war, are analysed in detail in Brian Simon, *The Politics of Educational Reform, 1920-1940*, London 1974; see especially Chapter 6, 'Consolidating the Pyramid: Differentiation and Classification', pp.225-50.

5. Brian Simon, *Intelligence Testing and the Comprehensive School*, London 1953, p.12, reprinted in Brian Simon, *Intelligence, Psychology and Education, A Marxist Critique*, London 1971.

6. See, for instance, *Transfer from Primary to Secondary Schools, Report of a Consultative Committee appointed by the Executive of the National Union of Teachers*, London 1949.

7. *Hansard*, House of Commons, 17 February 1953, Cols. 311-12.

8. A.B. Clegg, 'Some Problems of Administration in West Riding Grammar Schools', University of Leeds Institute of Education, *Researches and Studies*, No. 7, January 1953, p.9.

9. *Journal of the Institute of Education of Durham University*, Vol.4, No.23, May 1953 (article on 'The Scholarship').

10. A.Greenough and F.A. Crofts, *Theory and Practice in the New Secondary Schools*, London 1949, pp.7-9.

11. The Editorial Board consisted of several well-known Labour supporters including H.L. Beales, G.D.H. Cole, R.H.S. Crossman and Kingsley Martin; the other members were Noel Annan, Lord Simon of Wythenshawe and Barbara Wootton.

12. *Political Quarterly*, Vol. XXII, No.4, October/December 1951, pp.317-20.

13. Eric James's *Education for Leadership* (1951) itself contained a strong polemic against the comprehensive school and, using Plato and Karl Mannheim as the main authorities appealed to, reiterated and developed the argument already partially elaborated in *The Content of Education* (1949) and earlier articles. See pp.126-7.

14. 'For it is here', the editorial continues, referring to secondary modern schools, 'that the children of good intelligence can be educated in a way which will develop his general ability to understand the world in which we live, to enjoy a fuller life, and to appreciate cultural activities, without being forced to pursue intellectual and technical achievements beyond his capacity.' Unexceptional rhetoric, perhaps, if grammatically flawed.

15. *Political Quarterly*, Vol. XXIII, No.1, January/March 1952, and Vol. XXIII, No.2, April/June 1952. The *Times Educational Supplement*, under a new editor (Walter James) claimed that this contribution to the debate 'is welcome as a valuable proof that opposition to the comprehensive school is becoming general in men of sense in all parties', 12 October 1951.

16. *Listener*, 16 November 1950.

17. The National Foundation for Educational Research was established in 1947 following the 1944 Act which legitimised local authority expenditure on research. 50 per cent of its funding was contributed by local authorities, the rest by the Ministry of Education. At this stage it saw its main function to be to service local authorities' selection examination requirements. Very little specifically *educational* research was undertaken.

18. Stephen Wiseman, 'Higher Degrees in Education in British Universities', *British Journal of Educational Studies*, Vol.II, No.1, November 1953.

19. Peter Wann, 'The Collapse of Parliamentary Bipartisanship in Education, 1945-53', *Journal of Educational Administration and History*, Vol. III, No.2, June 1971.

20. Sidney Pollard, *The Development of the British Economy, 1914-67*, 2nd edn., London 1969, pp.43ff.

21. Britain's relative economic decline, of course, has its origins much further back – becoming evident already from the 1860s. But this raises much more fundamental issues than can be explored here. For a penetrating study of Britain's consistent, and long-term, relative educational backwardness, see Andrew Green, *Education and State Formation*, London 1990.

22. Pollard, op.cit., p.500.

23. According to Seldon, Churchill appointed Butler reluctantly, surrounding him with safeguards due to his lack of experience in financial matters. Anthony Seldon, *Churchill's Indian Summer, the Conservative Government 1951-55*, London 1981, p.154.

24. At the time of writing these have been available at the Public Record Office (under the 30 year rule) up to 30 December 1958.

25. An aspect of Butler's activity not mentioned by Anthony Howard in his (official) biographical study, *RAB, a Life of R.A. Butler*. His Chapter 12, 'High Noon at the Treasury' covers this period. For Butler's appointment as Chancellor, pp.178-79. Seldon, op.cit., p.272, also lets Butler down lightly, only saying that he was, 'perhaps surprisingly not as enthusiastic in support of resources for education as might have been expected' – a serious misjudgement.

26. Simon, *The Politics of ...* pp.46-7.

27. For Cabinet discussion on these issues, CM(53)46, 28 July 1953, and report of Committee of Ministers on supply expenditure, CP(53)61.

28. The only positive initiative under discussion at Cabinet level related to a proposed major extension of Imperial College, London and possible parallel developments at Glasgow and Manchester. For Lord Woolton's memo 'Higher Technological Education', CP(52)56. Woolton was Lord President of the Council.

29. CM(51)16. The timing of circular 242, said Churchill, 'had been unfortunate. No further announcements of policy affecting major items of expenditure should be made without the authority of the Cabinet.'

30. The severe cost limits imposed enforced new, more economic building techniques and the development of school building consortia. See Stuart Maclure, *Educational Development and School Building: aspects of public policy 1945-73*, London 1984.

31. CM(51)19, 20 December 1951.

32. *TUC Report, 1952*, pp.163-4.

33. PRO ED136/892, letter from Horsbrugh to Butler, 17 October 1952.

34. PRO ED136/889, Treasury memo, 31 December 1952.

35. PRO ED136/890, Chancellor's letter, 7 October 1953.

36. For the Swinton Committee, PRO CAB 134/783 and 134/784. On the Superannuation Bill, ED136/896. For the superannuation issue, P.H.J.H. Gosden, *The Evolution of a Profession*, Oxford 1972, pp.132-53.

37. PRO ED136/896, memo, Flemming to Horsbrugh.

38. PRO CM(54)9, 7 July 1954.

39. *Economist*, 21 March 1953.

40. *Education*, 1 February 1952.

41. Ibid., 23 November 1953.

42. *Manchester Guardian*, 12 December 1951.

43. *Schoolmaster*, 17 January 1951.

44. *Reynolds News*, 13 January 1952. Tomlinson's closing months were clouded by his perception of the real meaning of the government's economies in education. 'It was a particularly bitter pill', writes his biographer, 'that the Chancellor of the Exchequer who had piloted the 1944 Act through Parliament should be concerned in these economies.' 'Mr Butler's murder of his own child', he said, 'would prove disastrous for the country and for the Conservative Party.' Fred Blackburn, *George Tomlinson*, London 1954, p.202.

45. *TUC Report, 1952*, pp.163-65.

46. *Education*, 1 February 1952.

47. Ibid., 25 April 1952.

48. *Social Service News* (Labour Research Department), May 1953.

49. The TUC protested against the continuing economies in education in 1953 and 1954 in each case passing a strong resolution unanimously after a Congress debate. *TUC Report, 1953*, pp.172-4, 314-8; *TUC Report, 1954*, pp.337-8.

50. Quoted in *Education*, 26 June 1953 from *Report of the Select Committee on the Estimates*, June 1952.

51. Ibid., 26 February 1954.

52. *Social Service News* (LRD), August 1953.

53. *Times Educational Supplement*, 26 June 1953.

54. *Education*, 2 June 1953. For a general discussion of this, and related issues, John Vaizey and John Sheehan, *Resources for Education*, London 1968, passim.

55. 'Central' schools, selective schools within the elementary system, had been widely developed by the London County Council in the inter-war period. They aimed to retain pupils to the age of 15, and normally embodied an industrial or commercial bias in the curriculum.

56. *London Comprehensive Schools: A Survey of Sixteen Schools*, London County Council, 1961. For the popularity of these experimental schools, Brian Simon, *The Common Secondary School*, London 1955, p.85.

57. Margaret Cole, *What is a Comprehensive School? The London Plan in Practice*, London 1953, p.4.

58. *Hansard*, House of Commons, 24 July 1951, Cols. 228, 491.

59. For this episode, see Peter Wann, op.cit.

60. In 1952 a motion deploring the attempt to replace the tripartite divisions in secondary education was carried with one dissentient. In 1953 a motion opposing comprehensive schools, proposed by Angus Maude, was carried unanimously, Seldon, op.cit., p.276.

61. Kidbrooke was approved as a school 'which will serve a definite catchment area from which *all* children of secondary school age will normally attend' (my emphasis, B.S.), *Education*, 12 March 1954.

62. Alexander's argument was based on the potential wastage of resources resulting from this procedure. Ibid.

63. *Observer*, 12 September 1954. The speech is described as 'injudicious'.

64. *Hansard*, House of Commons, 10 November 1953.

65. *Times Educational Supplement*, 5 March 1954.

66. Ibid.,7 May 1954, 12 March 1954.

67. Ibid., 11 June 1954. The Bec school had 450 boys on roll. The LCC wished to extend it by providing a further 1,500 places on the same site.

68. *Schoolmaster*, 28 November 1952. Anglesey had planned this transition already before the war. The alternative would have been to have built new secondary modern schools and one technical school (boarding) alongside the four existing grammar schools. This would clearly have been uneconomic.

69. For the Isle of Man's initiative, *Manchester Guardian*, 11 May 1953, article on the historical background and early developments.

70. David Rubinstein and Brian Simon, *The Evolution of the Comprehensive School, 1926-1972*, London, 2nd edn., 1973, pp.69-70.

71. *Education*, 11 December 1953.

72. J.H.P. Oxspring to Lady Simon of Wythenshawe, 17 November 1953 (in the author's possession). The three schools referred to were situated at Willenhall, Tettenhall and Rowley Regis. All three opened in September 1955.

73. See *The New Secondary Education*, p.24.

74. *Education*, 8 May 1953.

75. C. Burt (ed.), *How the Mind Works*, London 1933, pp.28-9.

76. P.E. Vernon, 'Intelligence Testing'. *Times Educational Supplement*, 2 January 1952, 1 February 1952; see also ibid., 12 December 1952, 26 December 1952 and 24 April 1953 for discussion and further articles on this issue.

77. The material in this paragraph is taken from Brian Simon, *The Common Secondary School*, London 1955, pp.52ff. See also Robin Pedley, *Comprehensive Education*, London 1956, pp.43ff.

78. A reviewer in the *Times Educational Supplement* characterised the book as 'a formidable indictment of the theory and practice of intelligence testing', concluding that 'the case stands up'; that, therefore, the arguments advanced 'should draw a reply from the defence, and the reply should be couched in language as comprehensible as that of the prosecution', *Times Educational Supplement*, 15 January 1954. One responsible reviewer (from the National Foundation for Educational Research), on the other hand, felt able to dismiss the book as 'too silly to merit rational discussion, except perhaps in the pages of a journal devoted to psychotherapy' (A.F. Watts, *Journal of Education*, March-April 1954).

79. L.S. Hearnshaw, *Cyril Burt, Psychologist*, London 1979, p.241. See also pp.109, 118, 227-8.

80. The following paragraphs are based on the 1953 *Labour Party Conference Report*, pp.166ff. See also Rodney Barker, op.cit., pp.94-7, and Michael Parkinson, *The Labour Party and the Organisation of Secondary Education, 1918-65*, London 1970, pp.71-5.

81. The debate included discussion on an amendment to *Challenge to Britain*, concerning the public schools. This, in contrast to that on comprehensive education, revealed an almost total lack of clarity – or agreement – as to policy. The amendment, which proposed immediate abolition, attracted little support and was defeated.

82. CP(54)252, Report of Committee on Civil Expenditure (Swinton Committee), Memorandum by Chancellor of the Exchequer, 23 July 1954. Butler's memo concludes with a quotation from the *Economist* (3 July 1954). 'The miracle has happened – full employment without inflation, and this despite the heavy burden of defence, the rising burden of the social services, and some reduction in taxation.'

83. PRO ED136/856, Florence Horsbrugh to Secretary, 15 October 1954.

84. David Eccles had been Minister of Works since the formation of the government. For Horsbrugh's departure, Peter Gosden, *The Education System Since 1944*, Oxford 1983, p.16, and Seldon, op.cit., pp.272-3. 'I am very sad to have left the Ministry,' she wrote to Lord Woolton.

85. CP(54)343, Education Policy: Memorandum by the Minister of Education, 12 November 1954. The next two paragraphs are based on this source.

86. CM(54)80, 29 November 1954.

87. Ibid.

88. And to class advantage. The budgetary increase in 1955-56 was planned to cover a number of measures relating to educational benefits for the middle classes. People with incomes of £1,250 – £3,000, Eccles wrote to Butler (20 January 1955) have been 'pressing me hard about educational benefits of one kind or another' (e.g. scholarships for university students, boarding education for service personnel, etc.). Eccles asked for a talk with Butler on taxation policy for this section of the population – including 'any talks in which I may be involved with spokesmen of the public schools'. Indeed at this time the Ministry worked out the costs of an 'Assisted Places Scheme' (so-called), involving state fee payments for 10 per cent of places at fifty schools (cost equals £300,000); a forerunner of the 1981 Education Act scheme which must have been pigeonholed. PRO ED136/859.

89. *Schoolmaster*, 7 January 1955.

90. Ibid., 22 April 1955.

91. PRO ED136/861

92. This is a reference to material in note 88.

93. CP(55)6, Secondary Education, Memorandum by the Minister of Education, 20 April 1955.

94. I have no evidence that this paper was ever discussed in Cabinet. It was probably simply circulated for information.

95. New towns in fact became a focus for comprehensive developments in the late 50s

and early 60s; for instance, Crawley, Harlow, Kirkby and later Milton Keynes developed comprehensive systems.

96. Rubinstein and Simon, op.cit., p.73.
97. *Times Educational Supplement*, 6 January 1956.
98. Ibid., 1 July 1955.
99. Ibid., 4 February 1955.
100. *Higher Education Journal* (NUT). Autumn 1955, p.5. For a useful summary of London developments to 1958, Raymond King, 'The London School Plan: the present stage', *Forum*, Vol. 1, No. 1, Autumn 1958.
101. *Journal of Education*, October 1955.
102. *Education*, 25 February 1955.
103. CP(55)57, for Butler's memorandum, discussed on 5 July 1955, CM(55)20.
104. PRO ED136/894 for Butler's letter to 'Dear David', of 3 August 1955. On 26 July 1955 Butler spoke on the economic situation in the House of Commons, outlining the government's attitude to expenditure by local authorities and nationalised industries.
105. Ibid., Eccles to Butler, 10 August 1955.
106. Ibid., Butler to Eccles, 26 September 1955.
107. Ibid., Butler to Eccles, 2 November 1955.
108. Ibid., Eccles to Butler, 3 November 1955.
109. Ibid., Butler to Eccles, 4 November 1955.
110. CM(55)45, 6 December 1955. The Treasury survey is CP(55)188. 'Social Services Expenditure', memorandum by the Chancellor of the Exchequer, 3 December 1955. CP(55)189, 'School Meals Service', memorandum by the Minister of Education, 5 December 1955. The Treasury survey is mainly concerned with achieving further reductions in taxation. Educational and other social service expenditure should be reduced. 'If early decisions are made, it would be possible to slow down the rate of expansion, e.g. by a slower intake of teachers, slower development of the National Health Service', etc.
111. A reference had been made in the Queen's speech to the expansion of facilities for technological education. Hansard, House of Commons, 6 May 1955. A debate on scientific manpower took place on 21 July 1955. Ibid., 21 July 1955, Cols 579ff. The motion, moved by Austen Albu, was replied to by David Eccles.
112. CM(55)23, 14 July 1955.
113. PRO ED136/870. 'Technical Education, paper leading up to Cabinet paper', December 1955. For the Imperial College initiative, see note 28.
114. PRO ED136/870, Eccles to Secretary, 7 November 1955.

4 Background to Break-out, 1956-1960

1 Beginnings

1956 was in some respects an ominous year. Anthony Eden, who started his period of office with high hopes for the future, resigned as Prime Minister suffering ill-health but discredited as a result of the Suez adventure, early in January 1957. In Eastern Europe, Soviet invasion of Hungary, following Khrushchev's revelations at the 20th Congress of the CPSU, led to some extent to a political realignment on the left in Britain. Nevertheless, basic economic and social change continued to find their reflection in new and more urgent demands and pressures on the system of education. Seeking the origins of the educational breakout of the 1960s one is led inevitably and precisely to this year – 1956.

It was in this year that the Scientific Manpower Committee (an official forecasting body) first recommended a radical expansion in the output of scientists and technologists from universities and technical colleges – from the 1955 figure of 10,000 to 20,000 by the late 1960s.[1] The numbers game had begun. This target was accepted by the government, action taken, and numbers of full-time students in both pure and applied science in fact increased from 28,000 in 1954-55 to 40,000 in 1959-60. At the same time (1956) the Prime Minister gave expression to the new acceptance in government circles of the need to mesh in with the scientific revolution, implying support for educational advance. In a speech at Bradford in January he said:

> The prizes will not go to the countries with the largest population. Those with the best systems of education will win. Science and technical skills give a dozen men the power to do as much as thousands did fifty years ago. Our scientists are doing brilliant work. But if we are

to make full use of what we are learning, we shall need many more
scientists, engineers and technicians. I am determined that this
shortage shall be made good.

A year later (1957) the Soviet Sputnik seemed dramatically to
underline how far science and its application had gone in the
Soviet Union. By this time there was a growing (if tardy)
realisation that action was urgently necessary.

The quotation from Eden's speech prefixed David Eccles'
White Paper on *Technical Education* (Cmnd. 9703) which
Eccles had been preparing at the end of the previous year, and
to which he gained full Cabinet approval. Published in
February 1956, this was the first, decisive step marking the new
approach. Arguing that modernisation across the whole of
industry was essential, the White Paper identified 'an intense
and rising demand for scientific manpower', as well as for
technicians and craftsmen to support them. An appendix on
the USA, USSR and Western Europe detailed a clear
superiority on the part of the Soviet Union in particular in the
output of engineers and technicians. 'The technological
challenge of other countries,' wrote Sir Francis Simon in a full
page critical evaluation of the White Paper in the *Sunday
Times*, 'particularly Russia, seems at last to have brought the
government to realise the magnitude of the problem; they
intend to spend about £100 million on technical education
within the next year.'[2]

The White Paper outlined a streamlined, rationalised, and in
a sense elitist structure to be developed *alongside* the
universities. Colleges of Advanced Technology (CATs) were to
be brought into being and a strategy laid down for the
reorganisation of the technical college world generally.

CATs were to focus on advanced level courses, including
post-graduate work and research. All such work would attract
the 75 per cent grant which had been spread among a variety of
institutions for their advanced courses for some years. Circular
305 which followed (in June 1956) attempted to define
precisely the respective functions of (a) local colleges, (b) area
colleges and (c) regional colleges, to which this new fourth
level, the CATs, was now to be added: eight regional colleges of
technology were now so designated. Here, then, was the
beginnings of an important new initiative covering the whole
field of technical (and further) education, even though nothing

was said about implementing the county college sections of the 1944 Act.

Discussion and new forecasts about the expansion of universities also got under way in the mid-to-late 1950s, and indeed from 1956 numbers began to rise – for the first time since 1950 (see Appendix Table 14, p.597). A series of 'managed' debates in the House of Lords between 1956 and 1960 brought out Britain's relative backwardness – it was at the close of the May 1960 debate, on a motion moved by Lord Simon of Wythenshawe proposing an inquiry into the whole field, that the government spokesman, Lord Hailsham (Minister for Science), gave a half promise of action on this front, resulting a year later in the appointment of the Robbins Committee.[3] Another government spokesman, Lord Dundee, in the debate of 1960, sketched in the background of restrictions since the Second World War. For the first ten years, he said, very severe building rationing and restrictions operated, lifted only in 1956. University building grants were limited to £4 million a year. In 1957 they rose to £10.5 million and in 1960, provisionally, to £15 million.[4]

Forward planning by the University Grants Committee now led to advice to the government that places needed to be substantially increased by the late 1960s – to a least 124,000 or perhaps 135,000. This expansion, the committee held, could be achieved within existing universities together with one new one, at Sussex.[5] This was the first serious official proposal for expansion.

It seems clear that the main immediate pressure came from the area of demand. This was dramatically brought out in the Crowther Report of 1959.[6] In a special 'crisis' chapter, this pointed out that a critical situation was rapidly developing in terms of the availability of university places for qualified students. Immediate and drastic action was necessary. The unexpected increase in the number of pupils staying on voluntarily at school meant that more and more were passing the necessary examinations and qualifying for university (this was *before* the birth-rate increase reached the eighteen-year-olds). But places available remained static. In 1955, for instance, of candidates for universities, between 80 per cent and 85 per cent were qualified, but only 60 per cent gained places. Asking what the position would be like in ten years' time (1969), when the sharp increase in the birth-rate following the Second World War would result in many more eighteen-year-olds, while a higher proportion would be likely to stay on longer at school, the Crowther Report argued the need for a rapid build-up of university places, well above the numbers already planned: 'The disparity between the increase in the size of the field and the number of available places is so great that an intensification of the fierceness of the competition to get into the universities seems virtually certain.' This increased competition, which was already having serious negative effects in the sixth forms, 'is going to get more severe, and perhaps much more severe'.[7]

It seems clear that this argument was very influential. In a period of relative prosperity and full employment a government would be particularly sensitive to demands of this kind, especially since the main social classes involved – middle and professional, who proved to be the main beneficiaries – carry a good deal of political weight. Indeed, we are already moving into a period when the expansion of higher education as a whole is determined, superficially at least, on the basis of demand. This pressure 'from below' now linked with the pressure from above (as it were) to increase the output of scientists, and engineers in particular, to keep up with other advanced industrial countries, and with the actual growth of new 'high technology' industries requiring an increase in the output of trained scientific manpower.

This, then, is the point at which planning for expansion within higher education as a whole got under way. In the summer of 1959 the UGC reviewed the situation in the light of fresh evidence about 'the trend' (the increase in the proportion staying on to the age of seventeen or later). The committee increased its target by 35,000 to 40,000, giving a new target of 175,000 students by the late 1960s.[8] The committee again said that this increase could take place within existing universities but now added that a contribution would be needed from new universities. The government now approved plans for two more new universities (at York and Norwich) in addition to that at Sussex, which was already accepted and where planning was now underway.

In the summer of 1958 the UGC set up a sub-committee on new universities. By this time the idea of new universities had caught the popular imagination, and applications to be the centre of a new university began to pour in – from Essex,

Gloucestershire, Kent and Warwickshire in 1959 and, trespassing into the first year of the next decade (1960-61), from Bournemouth, Chester, Lancaster, Plymouth, Stamford and Swindon. Approaches were also made from Stevenage and Whitby, and from six Scottish centres.[9] The whole expansion issue now became self-accelerating. By July 1961 seven new universities had been authorised, each originally planned for about 3,000 students, with the possibility of expansion.[10]

But it was not only in universities that things were now on the move. In 1957 the decision was taken to extend the length of the teacher-training college course to three years to take effect from 1960.[11] Originally the hope was that, due to the expected decline in the number of pupils in primary schools in the early 1960s, this extension would not cause difficulties in the supply of teachers. There was to be no increase in recruitment, so output would be reduced by one-third, but this could be assimilated. However, things turned out otherwise. Partly because of a new upturn in the birth-rate, as well as the 'unexpectedly large increase' in the numbers staying on beyond the age of fifteen, many more teachers were required in the 1960s than expected when this decision was taken. The result was a crash programme of expansion, which started in earnest in 1959, when the colleges were suddenly told to expand by 50 per cent. The number of students at these colleges increased from a total of 33,000 in 1957-58 to 55,000 five years later (1962-63); this expansion increased apace throughout the 1960s.[12] So here also, and for different reasons, things were on the move.

Expansion at the advanced level in technical colleges, as we have seen, was provided for in the 1956 White Paper. This 'alternative route' to higher education now began to develop from what had been vestigial beginnings in the earlier 1950s. After 1956 students could now prepare for the new 'Diploma of Technology'. In a sense, it was here that expansion was swiftest, as a result of thousands of individual decisions taken in the 1950s. In this area, the number of full-time students more than doubled between 1957-58 and 1962-63 (that is, in five years) from 13,000 to 31,000.[13]

By the early 1960s, then, well before the Robbins Committee reported in 1963, expansion across the whole field of higher education was under way. By 1962-63 the universities had reached a total of 131,000 students (from 85,000 in 1955).

Technical colleges had 31,000 full-time students following 'advanced' courses, while teacher-training colleges reached 55,000 students. This gives a total of 217,000 students in all full-time higher education in Great Britain in 1962-63 and reflects the rapid increase in student numbers over a period of five years from a total of 148,000 in 1957-58, an increase of nearly 50 per cent.[14]

2 Conflict on Secondary Education

Within higher education, the decision had already been made by the end of the 1950s to accede to growing demand – if tardily and somewhat reluctantly. The case for such an expansion – and the pressure for it – was clear. With the aid of Eccles's measures, mentioned earlier, the main benefits would accrue to the middle and upper classes, so reinforcing the existing social structure. At the same time action would be taken, and be seen to be taken, to meet even more tempestuous developments abroad – in the Soviet Union in particular, but also by Britain's trade rivals in the Western world. The 'clamorous demands of industry' might be met, and Britain put on the road of exploiting the scientific know how for which she was famous. But within the field of secondary education, those in authority perceived things rather differently.

Similar pressures were insistently showing themselves at lower levels – and here they met with a continuing resistance. Eccles' policy of obstructing the move to comprehensive education was carried through equally relentlessly first by Lord Hailsham, who held the post for eight months, and then by Geoffrey Lloyd who was appointed minister in September 1957. In December 1958, again just before a likely election (October 1959), Lloyd used R.H. Tawney's title to launch a new White Paper, *Secondary Education for All: A New Drive*. Although a five-year £300 million programme of new school buildings was announced which aimed at finally completing reorganisation, this 'reorganisation' was still to be on Hadow lines, laid down over thirty years earlier; that is, the bulk would be for new secondary modern schools, which were now belatedly encouraged to provide examination courses for some of their pupils (a tactic now popular to cope with the 'bulge' and avoid building more grammar schools). Secondary modern schools, it was now argued, should 'provide a full secondary education for each of their pupils in accordance with his [*sic*] ability and aptitude.'

In what seems now like a last-gasp defence against comprehensive education, the White Paper argued strongly against this solution. It would be wrong to impose a uniform pattern of secondary education. Schools are shaped historically by local circumstances and the result should be variety. Experiment with comprehensive schools would be permitted only in two situations, the White Paper announced, echoing Eccles's guidelines: in country districts with sparse populations, and in new housing estates where there were no existing schools with a well-established tradition as grammar, technical or modern:

> But it is quite another matter when a local authority proposes to bring to an end an existing grammar school ... simply in order that a new comprehensive schoool may enjoy a monopoly of the abler children within its area. It cannot be right that good existing schools should be forcibly brought to an end, or that parents' freedom of choice should be so completely abolished.

This highly aggressive and totally unsympathetic formulation reflects the sharpness that now entered this controversy.[15]

This arose, without a doubt, from the unceasing pressures on this issue from below; comprehensive education was originally very much a grass roots issue, one supported and propagated by local organisations – trades councils, some local Labour Parties (though by no means all at this stage), Communist Party branches, some local NUT associations and Co-operative organisations. At this stage there was no general monitoring of this movement, but the newly founded educational journal *Forum*, in 1959 commissioned a series of articles from different regions analysing developments.[16] These indicated a rapid build-up of pressures and developments. London, of course, led the way. In 1954, as we have seen, Kidbrooke had been opened as a comprehensive school; but by the end of the next year another five were in existence. In 1956 ten more were added, with five each in 1957 and 1958 – a total of 26 schools.[17] In 'seven note-worthy years', wrote Raymond King, the well-known head of Wandsworth, looking ahead (in 1958) to 1961, 'London will have opened some 40 per cent of the comprehensive schools envisaged in the London Plan.' To teach in a London comprehensive, he added, is 'an exhilarating experience' – an approach reinforced by his staff.[18]

The *Forum* round-ups in these years reported a strong tendency to reject tripartitism in South Wales and aim boldly at a comprehensive system.[19] At Newport the decision was taken in 1958 to move over to a fully comprehensive system by 1960 (all the schools needed replacement). At the May elections in that year the Tories made opposition to this policy their chief plank. The result was the election of four new Labour councillors. Though the full plan was rejected (by Edward Boyle – the 'destruction' of a grammar school was inadmissible),[20] two comprehensives were allowed (Duffryn and Hartridge High Schools). In 1958 Swansea now drew up a new plan, involving the transformation of existing 'multi-lateral' schools (found too restrictive) to full comprehensives. Cardiff councillors had (in 1959) recently visited Leicestershire where the two-tier comprehensive system was now under way. In Glamorgan a long-standing Labour authority, whose early proposals for comprehensive schools had been rejected by Tomlinson as 'too small', had obtained approval for a school at Treorchy and two more on new housing estates – including the well known Sandfields comprehensive school ar Port Talbot.[21] The authority there was planning to abolish the 11-plus in July 1959; another school was planned for Porthcawl.

These developments covered the industrial area of South Wales, but should be seen in the wider context of Welsh resistance to tripartism. As well as Anglesey's comprehensive system, now well established, Pembrokeshire had adopted a policy of bilateral schools, while Carmarthenshire, Breconshire (and other authorities) – all predominantly rural areas – were all establishing some comprehensive and bilateral schools. In sum two of the four Welsh county boroughs were, in 1959, developing comprehensive systems while elsewhere there was a growing stress on the comprehensive solution. It seemed that Wales could lead the way to the abolition of the 11-plus, concluded the *Forum* survey, and in the development of a national system of comprehensive secondary schools.

A report from the West Midlands in the same journal referred to the three Staffordshire schools mentioned earlier, and the planning of three more at Willenhall, where no grammar school existed. Two large comprehensives were already at work at Birmingham, Great Barr and Sheldon

Heath while further schools were planned. At Coventry, seven of the planned comprehensives were already in operation; Walsall, which 'had long been comprehensive-minded' had the Joseph Leckie School in operation, and had just opened another (T.P. Riley School). At West Bromwich the Churchfields comprehensive school, opened in 1956, had adopted an unusual and highly successful recruitment policy.[22]

From Yorkshire Robin Pedley reported on Bradford's plan for the building of nine comprehensives over the next twenty years (a plan that was to be overtaken by events). Leeds had received approval for two new comprehensives on new housing estates (Holbeck and Cross Green) to add to Foxwood and Allerton Grange, established in 1956 and 1958 respectively. Sheffield, later to be a bastion of comprehensive education, was awaiting permission to transform a secondary modern to a comprehensive school; East Riding had developed a first comprehensive for 900 pupils at Withernsea. Hull, which had recently opened two large establishments, each offering grammar, technical and modern schooling, included three new comprehensives, each for 1,440 pupils, in its five-year building programme. The North Riding, which had had its original proposals vetoed as 'too small' (see p.109), was developing bilateral grammar/modern schools, as at Easingwold. Pedley, summing up the situation in Yorkshire in 1959, felt that the county had, in fact, been slow to react to the challenge of new evidence (see Chapter 6) and contrasted the inaction of several Labour-controlled authorities with 'the avowed policy of the Labour Party': Labour controlled ten of sixteen local authorities, 'but very few of these are as yet showing the kind of initiative in planning a comprehensive system that a Labour minister will presumably expect if he finds himself in office later this year.'[23]

Another report a year later (1960) from Bristol and the West found little development except in Bristol itself, where the authority when under a Labour administration had developed ten schools described as 'county secondary schools, with grammar and modern streams' – seen as 'an interesting development in the direction of comprehensive education'.[24] The Labour group in Bristol included a strong and early proponent of comprehensives – St John Reade.[25] Later, Bristol also was to develop as an early centre for comprehensive education (within the maintained system, of course). This group of early reports included a survey of developments in four New Towns – virgin territory in most cases, even according to the Eccles guidelines. At Crawley (Sussex) the establishment of the well-known Sir Thomas Bennett School in 1958 'exemplifies the trend away from tripartitism in Crawley' while another three comprehensives were under way. In Harlow (New Town) six bilateral schools were planned, to operate in pairs (these later became fully comprehensive); on the Kirkby Estate outside Liverpool, all four schools serving the area were, by 1960, fully comprehensive, while at East Kilbride New Town, outside Glasgow, Judith Hart (elected as MP in 1959) reported Duncarig, the new comprehensive designed by Basil Spence, to be already severely over-crowded.[26]

These reports do not, of course, cover the country; they do, however, give a fairly representative picture of developments by the end of the decade – and convey something of the atmosphere of the time. Among the greater industrial cities of the Midlands and North with one or more such schools were, as we have seen, Birmingham, Leeds and Sheffield, to which should be added by now Manchester and Nottingham. In Scotland also there had been new developments. Glasgow, which had opened its first two purpose-built comprehensives in 1954 had, by 1962, 22 such schools of two types: For pupils aged from twelve to sixteen and those between the ages of twelve and eighteen. In the rural and small town areas of Scotland, also, there had been developments, though these were based on the long historical tradition, north of the border, of the 'omnibus' (or 'all-in') school.

One English county development deserves special mention at this point, since its example was highly influential at a crucial stage. This is the Midland county of Leicestershire.

In the autumn of 1957 Stewart Mason, Director of Education, launched his 'Leicestershire Experiment and Plan', as he called it. This was the more unexpected since Leicestershire was a Conservative authority – governed by representatives of the traditional county families it was, in fact, almost feudal in its nature, though with a reputation for educational advance. The Leicestershire plan was an ingenious solution to the problem of making an immediate transition to comprehensive education utilising existing buildings, and in fact retaining existing, though transformed, schools, both grammar and modern. This was the two-tier system, by which modern schools, recruiting all children in their locality, now became comprehensive 'high' schools, (eleven to fourteen) while the grammar schools, becoming comprehensive 'upper' schools (fourteen to eighteen) recruited all pupils from their feeder high schools. The scheme was originally brought into being in two specific areas in the county; if judged successful, it was to be extended through a series of stages, to cover the county as a whole.[27]

Mason always held that this brilliant idea came to him suddenly while shaving – consistently denying that he owed anything to Robin Pedley, who had been arguing for a similar change to a two-tier system very publicly for several years – and from the base of a local university at Leicester.[28] However that may be, Pedley, who had been called for a discussion about his ideas by Eccles in 1956 (which indicates some softening on Eccles' part), states that Hailsham, now Minister, decided that this Leicestershire re-organisation could go ahead without the need for ministry approval or disapproval.[29] This decision was made on the grounds that no existing school was being closed, nor was any existing school threatened with either extinction or 'assassination'. The way was clear, then, for this development, which had the full support of the County Council and its Education Committee (Sir Robert Martin, a highly prestigious county – and national – figure, and a strong supporter of the scheme, was chairman of both!)

As the Leicestershire scheme got under way, immense interest was aroused among local authorities up and down the country, many of which were now anxious to introduce systems of comprehensive education but could hardly envisage the possibility of new, purpose-built, all-through (eleven to eighteen) comprehensive schools for all their secondary pupils. From Cardiff, as we have seen, from Manchester, from many other areas now increasingly concerned to find a viable solution to their problems, delegations of councillors came to see the Leicestershire Plan in operation. It seemed as though this initiative might open the flood gates, so long and so effectively kept dammed.

By the end of the 1950s, then, there was some development. But, although it might appear that a rapid swing to comprehensive education had now started, in fact by 1960 there were only 130 such schools in existence, catering for less than 5 per cent of secondary school pupils – while the Eccles criteria remained as the official guidelines, development was bound to be severely limited. (See Appendix Table 6a, p.586). However the potential for a rapid break-out was now clearly there while the significant new factor was not so much the number of schools established as the example that had been set, at a time when, due to inevitably increasing pressures, it was becoming more and more difficult to maintain confidence in the process of selection. Here, two important publications towards the close of the decade had a profound impact, if particularly on professional educators, teachers and administrators.

The first of these was a report by a specially appointed committee of leading psychologists on the whole issue of intelligence testing and selection. There had been mounting concern, among psychologists and others, about the way in which specific instruments and theories were being used to legitimate a school system of which many were increasingly uneasy. *Secondary School Selection*, published in 1957, set out to reply to the criticisms that had been made but, in so doing, modified the theory in significant ways. In particular this report, under the influence of its chairman and progenitor (P.E. Vernon) explicitly rejected the theory of total genetic determination – and so distanced itself from the classic theories of Cyril Burt. Intelligence, the committee held, could certainly be influenced by the environment and by upbringing. It followed, then, that it was not appropriate to sort young children into A, B and C streams within primary schools. Further, early selection to different types of secondary school was also to be deprecated. 'Any policy involving irreversible segregation at eleven years or earlier is psychologically unsound, and therefore ... in so far as public opinion allows – the common or comprehensive school would be preferable, at least up to the age of thirteen.[30]

This was certainly an extremely important concession since it struck at the base of the main theoretical support for the divided system which had retained its hegemony throughout the inter-war period and later. However a further blow to supporters of the divided system was in store from an equally impeccable, professional source. In 1958 the National Foundation for Educational Research published the first serious, large-scale and well-designed research report on the actual practice of selection and its results. Briefly, the authors (D.A. Pidgeon and Alfred Yates) concluded that, even utilising the best selection procedures yet devised, at least 10 per cent of children in any age-group would be wrongly allocated. This meant that, in an average age cohort in the 1950s, some 60,000 children were inevitably 'selected' for the wrong type of school. Since there was no serious possibility of further improving 'techniques of allocation', comprehensive, multilateral, or some more flexible structure, the authors suggest, was desirable.[31]

This sort of critique of the system was reflected in the generally highly progressive report of the Central Advisory Council for Education (England) entitled *15-18* (The Crowther Report). This argued for an extended school life for all and, while not overtly embracing the comprehensive solution, criticised the rigidity of the established system preferring the evolution of more flexible forms of organisation. This was published in 1959. It was in this same year that C.P. Snow's famous lecture on *The Two Cultures* (which sold 100,000 copies in a few years) finished with a strongly critical attack on 'the rigid and crystallised pattern' of English education.

As the defence of the selective system began to crumble, so the campaign (as it was) for the defence of the grammar school now took even sharper forms. In *The Essential Grammar School*, Harry Rée, then head of Watford Grammar School, reiterated Eric James's arguments in the new context. It was essential to educate 'gifted' children together in a single separate school. The grammar schools provided a specific avenue to social mobility for bright working-class children. They contain children from 'rich and varied backgrounds'. Secondary modern schools were well adapted for the education of the ordinary child. Reflecting the new confidence of the grammar schools after the demoralisation following the 1944 Act, and, in effect, arguing strongly against the 'public' schools as incapable of providing an effective education in the new situation, Rée also totally rejected the comprehensive solution (requiring schools of 5,000!) and concluded that it was the local grammar schools which were now taking over the public school traditions 'inspired by Dr Arnold'. This idea of education 'springs ... from a Christian tradition peculiar to this country ... now the grammar schools are taking over'. Only 'an act of blindness' could interrupt their course.[32] Rée's book was the forerunner of a sustained, and in a sense unscrupulous campaign by the leading associations of grammar school teachers who now saw their position, and their schools, under threat. In 1958 the Incorporated Association of Head Masters (which united maintained grammar, direct grant and some public school headmasters) issued a statement entitled *The Grammar School: A Reply to the Labour Party's Educational Proposals*. This argued passionately that the grammar schools must remain inviolate. The Incorporated Association of Assistant Masters (uniting male teachers from the same group of schools) in a leaflet entitled *Comprehensive Secondary Education*, issued at the same time, concluded that the nation should resolutely resist any development which might destroy or damage the grammar school. A year later the 'Joint Four', as the secondary organisations were called (two male, two female), published *The Organisation of Secondary Education*, a sustained polemic against the comprehensive and for the grammar school. It was, of course, the contention of Raymond King and other experienced grammar school heads who supported the change to comprehensive education that, far from destroying the grammar schools, the transition meant the extension and transformation of these schools to meet the needs, and the nature, of the entire secondary school population. However among certain groups the matter had by now gone beyond rational argument.

The 1958 White Paper *Secondary Education for All: a new drive* was, of course, well received by the 'grammar school lobby', as it now came to be called. And so were the continuing decisions by succeeding Ministers of Education when faced with local plans for comprehensive education. As mentioned earlier the proposal at Newport (Monmouthshire) to replace the city's twelve modern, one technical and four grammar schools by four comprehensives, with the aim of abolishing selection throughout the city by 1960, was rejected by the Minister in 1958. The education committee, in reply, reaffirmed their intention 'in keeping with their powers' to move towards the abolition of the 11-plus and the segregation of pupils and to establish the full comprehensive system as and when opportunity offers.[33] Early in 1959 Geoffrey Lloyd, rejecting a proposal to establish a comprehensive school at Darlington, continued the imposition of what increasingly appeared to many as a doctrinaire and unimaginative policy of negation.[34]

3 The 1950s Assessed

Conflicts over the shape and structure of secondary education clearly reflected sharpening differences over objectives within this field. On the one hand a grass-roots movement, which found expression in the policies of such authorities as Manchester, London, Walsall, Darlington and elsewhere was fighting to break through the crystallised structure and open up the whole field of secondary education to new institutional forms which it was expected, would enhance opportunity and make a reality of the 1944 Act's promise of secondary education for all. The driving force here at this stage was the Labour movement in its broadest sense – the trade unions, the Labour and Communist parties, the Co-operative Union and, of course, locally the trades councils and local Labour parties in particular who controlled many local authorities. Social forces represented by Conservative governments (and civil service) on the other hand, had different objectives. Their strategy was equally clear on this the most sensitive issue in education. It was to maintain, and reinforce, the divided (or 'tripartite') structure within secondary education, to strengthen the selective system, and to make only such modification within it as to render it acceptable in the new conditions to parents in general. This was the significance of the alternative strategy of building up the secondary modern schools by encouraging advanced (examination) courses, and the Eccles policy of embodying vocational-technical courses within them. Outside the maintained system, steps were also taken, as we have seen, to strengthen the 'public' schools vis-a-vis the state system, and to ease the way for the middle and upper classes in terms of greater assistance towards access to higher education.

Throughout the decade, which started with nearly two years of increasingly demoralised Labour rule, followed by eight years of Conservative government, (the Tories won their third successive electoral victory in October 1959), a very tight control over the educational (particularly the school) system was retained. It is the case that educational expenditure, as a proportion of gross domestic product (GDP) rose gradually from under 3.0 per cent to 3.6 per cent in 1960 (see Appendix Table 15, p.599) But this was largely the result of the increase in the total number of pupils by over one million (to which another million were to be added in the next decade). Indeed in 1953, as noted earlier, W.P. Alexander argued that expenditure per pupil was *less* than it had been in 1938 (in terms of purchasing power), while PEP (Political and Economic Planning) in the same year, reached the conclusion that such expenditure in real terms had remained approximately stable over this period.[35] (It may be that there was a marginal increase in expenditure per child by the end of the decade, in line with the degree of economic growth now achieved). There was, in fact, a slight decline in the pupil-teacher ratio (from about 26.8 to 25.1) during the decade though there were still very many over-large classes (see Appendix Table 4a, p. 581). A key feature of the decade, however, was the increase in the number of pupils staying on at school until the age of seventeen – this nearly doubled from about 24,000 in 1950 to 46,000 in 1960 – and it was, of course, this (known as the 'trend') that led to the bottle-neck at the age of eighteen and the sudden expansion of higher education. Similarly, the number of students in full-time further education more than doubled during the decade (from 50,000 to 113,000), while, after the freeze in the early 1950s, the number of university students increased from under 85,000 to 108,000 (in 1960). (See Appendix Table 14, p. 597.)

While there was some expansion, then (particularly during the last years of the decade), restrictive overall policies ensured that there was no increase in educational opportunity during the 1950s – rather the reverse. Using the same indicator as in Chapter 2 (p. 142) – the proportion of the thirteen-year-old age cohort in selective and non-selective schools – we find that the percentage gaining a selective place (grammar and technical, plus grammar-technical streams in bilateral and multilateral schools) fell from 23.0 per cent in 1950 to 22.9 per cent in 1961. Grammar school places, as a proportion of all 'maintained' secondary school places, rose from 19.6 per cent to 19.7 per cent during the decade, while technical school places fell from 3.4 per cent to 3.2 per cent. In 1961, 11 per cent of 13-year-olds were either in comprehensive (5.3 per cent) or 'other' secondary schools (5.9 per cent),[36] and these have been excluded from the calculations (above) as regards secondary school opportunity, since their pupils cannot be placed in any of the three categories (grammar, technical, modern). Generally, then, these figures indicate that there was *no* increase in educational opportunity, as measured by the criteria given above, during the 1950s (see Table 4.1). In fact, 1960 marked the high point in the abortive expansion of secondary modern schools; their decline started now. It also marked the high point in numbers of technical school pupils, with just over 100,000; these also started their decline (see Appendix Table 5a, p.583).[37] Grammar schools, which had certainly expanded, more particularly in the latter half of the decade (though not as quickly as the growth in the relevant age cohorts), were to reach their peak three years later, in 1963. Comprehensive and 'other' secondary schools expanded rapidly, especially after 1955, but these formed a relatively small proportion of the nearly 3 million pupils now in secondary education. Finally, the number of children aged thirteen still in all-age schools (where they could not receive a 'secondary' education) dropped from about 90,000 (18 per cent) in 1950 to 26,000 (3·8 per cent) in 1961.

Table 4.1

Local   Authority   Maintained   Schools,   England   and Wales, Distribution of Pupils aged Thirteen

	1950		1961	
	Number	Percentage	Number	Percentage
Modern	290,812	58.6	496,781	73.2
Grammar	97,067	19.6	134,451	19.7
Technical	17,327	3.4	21,876	3.2
All-age	89,564	18.2	25,731	3.8
Comprehensive	2,092	0.4	36,043	5.3
'Other'	—	—	40,193	5.9
Modern plus all-age	380,376	76.8	522,512	77.0
Total	494,770[a]		755,119[b]	

[a] Excluding comprehensive.
[b] Including comprehensive and 'other'.
Sources: Education in England and Wales, Report and Statistics, 1950; Statistics of Education, Part I, England and Wales, 1961.

The analysis so far made focuses on overall national figures only. Data gathered for the Robbins Report on Higher Education (1963), however, referring to 1960, enable a deeper penetration into the massive variations concealed by such an analysis. These made it dramatically clear that the sharp inequalities in education in England and Wales were due to three main factors: differences in social class, in sex (or gender), and in geographical location. Where these advantages (or disadvantages) reinforced each other, real differences became enormous. At their maximum, these showed that the opportunity to reach full-time higher education for a middle-class boy living in Cardiganshire was roughly 160 times as great as that for a working-class girl living in West Ham.[38] In other words, by this period, enormous regional and other differences in opportunity had been allowed to develop. The proportion of sixteen-year-olds in maintained schools (as a proportion of thirteen-year-olds in these schools three years earlier) varied from 15·3 per cent in the 'northern' region to 28·6 per cent in the 'south-eastern' region.

Gross regional variations, therefore, were one important aspect of educational inequalities, but, as was now at last beginning to be realised, so was gender. In 1961 nearly three times as many men entered universities as women; for full-time study at technical colleges, four times as many. Only the training colleges had a preponderance of women over men. Opportunities in certain fields requiring higher education were still very restricted. Nearly four men were training as doctors for every one woman; the same proportion held good for pure science at the universities. The most striking figure was perhaps that for the technological faculties of universities, where there were 32 men for every woman.

Looking further back we find that girls tended to leave school earlier than boys; of boys and girls with five or more 'O' levels, ten boys stayed on at school to every eight girls. 51 per cent of these boys obtained three or more 'A' levels compared to only 34 per cent of the girls. Evidently, then, severe inequalities clearly existed by 1960-61 between men and women as regards educational opportunities generally.[39]

However what was now becoming abundantly clear, partly as a result of earlier studies by sociologists, was that the most important, the most pervasive and intractable of the three factors leading to inequality was the class factor – this because it is all-inclusive, affecting everyone wherever they live and of whatever sex. A great deal of evidence had been gathered during the 1950s highlighting class inequalities and making clear how deep seated and enduring these were proving to be.[40]

The overall class analysis made by the Robbins Committee, but referring to 1962, showed that 45 per cent (or nearly half) of those from higher professional families were successful in obtaining full-time higher education; 10 per cent of those whose fathers were in clerical jobs; 4 per cent of children of skilled workers, and only 2 per cent (or one in 50) of children of semi-skilled or unskilled workers who comprised, in fact, about 22 per cent of the total population.[41]

The class factor was already being recognised as deep seated and enduring. Evidence was accumulating that the percentage of entrants to grammar schools from the working class had actually *fallen* during the 1950s.[42] W.D. Furneaux, who published *The Chosen Few*, a study of selection for the universities in 1961, referred later to 'the extraordinary stability in the picture of differentials in social class attainment, not only over the past ten years but over the past fifteen or twenty'. 'In fact', he added, 'we have a social class structure which, as things stand, is virtually self-perpetuating.' He concluded, 'Unless we have done something about initiating social change then we shall be in the same position in fifty years' time as we are now.'[43] These have proved (at least after thirty years) to be prophetic words.

It was partly a growing consciousness of Britain's relative backwardness which, as we have seen, began towards the end of the decade to penetrate even the Tory Cabinet and government, that sparked new plans for expansion both within technical education and at the universities. The particular target at that time was the Soviet Union – but also Britain's 'Western' competitors. As stated at the start of this chapter, although Britain achieved a slow but steady rate of economic growth, she was far outstripped in this by most comparable advanced industrial countries during the decade – in particular by the USA and USSR, but also now by Germany, France, and, in the far East, by Japan. Even the moderate expansionist policies of the final years of the decade were to leave Britain yet further behind, whilst little or nothing was achieved in terms of allaying the obstructive forms of regional, class and gender differentials which acted as a break on the development of the human potential available. The crystallised pattern, criticised by C.P. Snow, embodied and froze these obstructive forces.[44]

Throughout the 1950s the traditional institutions of the country retained their hegemony which, indeed, was deliberately reinforced. The universities (dominated by Oxford and Cambridge), the public schools and the grammar schools (including the direct grant variety) persisted unchanged. In 1955, for instance, the FBI established a development fund contributed by industry to finance modern scientific laboratories and equipment specifically for independent schools. The 'new' technical 'alternative system', as beginning to be constructed by Eccles and promoted by the Crowther Report, was to be established *alongside* the traditional structures whose hegemony was not thereby threatened.[45] The long conflict and controversy over technological awards, which ran through all this period and continued later, was symptomatic of contemporary attitudes, and of the determination of existing institutions to retain their primacy – or monopoly – in this case of degrees.[46] No fundamental restructuring in the field of education was envisaged.

But, as we have seen, there were points of growth, of development. These had been contained, relatively effectively. But they were expressive of deep seated social factors which now began to exert unexpected strength and force.

The first of these was the demographic trend. The birth rate, which had declined steadily from the 1890s, suddenly shot up during the war, as we have seen. More children meant more teachers and more *young* teachers – more teacher trainers, more students in colleges and universities became a necessity. This was a new experience for this country – in recent times at least. Of course they could be squeezed into the old mould – and such was the intention. For a few years this was successful; but other factors rendered this policy untenable.

The chief among these, as suggested at the start, was the more or less rapid transformation in social structure consequent upon the beginnings of the third industrial revolution – the expansion of industries with a high scientific – technological component and the resulting growth of what we might call intermediate social strata, together with the clear reduction in manual working-class occupations. The 1950s, for instance, saw a massive run-down in the coal industry and other basic industries were similarly affected. Skilled workers and the so-called 'new middle class' brought with them new educational aspirations, aspirations which could not be contained within Snow's 'rigid and crystallised pattern'. They also, I would suggest, now began to espouse education as a means of maintaining or enhancing status (what sociologists refer to as 'cultural capital'), as indeed the professional section of the middle classes had always done. Their attitude to education and what it could achieve tended to be positive. So a new and more far-sighted educational ideology began to develop and exert an influence. From around the mid-to-late 1950s these factors fused with the demographic trend to develop a self-acceleration sufficient to burst the bonds that held things so tightly controlled. First, the universities, strongly guarded in the late 1940s, then the whole field of secondary education and, to some extent, that of technical education felt this pressure now in a new form. This was sufficient, at least by the early 1960s, to allow space for a sustained assault on the defensive bastions which had been so carefully erected in the 1950s and before.

Notes and References

1. *Scientific and Engineering Manpower in Great Britain*, HMSO 1956.

2. *Sunday Times*, 4 March 1956. Sir Francis Simon, a distinguished physicist, was Lee Professor of Experimental Philosophy and Head of the Clarendon Laboratory at Oxford. He died in October 1956.

3. *Hansard*, House of Lords, 11 May 1960, Cols 648ff. Lord Simon's motion, and supporting speech, specifically proposed a committee of enquiry 'to work for 3 or 4 years to consider the next 20 years, or even the period up to the year 2,000'. For Simon's activities in this field, Mary Stocks, *Ernest Simon of Manchester*, London 1963, pp.165ff.

4. Ibid.

5. Ibid., Col. 651.

6. *15-18, Report of the Central Advisory Council for Education – England* (the Crowther report), Vol. 1, HMSO 1959.

7. Ibid., pp.285-95.

8. *Hansard*, House of Lords, 11 May 1960, Cols. 652-3.

9. University Grants Committee, *Returns from Universities and University Colleges, 1959-60*, HMSO 1961, p.6.

10. University Grants Committee, *University Development 1962-1967*, HMSO 1968, Cmnd 3820, p.49.

11. This was proposed by Lord Hailsham as Minister in a memo dated 16 May 1957, CP(57)123, and eventually approved by the Cabinet, CM(57)42 and later. The decision was reaffirmed when, only one year later, a teacher shortage was expected, requiring emergency measures. Minister of Education memo to Cabinet, CP(58)149.

12. Richard Layard, John King and Claus Moser. *The Impact of Robbins*, Harmondsworth 1969, Table 2, p.23 (reproduced on p.260).

13. Ibid.

14. Ibid.

15. *Secondary Education for All: A New Drive*. Cmnd 604, December 1958, pp.5-6. The politics of this White Paper deserve an article in themselves. The initiative was originally taken by Eccles (memo entitled 'A Further Advance in Education', 7 December 1956, CP(56)278), who argued the importance of educational advance in the post-Suez era. This initiative was endorsed first by Hailsham (Cabinet memo, CP(57)23), but it then fell to Geoffrey Lloyd to carry it through. A draft was presented to Cabinet on 25 November 1958. This contained several positive references to comprehensive schools while basically rejecting these as a solution. At the Cabinet meeting (CM(58)82, 25 November 1958) these references 'to the value of comprehensive schools' were criticised – they 'might expose the government to political embarrassment'. As a result the 'embarrassing' paragraphs were cut out and other offending paragraphs rewritten for the final draft, which reflected the hard line defined in the text. Ironically the parallel Scottish circular took comprehensive education for granted. The Cabinet papers, which are prolific, bring out very clearly the *political* importance attached to this initiative – particularly in countering Labour party policy on this issue – see especially minutes of the Cabinet's Educational Policy Committee (CAB 134 1663), 4th meeting, 9 July 1958.

16. Founded as an independent journal in the autumn of 1958. *FORUM for the Discussion of New Trends in Education* was dedicated to promoting the transition to comprehensive education and the modification of streaming in junior schools. It was established by Robin Pedley, Brian Simon and Jack Walton – the former then both lecturers at the University of Leicester, the latter a local teacher (later Professor of Education at Armidale, New South Wales).

17. Some of these were 'County Complements' – associated with voluntary aided or controlled grammar schools to form comprehensive units.

18. One member remembered later 'the staff-room frequently half full of young teachers excitedly talking shop at six in the evening when the school keeper (an appointment as happy as that of most of the teaching staff) came round to chivvy us out'. Roy Waters, quoted in Brian Simon, *Does Education Matter?*, p.166.

19. 'Report from South Wales', Joan Simon, *Forum*, Vol. 1, No.2, Spring 1959.

20. Sir Edward Boyle had been appointed Parliamentary Secretary to the Ministry of Education on 18 January 1957, retaining the post until 21 October 1959. He was appointed Minister of Education on 13 July 1962. In the April 1964 re-organisation he became Minister of State for Education.

21. At Sandfields, 'All the staff seem young, full of enthusiasm and bursting with plans which it would need a separate article to outline,' wrote *Forum*'s reporter, Joan Simon, op.cit.

22. B.F. Hobby, 'Report from the West Midlands,' *Forum* Vol.1, No.3, Summer 1959.

23. Robin Pedley, 'Report from Yorkshire', *Forum*, Vol. 2, No. 1, Autumn 1959.

24. H. Knowlson, 'Report from Bristol and the West', *Forum*, Vol. 2, No. 3, Summer 1960.

25. St John Reade had been a teacher at a public school (Clifton) before the war.

26. *Forum*, Vol. 2, No. 2, Spring 1960, articles by John Merrick (Crawley), Sheila Hiller (Harlow New Town), S. Bury (Head of Brookfields, Lancashire's first comprehensive, on the Kirkby Estate), Judith Hart (East Kilbride New Town).

27. For the origins of the Leicestershire initiative, D.K. Jones, *Stewart Mason, The Art of Education*, London 1988, especially Chapter 3, 'The Comprehensive "Experiment" '. For an analysis of the Leicestershire Plan in its full development, Brian Simon, 'Education in Leicestershire', Chapter 21 in N. Pye (ed.), *Leicester and its Region*, Leicester 1972.

28. For instance, in *Comprehensive Education, A New Approach*, London 1956, a book which received wide publicity at the time. Pedley had already argued for a two-tier system in *Comprehensive Schools Today*, London nd 1955?, based on articles published in *Education* in October 1954. This survey included comments by leading educators including H.C. Dent, Eric James, and, from local authorities, Harold

Shearman and W.P. Alexander. It was published by the Councils and Education Press, of the Association of Education Committees.

29. Robin Pedley, 'Report from Yorkshire', *Forum*, Vol. 2, No. 1, Autumn 1959, p.24. On this issue, Edward Boyle has written, 'David Eccles arranged a debate on this subject between Dr Pedley and officers of the Ministry, shortly before his departure [January 1957]; and Stewart Mason's "Leicestershire scheme", the first experiment with middle schools, made its (deliberately) cautious beginning in April 1957'. *Journal of Educational Administration and History*, Vol. 4, No. 2, June 1972, p.30.

30. P.E. Vernon (ed.), *Secondary School Selection*, London 1957, pp.43-4, 53. It is interesting to note that Hans Eysenck was a member of this committee.

31. Alfred Yates and D.A. Pidgeon, *Admission to Grammar Schools*, (NFER), London 1957, pp.191-3.

32. Harry Rée, *The Essential Grammar School*, London 1956, pp.18ff, 39-40, 83-4. Rée later became a strong supporter of comprehensive education.

33. *Education*, 12 September 1958.

34. *Times Educational Supplement*, 17 April 1959.

35. *Education*, 26 June 1953; *Times Educational Supplement*, 26 June 1953.

36. 'Other' secondary schools were largely bilateral schools, which could not be categorised either within the tripartite pattern, nor as comprehensive.

37. It will be remembered that the Eccles policy of 1957 included the announcement that no further technical schools were to be built except where a very strong case could be made. The decline in the number of technical schools in the 1960s was largely due to the integration of those that existed into comprehensive schools.

38. Brian Simon, 'Inequalities in Education' in *Intelligence, Psychology and Education*, London 1971, pp.166-76.

39. Ibid.

40. Both the Central Advisory Council (England) reports, *Early Leaving* (1954) and *16-18* (the Crowther report, 1959), contained a mass of such evidence. Specialist studies include A.H. Halsey and L. Gardner, 'Selection for Secondary Education', *British Journal of Sociology*, March 1953, and J. Floud and A.H. Halsey, *Social Class and Educational Opportunity*, London 1956.

41. *Higher Education* (the Robbins Report), Cmnd 2154, HMSO 1963, Table 21, p.50. In addition, 19 per cent of those from 'Managerial and other professional' families reached full-time higher education.

42. Claus Moser, quoted in Simon (loc.cit., note 38 p.171).

43. W.D. Furneaux, *The Chosen Few. An Examination of Some Aspects of University Selection in Britain*, Oxford 1961. The quotations in the text are based on this study. Simon, loc.cit., note 38, p.171.

44. In November 1962 Harold Macmillan addressed a memo to both the Chancellor and his Deputy (Butler) entitled 'The Modernisation of Britain'. This stressed Britain's relative backwardness as compared with 'our commercial rivals' and sketched important counter-measures. There is no evidence of effecive further action. Indeed it is abundantly clear, both from Alistair Horne's two volume biography and Macmillan's own multi-volume memoirs that Macmillan himself, when Prime Minister (1957-63), took no serious interest in educational issues – leaving policy and action to his Ministerial team. He did, however, take great delight in his election as Chancellor of Oxford University in 1960, and in the subsequent exercise of that office. Alistair Horne, *Macmillan, 1957–1986, Volume Two of the Official Biography*, London 1989.

45. Eccles's alternative plans for secondary modern schools, it will be remembered, were designed to develop new patterns without changing or threatening existing structures – a point he specifically made in his memo to the Cabinet (see pp.185-6).

46. See Harold Silver, *A Higher Education: The Council for National Academic Awards*, London 1990.

Part II

5   The Break-out
in Higher Education

The educational tide is rising throughout the world. From China to Peru the flood of new pupils, the rise of educational expectations, the demand for teachers has, since the late 1940s, become a dominant social fact – perhaps *the* dominant social fact in all contemporary societies.[1]

This comment, published early in 1963 in a review of three French books on education in a literary journal, is sufficiently characteristic of the feeling of the time to warrant giving it pride of place in the introduction to this chapter. In the early 1960s a whole concatenation of circumstances was coming together reinforcing the enhanced value now set on education – by individuals, groups and by governments. We are now entering a decade marked by striking advances across the whole field of education – including the unprecedented act of drawing up a full, twenty-year plan of development of higher education in Britain; by decisive steps towards the transform-ation of the publicly maintained system of secondary education – in this case as a result of a popular grass roots movement from below; and by the emergence of the hitherto obscured field of primary education into the full light of day. With radical changes taking place in each of these three main sectors roughly at the same time, it is no wonder that the 1960s are, and must be evaluated as a formative, and indeed unique, 'moment of change' within British education.

The pressures leading towards the 'break-out' in the 1960s, as we have seen (Chapter 4), first become insistent within the field of higher education in the late 1950s – even if the first signs of parallel developments within both secondary and primary education were, by then, also apparent. But we are now entering a period when the economy was beginning to take off, when aspirations were rising – related both to the knowledge explosion and the emergence of new, science-based industries of the 'third industrial revolution' – and when governments began to value education on a quite new level.

This latter development, which was, of course, of crucial significance in terms of resource allocation, was the result of two main factors. First, recognition that educational growth, particularly in the field of science and technology, was an essential aspect of economic growth; 'human capital theory' begins now to take off, and is used to legitimate enhanced educational expenditure – now seen as 'investment'. Second, a growing acceptance of the views popularised by Anthony Crosland in the mid-1950s that the redistribution of incomes, through social but specifically educational policies, could, in a period of economic growth, act as a palliative to social problems, stabilising the 'mixed economy' through a drive towards equality. 'Egalitarianism' was to replace socialism as an objective – or, rather, to be seen as identical. These two approaches – that derived from human capital theory and its egalitarian counterpart did not, in a period of economic growth, appear contradictory. Around each, a broad consensus might be established and indeed was established in the outlook and policies of Edward Boyle and Anthony Crosland, Tory and Labour respectively, the two dominant ministers (or secretaries of state) during the early formative, or decisive years of the 1960s (1962-66).

Of the impact of the first of these, a good example is Douglas Home's instant and very public (televised) welcome and acceptance of the Robbins Report on the day of its publication (23 October 1963) – only five days after he took over as Prime Minister from Harold Macmillan. Of the second, government acceptance and (under Labour) support for the move to comprehensive secondary education and, in particular, acceptance of a policy of positive discrimination as recommended by the Plowden Committee in 1967 (Educational Priority Areas). Acceptance of both policies required increased expenditure on education – over and above that required as a result of increases in the birth rate. In fact, between 1960 and 1970, educational expenditure, calculated as a proportion of gross domestic product (GDP), increased by nearly 50 per cent.[2]

The 1960s break-out forms the subject matter of this and the following two chapters. It did not take place without generating contradictions and struggles, sometimes very sharp, as we shall see. Nor was all plain sailing, especially towards the end of the decade. Advance, changes, even transformation in the three main sectors covered (higher, secondary and primary) were, of course, related and affected each other; attempts will be made to clarify these relations and their importance. In this chapter, however, the focus must be on higher education, and, at the start at least, on the universities.

1 The Robbins Report and its Significance

The Background

'In the mid-Fifties', writes E.G. Edwards in *Higher Education for Everyone*, there occurred 'a sudden break in the continuity of the long-term trend' (in terms of recruitment to higher education). 'From then on, for the next fifteen years, there was an extraordinary unpredicted and unpredictable explosion in university and higher education expansion, common to all the countries of the advanced world.'[3] The author's chapter on this issue is entitled 'The Student Explosion of the 1960s'.

We have already examined, if briefly, the start of this expansion. Between 1957-58 and 1962-63, a period of five years, the number of students in full-time higher education in Great Britain had already increased by nearly 50 per cent (from 148,000 to 217,000). The universities had expanded by nearly 30 per cent (from 103,000 to 131,000), the training colleges were experiencing a crash programme while full-time advanced students in technical colleges had more than doubled (13,000 to 31,000, see Table 5.2, p.260). Annual recruitment rates in each of the three sectors, and in these combined, indicated the speeding up of the rate of expansion, having a long term cumulative effect.

The pressure for a high level enquiry into the whole field was sustained for many years – finding expression particularly in the series of debates in the House of Lords already mentioned. Finally, as we have seen, the need for such a step was conceded (by Lord Hailsham, in May 1960). The whole system was burgeoning, but in a 'spontaneous', uncontrolled manner. In any case there was no 'system' as such – institutions, on various levels, had 'just growed' like Topsy. Alongside the traditional universities, new institutions were emerging – especially the technical colleges, following Eccles's initiatives. The impact of the post-war birth rate bulge was now (1960) about to hit higher education, an influence enhanced by what was known as 'the trend' – the increase in the proportion of each age group staying on at school. In these circumstances, what should be the pattern of the evolving institutions? How should they be financed? What should be their relations to each other? These were questions which now urgently demanded a solution.

What form should the enquiry take? There were those who argued for a royal commission, so symbolising the importance of these steps. There were those in universities, apparently, who feared this action, believing that a royal commission, like its Victorian predecessors, might lead to over-radical action.[4] In the end the decision was to set up a departmental committee appointed by the Treasury, but 'supra-departmental', as John Carswell puts it, 'in that it was appointed by the first lord of the Treasury, namely the prime minister' – an arrangement which is, apparently, unique.[5] The committee's appointment was finally announced in February 1961, nine months after Hailsham's acceptance of the idea. It was to report within two and a half years – in October 1963. Given the massive amount of evidence received, and in particular of research undertaken, this was a considerable achievement.

It is worth noting at this stage that the terms of reference of the committee said nothing specific about expansion. Their emphasis, as John Carswell has pointed out, was 'on the need to review the *pattern* of higher education', and the final report itself focuses also on institutions and 'machinery of government'.[6] For the Treasury, then, this was the important issue to get settled. 'So far as *expansion* went,' writes Carswell (the chief official responsible for university finance), the Treasury felt that having, in the period 1957-60, agreed to 'almost everything' the university grants committee had asked, 'nothing very fearful need be expected'. 'No direct invitation to consider further growth was extended in the terms of reference.'[7]

If these sentiments represented Treasury thinking at the time of the appointment of the Robbins Committee, by the time it reported all was changed. It is certainly the case that a great deal had been achieved by the university grants committee between 1957 and 1960 – a substantial increase in university salaries, approval for the designation of seven new universities, an increase in capital programmes (from £12,000,000 to £15,000,000 a year from 1960), while the so-called 'quinquennial settlement' of 1957 had been reopened, at the request of the UGC, to provide additional funding necessary for the 8,000 extra students expected over and above those originally planned. In 1959, as we have seen, the UGC's target of 135,000 students by the mid-1960s was raised to 175,000 'by the late 1960s or early 1970s', and capital programmes were again raised – this time to £25,000,000.[8] No doubt, in these circumstances, the Treasury felt that a period of stability would now supervene when attention could be turned to problems of administration and control.

It was not to be. The student expansion of the late 1950s only heralded the explosion of the 1960s. It continued at roughly the same rate during the two to three years the Robbins Committee itself was sitting (1961-63), and, for the next four or five years took off at an even faster rate (see Appendix, Table 14a, p.597). The build-up and expansion of higher education had by now become a social trend having wide popular support. This was made abundantly clear in the mass of documentary 'evidence' from social, political and educational organisations of all kinds and levels which now poured into the offices of the Robbins Committee.[9]

The issue that emerged most strikingly in the evidence published at the time (mostly in the late summer and autumn of 1961) and reported in the media was widespread agreement on the need for large-scale expansion. The theory of a strictly limited 'pool of ability' received little or no support – for instance, the National Union of Teachers, then by far the largest and most representative teachers' organisation, went out of its way specifically to denounce this conception which, until recently, had dominated all thinking about education; instead it focused attention on the waste of human resources caused by 'the inadequate provision of education generally and higher education in particular',[10] a standpoint strongly supported by the Trades Union Congress, which made a number of radical criticisms of existing educational opportunity including an analysis of its class basis.[11] The NUT made no estimate of the total numbers requiring higher education in the future, but others did. The Communist Party, which had kept developments in higher education under review consistently since the war, argued for an increase to some 350,000 or 400,000 students in all types of higher education by the mid-1960s,[12] was perhaps the most radical, but the Fabians and the National Union of Students both envisaged a student population of some 700,000 by 1980,[13] while the Association of Education Committees (local authorities) looked to a total of 500,000 (though giving no date).[14] Even the Headmasters' Conference (public schools) suggested a target of 250,000 in universities alone.[15] The most conservative proposals were those by the vice chancellors and the Association of University Teachers (AUT) – in that order. The vice chancellors did not want any expansion above 175,000 (in universities alone) in the next ten years, while the AUT wanted no more than 200,000 in the universities by 1980; that is, they proposed that the universities should scarcely double their size in the next twenty years.[16]

Several of the bodies submitting evidence recognised that expansion on the scale proposed required a reorganisation of the structure of higher education as a whole, and this, of course, was the key question the Robbins Committee had been asked to review.

The crucial issue here was the relation between universities, technical colleges and training colleges. Were these to remain, as the Communist Party put it, 'separate, rigidly demarcated "types" of institutions', or was there to be a move towards 'an integrated system of institutions of equal status?' This latter view was strongly supported by the TUC which declared itself as 'strenuously opposed' to the development of a 'tripartite' system of higher education – training colleges, technical colleges and universities forming a threefold pattern of separate types of institutions. Instead they believed that all institutions of higher education should have university status, and looked forward to the development of a 'comprehensive system of higher education' which should constitute a coherent whole.

Other bodies were more cautious. The AUT, for instance, proposed that the newly established colleges of advanced technology should be brought fully into the university system; they did not, however, envisage any relations with technical colleges other than Colleges of Advanced Technology (CATs).

The development of CATs as universities, giving their own degrees, was supported also by the vice chancellors and by the ATTI (Association of Teachers in Technical Institutions).[17] Several organisations also suggested either that the three year training college course as just introduced should exempt students from part of the requirements for a first degree, or that these students should be permitted to take a university degree while studying at the college. It is, perhaps, worth noting, in view of future developments, that the principals of the colleges of advanced technology appeared as strongly opposed to any merging with universities. They wanted the right to give their own degrees (including higher degrees), to develop new faculties in pure science, social science, 'other studies', as well as applied science and engineering, and in general demanded equality of status and conditions with the universities, while remaining completely separate from them.[18]

A good deal of attention was paid in the published evidence to the control and co-ordination of higher education as a whole. The TUC proposed that responsibility for the whole field of higher education should be transferred to the Minister of Education.[19] The ATTI proposed that the UGC be superceded by a grants committee 'more broadly representative of national interests and responsible for financing the whole field of higher education', directly responsible to a minister of Cabinet rank. The establishment of a national council for higher education concerned with the financing and planning of the whole system, together with regional councils to facilitate decentralisation and regional planning and co-ordination, was proposed by the Communist Party. No other proposals quite took this form, although the Association of Education Committees wanted regional councils to finance and control the lower stream of higher education. The Fabians, however, argued for a complete overhaul of the administrative structure and the setting up of national and regional authorities; what was needed was 'a viable unified system of administration of higher education'. As was to be expected, the vice chancellors, however, gave a strong warning against any tampering with the University Grants Committee which must, they argued, remain in being for university finance alone. The general trend of opinion, however, as reflected in the evidence, was towards a more unified system of administration. This was supported in the Treasury's evidence to the Robbins Committee where it was argued that it would not be appropriate for the Treasury to assume departmental responsibility for CATs 'or to be in the lead in co-ordinating higher education as a whole'.

> It follows that a unification of responsibilities for universities and CATs (and, a fortiori a wider unification of responsibility for higher education) could be brought about only by a change in ministerial responsibility for the universities.[20]

Many other issues were, of course, discussed in the evidence submitted (for instance the whole issue of opportunities for women in higher education – by Bedford College and others). The National Union of Students and the AUT, for instance, as well as the Communist Party, devoted considerable attention to the content and methods of education. In general the most 'progressive' standpoints were expressed by organisations connected with the labour movement (the TUC, the Communist Party and possibly the Fabians), and from the teachers (NUT and ATTI, though not from the grammar school and public school headmasters). As was pointed out at the time this indicated a line-up that had achieved considerable educational advances in the past. The most conservative evidence came from the vice chancellors (who appeared to want as little change as possible) and, regrettably, from the AUT. Several organisations, however, did propose a closer relation between the universities, technical and training colleges, and this now emerged as the key issue in any advance.

The thinking and public discussion which accompanied the formulation and publication of this 'evidence' itself contributed to transforming the atmosphere while the committee itself was sitting, so preparing the ground for sympathetic reception of the radical nature of the committee's report. In October 1961 the first new university – Sussex – opened its doors while active preparations were now taking place in relation to the other six new universities. An ethos of expansionism was now emerging – supported also by the Conservative government which, holding power uninterruptedly since 1951, was running into serious internal difficulties yet attempting to appear as an apostle for 'modernisation'. The resources required, as we have seen, were made available, if only after a series of sharp battles within the civil service. It was, however, to be the

Labour Party which now saw its chance and seized its opportunity.

There were to be two phases in this move. First the appointment and report of a study group on higher education, and second, the sharp focus at the 1963 Labour Party conference, held in September/October 1963, on the crucial 'statement of policy' entitled 'Labour and the Scientific Revolution'. We may take each of these in turn.

'Higher Education is facing a crisis of unprecedented severity, and, if disaster is to be averted, vigorous action will be essential the moment a Labour government is returned to power.' In these dramatic terms, Harold Wilson launched the 'Taylor Report', the product of the study group appointed by Hugh Gaitskell in March 1962. The committee, which included Anthony Crosland, John Vaizey and other Labour educationists and MPs, worked quickly, reporting in the late summer of 1963 – before the annual conference. Benefiting, as the group acknowledge, from much of the written evidence submitted to Robbins, the study group came out with a generally radical, forward looking policy of advance.[21]

'There must be a rapid and continuing expansion of higher education, on a scale never before contemplated,' runs the introduction. Higher education should be 'a right for all able young men and women, regardless of their families' class, income or position'. Further, 'a nation's primary asset' is the brainpower and skill of its scientists and engineers, research workers and technicians, administrators and professional men and women. The human capital theory is projected in popular terms: 'Economic expansion is only possible if university and technological education expands rapidly and continuously to provide the necessary brainpower and skill.' Segregation between institutions of varying status persists but must be overcome; 'university status' they argue, 'should be conferred on a wide range of institutions' at present excluded.[22]

The committee proposed a short-term 'crash' programme, and a long-term plan; the former to get over the immediate problem of shortage of places, the latter as a plan for the future. Over the next twenty years 'we shall need about seventy universities in England and Wales and about ten in Scotland' – rather more than twice the number then existing. With 80 universities, the highest projections for expansion (700,000 students) could be met, but this means finding sites for 'about forty-five new universities in Britain'.[23]

The bases for these new universities would be found in existing institutions which, upgraded and with additional resources, would become university institutions. These include all existing colleges of advanced technology which should become full universities 'forthwith', a number of existing regional technical colleges and all teacher training colleges (three modes of their development into university institutions are proposed). To equalise the status of university institutions a quota system determining entry is proposed (chiefly as a means of reducing the 'exaggerated prestige' attached to Oxford and Cambridge).[24] Finally the study group came down in favour of the transfer of responsibility for higher education as a whole to the minister of education. There would, however, be a 'national university development council' as an overall planning body, as well as 'regional university grants commissions' responsible for implementing the national plan within each of the major regions.[25]

Such a programme, the group argue, will not be cheap; 'viewed realistically', however, 'it is no more and no less than a matter of national survival'. Inevitably there would have to be 'substantial new capital and current expenditure'. The expansion of higher education, it is again reiterated in conclusion, 'is in itself an essential pre-requisite to further long term growth and economic expansion.'[26]

This report, later to be repudiated in terms of policy by one of its signatories (Crosland), was appropriately published a few weeks before the 1963 annual conference of the Labour Party – at which a sustained attempt was made to take the high ground as the main 'modernising' party, in terms of science and technology and its application through education. The succinct policy statement 'Labour and the Scientific Revolution' was debated at the conference and unanimously approved, with acclamation.[27]

'A nation's success in applying science to industry depends first and foremost on its education system,' it is stated, but stop-go economic policies have prevented rational planning. The first and overriding need is 'a major expansion in our universities'. Targets are spelt out – an additional 150,000 places as a minimum with the resources and buildings necessary for a major thrust forward. Universities must be deliberately sited so that they are 'in close and continuous touch with the life and needs of the nation'. Barriers must be broken down between academic institutions, between scientists in industry and the universities and those in government. The CATS must immediately be raised 'to full university status', but the weight of the new expansion programme 'must clearly fall on existing universities'. In particular research must be developed; scarce resources of scientific expertise must no longer be concentrated on military research and development. Instead our universities and technological institutes must become 'the home of first class higher education and research'. To achieve this 'is well within our means'. 'A new deal for the scientist and technologist in higher education, a new status for scientists in government, and a new role for government sponsored science in industrial development are the three essential requirements for reviving the economy'.

There needs also to be mass participation in planning – this is essential in the new age of the computer and automation which, without planning, 'equals chronic unemployment'. Adult training and retraining facilities are urgently necessary to avoid technological redundancy. A new level of leisure will be available for all and this also must be provided for. 'The central feature of our post-war world is the scientific revolution,' opened the statement. It closed with a vision of the future:

> The prospect that the scientific revolution opens before us is a working life which is secure and interesting, in a society where machines are subordinate to man; a world in which hardship and suffering are progressively eliminated and the whole range of man's culture is available to enrich the lives of all. This is the true socialist vision which, in the past, want and ignorance have held from our grasp.

It was in his major speech presenting this statement to the conference that Harold Wilson, who had succeeded Hugh Gaitskell as leader only a year earlier, made his famous statement referring to 'the Britain that is going to be forged in the white heat of this [the scientific, B.S.] revolution'. Here again major emphasis is put on plans for higher education. The Taylor report has been of high importance. 'They recommend, and we accept, a crash programme ... to make fuller use of existing universities and colleges of higher education.' 'They propose, and every one of us must accept, a tremendous building programme of new universities.' These, or some of them, should be sited in industrial areas 'where they can in some way reflect the pulsating throb of local industry', and where they can work in partnership 'with the new industries we seek to create'. A new ministry of higher education must become 'the focal point' of planning. A 'university of the air' must also be created.[28]

Harold Wilson's speech was a major contribution at this particular point in time (and deserves re-reading and serious consideration). It included rhetoric and rhodomontade, as most 'conference' speeches do; but it presented a vision, or perspective, of the meaning and significance of the scientific revolution and the conditions for its redirection – or exploitation – in the interests of all. Missing, perhaps, was a specific analysis of the social or structural changes necessary to realise the perspective put forward; and this, of course, was to become increasingly apparent over the years. Nevertheless Wilson's speech, and the enthusiastic and supportive debate which followed it, undoubtedly made a massive impact, influencing public opinion and no doubt convincing many of those involved in industry and the universities as scientists, administrators, technicians and technologists that the Labour Party really was a modernising party; that it had a clear policy for science, technology and education; and that the future was safer in its hands than in those of the Tories.

The Robbins Report

Just three weeks after the Labour Party conference, on 23 October, the report of the 'Committee on Higher Education' (as the Robbins report was officially called) was published. As already indicated, it was welcomed enthusiastically in all quarters, almost without exception; and in particular by the new Prime Minister, Douglas Home, who assured the nation on television that very evening (holding aloft a copy before the cameras) of the government's full and enthusiastic acceptance, in principle, of the report as a whole. The Robbins era had begun.[29]

First, a few words on the committee itself which had been appointed by Harold Macmillan as Prime Minister, though clearly on the advice of Treasury officials (then responsible for the universities) and in particular of Sir Keith Murray, the genial, expansionist and highly effective chairman of the UGC.[30] Robbins himself, a traditional but distinguished economist from the London School of Economics, as the chairman, came from the university world, as did six of the other eleven members. The most forceful of these was Sir Philip Morris, vice chancellor of Bristol University, who came originally from the world of local authority administration (Kent) and had played a leading part in the development of army education, including the innovative Army Bureau of Current Affairs during the war. Others included Sir Patrick Linstead, rector of Imperial College, London, Professor James Drever, psychologist and later (1967) principal of the University of Dundee, a professor of accounting and business methods at Edinburgh (Sir David Anderson), Helen Gardner, fellow of St Hilda's College, Oxford, and Lionel Elvin, principal of the London University Institute of Education. There were in addition two industrialists, Sir Edward Herbert, a shipbuilder (already old when appointed, he died before the report was published), and R.B. Southall from British Petroleum. Neither seems to have made any serious impact on the committee's thinking or procedures.[31] This could not be said of Harold Shearman, then chairman of the education committee of the London County Council, firmly based in the Workers' Educational Association and a strong proponent, incidentally, of comprehensive secondary education. 'He was not usually argumentative or disputatious,' writes Carswell, 'but he saw clearly the ground on which he was bound to stand.'[32] The schools were (oddly) represented only by two teachers from public schools – none from the state system. These were Dame Kitty Anderson, head of the historic North London Collegiate, and Anthony Chevenix-Trench, head of Bradfield when appointed who became head of Eton while the committee was in session.

The balance of the committee is important in terms of its report. It was overwhelmingly university-orientated from the start. In particular there was no single representative of the burgeoning world of the technical colleges, an 'oversight' that was to lead to difficulties later.[33] But neither, for that matter, was there any representative, or anyone who had experience of teaching in a training college (though Lionel Elvin, through the London Institute, had close relations with these). Nor, as already remarked, was there a single teacher or representative of teachers from the maintained (or state) system which fed into higher education across the board. It was, in fact, a

Conservative-appointed, university-dominated body. The radical nature of its proposals and general outlook, then, are all the more striking as symptomatic of the surge of advanced liberal thinking at this period. It should also be remembered that the expansion of higher education was seen largely in university terms by almost everyone at this time – the Taylor Report, already discussed, and signed by such later proponents of 'binary' as Crosland and Tyrrell Burgess being a case in point. According to Carswell, who sat in on the committee as Treasury assessor, there was an 'inner, unofficial group within the committee' who made the running. This consisted of 'the chairman, Morris, Linstead and Murray' (not actually a member, but chairman of the UGC and an 'assessor'). The main themes of the report – 'expansion, autonomy and the generalisation of the university model', he continues, 'are theirs'.[34]

Central to the whole thrust of the report, as Carswell suggests, was legitimisation of a policy of massive expansion across the whole field of higher education. Arguments favouring the concept of a restricted 'pool of ability', based on biological (genetic) factors, though now beginning to be questioned, had long held the field. Legitimisation of expansion involved a confrontation with these theories and their rejection. To assist with this, the committee sponsored 'evidence' from two leading analysts, one psychological the other sociological. Professor P.E. Vernon, from the London University Institute of Education, was asked to submit evidence on mental measurement and the distribution of 'Intelligence', while Jean Floud, who had already made her name as a leading sociologist of education, tackled the issue of wastage of ability and its sociological determinants.

In July 1961 Vernon, then the leading educational psychologist in the country, submitted his memorandum. This, he wrote, contests the view – widespread among educationists – that there exists in the population a fixed distribution or 'pool' of intelligence, which limits either the numbers of individuals capable of higher education, or the educational standards that can be achieved by groups of pupils or students of given IQ level'.[35] Briefly describing the theory (that on a typical intelligence test, the proportion obtaining IQs of 130 or over is 2.5 per cent, of 120 and over 9 per cent, so that the 'pool' is precisely limited at each level), Vernon adds, 'I wish to state categorically that this reasoning is unsound, and that no calculations of the numbers of eligible students can be based on tests of intelligence or other aptitudes.'[36]

Vernon's arguments supporting this approach are complex and perhaps too detailed to enter into here. Measured intelligence (IQ), he says, as well as 'scholastic achievement', 'fall far below potentiality'. Researches in Sweden and the USA indicate that the actual experience of a full secondary and higher education raises IQ by some twelve points compared with those of equal IQ who leave school early. Further, tests are very poor predictors of degree results (correlations in Britain worked out at about +0.20), adding that, if only the top 5 per cent on IQs were admitted to universities 'we should miss more than half of those who are really the most able'. As a criterion of admission, he adds, IQs are 'almost as weak' as height (university students are taller than most of the population). Both in the USA and the USSR 'much larger proportions of the adolescent population are tackling advanced secondary school subjects than in the United Kingdom'; the proportion of the population undergoing higher education also varies in different social and ethnic groups – it cannot be held that these proportions are 'fixed by some immutable distribution of intelligence'.

The supply of students, then, cannot be determined by a formalistic calculation. It depends on a variety of social and educational factors (which Vernon lists). It is not, therefore, possible to set limits to the supply of students, though Vernon suggests that, in the current context (social and educational), 'There seems little reason why something like 15 per cent of the population should not be capable of work of university standard.' This, he argues cogently, need not lead to any lowering of standards, or increased failure rate, at the universities. (An expansion to 15 per cent would have meant at least a doubling of the number of university students.[37])

Jean Floud, in her contribution, was at least equally outspoken. In her view the idea of 'intelligence' as a factor determining future attainment (and therefore the concept of a 'pool of ability') 'is scientifically virtually valueless'; it is no more than a postulate, not observable empirically, and lacking any explanatory value. Measured intelligence (IQ) she adds, is 'the result of a cumulative process of development which is not unilinear throughout childhood, which proceeds at an irregular pace, does not stop at any particular age, and is susceptible to a striking degree to environmental influences'.

It is, therefore, impossible, in her view, to use 'intelligence' level, or for that matter GCE examination results, as predictors of university success. If all capable of achieving success in GCE 'O' level exams (five passes) are regarded as potential university students, then 50 per cent of each age group must be 'selected' to take them – an immense borderzone therefore exists for higher education. Until we understand better the conditions making for 'success' at the university it is impossible to estimate the numbers who should be so selected. The supply of potential students, Floud argued in essence, is a function of 'social change and social policy' – and can be altered by changes in that policy. The primary sector of education developed after 1870, the secondary sector in the first half of this century; the problem of developing the tertiary sector in succeeding decades is in principle similar. Fundamentally it is a problem of supply and demand. 'What only the few could do yesterday the many can do today.' The question of the quality of the population in any psycho-genetic sense, she concluded, 'is as irrelevant today as it was then. There is no iron law of the national intellect imposing an upper limit on the educational potential of the population.' The whole dispute about 'intelligence', she implied, is purely ideological.[38]

It is partly on the basis of this expert evidence, but also on their own statistical analyses and enquiries, that the Robbins Committee totally rejected the concept of a strictly limited and biologically determined 'pool of ability'. If there is to be such talk, they conclude, 'it must be of a pool which surpasses the widow's cruse in the Old Testament, in that when more is taken for higher education in one generation more will tend to be available in the next'. In short, they add:

> We think there is no risk that within the next twenty years the growth in the proportion of young people with qualifications and aptitudes suitable for entry to higher education will be restrained by a shortage of potential ability.[39]

The way was clear, in terms of the availability of student supply, for the massive expansion circumstances and the time seemed to demand.

As is well known, the Robbins Committee rejected what

Table 5.1
Home and Overseas Students in Full-time Higher Education:
Past Trends and Future Needs Great Britain, 1924-25 to 1985-86

	Thousands
1924-25	61
1938-39	69
1954-55	122
1955-56	128
1956-57	137
1957-58	148
1958-59	160
1959-60	170
1960-61	179
1961-62	193
1962-63	216
1963-64	238
1964-65	262
1965-66	290
1966-67	312
1967-68	328
1968-69	335
1969-70	339
1970-71	344
1971-72	356
1972-73	372
1973-74	392
1974-75	412
1975-76	433
1976-77	453
1977-78	475
1978-79	499
1979-80	528
1980-81	558
1981-82	(596)
1982-83	(627)
1983-84	(655)
1984-85	(678)
1985-86	(697)

Notes: 1. Figures for 1924-25 and 1938-39 are estimated.
2. Figures for 1954-55 to 1962-63 represent actual numbers (1962-63 data being provisional).
3. Figures for 1963-64 to 1980-81 are recommended.
4. Figures for 1981-82 to 1985-86 are estimates of places likely to be needed but are not put forward as recommendations.

Source: Higher Education (Robbins Report), Table 30, p.69.

might be called 'manpower planning' in its estimates of future expansion, largely on the grounds that changing demand for specific forms of labour was (generally) unpredictable (the demand for teachers was an exception here), and that, in any case, as in the Soviet Union, 'there would always be use for people who had been trained to the limit of their potential ability'.[40]

The committee's estimate of future numbers is, therefore, based on a complex set of factors relating to the likely demand for higher education on the part of students. After considering trends in the size of the relevant age groups (eighteen-year-olds – then rapidly increasing), the proportion of each age group likely to reach the level of attainment appropriate for entry (also increasing annually), the proportion of those so qualified likely to enter higher education, as well as likely developments in length of study and the provision of places for foreign students, the committee finally produced a table giving an estimate of the total number of students in full-time higher education covering the next seventeen years (that is, to 1980-81) with provisional estimates for five years more (1985-86). This table (5.1), reproduced on p.237 (and covering actual numbers since 1924-5), indicates that the Robbins committee planned a doubling of student numbers over a period of fourteen years (to 1977-78), and almost a tripling (697,000) by 1985-86.[41]

Expansion requirements for the next ten years, the committee reported, 'demonstrate the need for urgent action'; but the solution of these problems 'will not be symptomatic of a passing crisis to be met by temporary expedients'. On the contrary, they will rather mark 'the dawn of a new era in British higher education'.[42] The committee's main guiding principle, 'assumed as an axiom', was that 'courses in higher education should be available for all those who are qualified by ability and attainment to pursue them and who wish to do so.' On this 'general principle ... we hope there will be little dispute'.[43]

What of the structure of the system the committee proposed to cope with rapid and massive expansion? It was certainly university-oriented – fundamentally, Robbins proposed a unitary system of university institutions. By 1980-81, the committee recommend, 346,000 of the total of 558,000 places should be provided in universities. Existing universities should expand, seven new universities had already been founded, the colleges of advanced technology should be given university status, but even so there would be a shortfall of 50,000 places. The committee, therefore, recommended the foundation of a further six new universities with a total capacity of 30,000 students by 1980. Further, university status should be given to some of the present regional colleges, central institutions (in Scotland) and colleges of education, to cover the remaining 20,000 places required.[44]

But the university principle went further than this. In view of the projected demand for teachers, the committee estimated that, in 1980-81, a total of 146,000 places would be required in teacher education in Great Britain as a whole. But all these would also, according to their proposals, be brought within the orbit of the universities, administratively, financially and academically. The universities, they proposed, should develop 'schools of education' of which the colleges (now to be called colleges of education) should be an integral part. Local authorities would continue to play an important role, but the committee did not believe the colleges could develop in the ways they advocated 'unless they are accorded collectively within the university orbit a sufficient degree of autonomy'. This, they held, could only be achieved through establishing the closest links with the universities, as integral parts of the system, in the way they proposed. This proposition, widely welcomed by college staff and principals, was the subject of a strong 'note of reservation' by Harold Shearman, to which we will return later.[45]

What of technical and higher technological education – an area where the Robbins committee's proposals were later criticised, and in which, admittedly there was little expertise on the committee (with the exception of Linstead). Here a major recommendation was for the development of five (later six) SISTERS (Special Institutes for Scientific and Technological Education and Research) – a British equivalent to the famous Massachusetts Institute of Technology and the Technical High Schools at Zürich and Delft; these should be developed from existing centres – Imperial College in London, Manchester College of Science and Technology, and that at Glasgow (Royal College of Science and Technology). One should be an entirely new foundation, the fifth developed from a selected College of Advanced Technology.[46] Another major recommendation (as we have seen), in line with many of the proposals received, was for the immediate designation of the ten existing CATs as full (technological) universities. So far so good. As for the general system of further education, however, the committee are somewhat vague in their proposals. The 25 regional colleges could develop in a variety of ways, 'some may follow the colleges of advanced technology and attain university status'. The work of the 160 or more area colleges is also discussed. The major proposal, however, is that the existing national council for technological awards should be replaced by a council for national academic awards (CNAA) which should have degree giving powers, and so serve the regional and area colleges who should be encouraged to develop degree level courses (as several already had, working for London University external degrees). These proposals, the committee conclude, 'should together give a new impetus to the development of vocational higher education in Great Britain and, in particular, should remedy weaknesses in the nature and organisation of technological education and research.'[47]

The remaining main recommendations can be briefly set out. On the crucial issue of control and finance the committee rejected recommendations for a regional structure of control. They came down very firmly for an enlarged, and strengthened, university grants committee, to be called the university grants commission.[48] This should have general oversight over the 60 or so universities in Great Britain (with enlarged responsibilities in relation to training colleges) they expected to be the total by the end of the seventeen-year period planned for – these would be 'autonomous' and self-governing, but operating within the 'broad policy on higher education' that must be 'the concern of the government and of parliament'.[49] The committee also rejected the proposition that there should be a single secretary of state for education with responsibilities covering all sectors (as proposed, for instance, by the Taylor Report). There should be another specific ministry for higher education, to be known as the Ministry of Arts and Science, which would assume the existing responsibilities of the Lord President in his capacity as minister for science. His or her main responsibility would be 'for the autonomous institutions ... suitable for control on the grants committee principle'.[50] Whether there should be one or two ministers of education became a highly controversial issue following the report's publication.

Finally the committee, assessing education as an *investment* yielding positive returns, favoured the full grants system to students as originally proposed by the Anderson committee (see note 4), rejecting the concept of loans as a main means of finance. They drew attention to the minority representation of women at universities, seeing here a large reserve of unused potential ability. Finally the committee deplored (but rather politely) the hegemony of the ancient universities and drew particular attention to the very high proportion of public schoolboys who made up their (male) student body – suggesting these universities reform themselves on these and other particulars.

From Robbins to Binary

The publication of the Robbins Report, and the government statement that followed it one day later, inaugurated what Carswell calls 'the Great Plastic Period' when 'lumps of raw flesh', (as a senior civil servant put it) were 'being hurled about'.[51]

> The public mood was one in which great numbers of things which in a normal period would take years to settle, if they could be settled at all, could be decided for good or ill in almost no time. The press, the public, the political parties, were full of enthusiasm for higher education, especially university education. Money flowed in abundance'.[52]

Both Labour and Tory, reflecting this aroused public opinion, were vying with each other for leadership of the expansionist movement. Everything seemed possible.

As already made clear, the Conservative government immediately announced its total support for the main recommendations of the Robbins committee in a White Paper announcing a ten-year plan at an estimated cost of £3,500 million. Accepting the Robbins principle that courses in higher education should be available for all those qualified who wished to follow them, the government accepted the committee's calculations as to the number of places needed, in universities and in higher education as a whole, and these projections were officially adopted as government objectives for 1967-68 (328,000) and for 1973-74 (390,000) respectively. The proposal that the colleges of advanced technology (and certain Scottish institutions) should have university status was also accepted, as well as certain other recommendations concerning specific institutions.[53] The proposal to establish a council for national academic awards was also accepted, as was the proposal that an independent body on the lines of the UGC be established as the channel for the government's financial support for autonomous (university type) institutions.[54]

The publication of the Robbins Report was followed by a full-scale two day debate in the House of Lords, which took place on 11 and 12 December. On a motion by Lord Taylor, chairman of the Labour Party's committee which produced *The Years of Crisis* (the Taylor Report) a few months earlier, the motion drew attention 'to the need for immediate and long-term action'. Over twenty speakers in the debate, including Lords Todd, McNair and James, the Archbishop of Canterbury and the Bishop of London, all expressed their support for the committee's recommendations, which, said Lord Taylor, 'were in almost every respect identical with' the Labour Party's own report. He expressed surprise at the speed with which the government had accepted them. During the debate Lord Robbins himself spoke eloquently in defence of his committee's recommendations. For the government, David (now Lord) Eccles and the Earl of Dundee reiterated their support and agreement, the latter recalling that it was towards the close of the 1960 debate that the appointment of just such a committee had been announced.[55]

From now on, events began to move at an even more tempestuous rate. The 'political convulsion'[56] that followed Harold Macmillan's sudden resignation as Prime Minister on 13 October 1963 may have eased the road for the expansionists. Alec Douglas Home (formerly the Earl of Home), who succeeded him, clearly saw the need to throw his weight behind what was now becoming a broad popular movement. The general election, which took place in October 1964 resulting in a wafer-thin majority for Labour, probably did not greatly alter the rate of development except, perhaps, to accelerate things even further in the immediate aftermath. But, during the full year after Robbins reported, the Conservative government pressed ahead with a series of decisions promoting the immediate expansionist policy advocated by the Robbins committee.

The White Paper accepted in full the main thrust of the Robbins recommendations as regards expansion. This involved implementing the committee's emergency, short-term 'crisis' programme to 1967-68 – the provision of an extra 57,000 student places within four years.[57] A major building programme was undertaken immediately to equip the CATs effectively as full universities with an expanded student intake. This involved substantial extensions at most of the CATs, while three of these were to be developed as university institutions on entirely new sites (Brunel at Uxbridge, Bristol at Bath, Battersea at Guildford) – each of these massive undertakings being equivalent to the building of the new 'green field' universities such as Sussex, Lancaster and Essex. The decision was made that the CATs (and Heriot Watt) would be transferred to funding through the UGC on 1 April 1965. The target was that these institutions should comprise 19,000 full-time and sandwich students by 1967-68.[58]

Resources were also made available for the universities on a generous scale – in February 1964 substantial increases in recurrent (annual) grants were announced (of £3.5 million in 1964-65 up to an extra £9.8 million in 1966-67, the last year of the 1962-67 'quinquennium'), and in capital grants, which were increased by £15 million (in terms of value of building projects) in 1964 alone, with further substantial increases announced for future years.[59] In July, after consulting the UGC, the government announced authorisation of a single new university for Scotland (as proposed by Robbins) at Stirling. The establishment of the University of Strathclyde (from the Glasgow Royal Institution) was also announced that summer (in August), while in May the go-ahead had been given for the foundation of two new business schools (as proposed by Robbins) and, for that matter, of a new medical school at Nottingham University (in July).[60] The College of Aeronautics and the Royal College of Art were also brought within the university complex.[61] As the DES reported, seven new universities had been founded since 1958; during 1964 two of these, Essex and Lancaster, recruited their first students. The UGC was now strengthened on the lines of the Robbins recommendation by the appointment of ten new members, some with a particular knowledge of technological education, in view of the recruitment of the CATs within the university world, and by a strengthening of its secretariat.

On the issue of the six further new universities the Robbins committee had argued were essential to meet projected student growth, the White Paper had stated that both this proposal, and that concerning the promotion of other institutions as universities, would be considered later in connection with the formulation of a ten-year plan. Applications for acceptance as sites for these projected (or possible) new universities continued to pour in; the DES reported over 50 such applications, including seven from Scotland. At this stage all still seemed possible. However on the Robbins proposal to create five super-institutions (the SISTERS) the government prevaricated – asking the UGC for further advice.[62] Finally, in September, the council for national academic awards was established.[63] In the college of education world, expansion was pushed ahead – recruitment of students increased, a mass of building projects (37) were underway with the stated aim of providing 80,000 places by 1970-71.

During the year, however, two important government decisions were taken in direct opposition to the Robbins proposals – one by the Tory government and one by Labour. Early in February, 1964, only three months after publication of the report, the Prime Minister (Home) announced that, 'after taking full account of the views that had been expressed', he had concluded that the right course to follow as regards ministerial responsibility 'was to have a single minister with total responsibility over the whole education field'.[64] By this announcement, the Robbins argument that there should be a separate minister of arts and science responsible for the University Grants Commission was rejected. This solution (a single minister covering the whole field of education) had been strongly pressed by Harold Shearman, the single dissentient on the Robbins committee, but one having a broad experience of the school system. In a sense, this decision can be seen, in retrospect (as it was seen at the time), as a blow against the prestige, and the independence, of universities.

The Prime Minister announced that, from 1 April 1964, a Department of Education and Science would be established as a single department but with two distinct administrative units, one responsible for schools, the other for science and, through the UGC, for universities. There would, then, be one secretary of state assisted by two ministers of state, one responsible for each unit, but both accountable to the secretary of state. At this point in time, Sir Edward Boyle had been Minister of Education (from July 1962), while Lord Hailsham had been Minister of Science since the ministry's creation in October

1959. Hailsham had, of course, also been a major contender for the leadership of the Tory party in the hiatus of October 1963 following Macmillan's resignation.

On the creation of the new department, Boyle is said generously to have stood down. In any case the first secretary of state was to be Hailsham, now, however, known as Quintin Hogg. Boyle was appointed Minister of State for Education (with a seat in the Cabinet), and a second minister (for higher education and science) appointed, Lord Newton. During 1964, then, there were three ministers or secretaries of state responsible for education: Edward Boyle (until 1 April), Quintin Hogg (Hailsham) for the next six and a half months, and Michael Stewart after the Labour victory of October.

It was the Labour government that took the second decision in this year involving rejection of a major Robbins recommendation – that concerning the transfer of administrative control of colleges of education to universities within the proposed 'schools of education'. Once again the government was to prefer the arguments in Harold Shearman's 'Note of Reservation' to those of the main body of the committee. Early in December 1964 Michael Stewart announced that, while the government agreed that the relationship between universities and colleges should be extended in the academic sphere through the development of 'schools of education', the colleges should not be handed over administratively and financially to the universities – at least at the present time, when the colleges were engaged 'in a very large and rapid expansion' and when the problems of teacher supply 'were especially difficult'.[65] In a sense it could be argued that the local authority lobby, then powerful (the 'partnership' still existed), had won in a power battle with the universities.[66] The decision probably did not affect the build-up of teacher supply; but it did strongly dent the Robbins committee's vision of a unitary system of higher education. On this issue, Lord Robbins permitted himself a dignified protest.

> It must be a matter of profound regret that a government which claims to be progressive, aided and abetted by the University Grants Committee which has certainly not yet risen to the level of the new opportunities with which it is confronted, should have chosen this poor-spirited solution to this very important educational problem.[67]

In spite of these developments, which to some seemed ominous, generally at the end of 1964, or rather more than one year after the publication of Robbins's epoch-making report, the wind seemed set fair for a planned, continuous and massive expansion across the whole field of higher education. Writing a full generation later (in 1987), Sir Albert Sloman, Vice Chancellor of the new university at Essex which, recruiting its first students in 1964 was originally planned to allow expansion up to 10,000 students, wrote that, 'It is extraordinary, quite extraordinary, but when you look back nobody in their senses could do other than think that it was a good thing to expand. No government,' he goes on, 'would have done other than be generous in its funding of universities. The towns and counties were falling over each other to have a university. It is quite extraordinary,' he added, 'that within a decade, all that turned sour.'[68]

Indeed, for a brief halcyon period, all things seemed possible. Sloman's initial vision of Essex's full development was as a new type of university, untramelled by traditional structures and procedures, developing as an internationally renowned centre of excellence in particular for high level research and study in the social sciences. Several of the new universities initially were determined to break down the system of specialised and isolated departments through the establishment of cross-disciplinary schools as at Sussex, where this structure was deliberately developed as central to new forms of internal organisation. New institutions brought new enthusiasms; new thinking, new procedures, a new commitment. Older universities, through expansion, were also able to strike out in new directions. The ossification of the past seemed broken. Nor was it only the universities which took heart from the new conditions – the colleges of education, now with the new three year course and, following Robbins, the new four-year BEd, while certainly bringing problems, were themselves striking out in new directions, requiring new thinking, new procedures, while the technical college world also benefited, even if, in their case, the main thrust of development seemed to many to pass them by. This, then was the climax of the whole movement for expansion and development across the board in the field of higher education – a movement which had, by now, gradually gathered pace from the late 1950s. At this specific point in time it seemed that the unitary system of higher education, consisting of a complex of institutions of similar status, was now being brought into being, and even as if nothing could stop it. But to the discerning, the key decisions taken in 1964, already referred to, indicated some of the strains to which such a policy began now to give rise. These marked 'the rift in the lute', as John Carswell entitles his chapter on underlying divisions, only now becoming apparent.

2 Binary and Beyond

The Inception of Binary

It was on 27 April 1965 that a sledgehammer blow was aimed at the Robbins conception of a unitary system of higher education. This took the form of a powerful, even aggressive and highly prescriptive speech by Anthony Crosland, who had at that time been Secretary of State for Education and Science for three months. Delivered at Woolwich Polytechnic to the ATTI (Association of Teachers in Technical Institutions) Crosland here announced the pure doctrine of what has been known ever since as the binary system, and the full support of the government for such a pattern.

The government, he said, accepted the Robbins view that, in place of the 'largely unco-ordinated activities and initiatives of the past' there must be 'a system' of higher education. This system, he went on (making no further reference to Robbins), 'must be based on the twin traditions which have created our present institutions.' These are broadly of two kinds.

> On the one hand we have what has come to be called the autonomous sector, represented by the universities, in whose ranks, of course, I now include the colleges of advanced technology. On the other hand we have the public sector, represented by the leading technical colleges and the colleges of education.

The government, Crosland announced, accepted 'this dual system' as being fundamentally the right one. Each would make 'its own distinctive contribution'. The alternative of a unitary system, he claimed, involved hierarchic organisation on the 'ladder' principle 'with the universities at the top and the other institutions down below'. Such a system, Crosland argued, 'would be characterised by a continuous rat race to reach the first or university division and a certain inevitable failure to achieve the diversity in higher education which contemporary society needs.'

Four basic reasons were given for this solution. First, vocational, professional and industrially-based courses at various levels required 'a separate sector' ('with a separate tradition and outlook') for their development. Second, a university monopoly of degree-giving, combined with selective transference of institutions into the university system, would mean that the public sector 'becomes a permanent poor relation perpetually deprived of its brightest ornaments' and with 'a permanently and openly inferior status'. This would be bad for morale and standards. Third, a substantial part of the system of higher education 'should be under social control, and directly responsive to social needs'; and finally, in a highly competitive world relying more and more on professional and technical expertise, we needed to develop high level scientific-technological institutions on a par with those in other countries. 'Let us now move away', said Crosland, now relying on an egalitarian rhetoric, 'from our snobbish, caste-ridden hierarchical obsession with university status'.

The tone of Crosland's speech was highly and presumably purposely provocative. The universities, presented as 'pursuing learning for its own sake' were contrasted with a 'relevant', vibrant 'public sector' deserving of public support. In the course of the speech, Crosland announced the government's decision that there should be no new universities or accessions to university status 'for about ten years' (in fact, with the exception of the Open University, provided for in Crosland's speech, and the private university of Buckingham, there have been none since). In practice, as Carswell has noted, this policy declaration both put an effective barrier against technical college aspirations to autonomy but also did a great deal more than this 'by fortifying and adorning the barrier with institutional doctrines which constituted a kind of Robbins in reverse.' A 'low' rhetoric now confronted the 'high' rhetoric of the report, and 'the government adopted them both'. A shadow was cast on the universities; sterotypes emphasised. The Robbins Report's vision that the universities should constitute the national system of higher education 'was muffled and impaired by the Woolwich speech', if not destroyed.[69]

The announcement of the binary policy in these terms led to a crescendo of criticism – not only from the universities and university representatives, but also from many who saw the

Robbins concept of a unitary system as the basis for a broad based democratic advance. The vice chancellors' committee later put on record that there had been 'no consultation whatever with the universities' before the 'original and rigid theory of the binary system was promulgated by the government'.[70] Many within the Labour Party and on the left generally were shocked by what they saw as the imposition of a brutal, divisive policy in higher education – one which certainly was hardly foreshadowed by the Taylor Report of which Crosland had been a signatory. As we shall see, Lord Robbins himself was moved to condemn the new policy as a whole in a House of Lords debate in December.

Crosland later, while accepting responsibility, claimed that he was pushed into making his Woolwich speech prematurely by his 'officials'. Talking to Maurice Kogan about this episode some five years later he said that when he began his work as secretary of state, 'I made an appalling blunder,' from which he learnt a lesson he would never forget. Making the Woolwich speech broke a rule he had made (and announced) to make no pronouncements on major policy for his first six months. He should not, he said, have accepted the advice to do it, and his officials should not have advised him to make it. Every change he made in the draft made the speech worse.

'It came out in a manner calculated to infuriate almost everybody you can think of ... and did considerable harm to the policy.' While Crosland was 'utterly convinced that the policy was right', the speech 'put people's backs up quite unnecessarily'. 'Were you bounced by officials?' asked Kogan. 'They wanted to get the policy on record as soon as possible,' answered Crosland.[71]

The *éminence grise* who apparently successfully pressurised Crosland 'to get the policy on record' (and the speech was immediately issued as an 'administrative memorandum', giving it (some) statutory force, at least as an expression of government policy) was Toby Weaver. As deputy secretary at the DES responsible for (public sector) higher education since 1962, there is no doubt that he strongly pressed the binary policy, which, of course, strengthened the position of the DES in the control of higher education *vis-à-vis* the universities[72] – as also the creation later of the polytechnics within the public sector to parallel the universities. In Weaver's own analysis, however, things are presented as having developed pragmatically.

Policies do not happen through setting objectives and pursuing them in a linear direction (Robbins). 'The policy business is a very human business and much more like a game.' Binary had 'come about because the government had been faced with a "policy vacuum" as a result of the decision not to take the colleges of education out of the local authorities and DES.' Both Conservative and Labour governments, who had adopted this policy, had, therefore, dismantled the Robbins idea; Crosland had been the first 'to look over the fence' and see 'the much undervalued system of post-eighteen education started by public authorities ... and waiting to be developed.' A second factor 'was a decision on resources' and the need to concentrate these for higher level courses. So 'the binary system was born.'[73]

Binary clearly appealed to the DES – anxious to enhance its control over the developing system of higher education; hence the pressure on Crosland and insistence on getting the policy 'on the record' at a crucial moment. It appealed to the ATTI, which provided an ideological justification for its development in terms of a practicist instrumentalism, together with a petit-bourgeois radicalism which found expression also in Crosland's speech. It was, in fact, to the annual conference of the ATTI that Crosland delivered the Woolwich speech. It appealed to the local authorities, sensitive (since the removal of the CATs) to the loss of further colleges to the university system.[74] It appealed also to the Conservative Party and was in fact a policy of consensus. Edward Boyle went out of his way publicly to support the binary policy shortly after its announcement in a commons debate.[75] Though later when a university vice chancellor, he seemed less certain.[76] It further had the support of what Weaver called Crosland's 'associates' – the group of like-minded 'egalitarians', with whom he discussed policy informally, particularly Tyrrell Burgess, whose writings on this issue Crosland specifically recommends in his talks with Kogan.[77] Within this complex field a whole orchestra of support for the DES line was brought together. So the binary system was created and is still with us. It was also, of course, a cheaper (more 'cost-effective') way of achieving growth in higher education than expanding universities as proposed by Robbins. Government (DES) controls were also greatly stronger in the field of further education than in those of both universities and schools (at that time).

A Plan for Polytechnics

In the House of Lords (and elsewhere) Lord Robbins again made his own dignified, and weighty protest.[78] The government's decision about colleges of education he regarded as 'profoundly unfortunate' – here he developed his views, and those presented in his report, at considerable length, holding, as he did, that this was a reform of great significance. But the government's decision, he continued, is now clearly part of 'a much wider policy', which is 'deliberately intended to take us in a direction completely different from – indeed completely opposed to – the conceptions underlying [his] report'. The secretary of state has 'proclaimed an internal separation between the autonomous universities and the rest of the system' – all this 'is diametrically opposed to the conceptions which inspired our recommendations'. His committee had recognised the need for 'diversity both of academic and administrative forms', but 'we conceived of the system as unitary' in the sense that it was 'flexible and evolutionary' and that 'it contained no unnecessary barriers or limitations on growth and transformation'. The philosophy of the binary system, Robbins claimed, 'negates all this'. It creates barriers, prevents new experiments, new organisational forms and especially union between related institutions. All such suggestions are ruled out. Extending his critique to the arguments presented in favour of binary (e.g. social control), Robbins finished by pointing to the 'supreme paradox' that a government 'pledged to abolish artificial hierarchy and invidious distinctions in the schools' should at the same time be 'actively engaged in preventing the elimination of artificial hierarchies and invidious distinction in higher education'. The secretary of state should take note of 'the atmosphere of frustrated plans and disappointed aspirations' which has followed his recent decision, and think again 'long and earnestly' before continuing a course 'which can bring no pleasure of benefit to any but a few snobs at the centre and bullies at the periphery'. This was a fine and impressive performance which hardly got the considered response it merited from government representatives.[79]

Approximately a year later, Crosland took the opportunity of a visit to the new University of Lancaster to calm the simmering criticism of binary in a speech overtly appreciative of universities and couched in less aggressive and more rational terms. The policy, however (now taking new institutionalised form) was reiterated, though softened. He hoped he had said enough to make it clear, said Crosland towards the close of his speech, that he did not want any rigid line between the sectors – quite the contrary. 'I think these fears partly arose because "binary" is possibly not the best word to describe the system of higher education that we have in this country, and you will notice that I have tried to avoid it.' Our system, he said, is better described as 'strikingly varied, plural and diverse'. This 'is thoroughly healthy, and we should seek to preserve it'.[80] Within this exercise of obfuscation, however, very active steps were underway to strengthen and expand the 'public sector' vis-a-vis the universities.

The next thing 'after enunciating binary' writes Susan Crosland, in her biography, 'was to determine where to move from there'. With the help of Weaver and others Crosland now 'invented' the polytechnics as a makeweight to the universities – 'which took courage, was revolutionary, and was right', as Weaver apparently said.[81] However that may be, the White Paper, *A Plan for Polytechnics and Other Colleges*, (Cmnd 3006) was published in May 1966 – that is, just over a year after the Woolwich speech. This was presented as a logical step in the development of the pattern of further education since Eccles' original white paper of 1956 had introduced the four-tier system described earlier (in Chapter 4). Attention was drawn in the introduction to the fact that the CATS had been transferred (after Robbins reported) to the university sector, and to the establishment of the CNAA to provide degrees for students in non-university institutions. The government was engaged in 'an even greater expansion of higher education' than forecast in Robbins, and had announced 'their intention of developing a distinctive sector of higher education within the further education system to complement the universities and colleges of education'. This was to be achieved 'by concentrating full-time courses of higher education ... in a limited number of strong centres' – the proposed new polytechnics. The aim of concentration was clearly stated and reiterated – full-time advanced and degree students were too widely dispersed among 25 regional and more than 30 area and about 100 other colleges. What was needed was 'to concentrate expensive resources in few centres'. These would comprise both full-time and part-time students – and students at all levels: 'As comprehensive academic communities they will be expected to cater for students *at all levels* of higher education.'

This document is short and largely administrative – there is no serious discussion about the specific educational features of the proposed polytechnics, though stress is placed on the need to cater for part-time students, those requiring courses below degree standard, as well as full-time degree students – hence Crosland's description of them as 'comprehensive' colleges. In effect, however, and as the White Paper makes clear, this was a further step in the process of rationalisation – 'The object will be to reduce substantially the number of colleges engaged in full-time higher education,' though non-polytechnic colleges could continue to offer such courses for approval. In essence, by a process of merging individual, and hitherto separate colleges, the object was to create large institutions, with a minimum of 2,000 full-time students (and at least another 2,000 part-time); these would provide a sound base for further development later. An appendix listed preliminary proposals for the establishment of polytechnics throughout England and Wales. A year later (April 1967) Crosland confirmed the White Paper's provisional list of 28 polytechnics, with the possibility of two more, at Stoke and Preston. Detailed schemes of development were now asked for, while guidance was sent 'on the points on which I will wish to be satisfied before actually designating a polytechnic'.[82] This dealt in some detail with the government and academic organisation of polytechnics, and generally gave guidance for the preparation of schemes. Here we see in practice one of the main advantages of binary for the DES. 'We could lay down that we would follow a binary policy,' Crosland told Maurice Kogan during their discussions, 'choose the polys and say broadly what sort of courses they should follow.'[83] Here, DES control seemed absolute, though in practice things hardly worked out that way.

The policy meant rejection of proposals for mergers across the binary line, at least for the time being. The new University of Warwick and Lanchester College of Technology (located in Coventry) had made such a proposal in March 1965, to be firmly rejected by Crosland (DES). This 'would run counter to government policy' and 'might prejudice the lower level and part-time work of the Lanchester College'. That had certainly not been the original intention, but this and like innovations (referred to by Robbins in his speech) were not, at this stage, to be given the go-ahead.[84] In any case, Lanchester College was already clearly marked down, in the minds of DES officials, as a future polytechnic, and was so included on the White Paper's provisional list. This merger proposal was a post-Robbins phenomenon, and indicates, perhaps, the kind of direction a Robbins type system would have taken, had the binary decision not been taken.[85]

The polytechnic proposal, of course, went ahead – early in 1969 Edward Short, now secretary of state, formally designated the first three of these as full blown polytechnics – at Hatfield, Sheffield and Sunderland.[86] These became 'operational' in January 1969. All 30 had been designated by 1973.

3   Developments in Higher Education, 1965-70

To 1967-68

The imposition of the binary policy, while putting a stop to the establishment of any new universities, did not halt the rate of expansion in student numbers across the whole field of higher education. Its structural effects, however, proved to be long term. The universities – or their representatives – objected, protesting at the total lack of consultation that preceded Crosland's Woolwich speech, and pointing to the dangers inherent in creating two parallel systems with the likelihood of much overlapping, and hence inefficiency and confusion.[87] Lord Robbins continued his campaign for a unitary system[88] – perhaps all was not lost; the vice chancellors, however, clearly felt that the binary system was here to stay – whatever second thoughts had 'blurred the outline of the arguments' used by Crosland at Woolwich, they reported, 'the underlying intention' of the binary system 'has remained the touchstone of thinking in the department of education and science'. Here binary was recognised as a civil service policy, a position since publicly confirmed by the leading official involved – Toby Weaver.[89]

Colleges of education. It was within this new (or some would say traditional) structure that expansion continued at a varying, but generally explosive rate across the three sectors in the mid-late 1960s. In April 1965 Crosland launched his fourteen-point emergency programme to solve the intractable problem of teacher shortage. This was a dramatic and ambitious plan – according to John Vaizey he set out to expand the teacher training system 'further and faster than his officials wished'.[90] A major aim was the reduction of class sizes ('I mean the actual teaching groups'), to the so-called (because not implemented) 'statutory limit' of 30 in secondary schools and 40 in primary schools. Some 2,000,000 children, Crosland stated, were in over-size classes according to these criteria. But this reform was to be carried through when an extra 1,000,000 children would come into the schools 'over the next five years' (70 per cent of them in primary schools), and yet another 1,000,000 between 1970 and 1975; an increase of 200,000 a year for the next ten years. Three-quarters of this increase was due to the rising birth rate, the rest to the decision (already taken but to be abrogated) to raise the leaving age to sixteen in 1970. This, said Crosland, 'is a daunting prospect'. The problems of teacher supply were compounded by the enormously high wastage rate, particularly among women teachers (and exacerbated 'by the increasing tendency for earlier marriage'). Two teachers were 'wasted' for every three recruited. What was needed was roughly to double the number of teacher-training places from 60,000 (in 1965) to 110,000 (in England and Wales) by 1973. It was to move rapidly towards this target that Crosland outlined his fourteen points, involving full utilisation of all accommodation, the establishment of annexes, the establishment of several new day colleges, the possibility of introducing 'box and cox' schemes, and other methods of increasing output. This was a crash programme, demanding a lot from the existing colleges, but holding out a positive perspective of improved conditions for the mass of teachers through a *reduction* in class sizes at a time of population expansion.[91]

'If there were a prize to be awarded for expansion,' wrote Claus Moser and others in 1969, 'it would have to go to the colleges of education.'[92] Unlike the further education colleges (whose expansion was proportionately greater, but numerically smaller) they could not expand by using space previously occupied by non-advanced students; nor were many new colleges founded. The earlier expansion (the so-called '80,000 place programme', announced in 1962) aimed at reaching this figure by 1970-71. The Robbins committee had accepted this target (for 1969), but recommended 'a further steep rise' to 110,000 places by 1973-74.[93]

In fact the Robbins target had already been greatly exceeded by 1967-69 – by about 26 per cent. This was the direct outcome of the Crosland initiative, itself derived from a report of the National Advisory Council on the Training and Supply of Teachers which brought out very clearly the need for decisive action.[94] By this time (1967-68), then, the colleges of education (in England and Wales) had in fact expanded to a total of 94,800 students as compared with the Robbins target estimate of 75,200.[95] This was achieved without any reduction in standards of entrants.

Further education. If the growth in the number of students preparing as teachers had, by 1967-68, far exceeded the original Robbins targets, the same was true – indeed the actual expansion was even greater – of full-time advanced students within the whole, confusing field of further education (technical colleges, art colleges, the early polytechnics, etc.) These colleges, of course, catered for an enormous variety of post-school education, both part and full-time, at all levels; but here we are concerned only with what has been called 'the academic tip of this iceberg' – those taking so-called 'advanced' courses above GCE A level or the Ordinary National Certificate (ONC). These included both full-time and part-time students in a ratio, then, of about one to three. When the Robbins Committee reported (1963) there were 36,000 full-time advanced students within this system (nearly a threefold increase, incidentally – from 13,000 – since 1957-58). In 1967-68 this total, which Robbins predicted would, at this point, rise only to 47,000, had in practice reached the massive total of 71,000 – almost doubling in four years, though these students were then spread over a large number of institutions. This expansion was entirely unexpected. It reflected the ongoing exponential demand for higher education, as well as the circumstance that, although universities were rapidly expanding, their *overall* share of students within higher education as a whole was, at this stage, marginally declining. In fact, the field of further education (including polytechnics, but these had hardly started) was now acting as a safety valve for higher education, 'mopping up the demand not satisfied by other sectors'.[96]

In a purely logistical sense, expansion was easier, and probably cheaper, in these colleges than in universities and colleges of education. Facilities already existing could be transferred to meet the needs of full-time advanced students, whereas elsewhere new facilities had to be provided. Equally important, as has been pointed out, was the method of financing this expansion, by which all such expenditure by specific local authorities was 'pooled', and the liability for it apportioned between authorities as a whole according to a specific formula. An authority expanding rapidly by this means would, therefore, after the final reckoning, 'bear only a tiny part of the extra cost, most of which will be borne by other authorities which had no share in the original decision'.[97] However this may be, and in spite of the existence of certain controls, 'broadly speaking' (it was written at the time) 'there is little to discourage individual local authorities from expanding further education to the limits of students' demands for places.'[98] To all intents and purposes, then, there existed at that time an open system in the provision of places.

As in other areas, there were important innovations here also, in terms of changes in the procedures and content of education – in particular, the development of 'sandwich' courses involving alternation between periods in industry and college on the part of the student in the case of vocationally oriented courses. The newly instituted Council for National Academic Awards (CNAA), which now offered degrees to these colleges and polytechnics, encouraged the new thinking involved. A great deal of energy was devoted to the design of such courses, which now took the place of the traditional degree level work leading to the London University external degrees.

So, only four years after Robbins, advanced work in the colleges was burgeoning – far beyond what had been either planned or expected. It was this development, of course, which lay behind Crosland's polytechnic decision already discussed. This unexpected expansion provided the fuel enabling DES officials to press the binary claim – even if, as we have seen, they could hardly argue that they (the DES) had exercised any foresight themselves in the planning of these developments (unless benevolent *laissez-faire* is acceptable as a means of policy formation).

The universities. The largest share of the expansion, in the five years following Robbins, took place, as planned, in the universities, although these accounted for less than half of the total expansion in higher and advanced further education. Nevertheless, the number of full-time students in universities rose from 140,000 in 1963-64 to 200,000 five years later, an increase of 60,000. Here the expansion that actually took place closely followed the Robbins proposals (to 197,000 in 1967-68). Indeed, of the three sectors, this was the only one which was not largely exceeded four years later.

The increase in overall demand, which greatly exceeded the Robbins projections during these years, was immediately due to the unexpectedly large increase in the number qualifying for higher education by acquisition of two A levels. This began to mount at an accelerating rate precisely from 1963, and this could hardly have been foreseen by the committee which, in any case, did not wish to alienate support by making assumptions which might have been criticised as over-optimistic. In the outcome, the committee under-estimated this increase (in 1967) by as much as 26 per cent (a total of 16,000). This, of course, resulted in increased pressure on all institutions of higher education, but especially universities. It also meant that, in spite of overall continuous expansion, the percentage of qualified school leavers obtaining a place at university had, by 1967, actually declined by as much as 10 per cent since 1961.[99]

Immediately after the Robbins Report was published, the UGC wrote to all universities asking 'what they could do to help achieve the new target, and how much it would cost them'. What was needed was the 40 per cent increase just mentioned. In spite of the anti-expansionist views earlier expressed by the Vice Chancellors Committee and AUT, when addressed individually the universities offered expansion to a total of 217,000 by 1967-68 – that is, 20,000 *more* places than the figure proposed by Robbins and accepted by the government. This 'magnificent response' apparently 'consider-ably surprised those who hold a general belief that universities are impervious to social need'. If other sectors expanded faster, this, as has been pointed out, was 'by the wish of the government and not of the universities'.[100]

Where did the bulk of the expansion that was finally accepted for 1967-68 actually take place? Although it may seem surprising, not in the new universities, nor in the CATs (which acquired university status finally in 1966-67). Of the total of extra students admitted between 1962-63 and 1967-68 (69,000), 25,000 were accommodated within the older English civic universities (such as Manchester, Leeds, etc.). The new universities now (1967-68) accounted for 12,000: the former CATs for 10,000, London for 6,000, Wales for 3,500 and Oxford and Cambridge together only for 2,500. Scotland's student numbers increased by 10,000.

The Robbins Committee had based their proposals on the assumption that the universities should cater for 60 per cent of all students in advanced higher education but it is here, as we have seen, that things went awry. The quicker rate of actual expansion in colleges of education and within further education meant a steady decline in the proportion at universities from 59 per cent (the actual figure in 1963-64) to 53 per cent four years later – in 1967-68. By this latter date, then, nearly half of all students in higher education were outside the universities proper – those in colleges of education had, of course, been denied this (university) perspective by the decision of 1964. Since Crosland's Woolwich speech (1965), and subsequent action, the binary system had been imposed. While this drew a sharp line between the so called 'private' (a misnomer in fact) and the 'public' sectors, by 1967-68 it was too early to evaluate its implications in terms of growth, and relationships.[101]

Two further points may be made. The first indicates the difficulties of planning. Robbins had proposed that two-thirds of the extra places provided in universities should be in science and technology. In fact only 37 per cent of these, by 1966-67, were provided in science (though if the CATs are included, 43 per cent). The extra demand centred disproportionately on the areas of arts and the social sciences, so that overall proportions finally achieved by 1967-68 differed considerably from those predicted (and planned for). This so-called 'swing from science' was investigated by the Dainton Committee which proposed an active policy to counter this movement in the schools, as also, later in the Swann Report (1968) which recommended a broadening of university degrees as multi-disciplinary.[102] In the meantime the universities necessarily adapted themselves to meet the main thrust of the new demands.

The second issue relates to gender. The 1960s saw a gradual

Table 5.2
Students in Full-time Higher Education, Great Britain, 1957-58 to 1967-68

Number of students (thousands)

	Universities (including former CATs)		Colleges of education		Further education		All full-time higher education		Percentage of students in universities	
	Actual	Robbins	Actual	Robbins	Actual	Robbins	Actual	Robbins	Actual	Robbins
1957-58	103	–	33	–	13	–	148	–	69	–
1962-63	131	–	55	–	31	–	217	–	60	–
1963-64	140	142	62	59	36	36	238	238	59	60
1964-65	154	156	71	66	43	39	267	262	57	60
1965-66	169	173	82	74	51	42	302	290	56	60
1966-67	184	187	95	80	59	45	339	312	54	60
1967-68	200	197	106	84	71	47	376	328	53	60
Percentage growth 1962-63 to 1967-68	53	50	93	54	129	51	74	51	–	–

increase in the proportion of women students in universities – from just over 24 per cent in 1958-59 to nearly 28 per cent ten years later. In fact at this stage a much smaller proportion of young women with A levels went to university than was the case with young men – 44 per cent compared with 67 per cent.[103] As in the case of social class (as we will see shortly) gender differentials have proved hard to eradicate, though the trend towards an increase in the proportion of young women within higher education has been sustained.

Table 5.2 (from Layard, King and Mosers' very useful Penguin education special, *The Impact of Robbins*, effectively summarises developments across the board relating to the expansion of the number of students in full-time higher education in Great Britain as a whole over the four years 1963-64 to 1967-68. The table is of particular value in that, in each of the three sectors, it compares what actually happened (in terms of numbers) with the Robbins projections.

The table makes clear that, only four years after the report was published, the actual number of students had increased far beyond the Robbins target (to 376,000 rather than 328,000, an overshoot by nearly 50,000). Colleges of education accounted for 22,000 of these and those of further education for as many as 24,000. Only the universities were more or less on target, but, as we have seen, this was due to specific government policy, which firmly held down their rate of expansion to the Robbins targets. The consistent annual reduction in the proportion of places held by university students, already mentioned, is reflected in the right-hand column. The last line in the table also clearly indicates the extraordinary disparities in the rate of growth of the three sectors, even if the Robbins committee had predicted, and proposed, fairly even growth across all three. These five years (1963-67) were, in fact, the period of most tempestuous growth in higher education in the country's history.

The End of the 1960s – to 1970-71
But in fact growth was to continue at an unexpectedly high rate through the closing years of the decade – and later into the early 1970s, as we shall see in the next chapter. In 1969-70 expenditure on education, at roughly £2,300 million, exceeded defence expenditure for the first time in the history of the country, now reaching nearly 5 per cent of GDP (see Appendix

Table 5.3
Students in Full-time Higher Education, Great Britain, 1962-63 to 1970-71

Number of students (thousands)

	Universities (including former CATs)		Colleges of education		Further education		All full-time higher education		Percentage of students in universities	
	Actual	Robbins	Actual	Robbins	Actual	Robbins	Actual	Robbins	Actual	Robbins
1962-63	131	–	55	–	31	–	217	–	60	–
1967-68	200	197	106	84	71	47	376	328	53	60
1970-71	228	200	119	96	96	48	443	344	52	60
Percentage of growth 1962-63 to 1970-71	74	53	116	75	210	55	104	59		

Source: Figures for 1962-63 and 1967-68 from Layard, King and Moser, *The Impact of Robbins*, as in Table 5.2, p.260; those for 1970-71 ('actual') from W.A.C. Stewart, *Higher Education in Postwar Britain*, Tables 16.1 and 16.4 (for England and Wales) and *Scottish Education Statistics*, 1971 and 1973.

Tables 15 and 16, pp. 599-601). Expenditure on higher education, at nearly £500 million in 1970, of course contributed to this growth. As the decade drew to a close there was no indication of a slow-down in the rate of advance nor in the strength of the insistent demand. Even the warning of a now declining birthrate (which had clear implications in terms of teacher supply) was, surprisingly, only partially recognised at a very late stage.

In the previous section actual developments to 1967-68 were compared to the Robbins projections, and, to clarify the situation at the end of the decade a similar procedure will be adopted, starting, this time with the universities. Because of a substantial decline in the size of the eighteen-year-old age cohorts (from 963,000 in 1965 to 724,000 in 1970), Robbins had envisaged that there would be a 'plateau', or levelling off, in demand over these years, proposing an expansion of only 7,000. In 1970-71, therefore, Robbins had proposed provision of 200,000 places in Great Britain as a whole – only slightly above the 1967-68 figure, and, in fact, the total actually reached in that year. But universities continued to expand – by nearly 6, 4 and again by 4 per cent in each of the three years to 1970-71. As indicated in Table 5.3, therefore, the total number of full-time students in universities now reached 228,000 – more than 10 per cent more than predicted.

Moving now to the colleges of education we find, according to Stewart, that the DES actually 'had no reliable figures' as to numbers 'quite simply because the activity in teacher education in the late 1960s was prodigious with emergency crowding in many places to reach 130,000 by 1972-73'. This seems an extraordinary admission. A census completed in 1968 by the DES found that there were already between 115,000 and 116,000 in the colleges 'in constant shift and movement and in some places only just in administrative control' (!!) At this stage the planned total had been 110,000 (itself well above the Robbins projection for that year). The birth rate had, in fact, started to decline in 1965, and, while a single blip would not have been important, consistent decline year by year thereafter (as actually happened, see Appendix Table 1, p.575) might surely have made some impact on DES planners. The DES, however, was still, in 1970, proposing a teacher training population of about 130,000 by the middle 1970s (the figure proposed for England and Wales by Robbins). Disaster was to fall on these colleges later, as we shall see, masterminded by the DES officials in charge of this branch. If this is a tale of culpable confusion in high places, it meant, of course, that the build-up of the colleges continued throughout the late 1960s. Assuming the DES (and Scottish Education Department) published statistics are correct, the total number of students here had, by 1970-71, reached 119,000, compared with the 96,000 by this date predicted by Robbins. Here again actual developments overshot the Robbins figures by, in this case, nearly 20 per cent.[104]

Finally, in terms of this analysis of growth in full-time higher education, these is also the whole field of 'further education' where, as we saw earlier, growth was the most rapid of all the three sectors in the mid-1960s, if from a smaller base. Full-time advanced students were now (1970-71) beginning to be concentrated in the new polytechnics, but there were many elsewhere. In fact, overall, growth continued in this sector with extraordinary rapidity. The 71,000 such students of 1967-68 reached 96,000 three years later (an increase of over 8,000 a year). As compared with the Robbins projections, which again predicted level pegging during these years due to the decline in the size of the age cohort, growth here far overshot the target, reaching over 200 per cent compared with the 54 per cent proposed. Perhaps this specific development is the most remarkable of all.

If we summarise the situation, as before, we find that the actual total in full-time higher education in 1970-71 reached 443,000, compared to the Robbins projections of 344,000. The percentage growth from 1962-63 now reached 104.1 The Robbins prediction, at 58.5, was by now left far behind.

But if we are considering higher education as a whole in the 1960s, this was not all. There is the parallel growth in part-time students taking advanced courses equivalent to the full-time students to consider. These courses were available in technical colleges, art colleges and later also in polytechnics. The statistics (relating to England and Wales alone) show growth here also, though not as rapid as for full-time students (a relative shift towards the latter took place during the decade). There was, however, significant growth here also – from a total of 77,490 in 1960-61 to 109,470 in 1970-71, an increase of approximately 32,000 (or 41 per cent). If Scotland is included the 1970-71 figure rises to 120,630.[105]

Finally, there is the Open University which, if it recruited its first students in 1971 (19,581 of them, selected from over 40,000 applicants) must surely be assessed as a 1960s initiative. First announced 'as a firm commitment of the incoming Labour government' in September 1963, planning got seriously under way with the appointment of Jennie Lee as Minister for the Arts with a specific responsibility here early in 1967.[106] A planning committee was then appointed (under Sir Peter Venables) which reported in January 1969. On 30 May that year a royal charter was granted, in the nick of time as things turned out. Senior staff were appointed from early 1969; new type courses involving extremely innovative pedagogic means were designed, and in October 1971 the university got under way. The aim was to provide university education to normal degree standards for those who had 'missed out', and were prepared to undertake serious part-time study at home under the close guidance provided. Equivalent, in size, to perhaps seven new universities (though the direct comparison cannot be made), the Open University was now launched on its astonishingly successful career, soon acquiring an international reputation of the first order.[107]

Whatever the criticisms, problems, even disorders that arose, it can hardly be denied that advances in higher education in the 1960s were of major significance for the future of this country.

Notes and References

1. *Times Literary Supplement*, 15 February 1963.

2. W.F. Dennison, *Education in Jeopardy, Problems and Possibilities of Contraction*, Oxford 1981, p.9. See Appendix Table 15, p.599.

3. E.G.Edwards, *Higher Education for Everyone*, London, 1982, pp.51-2. Edwards had recently retired as Vice Chancellor of Bradford University when this book was published. It contains a detailed historical analysis of long term trends in higher education, together with a critique of contemporary tendencies.

4. This solution had been strongly pressed, for instance, by the Labour Party which had announced its intention of appointing such a Commission if and when returned to power (in *Learning to Live*, 1958, an educational policy statement). See also Graeme C. Moodie, *The Universities: a Royal Commission?* Fabian Research Series 209, September 1959, and Lord Simon of Wythenshawe, 'A Royal Commission on the Universities?', *Universities Quarterly*, Vol. XIII, No. 1, November 1958. This proposal was discussed in Cabinet in 1958, and rejected in favour of an enquiry into student awards. This, the Anderson Committee, appointed in 1958, reported in 1960 (*Grants to Students*, Cmnd 1051), proposing a uniform national system of entitlement conditional on the achievement of two A levels (GCE) and acceptance by a university.

5. John Carswell, *Government and the Universities in Britain*, Cambridge 1985, p.27.

6. The Treasury Minute of Appointment defines the Committee's function as 'to review the pattern of full-time higher education in Great Britain and in the light of national needs and resources to advise Her Majesty's Government on what principles its long-term development should be based. In particular, to advise, in the light of these principles, whether there should be any changes to that pattern, whether any new types of institution are desirable and whether any modifications should be made in the present arrangements for planning and coordinating the development of the various types of institutions.'

7. Carswell, op.cit., p.19.

8. Ibid., pp.17-8. The seven new universities approved by the close of 1960 were those at Brighton (Sussex), York, Lancaster, Warwick (Coventry), Essex (Colchester), Kent (Canterbury) and East Anglia (Norwich). Developments in this period are reported in *Interim Report of the University Grants Committee for the Years 1957-1961*, Cmnd 1961, April 1962.

9. Over 400 documents of written evidence were received. These are available at the Public Record Office and elsewhere (e.g. London School of Economics Library). The Committee published only the records of the oral evidence they received and the written evidence on which this was based, together with a small number of other memoranda they received. Several of the major documents were, however, published by the organisations producing them.

10. NUT Memorandum, *Higher Education, Evidence – Part One*, Vol. B, pp.710ff.

11. TUC Memorandum, Ibid., Vol. E, pp.1438ff.

12. *The Development of Higher Education in Britain*, evidence presented to the Robbins Committee by the Communist Party, July 1961.

13. *The Structure of Higher Education*, by 'A Fabian Group', Fabian Tract 334, October 1961; *Memorandum to the Committee on Higher Education*, National Union of Students, June 1961.

14. AEC Memorandum, *Higher Education, Evidence – Part One*, Vol. C. pp.758ff.

15. HMC Memorandum, ibid., Vol.B, 630ff.

16. Committee of Vice Chancellors and Principals, Memorandum, ibid., Vol. D, pp.1126ff and 1146ff. *Submissions to the Committee on Higher Education*, Association of University Teachers, 1961.

17. ATTI Memorandum, *Higher Education, Evidence – Part One*, Vol. B, pp.588ff.

18. Committee of Principals of Colleges of Advanced Technology, Memorandum, ibid., Vol. C. pp.779ff.

19. Responsibility for universities, of course, then lay with the Treasury, the Lord President of the Council being its Parliamentary spokesman.

20. H.M.Treasury Memorandum, *Higher Education*, Evidence – Part One, Vol. F, pp.1956ff.

21. *The Years of Crisis, Report of the Labour Party's Study Group on Higher Education*, Labour Party, n.d. (1963).

22. Ibid., pp.7-9.

23. Ibid., p.26.

24. Ibid., pp.29-32, 37.

25. Ibid., pp.43-5.

26. Ibid., p.47.

27. 'Labour and the Scientific Revolution' is printed as Appendix II of the *Labour Party Conference Report*, 1963, pp.272ff.

28. *Labour Party Conference Report*, 1963, pp.133ff.

29. Quintin Hogg (Viscount Hailsham) characterised the report as 'the most important document since Beveridge'; Sir Geoffrey Crowther called it 'one of the most remarkable state papers of our time' (both quoted by Stuart Maclure, *Observer*, 30 October 1965). The only serious note of opposition surfaced two months later when the *Times*, then a paper of some moment, launched a bitter attack in three first leaders on successive days, (4, 5 and 6 December 1963). This was a premeditated and carefully prepared action, not 'a mere critical stand, but a root and branch onslaught'. Iverach Macdonald, *History of*

the Times, London 1984, Vol. V, pp.371-2.

30. 'In manner large, benevolent, persuasive, in action almost inexhaustible, he was a convinced and consistent expansionist.' Carswell, op.cit., p.14.

31. 'Though industry had three seats on the committee, its voice was little heard.' Ibid., p.31.

32. Ibid., p.31.

33. Ibid., p.31. 'By an oversight which turned out to be important, there was no member drawn from the world of the technical colleges'. Carswell, in a chapter entitled 'Picture of a Committee', op.cit., pp.27ff., discusses the personnel of the committee (and its helpers or assistants) in some detail. He himself acted as assessor to the committee from the Treasury in the later phases (p.29).

34. Ibid., p.33.

35. P.E. Vernon, Memorandum, *Higher Education Report* (Robbins Committee), *Evidence, Part II* (documentary evidence), pp.170-8.

36. Vernon adds, 'though they could conceivably be based on tests or surveys of aspirations, interests and social attitudes in the population'. Ibid., p.171.

37. Ibid., pp.174.

38. Jean Floud, Further Memorandum, Ibid., pp.50-7.

39. *Robbins Report*, p.54.

40. Ibid., p.74. The discussion on the difficulties of manpower planning is on pages 71-4.

41. For this discussion, ibid., pp.54-70.

42. Ibid., pp.69-70.

43. Ibid., p.8.

44. Ibid., pp.152-5. The Robbins Committee was concerned with Great Britain as a whole.

45. Ibid., pp.157, 119; for the note of reservation, pp.293-6.

46. Ibid., pp.128-30.

47. Ibid., pp.137-46.

48. Ibid., pp.238ff.

49. Ibid., p.244.

50. Ibid., pp.250-2. At the time the Robbins Report was published, Viscount Hailsham (Quintin Hogg) was both Lord President of the Council and Minister for Science, a post that had been established by Harold Macmillan after the 1959 election. For Hailsham's (unrevealing) comments on this appointment see Chapter 27. 'Science and Technology', in Lord Hailsham. *The Door Wherein I Went*, London 1975. On the Robbins report the author comments 'I remain wholly impenitent about having embraced it with open arms … big decisions like this need to be taken with the heart rather than the head.' pp.147-8.

51. Carswell, op.cit., p.52. The civil servant was Sir Maurice Dean, of the Treasury. The government statement was published as a White Paper, *Higher Education*, Cmnd 2165, in November 1963.

52. Carswell, op.cit., p.52.

53. For instance, for a new university in Scotland (eventually Stirling), for 'a completely new technological university', and concerning the further development of Imperial College, the Royal College of Science and Technology at Glasgow, and the Manchester College of Science and Technology.

54. On the recommendation that six new universities be established, the government prevaricated. This would be considered later, as also the proposals for organisational change (in terms of departmental responsibilities).

55. *Hansard*, House of Lords, 11 and 12 December 1963.

56. The phrase in Carswell's op cit., p.61, perhaps reflecting civil service experience. Lord Hailsham, the Minister for Science (and responsible for universities), threw himself into the campaign for the leadership of the Tory party, abjuring his peerage in the process.

57. See the final chapter of the Robbins Report, 'The Short-term Emergency', pp.257-64.

58. *DES Report*, 1964, p.86.

59. Ibid.,pp.89-90.
60. These fell outside the Robbins committee's purview, but had been recommended by the University Grants Committee.
61. *DES Report*, 1964, pp.86-7.
62. Ibid., p.88.
63. Ibid., p.64.
64. Ibid., p.84.
65. Ibid., p.73-4. According to Stuart Maclure (*Observer*, 30 October 1965) this decision announced by Michael Stewart, 'had already been reached by Hogg and Boyle'. They also agreed with the Labour government's rejection of the Robbins proposals relating to the SISTERS.
66. Carswell, op.cit., pp.70-1.
67. Letter to the *Times*, December 1964.
68. *Independent*, 30 July 1987.
69. Carswell, op.cit., pp.70ff. The author says that it was only too easy for the hearer of the Woolwich speech to see the universities as somehow placed in isolation, seeking after truth, pursuing learning for its own sake, and getting a lot of money for it (e.g. Oxford and Cambridge). The new institutions were presented as 'relevant', 'responsive', 'socially controlled', it being implied that these qualities did not characterise the universities. It is ironic, Carswell suggests, to note that the DES was in fact able to exercise a far stricter control over the universities than the polytechnics in the early 1980s.
70. *Report on the Quinquennium 1962-1967*. Committee of Vice Chancellors and Principals, p.8.
71. Maurice Kogan, *The Politics of Education*, Harmondsworth 1971, pp.193-4.
72. Susan Crosland puts it like this: 'Toby Weaver was now the senior official concerned with higher education. He proposed the binary policy to Tony. Tony seized it, amended it, and made it his own.' Susan Crosland, *Tony Crosland*, London, 1982, p.159. Sir Toby Weaver's own interpretation of his motives in pressing the binary solution are presented in 'The Prophet who had his Way', by Peter Scott, (based on an interview after Weaver's retirement). *Times Higher Educational Supplement*, 10 February 1978. One of the main results of this policy, Weaver claims, has been 'to protect the universities from their own ambitions to adopt a more popular role … to preserve a classical and perhaps rather idealistic vision of the university'.
73. 'Wicked Sir Toby on the Birth of Binarism', report of a talk at a seminar, *Education*, 20 August 1976. For Weaver's publicly expressed views at the time (at a meeting of Chief Education Officers and others), see *Education*, 20 August 1965. For a full and recent statement and interpretation, see Toby Weaver, 'Policy options for post-tertiary education', *Higher Education Review*, Vol. 14, No. 2, September 1982.
74. Resolution of the Association of Education Committees: 'The association fully supports the concept of a binary system in higher education'. *Education*, 9 July 1965.
75. 'There is a wholly false idea gaining ground that all right thinking educationalists except a few tiresome people in Curzon Street [the then location of the DES, B.S.] think that we ought to have a unitary system of higher education. This has not been the policy of successive governments of this country. It is not the view of … Mr Hogg or myself.' This statement was immediately welcomed by Crosland ('handsome assistance'); 'it will be very helpful, if they [regional colleges] do not think that merely by a change in government their position is likely to be altered. I am much obliged to [Edward Boyle] …'. House of Commons debate report, *Education*, 7 May 1965.
76. Kogan, op.cit., pp.128-9. 'The binary system, as we have it today, is inherently unstable.'
77. On the need for institutions catering not only for degree level students, 'but for the part-time student, the sub-degree course, etc.', Tyrrell Burgess 'has put the case better than anyone else' (Crosland in Kogan, op.cit., p.195). Tyrrell Burgess, 'whose writing on education was respected by Tony, characterised the Robbins view as "a kind of club with universities as full members, the colleges of education as associate members, and

regional colleges on a gratifying waiting list" '. Susan Crosland, op.cit., pp.158-9.

78. *Hansard*, House of Lords, 1 December 1965, Vol. 270, No. 12, Cols. 1249ff. This speech, and that made in the Lords debate of 11 December 1963, are reprinted in Lord Robbins, *The University in the Modern World*, London 1966. Other papers on higher education are included.

79. Lord Longford, government spokesman, in reply was merely frivolous. C.P. (now Lord) Snow also replied weakly.

80. Speech reported in the *Teacher*, 27 January 1967.

81. Crosland, op.cit., p.159.

82. Parliamentary statement by Secretary of State for Education and Science, 5 April 1967, issued as Administrative Memorandum No. 8/67.

83. Kogan, op.cit., p.193.

84. *Education*, 3 September 1965.

85. The proposal was that the university would appoint a director of industrial and extramural studies, a new post with professorial status. The work of the college would be continued as university work. 'These proposals are seen as an exciting opportunity of creating a new university broadly based in arts, social studies, and science and combining a strong technological side,' said the statement proposing the merger. Ibid.

86. *DES Report*, 1968, p.22.

87. Committee of Vice Chancellors and Principals, *Report on the Quinquennium 1962-67*, p.8.

88. For instance, see the *Listener*, July 1967 (interview).

89. *Times Higher Education Supplement*, 11 November 1983, 'Toby Weaver on Inevitability of a Binary Policy'.

90. John Vaizey, 'Anthony Crosland' in *In Breach of Promise*, London 1983, p.89.

91. 'The Teacher Shortage: Mr Anthony Crosland's 14 Point Plan', *Education*, 23 April 1965.

92. Richard Layard, John King and Claus Moser, *The Impact of Robbins*, Harmondsworth 1969, p.65 (chapter on 'The Colleges of Education').

93. Ibid., p.65.

94. NACTST, ninth report, *The Demand for and Supply of Teachers, 1963-1986*, HMSO 1965.

95. Layard, King and Moser, op.cit., pp.65-6. In Scotland, the actual number of students in colleges of education in 1967-68 was 10,800 compared to the 9,000 estimated by Robbins.

96. Ibid., p.71. See Chapter 9, 'Further Education' for a succinct analysis of this phenomenon.

97. Ibid., pp.71-2. According to the authors, it was rumoured that, 'when this was expounded to an incoming Secretary of State, he refused to believe it was true'. Ibid., p.71.

98. Ibid., p.72.

99. Ibid., p.43. For a thorough discussion of 'the upsurge at A level', see the chapter (3) of that title in Ibid., pp.31-40.

100. Ibid., p.41.

101. For an intelligent contemporary evaluation, Chapter 7, 'The Binary System' in ibid., pp.61-4.

102. Council for Scientific Policy, *Enquiry into the Flow of Candidates in Science and Technology into Higher Education*, HMSO 1968, Cmnd 3541 (the Dainton Report); Committee on Manpower Resources for Science and Technology, *The Flow into Employment of Scientists, Engineers and Technologists*, Report of the Working Group on Manpower for Scientific Growth (the Swann Report), HMSO 1968, Cmnd 3760.

103. W.A.C. Stewart, *Higher Education in Postwar Britain*, London 1989, Table 15.7, p.279.

104. This analysis relating to the DES is derived from Stewart, op.cit., p.312, and from Leonard Cantor, 'Public Sector Higher Education: 1945-85', Chapter 16 of Stewart, op.cit., p.303.

105. Cantor, op.cit., p.300, table 16.1; p.301, table 16.2.
106. Harold Wilson, foreword to Walter Perry, *Open University, A Personal Account by the First Vice Chancellor*, Open University Press, 1976, p.xi.
107. Walter Perry, op.cit., passim.

6 The Break-out in Secondary Education: The Comprehensive School

1 Developments to the Issue of Circular 10/65

The Local Authority Surge, 1963-64

Although, from 1960, an enormous expansion of higher education was under way, within the secondary schools, where reorganisation was held rigidly within the Eccles formula, stagnation was the order of the day, and this in spite of the advances (and mounting frustrations) recorded in Chapter 4. The 1958 White Paper, a clear statement of government policy, held all in thrall. Secondary modern schools were to develop specialist sides (or strengths). This would take the steam out of the 11-plus; the grammar schools would be preserved.

But, as Edward Boyle wrote later, this 'alternative' policy came too late.[1] Eccles had been right to issue his warning to the Cabinet in 1955 that the 11-plus was becoming a critical political issue. In the late 1950s and early 1960s pressures were building up from all parts of the country, but perhaps particularly from the great conurbations in the North. It was becoming clear by now that a social movement of some significance was under way – reflecting increased aspirations and mounting frustration on the part of parents (including new social strata emerging from technological change) and the local authorities representing them. When he returned to education as minister in July 1962, Boyle wrote later, 'It was clear to me ... that support for the development of secondary education along comprehensive lines was gaining considerable momentum.'[2]

Looking back, it is now clear that 1963 was the crucial moment of change. In this year the two great cities of Manchester and Liverpool set the pace, showing their absolute determination to make the change. Manchester, having a large Labour majority, and having been frustrated in its efforts to reorganise at Wythenshawe a few years earlier (see pp.186-7), adopted an unusual procedure. A tightly framed resolution was presented to a full meeting of the city council in July, eventually carried by 62 votes to 25. This *instructed* the education committee to 'prepare and present to the council within six months proposals for converting all county secondary schools, and such other appropriate schools as may wish to participate, into comprehensive schools'. There was to be no more prevarication.[3] The stated aim was 'to abolish the practice of selection by 1965'.

Thirty miles away, in Liverpool, similar developments were under way. Here a Labour majority, in control from 1955 to 1961, had brought one comprehensive school into being (Gateacre) and had plans ready for four others when, in May 1961, control was lost to the Conservatives. Two years later, when Labour returned, a decision was immediately made to plan the transformation of the entire system. In July 1963, (as at Manchester) the city council approved recommendations of the education committee that this committee,

> believing that comprehensive schools afford the greatest possible opportunities to boys and girls of all degrees of ability, affirms that it is its intention that a comprehensive system of secondary education shall be established in Liverpool, and that the county secondary schools shall be reorganised accordingly at the earliest possible date, and as a consequence the 11-plus shall be abolished, and instruct the secondary education sub-committee, as a matter of urgency, to prepare a scheme directed towards these ends after consultation with the teachers.[4]

By October that year the Director of Education had presented a report to the education committee on the various ways in which this resolution might be implemented. Both Manchester and Liverpool were determined to press ahead as quickly as possible. Both intended that their schemes should be fully operational at the start of the school year in September 1965.

Other areas were not far behind, and in the country as a whole a veritable explosion of grass-roots activity was under way – though no one, as yet, assessed, or was even aware of, its extent and significance. In Sheffield the Labour group, which had a large majority on the city council, decided in 1962 (to quote from an official memorandum) 'to move as quickly as possible towards a more comprehensive system of secondary education with the aim of abolishing segregation at 11-plus.' This was to be achieved in turn in each of the three zones into which the city was divided. In October 1963 Bradford city council resolved to end all selection at 11-plus and at the same time authorised reorganisation of schools to make this possible. An intensive programme of public meetings on the proposals attended by over 9,000 parents was immediately carried through.[5] At this time also the West Riding, now 'firmly oriented towards a comprehensive system', was pressing its 'middle school' (nine to thirteen) variant, soon to be successful. A survey of developments in the summer of 1964 concluded that 'There is a major educational change under way in Yorkshire.'[6]

But in Lancashire it was much the same. In July 1964 the prestigious Lancashire Education Committee responsible for 29 districts – each comparable in size to the average county borough, and covering a total population of over 2,200,000 – resolved on the introduction of comprehensive forms of organisation. At the same time, in addition to Manchester and Liverpool, the great bulk of the county boroughs were by now considering making the change. An illustration of the temper abroad by this time, runs a report, is a phrase by the chief education officer for the county (Lancashire) when welcoming the passing of the 11-plus, that 'archaic monstrosity' whereby little boys and girls are allocated to schools like apples to baskets. A *'Re-appraisal'* of the position in Preston, published over the name of the chief education officer of that city, in April (1964) was prefaced by a recent finding of the United States Supreme Court:

> We conclude, that in the field of public education the doctrine of 'separate but equal' has no place. Separate educational facilities are inherently unequal.[7]

In his 'Reflections' on this period, Edward Boyle, then Minister of Education, recalls that, by 1963, his officials estimated that 90 out of the total of 163 local education authorities in England and Wales 'had in a few cases completed, or else were working on, reorganisation schemes which they wanted to implement for the whole, or a part of their areas'. Furthermore, he added, since many of these were not Labour-controlled, their plans 'could not simply be written off as politically motivated'.[8] In November 1964, a few days after the General Election of that year, a telephonic survey by the *Sunday Times* indicated that, of the 149 authorities (in England) 120 were considering or were introducing some reorganisation. 65 had already established some comprehensive schools. '11-plus is Going Fast' headlined the paper. 'The Comprehensives Move In'.[9]

As we have seen, the new minister (Boyle), who succeeded Eccles (second term) in July 1962, was soon made aware of the strength of this movement, and, unlike his predecessor, although constrained by Conservative tradition and thinking, reacted warily but sympathetically.[10] With a traditional upper-class education (Eton and Oxford), Boyle was a man with unusually wide interests, cultured, civilised and knowledgeable; his approach and attitude is perhaps better described as whiggish than 'Liberal-Tory' (the usual description) – a supporter of reform from above. Boyle had a difficult furrow to hoe, given, as he put it later, 'the political and educational significance of the most prestigious grammar schools to a Conservative government'.[11] Recognising the force of the movement for secondary re-organisation, and increasingly sympathetic to its objectives, he clearly saw his function partly in terms of educating the Conservative Party to accept this degree of educational change – and here he had a certain success at party conferences in 1962 and 1963. At the crucial period of change in the summer of 1963, Boyle announced at the annual conference of the Association of Education Committees that he thought the time had come 'to abandon the idea of the "bi-partite" system … as the "norm", compared with which all other forms of organisation were to be thought of as "experimental",' and that in future any proposals (under Section 13 of the 1944 Act) submitted for approval would be decided as 'strictly on educational grounds.'[12] So the Eccles criteria at long last were laid to rest. This announcement, of course, encouraged local authorities to feel that proposals for re-organisation now at least had some chance of success. In the early autumn of 1964, further, Edward Boyle persuaded the Prime Minister Douglas Home, as soon as the October date of the General Election was announced, to make time immediately for a parliamentary Bill already in preparation that would make the middle school solution to comprehensive organisation legally possible. 'I suppose you might call the 1964 Act,' he said later, 'my parting gift to the ministry.'[13]

By the summer of 1964, then, things were moving fast. As indicated in Chapter 5, Labour had made an impressive bid for the high ground in its policy statement 'Labour and the Scientific Revolution' which formed the focus of debate at the party conference in the preceding September, and to some extent won the nation's attention. Committed now to comprehensive re-organisation, the party had pledged itself at this conference 'to give highest priority in finance and resources to education' and 'to set up a universal system of comprehensive secondary education and to abolish the 11-plus'. The means by which this should be done reflected a greatly increased determination. 'This could be most easily achieved by converting existing permissive legislation into compulsory legislation binding upon the local authorities.'[14]

Commitment of the party by conference decision, however, did not necessarily mean full commitment to such a reform by a future Labour government. This had already been evident, precisely in this sphere, during the 1945-51 Labour government' terms of office, as we have seen (Chapter 2). This difference in intentions, between party and government, was to dog the whole comprehensive movement in the years ahead.

Nevertheless the conference decision of 1963 seemed to imply a decisive move towards comprehensive education if and when Labour returned to power, which now began to seem probable. The national focus on education was enhanced at this time by the publication, first, of the Central Advisory Council's report *Half our Future* (the Newsom Report), concerned with the education of pupils aged between thirteen and sixteen 'of average and less than average ability'[15] and a few weeks later, of the Robbins report. It was in his foreword to the Newsom Report that Boyle coined his famous phrase relating to human potentiality – and its connection with the doctrine of fixed 'intelligence'. 'The essential point', he wrote, 'is that all children should have an equal opportunity of acquiring intelligence, and of developing their talents and abilities to the full.' As we have seen, the Robbins Report also rejected the fatalistic theories of the past concerning human development. So, a new phase now opened out.

The Robbins Report was, as we have seen, immediately and enthusiastically welcomed by Douglas Home who took over as Prime Minister from an ailing Macmillan only a few days before publication. Education was clearly seen as a vote-winner, and here Labour now had the edge. Yet, in spite of the virtual disintegration of the Macmillan government over the last year due to the handling of the Profumo scandal, the 'night of the long knives' and other difficulties, Labour was victorious only by a whisker. Polling only 200,000 votes more than the Tories, they gained thirteen more seats but, with nine Liberals returned, their overall majority was precisely four.[16] This, of course, was to be rectified later (March 1966), but at this stage the situation was tenuous. In most areas of sensitivity, the government hastened slowly.

This was certainly the case, as far as the new Labour government was concerned, with comprehensive education – in spite of the groundswell noted earlier. But as the weeks passed and yet more local authorities fell into line, government confidence gradually increased. Here was an issue around which, it began to appear, a new consensus might be achieved. It was also one of the few issues on which Labour had a clear policy – or so it seemed. To some, indeed to a future Secretary of State for Education, Anthony Crosland, comprehensive reorganisation was *the* chief means of moving towards a greater egalitarianism within a 'mixed' economy. It was certainly not seen officially, by the Labour government, as an essential adjunct to the transition to socialism – nor, as it soon became clear, were socialist measures of any kind envisaged. As Wilson's first one hundred days rolled by, pragmatism became the order of the day.

Labour's Action: Circular 10/65

The new parliament met early in November 1964, and only a few days later the new Secretary of State, Michael Stewart,[17] took the opportunity to make a clear statement. 'It is the government's policy', he announced, 'to reorganise secondary education on comprehensive lines. The method and timing of reorganisation', he went on, 'must vary from one area to another.' In a reference to Labour's manifesto which had promised 'Grammar school education for all', he concluded that one aim of the government's comprehensive policy was to preserve 'what we all value in grammar school education' for those children who now receive it 'and make it available to more children.'[18] So, from the start, official 'Labour' policy was presented as essentially conciliatory and moderate – a far cry from the objectives some held of a fundamental transformation of the system in line with democratic objectives.

A few days later a full debate on a Tory motion (moved by a Bristol MP) deploring 'the wholesale abolition of direct grant and maintained grammar schools' provided the occasion for a defence of the new government's policy. In a well argued speech, drawing on the experience of two London comprehensives which had developed from grammar schools (Mayfield and Wandsworth) as well as on Leicestershire, Stewart claimed that already 68 local authorities, covering 63 per cent of the secondary school population, were either implementing or examining concrete proposals for reorganisation, while another 21 were contemplating reorganisation. These authorities were 'of all political colours and of none'. In order to avoid too great a degree of local variation 'it was now right for the central government to give a clear lead'. Claiming that he was only anticipating what Sir Edward Boyle would have done within perhaps twelve or eighteen months he concluded that, in the government's view, 'We ought now to accept that reorganisation of secondary education on comprehensive lines should be national policy.'[19]

'Thoughtful and in some ways reassuring', was how the *Times* characterised Stewart's speech; 'thoughtful and conciliatory' was the *Guardian*'s evaluation, though the *Sunday Times* regarded it as 'equivocal', while congratulating the government on its cautious approach.[20] The Tories were worried that the popular surge now emerging – indeed accelerating – might bring not only the maintained but also direct grant grammar schools toppling down – the world turned upside down.[21] All this and other fears came out in a combative speech by Quintin Hogg as the main Tory speaker (with Boyle) in a major debate in the House of Commons late in January 1965. Local authority plans were 'a series of precipitate, makeshift proposals ... seeking to cram into a system which was designed for quite another purpose comprehensive schemes simply for the purpose of claiming to have abolished the 11-plus'. Above all coercion should not be used – 'a single unitary principle of reorganisation ... would undermine the whole philosophy of the 1944 Act'. It would 'bring back the bitterest political antagonism into education'.[22]

To all this, Stewart gave another 'moderate', but in some respects hard hitting response, again stressing the widespread nature of the change and the main arguments in its favour. By this time it was clear that the government had decided to take action, and the general form of that action. Indeed a few days earlier the Cabinet had agreed to Stewart's proposal 'to issue a Circular to local education authorities' calling on them 'to submit plans ... for the reorganisation of their secondary schools on comprehensive lines'. Answering questions just before the January debate, Stewart took the line (agreed in Cabinet) that there would be a very large measure of 'willing cooperation' from local authorities and that he 'would not ask the House for legislation unless it proved essential for the continuation of the comprehensive policy'.[23]

A 'heated debate in the Lords' a few days later rounded off this flurry of parliamentary activity. Here, true to type, David Eccles (now ennobled) 'raised the temperature ... by asserting that the doctrine of uniformity expressed in the demand for a complete system of comprehensive schools affronted both Christian and human ideals'. The individual 'was sacrificed to society' and the parent 'silenced by the politician'.[24]

In this debate comprehensive education got rather short shrift from the combination of Tory ex-ministers, grammar school proponents and others to whom it was anathema. Local education authorities, said Lord Newton (a Tory ex-minister) 'are, without any encouragement, pressing ahead with experiments almost certainly too fast'. (It was this powerful, uncontrolled pressure from below that Tories found especially disturbing.) Florence Horsbrugh also now ennobled, while actually claiming credit for Kidbrooke, reiterated again and again that the government should 'stop and think' – 'It is the question of hurry which is causing me very great anxiety.' The government should 'keep their minds open and take no decision for the time being'. A major contribution, as might be expected, was also made by Eric James (also by now ennobled), who reiterated the arguments in his earlier polemical writings (see pp.126-9). In this debate the government's case was made by C.P. (now Lord) Snow, whose authority was somewhat dented by his forced admission (when challenged by Eccles) that his own son was being educated at Eton – for which he was accused as being one of those 'whose private conduct labels them as humbugs'.[25] A refreshing breath of reality did intrude itself into this debate, however, in the contribution by Lord Gardiner (the Labour Lord Chancellor).

Though this was not his subject he had been provoked, as he said, by a remark of Lord Newton's that no one really knew whether the Leicestershire Plan was a success. Attending a local government boundary enquiry at Leicester a few weeks earlier, he found that, though only a few people were expected, the only hall available was the very large concert hall (this was the De Montfort Hall). 'This was taken, and it was packed out with thousands of people ... the vast majority were parents and they were hopping mad because in the city they had secondary and grammar schools whereas the county had comprehensive schools.' Some of them 'had sold their homes in Leicester in order to get away from the city education system and the 11-plus and give their children the advantages of a comprehensive school education, and now they were being threatened with being put back into the city again'. Of course, he added, 'I had always known that the 11-plus was not very popular but I had never known before the extent it was both hated and feared.' Perhaps, he concluded, they were right.[26]

Immediately following the House of Commons debate towards the end of January there was an important change of personnel. Michael Stewart, who had piloted the first debates and discussions in the House of Commons in a conciliatory, somewhat ambiguous but nevertheless tough-minded way, was transferred to the Foreign Office where Gordon Walker's tenure, in face of his failure to gain electoral support and win a seat in parliament, could no longer be condoned. Stewart's successor, Anthony Crosland, who, as we have seen, had made his name as an ideologist promoting a revisionist, social democratic perspective, now took his place as Secretary of State for Education and Science. Crosland had made his support for the comprehensive solution (and his conviction that the public schools were a chief bastion of class society) abundantly clear in earlier writings.

In the meantime the grass roots, local authority swing to comprehensive education, based on the movement of opinion that Lord Gardiner had so graphically illustrated, proceeded with added momentum. In January 1965, while parliament was debating, several new authorities announced plans and discussions aiming at comprehensive reorganisation. At York, a working party of sixteen teachers started work on a plan for the city, following a detailed report by the chief education officer completed just before he died in November 1964. The working party's conclusion, the *Times* reported, 'could mean the abolition of York's four grammar schools in favour of a comprehensive system'. 'Socially and economically', the Chief Education Officer (CEO) had reported, 'the present system cannot be defended'. Among supporters of the proposal, the paper reported significantly, was Professor H. Rée, now Head of the Education Department of York University and a co-opted member of the education committee.[27] It will be remembered that only ten years earlier, Harry Rée had been a leading opponent of the comprehensive school. Other authorities now preparing plans included Wakefield, Middlesbrough, Southend and Birmingham.

While in both Liverpool and Bristol the authorities continued to elaborate on and clarify their plans, in both areas 'parents' action committees' were formed to fight the proposals – so originating a form of action that became general, if largely ineffective, in the years to come. Public meetings, demonstrations, deputations, telegrams became the order of the day as these groups of parents, often the alumni of particular local grammar schools, pressed their case. 'Please consider public statement to reassure Liverpool and Bristol parents that local irresponsible extremists' local council educational proposals will not be condoned by Labour Minister of Education,' was the telegraphic result of the co-operation of both these organisations immediately on Harold Wilson's move to Downing Street in October – an example of a pressure that attempted to counter the broader based popular movement on which the transition was founded.[28] Grammar school headmasters continued, through their organisation, to express an intransigent opposition.[29] But such expressions of view were no longer able to do more than perhaps deflect the drive towards a more basic school reorganisation.

In the meantime Crosland was making clear, in a series of speeches, that plans for the issue of a Circular to local authorities were under way, while stressing, as he put it, that it was no part of the government's intention 'to seek to impose destructive or precipitate changes on existing schools', nor to approve 'any old makeshift scheme'. The object was 'to give impetus and direction' to the process of change and to ensure that 'the objective of a non-selective pattern of secondary education should be firmly declared'.[30] In March, at a Labour Party conference at Lincoln, Crosland, as well as devoting a long section of his speech to the need for action on the public school issue (see below), outlined in some detail the five different ways in which local authorities were planning the change and made it clear that the Circular would not 'prescribe one form as universally applicable'.[31] The draft Circular was now expected to be issued shortly and, at the end of March, Crosland made it clear that it would not impose any solution. 'I regard compulsion as an academic question at the moment', he stated in the House of Commons. 'I am perfectly confident that local authorities will respond voluntarily and cooperatively to our request to submit plans.'[32] Finally the draft Circular was issued confidentially to educational bodies towards the end of May and the final draft published on 14 July 1965.

So, in the end, the government eschewed compulsion – a decision that was to lead to difficulties later; further, in *requesting* the submission of plans, the Circular outlined the different methods that would be acceptable, though expressing a preference for the all-through eleven-to-eighteen school. Authorities were given one year to make their submissions. In this sense the procedure used was that originally proposed at the 1953 Labour Party conference, and *not* that accepted at the 1963 conference which proposed a statutory measure involving compulsion. The Circular also stated that no extra money would be available to assist reorganisation before 1967 – a decision hardly reflecting a serious determination to bring about a fundamental change in the structure and direction of secondary education.

Characterised in the *Guardian* as an 'amiably toothless tiger' (by Peter Preston), as a 'vague and permissive document' in the *Times Educational Supplement*, but as 'regrettably dictatorial in tone' in the *Daily Telegraph*, this statement that comprehensive secondary education was now national policy was, in a sense, and for all its weaknesses, epoch-making.[33] Now at last, it seemed, to those supporting the move, the way was clear to develop a more genuinely popular, and democratic, system of education, embodying the ideals of the early comprehensive pioneers. Nevertheless it was already clear that further battles lay ahead.

Early in the autumn of 1965 a well organised pressure group of comprehensive supporters was formed to monitor developments and to press for radical change – the Comprehensive Schools Committee (CSC).[34] The editorial of the first number of its bulletin was headed 'What Sort of Schools Does Mr Crosland Want?' The group argued, and with reason, that the future pattern of comprehensive education would be determined, 'not by the Circular, nor by the initial plans submitted by the LEAs'. It would be determined by the secretary of state's decision as to 'which plans he accepts and which he rejects'.

And what had Crosland actually done? Liverpool's proposals were rejected, as also those of Luton and Stoke-on-Trent.[35] All three plans had proposed grouping schools together to form comprehensive units as the most practicable way of making the transition in existing buildings (London had made extensive use of this system). All three authorities were told to think again. On the other hand, Crosland accepted the Doncaster plan, and those of three other authorities which involved a common school for the ages eleven-to-thirteen followed by the 'choice' of (i) a school to prepare for A level GCE involving a promise to stay to eighteen, and (ii) a 'lower' or 'modern' school for the rest – a system which, according to the Comprehensive Schools Committee, simply reinforced and crystallised existing class divisions. Of the seven schemes considered in the last six months, the CSC claimed in the autumn of 1965, four of the latter type had been accepted, 'while the three genuinely comprehensive schemes have been, to all intents and purposes, rejected'. The actions of the DES in the future, then, 'deserves the closest attention'.[36] Evidently, then, the battle was hardly over.

2   New Developments, 1965-70

The Swing Accelerates
In spite of these difficulties 'at the top' (as it were), following the issue of Circular 10/65, the conditions now existed for a rapid transition to comprehensive education, though, as a result of the decision not to legislate, the crucial decisions would have to be made locally, within and by each of the then existing 163 local authorities responsible for their 'systems'. Each of these was now officially 'requested' to submit a plan within a year for acceptance, or otherwise, by the secretary of state. A special department within the DES was charged with

monitoring plans as they came in, and advising the secretary of state (Crosland).

Initial responses in the autumn of 1965 showed a diversified picture. Of the 163 authorities, 50 intended to have, or were already operating fully comprehensive schemes. About twenty were, at this stage, unwilling to consider comprehensive reorganisation, while of the remaining 80 about half had set up working parties with the task of producing plans (some with less enthusiasm than others), while the other half appeared to be tackling reorganisation in a piecemeal manner – that is, planning to recognise rural areas but not towns, to build comprehensives in new areas but not to reorganise in old ones, or to introduce one comprehensive 'experiment' in a selected part of their area. Already a considerable variety in the structures proposed was clearly evident – all the options under 10/65 were being considered.[37]

The situation was, however, transformed by the General Election, called by Harold Wilson on 31 March 1966 – after seventeen months in office. The tenuous majority gained in October 1964 was clearly restrictive and, during this honeymoon period, the government's popularity and support had grown. The Labour manifesto gave particular prominence to the government's plans for comprehensive reorganisation and to its intention to take measures to ensure the 'integration' of the public schools into the national system – a commission to make recommendations on this question had already been appointed, in December 1965. This election recorded a significant swing to Labour who gained 48 per cent of the vote, compared to 42 per cent for the Tories. In the Commons Labour's majority over the Conservatives was now more than 100, with the prospect of a full five-year term ahead. The spring local elections also resulted in sweeping gains – the bulk of the local authorities now (unusually) reflected the political outlook of the government. The election had been preceded by a new Circular, 10/66, published only a fortnight earlier, which announced that capital grants for new secondary buildings would be available only for projects compatible with comprehensive reorganisation. By this time the atmosphere had changed – though as we shall see, sporadic local actions continued, largely organised by local grammar shools threatened by reorganisation. There were to be no more sour debates in parliament. This, in fact, was a moment when the government could have introduced legislation to speed the transition, having wide popular support and a powerful Parliamentary majority. The inevitability of change was becoming generally recognised.

This was evidenced in three main areas – among local authorities, among the teachers and among parents. We may examine these in turn.

Local authorities. There was, of course, resistance among a few Conservative-dominated authorities which were determined to make no change, and which relied, correctly as it turned out, on the fact that Circular 10/65 merely made a request, and certainly carried no statutory force. By the autumn of 1965, twelve authorities took this stance, either declining to submit plans, or indefinitely postponing them, while some (including Kingston-on-Thames and Richmond in Surrey) submitted plans announcing their intention to keep selection at the age of eleven.[38]

Over the next few years, however, this hard core was further reduced, though several authorities relied on persistent delaying tactics to hold up change. In the outcome, the great bulk of the authorities, Labour and Tory, finally did respond positively to the Circular.

But this involved a process in which attitudes changed. Edward Boyle was fond of pointing out that, while some Conservative authorities – for instance, Leicestershire[39] – had brought comprehensive schools into being in some parts of their areas (more particularly certain shire counties), some Labour-controlled auhorities in urban areas stoutly resisted the move, even though it had now long been official Labour policy. These were authorities, such as the city of Leicester (then responsible for education), where Labour policy was controlled by what may be described as Labour's backwoodsmen – city aldermen, locally prestigious, closely involved with local grammar schools (often as long-standing chairmen of governing bodies) which they continued to see as the jewels in the crown of their local systems.

This approach was, of course, rooted historically in the thinking and outlook of the 1920s and 30s, when Labour fought a long battle to open up the grammar schools to the working class – an approach which, as we have seen (Chapter 2) extended into the post-war period. Proponents of comprehensive education within the Labour Party represented a new tide in educational thinking which began to make an impact locally in the late 1950s and early 1960s. In areas like Manchester, Liverpool, Bristol, Sheffield and Bradford, as we have seen, these achieved hegemony within the Labour Party at this time, but in other areas, with less radical traditions, the process took longer, and sometimes entailed years of bitter struggles within the Labour Party itself before the grip of the old guard was broken and the new pro-comprehensive elements began to supplant them in their policymaking role and in positions of responsibility. This was very much the position in Leicester, Birmingham and other Midland cities as well as in the North-East.[40] By 1964 or 1965, however, the bulk of the Labour authorities were in the hands of enthusiastic supporters of secondary reorganisation, and, as Crosland later pointed out, at the time of the issue of 10/65 the great bulk of local authorities were under Labour control.[41]

The teachers. What of the teachers? From the start there had been a small core of enthusiasts who to some extent made the running both in the early schools and the professional organisations; these included such distinguished leaders as G.C.T. Giles and Raymond King (both grammar school heads), Margaret Clarke (NUT executive and head of Peckham), Nan Macmillan (President of NUWT 1939-41 and head of Silverthorne in Southwark), the well known historian George Rudé (AMA and Holloway in London) and many of a younger generation. These, some of them Communists, some Labour, others uncommitted politically, flocked into the early schools, experimental and otherwise, and clearly influenced professional colleagues, both in the grammar school teachers' organisations and within the National Union of Teachers. Reorganisation, however, raised difficult questions relating to the professional interests of teachers – the issues of salaries, career prospects, redeployment and consultation – while the bulk of the teachers, both primary and secondary, had a long historical experience of assimilation to their role within the divided system.

This took time to overcome. The main grammar school associations, as we have seen, took the lead in mounting a campaign for the defence of these schools in the late 1950s, spurred on by David Eccles. The NUT, through the 1950s and early 1960s, was quiescent on this issue – in effect rejecting the comprehensive solution, though this approach was contested in both organisations. The publication, by the NUT in 1958, of a serious and authoritative study by leading comprehensive school headteachers (*Inside the Comprehensive School*) significantly marked a growing interest in the educational issues involved.

But it was in the 1960s things began to change – and with some rapidity. Already in 1960 the Assistant Masters' Association, which now had members teaching in comprehensive schools, published a sympathetic and objective report, *Teaching in Comprehensive Schools*, based on the experience of members serving in such schools. In 1967 a second report was published, based on information 'provided by a greater number of members', many of whom had now had 'much longer experience'. The tone of this report is far removed from the over-excited contributions of grammar school proponents in the 1950s and earlier. The purpose of the publication is defined as to assist grammar school teachers 'to know as much as possible about what serving in a comprehensive school means so that they can offer constructive criticism of plans involving their own schools'. Opposition to change, because it means disturbance, it is stated, 'is both unworthy of a profession and certain to be ineffectual'.[42] The publication itself was a useful, informed and thoughtful compilation covering all aspects of comprehensive school structure, curriculum and teaching written by teachers working within the schools.

The most important organisation, however, was the NUT[43], the majority of whose members were (and are) primary teachers, but with a substantial minority within the secondary schools. As we have seen, leading NUT executive members, like Giles and Margaret Clarke, were comprehensive supporters, but, as an organisation, support for reorganisation was first carried as a conference resolution at Easter 1965 – that is, only shortly before the issue of Circular 10/65.[44] This resolution was worded warily, and, perhaps, diplomatically.[45] A year later, however, in 1966, a strong resolution affirmed 'support for the reorganisation of secondary education under a system of comprehensive schools' and specifically declared the union's opposition to systems 'of so-called comprehensive education' which involved 'a measure of selection of pupils at 13-plus and 14-plus for entry into different schools' – a specific attack on schemes of the Doncaster type which Crosland had recently accepted. The NUT now clearly stood 'for the elimination of the selection principle' and was to maintain this approach consistently thereafter.[46] Indeed, following the publication of the first Black Paper (1969) attacking comprehensive education, the NUT Conference called on the government to ensure the universality of the transition by legislation 'abolishing selection for secondary education', adding that this could only be achieved 'by incorporating the grammar schools and other selective secondary schools into the comprehensive system, thereby creating a unified system for all children'. Conference believes, the resolution goes on, 'that the continued existence of the grammar schools completely nullifies all attempts to create a fully comprehensive system'. Having in mind those authorities still refusing to make the change, the Secretary of State was called on 'actively to intervene forthwith and demand that local education authorities present comprehensive schemes of secondary reorganisation immediately ...'[47] This was the background to Edward Short's abortive Bill of 1970 which will be discussed later. It does, however, graphically represent the growing feeling among the mass of NUT members of the urgent need for action. Through the 1960s, then, the bulk of the teaching profession, and this gradually included more and more ex-grammar school teachers, swung generally towards solid support for the move to comprehensive education.

The parents. Parental opinion – and its shifts and moods – is harder to evaluate; after all, this constituency runs into millions. That there was a groundswell of frustration with the 11-plus emerging as a great wave of public opinion in the early 1960s is clear enough – and hardly disputed; it was this, after all, that lay behind the whole movement for comprehensive education and expressed itself in the urgency and determination shown in the original resolutions of the Manchester and Liverpool city councils, as elsewhere. But parental opinion cannot easily find organisational form, except, perhaps, around specific local issues.

This is why a high profile was taken, initially, by parents organised by individual grammar schools 'threatened' by reorganisation – in the form of 'save our schools' committees, preservation societies and the grammar school action groups. Fighting funds and fighting associations of prestige grammar schools were fully operational wherever local authority planning of reorganisation looked like taking place. In towns like Leicester, Flint, Liverpool, Enfield, Ealing, Bexley, Dudley and many more, these organised. The grammar schools themselves were the actual centres of these campaigns. Head teachers provided facilities for meetings and urged parents to sign or circulate petitions. Parents with children in grammar schools, and old boys' and old girls' associations spearheaded local campaigns against reorganisation.[48] While these activities were inevitably temporarily effective – even influential – in holding up change, in the nature of the case they equally inevitably faded away once reorganisation was accomplished.

On the other side an important role, both locally and nationally, was played in the mid-late 1960s by another pressure group uniting parents with others – the Confederation for the Advancement of State Education (CASE). Originating as local pressure groups in the period 1960-62 concerned to fight for greater resources to improve the quality of local, particularly primary, schools, some 26 such groups united in 1962 to form the national organisation. Supported, in particular, by Edward Boyle as an expression of parental views, a representative from CASE was appointed (by Boyle) on to the Plowden Committee (in 1963), together with another from a 'consumer association', the Advisory Centre for Education, (ACE); this was Michael (later Lord) Young.[49]

Both CASE and ACE quickly moved to strong support, not only of state (as opposed to private) education, but of fully effective comprehensive systems which CASE espoused officially in 1966. Local CASE branches actively supported the move to reorganisation while nationally CASE pursued the same policy.

> There was a CASE representative on the Plowden Committee on Primary Schools, CASE made a substantial contribution to the fight for comprehensive reorganisation. It helped to put parents clearly and indelibly on the education map. Vigorous, effective and well publicised local campaigns gave credibility to the national voice.[50]

CASE was a well organised, serious, largely middle-class, parental pressure group which threw its weight behind comprehensive reorganisation at a crucial moment. It represented that section of the 'new middle class' that rejected private education and instead was determined to shape the national system to its own wishes. This, in its view, involved rejecting selection – and this is what was particularly significant in the stand they took. No doubt this support eased the transition. The main swing of parental opinion had, however, developed earlier – well before CASE espoused the cause.

Public opinion polls are perhaps the best measure of parental attitudes. What can be gleaned from these? From the beginning of the transition these showed that comprehensive schools enjoyed majority support, while anti-comprehensive opinion during the 1960s stayed fairly steady around the 20 per cent mark, the proportion of the national population taken into the grammar schools. Further, public support rose steadily as comprehensive schools were introduced into specific areas – a survey done in 1967 indicated that support for comprehensive schools rose to 73 per cent in areas where comprehensive schools had been introduced, to 85 per cent in areas where those questioned had children in comprehensive schools.[51]

The shift of opinion in the 1960s, then, appears decisive – as a deep-rooted change. The great bulk of the local authorities, of the teachers, of public opinion and parents generally – but particularly those closely involved – were now strongly supportive of the movement. A new literature was burgeoning around the comprehensive school. In 1963 Robin Pedley published a popular Penguin, *The Comprehensive School*, written for parents and the general public. This was reprinted five times during the 1960s alone. Nevertheless, there was still a minority opposition increasingly frustrated as the movement gathered pace. This was to erupt in various forms in the future.

Winning the ideological battle. There developed, then, by the mid-1960s, widespread popular support for the need for structural change – based on anger and frustration about the 11-plus, and the divided system of which it was the symbol and expression. To this, the comprehensive school, in one form or another, seemed the only rational solution. What was being expressed was a popular revulsion from the selective system of functional school types deriving from the thinking of the 1920s and 30s, and developed in a new form in the 1940s and 50s.

But this popular movement coincided in the 1960s with the movement of ideas reinforcing the desire to open up new opportunities, and to broaden perspectives for young people of secondary school age. It was in the work of psychologists, sociologists and economists in particular that these views found expression.

Deterministic theories no longer held the field in psychology – theories which for long had provided the main legitimisation of the divided system. Indeed instead the concept of the educability of the normal child – and, for that matter, of the 'sub-normal' – began to gain widespread acceptance, both within the teaching profession and outside.[52] As we have seen, the Robbins committee overtly rejected the concept of a strictly limited pool of ability. Their view, reinforced by the 'evidence' provided by Philip Vernon, was informed by a belief in human potential and the need to provide the conditions for its release. Reflecting this changed outlook, Edward Boyle's introduction to the Newsom Report, also of 1963, placed the emphasis on equalising children's opportunities 'to acquire intelligence' which was not, in this formulation, seen as a genetic 'given'. This view was strongly reinforced, as we shall see in the next chapter, in the Plowden committee's assessment (1967) which stressed the importance of the child's interaction with its environment as the main factor determining development, intellectual and other. At this time the concept that a child's development was the resultant of its activity within a controlled environment (schooling) began to be influential – a standpoint developed by leading Soviet psychologists whose work now began to make an impact both in Britain and the United States.[53]

It was work (thinking) of this kind which led to the new emphasis on educability; and which therefore directly reinforced the view not only that children should not be segregated at an early age into different types of school, but also that more open and flexible school structures were required to meet the needs of children – or to provide the conditions to maximise the realisation of potential. This clearly had implications not only for the structure of the system as a whole, but also for the internal structuring of individual schools.

But at this stage it was not so much the psychologists as the new breed of sociologists who were making the running. Sociological studies, as we have seen, had already brought out clearly the extent to which the divided secondary system discriminated against children of working-class origin and, conversely, favoured the middle-class child. Studies of educational opportunity had already revealed that the 1944 Act, which was intended to ensure equality of opportunity, had in fact made no more than a marginal change in the situation. A series of studies of this character were drawn on by Jean Floud who presented this argument with great force in her evidence to the Robbins committee – as we saw in Chapter 5. From analyses of this kind emphasis had begun to be placed on the immense 'wastage' of ability through the school system first fully brought out both in *Early Leaving* (1954) and in the Crowther Report of 1959, and later developed authoritatively in a series of sociological studies.[54] Leading sociologists, for instance, A.H. Halsey and Jean Floud, were themselves strong supporters of the comprehensive school, seeing it as a means of enhancing social mobility and of moving towards a more egalitarian society – and so of reducing 'wastage' and strengthening the economy. Anthony Crosland was himself well versed in the literature of the sociologists – particularly their educational analyses – and also an overt 'egalitarian'. It was at about this time that sociologists achieved a kind of hegemony in their theoretical contributions to the ongoing educational debate; nor was it an accident that Crosland appointed Halsey as his personal adviser when at the DES (the first of such 'political' appointments). Sociologists could make a practical as well as a theoretical contribution.[55]

The third field of analysis where work now began, if perhaps obliquely, to power the comprehensive movement, was again a new area – the economics of education, until now a relatively untilled field. Here the impetus sprang from the so-called human capital theory, which saw economic growth as, in part at least, a function of investment in education. Such views led naturally to support for the expansion of education right across the board, and, linking with sociological theories concerning 'wastage', pointed also to support for comprehensive education as a means of maximising economic outcomes. The 1960s saw the publication of a large number of books and articles which successfully established this field of analysis both as a branch of economics itself, and as a specific area of applied study. The leading exponent here in the 1960s was John (later Lord) Vaizey, an extremely prolific writer and analyst, who fully supported the swing to comprehensive education.[56] Another, Maurice (later Lord) Peston, now also began to make an impact in this field.[57]

It was these, apart from educationists and politicians, who by the mid-1960s were making the running in the theoretical debate or argument, which is, of course, unceasing. Those presenting an elitist view, favouring the selective structures of the past, were, as it were, shouldered aside, their standpoint rejected as irrelevant to the needs of the times and obsolete in their thrust. Indeed in the mid-1960s, so complete was the hegemony of those supporting the transition to comprehensive education, that there was little engagement or debate between the two sides. The opposition was, of course, to break out in a frustrated rage with the publication of a first Black Paper, in 1969, though this, in fact, was motivated by the student upsurge of 1968 rather than by developments within secondary schools.[58] The Black Paperites were, however, very soon to concentrate their fire precisely on comprehensive education (see Chapter 8, pp. 396-401).

Apart from – or perhaps related to – these movements of opinion and popular support, were actual developments within comprehensive schools themselves. At this period those who wished to teach in them – particularly the new, purpose-built schools which recruited a new staff – were, perhaps, of a rather special and unusual breed. 'At 29 I was one of the older staff,' writes a teacher then at Abbey Wood in London, a new school (in 1961):

> Most of the staff were straight out of college or university and most were committed to comprehensive education. The intellectual level was very high, not perhaps in terms of class of degree, but in terms of intellectual curiosity ... it was all a very exciting period – there was certainly something about Abbey Wood which we all felt and which engraved itself on our consciences.'[59]

This enthusiasm and commitment among the teachers of the early comprehensives must account partly for their success.

Another factor which advanced the thrust to comprehensive education at this stage was mounting evidence of their effectiveness in terms of the traditional criterion of examination successes. Early surveys carried out by Robin Pedley indicated that comprehensive schools which were (i) genuinely comprehensive (i.e. not creamed) and (ii) had been in existence long enough to have provided all the secondary education for their students, achieved better results than schools within the divided system. Some comprehensive school results, now becoming known, were, indeed quite remarkable, e.g. the Thomas Bennett school at Crawley. The fear that reorganisation would lead to a decline in standards already appeared illusory.[60]

Finally, the 1960s was a period of expanding school population. Between 1960 and 1970 secondary school numbers rose by over 300,000, though the biggest expansion, 700,000, now hit the primary schools (see Appendix Table 2a p.576). Education generally was necessarily an expanding industry, and the comprehensive movement gained from this. New buildings were required embodying new conceptions of the nature and purpose of education. Purpose-built comprehensive schools of varying types sprang into being: middle schools (nine to thirteen) high schools (eleven to sixteen) upper schools and all-through comprehensives. The leash was taken off the DES's architects' unit. Since 1958 these had been confined to designing (and building) only grammar schools (in the secondary field). In 1964 this key unit designed its first comprehensive school. The character of these new, sometimes very unusual buildings often caught the public imagination.[61]

Winning the comprehensive battles. Nevertheless a vociferous minority remained unreconciled to the change, and continued to fight the battle for the grammar schools and oppose reorganisation. These struggles took place both locally and to some extent on the national stage – in particular by a substantial minority at Conservative Party conferences in the late 1960s.

In the autumn of 1965 a few months after the issue of 10/65, an attempt was made to give cohesion to local protests by the formation of the National Education Association. This was the outcome of a private meeting in Middlesex attended by some 60 representatives from parents' protest committees and old boys' associations as well as headmasters and school governors. The aim was to pilot local opposition and if necessary take legal action against local authorities. Up to this time, reported the *Times Educational Supplement*, 'the fiercest outcry' against the transition had come from Bristol, Luton and northern cities such as Manchester, Liverpool and Sheffield. The moving spirit, however, was an industrial consultant in London, chairman of the Old Hamptonians

Grammar Schools Committee.[62] But in the nature of the case, support tended to drop away once the immediate traumas of local reorganisation were survived. The NEA made no effective impact on the national scene.

Early in 1966 a number of authorities, mainly Conservative-controlled, made the headlines with decisions that appeared to defy the Circular's 'request'. 'Surrey on brink of education revolt', reported the *Guardian* in January 1966, following the next day with 'Worcester to keep 11+'. 'Bournemouth Holds Out' reported the *Times Educational Supplement* in December 1965. 'More may reject comprehensives ... other authorities are expected soon to join Surrey and Bournemouth in opposing government plans to introduce comprehensive education on nation-wide scale' (*Sunday Times*).[63] 'Croydon Joins the Rebels', headlined the *Teacher* later that month, 'More Authorities Reject All-out Comprehensives'. This was, of course, just the moment when decisions had to be made, and too much should not be made of this scurry of opposition. By this time only some half-dozen education authorities were in open revolt against the Circular – of a total of 163. Nevertheless these moves indicated that there was not, as yet, the national consensus Michael Stewart had hoped for two years earlier.

In a sense, the real crunch came a year later – in the spring of 1967. The initial surge of support for Labour, epitomised in the 1966 General Election result, was on the wane, and the more typical pattern of opposite central-local electoral results reasserted itself. Labour lost heavily in the municipal elections, the Tories gaining a landslide victory. Cities like Manchester and Liverpool changed hands while the Tories won control of the Greater London Council – 'the really shattering result' was the Inner London Education Authority (ILEA). 'Winning these exceeded the wildest Conservative hopes.'[64] If there was a real, popular movement in support of the divided system, now was the time for it to exert its power.

But, as the Comprehensive Schools Committee commented, these election results could hardly be interpreted as a hostile verdict on comprehensive reorganisation. 'In fact there is no evidence', they concluded, 'that this issue contributed to the anti-government swing: rather the reverse.' In London the Conservatives 'had deliberately played down the issue because their own poll provided powerful evidence of the popularity of the comprehensive idea'. Indeed Richmond, where the Conservative council had been making a particularly strong stand against comprehensives, 'had the lowest swing of all the London boroughs'.[65]

At Manchester, where the struggle had been particularly sharp, the new Conservative council decided immediately that they would not stop comprehensive reorganisation, due to start that September. 'The plan was approved by Whitehall last Autumn,' said Kathleen Ollerenshaw, now chairwoman of the Education Committee. 'Appointments have been made, parents have made their choice, and letters are now ready for being sent out to parents. We shall have to see how it works,' she added, 'and also see if we ought to reintroduce one or two selective schools.'[66] No such action, however, followed. In Bristol, where the Conservatives also gained control, the new council contented itself with restoring the free places at seven local direct grant grammar schools which Labour had earlier abrogated. There would be no general attack on the city's burgeoning system of comprehensive schools.[67] In London the defenders of the grammar schools were only now reported as beginning to take up 'what looks rather like last-ditch stands' in their opposition, not now to a Labour-controlled ILEA, but 'to the more liberal Conservatives who are now in control'. Christopher Chataway, the new 'leader', no doubt sensitive to opinion poll results, had no intention whatever of reversing the carefully planned development of London's comprehensive schools.[68]

However, as mentioned earlier, the 'last-ditchers' mounting frustration found expression at the Tory Party conference in both 1967 and, more particularly, 1968. Of course this was a particular constituency, concerned with the political battle and not necessarily directly involved as individuals in coping with the very real – and responsible – problems of providing systems of education for local populations. It was to these latter sections of the party that Edward Heath, now leader, offered support in a major policy statement to the Conservative National Advisory Committee on Education in June 1967. In a speech regarded as a vindication of the line Boyle, as official opposition spokesman, had been taking, and as an answer to criticisms from right-wing Conservatives who claimed he had not given a lead, Heath emphasised his position. 'I want to make it clear', he said, 'that we accept the trend of educational opinion against selection at 11-plus. If the transfer from primary to secondary education is now to be made without selection, this is bound to entail some reorganisation of the structure of education.'[69] This change of heart, as we shall see, proved only temporary.

At the Conservative Party conference in October that year, however, what one journal described as 'evidence of uneasiness among the rank and file' at the 'sophisticated' line taken by Boyle and now by Heath surfaced clearly. Tory policy was described as 'ill-defined and ambiguous'; parents wanted to know 'Are we going to fight their battles or not?' Conservatives should take far more notice of parents and 'much less of idealists and pundits'. The conference should make it clear to the shadow Cabinet that the party 'wanted to preserve the grammar schools' while also raising standards in secondary modern schools. The substantial (minority) vote of 816 was registered against the official (innocuous) motion.[70]

A year later, spurred on by a powerful 'save-the-grammar-schools' speech by Angus Maude, Stratford-on-Avon's MP (who received a standing ovation), the conference ensured the addition to another relatively innocuous motion of a strongly worded addendum condemning the government's attempts to force on local education authorities reorganisation schemes 'calculated to destroy established grammar schools and to lower academic standards'. Clear and unequivocal support should be given to authorities which sought 'to resist government blackmail and preserve their grammar schools from senseless destruction'. Local authorities, said Maude, had been 'bullied, bewildered and blackmailed' into believing that they had no alternative but to 'destroy' established grammar schools. Unless the Conservative Party stood up for the grammar schools, Maude claimed, they would lose votes at the next election. In his reply to this fiery debate, Boyle trod a delicate political line, finishing by saying that while he would join willingly in the fight against socialist dogmatism, 'do not ask me to oppose it with an equal and opposite conservative dogmatism'. It was, in the circumstances, a courageous speech, but the debate underlined a division within the Conservative Party which was to find expression in the next decade.[71]

The position at the end of the 1960s. The excitements and calls to battle – so popular at Conservative Party conferences – were far removed from the actual problems local authorities, Tory and Labour, faced in the shire counties and in the large industrial cities. Election oratory of this kind did not, in fact, result in the kind of challenge locally Angus Maude had called for, although it probably slowed things down in certain areas and encouraged recalcitrant authorities to dig their heels in deeper. But in Manchester, for example, the Conservatives were now happily administering the transition; in London, under Chataway, plans for the transformation of more grammar as comprehensive schools, which differed little from Labour's plans, were accepted by Ted Short (now minister).[72] In Leicestershire the county triumphantly completed reorganisation throughout its area precisely in 1969, finally abolishing the 11-plus – the first English county to do so. If, for some, too slowly and hesitantly, the comprehensive band-wagon rolled on. An assessment by David Donnison (who followed Newsom as Chairman of the Public Schools Commission) summed up the situation as he saw it in the summer of 1970:

> Reorganisation is difficult, resources are scarce, and the whole process will take at least 20 years to complete. But nothing can reverse the drive to give young people a more equal start in life, and to enable more and more of them to take their education further. First pioneered by the local education authorities, reorganisation is now supported by steadily growing majorities – particularly among younger parents and particularly in places that have comprehensive schools.[73]

The comprehensive reform, however, received a serious setback in January 1968 when, as part of the package of economy measures decided by the government to meet a sudden financial and economic crisis, the Cabinet decided to postpone the raising of the school leaving age to sixteen for two years – from 1970 to 1972. The proposal was sharply contested in Cabinet where Gordon Walker, though now Secretary of State for Education and Science, gave his full support to Roy Jenkins who, as Chancellor, had proposed the measure (his arguments 'were quite disgraceful' according to Tony Benn, who had just joined the Cabinet).[74] The argument in Cabinet was won by one vote. The immediate negative effect of this decision was the substantial delay it caused in the provision of building which could have assisted reorganisation. The equivalent delay in the provision of a full five-year course for all in comprehensive (and other) secondary schools also blunted perspectives at that time. For some, however, especially those at the grass roots, this decision strengthened determination to press ahead and ensure success for the transition.

This expressed itself with considerable force at the Labour Party conference in the autumn of 1968. Here, dissatisfaction with the rate of progress was reflected in a number of resolutions from constituency parties as well as in a statement of the national executive which emphasised the 'educational divisions and privileges' that still abounded, affirming that the comprehensive system now being established 'is far from full achievement'. It would require a strong impetus 'to prevent it ossifying into the still selective bilateral system'. One of the things we really must do, said George Brown, to loud applause, 'is to make the comprehensive educational system really valid and really universal'. As a result of the 1968 municipal elections, Labour majorities now existed in only eighteen local authorities even if, as we have seen, this was not resulting in an actual reversal of the swing.[75] The concern of delegates for more rapid and decisive action, however, expressed itself in the proposal from local constituency parties for the introduction of a new Education Act making the provision of non-selective secondary education a statutory duty.[76] It was against this kind of measure that Maude was arguing at the Conservative Party conference.

In fact the government now, if belatedly, began to plan such a measure – in so doing responding to local and party pressures. But before we deal with this it will be as well to take stock. Just what had been actually achieved, on the ground, since the issue of Circular 10/65?

Table 6.1 gives the official (DES) figures for this period.[77] This indicates that the total number of 'comprehensive' schools of all types had increased from 262 in 1965 to 748 in 1968 and was to increase further to over 1,100 in 1970. The proportion of the secondary school population in these schools reached 20 per cent in 1968 and was to top 30 per cent only two years later. (These figures of course apply only to pupils in *maintained schools* – if private, independent or 'public' and direct grant schools are included the proportion of the relevant cohorts in comprehensive schools drops considerably.)

It is not necessary here to make a detailed analysis and breakdown of these figures into different types of school, but generally speaking, something over one third of the comprehensive schools existing in 1970 were eleven/twelve-to-eighteen

Table 6.1
Growth of Comprehensive Schools in England and Wales, 1950-70

Year	1950	1955	1960	1965	1966	1967	1968	1969	1970
Number of Schools	10	16	130	262	387	507	748	960	1,145
Percentage of secondary-school population in comprehensive schools	0.3	0.6	4.7	8.5	11.1	14.4	20.9	26	31

Note: For 1960 to 1968 percentages given by Minister of State for Education and Science, House of Commons, 15 May 1969. Percentages for 1950 and 1955, and numbers of schools from 1950 to 1970, derived from, or given in, DES, *Statistics*, Vol.1, p.viii, 1968, and Vol.1, 1970.

'all-through' schools, about a third were schools feeding a separate sixth form or tertiary college (including eleven/twelve-to-sixteen schools co-existing with eleven-to-eighteen schools and feeding their sixth form students into the latter), and about a quarter were two tier schemes with a break at thirteen or fourteen (as in Leicestershire). 5 per cent were in one or other of the 'selective interim' schemes as at Doncaster.[78]

But how many of these were 'genuinely' comprehensive – that is, recruiting all, or nearly all children living in the locality who attended maintained schools, or, in other words, were not 'creamed' by having to co-exist with local grammar schools? The answer is, very few. Over half of all comprehensive schools (including those in London and Coventry) co-existed in 1968 with local grammar schools; in only 43 per cent of cases were comprehensive schools the only ones available. The latter schools nationally had larger sixth forms and a substantially larger proportion of the top 20 per cent of the ability range, though their exam results were, interestingly, only marginally superior.[79] Such analyses were not offered by the DES which classed all 'reorganised' schools as comprehensive. Ministers also tended to exaggerate success rates in their public statements.

Proponents of reorganisation were far from happy with the situation. Caroline Benn, representing the views of the Comprehensive Schools' Committee, asked, in the late autumn of 1968:

> Is it good enough that only one quarter of secondary school pupils should be in comprehensive schools almost five years after the government was elected with a clear mandate for national reorganisation, almost four years after that policy was implemented by Circular 10/65, and a full quarter of a century after the introduction of comprehensive schools into Britain by local education authorities?'[80]

Further there were doubts whether the momentum now achieved could be maintained, particularly in relation to the educational cuts enforced by the government in that year, including the Cabinet's decision to postpone the raising of the school leaving age until 1972.

Grass-roots pressure on the leadership finally impelled the government to introduce a bill outlawing selection – in theory at least. At the 1968 Labour Party conference Alice Bacon, replying to the debate on education, informed her audience that the government intended to equip themselves with powers to compel laggard authorities to go comprehensive, though not before the Maud Report on local government reform was published.[81] 'Government Prepares to Force Issue on All-in Schools', headlined the *Times*, 'delegates cheered the decision'. In fact, however, the decision had been that a new all embracing Bill would be presented following the Maud commission's report expected soon, which would update the 1944 Act in several respects and pass through parliament in the 1969-70 session – in the government's last year.[82]

However, as things turned out, a legislative measure was prepared dealing only with non-selective education. A situation had by now developed which was clearly unsatisfactory. Although only a handful of authorities were refusing to act, the approach of others appeared deliberately time-wasting and half-hearted. In 'The Case for Legislation: Six Reorganisation Stories', the Comprehensive Schools Committee analysed the fudging and prevarication resulting in long delays and failure to reach decisions in the case of Birmingham, Kent, Brighton, Gloucester, Bolton and Halifax – in all of which five years of discussions had failed to produce acceptable plans – or even any plans at all.[83] Circular 10/65 had, as things turned out, 'only been half successful, and in reorganisation', wrote

Caroline Benn, 'half success is particularly unacceptable'. It was unsatisfactory to have 'some authorities with the bi-partite system and the 11-plus, while others had fully comprehensive systems'. It was even more unsatisfactory 'to expect comprehensive schools to develop and flourish' in areas where grammar school sectors were also being maintained.[84] Hence the recognition of the need for legislation to 'redefine' secondary education and abolish the 11-plus – a decision finally announced late in 1969. Short's (short) Bill was laid before parliament early in 1970. Although this Bill had certain weaknesses, allowing selection in certain fields and giving no final date for the submission of the plans demanded [85] – its general effect would certainly have been to impose the duty of developing non-selective systems on all local authorities in England and Wales. The Bill was given its second reading in the House of Commons early in February 1970. It fell victim, however, to Wilson's decision to call a general election in June 1970, nine months before the government would have run its full course. The omens (in the form of opinion polls) were good. In spite, then, of the Labour government's failure to act more decisively on this issue since gaining power over five years earlier, there seemed every prospect that, soon after the assembly of the next parliament, comprehensive education would become a statutory duty.

Internal Developments within Comprehensive Schools

A sea of tripartism. The relative success of the movement to restructure local 'systems' of secondary education has been outlined in the last section. The force behind this movement, as we have seen, derived from the popular determination to get rid of the 11-plus through the establishment of the single secondary school. But this movement generated a wider objective – that of overcoming the process of selection itself, particularly during the early years of secondary schooling – during the 1960s, between eleven and fifteen. Many of the early supporters of the comprehensive school believed it to be both necessary and possible to create the single unified ('genuinely') comprehensive school which offered all its pupils not only common educational experiences, but access to the main fields of knowledge and skills. This implied that, to the age of fifteen or at least thirteen, the comprehensive school should be undivided in its internal structure and pattern – that the classical system of streaming inherited from the past should be rejected, or greatly modified, in favour of new forms of grouping whereby each class should, as it were, reflect the make up of the whole of the local community – intellectually, socially, and in terms of gender and ethnic origin.[86]

But, given the very gradual transition to comprehensive education, and the demands made on these schools by a socially divided society, the implementation of this objective met with difficulties. Sociologists argued that the schools could not transcend the insistent requirements of the existing occupational structure which acted to force differentiation within comprehensive schools.[87] Others, however, including sociologists with a different approach, argued that, by transforming their internal structure, schools could influence social change and assist in the struggle for a more egalitarian society.[88] Those who approached the issue from the angle of Marxism held that the school system had a certain relative autonomy – or space – which allowed it scope, even within a capitalist society, to establish new forms antagonistic to that society. These, of course, were theoretical analyses – not the less important for that, since conviction in either direction determined action, and therefore outcomes.

The first fully comprehensive schools were established in what can best be described as a sea of tripartism, when the values which underlay this system, derived from the thinking of the 1920s and 1930s, greatly predominated. At Holyhead in Anglesey, which can be identified as the first fully comprehensive school in terms of intake (1949), the school's inner structure was based, as its head, Trevor Lovett, explained in 1956, on the Hadow principle of 'progressive differentiation'. The first year was seen as diagnostic, though even at that stage the children were divided into streams on the basis of seven or eight tests given shortly after entry. Thereafter an elaborate system of differentiation was brought to bear, segregating the more advanced from the average and these from the more backward who left at fifteen. Holyhead school appeared as a beacon to comprehensive supporters in the late 1940s. It showed beyond a doubt that such schools were viable. But it did so at the cost of accepting the ideology of the divided system from which it emerged.[89]

The then hegemonic values embodied in the divided system

ensured that comprehensive schools, as they gradually came into being in the 1950s and early 1960s, were forced to 'prove' their viability through achieving examination results at least as good as those prevailing generally. This was then seen as a condition of success, and, as we have seen, this target was, in general, achieved. Success here, in the circumstances of the time, should not be under-estimated, but it was, of course, achieved at a cost. Concentration on the more academic students at the expense of the majority involved importing within the single secondary school values and practices characteristic of the divided system that comprehensive education was intended to overcome.

These practices were reinforced by the examination system which, as we saw in Chapter 2, can be a potent weapon in terms of social engineering. The comprehensive reform did not carry with it, as an essential aspect, examination reform, and, due to the pragmatic way in which comprehensive schools only gradually became established, it was difficult to see how this could have been done. The General Certificate of Education (GCE), brought in in 1951, was clearly and specifically designed as a grammar school examination – readers will remember the radical steps taken in the late 1940s to ensure that secondary modern pupils should not be permitted even to enter. As comprehensive schools came into being, this remained, until 1965, the only officially accredited examination opening the way to higher education and the professions. The result was that grammar school procedures, in terms of teaching and learning, and overall curricula, were transferred wholesale, and without serious modification, within the comprehensive schools. In a sense, then, the structures of the bipartite system were recreated *within* comprehensive schools.[90]

A consistent struggle was waged, by teachers in comprehensive schools, against this development with the aim of developing more unified structures – this will be referred to shortly; but things moved rapidly in the 1960s and to understand the context of this struggle new developments in examinations which now took place need consideration.

The pressure from secondary modern schools to enter pupils for GCE had risen greatly in the late 1950s – by 1958 over a quarter of such schools entered candidates.[91] The result seems to have been yet another panic over this whole issue. In July

1958 the Secondary Schools Examinations Council (SSEC) appointed a sub-committee to advise and report. In presenting this report the chairman, Robert Beloe, stressed the committee's consciousness of the need for speed. 'As our study has progressed,' he wrote, 'we have been increasingly aware of the urgency as well as the complexity of the problems confronting us. We have, therefore, pressed ahead with all possible speed to present our report.'[92]

The committee, which reported in 1960 to the SSEC, and so to David Eccles, now again Minister of Education, proposed the establishment of a new examination eventually known as the Certificate of Secondary Education (CSE). The committee, of course, reported when the divided system of secondary education, firmly supported as official policy by the government, seemed to those in authority fully entrenched, and *before* the swing to comprehensive schooling of 1962-63 got underway. The committee's report, in fact, reflected official thinking at that particular moment in time in its recommendations. These were, first, that for the top 20 per cent of the total sixteen-year-old age group GCE O level provided an appropriate objective (i.e. those in selective schools), and second, that the new examination proposed should be designed for the next 40 per cent – these were divided into the top 20 per cent who could be expected to pass in four or more subjects and the next 20 per cent who 'might attempt individual subjects'.[93] No examinations were proposed for 'the bottom 40 per cent'.

This new examination, CSE, was brought in in 1962, so that students first sat the examination in 1965. Thus an anomalous situation was created. Just at the point when the drive towards comprehensive education became almost a nationwide consensus, with government support, a new examination was established which, while embodying certain progressive features,[94] imposed a threefold division within comprehensive schools. Students, at least between the ages of thirteen or fourteen and sixteen had to be categorised and taught in three main groupings comprising those aiming at GCE, at CSE, or at nothing (in terms of an examination).

All this can be seen, perhaps with hindsight, as a direct product of the way in which the Labour government acted. The original decision not to legislate for a nation-wide change, but instead to 'request' local authorities to submit 'plans', reinforced by the subsequent failure following the 1966 election, ensured the piecemeal, gradual process of transition that in fact ensued. No overall planning for this change, no serious thinking through of its implications on a national basis ever took place, either now or, as we shall see, later. At no point, for instance, was any official thought, enquiry or study made as to what should comprise an appropriate curriculum for the new comprehensive schools now coming into being.[95] Nor was any attention given officially to determining an appropriate examination. All this was in sharp contrast to the way a like transition was, during these years, being carried through in Sweden, where all these factors were indeed taken into account in a rolling reform that moved consistently from one stage to the next. In practice the new (comprehensive) system was forced to exist alongside the old, and it was the old system that was supported by the superstructure of exams, salary differentials and the like. The net effect of all this was to impose a differentiated structure on comprehensive schools which was precisely what these schools were supposed, and expected, to overcome. This contradiction imposed great difficulties on heads and teachers within these schools, contradictions which sharpened as the movement gathered pace through the 1960s.

Dramatic expression was given to the growing frustration felt by comprehensive heads on this issue in the response of a sample to an enquiry on this and other matters in 1968. Already by this time it had become evident that the comprehensive school required a single examination for all (or most of) its students at sixteen – an objective that would unify the school and its teaching. The sample open-ended enquiry referred to covered many important areas of comprehensive practice, but the question asking whether the head had 'any views about external examinations and their place in the comprehensive school? e.g. whether CSE should replace GCE in some subjects?' revealed 'a strength of feeling beyond that released by any other question'.[96] The strongest views were expressed by the majority of the respondents who stressed the need to replace the two examinations by one; in most cases the new CSE was favoured, very often mode III which allowed schools to develop their own syllabuses and carry through their own assessment, subject to external moderation. A sample of these responses gives a flavour of the feeling on this issue:

The CSE/GCE position is gradually becoming intolerable.

I look forward to the day when CSE (preferably Mode III) will replace GCE 'O' level.

The two O-type examinations is one too many – either GCE O-level should go or CSE should. I would prefer to retain CSE.

GCE O-level and CSE should merge.

CSE for all.

CSE should completely replace GCE at O standard.

CSE should replace O-level in all subjects in the comprehensive school.

Scrap O-level!

They are a menace. The existence of two examinations designed for pupils of different ability is a major stumbling block. O-level and CSE should both be replaced by a new internally assessed, externally moderated exam (based on Mode III CSE method).[97]

By the end of the 60s, however, nothing along these lines had yet been achieved though in fact the Schools Council (see later), which had started work on a common exam system in October 1967, recommended in July 1970 that such an exam should be instituted. However the long saga of resistance and prevarication to this proposal was now only to start – it was to be nearly another *twenty years* before anything was done, as we shall analyse in the two final chapters. The retention of a divisive structure within comprehensive schools was a strongly fought and effective strategy on the part of what is generally referred to as 'the Establishment' (civil service, universities, etc.), but aided, it must be said, by important members of the Labour government, including Secretaries of State for Education in the 1960s and more particularly the 1970s, who retained an elitist approach and were less than enthusiastic supporters of a radical reform. The retention of such divisive practices *within* comprehensive schools formed, as it were, a second, strongly fortified line of defence of existing structures – and so of the status quo.

Comprehensive heads and teachers, however, who wished to realise the full significance of reorganisation, were forced to discover means of fighting back against these externally imposed divisions. This involved strategic manoeuvering within the space provided, in spite of itself, by the new examination structure. One solution, envisaged by some schools, is suggested in the quotations above. This was simply to abolish GCE unilaterally, as it were, within the single school, and to enter pupils for CSE only. Since grade 1 CSE was accepted officially as equivalent to a GCE pass this meant that in theory a student with sufficient grade 1 passes could qualify for the universities and professions. A further possibility was that all, or nearly all students (including many of the 'bottom 40 per cent') could be entered for CSE in certain subjects. So a single exam might be created within the maelstrom and external divisive pressures resisted. The survey, previously mentioned, but this time of *all* existing comprehensive schools in England and Wales in 1968 indicated that as many as 199 out of a total of 661 schools stated that, in certain subjects, *all* pupils hoping to sit for an external exam in these subjects would from 1969 onwards sit the CSE rather than GCE.[98]

Other possibilities involved negotiating similar GCE and CSE syllabuses with complaisant examining boards. This was complex and involved a good deal of shopping around in the case of each individual subject and in some of the most important was impossible of achievement. But schools which wished to develop a common curriculum, or core, for all their pupils, sometimes made heroic efforts, not without success, to 'bend' the system to their objectives.

Streaming. However the really crucial issue, which emerged with great force in the mid-1960s, was that of streaming, an issue which was, of course, closely connected with the nature of the examination at the age of sixteen or later. The concept of the non-streamed comprehensive school, at least between the ages of eleven and fourteen had, as we have seen, been there from the start.[99] The early London 'interim' schools had attempted to reduce fine differentiation of this type, and the LCC's first official publication on inner school organisation, *The Organisation of Comprehensive Secondary Schools* (LCC, 1953) had specifically recommended that, in the less 'academic' subjects, pupils of varying levels and abilities should work together in the same forms. However for the more difficult subjects it was accepted that pupils should be allocated to different streams or sets, pursuing different curricula at different 'levels' – as at Holyhead.

The first task for the more advanced teachers was to propagate both the idea, and the viability, of a *common* curriculum for all pupils in the main school subjects. Historically, of course, quite different approaches were considered appropriate for children in different types of school, elementary and secondary before the 1944 Act, grammar and 'modern' thereafter. The very idea that *all* (normal) children could and should follow a similar curriculum was new and, in a sense, revolutionary. Much thinking went into this and positive experiences gained which indicated the viability of this approach. At this stage – in the mid-late-1950s – the London schools were to the fore in this approach. A series of studies covering history, English, science, mathematics, languages and geography, drawing largely, if not entirely, on London experiences, was published already in 1957.[100]

Following the shift towards common syllabuses in the main subjects, the issue of grouping was now clearly raised in a new way. The mid-1960s was the point at which the revulsion against streaming in primary schools reached it height, as will be analysed in the next chapter – the transition at this point to non-streamed structures in these schools was extremely rapid. It was inevitable that the practice of streaming, prismatic or otherwise, at the ages of eleven, twelve and thirteen now also came under fire – particularly from experienced teachers in comprehensive, as well as in secondary modern and grammar schools. There was growing evidence that the act of streaming itself predetermined a child's development.[101]

In the summer of 1965, the independent educational journal *Forum* published the results of a study of three years experimental work in the lower forms of a Coventry comprehensive school, of which the author D. Thompson was head. This chronicled a three stage, experimentally backed, transition to complete non-streaming (or 'mixed ability' grouping), concluding that this structure was not only viable but educationally necessary – in the sense that only such a structure could allow children's abilities to be revealed. Streaming, Thompson concluded, conditions pupils to a level of response this form of organisation sets for them, and which the authorities and the pupils 'come to believe is a measure of their "innate ability" '. Such, he concluded, '*is the true nature of streaming*'.[102]

Thompson's article, published two months before the issue of Circular 10/65, aroused a great deal of interest among comprehensive school teachers and heads. Here was a well-established, all-through eleven-to-eighteen comprehensive school in an urban area deliberately breaking new ground and pioneering a new approach to comprehensive education. Nor could anyone accuse this school of embracing a sloppy, ill-thought-out progressivism. On the contrary, the head saw himself, in a sense, as a latter day Thomas Arnold. Gowns were worn, discipline stressed, hard work, class teaching and homework were the rule. The breakthrough was specifically related to a new assessment of educability and consequent questioning and transformation of inner school structures.

The high point in the movement towards non-streaming in the comprehensive school came one year later, in June 1966. At an over-subscribed conference on the issue, organised jointly by *Forum* and the Comprehensive Schools Committee, 400 teachers assembled for a thorough discussion of the whole question. Chaired by Raymond King, lately of Wandsworth School, head teachers – Miss E.M. Hoyles of Vauxhall Manor, a London comprehensive, Michael Tucker, head of Settle School, West Riding, and heads of department, Derek Roberts, geography, of the David Lister comprehensive at Hull, Donald Reid, biology, Thomas Bennett School at Crawley, Elizabeth Allsopp, English, at Vauxhall Manor and others – discussed the process of unstreaming as they had experienced it, highlighting its problems and their solutions. The atmosphere generated at this conference, held shortly after Labour's electoral victory in March was exceptionally positive – almost electric. It seemed, at this particular moment in time, that a basic transformation of the whole system of secondary education was a real possibility.[103]

That this response reflected what was becoming a nationwide movement was evident from its immediate follow-up in a number of areas. Well attended full day conferences were held at Nottingham, Gloucestershire, Bedfordshire and Exeter – organised by universities and local authorities; others were planned in Reading, York and elsewhere whilst a number of study groups were set up in London, Leicester and elsewhere.[104] *Forum* continued to focus on the issue and published many articles on the theory and pedagogy of teaching non-streamed classes in succeeding years.[105] Just at this time (1967) David Hargreaves, in *Social Relations in a Secondary School*, published the first ethnographic analysis of the actual impact of streaming on pupils' attitudes, particularly in the alienation of those relegated to low streams. This made a big impact at the time, and was seen as having serious implications for the inner organisation of comprehensive schools.

Surveys carried out in 1968 and 1971 indicate the growing transition to more flexible forms of grouping within comprehensive schools, though also the tenacity with which older forms were retained. The 1968 survey (of all comprehensive schools in Britain previously referred to) showed that 22 per cent of schools used one or other form of mixed ability grouping for first year pupils, while just under 20 per cent used classical (or prismatic) streaming. Three years later, in 1971, schools using mixed ability grouping in the first year had risen to nearly 35 per cent, while those using streaming had dropped to just under 5 per cent. The most popular system was banding – then probably a transitional mode between strict streaming on the one hand, and full non-streaming on the other.[106]

Evidently a conflict was developing in the late 1960s between those forces committed to a full reform – and to opening up the secondary school system in a new way – and the more traditional forces which wished to emphasise the potentialities of the comprehensive school for the introduction of a more refined – or sophisticated – selective process than was possible within the true structures and procedures of the 11-plus. This difference, or conflict, was highlighted in 1969 by the sociologist, Dennis Marsden, in an analysis in which he isolated two opposing concepts of the comprehensive school – the 'egalitarian' and the 'meritocratic'. 'While what may be called the "meritocratic school" seeks primarily to maximise the academic attainments of children from all social backgrounds', he wrote, 'the "egalitarian school" also lay stress on broader educational aims and is intended to become a solvent for inequalities and social tensions in society.' Proclaiming himself an egalitarian in this sense, Marsden warned against the power and influence of the meritocrats. Even if legislation is brought in (as the government was now to attempt), this could not in itself represent 'the achievement of the comprehensive principle in education', he concluded. 'We are just coming to realise how hard the fight will be'.[107]

3 Teachers and the Curriculum

The 1960s are commonly assessed as marking a striking growth in teacher autonomy, especially in relation to the curriculum. Certainly these years saw a rapid and very substantial increase in the size of the teaching profession itself – as also of the colleges of education which, in this decade, were transformed from a set of small, tightly controlled 'total' boarding establishments to large, loosely organised institutions in new, brash buildings pullulating with students who now spent three years on their course – some of them four.

The concept of teacher autonomy is fraught with difficulties; it can be (has been) argued that this may be simply a sophisticated means of exercising control – indirectly rather than directly.[108] However that may be, the received (and official) view of the 1960s was that the curriculum (or what went on in schools) was the specific responsibility of the *teachers* – not of the local authorities (though their role here was unclear) and certainly not of the state – or the central government. This was an essential factor underlying the functioning of the 'partnership', extolled by Lester Smith (see pp.159).

This approach was stressed, for instance, by Crosland shortly after his period of office. 'The only influence', he said, speaking of the secretary of state's impact on the internal organisation of schools and the curriculum, 'is the indirect one that is exercised through HMIs', and through sponsored research projects. 'The nearer one comes to the *professional* content of education, the more indirect the minister's influence is', adding, 'and I'm sure this is right.'[109] Indeed, as late as 1975 the same approach is reiterated as totally self-evident, in the introduction to a study of the Schools Council. Published just a year before James Callaghan's Ruskin speech altered the atmosphere (see pp.447-51) the editors state with ringing confidence that:

It is remarkable how firmly entrenched now is the purely twentieth century dogma that the curriculum is a thing to be planned by teachers and by other educational professionals alone and that the State's first duty in this matter is to maximise teacher autonomy and freedom.[110]

This whole issue arose as a result of yet another initiative by David Eccles – pursuing his aim of 'modernisation'. In the debate in the House of Commons on the Crowther Report in March 1960, Eccles expressed his concern that parliamentary debates on education were normally confined to bricks and mortar, and organisation. It was his intention, he said, 'to try to make the Ministry's voice heard rather more often and positively and no doubt more controversially' on what was being taught in schools and training colleges. In effect he proposed that the central authority should venture into what he cleverly described as 'the secret garden of the curriculum' – a phrase which was to stick.[111]

Not until two years later (divisions within the ministry are said to have delayed progress) was action taken. In February 1962 the formation of a Curriculum Study Group was announced comprising a small group of officials and HMIs (together with Jack Wrigley, a professor of education) with a brief of 'thinking about the educational process' and 'placing before our partners ... a range of possible solutions to future problems'.[112]

It is of historical interest that this announcement at this particular moment in time led to the most almighty row. The 'partnership' system, whether a fiction or not, was now at its height, and both Alexander (for the local authorities) and Ronald Gould (for the NUT – then by far the largest teachers' union) were totally determined to defend their constituents and what they saw as their rights. Together they made a formidable duo. The whole initiative relating to the Curriculum Study Group had developed secretly and there had not even been a pretence at 'consultation'. Gould thoroughly objected to the unilateral intervention of the ministry in an area which had by now been recognised as the teachers' professional concern. Alexander saw in the initiative a bid to alter existing power relations – he threatened, in effect, to break off relations unless an acceptable solution could be found. A representative body, comprising local authorities, teachers and other educational agencies should be established. 'If the minister wanted the co-operation of local authorities and teachers, he must set one up.'[113]

So, after two further years of negotiation and enquiry, the 'Schools Council for the Curriculum and Examinations' was brought into being on 1 October 1964 (the minister responsible being Quintin Hogg). The first chairman was Sir John Maud, permanent secretary of the ministry of education in the 1940s (see Chapter 2) – a prestigious appointment, stressing the importance attached to this post and the new organisation. The scope of its responsibilities, its organisation, finance and structure generally took the form recommended by a committee (the Lockwood Committee) set up by Edward Boyle in May 1963.[114] Financed equally by the ministry and local authorities, it originally took over the personnel of the Curriculum Study Group as its secretariat. Its function was defined as advisory only.

The main point to stress here is that, from the first, teachers' representatives were deliberately accorded a majority on the governing council (of 75), and on all the main committees except finance – this indeed was written into the original constitution.[115] The whole ethos of the Schools Council – as articulated in the Lockwood Report recommendations – overtly stressed the responsibility of individual schools and teachers in evolving their own curriculum. The first and main recommendation, drafted by Derek Morrell, the energetic, idealistic and unusual ministry official originally responsible, stressed this very precisely:

> We reaffirm the importance of the principle that the schools should have the fullest measure of responsibility for their own work, including responsibility for their own curricula and teaching methods, which should be evolved by their own staff to meet the needs of their own pupils. We believe, however, that positive action is needed to uphold this principle.[116]

The principle was reiterated three times in the fourteen pages of the Lockwood Report.

The importance of the Schools Council, it may perhaps be argued, lay more in its acting as a symbol of the ideology of 'teacher control' and even 'autonomy' than in anything it actually did – or than any specific influence it actually had on either the examinations or the curriculum during the 1960s. It appeared to crystallise the historically determined 'partnership' concept of educational administration and control, overtly devolving curriculum and teaching on to where, it was widely accepted, they professionally belonged – the teachers. For a profession which, unlike medicine, law, engineering, was not in any way self-governing, it was a clear and deliberate step aimed at enhancing both the self-image and the public image of the teachers. On the one hand it could be seen (or interpreted) as a step towards the incorporation of teachers into governing processes;[117] on the other as enhancing their scope for autonomous activity. If teachers took the latter direction, the potentiality for conflict with the authorities might be enhanced. In the meantime the Schools Council appeared as a striking victory of the idea of teacher, school and local autonomy as opposed to centralised direction, interference and top-down management.[118]

The Schools Council was born on the wave of the curriculum reform movement which had its inception in the modernising tendencies of the late 1950s – fuelled especially by the Soviet Union's dramatic first Sputnik of 1958. The first, large scale initiative here, in this case to drag science teaching into the mid-twentieth century, was taken by an independently funded body, the Nuffield Foundation. The crucial subjects of chemistry, physics, later biology were first tackled from 1958, later mathematics and modern languages. Two points might be noted here, first, this movement got underway while the divided system had almost complete hegemony – comprehensive education appeared to many no more than a tiny distant cloud the size of a small man's hand. These projects were directed specifically at the 'top 20 per cent' in grammar schools (and those in public schools) – not to the mass of the children. Second, Nuffield pioneered a process of curriculum reform specific to this country. Responsibility was given to teams of teachers picked from the schools (both public and maintained) for their innovative capacity, aided by university (and other) experts or scholars in these fields (e.g. Sir Neville Mott). No evaluation was built in (it was early days for that); what emerged was, ideally, an amalgam of the best of prevailing practice. The outcome was a curriculum 'package' – guidelines, suggested syllabuses, activities, a mass of special designed apparatus (especially for physics and chemistry – for a single school to equip itself for 'O' level Nuffield physics cost up to £3,000 – today, £30,000).

It was this latter approach to curriculum reform that was taken over by the Schools Council from 1964 (although

Nuffield continued to be involved in its own independent activities for several years). But at the start – and indeed for some years – the Schools Council continued to reflect the differentiated approach of Nuffield. One of its early products, *Society and the Young School Leaver* (Working Paper No.11, 1967) produced in preparation for the raising of the school leaving age to sixteen was very sharply criticised (in an article entitled 'Instruction in Obedience') by a philosopher of education as embodying a series of low grade activities for the 'less able' – or mass of working-class children. 'It would not be at all fanciful to see the major aim of the new curriculum as getting the ordinary child to accept his lot in life as inevitable and try to make the best of things,' wrote John White, of the London University Institute of Education.[119] The decision to launch this enquiry was made at the first meeting of the Schools Council, together with a decision to enquire into the pattern of sixth form curricula and examinations (Working Paper No.5, 1966). The tendency (or, in fact, practice) at the early stage was, then, to accept existing ability and structural differentials rather than to challenge them.

A mass of material flooded the schools from the Council from the start. During the first two years, for instance, about twenty documents were issued in three main series, firstly about a dozen Examination Bulletins mainly concerned with the new CSE – a major preoccupation, secondly a series of Working Papers offering suggestions for curriculum development projects and finally a series of Curriculum Bulletins recording developments in curricula and teaching methods. The Nuffield model was used in new subject areas – teams of seconded teachers from all sectors, backed by consultative committees. These drafted new programmes and materials which were tried out in selected schools, modified as a result of feedback from teachers and pupils, and subjected to more extensive trial before publication. This took the form not of textbooks, but of teachers' guides and related materials giving the teachers a range of choice for their lessons.[120]

The idea of curriculum development took off and penetrated the schools and whole local authority areas. GCE A and O level examinations were remodelled in line with the requirements of the Nuffield projects. The movement penetrated the schools particularly through the formulation of the new CSE syllabuses in each of their three modes – using mode III an individual teacher could develop his or her own syllabus legitimised through the regional board. An immense amount of time and energy was spent by teachers on these developments – particularly in the new comprehensive schools now coming into being.

The Schools Council encouraged the setting up of teachers' centres locally on a large scale – accommodation set aside (for the first time) where teachers from different schools could meet to discuss and hammer out new ideas and procedures; several hundred were in existence by 1970, usually with an innovative seconded teacher as warden, sometimes quite well equipped with resources.[121] In 1966 one of the pioneers of this work concluded that 'the future possibilities for this dynamic movement in curriculum development are enormous'. Though the cost was growing – 'the initial figure of £100,000 per annum for the preliminary work could well rise to £1 million per annum'.[122] The movement demanded also a big development of in-service work – where teachers could gain expertise in the application of new curricula.

The extent of this movement – of its actual penetration into the schools – should not, perhaps, be exaggerated. No doubt it affected certain areas more greatly than others – particularly where the local authority was supportive.[123] But that there was a general movement closely affecting the schools there can be no doubt. A certain aura of excitement developed in the late 1960s, particularly in the schools and among students at several universities and colleges. Of this period, Ted Wragg wrote in 1985:

> Yet the haunting memories of the excitement of the 1960s, for me the best decade for curriculum development, only underlines the odiousness of central demand for drab uniformity and lack of adventure in the 1980s.[124]

Such an outcome, at this time, seemed unimaginable.

An important, well funded project, symptomatic of the time, was the 'Resources for Learning' project financed by Nuffield. This focused both on the provision of new-type resources and technology and on the new pedagogy, based on the principle of independent learning. The thinking was basically of an advanced liberal character, emphasising the potential for individualisation at the secondary stage (and in this can be seen as complimentary to the main thrust of the Plowden Report

(1967) on primary education).[125] Several of those closely involved went on to implement the main ethos or recommendations of this project within the schools – Tim McMullen, for instance, was appointed the first principal of Countesthorpe College in Leicestershire, a new upper school (opening in 1970) whose design and internal structure embodied the advanced thinking of this project.[126] Other important projects at this time related to social studies or integrated humanities curricula which also developed new pedagogic means.[127] One project, which became famous (or notorious) was the Humanities Curriculum Project (HCP) directed by Lawrence Stenhouse together with an exceptionally talented team of teachers – fundamentally this also proposed new pedagogic means (the 'neutral chairman') to promote rational thinking and discussion on contemporary political, social and economic issues.[128]

It was often argued, later, that Schools Council curriculum reform projects were only marginally taken up in the schools themselves, though the evidence for this at this period is weak or non-existent.[129] However the Schools Council itself and its projects were one thing, the actual movement – even effervescence – in the schools (both primary and secondary) was another. It was the latter which took off towards the end of the 1960s, and, as we shall see, into the 1970s with considerable momentum and indeed elan, supported and to some extent underwritten, by the Schools Council, whose projects, if belatedly, now began to reflect developments in the schools themselves after the first stuttering and somewhat myopic beginning. By the end of the 1960s, as we have seen, a growing proportion of comprehensive schools were entering all their candidates in specific subjects for CSE – a teacher-controlled examination.[130] The universities, of course, continued to dominate the GCE boards – and therefore both examinations and content; and here the teachers' 'autonomy' remained very much a fiction – though even here there was some movement. But, generally, there was something of an explosion in the schools, related not only to the transition to comprehensive education, but to curriculum reform and change within the schools themselves.[131]

The underlying values and concerns of this early period of the Schools Council were, according to one of its senior officials (Maurice Plaskow), best summarised in an article by

Lawrence Stenhouse setting out what he saw as the necessary conditions for giving reality to the slogan 'secondary education for all'. He wrote in ringing terms:

> We need to establish a new climate of relationships with adolescents which takes account of their responsibility and is not authoritarian. Education must be founded on this co-operation, not on coercion. We must find a way of expressing our common humanity with our pupils, and we must be sensitive to the need to justify the decisions of authority to those affected by them. At the same time we need gradually to develop the capacity for independent study and enquiry with the flexibility of mind which this implies. In short, we need to transform our adolescent pupils into students.[132]

These were the humanist, basically liberal, far-sighted ideas gaining currency as educational objectives, and underlying aspects of the curriculum reform movement at the close of the 1960s. Among the teaching force, scope for involvement and action gave new opportunities to younger teachers to have their say and influence over curricula and teaching – many comprehensive schools brought with them new, more democratic internal forms and structures.[133] Among young teachers and perhaps particularly among students in the late 1960s there was a ferment of ideas and activity – we will examine in Chapter 8 aspects of the student movement or 'revolt' of 1968 to 1970. Many traditional ideas, values and practices were being called into question, and, for those preparing to teach, a considerable enthusiasm as to the possibilities of ensuring social change through educational change was clearly apparent. The enthusiasm and interest in radical solutions among the young was fed by a flood of easily readable, well produced and essentially questioning and stimulating books from, in particular, Penguin Education (of which, incidentally, Edward Boyle was a director). Neil Postman and Charles Weingartner's *Teaching as a Subversive Activity*, John Holt's *How Children Fail* (1969), Freire's *Education and Liberation*, Everett Reimer's *School is Dead* (1971) and several others were added to *The Hornsey Affair* (1969), Theodore Rosjak's *Dissenting Academy* (1969 in Penguin), Edward Thompson's *Warwick University Ltd.*, (1970), Cohn-Bendit and others' *The Student Revolt* (1968), Cockburn and Blackburn's *Student Power* (1969), Kozol's *Death at an Early Age* (1968). A.S. Neill, symbol of liberationist education, now gained a new lease of life, his books selling in huge quantities in the USA, Germany as well as in Britain. The National Union of School Students was now formed. Things were on the move. Many of the young students, having played a part, however minimal, in the student movement of those years, were ready, indeed anxious, for change. It was into this atmosphere that the first Black Paper, of June 1969, exploded like a bomb.

These developments among the students certainly led to an infux of young teachers with radical ideas (sometimes very confused) into the schools, but were, perhaps, peripheral to the schools and teachers as a whole.[134] But any assessment of the 1960s must record this as a period of decisive change in terms of teacher professionalism, control, self-image, and even autonomy. This was a period when governments evidently willingly loosened the rein, earlier tightly held (and later reimposed). Teacher training, for the bulk of the profession, had been lengthened to three and for some (with the BEd) to four years – the long fought for perspective of a graduate profession now seemed realisable. Above all, teachers were now seen as responsible for the curriculum – for what went on in schools. A response to this freedom – and responsibility – was the energy, sheer hard work, and creative thinking that was voluntarily given by thousands of teachers to curriculum reform and pedagogical change. In spite of all the crises and conflicts – over constantly eroding salaries, over reorganisation, over the continuing teacher shortage and the high turn-over rate in the schools, the 1960s can be seen, in a real sense, as the heroic period in English (and Welsh) secondary education. Fundamentally, it was the gains made during this phase which were later to be perceived as a threat – to be brought under control and curbed, whatever the cost.

4 The Public and Direct Grant Schools

The Public Schools

The Labour party's manifesto for the 1964 election promised action on two fronts in education – reorganisation of secondary education in terms of comprehensive schools, and 'integration' of the 'public' (private) schools within the state system. Both objectives were reiterated in the manifesto for the 1966 election, which resulted in a large majority. The government could legitimately claim that it had an obligation to carry both the measures, particularly after its endorsement in 1966 – in terms of British constitutional practice.

In the egalitarian, or radical atmosphere which developed in the early 1960s, the public schools stood out like a sore thumb. They had been fortunate to survive the criticism which found widespread public expression and support during the war years – as we saw in Chapter 1, their survival intact during this period owed a good deal to the sophisticated manipulative politics master-minded by R.A. Butler. Further the direct grant grammar schools, a category which overlapped with the traditional 'public' schools, were also exceptionally fortunate to survive unchanged – even the demand for the abolition of fees in schools which were directly funded by government was successfully resisted. Both types of school, as we have seen, were not in any way threatened by the post-war Labour government – both had survived this period, and, indeed, had been strengthened in terms of resources and financial viability.[135]

The position of the direct grant grammar schools became very clearly anomalous once the government had announced its decision to go comprehensive. How could a government, determined to abolish selection within the maintained system for which it was directly responsible, continue to fund to a very substantial degree, a group of 178 generally highly selective schools, variously scattered up and down the country as a result of historical and geographical (or demographic) circumstances? Clearly the situation had become both contradictory and illogical. This was already recognised in Circular 10/65 which expressed the hope that direct grant schools would enter into discussions (negotiations) with the relevant local authorities with a view to participating in the move to comprehensive education. The possibility of legislation to enforce such moves was no more than hinted at in the Circular – but it was there.

The public schools, however, having historically successfully preserved their 'independence' from the state were a different matter. Their 'integration' with the state system would be likely to be complex and difficult, to stir up powerful forces among the Establishment, and to involve legal and constitutional difficulties – that is, if the term 'integration' meant a radical change whereby the schools would participate fully in the development of local systems of comprehensive education. On this issue, in March 1965, Crosland went on record.

Rejecting the concept that 'integration' could be achieved through the entry of a few pupils from the state system (as had been proposed by the Fleming Committee), he announced: 'We must either have a proper reform or none at all.'[136]

Anthony Crosland had made his own position on the public schools very clear in a widely publicised and incisive article published in *Encounter* (in July 1961), and reprinted (with revisions) in his important personal manifesto *The Conservative Enemy*, subtitled 'A Programme of Radical Reform for the 1960s' (1962). In *The Future of Socialism* (1956) Crosland had argued his 'revisionist' thesis: to achieve a 'more just' (egalitarian) society, which, he claimed, should be the aim of socialists, redistributive taxation changes were necessary and, allied with these, educational reforms which would break down existing social barriers – primarily comprehensive education and the 'democratisation' of entry into the public schools. In *The Conservative Enemy*, Crosland claimed that a Labour government must give high priority to the reform of the public schools – these should be 'assimilated' into the state system.[137]

To 'examine' this whole issue, and make recommendations, recourse was had once again to the time-honoured (and time consuming) method of appointing a commission.[138] This was announced by Crosland in the House of Commons on 22 December 1965 – that is, some five months after the issue of Circular 10/65. Having established the commission, which he knew would take two years to report, Crosland (according to his wife's biography) 'turned his mind back to the reform that could be made now'.[139] In the inner recesses of the Cabinet, however, Crosland, when introducing his proposals for a commission, did so with the words: 'This is a strictly insoluble problem'.[140] It appears that from the first there was the lack of political will which would certainly have been necessary to carry 'a radical reform'. Was this move also to be an essay in political manipulation? And if so, in whose interests?[141]

The terms of reference were clear enough: 'to advise on the best way of integrating the public schools with the state system of education'. However a specific gloss was added which implied the schools' continued existence if in modified form. The commission was asked to pay special attention to creating 'a socially mixed entry', to moving towards 'a progressively wider range of academic achievement', and to ensuring 'the progressive application' of the principle that the public schools 'should be open to boys and girls irrespective of the income of their parents'. These, with hindsight somewhat confused objectives, and the terms of the reference as a whole, were drafted by Crosland.[142] The initial terms did not refer in any way to the direct grant schools.

By handing the problem over to a commission, the government both bought time and publicly divested itself of the immediate responsibility of determining the precise meaning of 'integration' and the methods by which it might be achieved. The chairman appointed, Sir John Newsom, provided, at this time, a prestigious figurehead, but not one noted for radical views on this, or other educational issues.[143] The vice-chairman, D.V. Donnison, Professor of Social Administration at the London School of Economics was, however, a serious social analyst and a strong supporter of comprehensive reorganisation. The bulk of the membership came from the educational establishment, mostly with knowledge, experience and involvement in independent schools.[144] There were two comprehensive heads (W.F. Hill of Myers Grove at Sheffield and H.G. Judge of Banbury School, Oxfordshire),[145] a token industrialist and trade unionist, two university 'liberals', Lord Annan and Bernard Williams, and three others (including the economist, John Vaizey). In terms of the politics of the period, and the evident intention to seek a compromise solution, the group was appropriately chosen. With one or possibly two exceptions, however, it hardly represented the social forces whose criticisms had forced (or led to) its appointment.

Concern had, however, developed among the public schools from the moment of the October election in 1964. It was already clear that action of some kind was on the agenda. At the Headmasters' Conference annual meeting held immediately before the election, the mood was conciliatory. 'We fly the flag of independence', said the Chairman, 'because we believe in the maximum choice for parents and not because we favour any form of class segregation.' It is not of our choosing, he went on, 'if our schools are delaying the disappearance of the kind of social distinctions which are anachronisms in a democratic society'. The socially divisive influence of the public schools, 'about which we have been hearing so much', can be exaggerated.[146] There is probably no institution more effective than a boarding school 'for revealing the irrelevance of class and exorcising it from the system'.[147]

Apparent readiness to co-operate, if only on terms acceptable to the schools, was the keynote at this stage. Before the appointment of the commission, however, as we have seen, Crosland had articulated his own views, especially on the divisive nature of the public schools, forcibly on several occasions and made it clear that he rejected 'the fig leaf school of thought' – 'the idea that the problem is solved and the battle won if the schools admit a derisory minority of children from the state system'. Speaking as a socialist minister, he concluded, 'I am determined that there should be less privilege, less hierarchy, and less aristocracy in our educational system.' He was, and always had been, 'an unrepentant egalitarian'.[148]

By 1966, however, resistance was hardening among the public schools. 'No surrender' headlined a press report of the HMC's autumn conference in that year, 'HMC Bare Their Teeth'; if words mean what they say, runs the report, 'the public schools were determined to surrender neither independence nor selection'.[149] The retiring chairman, head of Rugby, in his opening address, delivered a passionate outburst against the government's comprehensive policy. 'Never before', he said, 'have we found ourselves in the situation in which schools of high academic standard, whether independent, direct grant or maintained, are regarded as socially undesirable because of that very excellence.' No schools would contemplate taking in the whole spectrum of ability.[150] In effect the schools were now daring the government (and so, the commission) to take radical measures, and signifying their united opposition.[151]

The Public Schools Commission's report (a second 'Newsom' report) was published on 22 July 1968. This first report was confined to the independent boarding schools (the main group of traditional 'public' schools). The direct grant grammar schools (several being 'public' day schools) were reserved as the subject of a second report. In October 1967 the commission had been given an additional reference to advise on how these schools 'can participate in the movement towards comprehensive reorganisation' since by this time it had become quite clear that the direct grant schools were not co-operating with local authorities on the lines proposed in 10/65.[152]

The evidence accumulated underlined the class character of the public boarding schools, as already brought out, of course, in researches over several decades. Over 90 per cent of boarding pupils at boys' schools had parents in the professional and managerial classes.[153] In a chapter entitled 'Divisiveness – Boys' Schools', the commission make an acute and wide ranging analysis of the public school phenomenon and of its profound effect in terms of life chances. The public schools, it concluded,

> are not divisive simply because they are exclusive. An exclusive institution becomes divisive when it arbitrarily confers upon its members advantages and powers over the rest of society. The public schools confer such advantages on an arbitrarily selected membership, which already starts with an advantageous position in life. There is no sign that these divisions will disappear if the schools are left alone. They themselves deplore this. It is time we helped them to change a situation which was not of their making.[154]

But how were the schools to be so 'helped'? That, of course, was *the* crucial issue. It will be remembered that Crosland personally held that what was needed was 'a proper reform, or none at all'. A radical solution involved, not 'abolition', but 'assimilation' (a term Crosland also used) into the national system as it was then evolving. How did the commission deal with this issue?

It considered it. It is arguable, it reported, that all independent schools 'should be taken over and run by local education authorities'. This, it said, 'is by no means impossible'. Local authorities 'are well capable of maintaining and running ... any type of schools and to take over the independent schools would ... be no more than a marginal addition to their responsibilities'. A deliberate policy for taking the schools over would have to be carefully worked out, 'but', it insisted 'there is no intrinsic difficulty'. 'A single measure of legislation would enable all acceptable independent schools to be maintained by local education authorities either as county or voluntary schools as from a given date.' While boarding schools might be more complex this could easily be overcome. Local authorities already run many such institutions (e.g. colleges of education and boarding special schools). No constitutional difficulty would arise.[155]   Having set out this solution, and added that 'most of us' would not regard it 'as being in principle wholly wrong, either morally or educationally', the commission proceeded to reject it 'at this stage'. Four reasons are given.

1. Public opinion may not be ready to support this course.
2. The immediate cost to the Exchequer would amount to £60 million a year; this is 'considerable' and might lead to the postponement of other desirable reforms.
3. Local authorities, which gave evidence (with one exception) showed no disposition to take over independent schools.
4. There was no evidence that pupils with boarding needs could fill all the places that would become available.[156]

With this rejection of what might be called the all-out solution, the commission presented its own, pragmatic proposals. In effect these involved that the recruitment of 'at least half' of the total number of boarding pupils should be from the state system. These would be 'assisted' pupils, their fees paid by the state through the proposed Boading Schools Corporation.[157] The method by which this should be carried through is elaborated in some detail; but, in essence, this was the commission's main proposal. The public boarding schools would remain as independent institutions, recruiting half their pupils through the state system. A full chapter is devoted as to how these 'assisted' pupils would be selected (Chapter 12).

On publication, this report was greeted with a cry of horror which unusually, united all right across the political (and educational) spectrum. 'Has any educational report ever been so unanimously damned or derided as the Public Schools Commission's?' asked the *Times Educational Supplement* in an editorial comment. 'The press, right, left and centre, has said it is unworkable and hypocritical. The politicians say it will be shelved.' In a round-up of the press response, the journal first quoted the *Morning Star* (then reflecting Communist Party opinion) – the report is 'only fit for the dustbin'. Most of the dailies used more euphemistic language, but 'all either shouted, reflected or implied that the report was a very bad one – irrelevant, politically hypocritical and self-contradictory'. In an age besieged with reports and commissions, 'none has had such a cynical and concertedly negative response from all shades of journalistic opinion'.[158] The *Daily Telegraph* and *Daily Express* both rubbished the report – things should be left as they are; only the *Sun*, *Times*, *Guardian*, and *Financial Times* could bring themselves to a serious discussion, but all agreed that the proposals should not become law.

Educational organisations were also unanimously opposed. The NUT saw the report as 'disastrous' – to spend millions on the public schools (the assisted places scheme proposed would have cost £12 million a year) when the money was urgently needed to replace sub-standard primary schools would be totally irresponsible. The Comprehensive Schools Committee urged the government to reject the report out of hand. It should focus its energies on accelerating comprehensive reorganisation. The report opposes educational selection, but then demands more of it. The Confederation for the Advancement of State Education (CASE) claimed that the report's main recommendation is 'neither practicable nor desirable'. On the right, the Tory MP Angus Maude characterised the report as 'a very considerable waste of time', while the Headmasters' Conference and the Governing Bodies Association (public schools) found the report disappointing, criticising 'its doctrinaire rigidity', its wooliness of thought and its avoidance of problems. If implemented the proposals would 'destroy excellence'. If the scheme went through, claimed the *Times Educational Supplement* in a main leader, it would 'ruin' the public schools. 'Perhaps that is what some of the members of the Commission wanted' (a very doubtful charge, incidentally). The Commission 'certainly pay scant regard for the fee-paying parents. They would raise their fees, by withdrawing charitable status, and reduce what the fees purchase now by lowering academic standards and changing the schools' character.' 'It is a mad doctrinaire bargain,' the leader concludes, 'which no man in his senses would accept.'[159]

Apparently the report was on the agenda of the Cabinet meeting on 18 July (four days before publication). Of the three diarists present, two mention it. Raced through 'a massive amount of Cabinet business in a short time', wrote Barbara Castle.

> We disposed quickly of the first report of the Royal Commission [*sic*] on the public schools. None of us have a good word for it so we decide that it should be published on 22 July without any government announcement or not at all. It is pretty clear that in the end we shall decide not to proceed with it.

Tony Benn was disappointed:

The Public School Commission report was before us. 'Caroline [his wife, and the leading figure behind the Comprehensive Schools Committee] had done a great deal of work on this and given me a big brief but Harold didn't want to discuss it. It was agreed it should be published without government comment.[160]

Crossman, the third diarist present, makes no mention of the discussion, such as it was. It is apparent that Crosland, originally responsible for the decision to appoint the Commission and chief among Labour ideologists demanding reform through the 1950s and beyond, remained mum (if he was present); he was, of course, now at the Board of Trade, the secretary of state at the DES being Edward Short.

One influential individual, earlier research adviser to Crosland, who rejected the report, was the sociologist A.H. Halsey. In a long analytical article immediately after publication he reached the conclusion that the only possible solution was that rejected by the commission – abolition of the public schools 'by taking them over'. It was, he wrote, 'very doubtful' whether a Labour government 'will accept the integration compromise' nor would he himself. The commissioners, 'themselves produced overwhelming evidence of the grotesquely unjust consequences of the existence of the public schools in their present form'. They had also indicated that 'take-over' by local authorities was 'perfectly possible'. 'I advocate this solution.'[161]

But it was at the Labour Party conference that autumn that indignation at the commission's half-hearted recommendations boiled over in a remarkable display of feeling. The issue of the 'integration' of the public schools had been a matter for debate year after year. In 1967 a resolution urging immediate legislation 'to bring all public, direct grant and other fee-paying schools within the state system in the lifetime of the present government',[162] while widely supported from the floor, was in fact finally just defeated, but only after Alice Bacon, speaking for the executive, had appealed for it to be remitted on the grounds that the commission's report was shortly expected and that conference should reasonably wait. When the local party proposing the resolution refused to remit, the chairman 'very reluctantly' called a vote, resulting in the defeat of the resolution by 3,340,000 to 2,776,000.[163]

Alice Bacon had frankly expressed her own support for the TUC's evidence to the commission (arguing for full assimilation, or local authority takeover). At the 1968 conference, held a few week after publication of the report, a resolution rejecting the commission's findings was moved. 'We in this party totally reject the findings of the Newsom Committee,' claimed the mover (D. Heap). In a powerful speech which clearly gained wide support, the seconder recalled the previous year's debate. 'We were told we should wait, and if we did not like this report then we would know what to do with it. (Applause) The report is here, and we will have none of it.'[164] Several other speakers argued in a similar vein. In her response Alice Bacon presented the issue. The government, she said, 'has made no pronouncement about the Newsom Committee's report. We have said we want to hear public opinion'. But the executive committee 'believes that this conference and this movement is a large and important part of that public opinion (applause) and in accepting this resolution the national executive urges the conference to come out against the Newsom committee's report (loud applause)'. Now it was up to the secretary of state ('now the secretary of state knows what the opinion of this conference is on that').[165]

So there they were, after all that effort – a great conference victory had been won. But, realistically, those within the party who wanted change were now back to square one. The report's proposals were rejected. No others were substituted. It was Crosland's view, with hindsight, that the problem was still there 'and we shall eventually have to come back to it'.[166] But history seldom offers second chances.

The Direct Grant Schools

The problem of the future of the direct grant schools presented a second, possibly more tractable issue for the commission to deal with. As we have seen, a further reference covering these schools was given in October 1967. The, perhaps naîve, expectations expressed in Circular 10/65 as to their co-operative involvement in local schemes of comprehensive reorganisation were not working out in practice – at least as concerns the bulk of the more prestigious schools. In any case, Labour was committed to reconsideration of the whole principle of the direct grant. The contradiction between support for comprehensive reorganisation, and the direct financing by government of a highly selective group of schools had become acute.[167]

To tackle this second reference the commission was reorganised. Professor Donnison now took over the chair from Newsom. Eight of the original commissioners (including Donnison) remained, but eleven newcomers were appointed – some of whom were heads or ex-heads of direct grant schools. Local authority representation was, however, slightly increased, with three new members.

This commission made clear its total support for the movement to comprehensive education. What was of crucial importance for the country, it argued, was to create a new system which would enable more and more children 'to take their education to a point which enables them to go on learning and adapting throughout their lives'. Existing 'gross inequalities' must be overcome. Britain allows 'larger proportions of her young people to drop out of school at the ages of fifteen and sixteen than her neighbours and major competitors', and is 'already severely handicapped by this waste of talent'. An educational system 'which enables a minority of the most fortunate children to take their education a long way, while turning the rest out into the labour market as soon as it is socially tolerable ... is as obsolete as the industrial era from which it originated'. There is no time to be lost, concluded the commission, 'in creating the new system we need'.[168]

The commission's proposals and analysis were tightly argued, and based on a mass of research data published in a second volume. It was found, for instance, that 85 per cent of boarding pupils (both boys and girls) had fathers whose occupations were classified as 'professional and managerial (social classes I and II). For day-school pupils the figure fell to 58 per cent, but those with semi-skilled and unskilled fathers (social classes IV & V) comprised only 8 per cent (and even less in the case of boarding pupils – 1.3 per cent).[169] These figures underlined the social role played by the schools, and in particular put into question the very frequent assertions by supporters that their 'social admixture' is 'normally far greater than that found in other schools'. The 'duke and dustman' syndrome had been widely used in the schools' defence.[170]

The commission reached three main conclusions. First, that 'Day schools which received grants from central or local authorities or educate children whose fees are paid by these authorities must participate in the movement towards comprehensive reorganisation in some way that accords with local needs and plans.' Second, that arrangements for participation must be worked out between the schools and the local authorities 'on terms approved by the Secretary of State', and third, that fees should be abolished in day schools 'which depend mainly on central or local government for their support'.[171]

There was a difference of view as to the financial basis of integration – should the schools then be funded locally or nationally? Seven members recommended 'full grant status' (scheme A) – that is, direct national funding, eight proposed 'locally maintained' status (scheme B) – full local funding. The latter scheme clearly more directly met the needs – and spirit – of comprehensive reorganisation.[172] Both the chair and vice chair (Donnison and Annan) and two others held that either scheme was acceptable in principle.

The commission's report was published on 24 March 1970. As might be expected, press reaction was various. The *Times* dismissed the report as a 'candidate for limbo' and was critical of the ultimatum implying that direct grant schools 'must be gobbled up or hop off to the sanctuary of independence'.[173] The *Guardian*, on the other hand, gave the report an ecstatic welcome. 'Fresh and incisive', it was 'one of the best, most practical educational documents for years'. Donnison's team had 'diagnosed a real and urgent problem', the 'impossibility of fruitful coexistence between a state system of comprehensive schools and a rash of state-subsidised, rigorously selective direct grant schools'. These 177 'maverick schools', the *Guardian* concluded, 'must get into the central system or get out entirely, opting for the perils of total independence'.[174]

Just before this report was published, Edward Short, now Secretary of State, had introduced his 'short' Bill into parliament making planning for comprehensive reorganisation a statutory requirement. Now in late March the government welcomed the report, in contradistinction to its response to the public school report, and announced its decision to act on its recommendations. This, as of course was to be expected, was sharply attacked by Margaret Thatcher, now shadow minister for education; the direct grant schools, she urged, should 'hang on' until the Conservatives were returned at the next election. They would then set aside the commission's findings, seek to extend the direct grant system and possibly even re-open the direct grant list.[175]

What sort of a summary can be made of the developments in secondary education in the 1960s? These, in a sense, were contradictory. That there was a strong, popular surge towards comprehensive education is undoubted. And this was to continue. The form in which it was introduced, or, perhaps, facilitated by the Labour government ensured a relatively slow transition marked by innumerable local battles, by set-backs and advances. The opportunity to bring about a decisive transformation of the system was in fact lost. Among powerful members of the government a basic lack of will on this issue was clearly discernible (in 1964 Harold Wilson had himself announced that grammar schools would be abolished 'over my dead body'). Once again government policy, while in this case overtly giving effect to conference decisions, in practice failed to carry through the full reform proposed, promised and expected. The piecemeal nature of the progress achieved by 1970 ensured that the full value and implications of the change, as perceived by its progenitors, could not be realised.

Nevertheless there was progress – based often on local support and conviction, with a strong commitment by many teachers and authorities determined to ensure that the maximum gains possible were achieved, while popular pressure was now insisting on more decisive action in the form of legislation. In a sense, then, in this area, the end of the 1960s presaged a further break-out, this time involving a fuller comprehensive provision for the crucial sixteen to nineteen age group in the form, perhaps, of tertiary colleges now coming into being.

The struggle to unify the inner structure of comprehensive schools was also now coming to a head, with the Schools Council's proposal for a single examination for all at sixteen. At the same time the government's acceptance of the Donnison report, involving the integration of the direct grant schools into local systems and the abolition of the direct grant itself, was on the agenda. In spite of the public schools fiasco (and its importance should not be under-estimated), things were on the move.

But it was precisely at this moment that certain extraneous happenings began to dominate the educational scene – the student revolt (of 1968-70) and the specific response it elicited, the Black Papers. These form the subject matter of Chapter 8, concerned with the close of the 1960s.

Notes and References

1. 'The only possible means of preserving a bipartite system would have been the encouragement of GCE courses in all secondary modern schools *from the first*,' (emphasis in the original), Edward Boyle, 'The Politics of Secondary Schools Reorganisation: Some Reflections', *Journal of Educational Administration and History*, Vol. 4, No. 2, June 1972, p.31.

2. Ibid., p.32. Edward Boyle had been Parliamentary Secretary at the Ministry of Education from January 1957 (when Eccles left) to October 1959.

3. This procedure was adopted to ensure results. The crucial resolution was drafted by Norman Morris. In 1953 it had been Norman Morris who moved the key resolution on comprehensive education at the Labour Party Conference. A leading member of the National Association of Labour Teachers, Morris was the son-in-law of a Manchester Labour stalwart, Alderman Wright Robinson. For the resolution, see *Forum*, Vol. 6, No. 1, Autumn 1963, p.10. The Manchester Education Committee at that time included Frank Hatton (chairman), Dame Mabel Tylecote, Lady Simon of Wythenshawe, Maurice Pariser, Abraham Moss – a strong team (see *Times Educational Supplement*, 28 May 1965, 'Transition in Manchester', sub-headed 'Grass Roots Democracy').

4. See, for this resolution, 'Comprehensive Education: Reorganisation of City Secondary Schools', Report of Director of Education, City of Liverpool Education Committee, 1964. A leading role in the Liverpool decision at this time was played by John Hamilton (senior), a prominent figure for decades in Liverpool's educational (especially adult educational) activities, and by his son, John Hamilton (junior); also by Mrs Wormald, Stan Thorne and others.

5. Joan Simon, 'The Swing Towards Comprehensive Education: Sheffield and Bradford'. *Forum*, Vol.6, No.3, Summer 1964, pp.92-5.

6. Ibid., p.95.

7. Quoted in Joan Simon, 'The Swing Towards Comprehensive Education, 2. Lancashire'. *Forum*, Vol.7, No.2, Spring, 1965.

8. Boyle, op.cit., p.32.

9. *Sunday Times*, 8 November 1964. The survey listed all local authorities summarising the position in each (in England). The paper featured, on the same page as the survey, a photograph of the Bristol protest march on Whitehall (of 50 parents). The secretary of the newly formed Bristol Secondary Education Defence Association (Mr J.A. Scammell) is quoted as saying, 'The system of one child, one place, one school, is a rotten system, thought up by rotters'.

10. See his comments on the situation in Maurice Kogan, *The Politics of Education*, Harmondsworth 1971, pp.77-9 and 115-7.

11. Ibid., p.117.

12. Boyle, op.cit., p.34.

13. Kogan, op.cit., p.78.

14. *Labour Party Conference Report* 1963, pp.153ff.

15. This phraseology already sounded antique. The Central Advisory Council (England) was given its reference by David Eccles in March 1961 – as part of his efforts to legitimise secondary modern schools. Its report made little impact and was soon to be overtaken by events.

16. Labour gained 44.1 per cent of the votes to the Conservatives' 43.4 per cent. 317 Labour MPs were returned to 304 Conservatives and 9 Liberals.

17. An MP since 1945, by profession an adult educationist, Michael Stewart wrote of his brief period as Education Secretary in his autobiography, *Life and Labour*, London 1980 (Chapter 6, 'Entering the Cabinet').

18. *Times Educational Supplement,* 20 November 1964.

19. *Times*, 28 November 1964, Parliamentary report for Friday, 27 November 1964.

20. *Times*, 28 November 1964; *Manchester Guardian*, 28 November 1964; *Sunday Times*, 29 November 1964.

21. See the leaders in the *Times* and the *Sunday Times*, ibid.

22. *Times Educational Supplement*, 29 January 1965. The government's amendment was carried by 306 to 279, a considerable majority in the circumstances. The amendment firmly supported comprehensive education, adding that 'the time is now ripe for a declaration of national policy'.

23. Stewart, op.cit., p.132. Stewart here rebuts R.H.S. Crossman's interpretation (in his diaries) of Cabinet discussions on this issue, as, in some respects, 'pure invention' (p.133), see Richard Crossman, *The Diaries of a Cabinet Minister*, Vol.1, *Minister of Housing 1964-66*, London 1975, pp.133-5.

24. *Times Educational Supplement*, 12 February 1965.

25. Snow: 'May I reply to the noble Viscount's somewhat personal remarks? It is perfectly simple. It seems to me that if you are living in a fairly prosperous home it is a mistake to educate your child differently from most of the people he knows socially. I should not think it is right to impose whatever ideologies I have upon someone who may not have these ideologies.' This last, somewhat vacuous phrase apart, Snow's legitimisation of his action is a clear and 'perfectly simple' expression of the function of education in a class society, and illustrates the canker at the heart of the educational system in Britain as it actually exists.

26. *Hansard*, House of Lords, 10 February 1965, Vol.263, No.37.

27. *Times*, 8 January 1965. Harry Rée was to play an important part in the move to comprehensive education from this time on – and especially in the development of comprehensive schools as community schools.

28. *Times Educational Supplement*, 30 October 1964.

29. Report of Conference of Incorporated Association of Head Masters, *Times*, 1 January 1965.

30. Speech at Manchester, *Education*, 12 February 1965.

31. *Times Educational Supplement*, 12 March 1965.

32. *Times Educational Supplement*, 26 March 1965. Determination of the formulation of this aspect of Circular 10/65 is discussed in Kogan, op.cit., pp.188-92. Kogan states that much argument went on in the DES as to whether the Circular should 'request' or 'require' local authorities to prepare plans for comprehensive reorganisation. Prentice, now the junior minister responsible for schools, wanted 'require', the department's officials wanted 'request'. Crosland finally decided on 'request', which fitted his judgement of the 'general mood in the local authority world'. Asked by Kogan later if he regretted not taking statutory powers, he answered 'No'. Most authorities were then Labour controlled. Schemes were coming in fast. The DES could not have coped with a faster rate. But the situation changed later, when 'the disastrous electoral results of 1968 and 1969' put the Tories in power 'almost everywhere'. Crosland also told Kogan that the Circular existed in embryo when he was appointed. He redrafted it, and arranged that it be circulated to associations asking for written comments. Long meetings took place with the main bodies concerned. This consultation process 'took months and months'. Kogan also summarises the effect of this consultation exercise on the formulations in the Circular itself – for instance, that the two-tier system would be acceptable as a transitional phase, etc. Circular 10/65 is reprinted in J. Stuart Maclure, *Educational Documents*, 4th edn., London 1979, pp.301-7.

33. *Guardian*, 14 July 1965; *Times Educational Supplement*, 31 December 1965: *Daily Telegraph*, 22 May 1965.

34. The Comprehensive Schools Committee was launched at a press conference on 24 September 1965. Rhodes Boyson, then head of Robert Montefiore School (Stepney), and at that time a strong proponent of comprehensive education, chaired the meeting. Peter Townsend presented the arguments for comprehensive education. Margaret Miles spoke on the role of the new organisation and Brian Simon on the need for research. There was wide press coverage of the launch. The first issue of the organisation's Bulletin reported more than 100 letters a week, with dozens of requests for speakers and other forms of assistance. The information officer was Caroline Benn, whose energy and flair fuelled the whole movement.

35. Though a *selective* sixth form college was accepted at Stoke.

36. *Comprehensive Education*, Bulletin of the CSC, No.1, Autumn 1965. In the next issue of this journal, Norman Morris (Manchester) argued that the Secretary of State had to ensure the viability of reorganisation schemes in terms of availability of the necessary specialist rooms and facilities. 'Simply to rename a building, or a group of buildings 'comprehensive' without ensuring that the new school has the capacity and the facilities to provide comprehensive education is clearly deceptive and unhelpful,' though the department 'must be prepared to accept something less than the ideal'. Both Manchester and Liverpool, he added, suffered from having submitted their schemes 'before the department was ready to say what it might, or might not, accept'. Ibid., No.2, Spring 1966.

37. Caroline Benn, 'Reorganisation: The State of Play', *Comprehenive Education* (CSC Bulletin) No.3, Summer 1966.

38. *Comprehensive Education*, (CSC Bulletin) No.4, Autumn 1966.

39. Although whether this can be regarded as a Conservative authority in the normal sense is, perhaps, open to question. Many councillors sat as independents before local government reorganisation in 1972 fused the shire county with the city of Leicester resulting in overt politicisation.

40. The Birmingham Labour Party leadership was only finally won around 1964; Leicester took longer. Crosland addressed a Labour Party local government conference in 1964 which was important in this process.

41. Kogan, op.cit., p.191.

42. *Teaching in Comprehensive Schools, a second report.* The Incorporated Association of Assistant Masters, Cambridge 1967, pp.vii. 4-5.

43. The National Association of Schoolmasters (NAS) not then amalgamated with the Union of Women Teachers (UWT), was then the second largest union with 38,000 members – male and mostly in secondary modern schools. In the late 60s the NAS supported the move to comprehensive education.

44. The NUT Executive first indicated its support for comprehensive education in evidence submitted to the Plowden committee in 1964.

45. 'Conference, while supporting schemes of reorganisation that increase the educational opportunities afforded to children, affirms that': (i) teachers' career prospects need protection, (ii) consultation with teachers must take place, (iii) extra grants are needed to adapt buildings to new uses. *Teacher*, 30 April 1965.

46. Ibid., 22 April 1966.

47. Ibid., 18 April 1969.

48. Caroline Benn and Brian Simon, *Half Way There*, 2nd edn., Harmondsworth 1972, pp.75-6.

49. The Advisory Centre for education was first established in 1960 as a vehicle for 'consumer' views and centre for parental advice relating to education. Its leading spirit was Michael Young who founded the Consumers' Association and its well-known journal *Which?* – the educational counterpart being entitled *Where?* In 1961 Michael Young published his satire *The Rise of the Meritocracy*; later, with Michael Armstrong, *The Flexible School* and other writings generally supportive of comprehensive education.

50. Rick Rogers, 'CASE for Revival?', *Times Educational Supplement*, 13 January 1980.

51. *Half Way There*, p.80. See also the New Society Research Services national survey, *New Society*, 26 Otober 1967 and Stephen Hatch, 'Parents' attitudes to Comprehensive Schools', University of Essex, 1965.

52. Children previously regarded, and categorised, as 'ineducable' were now shown to be educable. Psychologists and research workers whose studies made this significant breakthrough included Neil O'Connor, Jack Tizard and Brian Kirman. See Neil O'Connor, *Speech and Thought in Severe Subnormality, An Experimental Study*, London 1963; Jack Tizard, *Survey and Experiment in Special Education*, inaugural lecture, Univerity of London Institute of Education, 5 December 1966, London, 1967;

L.J. Hilliard and Brian H. Kirman, *Mental Deficiency*, London 1967, and Brian H. Kirman, *Mental Retardation, Some Recent Developments in the Study of Causes and Social Effects of this Problem*, London 1968.

53. L.S. Vygotski's highly influential *Thought and Language* (a mistranslation, in fact), though written in the early 1930s, was translated and published in the United States (and England) in 1962, making an immediate impact. The creative work of A.R. Luria, A.N. Leontiev and others of the Vygotski school of Soviet psychologists was also now beginning to become available in such publications as Joan Simon (ed. and trans.), *Speech and the Development of Mental Processes in the Child*, London 1959, by A.R. Luria and F. Ia. Yudovich; Brian Simon and Joan Simon (eds.), *Educational Psychology in the USSR*, London 1963, and collections edited by Neil O'Connor and others. The importance of the work of Soviet psychologists at this time is due to the positive view they took as to the potentialities of human development through education, in contradistinction to the outlook of psychometrists in Britain (for instance Cyril Burt and Hans Eysenck) who generally held that genetic determination was absolute.

54. A leading publication, much used by students in the 1960s, was the reader *Education, Economy and Society*, edited by A.H. Halsey, Jean Floud and C. Arnold Anderson, New York 1961. Part III focused on 'The Selection Process in Education'. For the European dimension, *Ability and Educational Opportunity*, ed. A.H. Halsey, OECD 1961.

55. A.H. Halsey began a *New Society* article (17 June 1965) on 'Education and Equality' with the ringing declaration: 'Some people, and I am one, want to use education as an instrument in pursuit of an egalitarian society. We tend to favour comprehensive schools, to be against public schools, and to support the expansion of higher education.'

56. John Vaizey, *The Costs of Education*, London 1958, was an early work in this field, but see also Vaizey's *Education for Tomorrow*, London 1962 (a very popular book), and *Education in the Modern World*, London 1967. Enobled by Harold Wilson, Vaizey moved to the cross benches (from Labour) and then to the Conservative. Like C.P. Snow, he sent his son to Eton.

57. Mark Blaug, Maurice Peston and Adrian Ziderman, *The Utilisation of Educational Manpower in Industry, A Preliminary Report*, Edinburgh 1967; later publications included Maurice Peston and Bernard Corry (eds.), *Essays in Honour of Lord Robbins*, London 1972, and Maurice H. Peston, *Public Goods and the Public Sector*, London 1972.

58. Perhaps the most consistent, and serious, analyst continuing to present the case for elitism (or minority culture) was G.H. Bantock, whose *Education in an Industrial Society*, and *Education and Values: Essays in the Theory of Education* were published in 1963 and 1965 respectively. Bantock later became a contributor to the early Black Papers.

59. Letter to the author from David Rubinstein, head of history at Abbey Wood (ILEA); later university lecturer in social history, Rubinstein spent nine years teaching in London comprehensive schools.

60. Some doubts have recently been cast on the validity of the three surveys conducted by Robin Pedley in the 1960s. The main criticism is whether Pedley's surveys effectively compared like with like (a complex issue). See David Reynolds and Michael Sullivan, *The Comprehensive Experiment, A Comparison of the Selective and Non-selective System of School Organisation*, London 1987, pp.36-8.

61. For instance, in Leicestershire, where Stewart Mason (CEO) was closely concerned with the planning of several new innovative buildings embodying modern pedagogical conceptions, (e.g. the Countesthorpe, Desford, and Wreake Valley Colleges, and several high schools, for instance, Manor High School at Oadby). See his chapter on 'School Building' in Stewart C. Mason (ed.), *In Our Experience*, 1970, which gives a striking analysis of this development. See also, Donald Jones, *Stewart Mason, The Art of Education*, London 1988, Chapter 8, 'Building for the Future', and

Malcolm Seaborne and Roy Lowe, *The English School, its Architecture and Organisation*, Vol. II, *1870-1970*, London 1977, pp.186ff (for Leicestershire, pp.208-9).
62. *Times Educational Supplement*, 29 October 1965.
63. *Guardian*, 4 and 5 January 1966; *Times Educational Supplement*, 10 December 1965; *Sunday Times*, 8 January 1966.
64. *Education*, 21 April 1967.
65. *Comprehensive Education* (CSC), No.6, September 1967.
66. *Times Educational Supplement*, 19 May 1967.
67. Ibid., The Conservatives had promised to retain the remaining maintained grammar schools.
68. *Teacher*, 19 May 1967.
69. *Sunday Times*, 18 June 1967. The paper headlined its report 'Tories Must Accept Change in Grammar Schools – Heath'.
70. *Education*. 27 October 1967. To press matters to a vote at a Tory party conference is very rare. This was the first such vote since Harold Macmillan's 300,000 houses issue in 1951. Ibid.
71. *Times*, 10 October 1968.
72. For the ILEA, see Anne Corbett, 'Education, How Balanced?', *New Society*, 25 July 1968. Edward Short (later Lord Glenamara) was appointed Secretary of State on 6 April 1968, succeeding Patrick Gordon Walker, who had taken Anthony Crosland's place on the latter's move to the Board of Trade late in August 1967.
73. David Donnison, 'A Comprehensive Role for the Independent Schools', *Times*, 23 July 1970.
74. Tony Benn, *Office Without Power, Diaries 1968-72*, London 1988, pp.6-7. Other versions of this Cabinet discussion are given by R.H.S. Crossman, op.cit., Vol 2, London 1976, pp.636-67, and Barbara Castle, *The Castle Diaries, 1964-70*, London 1984, pp.348-50.
75. Anne Corbett, *New Society*, 11 July 1968.
76. *Teacher*, 4 October 1968.
77. DES criteria for the definition of comprehensive schools have been arbitrary and varied over time. For a discussion of this, Benn and Simon, *Half Way There* (2nd edn., 1972), pp.45, 459-60.
78. See *Half Way There* (2nd edn., 1972), Table 5.3, p.115. This book sums up the whole movement to comprehensive education to 1972. Each of these types of comprehensive school is discussed in detail in separate chapters. See also Table 6.2, p.119, 'Types of British Comprehensive Schools of Various Age Ranges', and 6.3, 'Types of Comprehensive Schools, 1968-72, England and Wales', p.125.
79. See *Half Way There*, Table 19.3, p.431. Chapter 19 analyses the problems of co-existence in some detail. The National Foundation of Educational Research's survey and report independently confirmed this analysis, see T.G. Monks (ed.), *Comprehensive Education in England and Wales*, October 1968. The *Guardian* commented on this conclusion (NFER), 'If a local education authority believes sincerely in comprehensive education it cannot logically maintain grammar schools as well.' 22 October 1968.
80. Caroline Benn, *Comprehensive Reorganisation Survey, 68-69*, (CSC) p.4.
81. *Labour Party Conference Report*, 1968, pp.239-40.
82. The *Guardian*, 16 October 1968. These plans, however, were modified. According to Tony Benn, Ted Short proposed in Cabinet in May 1969 that a major Bill should be presented in the next Parliament 'which would plan the education system for the next twenty-five years', to be preceded by a White Paper. In the meantime a Bill 'to compel local education authorities to submit comprehensive school plans' would be presented in the next session. Tony Benn, op.cit., p.168 (entry for 9 May 1969).
83. *Comprehensive Education* (CSC), No.13, Autumn 1969.
84. Caroline Benn, 'A New Education Act?', *Forum*, Vol. 11, No.3, Summer 1969.
85. It allowed selection for sixth form units or colleges, and in respect of pupils with ability (or aptitude) for music, dancing, 'or any other art'.
86. See, for instance, the views of H.C. Dent (p.54) and G.C.T.Giles (pp.95-6).

87. For instance, Julienne Ford, *Social Class and the Comprehensive School*, London 1969.

88. For instance, Dennis Marsden in 'Which Comprehensive Principle?', *Comprehensive Education* (CSC, No. 13, Autumn 1969). See also his *Politics, Equality and Comprehensives*, Fabian pamphlet, No.411, 1971.

89. T.Lovett, 'Comprehensive Years – Progressive Differentiation', *Times Educational Supplement*, 27 January 1956.

90. An extreme view was that of Michael Duane, ex-head of Risinghill School in London. In 1968 he wrote that 'the comprehensive school today is, at best, a grammar school combined with four modern schools (at worst, five modern schools) under one roof'. *Times Educational Supplement*, 12 July 1968.

91. *Secondary School Examinations other than the GCE* (the Beloe Report), 1960. Table 3, p.60.

92. Letter from the Chairman of the Committee to the Chairman of the Secondary Schools Examination Council, 4 July 1960, Beloe Report, p.v.

93. *Beloe Report*, pp.47-8. The committee stressed that the new examination 'should be largely in the hands of the teachers serving in the schools which will use them'.

94. Particularly procedures under 'Mode III', which allowed individual schools (or teachers) to design new-type forms of assessment (including coursework) and therefore gave scope for teacher-led curriculum development.

95. This failure contrasts with earlier practice. The 'Hadow' report, *Education of the Adolescent* (1926) discussed appropriate curricula for the proposed 'Senior' schools at some length. The Spens Report, *Secondary Education* (1938) contained several chapters specifically on the curriculum in grammar and technical schools. The Norwood Report, *Curriculum and Examinations in Secondary Schools* (1943) was concerned directly with the curriculum in grammar schools. Following World War Two, however, the focus changed. The Crowther Report, *15 to 18*, (1959) related only to students aged fifteen to eighteen. The Newsom Report, *Half Our Future* (1963) was concerned only with pupils in secondary modern schools. The main remit for the Central Advisory Councils in the 1960s was that given to the Plowden Committee, focussing on primary education. After completing this brief the CAC's never met again, and were abolished in 1986. The enquiry by the NFER, set up by Crosland in 1966, dealt only in a peripheral way with curriculum – in any case this body was not constituted to advise on the matter (see T.G. Monks, *Comprehensive Education in England and Wales*, NFER, 1968 and T.G. Monks (ed.), *Comprehensive Education in Action*, NFER 1970). For a full discussion of curriculum problems in the new comprehensives Clyde Chitty, *Towards a New Education System: a Victory of the New Right?*, London 1989, Chapter 1, 'The Evolution of a Grammarised Curriculum: 1944-1976'.

96. *Half Way There*, p.268.

97. Ibid., pp.268-9.

98. Ibid., p.573. A Table gives the percentage of these 199 schools stating this to be the case for each subject there listed.

99. See note 86.

100. Brian Simon (ed.), *New Trends in English Education*, London 1957. Part IV 'Towards a Common Education' included articles on each of the subjects mentioned in the text – that on a common history syllabus being written by George Rudé, the well-known historian then head of history at Holloway School, London.

101. An important research study by a Medical Research Council Unit, confirming this, published in 1964, was J.W.B. Douglas, *The Home and the School*, London 1964. This was based on data derived from a longitudinal survey of a representative sample of children, focussing on their development. Douglas concluded that 'streaming by ability reinforces the process of social selection ... Children who come from well-kept homes and who are themselves clean, well-clothed and shod, stand a greater chance of being put in the upper streams than their measured ability would seem to justify. Once there they are likely to stay and to improve in performance in succeeding years. This is

in striking contrast to the deterioration noticed in those children of similar measured ability who were placed in the lower streams. In this way the validity of the initial selection appears to be confirmed by the subsequent performance of the children, and an element of rigidity is introduced early into the primary school system'. Ibid., p.118.

102. D. Thompson, 'Towards an Upstreamed Comprehensive School', *Forum*, Vol. 7, No.3, Summer 1965, emphasis in the original. This was The Woodlands School, Coventry. Thompson's research was later written up and extended in 'Organisation in the Comprehensive School: an investigation into the effects on certain educational results of a transition from streamed to unstreamed forms of organisation in a large comprehensive school', unpublished PhD thesis, University of Leicester, 1973.

103. For a report of this conference, see 'Non-Streaming in Comprehensive Schools', by Ray Pinder, *Forum*, Vol.9, No.1, Autumn 1966; see also *Comprehensive Education* (CSC), No.4, Autumn 1966. A full transcript was also made of the proceedings.

104. *Comprehensive Education* (CSC), No.4, Autumn 1966.

105. For instance, Vol. 12, No.3, 'Teaching Unstreamed Classes'; Vol. 13, No.1, 'Mixed Ability Science'; Vol. 18, No.1, 'Mixed Ability Teaching: French, Science, Maths'; Vol. 21, No.3, 'Mixed Ability Teaching and Learning', etc.

106. *Half Way There* (2nd ed.,1972), Table 10.2, p.219.

107. Dennis Marsden, 'Which Comprehensive Principle?', *Comprehensive Education* (CSC), No.13, Autumn 1969. Marsden's article was criticised by Brian Simon and Albert Rowe in the following issue – see *Comprehensive Education*, No.14, Spring 1970; it was also the subject of a main leader in the *Times Educational Supplement*, 5 December 1969, and subsequent discussion by G.H. Bantock and Michael Armstrong. Ibid., 12 December 1969 and 26 December 1969.

108. See Gerald Grace, *Teachers, Ideology and Control*, London 1978, especially pp.97-100; John White, 'The End of the Compulsory Curriculum', in *The Curriculum: the Doris Lee Lectures*, University of London 1975. The critique of teachers as 'autonomous professionals' is central to the argument in the Centre for Contemporary Cultural Studies' *Unpopular Education, Schooling and Social Democracy in England Since 1944*, London 1981. See especially pp.89ff on the 1960s settlement.

109. Kogan, *The Politics of Education*, p.172.

110. Robert Bell and William Prescott (eds.), *The Schools Council: A Second Look*, London 1975, p.2.

111. The account which follows is based on Ronald Manzer, 'The Secret Garden of the Curriculum', in Bell and Prescott, op.cit., pp.9-15, and Arnold Jennings, 'Out of the Secret Garden', in Maurice Plaskow, ed., *Life and Death of the Schools Council*, London 1985, pp.15-39.

112. Jennings, op.cit., p.16. The model was apparently that of the Development Group in the Architects and Building Branch of the Ministry. This group was established in 1948 to pioneer the design and planning of new school buildings. Good descriptions of its work are Stuart Maclure, *Educational Development and School Building: Aspects of Public Policy, 1945-73*, London 1984 and, especially Andrew Saint, *Towards a Social Architecture, the Role of School Building in Post-War England*, London 1987.

113. Quoted in Manzer, op.cit., pp.11-12.

114. At this time Boyle, who frequently stressed his belief in and support for the 'partnership', was minister. In May 1963 he announced that a Schools Council would be established on the lines proposed by Gould and Alexander and set up a committee under Sir John Lockwood to make recommendations. The committee reported in March 1964, *Report of the Working Party on the Schools Curricula and Examinations* (the Lockwood report), HMSO 1964. For a recent assessment of the work of the Schools Council, see Peter Gordon, 'The Schools Council and Curriculum: Developments in Secondary Education' in Roy Lowe (ed.), *The Changing Secondary School*, London 1989.

115. On the Council of 75, 37 represented teachers' organisations, 2 the Headmasters' Conference and preparatory schools. Of these 37, seventeen represented NUT, four

the NAS, the remaining sixteen places being shared between six other teacher organisations. Local authorities had ten places, the DES three, the rest being split among various voluntary organisations and the field of higher education. The TUC and CBI had one place each.

116. Quoted by Jennings, op. cit., p.20.

117. See, for instance, Michael F.D. Young, 'On the politics of educational knowledge: some preliminary considerations with particular reference to the Schools Council', in Bell and Prescott (eds.) op. cit., pp.31-55, and Anne Corbett, 'Teachers and the Schools Council', ibid., pp.96-113.

118. But in fact many of the schools council's staff of about 50 were drawn from the DES and HMI. This, to Professor John F. Kerr, then closely involved, 'suggests a strong link with the Department, but it is contended that the full time staff must be genuinely the servant of the Council'. 'Introducing the Schools Council', *Forum*, Vol. 9, No.1, Autumn 1966.

119. John White, 'Instruction or Obedience?', in Bell and Prescott, op. cit.

120. J.F. Kerr, op. cit.

121. It was, for instance, a condition of participation in the trials of the joint Nuffield/Schools Council primary mathematics and science material that local authorities should provide such centres.

122. Kerr, op. cit., p.13.

123. For instance, Leicestershire, an area the author knows well. Teacher centres established in the county had wardens appointed of the calibre of Margaret Gracie and Emmeline Garnett (the latter later Principal of Wreake Valley – a Leicestershire upper school and community college). For Gracie, see Brian Simon (ed.), *Margaret Gracie, A Teacher for our Time*, Leicester 1983; her work and outlook epitomises the most positive features of the 1960s innovations.

124. *Times Educational Supplement*, 75th anniversary number, 1985.

125. See L.C. Taylor, *Resources for Learning*, Harmondsworth 1971, for an analysis and description by the project's director.

126. See John Watts, *The Countesthorpe Experience*, London 1977. For McMullen's educational outlook, I. McMullen, 'Flexibility for a Comprehensive School', *Forum*, Vol.10, No.2, Spring 1968, and 'Countesthorpe College, Leicestershire', *Forum*, Vol. 14, No.2, Spring 1972.

127. For instance, the 'Integrated Studies Project', based at Keele University. For this and similar Schools Council initiatives, Douglas Holly, *Society, Schools and Humanity*, London 1971, and *Beyond Curriculum*, London 1973.

128. The team was later established at the University of East Anglia as the Centre for Applied Research in Education (CARE), a centre which has been a main focus of teacher and school-based curriculum development work ever since.

129. For problems of dissemination, Jack Wrigley, 'Confessions of a Curriculum Man', in Plaskow, op. cit., pp.46-8. In 1972 the Schools Council set up a working group on dissemination which reported a year later.

130. The regional CSE examination boards, set up after the Beloe Report's recommendations were accepted, played a big part in the development of this examination.

131. And within primary schools – see Chapter 7. For a survey of the structure of the curriculum as it actually existed in comprehensive schools in 1968 see *Half Way There*, Chapters 10 to 12. Chapter 11 deals in some detail with the option system for pupils aged fourteen to sixteen, widely developed at this time.

132. Quoted by Maurice Plaskow, *Life and Death of the Schools Council*, pp.4-5. Stenhouse was writing on the objectives of the Humanities Curriculum Project – (Dialogue 5).

133. There is no space here to deal with this, or other important concomitants to comprehensive reorganisation. For material on new forms of organisation at this time, *Half Way There*, Chapters 14 (internal school organisation – year and house systems) and 15 (guidance, counselling, staff and school organisation).

134. Many, especially in London, were profoundly influenced by M.F.D. Young's *Knowledge and Control*, London 1971, which presented a relativist view of knowledge, legitimising practices which down-graded the value of traditional approaches.

135. See pp.64-5 and 135-9.

136. *Times Educational Supplement*, 1 March 1965. See also Susan Crosland, op. cit., p.142.

137. Crosland's conclusion here is 'We must either have a *radical* reform or none at all.' (my emphasis, B.S.) C.A.R.Crosland, *The Conservative Enemy*, London 1962, Chapter 11, 'The Public Schools and English Education', p.180.

138. The Labour Party's 1964 manifesto had included the undertaking to 'Set up an educational trust' to advise on the best way of integrating the public schools into the state system of education.

139. Susan Crosland, op. cit., p.142. 'There was no way for him to reform the public schools in 1965.' she writes. 'No one knew how it should be done – how to select free places; no detailed scheme had been worked out in opposition.' Hence the appointment of the commission.

140. Barbara Castle, op. cit., p.71.

141. Kogan: 'When you set up the commission did you really think it was going to come up with anything? Or did you regard it as a political move?' Crosland: 'It was a political move in the perfectly proper sense that we were committed to it by our manifesto.' Kogan, *The Politics of Education*, p.196.

142. Ibid., See also p.177 (where Crosland refers to the scepticism of DES officials about this whole initiative), and p.184 (on the 'sustained dialogue' he had with these officials about the terms of reference).

143. The Newsom Report (1963) has already been discussed (p.275). In 1948 Newsom published *The Education of Girls* which presented traditional views on the role of women and their education. (For an acute critique, Carol Dyhouse, 'Towards a "Feminine" Curriculum for English Schoolgirls: The Demands of Ideology 1870-1963', *Women's Studies International Quarterly* 1978, Vol.I.) Newsom was already Deputy Chairman of the Plowden Committee (Central Advisory Council, England) when Crosland appointed him Chair of the Public School Commission. He was, at this time, a kind of educational Pooh Bah.

144. Including T.E.B. Howarth, High Master of St Paul's School; J.C. Dancy, Master of Marlborough College (the latter had recently published a mildly critical book on public schools, *The Public Schools and the Future*, London 1963), and Dame Kitty Anderson, former headmistress of the prestigious North London Collegiate school, a 'public' school for girls.

145. In *A Generation of Schooling*, Oxford 1984, Harry Judge (a friend of both Crosland and Crossman) writes (unrevealingly) of the Commission's work, concluding that 'In the event, nothing was or could be done.' See pp.89-98.

146. The *Teacher*, 2 October 1964. The chairman was Dr Derek Wigram, head of Monckton Combe School, Bath.

147. *Education*, 2 October 1964.

148. Speech at a Labour Party area conference at Lincoln, 6 March 1965, *Times Educational Supplement*, 12 March 1965. Crosland took the opportunity here to set out his whole programme, including comprehensive reorganisation and public school reform.

149. *Times Educational Supplement*, 7 October 1966.

150. Ibid., And see the supportive leader in this issue headed 'Tougher'.

151. Two members of the commission attended this conference, Donnison and Vaizey. Ibid.

152. This additional task was set the commission by Patrick Gordon Walker who had succeeded Crosland as Secretary of State in August 1967.

153. Public School Commission, *First Report*, Vol. I, *Report*, p.56. Full details relating to social origins of pupils are given in Vol.II, *Appendices*, Appendix 6, Table 5, p.101. These indicate that the proportion of boarding pupils from social class IIIA

(non-manual) was 4 per cent, from class IIIB (manual) 1 per cent, and from social class IV (semi and unskilled) less than 1 per cent.

154. Ibid., pp.61-2. The Commission concluded that girls' schools 'are not as divisive as the boys' schools', their pupils being 'few in number', and later not wearing an old school tie, 'literally or metaphorically', ibid., pp.66-7.

155. Ibid., pp.76-77. See Chapter 9, note 89, for steps taken later by a Conservative government intended to frustrate any such measures in the future.

156. Ibid., pp.77-78.

157. Ibid., pp.8-9.

158. *Times Educational Supplement*, 26 July 1968.

159. Ibid., *Times*, 23 July 1968; *Education*, 26 July 1968.

160. Castle, *Diaries, 1964-70*, p.490; Benn, *Diaries, 1968-72*, p.91. Benn continues, 'It was a terrible report suggesting that 50 per cent of public schools should be opened to ordinary boys, but that would in fact limit intake to those of reasonably high ability – a ghastly document.'

161. A.H. Halsey, 'The Public Schools Debacle', *New Society*, 25 July 1968. Halsey claimed later that Crosland had opted for a Commission 'against my passionate advice'; letter to the author, 1990.

162. And 'to compel all educational authorities to reorganise secondary education on comprehensive lines'.

163. *Labour Party Conference Report*, 1967, pp.136-7.

164. Ibid., 1968, p.234.

165. Ibid., p.240.

166. Kogan, op. cit., p.197. Crosland was no longer Secretary of State for Education when the commission reported.

167. Direct grant schools fell generally into two main categories. Most were highly selective, but there was a group of Roman Catholic schools which served church members in local communities.

168. Public Schools Commission, Second Report, Vol.I. *Report on Independent Day Schools and Direct Grant Grammar Schools*, HMSO 1970, p.31.

169. Second Report, Vol. II, Table 22, p.200. 'Other non-manual' (Class IIIA) were 21.3 per cent. It should be remembered that these are *average* figures. If the Roman Catholic schools had been excluded the percentages from social classes IV and V (8 per cent and 1.3 per cent) would have declined substantially.

170. For instance a pamphlet entitled *The Direct Grant School* (comprising a memorandum prepared by the direct grant committee of the Headmasters' Conference, n.d., 1969-70?) starts with these lines: 'One example does not prove anything, but it is a useful illustration: 'There can be few schools in the western world', writes a direct grant headmaster, 'where the sons of a bishop, an MP and a vice chancellor can mix on terms of complete equality with the sons of a fitter, a cotton operative and an invalid widow on public assistance.'

171. *Second Report*, Vol. I, p.108. A minority held that 'a few of the most highly selective grammar schools ... should be enabled to continue as "super-selective" schools' taking 'the ablest 1 or 2 per cent of pupils'.

172. Scheme A proposal involved the establishment of a 'Schools' Grants Committee' to administer the funds nationally.

173. *Times*, 25 March 1970. Two days earlier the *Times* had published a three-column centre-page article by Peter Mason, High Master of Manchester Grammar School, strongly contesting the likely recommendations. All attempts to reach an 'accommodation', he argued, had 'foundered on the rock of dogma'.

174. *Guardian*, 25 March 1970. It may be worth pointing out that Mark Arnold Forster, officially listed in the Donnison report as 'senior leader writer, the *Guardian*', was one of the newly appointed members of the commission for their second report.

175. Paul Price, 'Comprehensive reorganisation and the direct grant grammar schools', *Aspects of Education* (University of Hull Institute of Education), Vol.35, 1986, pp.34-48.

7 Primary Education in the 1960s

The 1960s was the decade which finally put primary education on the map – as a major, and largely distinct sector of the national system of education. In August 1963 Edward Boyle re-constituted the Central Advisory Councils for England and Wales and gave each of them a new brief – 'to consider primary education in all its aspects, and the transition to secondary education'. Their essentially humanist, liberal, 'progressive' reports were published in January 1967 and January 1968 respectively. Of the two, the 'Plowden' (English) report is perhaps the best known; but the 'Gittins' report for Wales paralleled its ideology and recommendations. Both reports were lengthy and thorough, involving the collection and publication of a mass of research data. Both, as we shall see, were warmly welcomed across the widest spectrum of public opinion on publication.

The establishment of large and prestigious committees to investigate the neglected area of primary education naturally had an effect on the schools, stimulating new thinking and new approaches. Over 100 organisations submitted written 'evidence' to the Plowden committee – that is, formulated their views as to the present and the future; many of these also gave oral evidence. Over 200 individuals, many of them teachers, submitted written evidence and some of these also gave oral evidence. All this reflected and reinforced the ferment of activity now developing within the field of primary education. Just at this time the swing to comprehensive education was getting under way, and with it the gradual liberation of the primary schools from the fetters of the 11-plus. Established procedures, for instance, streaming, now began to be widely questioned. Indeed, so radical were primary developments in the 1960s, as perceived by some, that in 1969 the first Black Paper made these the major charge against the system, identifying 'the revolution in our primary schools' as the cause of the student unrest of 1968–69 – an interpretation that, as we shall see, could hardly stand up to serious analysis.

The focus on primary education was timely. By 1963 this type of school had in fact only a relatively brief history as a 'system' – dating from Hadow 'reorganisation' accepted as official government policy in 1928.[1] By the outbreak of war in 1939, just under half of the existing all-age elementary schools inherited from the past had been reorganised into primary and post-primary (or junior and senior) departments or schools. In the post-war era, as we have seen, 'reorganisation' was given some priority by both Labour and Conservative governments, but until the late 1950s this was a gradual and slow process (see Appendix Table 2a, p.576). Reorganisation, in fact, was only finally completed in 1972 – five years after the Plowden Committee reported. Ironically, it was just at this time that further structural changes began. The 'reorganised' system covered the ages five to eleven, either in two stages (five to seven and seven to eleven) or as a single school (five to eleven). Boyle's 1964 Education Act now ushered in the nine-to-thirteen middle school, while the Plowden Committee itself was to propose transfer at twelve instead of eleven.

1 The Early 1960s

The main features of primary education, as it existed in the early 1950s, have already been briefly described (see pp.151-9). By the early 1960s the stress on streaming and a rigid internal structure had mounted – a direct reflection of the increasingly competitive struggle for grammar, or selective school entry at eleven-plus. There is no doubt that this form of inner school organisation affected the great majority of pupils in primary school at this time. In January 1965, for instance, while approximately one-third of all primary schools had 100 or fewer children on roll, and were, therefore, not large enough to provide parallel classes for most age groups, these schools contained only about 12 per cent of the primary school population.[2] The bulk of the schools, situated in urban and suburban areas, were in fact large enough to allow streaming – many were organised as three or even four stream schools, as originally proposed (by Cyril Burt) in the 1931 Consultative Committee's Report, *The Primary School*.

In January 1961 there were a total of 4,132,542 children in primary schools in England and Wales (of whom 220,198 were in all-age schools). Full-time teachers in primary schools totalled 141,160. In 1970 the number of pupils had risen to 4,919,382 – and of primary teachers to 172,434 – increases of nearly 800,000 and 30,000 respectively.[3] The whole decade, then, saw a continuous and relatively massive expansion across the board. As we saw in Chapter 5, a consistent drive was sustained to increase the supply of teachers – more particularly in the colleges of education. For Anthony Crosland, on taking office, this was a major issue. By the end of the decade, recruitment in the colleges of education reached over 37,000 per annum (in 1969 and 1970) compared with 15,000 in 1960 and 1961.[4] As a result of this expansion, there was a slight decrease during the decade in the pupil-teacher ratio, and in the number of oversize classes, in spite of the continuous growth of pupil numbers. In 1960 nearly 20 per cent of pupils were in such classes – that is, with more than 40 pupils – a total of some 800,000 children. By 1970 this had been reduced to 6.7 per cent. The pupil-teacher ratio over the decade also declined.[5] In the circumstances this was a definite achievement.

Structural Rigidity in the Primary School

The almost complete hegemony of streaming in the early 1960s – in primary schools large enough to adopt this form of organisation – was dramatically, and convincingly demonstrated in an enquiry by an independent investigator, Brian Jackson. Sampling one-third of such schools he found that 96 per cent of those responding to his enquiries streamed their pupils – only 4 per cent did not. Half the children in the sample schools had already been graded before they arrived in the junior school. Almost three-quarters were streamed by the age of seven. 'By the final year' as Jackson put it, streaming was 'almost universal'.[6]

Allocation of children to specific streams was done by the teachers sometimes as a result of subjective judgements, school reports and tests, and sometimes on the basis of 'objective' tests of reading, arithmetic and spelling together with juvenile 'intelligence' tests. Sometimes a combination of some or all of these was used. Generally the most popular methods were 'internal', 'private to the schools concerned'.[7]

An important aspect of Jackson's analysis was his study of the relation between streaming and social class. It had long been suspected that children from middle-class families tended to be allocated to A streams, while those from manual working-class homes were allocated to C or D streams. This is precisely what Jackson found. The pattern was similar in two-stream, three-stream and four-stream schools, but because the latter show the situation most clearly, Jackson's table relating to four-stream schools is reproduced here.[8]

Table 7.1
Eleven-Year-Old Children: Fathers' Occupation in 228 Four-Stream Schools, 1962, Percentages

Father's occupation	'A' Stream	'B' Stream	'C' Stream	'D' Stream	
Professional and managerial	55	17	13	5	100
Clerical	40	32	17	11	100
Skilled manual	34	30	24	12	100
Semi-skilled manual	20	28	31	21	100
Unskilled manual	14	24	30	32	100
Percentage of children in each stream	30	28	25	17	100
Total number of children sampled		7,097			

As Jackson points out, in such a four-stream school 'the professional or manager's child has 95 chances in 100 of not being in the D stream, whereas a third of the labourers' children end up there, even though the numbers in this school class are relatively small'. Indeed the statistical pattern presented in this table shows how consistently the class factor operated in stream placement in terms of each of the occupational categories. The patterns for the two- and three-stream schools are also entirely consistent in this respect, the most striking (in terms of clear differentiation) being the two-stream schools.[9] Jackson, then, corroborated in this enquiry, conducted on systematic lines, not only that the practice of streaming in primary schools was, in the early 1960s almost universal, but also that the practice discriminated in favour of the higher occupational groupings and against the lower. He also culled the views of teachers on the subject, finding that 85 per cent of those responding favoured streaming, 9 per cent were hostile (and 6 per cent held 'mixed views'). Both heads and class teachers of all streams responded. On this sample, he writes, 'support for streaming was overwhelming from every type of teacher and school'.[10]

The strength of feeling on this issue came out very clearly in response to a question asking teachers who favoured streaming how they thought staff and pupils would be affected if the school were *unstreamed*. Nearly 40 per cent said morale would drop ('shattered', 'they would leave school', etc.); over 90 per cent held that standards would drop ('slump!', 'Lower. Bad money drives out good'); those sceptical of streaming were adversely characterised ('earnest reformers with no background who are disposed to accept slogans and emotionalism', 'extremists who pay homage to the idea of equal opportunity', 'ivory towered lecturers in education', 'the cranks of this world', etc.). Generally, Jackson concludes, 'the overwhelming majority ... wanted streaming'; in their view it made teaching 'less arduous' and served the needs of all children. 'Not to stream in a large junior school', wrote a Lincoln headteacher, 'would be the height of professional irresponsibility'.[11]

Jackson's investigation was carried out in 1962–63, the results published in 1964. The Plowden Committee had already been sitting for a year, and it was now beginning to be realised that this was *the* crucial issue that had to be raised in any transformation – or reconstruction – of the primary school. Streaming which, according to Jackson, had spread 'with barely credible rapidity' throughout the country as Hadow reorganisation was completed,[12] was the product of the selective system of secondary education and the pressures of the 11-plus. As criticism mounted of the latter, so it did of the practice of streaming – in spite of the certainties articulated by Jackson's teacher sample. The rate of change in this area proved so rapid as to be almost unbelievable.

The Swing Against Streaming
The build-up of the battle against streaming (and it *was* a battle) was two-pronged: it took place simultaneously in the

realm of theory and of practice. It had one advantage over the fight for comprehensive education – it could be introduced into, and by, the individual school – it comprised an internal, basically educational transformation, not a system-wide structural change. But, as we have seen, it was precisely here that the resistance was likely to be most powerful. There was, however, a countervailing element. In the smaller primary schools up and down the country, and especially in rural areas, teachers were already, and necessarily, teaching unstreamed (or 'mixed ability') groups.

The swing against streaming took off, originally very slowly, from the late 1950s. In 1962, it will be remembered, Brian Jackson found 4 per cent of his sample of schools – schools large enough to stream – were in fact unstreamed. This probably accurately reflects the situation at that time. In the mid-1950s for instance, three such schools in the city of Leicester deliberately abandoned streaming. The head of one of these, George Freeland, who commenced unstreaming as early as 1953, analysed and recorded his experience in a publication of 1957. He believed that, as a result, standards were raised and the school functioned more effectively as a social unit. 'As a result of the experience of the last three years,' he wrote, 'there are no doubts in my mind as to the desirability of non-streaming.'[13]

From this time, non-streaming began to be developed, as a deliberate policy, among a minority of junior schools. In the West Riding, in Hertfordshire and elsewhere, experienced heads deliberately – and carefully – made the transition. 'After four years without streaming,' wrote one such head, who made the transition in 1955, 'I have a happy and enthusiastic staff, all of whom prefer the present organisation; the standard of work has improved, and relations with parents are excellent.' The flexibility of the unstreamed school, he added, is of great help when putting new ideas into practice.[14] This, in fact, was the common experience of the early, non-streamed schools.

On the theoretical level, the case against streaming lay primarily in a growing realisation that the original stream placement, at whatever level, determined children's life chances – often from the age of seven or even earlier. Research now indicated that transfer between streams, contrary to general belief, was minimal (about 2 per cent); the great majority of children in fact remained in their original stream placement.[15] In a major research project published in 1964 (as we saw in Chapter 6, see note 101), Douglas confirmed what had already been suggested – that the act of streaming itself accentuated initial differences between children.[16] An unexpected research finding, confirmed by Jackson's investigation, showed further that summer-born children had substantially greater chances than others of being allocated to A streams – a finding later shown to be effective right through schooling up to the age of eighteen.[17] This was interpreted as being due to the fact that summer-born children had one, or sometimes two, extra terms in the infant school compared to the others. But the major argument against streaming was that it found its ideological justification within the 'classic' theories of mental testing – now coming under fire. The chief psychological proponent of streaming had been Cyril Burt, adviser to the inter-war Consultative Committee which strongly recommended the practice. As we saw in Chapter 4, in *Secondary School Selection* (1957) a working group of leading psychologists had attempted to reconstruct a modified theory, and these themselves directly rejected Burt's approach. The dangers of streaming, they reported, 'are obvious'. Children

> who are relegated to a low stream, to suit their present level of ability, are likely to be taught at a slower pace; whereas brighter streams, often under the better teachers, are encouraged to proceed more rapidly. Thus initial differences become exacerbated, and those duller children who happen to improve later fall too far behind the higher streams in attainments to be able to catch up, and lose the chance to show their true merits.

Junior school streaming, they concluded, should be abandoned.[18]

The link between non-streaming in the junior school and comprehensive secondary education must now be clear. Both movements were founded on a more positive educational premiss (in terms of children's potentialities) than was conceivable within the theory and practice of the divided system. 'The trend in the larger primary schools where numbers are sufficient to allow streaming has been to abolish it,' wrote Leicestershire's Director of Education in 1960, commenting on the impact of comprehensive reorganisation on the primary schools. 'In one of the two areas it is disappearing altogether, and in the other for the most part it only remains in the upper part of the junior school.'[19]

Of the teachers' reactions he wrote:

> Usually teachers in charge of unstreamed classes find it at first an uphill task, but afterwards they get used to it and say that they prefer it. Those who have no experience of this way of organising the work are apt to state categorically that it must retard the pace of the brightest children. Those who practice it assert that it advances them more quickly.

The increased flexibility which has resulted, Leicestershire's Director claimed, has led to experimental work in the teaching of science, the introduction of a second language, greater concern with creative writing, the arts, music and drama, while 'the most striking change of all is taking place in the teaching of mathematics'. 'The ozone of enthusiasm and the tang of enquiry are in the air,' concludes the author, 'and one can't help breathing them in.'[20]

The issue of streaming – or non-streaming – was by no means a purely organisational question; on the contrary, it raised fundamental questions relating to pedagogy – to the actual and central teaching-learning process. This was by now becoming apparent. Of the three schools in the city of Leicester which adopted non-streaming in the late 1950s, for instance, each developed different approaches, each of which could be related to a different theoretical stance. School A, for instance, overtly rejecting theories derived from mental testing, attempted, largely through class teaching, to bring the whole of the class along together, aiming at specific levels of achievement. School B, where the head was an ex-psychologist, held that each child's activity should be determined by his or her particular intellectual level, and so moved over to a system based on total individualisation. School C, however, held that the nature of the child's interaction with other children, and with the teachers, in problem-solving was the crucial aspect that needed development; here carefully structured group work was developed as a main approach, supported both by some class teaching and individualisation.[21] This whole issue of the pedagogy of the unstreamed class became, as we shall see later, a major issue.

Although by 1962 only a small minority of schools had moved deliberately to unstreaming and the development of new pedagogic means, a movement had in fact by now got under way. In November that year a conference, attended by over 200 teachers, was organised by the independent educational journal *Forum* which had been founded in 1958 specifically to encourage this movement (as well as that to comprehensive secondary education). Chaired by Raymond King the conference was addressed by John Daniels who presented research evidence, not confined to this country, bearing on the question, and by three heads of unstreamed junior schools, all members of the journal's editorial board.[22] This conference took place just a year before the Plowden Committee was appointed.

Connoisseurs of the Ministry of Education's annual reports – admittedly a somewhat esoteric pursuit – may have noticed the extraordinary change that overcame these in 1962 and 1963, when Edward Boyle was appointed minister. These now suddenly reflect a new enthusiasm, almost a new romanticism, especially in the general introduction signed by the minister. Education is undergoing profound changes; things are taking off. Children are healthier, more active, maturing earlier, knowing more of adult life. Education is a 'process'. In junior schools there is more active learning, more experiment in methods of grouping, in oral expression, in the learning of mathematics through participation – here there are new strivings in the classrooms, a new generation of teachers, a healthy stress on the creative contribution of the learner. In particular, the author (Boyle himself?) stresses the 'vigorous discussion' going on on the question of streaming and non-streaming. So important did the minister consider it that a special enquiry into the whole issue by the National Foundation of Educational Research had been commissioned.[23] This was in 1962 – a full year before the reconstitution of the Central Avisory Council and the start of its enquiry into primary education. The NFER were not, however, to complete their research until *after* the Plowden Committee had reported – by which time, as will be shown later, life had moved well beyond their original concerns.

2 *Plowden Gestation: Primary Education in the mid–1960s*

The Central Advisory Councils (England and Wales) were reconstituted (following completion of the Newsom report) and given their (very wide) briefs by Edward Boyle in August 1963. The England Council worked for well over three full years and reported, in an exceptionally weighty tome, to Anthony Crosland, now Secretary of State, in November 1966. Entitled *Children and their Primary Schools*, this was finally published on 10 January 1967.[24]

With Lady Plowden, then virtually unknown as an 'educationist', in the chair, the ubiquitous Sir John Newsom (ex-CEO Hertfordshire) served as her deputy. The team of 25 members included several academics and social analyists – for instance, David Donnison (later of the Public Schools Commission), recently appointed to his chair in Social Administration at the London School of Economics, Harold Rose, to be succeeded by I.C.R. Byatt, both LSE economists, J.M. Tanner, Reader and later Professor of Child Health and Growth at the Institute of Child Health, London University, and – an unusual appointment – Professor A.J. Ayer, Wykeham Professor of Logic at Oxford. A number of teachers were included (four from primary schools), as well as Mollie Brearley, the well known principal of the Froebel Institute at Roehampton, Miss E.M. Parry, an inspector from Bristol with a reputation for a progressive or innovative approach, and two 'consumer' representatives, one from CASE, the other, Michael Young, a sociologist and director of the Institute of Community Studies, chair of the consumer-oriented Advisory Centre for Education (the organisation which had, in fact, encouraged and sponsored Brian Jackson's streaming research) and, of course, author of *The Rise of the Meritocracy*.

A strong team of HMIs and DES officials assisted the council of which the best known was, perhaps, J.E.H. Blackie, the chief HMI for primary education, already known, through his publications, as a strong proponent of progressive methods. The secretary was Maurice Kogan, then a young civil servant, later Professor of Government at Brunel University and author of many books on the politics of education and educational change.

This was, in a sense, a powerful team, deliberately constructed (according to Kogan) to subject 'the hot knowledge' of the practitioner and practical administrator 'to the informed critique of the sceptical philosopher and professional social scientist'.[25] Whether this was actually achieved must be a matter of opinion.

The committee called for evidence and, as we have seen, received a massive response. Members visited primary schools in Denmark, France, Sweden, Poland, the USA and USSR; they also visited many schools in England and Scotland (as the Welsh Committee did in Wales). The committee formed itself into eight separate working parties to study different aspects in depth. Wide-ranging research projects were commissioned, to be published in a second volume. 465 papers on different subjects were received, quite apart from the evidence sent by outside bodies. In every sense the committee now embarked on a serious, thorough study of all aspects of primary education, as they had been asked. This was the first such official study since 1931. As suggested earlier, the activity to which the committee gave rise reflected back into the schools – in a sense, a dialectical process was now under way, gathering pace. We may, however, now leave the Plowden Committee to their deliberations in the bare emporia of the DES's Curzon Street headquarters. What was happening in the field?

Movement in the Schools
Once again it is difficult to recapture the mood and feel of the 1960s. Young teachers were now flooding into the primary schools – the product of the now rapid expansion of the colleges; since 1960 these now had a three-year course. Traditional forms of authority were now widely questioned; individual teacher autonomy grew, teachers being accorded, and taking responsibility for their own classrooms. Heads, less certain of their authority than earlier, were now less concerned with enforcing whole school policies, though there were certainly exceptions here. In the colleges the students tended to be fed with a mix of intelligence test theory (though now less dogmatically than earlier) and the theories of the Swiss philosopher Piaget (not necessarily contradictory, although Piagetian studies focused on *development*). The students, so prepared, as young teachers on completing their courses, now seized their opportunities in the schools to strike out in new directions – or so many thought.

What transpired was what appeared, at least on the surface, as an explosion of curriculum reform, accompanied by an extraordinarily rapid swing towards unstreaming – a system which now had the added advantage of offering the flexibility required for such innovations (as Stewart Mason had pointed out). One measure of the extent of this movement lies in the enormous success of the 'new maths' – the driving force behind which was an HMI, Edith Biggs. *Mathematics in Primary Schools*, a detailed handbook of analysis and suggestions, prepared for the Schools Council and published as Curriculum Bulletin No. 1 in 1965, had sold some 165,000 copies by its third edition in 1969. A teacher of immense energy and skill, Edith Biggs travelled the country, holding workshops, inducting young teachers in the new approaches, peopling teachers' centres with enthusiasts. Her work was seconded by the pioneering studies of Z.P. Dienes, a mathematician at Leicester University who developed quite new approaches to concept learning in mathematics, evolving new apparatus and a new methodology. Supported by far-sighted advisers in Leicestershire, Dienes profoundly influenced the scope and character of mathematics learning not only in the county, but nationally and internationally. These approaches were a far cry from the type of computational drill that had predominated in the primary schools almost since their inception.[26]

The 'new maths' became a central focus in primary-school curriculum reform from the mid-1960s. Building on the pioneering work of Edith Biggs, the Nuffield Foundation financed a major primary curriculum project from September 1964. Fourteen local authorities participated in the pilot projects, teachers' centres were established as a condition of such participation, publications issued and missionaries in the form of project personnel, local advisers and teachers travelled the country spreading the gospel and new approaches – all this reaching a peak of activity around 1968.[27] At about this time, the Nuffield foundation also funded a major primary-school science project, as well as another nationwide project in the teaching of French in the primary school. Although neither of these achieved the successes of the mathematics initiative, such projects added to the excitement of the time, which definitely penetrated the schools. Possibly for the first time in its relatively short history, primary education was now beginning to be seen as perhaps the major stage of importance within the whole educational cycle. Participation in one or other of these projects at that time not only carried with it a certain prestige – it also implied involvement at the edge of knowledge, in terms of a breakthrough in the understanding of children's learning, concept development and intellectual growth generally. The fact that a major government enquiry, known to be sympathetic to such developments, was sitting, only added to the general sense that things were on the move.

The 'new maths' was, of course, only one aspect of curriculum reform – science and French were others. But the move to more flexible, and informal, school and classroom approaches also eased the way, among at least a minority of schools, to a greater stress on more active approaches to learning and especially to more creative approaches than had been either possible or desired in the past. More scope was now given to children's writing – in the form of poetry, drama, art and craft and other forms – than was usual in the past. From the West Riding, Alec Clegg, the Chief Education Officer, published a remarkable collection of primary school achievements in the area of creative writing.[28] There was already, of course, a long-standing tradition of the encouragement of children's creative art in primary schools derived from the work of Marion Richardson and others before the war; this now also took off, accelerated by the very effective teaching of this subject in many colleges of education and art colleges. This was the period, also, when dance and dance drama of a modern, free type, penetrated both primary and secondary schools with very remarkable results – again the outcome of highly skilled professional teachers in the colleges.[29]

Later an attempt will be made to assess how far 'the revolution in the primary schools' (as it came to be called) actually penetrated the mass of the schools in the country – an extremely difficult undertaking, especially given that there were 20,000 of them (in England and Wales). At the time, however, it was the schools which espoused aspects of these new developments on which attention naturally tended to focus – especially when it was developments of this kind which tended to gain official support, both nationally and locally. As was perhaps natural, given the decentralised nature of educational administration that prevailed at this time, the impact of these new developments was felt more fully in some areas rather than others.

The main areas where what may be termed 'the break-out' within primary education was most advanced are generally held to be five – Oxfordshire, the West Riding of Yorkshire, Leicestershire, London and, in the case of nursery schools, Bristol. The first three, it will be noticed, (then) were shire county authorities, the others urban. It is also worth noting that all these authorities had espoused the cause of comprehensive secondary education by the 1960s; London had led the way here, but by the mid-1960s Bristol, Oxfordshire, and the West Riding had made advances while Leicestershire was actually to abolish the 11-plus throughout the county, so achieving full comprehensivisation, before the end of the decade. This was probably one important factor setting the context for the change within primary schools.

In each of these areas, a single individual may perhaps be identified as the focus of the change – arbitrary as the choice may appear. In Leicestershire and the West Riding, the directors of education, Stewart Mason and Alec Clegg; in Oxfordshire, Edith Moorhouse, adviser in charge of the county's primary schools from 1948 to 1964; in Bristol, Miss E.M. Parry, a local inspector (and member of the Plowden Committee); in London it is perhaps more difficult to identify a single individual but, if a choice must be made, it should probably fall on Christian Schiller, who retired as HMI for Primary Education (based in London) in 1955 but then, as Senior Lecturer in Primary Education at the London University Institute of Education, spread his teaching and outlook widely in the surrounding area.[30]

Clegg and Mason were, already in their time, both unusual characters – both wielded very considerable power (then possible for an administrator in a shire county); both were profoundly interested in the *processes* of education itself; both were extremely knowledgeable about all aspects and stages of education; both combined considerable authority with the ability, and deliberate intention, to decentralise decision making; both had a high regard for teachers – both held that the greatest rewards came from deliberately enhancing their autonomy and control (within the accepted county policy). Both had wide interests – in the fields of art, music, sculpture, literature. Both had clearly defined policies, in primary education and across the board; and finally, both successfully gained the full, consistent and unvarying support of their committees for their pioneering initiatives.[31]

Mason and Clegg each paid special attention to primary school developments in their areas, encouraging pioneering activity where they saw it as fruitful. Of the two, Clegg was probably the more visionary – in his deep understanding and faith in the transforming potential of education; though Mason, perhaps, achieved more in many specific developments

– especially in the field of art and music – that he successfully carried through.[32] Both were directors of a special breed – the conditions of the time gave each the scope he needed, and the opportunities to exploit their considerable abilities. Their careers encapsulate the positive features of the period. The particular concatenation of circumstances that brought such men to the fore at this particular time are not likely to be repeated.[33]

In a book published in 1968, two of Leicestershire's teacher leaders of this movement summed up what they saw as specific to the Leicestershire situation.[34] Each school, they say, 'is a self governing community within the larger scheme of education'. This is due to the way the authority extends 'both freedom and responsibility' to the head who in turn extends it to the staff. In return, the authority received 'loyalty, enthusiasm and co-operation' from the teaching staff. The line of thought so generated 'has produced a charged atmosphere where work with children is exciting and alive'. People are receptive 'to the exploration of new ideas' though everyone is encouraged 'to question "why" '. Further the final abolition of the 11-plus had removed the last barrier preventing schools from meeting the developmental needs of their children.

In addition the authority employed a body of 'advisers' who, no longer holding an inspectorial role of any kind, are welcomed into the schools and appreciated 'for the positive and constructive contribution they make'. These organised courses, discussion groups and workshops of all kinds. One such adviser specifically looks after probationary teachers in their first year, organising special courses for them on the educational methods used in the schools. As a result, young teachers 'are more effective and competent earlier in their careers' than in the past. Advisers also participate in the design and planning of new schools, consulting heads and teachers in the process. New schools are well sited and planned to be aesthetically pleasing, presenting 'high artistic standards'.

In the schools, original works of art by well known contemporary artists or sculptors are displayed 'alongside the work produced by the children'. Within the whole personnel of the authority there are high standards of friendly co-operation. Regular meetings take place within each locality of staff from the schools serving different age levels. The director organises meetings with all heads at each level where educational issues are discussed – such discussions are of a free and open character. In Leicestershire, the authors conclude, serving teachers are given every encouragement and financial backing to pursue all types of courses which lead to an improvement in their professional practice. New teachers are attracted to the county 'because of the obvious vitality of the education system'. The authority in particular welcomes teachers with initiative. This, then, 'is part of the background which has helped the swift evolution of educational progress' in Leicestershire's primary schools.

The Leicestershire background has been detailed at some length since this was certainly an important centre of new initiatives. Similar developments took place under Clegg in the West Riding – though this was very different in its geographical and industrial make-up, and also far larger. 'South Yorkshire', wrote Clegg later, 'in some respects is a grim area ... our first aluminium classrooms ... were very soon pitted by the industrial chemicals in the atmosphere, and the soot deposit near the pits is impressive'.[35] It was in primary schools in the pit villages that some of the most outstanding results were achieved in children's writing.[36] The point about Oxfordshire, said Lady Plowden later, referring to visits of her committee, 'as compared to the West Riding or Hertfordshire, was the sense of purpose, the groups of excited young heads all working together' – the result of years of creative activity by Edith Moorhouse.[37] 'People call it a golden age,' the latter said recently. 'It wasn't. There were great pressures. They were golden days because we made them golden days.'[38] In London Christian Schiller appears to have been an inspired teacher, perhaps something of an evangelist at least in his 'spontaneous' (but actually very carefully prepared) addresses. In October 1965 he addressed an HMI primary conference on the topic 'When a boy or girl is creative', closing with these words:

> When I look at our contemporary scene, full as ever of pressing problems, I am filled with wonder: wonder that so much in our teaching should have happened in the short spell of one working man's life and wonder at the possibilities, the powers of each boy and girl waiting to be released. It is a bright prospect.
>
> The light in the late afternoon, with its shadows, and colours of infinite gradation is like the light of sunrise.[39]

These five areas were, perhaps, not typical – they were

probably the most advanced in the country, nor would it be true to say that all the schools in these areas were equally pioneering. But that there was movement in the field, that new ideas and practices were being developed, is certainly true. There was also an effervescence in terms of inner-school organisation – 'family grouping', whereby two or more age groups were brought together,[40] the 'integrated day', which involved a basic restructuring of the curriculum as a whole,[41] a move towards a greater degree of 'open planning', involving the provision of greater space for movement and flexibility generally as opposed to traditional box type classrooms. Here the architects made what was often an impressive contribution.[42] 'There had been perhaps twenty or thirty years of triumphant progress by the primary schools in which it seemed that all that was good was happening through them,' wrote Kogan, Plowden's secretary in 1978:

> A powerful humanitarianism seemed to suffuse the best of the primary schools. To the visitor they seemed unbelievably good in their relationships between adults and children, able to elicit powerful interest on the part of the pupils, and yet still be highly productive in work that was both creative and skilful. The Plowden Report on Primary Education, [he added] celebrated the achievements of the primary schools in several hundred pages.[43]

Historical Origins of Primary Progressivism

Maurice Kogan refers to the period when Plowden was sitting as marking the outcome of 'twenty or thirty years' of 'triumphant progress in the primary schools'. This would date the progressive movement in the schools back to the early 1930s – and no doubt this deliberately places the inception of this movement roughly to the publication of the consultative committee's famous report of 1931.[44] Although this report advocated streaming, it also advocated an active approach to learning – and the need to broaden the whole concept of primary education to include dance, music, art and craft, the study of the local environment and so history and geography as well as the mastery of language and number. This was the period (following and resulting from reorganisation) when primary, and particularly junior schools were coming into being; there had, on the other hand, been a long tradition of separate infant schools (or departments) for children aged from five to seven.

The break-out of the 1960s, then, was certainly based on pioneering developments within the schools which had their inception earlier. In order to comprehend this movement, and its significance, it may be as well to look briefly at its historical origins – or at least some aspects of them.

In his fascinating study of the inter-war period Professor R.J.W. Selleck argued convincingly that a kind of watered-down progressivism had become the 'intellectual orthodoxy' among training college lecturers, HMIs and others by 1939.[45] Both the Hadow Reports of 1931 and of 1933 (on nursery and infant schools) had, of course, stressed a child-centred approach with the famous phrase 'activity and experience' central to each.[46]

What is less probable, however, is whether these sentiments were actually borne out in practice in the schools themselves at that time. Large classes (up to 50 or more) were then the norm; there was a considerable proportion of unqualified teachers, while continuous grinding economies as well as ancient and obsolete buildings made innovative initiatives difficult, if not impossible.

There were, however, already nodal points of change, grouped around certain pioneering educators and teachers whose influence now began to make an impact. Any choice must be arbitrary, but two areas may be singled out, those of art and movement.

In 1927 a remarkable collection of children's paintings was brought over from Vienna for a Save the Children fund exhibition. They had been produced under the tutelage of Franz Cizek, a Viennese who had been working in this field for many years. The works were striking – produced on large sheets of paper they were 'full of vigour and colour'. Some were 'incredibly detailed and stylised', others more impressionistic.[47]

This exhibition had an immediate popular appeal. The young HMI Christian Schiller bought a couple of the pictures and hung them in his nursery. Another visitor was Marion Richardson whose pioneering approaches to children's art now took off in her own teaching; again using large sheets of paper and a very wide variety of materials, her major aim was to stimulate the child's imagination and find the means of its expression. Marion Richardson, now perhaps chiefly remembered for her development of writing styles and patterns, later became an LCC inspector where she had scope for a wide extension of her influence.[48]

Another to be influenced was Robin Tanner, apprentice etcher and young teacher who, in the early 1930s developed an enormously wide range of teaching media and resources and got an extraordinary (to some unbelievable) response from his pupils.[49] One to be profoundly impressed (in 1932) was John Blackie, later assessor to the Plowden Committee and senior chief inspector for primary education.[50] Tanner became an HMI in 1935, working in Leeds, Bristol and elsewhere. In 1956 he moved to Oxfordshire where he was able to work in tandem with Edith Moorhouse, already for ten years in post as county adviser for primary education. The scene, then, was set for take-off.

Another area where an important break-through had been made before the war, bringing new conceptions of children's creative potentialities, was that of movement and dance. Here the original central figure was another central European, Rudolf Laban, who, as the leading figure in modern dance and movement in Germany, although actually a Czech, had been responsible for all the movement staged in connection with the 1936 Olympic games in Berlin. At a dress rehearsal, with 20,000 present, the Nazis objected, prohibited his work (defined as '*staatsfeindlich*') and banished Laban to a remote castle. Arriving in England finally in 1938 (to Dartington Hall where his pupil, Kurt Jooss, had his ballet), his influence spread rapidly, particularly after the war. His 'free' dance techniques were refined and applied to the school and education, profoundly influencing indigenous developments in this country (as acknowledged by Plowden), introducing dramatic and emotional elements within a carefully worked out structure.[51]

One brilliant teacher, who made movement the centre of the educational revolution at his slum school, hemmed in by industrial and other buildings in Birmingham in the 1940s, was A.L. Stone, who found movement and 'modern dance' to be the key that unlocked the absorbed interest and total commitment that he sought for his pupils and achieved. Stone's modest record, *Story of a School*, was published as Ministry of Education Pamphlet No. 14 in 1949 making an extraordinary impact, selling more than 60,000 copies.[52] The pamphlet covered movement, drama, art, children's writing, music and arithmetic – concluding with a short chapter on teaching which predicted Plowden's concepts. Already before his pamphlet was published, Clegg had recruited him (in 1947) as a county adviser for the West Riding, having retained 'a strong admiration for his original work in Birmingham'.[53] Another adviser Clegg recruited at this time was Diana Jordan, an ex-pupil of Rudolf Laban's who became the first Warden of Woolley Hall (a West Riding in-service centre for teachers working in the arts), while Basil Rocke, who had worked with Cizek, was another.[54] So the teams were built up in those areas which later took the lead in the 'revolution in the primary school'.

An important area where new approaches could germinate were the rural schools – though for the most part these were scarcely revolutionary. When Edith Moorhouse was appointed County Adviser for Oxfordshire in 1946 she had 178 schools to look after, of which about 100 contained only one or at most two teachers.[55] Her aim at first was to break down the physical isolation of the schools and teachers by organising group meetings, and then, seminars, poetry readings, visits to exhibitions, talks and discussions. Later, working with Robin Tanner, new approaches spread rapidly, young heads were appointed eager to widen the concept and scope of education, new courses run, workshops organised where the teachers themselves could try out new techniques, particularly in art and crafts; the support of a Conservative education committee was won partly by the astonishing exhibitions mounted and guided by the children themselves. The situation was gradually transformed, in spite of all the difficulties. By the early 1960s Oxfordshire was ready for the break out.

But it was from a small village school in Cambridgeshire, oddly enough, that the most striking single record of achievement was made. In 1963 Sybil Marshall published *An Experiment in Education*, describing her work in a tiny school of 26 children, their ages ranging from five to eleven. Extremely well written in a racy, informal but appealing style, the description of Sybil Marshall's activities and approach, as well as the quality of the children's activities – artistic, literary, dramatic, scientific – is in fact quite extraordinary and unusual. Here the work of a clearly brilliant teacher and educationist seemed to underline the creative potential of quite ordinary children. Published precisely in 1963, the year of Plowden's appointment, it meshed closely with the prevailing ethos, and helped to give it direction.[56]

If we attempt to sum up it may, perhaps, be said that there were three main sources for the primary school 'revolution'. First, the indigenous 'progressivism' which emerged in the 1930s, based to some extent on anglicised versions of Froebelian ideas, mixed with those of Maria Montessori and, especially, of Margaret McMillan. To some extent there was also an influence from the American philosopher and educationist, John Dewey. This somewhat undefined progressivism had been more influential in the area of rhetoric than in that of practice in the pre-war period. Nevertheless it formed the ideological orthodoxy by the late 1930s, as Selleck has argued.

Second, there were indigenous developments within the infant schools which, because of the early compulsory school starting age of five, are unique to Britain. It was here, if anywhere, that progressive ideas and informal structures were to some extent implemented before the war, to take off more rapidly after. Here Susan Isaacs' liberationist work at Malting House School (a private school) at Cambridge was important, as well as her own work at the London University Institute of Education. In the post-war period, this aspect was ably developed by Susan Isaac's disciple and successor at the Institute, Dorothy Gardner.[57]

Third, there were the, again indigenous, developments within the rural schools where streaming (and even the 11-plus) scarcely penetrated. This gave scope for pioneers and, as we have seen, these appeared and were able to exploit the possibilities.

There were other influences at work in the subsoil, as it were – the influence of evacuation, for instance, held by many to have forced teachers back on their own resources and so promoted creative thinking and new approaches.[58] There was also the gradual transformation of the general atmosphere – new conceptions of children's potential, a rejection of the fatalistic ideas of the past, and of procedures deriving from, and reinforcing these. But such general movements are more intangible – and speculative. The main point that needs to be made, in concluding this analysis, is that the soil had already been prepared, in some areas at least, for new growths within primary education. In the early 1960s these had begun to appear. By the time the Plowden committee finished its deliberations they were in flower. It may be worth pointing out that the main thrust of these new developments was in the area of affective, rather than cognitive education.

3 The Plowden Report and After

Publication, Theoretical Outlook and Proposals

The Plowden Report was published early in January 1967. It received a warm welcome right across the board – in the newspapers, the educational press and on television. Suffused, as it was, with a warm humanity ('at the heart of the educational process lies the child') it celebrated, as Kogan said, the achievements of the primary schools in several hundred pages. It was in fact to be the last of a long line of such enquiries. After the publication of this report, the Central Advisory Councils (for both England and Wales) were never to be reconstituted. The clause in the 1944 Education Act establishing them was finally repealed in 1986, a matter we will refer to later.

The report was virtually unanimous. There were a few 'notes of reservation' but not one on any of the central issues tackled.[59] Starting with a long theoretical chapter on children's growth and development a series of chapters (in Part 3) dealt with the home, school and neighbourhood – focusing on parents and their role, the concept of the community school, and specifically on proposals relating to 'educational priority areas'. A full chapter was devoted to immigrants and another to health and social services – in all these areas positive recommendations were made.

The bulk of the report, however, dealt with the structure of primary education, discussed its 'ages and stages', the impact of selection, problems of size and of the rural areas. Attention then focused, in an important series of chapters, on the curriculum and internal organisation of the schools – here the 'Plowden philosophy' was most apparent. Other chapters cover teacher training, staffing and related matters as well as school buildings, equipment and the general status and government of primary education. The long list of recommendations were both costed and prioritised in relation to the Labour government's 'National Plan' (later abrogated) which assumed an increase of about 25 per cent in expenditure on

Table 7.2
Plowden Report
HMI Categorisation of Primary Schools
Total Schools = 20,664

Category	Description	No. of Schools	Percentage of Primary School Population	Number of pupils
1	'In most respects a school of outstanding quality' 'Pacemakers and leaders of educational advance'	109	1	29,000
2	'A good school with some outstanding features' 'High quality, far above average, but...'	1538	9	–
3	'A good school in most respects without any special distinction'	4155	23	–
4	'A school without many good features, but showing signs of life with seeds of growth in it' 'Promising'	3385	16	–
5	'A school with too many weaknesses to go in category 2 or 3, but distinguished by specially good personal relationships' ('Often with large numbers of immigrant children')	1384	6	–
6	'A decent school without enough merit to go in category 3 and yet too solid for category 8' 'Run of the mill' schools	6058	28	–
7	'Curate's egg school, with good and bad features'	2022	9	–
8	'A school markedly out of touch with current practice and knowledge, and with few compensating features'	1309	5	–
9	'A bad school where children suffer from laziness, indifference, gross incompetence or unkindness on the part of the staff'	28	0.1	4,333

Constructed from Plowden Report, Vol. 1, pp. 101–2.

primary education in England and Wales over the five years 1964 to 1969. It could hardly be denied that the Plowden Committee had done its work, and very effectively.

The publication of the report accelerated the entire movement analysed earlier in this chapter. In an important sense it gave enormous encouragement to all that was most advanced in the primary scene. As Kogan later put it, it 'took on the exemplary function adopted by all previous consultative committees and central advisory councils. It laid out the best practices that could be found in primary schools with a view to encouraging others to follow them.'[60]

The committee had attempted an overall categorisation of all the primary schools in the country, carried through by HMI. As this is difficult to summarise, Table 7.2 has been constructed from the section of the report which describes the results of the survey.

What transpires is that 10 per cent of the schools fell into the two top categories of 'excellence' – of these the top 1 per cent were defined as 'in most respects a school of outstanding quality' – these were the 'pacemakers and leaders of educational advance'; while those in category 2 were schools 'with some outstanding features ... of high quality, far above average, but ...' (reservations expressed). It was the work of schools of these types which found reflection in the report – rather than the 'run of the mill' schools (attended by 28 per cent of the school population), or those 'with too many weaknesses' to go into a higher category, 'but distinguished by specially good personal relationships' (attended by 6 per cent).[61]

The timing of publication of the report has some significance. It took place less than a year after the Labour government had been returned with a greatly increased majority in the spring of 1966. The committee in fact reported to, and was warmly welcomed by Anthony Crosland, now Secretary of State. The economy seemed on an even keel, no one predicted the economic crisis that hit the country almost precisely one year later. Indeed this was the close of a period of full employment and, generally, uninterrupted economic advance extending now through the whole post-war period. It is clearly evident from its report that the committee's general perspective was one of continuous economic growth, full employment, enhanced affluence and the more or less inevitable emergence of a more egalitarian society where human potential, which the committee saw as unlimited, would find realisation. 'Unemployment has been almost non-existent since the war, except in some areas and for a small minority of workers,' it wrote. 'Incomes have risen, nutrition has improved, housing is better, the health service and the rest of the social services have brought help where it is needed.'[62] Most of the children, it added, 'are now physically healthy, vigorous, curious and alert'. This was, perhaps, the last point in time (1965–66) when such a general optimism expressed something of a consensus. This, then, was the context of the committee's deliberations – a context which finds reflection in the educational optimism of the committee's theoretical outlook, and of the practical proposals concerning the role of both teachers and pupils, and of classroom procedures generally.

It is to this area we may now turn, as most relevant to the analysis made in this book. Here the first (theoretical) chapter was important, since it legitimised what proved to be the main thrust of the report in terms of teaching – the need to individualise the educational process. The chapter stresses the uniqueness of each individual child – the 'enormously wide variability' in physical and intellectual maturity of children of the same age. This requires adaptability and flexibility on the part of the teacher. But, however wide this variation, children have one important characteristic in common, 'a strong drive' from a very early age 'towards activity in the exploration of the environment' (para. 45). This behaviour is 'autonomous' and is linked to the child's 'curiosity, especially about novel and unexpected features of his experience'. Development (or learning?) is interpreted as the resultant of 'the complex and continuous interaction between the developing organism and its environment' (para. 11). It is the nature of this interaction that, according to Plowden, enhances individual differences; even within members of the same family, it is held, such differences appear very early and lead to wide variation. Development generally is, therefore, the result of the interaction of an 'hereditary tendency and environmental factors' such as the level or degree of 'encouragement or discouragement' children experience (para. 52). In particular, mastery of language is seen as 'central to the educational process' (para. 55).

It is from this analysis, here very briefly summarised, that is derived the main thrust of the report as a whole – that individualisation of the educational process is the essential principle on which all educational strategy and tactics must be based. 'Individual differences between children of the same age', it is stated, 'are so great that any class, however, homogeneous it seems, must always be treated as a body of children needing individual and different attention.' However, the matter is even more complex than this. Intellectual, emotional and physical development all take place at different rates. A teacher, therefore, needs to know and take account of each child's 'developmental' age in all three aspects (para. 75). This, it transpired, was a tall order.

In a sense there was nothing strikingly new about these theories; they had formed the staple of advanced thinking for a long time, even if they were spelt out in a more detailed way here than previously.[63] But it is in the *consistent application* of these theories to practice that the Plowden Committee took things further than before. The committee, for instance, came out unanimously in favour of the abolition – or modification – of streaming within infant, junior and middle schools (para. 819). This is consistent with the theories just outlined concerning the enormous variability and, in a sense, unpredictability of children's development, and with the stress on the importance of environmental (or social) factors in its determination. If the child's educational (and other) experiences are seen as central to intellectual and indeed to overall development as the Plowden committee saw them, the categorisation ('streaming') of children according to their *existing* level of development at any one moment cannot be justified. Instead it is necessary, so far as possible, to provide a rich environment for all children, giving scope for the realisation of children's many-sided potentialities. The Plowden committee took this reasoning (if not spelt out exactly in this form) to its logical conclusion, both in its unqualified support for unstreaming, and (and very characteristically) in its insistence that 'the problem in the unstreamed class will be to translate into practice the principle of *individual learning*' (my emphasis, B.S.), (para. 824).[64]

It was entirely in keeping with this theoretical outlook, which was legitimised by reference to the work of the Swiss philosopher, Piaget, that the committee rejected full class teaching as the norm ('we would like to see less of it'), and proposed that the child's activity should be largely individualised, modified by resource to group work (although the committee were poorly advised here, and clearly did not recognise its complexity). They saw children as self-motivated, 'curious', enquiring by nature. Perhaps I can repeat here an attempted summary – or a general sketch – of the ideal Plowden type teacher (and pupils) written some years ago but since accepted as accurate by sympathetic post-Plowden analysts. The attempt is to reconstitute the Plowden ideal of class teaching, derived from the report as a whole. In this ideal class:

> The children are active, engaged in exploration or discovery, interacting both with the teacher and with each other. Each child operates as an individual, though groups are formed and reformed related to those activities which are not normally subject differentiated. The teacher moves around the classroom, consulting, guiding, stimulating individual children or occasionally, for convenience, the groups of children which are brought together for some specific activity or are 'at the same stage'. She knows each child individually, and how best to stimulate or intervene with each. In this activity she bears in mind the child's intellectual, social and physical levels of development and monitors these. On occasions the whole class is brought together, for instance for a story or music, or to spark off or finalise a class project; otherwise class teaching is seldom used, the pupils' work and the teacher's attention being individualised or 'grouped'.[65]

This, then, is the pattern of what came to be known as the 'informal classroom' – in strong contradistinction to the mechanistic teaching modes of the past. It was this approach which now received a powerful, official accolade.

If these were the chief pedagogical implications – indeed recommendations – of the Plowden Report, in terms of broad educational policy there were a number of proposals – in fact together these totalled 197. Here we can focus only on the most important. The first, to which the committee itself gave priority, are the proposals relating to educational priority areas – those 'most severely handicapped by home conditions'. Here there should be a policy of positive discrimination whereby greater resources and assistance should be given to these specific areas – no class above 30, salary increments for teachers, generous provision of teachers' aides (qualified teacher assistants), priority for buildings, extra books and equipment, expansion of nursery education, links with colleges, teacher centres, the development of community schools and so on. Research programmes should also be started to discover effective systems and to inform planning for later, long-term developments.[66]

Second, the committee proposed a massive expansion of nursery education where 'a start should be made as soon as possible'. This should be available from the age of three – detailed proposals are made relating to staffing and conditions.

Third, the committee proposed that community schools be developed in all areas, if especially in educational priority areas; parents should be much more closely involved with the schools and invited to give assistance.

Many proposals are also made on health and the social services and, of course, on internal school organisation. The 'first' (infant) school should cover three years (five to eight), followed by a four year junior school (eight to twelve). A number of proposals are made about teacher training where 'a full inquiry' is suggested. The final recommendation (No. 197) directed to 'LEAs and DES' provocatively sums up the committee's championship of the primary schools. 'All unnecessary and unjustified differences of treatment', it states boldly, 'should be eliminated.'[67] Of all these recommendations, those relating to educational priority areas and to nursery education were to prove the most important in terms of future policy developments.

Post-Plowden Developments, 1967–70

In 1970 the NFER finally produced its report on streaming – *eight years* after it was originally commissioned. Admittedly two interim reports had been submitted to the Plowden committee.[68] These were generally inconclusive and contained no positive advice, apart from stressing that 'substantial proportions of teachers are in favour of streaming' – only relatively few 'firmly committed to the opposing view'. The researchers concluded, rather rashly as things worked out, that 'this finding must be stressed at a time when some writers suggest that the death knell of streaming has already sounded'. Adding that parents and teachers generally preferred streaming they warned that 'any universal change recommended may meet with considerable opposition' – particularly since the attitudes for or against seem to form part of a whole syndrome of views, practices and beliefs.[69] By the time the substantive study had been published, the significance and potential importance of the report was long over – the research, though well intentioned, had missed the bus.[70]

The reason for this is that, contrary to the researchers' predictions, the schools themselves were taking their own decisions and, it appears, virtually unanimously decided to move to more flexible structures than could be allowed for under the rigid streaming system inherited from the past. Such, at least, is the evidence of research studies completed following Plowden. A survey of two local authorities in the Midlands carried through in 1970, for instance, found that the vast majority of the primary schools were, in fact, by now unstreamed. Five years later a study of all primary schools in Lancashire and Cumbria found only 13 per cent streamed. Finally in 1978 an HMI survey covering England as a whole found only 4 per cent of children in nine-year-old classes in the survey were streamed.[71] Within a mere fifteen years, then, the position Jackson (and, incidentally, the NFER) found in 1963 was totally reversed.[72] It seems clear enough that the swing to unstreaming (or 'mixed ability grouping') as a principle of school organisation was the one chief characteristic of the so-called 'primary school revolution' which cannot be gainsaid.

It was at about this period that the 'primary school revolution' in Britain aroused enormous interest in the United States where an attempt was being made to loosen up traditionally didactic procedures through the development of what was then there known as 'the Open School'. Teachers from Leicestershire and elsewhere had already been organising workshops in various states across the Atlantic for some years, and the flexible, informal structures of the more advanced schools in Britain were becoming well known. During the mid-late 1960s a considerable number of more or less distinguished American educationists visited this country, toured the key areas of the break-out and then wrote about their experiences, generally focusing on the concepts and practices of advanced British schools as models from which Americans could learn with advantage.

The key series of articles that started off this entire movement, were written by Joseph Featherstone, and published in the *New Republic* (a liberal weekly journal of which he was associate editor). These were printed under the heading 'The Primary School Revolution in Britain' and appeared in 1967, the year Plowden was published. Featherstone's articles comprised a powerful statement of support for advanced British practice which, he held, could provide valuable insights for American educators. These were reprinted with other articles in a book entitled *Schools Where Children Learn* (1971). Featherstone also wrote the introductory volume to a series entitled 'British Primary Schools Today' (1971) – a co-operative venture by American and British educators aiming to publicise modern procedures on both sides of the Atlantic.[73] 1970 saw the publication of Charles Silberman's *Crisis in the Classroom: The Remaking of American Education*, a project massively funded by the Carnegie Corporation. Over 100,000 copies of the hardback edition were sold together with 240,000 of the paperback; the book was also awarded seven prizes and received worldwide publicity. This drew greatly on the author's British experience, even if this was of a somewhat subjective, episodic character.[74] The same year (1970) saw the publication of Vincent Rogers' *Teaching in the British Primary School*, again produced for American readers but contributed to, in a series of articles, by the leading British educators with experience of the primary school. This carried a strongly adulatory introduction by Rogers, Professor of Education at the University of Connecticut and a convinced proponent of new forms of education. 1971 saw the publication of Lisa and Casey Murrow's *Children Come First*, sub-titled 'The Inspired Work of English Primary Schools', also based on descriptions of activities in selected schools, while in the same year Lillian Weber's useful and comprehensive *The English Infant School and Informal Education* was also published in England. This, actually worked on mainly in 1965–66, differs from the others in that it focused very specifically on the infant school which Lillian Weber saw as the centre of the drive towards what she describes as 'informal education'.

It is certainly the case that some of these writings were propagandist in character and tended, therefore, to convey what was perhaps a rosy-hued version of developments in British primary schools in general. The common tendency of these authors, who visited many schools, predominantly in the main geographical areas already discussed, was to identify with these developments and processes and to persuade fellow Americans of their viability. 'I visited these two schools in

Oxfordshire', wrote Vincent Rogers, 'I have not been quite the same since.'[75] Silberman's influential book is built up largely of vignettes of teacher and pupil interaction or activities, derived from visits again to selected, or recommended schools. He claimed that 'in every formal classroom that I went to visit in England, children were restless, were whispering to one another when the teacher was not looking, were ignoring the lesson or baiting the teacher or annoying other children,' while in the schools organised on the basis of informal schooling 'the joyfulness is pervasive; in almost every classroom visited, virtually every child appears happy and engaged. One simply does not see bored or restless or unhappy youngsters, or youngsters with the glazed look'.[76] Featherstone, although he uses the term 'revolution in the primary schools', is careful to underline that it is Plowden's 10 per cent 'best' ('outstanding') schools that he is talking about, and, as far as junior schools generally are concerned, makes clear that many of these are as arid, poverty-stricken and dull as he perceived most American education to be. For him, however, as with Vincent Rogers and, of course, Plowden, it is the 'best' schools that represent the trend, to which other schools are likely, given time and encouragement, to approximate.[77]

I have argued elsewhere that this phenomenon – the surge of enthusiasm for new developments within the British primary school – may be more significant as part of the American history of education than the British.[78] At this moment in time the Americans were experiencing a severe crisis within their schools – and looking for radical solutions. On the other hand the evidence presented often gives a vivid – and highly sympathetic – picture of contemporary developments in the most advanced schools. Ironically these assessments from across the Atlantic appeared just at the moment the first Black Paper spattered a load of black ink over these very practices.[79]

Reverting to this country, publication of the Plowden Report (which sold nearly 70,000 copies in a year) was quickly followed by the publication of John Blackie's *Inside the Primary School*, a popularisation of Plowden written officially and published by HMSO in 1967. Blackie, Senior Chief Inspector for Primary Education and assessor to the Plowden Committee (who had, however, retired in 1966), was then not only the most authoritative writer on primary education but a very strong proponent of the Plowden ideology and general outlook. Indeed the role of HMIs in this whole movement was clearly important and is a topic worthy of further study. *Inside the Primary School* was reprinted in 1968, 1969 and 1972 and, according to the author, in 1974 'has sold 70,000 copies in the UK and USA'. A separate American edition was also published in 1971.[80] Blackie's book was intended for parents and the general public but, he said, 'has proved popular among teachers'.

The swing towards informal, Plowdenesque teaching approaches clearly continued in the years immediately following publication of the report. Within a couple of years, however, a critique was launched from a relatively prestigious centre calling into question some of the leading assumptions behind the report's ideological – or theoretical – stance.[81] This is an issue to which we will return. In the meantime, what actions were taken by the government of the day to implement some, or all, of the committee's recommendations?

In the DES's annual report for 1967 Gordon Walker, now Secretary of State, referred to the publication of the Plowden Report which, he said, received 'an immediate and general welcome for its general tenor and philosophy'. The government accepted the proposal that national policy should adopt the principle of positive discrimination, and had allocated £16 million for school building in Educational Priority Areas – to be spread over two years. However the pressing economic situation made it necessary to proceed carefully in relation to recommendations involving substantial expenditure – on these matters consultations were proceeding.[82] A year later (1968) the government announced new proposals to initiate an urban programme of £20 to £25 million over four years, the bulk of which was earmarked for education.[83] By 1969, when Phase 2 of this programme was under way, a special drive was directed at improving nursery education – over 5,000 new places were expected to result.[84] Much could be done to implement the curriculum recommendations of Plowden with little expenditure, the Secretary of State assured educationists in 1968. An individual initiative by the sociologists A.H. Halsey and Michael Young secured (minimal) funding for the important EPA 'action research project' based on Plowden recommendations. This, operating from 1968 to 1971 in five areas, led to further developments in the 1970s.[85]

Together these measures can hardly be described as the great step forward Plowden had hoped for. Economic difficulties were, however, increasingly pressing. The advances already achieved, while exposing some weaknesses, seemed generally to form a firm base for the future.

4 Teacher Training in the 1960s

Looking back on the impact (or outcomes) of the Plowden Report twenty years on, Lady Plowden argued that the actual date of publication of the report had been unfortunate. It seems, she wrote, 'that our report could not have come out at a worse time'. She was not referring, here, to the sharp economic crisis that hit the country in the autumn of 1967, with resulting expenditure cut-backs by the government which hit education as well as other spending departments (postponement of the raising of the school leaving age, etc.). What she singled out, with hindsight, was the 'vast increase' in the number of teachers needed in the primary schools – a product of the rapid, and unexpected birth rate increase in the late 1950s and early 1960s. This meant huge numbers of young teachers entering schools that were already overcrowded. These conditions, she argued, militated strongly against the chance of effective implementation of the Plowden ideals.[86]

The crash programme to produce enough teachers to cope with the schools' needs has already been discussed (Chapter 5). With just under 30,000 students on initial training courses in training colleges in 1958, the total rose to over 107,000 in 1970.[87] The three-year course, long fought for in the profession, had been brought in in 1960 when an actual decline in school child numbers had been expected, and this, of course, exacerbated difficulties of supply. In 1958 the great bulk of the colleges were small, single-sex institutions, the majority being church-controlled (98 of the total of 140 colleges had fewer than 250 students). By 1970 22 colleges had over 1,000 students, and 66 over 750. The bulk of the colleges of education, as they came to be called after Robbins, were now large, mixed, and generally under secular control – of the expanded total of 157, 105 were local authority colleges, 52 voluntary.[88] From the tightly controlled, closed institutions inherited from the past, the colleges had been transformed with considerable rapidity into the predominantly large, secular and open institutions typical of the late 1960s and early 1970s. There were concomitant changes. Properly constituted and independent student unions were finally accepted (after a long resistance by some colleges), and separate, democratically controlled governing bodies (including staff and student representatives) established.[89] These were all, certainly, important gains.

But this crash expansion presented the colleges with real difficulties, as may be imagined. There was, first, the problem of designing a viable three-year course – to take the place of the traditional pot-pourri of courses which had comprised the crash two-year course originally designed to produce elementary school teachers in Victorian times. To this was added, after 1963, the more complex task of designing a four-year degree course (for the original BEd), at first for a small minority of students opting (and selected) to stay for a fourth year. While the planning involved in these changes was under way, a major issue was the recruitment of staff to undertake the expanded training commitment. Perhaps inevitably, in the circumstances, preference went to secondary grammar school teachers who could contribute to the specialist subject teaching now required in institutions whose academic quality was being upgraded. This resulted in a strengthening of the academic (subject) departments in line with the development of colleges as part of the system of higher education as envisaged by the Robbins committee. But these tutors had no experience of the primary schools where the bulk of the output of the colleges actually taught.[90] The study of education and its practical application in teaching was the responsibility of the overburdened education department in the colleges whose prestige *vis-à-vis* the academic departments, now began to slump.[91] But here, also, similar changes, which had adverse implications in terms of teachers' classroom practice, were also under way.

In March 1964 a high-powered (academic) conference was held, organised jointly by the Ministry of Education and university and college professors and lecturers to discuss 'the education course in the training of teachers'. 'The whole educational system of this country seems to have reached a state of fluidity which makes far reaching changes possible,' said C.J. Gill, Chief Inspector at the DES. 'Traditional ways of organising education, of teaching children and of training teachers, are being challenged,' he continued; new demands are being made on teachers, local authorities are abandoning the 11-plus, comprehensive reorganisation is taking various forms. 'In all this welter of change and projected change', he went on, the training college course needed reconsideration. There is no doubt that 'We are entering into a new phase in education in this country.'[92]

It so happened that, just at the moment when the mass of primary schools, through their own initiative, were moving over to non-streaming and finding their own solutions to the new pedagogic problems so arising, this conference effectively swung the whole area of teacher education firmly and effectively in what proved to be a highly academic groove, in which the main emphasis of studies in education in the colleges focused on the 'disciplines' (philosophy, history, psychology, sociology) held to underlie 'education' as a 'field of study'.[93] The main attack, or critique, on existing practice was launched by Richard Peters, a proponent of the 'revolution in philosophy' (involving 'the disciplined demarcation of concepts and the patient explication of the grounds of knowledge and conduct'). In a phrase which became notorious, Peters ridicules the 'undifferentiated mush', often perpetrated under the heading of educational theory. What was necessary was to identify the various disciplines which underlay, or contributed to, the study of education – now referred to as 'the three foundation disciplines' (history was here ignored). Gill himself had called for 'a rigorous theoretical basis' to be given to the students' work. This call was echoed by Peters and by other participants – Stephen Wiseman demanded courses in psychology which, 'in rigour of methodology' would bear comparison with any other university studies. Here also the new discipline of sociology flourished, now (perhaps belatedly) accepted into the canon of the 'foundation disciplines'.[94]

Following this lead, which exploded with considerable vigour, colleges of education (and universities) rapidly appointed specialist philosophers, sociologists, historians, to expanding education departments – many the products of new diploma and higher degree courses mounted at universities. Courses provided by these departments for their students reflected the 'disciplines' approach. Each became established, later setting up societies, publishing journals, organising conferences. The study of education was coming into its own.[95]

From the standpoint of the academic study of education there can be no question that this whole movement marked an important advance. The philosophers did clarify relevant concepts; historians elucidated developments; sociologists illuminated the role of class and language within institutions and systems as a whole. The whole field of the study of education was perceptibly moved on to a higher level. But there were negative effects as well. These studies did not and could not directly contribute to the practice of teaching. Their focus was remote from the classroom. They were unconcerned with pedagogy – with the production of highly skilled classroom practitioners. In this they followed a long-standing tradition in English educational studies.[96]

The result was that, just at the moment when a penetrating pedagogic guidance was required by trainee teachers, both in the primary and to some extent in the new type secondary (comprehensive) schools, it was scarcely forthcoming. Responsibility for students on school practice was spread among subject specialist teachers (whose experience was largely secondary) and by lecturers in education departments in colleges now increasingly staffed by subject specialists within the fields of education. There were, however, in most colleges, 'curriculum' specialists with primary school experience, though their status and function was variable; nor was there an effective functional arrangement between college lecturers who visited students on teaching practice, the teachers whose classes they used for practice and the students themselves. Finally, the actual practice of teaching was not illuminated by theoretical insights – nor by a body of knowledge easily available to the students. Teaching, as an art and (or) a science, fell between several stools – was no one's central responsibility. At this period, few research studies penetrated the classroom. The universities in the 1960s, responsible for training only a small minority of the total teacher output, concentrated almost entirely on the secondary age range, largely preparing grammar school teachers in the traditional way, or, as comprehensive education spread, subject specialist teachers for the new comprehensive schools. Only four universities trained a small number of primary teachers.

This is not by any means to say that the colleges of education, beset as they were with logistical problems on a massive scale, and with the restructing due to the three-year course and the new degree did not, overall, rise to the occasion with remarkable success. So enormous was the influx of students that, at one time in the late 1960s almost every primary class in the country accepted one or more students for practice – the colleges could not pick or choose to which schools to send their students; certainly they could not conceivably have concentrated them in Plowden's 10 per cent 'best' schools. Nearly all schools had to be used, often in remote areas. The students inevitably imbibed practices and attitudes characteristic also of the 'run of the mill', and 'curate's egg' schools (as characterised by the Plowden survey) which, of course, formed the majority.

Further, there is no doubt that some colleges – or sometimes specific departments within colleges – made an enormous contribution to the more positive changes brought about in the 1960s. In the West Riding, for instance, Woolley Hall, a centre for the continuing education of teachers, developed very close links with advanced primary schools, while Bretton Hall acted as a focus for the promotion of art, music, movement and craft which Alec Clegg sought so effectively to encourage. These are only specific examples of what was a widespread movement. It does not, however, detract from the general picture; involving lack of guidance in the crucial area of all purpose class teaching – the means by which primary education was and is carried on in this country.

In the circumstances it was perhaps inevitable that criticism of teacher training began to express itself increasingly in the late 1960s. The Plowden Committee devoted a chapter to the issue, expressing 'disquiet' at the level of academic qualifications of students, at the shortage of qualified lecturers in education departments and related matters (para. 961). Although they had received many favourable comments on the work of colleges and departments of education, there had also been much criticism (para. 971). The committee concluded that there should be a full enquiry into the whole subject of the training of teachers – a recommendation that was to be put into effect in 1971. In 1969–70 a House of Commons Select Committee examined the problems of teacher training, publishing extensive evidence from the teacher training world. In February 1970 Edward Short, as Secretary of State, invited Area Training Organisations to conduct detailed reviews of current procedures. An organisation for radical reform, mostly promoted by teacher educators themselves (including Harry Rée) with the scarcely eupheuistic acronym SPERTT, (Society for the Promotion of Educational Reform Through Teacher Training) was established in 1969. This gained considerable media publicity but was itself short-lived. Generally it began to appear by the end of the 1960s that teacher education would be high on the agenda for structural change.

5 *The Primary School Revolution: Myth or Reality?*

In the 1970s, as we shall see, a sharp backlash developed against the hegemony, as some perceived it, of 'progressive' methods in the primary schools. Indeed this was first publicly, and widely expressed in the first Black Paper of 1969 already mentioned. Here the suggestion was made that the roots of the student unrest which broke out in 1968 were to be found within the primary school. 'I sometimes wonder whether this philosophy', wrote Timothy Raison, a member of the Plowden Committee, editor of *New Society* (and later a Tory MP), 'does not owe at least something to the revolution in our primary schools.'[97] Taking up this point, the editors (C.B. Cox and A.E. Dyson) in their lead article entitled 'Progressive collapse', continued the analysis:

> Influenced by a variety of psychologists from Freud to Piaget, as well as by educational pioneers from Froebel onwards, these schools have increasingly swung away from the notion (which characterises secondary education) that education exists to fit certain sorts of people for certain sorts of jobs, qualifications and economic roles, to the idea that people should develop in their own way at their own pace.

'Competition', they continued, 'has given way to self expression. And now this has worked its way up to the student generation.'[98] The introduction of 'free play methods in primary schools', the editors claim at the start, is one of the 'revolutionary changes' that have taken place in English education. 'The new fashionable anarchy', they conclude in the letter to Members of Parliament, 'flies in the face of human nature', for it holds that 'children and students will work from natural inclination rather than the desire for reward'.[99] So the idea was planted, already at the close of the 1960s, that the student unrest, then at its height, was the linear (or direct) result of the new ethos and practices within primary education.

In view of this it is historically important to attempt an objective assessment of the extent and nature of the changes of the 1960s difficult though this may be.

In the first place, this hypothesis seems historically inaccurate, if only in terms of chronology. If the student unrest, or revolt, of 1968–69 was partly due to the primary school 'revolution', that revolution must be dated back at least ten or fifteen years; that is, to 1958 and earlier, when the students at the London School of Economics, Hornsey College of Art and elsewhere would have been in primary schools being inducted into their anarchistic attitudes. But, as we have seen, in 1958 the 11-plus examination was still the rule throughout the country, Leicestershire's reorganisation was only just beginning in two isolated areas of the county, only 150 comprehensive schools were in existence; the move to abolish streaming in primary schools was in its very first stage. The students of 1968 were, in fact, the products of the streamed, divided, hierarchic system which only began to be transformed in a significant way in the mid-1960s. They were, in fact, products of the very system the Black Paper writers looked back to with such cloying nostalgia.

In his *Inside the Primary School* (1967), Blackie, who had been senior chief inspector for primary schools, confirms this analysis. Asked by foreign visitors to arrange visits to 'activity' schools, HMIs, to whom the request was referred, 'found great difficulty in discovering any'. Change *was* taking place in the period 1947–53, but 'slowly, cautiously' and, as he puts it, 'sensibly'.[100]

Clearly there had been important, and generally very positive changes. Of these the rapid transition to non-streaming was, as already pointed out, probably the most important and widespread. But how far this led to the hegemony of anarchistic and 'free play' methods is quite another question. Certainly an emphasis on creative activities – in art, craft, music and movement – did powerfully emerge in certain areas (for instance, Oxfordshire and the West Riding); there was also something of a swing towards a greater focus on practical activities and 'discovery' methods in learning – for instance, in mathematics – and a new concern to exploit the school's setting in environmental studies. But evidence for the widespread adoption of 'free play' methods is hard to find.

For the Plowden Committee the HMIs, it will be

remembered (see p. 364), found a total of 10 per cent of 'excellent' schools, while about a third (including these) were 'clearly good' and another third 'run of the mill' and 'bad'.[101] Only the top 10 per cent could be equated with schools in which the primary school 'revolution' had taken place. Another HMI survey for the committee found 21 per cent categorised as 'good' and 'very good' in the sense that these schools were 'in line with modern educational trends'.[102] Conversely nearly 80 per cent were not regarded as impressive on these criteria. It seems, then, that the extent of the 'revolution' may have been exaggerated by its opponents. Perhaps the impression was given, following the publication of Plowden, that 'progressivism' was winning all along the line. The reality, however, was otherwise.

This conclusion derives support from the first systematic study of the actual organisation of junior school classrooms, a study undertaken in 1971.[103] As already mentioned, this study, which was carried out in two Midland areas, one of which had gone comprehensive, the other not, found little or no streaming; instead the modern 'informal' classroom organisation and layout was the rule. The teachers, however, maintained a very precise control over their pupils' activities. 'Some of the results', reported the author, '... question widely held beliefs about the "primary school revolution".' In spite of the relatively informal classroom layout adopted, 'there was so much evidence of tight teacher control over such matters as where children sit and moved that it seems highly doubtful that there is much opportunity for children to choose or organise their own activities in most classrooms.' These conclusions were supported by another survey of a different character carried through in 1970.[104] It concerned the way teachers who had adopted the technique known as 'the integrated day' – then considered as a way-out, 'progressive' approach – organised and controlled their classrooms. But here again the same conclusion emerged; namely, that the bulk of the teachers using this approach in fact normally maintained a tight control over the children's activities. Two or three years later Neville Bennett, surveying primary classrooms in the North-West, found only 9 per cent of teachers who could be characterised as 'progressive' in the Plowden sense – that is, met the Plowden criteria relating to progressive education.[105]

There is no doubt that some of the changes in primary

education in the 1960s were perceived as a threat by those brought up in the grammar school tradition, and who saw this as embodying all that was of value in education. It seems, however, that the grounds of their concern had little basis in fact. The whole critique, indeed, calls for analysis not so much on the educational as on the political level. For some, it was the social order itself that was threatened, and that required defence. This issue will be discussed in the next chapter.

Notes and References

1. For a brief resumé of the evolution of the primary school, Maurice Galton, Brian Simon and Paul Croll, *Inside the Primary Classroom*, London 1980, Chapter 2.

2. *Children and Their Primary Schools* (the Plowden Report), HMSO 1967, Vol.I, p.167 and Table 8, p.114.

3. See the DES annual reports, *Education in 1961*, p.135; *Education and Science in 1970*, p.12.

4. Ibid., (1961), p.58; (1970) p.27. A proportion of these, of course, went into secondary teaching.

5. Ibid., (1961), p.8 (1970) pp.24–5, see Appendix Table 4a, p.581).

6. Brian Jackson, *Streaming: An Education System in Miniature*, London 1964, pp.14–6. Jackson identified 2,982 schools in England and Wales large enough to stream; his sample of one-third covered 964 schools, of these 660 replied. The enquiry was not popular among certain local authorities.

7. Ibid., pp.17–9.

8. Ibid., Table 8, p.21.

9. Ibid., Table 6. This indicates that, in two-stream schools, 73 per cent of pupils with professional and managerial fathers were allocated to the A stream, only 27 per cent to the B stream. The figures for pupils with unskilled manual workers as fathers are reversed: 39 per cent are allocated to the A stream and 61 per cent to the B stream.

10. Ibid., p.31. 217 replies came from heads, 438 from class teachers.

11. Ibid., pp.33–44.

12. Ibid., p.150.

13. George Freeland, 'Purpose and Method in the Unstreamed Junior School' in Brian Simon (ed.), *New Trends in English Education*, London 1957.

14. E. Harvey, 'Unstreaming a Junior School', *Forum*, Vol.2, No.2, Spring 1960, reprinted in Brian Simon (ed.), *Non-Streaming in the Junior School*, Leicester 1964. This publication includes several articles by heads and others on the transition to non-streaming in junior schools. It also contains the *Forum* Editorial Board's evidence to the Plowden Committee on this issue.

15. *Non-Streaming in the Junior School*, p.17.

16. J.W.B. Douglas, *The Home and the School*, London 1964, p.118.

17. Donald Thompson, 'Organisation in the Comprehensive School', unpublished PhD thesis, University of Leicester, 1973.

18. P.E. Vernon (ed.), *Secondary School Selection*, p.43.

19. S.C. Mason, *The Leicestershire Experiment and Plan*, London 1960, p.20. The Leicestershire Plan was originally introduced in two specific areas – Wigston and Hinckley.

20. Ibid., p.20.

21. This paragraph is derived from personal classroom observations by the author in the late 1950s.

22. See Edward Blishen, 'Conference on Non-Streaming', *Forum*, Vol.5, No.2, Spring 1963. A second conference was held in April 1964.

23. *Education in 1962*, pp.2, 19–20.

24. The parallel 'Gittins report', *Primary Education in Wales*, equally weighty, was published a full year later, on 25 January 1968 (although it bears the date 1967). The Central Advisory Council for Education (Wales) was constituted some months later than the English Council, but given identical terms of reference.

25. Maurice Kogan, 'The Plowden Report Twenty Years On', *Oxford Review of Education*, Vol.13, No.1, 1987.

26. For this movement, see Bob Moon, *The 'New Maths' Curriculum Controversy, an International Story*, London 1987, especially Chapter 6. For Dienes' contribution, ibid., pp.55, 102, 167, 213; and see Z.P. Dienes, *Mathematics in Primary Education*, UNESCO (report), 1966.

27. Moon, op.cit., pp.121ff. For the origin of teachers' centres linked with the Nuffield Mathematics Project, Geoffrey Matthews, 'A Beginning of Teachers' Centres', in R.E. Thornbury (ed.), *Teachers' Centres*, London 1973. For a full evaluation of this movement, Dick Weindling and Margaret I. Reid with Peter Davis, *Teachers' Centres: A Focus for In-service Education? Report of the Schools Council Teachers' Centres Project*, Schools Council Working Paper 74, London 1983.

28. A.B. Clegg (ed.), *The Excitement of Writing*, London 1966.

29. At the City of Leicester College of Education, for instance, Vi Bruce, a very talented and committed teacher (and friend and ex-colleague of Alec Clegg's in the West Riding), devoted years of work and activity to this area, finally overcoming resistance to its inclusion as degree work (for the BEd) of a traditional Senate at Leicester University by a brilliant display of her students' work. She, and others like her, sent out to the schools hundreds of highly skilled practitioners.

30. For Schiller, see Christopher Griffin-Beale (ed.), *Christian Schiller in his own Words*, privately printed, 1979. Also Peter Cunningham, *Curriculum Change in the Primary School Since 1945*, London 1988, pp.57–62, and especially, for a vivid picture of Schiller as a young man, Robin Tanner, *Double Harness*, London 1987, pp.101–2, 141. (No man, Tanner concludes, 'has influenced primary education in our time so much as he'.)

31. For Mason, see Donald K. Jones, *Stewart Mason, the Art of Education*, London 1988, *passim*, but especially Chapter 6, 'Primary Schools and Progressivism'. See also Donald K. Jones, 'Planning for Progressivism: The Changing Primary School in Leicestershire Authority During the Mason Era, 1947–71' in Roy Lowe (ed.), *The Changing Primary School*, London 1987. For a detailed analysis of developments in Oxfordshire and the West Riding, with a special reference to the role of the Directors of Education (Alan Chorlton and Alec Clegg), see Leonard Marsh, 'Case Study of the Process of Change in Primary Education, Oxfordshire and the West Riding, 1944–72', unpublished PhD Thesis, University of York, 1987. For Alec Clegg, see four autobiographical articles in *Times Educational Supplement*, September–October 1974; also Peter Cunningham, op.cit., pp.49–57.

32. Donald K. Jones, *Stewart Mason*, Chapters 4 and 5.

33. Both directorships covered relatively long periods; Mason was appointed in 1947, retiring in 1971; Clegg's reign lasted from 1945 to 1974.

34. 'The Leicestershire Scene', Appendix A in Mary Brown and Norman Precious, *The Integrated Day in the Primary School*, London 1968, pp.136–9. The authors were heads of an infant and junior school respectively.

35. Alec Clegg, 'A Subtler and More Telling Power', *Times Educational Supplement*, 27 September 1974.

36. See A.B. Clegg, *The Excitement of Writing*.

37. *Times Educational Supplement*, 15 November 1985.

38. Ibid., For Edith Moorhouse's own version of developments in Oxfordshire, *A Personal Story of Oxfordshire Primary Schools*, privately printed, 1985.

39. Christopher Griffin-Beale, op.cit., p.80. This was not only rhetoric. As a young HMI in 1926, Schiller was sent to Liverpool and found a room near the docks. 'What I found was horrifying. At one school there were 81 children in a single class, fully a

third sitting in a coal hole. Families of six or more children lived in a single room. Schools consisted of long halls in which perhaps five classes, each one of them with more than 50 children in them, occupied the same four walls, so that the accent was on strict conformity, silence and absolute obedience if chaos was to be kept to a minimum.' Willem Van der Eyken and Barry Turner, *Adventures in Education*, Harmondsworth 1969, pp.104–5.

40. Lorna Ridgway and Irene Lawton, *Family Grouping in the Infants' School*, London 1965.
41. Mary Brown and Norman Precious, op.cit.
42. Stuart Maclure, *Educational Development and School Building: Aspects of Public Policy 1945–73*, devotes special attention to the 1960s in Chapter 6, 'The Changing Face of Primary Education'. See also Peter Cunningham, 'Open Plan Schooling: Last Stand of the Progressives?' in Roy Lowe (ed.), *The Changing Primary School*, London 1987; Andrew Saint, *Towards a Social Architecture, The Role of School Building in Post-War England*, New Haven and London 1987, and Malcolm Seaborne and Roy Lowe, *The English School, Its Architecture and Organisation*, Vol.II, 1870–1970, London 1977, especially Chapter 11, 'The Design of Post-war Primary Schools'.
43. Maurice Kogan, *The Politics of Educational Change*, London 1978, pp.55–6.
44. *The Primary School*, HMSO 1931.
45. R.J.W. Selleck, *English Primary Education and the Progressives, 1914–1939*, London 1972, p.156.
46. 'The curriculum is to be thought of in terms of activity and experience rather than of knowledge to be acquired and facts to be stored'. *The Primary School*, 1931, p.93; *Infant and Nursery Schools*, 1933, p.183.
47. Willem van der Eyken and Barry Turner, op.cit., p.97. For Cizek, see Richard Carline, *Draw They Must, A History of Teaching and Examining in Art*, London 1968, pp.158ff.
48. Eyken and Turner, op.cit, pp.98ff.
49. Ibid., pp.103ff. For Robin Tanner see also Peter Cunningham, op.cit., pp.192ff., and his own autobiography, *Double Harness*, one of the most remarkable books covering this movement.
50. Willem van der Eyken and Barry Turner, op.cit., pp.108, 113. Peter Cunningham, op.cit., pp.62ff.
51. For Laban's own definition of aims and techniques, Rudolf Laban, *Modern Educational Dance*, London 1948. See also, S. Thornton, *A Movement Perspective of Rudolf Laban*, London 1971 (from which the Olympic games incident is taken); Valerie Preston, *A Handbook for Modern Educational Dance*, London 1963; Betty Redfern, *Concepts in Modern Educational Dance*, London 1973; Joan Russell, *Creative Dance in the Primary School*, London 1965. For the Plowden Committee's assessment, *Plowden Report*, Vol.I, pp.256–7.
52. Alec Clegg, 'A Subtler and More Telling Power', *Times Educational Supplement*, 27 September 1974.
53. A.L. Stone was head of Steward Street Junior School, Birmingham (see P.H.J.H. Gosden and P.R. Sharp, *The Development of an Education Service, The West Riding, 1889–1974*, Oxford 1978, p.198, and Peter Cunningham, op.cit., pp.150–1).
54. Ibid.
55. Edith Moorhouse, *A Personal Story of Oxfordshire Primary Schools, 1946–1956*, privately printed, 1985. See also van der Eyken and Barry Turner, op.cit., pp.115ff., and Peter Cunningham, op.cit., pp.184ff.
56. Sybil Marshall, *An Experiment in Education*, Cambridge 1963. It is interesting to note that the author acknowledges no specific influences on her educational thinking and activity – except a single anonymous local authority art adviser during her first appointment elsewhere.
57. Susan Isaacs' most important books, *Intellectual Growth in Young Children* and *Social Development in Young Children* were published in 1930 and 1933 respectively. See D.E.M. Gardner, *Susan Isaacs: The First Biography*, London 1969. See also

D.E.M. Gardner, *Experiment and Tradition in Primary Schools*, London 1966. For infant school developments, Lillian Weber, *The English Infant School and Informal Education*, London 1971.

58. See Weber, op.cit., p.166, on evacuation.

59. That by A.J. Ayer and five others, recommending that religious instructions cease to be an obligatory part of the curriculum is the one of most general interest. There was also one dissentient (a female head) from the recommendation that corporal punishment be abolished in primary schools. *Plowden Report*, Vol.1, pp.489–93.

60. Maurice Kogan, *Oxford Review of Education*, Vol.13, No.1, March 1987, special number entitled 'Plowden Twenty Years On', A.H. Halsey and K.D. Sylva (eds.).

61. *Plowden Report*, Vol.1, pp.101–2. The categorisation of primary schools was master-minded by John Blackie.

62. Ibid., Vol.2, p.29.

63. Their validity was shortly to be questioned, especially in R.S. Peters (ed.), *Perspectives on Plowden*, London 1969 (see note 81).

64. *Forum*'s Editorial Board had presented written 'evidence' to the Plowden Committee – making a strong case against streaming. The Board was invited to present 'oral' evidence – that is, to be interrogated on the evidence, or to extend it. The three members present (two were junior school heads, the third, the author) soon realised that what the bulk of the committee wanted was that we should succeed in winning Professor A.J. Ayer to our standpoint. A lengthy interchange took place during which the *Forum* approach was subjected to analysis by the Wykeham Professor of Logic. At the close, all appeared satisfied – in any case no 'note of reservation' was formulated on this specific issue. For the *Forum* evidence, *Forum*, Vol.7, No.1, Autumn 1964.

65. Galton, Simon and Croll, op.cit., p.49.

66. *Plowden Report*, Vol.1, pp.464–6.

67. Ibid., p.482.

68. An abridged version of these reports was published in the *Plowden Report* Vol.2, Appendix 11. For the main, final report, Joan C. Barker Lunn, *Streaming in the Primary School*, Slough 1970.

69. *Plowden Report*, Vol.2, p.571; see also Barker Lunn, op.cit., p.56.

70. The NFER study contains interesting (historical) data. It confirmed Brian Jackson's conclusions relating to discrimination by social class and month of birth, and concerning the infrequency of transfer between streams. It did not discover any appreciable differences in academic achievement between streamed and unstreamed schools. Barker Lunn, op.cit., pp.57ff, 82ff.

71. Deanne Bealing, 'The Organisation of Junior School Classrooms', *Educational Research*, Vol.14, 1972, pp.231–5; Neville Bennett, *Teaching Styles and Pupil Progress*, London 1976, p.58; *Primary Education in England: a Survey by H.M. Inspectors of Schools*, HMSO 1978, p.28.

72. In 1963 the NFER had great difficulty in locating sufficient non-streamed schools to make up the matched pairs they required. They finally found 'about eighty', 'probably all the schools in the country that could be classified as such at that particular time'. Barker Lunn, op.cit., p.20.

73. This series of small paperbacks, published by Macmillan, included *An Introduction*, by Joseph Featherstone (1971), and 22 further booklets covering the whole field of contemporary practice in primary education. The initiative was carried through under the auspices of the Anglo-American Primary Education Project, the 'British Directorate' including John Blackie, Mollie Brearley and Maurice Kogan (project co-ordinator).

74. Silberman followed this up by publishing, in 1973, the *Open Classroom Reader*, another massive compilation drawing heavily on British writers.

75. Vincent Rogers (ed.), *Teaching in the British Primary School*, London 1970, p.v.

76. Silberman, op.cit., 1970, pp.228–9.

77. Featherstone, op.cit., pp.13–5.

78. Brian Simon, 'The Primary School Revolution: Myth or Reality?' in Brian Simon

and John Willcocks (eds.), *Research and Practice in the Primary Classroom*, London 1981.

79. The reference is to the cover of the first Black Paper, which represents a mass of ink blots besmirching a child's drawing of children. C.B. Cox and A.E. Dyson (eds.), *Fight for Education* (Black Paper 1), London n.d., 1969.

80. John Blackie, *Changing the Primary School: an integrated approach*, London 1974, p.106.

81. In R.S. Peters (ed.), *Perspectives on Plowden*, leading members of the academic staff of the London University Institute of Education, including Peters himself and Robert Dearden (philosophy), Brian Foss (psychology), and Basil Bernstein and Brian Davies (sociology), together with the Principal, Lionel Elvin, launched a severe critique of the theoretical stance informing the Plowden report.

82. *Education and Science in 1967*, pp.9–10. In a statement in November, 1967 Gordon Walker listed some of the steps being taken to implement Plowden. These included an improvement in teacher supply, accelerated school building, action on environmental and curricular issues. Ibid., p.10.

83. *Education and Science in 1968*, p.10.

84. *Education and Science in 1969*, p.9.

85. Its inception is referred to in A.H. Halsey, and K.D. Sylva, 'Plowden: History and Prospect', *Oxford Review of Education*, Vol. 13, No.1, 1987. For an analysis of this entire initiative, George Smith, 'Whatever Happened to Educational Priority Areas?', ibid. See also, for a blow by blow account of developments, A.H. Halsey (ed.), *Educational Priority, EPA Problems and Policies*, Vol.1, *Report of a research project sponsored by the Department of Education and Science and the Social Science Research Council*, HMSO 1972, pp.vii–xi, and Chapter 3, pp.31ff., 'The Governmental Response to Plowden'.

86. Bridget Plowden, ' "Plowden" Twenty Years On', *Oxford Review of Education*, Vol.13, No.1, March 1987.

87. Joan Browne, 'The Transformation of the Education of Teachers in the 1960s' in Edward Fearn and Brian Simon (eds.), *Education in the Sixties* (Proceedings of the 1979 conference of the History of Education Society, London 1980).

88. Ibid., pp.61–2.

89. Ibid., pp.67–8. This was a result of the *Report of the Study Group on the Government of Colleges* (the Weaver Report), HMSO 1966, and subsequent legislation (Education Act No.2, 1968).

90. In 1960 the so-called 'Balance of Training' Circular (Ministry of Education College Letter 14/60, October 1960) insisted that 85 per cent of student output from the colleges should be trained for primary teaching, only 15 per cent for secondary (though this was later modified). Ibid., pp.65–6.

91. Browne, op.cit., pp.68–9 refers to a study by M.D. Shipman which showed that, from the late 1950s, 'The expanding academic departments began to get the upper hand, a tendency that was reinforced by the three year course and the beginning of degree studies.'

92. Conference on the Course of Education in the Education of Teachers, held at Hull University, 16–21 March 1964 (mimeo, archives of the Universities Council for the Education of Teachers).

93. The classic rationale for this approach is Paul Hirst, 'Educational Theory', Chapter 2 of J.W. Tibble (ed.), *The Study of Education*, London 1966.

94. Hull University Conference Report, Mimeo, pp.3, 9–10.

95. A Philosophy of Education Society was established in 1966 and a History of Education Society in 1967. For this movement, Brian Simon, 'The Study of Education as a University Subject', *Studies in Higher Education*, Vol.8, No.1, 1983.

96. See Brian Simon, 'Why No Pedagogy in England?' in Brian Simon, *Does Education Matter?*, London 1985.

97. The Black Paper was quoting an article by Raison in the *Evening Standard*, 15 October 1968. This was concerned with student actions at the Hornsey College of Art.

C.B. Cox and A.E. Dyson, *Fight for Education* (Black Paper 1), London n.d. 1969, p.5.

98. Ibid., p.6.

99. Ibid., p.1.

100. John Blackie, *Inside the Primary School*, HMSO 1967, p.11.

101. *Plowden Report*, Vol.1, pp.101–2.

102. Ibid., pp.18–9. These were defined as (i) 'permissive discipline', (ii) 'provision for individual rates of progress', (iii) 'readiness to reconsider the content of education', and (iv) 'awareness of the unity of knowledge'.

103. Deanne Bealing, op.cit., pp.231–5.

104. P.R. Moran, 'The Integrated Day', *Educational Research*, Vol.14, November 1971, pp.65–9.

105. Neville Bennet, op.cit., pp.37ff.

8 The End of the Decade: New Polarities

1 New Perspectives

If there had been setbacks – postponement of raising the leaving age, economic cutbacks, the public schools fiasco, perhaps the binary structure imposed on higher education – there had, on the other hand, been important advances in education during the 1960s; indeed, in some senses, of historic significance. Although defined, in a book published in 1972, as 'The Decade of Disillusion', this related to the growing concern, especially among young people, with what was increasingly seen as the unprincipled pragmatism of the Labour government; its failure to move in any significant way towards socialism (however defined), and in particular with its role in the long drawn-out agony of the Vietnam War.[1] The early drive and idealism, crystallised in Harold Wilson's 1963 speech, had by now been lost. Towards the end of the decade the government was perceived as temporising on one issue after another – both in terms of foreign and of economic policy. On the other hand a record of liberal legislation relating particularly to home affairs had been achieved. In spite of disillusion, particularly among the left (and perhaps especially among students), Labour could still count on widespread support. The prospect of a political renewal still retained its potency. This related closely to new perspectives for educational change.

The world of education boomed during the 1960s – if simply in the sense that there was a great deal more of it at the end than at the start. In the book just cited, Brian MacArthur, a leading educational journalist, argued that, 'although educationists ... always look to the debits rather than the credits, there is no doubt that the 1960s was a decade of real achievements.'

These 'easily outweighed the disadvantages of over-enthusiasm'. 'If the past teaches any lessons', concludes the author, it is that 'expansion in education is irresistible and that somehow, however late, it is usually achieved.'[2]

Positive achievements were not, however, confined only to expansion, as we have seen. Within secondary education the thrust towards the transformation of the system, now having broad, popular support, was reaching a decisive stage. Already the unification of the comprehensive school through modification of its internal structure appeared as a realisable perspective, though this was an area of increasing contention. Here the probability of a leaving age of sixteen (although postponed) together with the growing movement towards the single examination for all (the Schools Council had been working on this since 1967) provided a realistic perspective by which an appropriate education for all to sixteen might be achieved.

These advances had opened the way for a new emphasis on primary education, embodying a decisive shift away from the rigid structures and teaching methods inherited from the past, and, however fitfully, reflecting the new, perhaps more relaxed but certainly more humanist ideals of the 1960s. Here again new policy initiatives seemed to open new perspectives – particularly official acceptance of the concept of positive discrimination, by which a greater than average proportion of available resources was to be channelled to children living in areas of greatest need. The focus of both sets of initiatives, within primary and secondary education, was on finding the means by which local systems could best provide for *all* the children for which they were responsible – the key objective of local government in this, its central area of involvement.

The greatest area of advance, in terms of expansion, was, of course, within the field of higher (and further) education. This has been documented in Chapter 5. In an important sense the 1960s will be remembered as the Robbins decade, when the targets even of that ambitious plan were substantially exceeded, even if the division crystallised in the binary system was, more or less harshly, imposed. If this was to create problems for the future it did not, in fact, halt the rate of advance, nor was it intended to. Its objectives were more concerned with cost and control, as Crosland originally made clear. The rapid expansion was not, however, accompanied by any easing of access for working-class students – rather the opposite; it was the new middle and professional classes who benefited most.[3] Even so, it was university (and college) students who, at the close of the 1960s, most dramatically expressed their alienation from existing social norms and government policies.

There was, then, advance across the board – some of which was beginning to take place at an unprecedented rate (for instance, the swing against streaming in the primary schools). The partial autonomy of education, as a social and civic function, is here apparent – Brian MacArthur's assessment, cited earlier, defining education as an area of definite achievement whatever the general failures of the period, has force. Here was a social movement of some significance whose roots must be sought in the new aspirations deriving from fundamental economic and social change, the consequence itself of scientific and technological developments underlying the third industrial revolution. In the politically necessary attempt to meet these new demands, governments in the 1960s, starting during the Macmillan period (and earlier), siphoned an increasing proportion of what was a growing national income to enhanced public expenditure. Budgetary expenditure on education, both in total, and as a proportion of public expenditure, rose consistently; as a proportion of GDP it also rose, for the first time exceeding defence expenditure (see Appendix Tables 15 and 16, pp.601-2).[4] Even so, resources were, of course, limited – particularly after 1968. In many areas (for instance, nursery education, provision for the sixteen- to eighteen-year-olds) Britain continued to lag far behind most comparable advanced industrial countries. Indeed, on certain crucial indicators, Britain's relative backwardness was, during this decade, yet further exacerbated.[5]

2 *The Student Revolt*

It was in the area of most rapid development – higher education – that a series of dramatic (and, for some, highly traumatic) events now took place which shook the established order and which, if obliquely, provided the spark for a new polarisation within the whole field of education. The student upsurge, or revolt, which reached its height in the early summer of 1968 provoked, within a few months, a backlash crystallised in a new form – the publication of a series of 'Black Papers' on education. These, while first targeting the students, their character, activities and demands, soon swivelled their guns on to a general critique, largely hostile, of new trends in education generally – specifically comprehensive schools, the movement to non-streaming, and what they defined as 'progressive' education. The first two Black Papers were published in 1969, when the Labour government was still in office. The third, welcoming the return of the Tories, in November 1970. The actual impact of the Black Papers, a clear attempt to obstruct or halt the developments outlined in the last section – is difficult to estimate, and appears to have been delayed (as the next chapter exemplifies). But both the student actions and the Black Paper response certainly had their effect – these events can hardly be ignored in a study of the history of education in the twentieth century.

A great deal has been written about the student protest movement, for such it was, of the late 1960s.[6] It was, of course, an international phenomenon, stretching across continents, finding expression primarily in the United States (where it had its inception), Germany, Italy, Yugoslavia, Japan, and, of course, in France (where through combined action with sections of the organised working class, revolution seemed to some a clear possibility). The high point was reached in the early summer of 1968, when the Sorbonne was taken over, and mass demonstrations through the centre of Paris became a daily occurrence. A new generation of student leaders emerged, militant, anarchistic in outlook, gaining mass support – Daniel Cohn-Bendit in Paris, Rudi Dutschke in West Germany (where the Free University of Berlin was controlled by the Sozialistische Deutsche Studentbund and many universities brought to a halt), and, in the United States, Bill Hayden and others, leaders of Students for a Democratic Society. At this point also Columbia University in New York was occupied while all over the United States parallel developments took place. Indeed the whole movement had its origin in student actions at Berkeley in California as far back as 1964, on the issue of free speech and the proper use of university land.

Explanations of this phenomenon, which appears as very specific to this particular generation of students, are many and various. They relate specifically to the feeling of helplessness, indeed alienation, of the young in a world then seemingly inexorably divided into two opposing parts, both armed with nuclear weapons threatening mass destruction – a tension sharpened in the growing intensity of the Vietnam War, which (in the Western world) of course most directly affected young people in the United States. Allied to this was a growing antagonism to increasing governmental power and its exercise by new technocratic methods seemingly allowing less and less opportunity for the citizen to influence public affairs; many resented manipulation by the mass media (as they saw it), withdrawing into themselves and living their own lives as they thought fit – a tendency enhanced by the existential philosophers, then dominant in France and elsewhere. Further, in contra-distinction to the radical student movement of the 1930s, 'all the inherited ideological concepts had lost their credibility' – those supporting the liberal (capitalist) state, *and* those pointing the way to socialism (the Soviet invasion of Czechoslovakia in August 1968 naturally confirmed this rejection). As one well qualified observer has put it, the search for alternatives now 'led the youth … to ideological fragmentation and to borrowing from various ideological traditions distant in space and/or time. It led them to either resignation or violence. Both reactions stem from a rejection of the Establishment.'[7]

But, due to their greatly increased numbers, students now had a new importance socially – even politically. In Britain the Latey Report (July 1967), proposing that the age of majority be lowered from twenty-one to eighteen, led the Cabinet to support the proposal for votes at eighteen. This was carried on a free vote in the Commons on 26 November 1968, the Bill gaining Royal Assent in the next year. This was an important new factor in the situation. As adult voters, students were now hardly *in statu pupillari* as in the past. This now began to influence the situation, in Britain at least.

The universities on the Continent, however, now crammed with students, with few facilities, had changed little in their form of government and control over the centuries. These, seen by the student leadership as arms of a hostile and morally objectionable state, now came under attack; change was demanded, in objectives, in teaching, in procedures generally. When this was not forthcoming, the students resorted to direct action – the strike, and, more effective, the sit-in (and in some cases violence). Within the universities the students found they had considerable power; especially since action aimed at democratising the universities 'gained more mass support than any others'. Indeed this was the area where student actions finally won definite concessions in several European countries as in the United States.

It was in May 1968 that the student protest movement reached its climax in Britain with militant action at the London School of Economics where the first sit-in had taken place a year earlier (March 1967). Although the movement in Britain never approached the scale, nor the level of violence, reached on the continent and in the United States, nevertheless this action at the LSE triggered similar action elsewhere which continued, with greater or lesser moments of confrontation, through the rest of 1968, into 1969 and even later. The action was confined largely, but not entirely, to universities (the polytechnics hardly existed, the colleges of education were little affected), but over 1968-69 the universities of Essex, Birmingham, Manchester, Leicester, Oxford, Bristol, Sussex, Warwick and others experienced mass student disaffection and confrontation.[8] Outside the universities the most striking actions, perhaps surprisingly, were those carried through at two art colleges, Hornsey and Guildford – in the latter case the students (270 of the total of 300) carried through what Jack Straw, then NUS president, called 'the longest sit-in in British history'. The key issue was the nature of art education – the Guildford students, again according to Straw, initiated by this action 'one of the most significant and dynamic contributions to the development of art and design education since the war'.[9] Similarly the long teach-in which began at Hornsey on 28 May 1968 was also mainly concerned with education – 'it was a long and careful examination of the prevailing theory and practice of education in art and design', extending far beyond the college and leading to a national conference on the subject. It was, its supporters wrote later that year, 'the nerve centre of the revolution'.[10]

But both these actions involved confrontation, disruption, the actual closure of the institutions and much agony for all concerned. The same was true, and on a much larger scale, in those universities that were the focus of the student protest. Chief among these, in the heady summer of 1968, were the LSE as already mentioned (where matters had been simmering since October 1966, with the appointment as director of Dr

Walter Adams, seen as a racist) and the new University of Essex where, in May 1968, the students took over the university for 48 hours. Here the issue sparking action was the visit of a lecturer from Porton Down, a centre for research in chemical warfare. In Bristol, where action followed later that year, the student demand that the union building should be made available to non-students, rejected by the university authorities, formed the *casus belli*. As Eric Ashby and Mary Anderson point out in their study of this phenomenon, *The Rise of the Student Estate in Britain*, each of these spark points embodied moral causes, 'to reject racial discrimination: to condemn war; to renounce privilege'. The authors continue (analysing the tactics of militant students as they saw them):

> If the first cause had less moral content than these, then it must proclaim some denial of rights, such as representation on university boards or committees, though the danger about these is that if the demands are reasonable the rights may be negotiated and the protest will collapse. So the demands must be in the form of an ultimatum (representation to be granted within a week) or must be certain to be rejected ('equal and democratic staff-student-worker control of all college and university organisations' as one manifesto put it).[11]

If this appears cynical, it fairly represents the tactics of the most militant groupings who gained control of the protest movement at certain institutions at specific times. But, as has already been made clear, the overall thrust of the movement in Britain was a determination by the students to achieve some degree of control over their own lives and especially of their education, both in terms of content and method. This had, in fact, been a long-standing student demand, first raised with some force by the student movement of the late 1930s.[12] But, until the late 1960s, little or nothing had been achieved. Students had neither any direct say nor representation on university senates and councils (the major governing bodies), nor had they achieved any representation on faculty boards and/or departmental committees. Before 1968 they were, in fact, totally excluded from any role in the government of universities (and of most colleges). It was to bring about a change here that the great bulk of the students took action, whatever the spark that ignited the conflagration. A sense of the breadth of this appeal can be gained from the support declared by the Federation of Conservative Students which, in October 1969, supported the freedom of students to stage sit-ins ('if they do not violate the rights of others') and appealed for more student representation on the governing bodies of universities and colleges.[13]

In what was described (in the *Times*) as 'a pugnacious attack' on administrators in universities and colleges in the first Granada Guildhall lecture, in October 1969, Jack Straw, then President of the NUS, expressed the view of 'moderate' students, now fighting to retain hegemony. Straw began his speech in uncompromising terms:

> I am here tonight to attack the last great unreformed institutions of our time – the universities and colleges of higher education. I am here to accuse them of failure: of failure themselves to institute the necessary reform of their own structures; of failure to apply their own professed ideals and methodology to themselves. [Democratic involvement, he added,] is not just a nice idea; it is now a necessity. For the educated man (sic) of the future must be able to dominate and control the constant change which technology will force upon us.[14]

In the House of Commons a select committee was now investigating the whole issue; its report, 190 pages long, accompanied by six volumes of evidence, was published in 1969.[15]. Already in 1968 the Vice Chancellors' Committee and the National Union of Students together negotiated an agreement covering many of the student demands – this statement was issued on 7 October 1968. This document, according to Ashby and Anderson, is 'of historical importance', not so much because of its content 'as because it is an affirmation on behalf of senior and junior members of universities that they are partners in the educational system under a voluntary discipline of scholarship'. Students are not 'customers purchasing degrees, nor wards under guardianship, and certainly not enemies'.[16]

When these words were written all was not over. Other confrontations were to come. But, gradually, both universities and colleges did reform themselves. Committees were set up (for instance, the Hart Committee at Oxford), enquiries conducted (at Cambridge, Warwick, Essex, Lancaster, Stirling, Birmingham and the LSE). New procedures developed, a new sensitivity – to the nature and outlook of students – generalised. Perhaps reluctantly, student representatives were admitted to senates, faculty boards and other key committees. Far from disrupting things, generally their contribution was found to be constructive.[17] The universities, said Sloman, Essex Vice-Chancellor, in a follow-up Granada lecture in 1969, 'need as never before, to draw their students into full and participating membership of a single cohesive community'. Such, then, was the ethos of the time. But to some, the student action carried with it a fundamental threat to the social order as a whole. We may now examine, in some detail, the most striking response to the student movement of the sixties – the Black Paper phenomenon, already briefly referred to in earlier chapters.

3 The Backlash: The Black Papers

The first Black Paper, published in March 1969, is perhaps best seen (and most sympathetically) as a somewhat hysterical response by university teachers to the student upsurge of 1968. Conceived, apparently, during a stroll on Hampstead Heath by its two editors, Brian Cox and A.E. Dyson (both from university departments of English literature), it expresses, sometimes very vividly, the sense of outrage felt by those who had, in a very real sense, seen their world turned upside down. The responsibility was not theirs, but the students'; indeed, as we have seen, special prominence was given to the primary schools (and so their teachers and mentors), even if this interpretation could hardly stand up, either logically or historically. Some scapegoat, however, had to be found outside the universities proper (that is, their teachers and administrators). Hence the broadening of the attack, as further Black Papers were published, from the students to the schools that produced them – comprehensive secondary education (though at this point, only a tiny proportion of university students came from these schools), 'progressive' education generally seen as leading to 'anarchy', the primary schools once again.

In the first Black Paper, thirteen of the total of nineteen separate contributions were concerned directly with the universities – and their students in particular; three dealt with secondary education, one only with primary schools while two ranged more generally. Of these, that by the Tory MP Angus Maude was given pride of place. This, a general attack on the 'ideology of egalitarianism', saw the main threat to the quality of education at all levels as stemming from this outlook. The egalitarian dislikes any process 'which enables some children to emerge markedly ahead of their fellows'. In the name of 'equality of opportunity', this leads to the destruction of schools 'which make special efforts to bring out the best in talented children'. It is, then, a recipe for disaster. We must, Maude concludes, 'reject the chimaera of equality and proclaim the ideal of quality'. The egalitarians, whose ideals of 'social justice' are prescriptions for mediocrity and anarchy, 'must be prevented from having any control over the education of the young'. Dons and school teachers must 'do battle against the enemies within their own gates'. The Trojan horse of egalitarianism 'has already been dragged deep into their citadel'.

If this general critique reflects the specific tone which characterised the Black Papers, the university contributors took it further and broadened the attack.[18] William Walsh, Professor of English Literature at Leeds University, utilises a Lawrentian sexual imagery in his denunciation of the students' demand for 'dialogue'. The current notion of this concept, he sees as 'a stark mutual invasion, a simultaneous rape' – the New Left 'sees knowledge as dialogue, the product of naked confrontation (or mutual stimulation)'. This concept of knowledge, he concludes, 'seeks to reduce human experience to a trauma of birth without inheritance or transmission, a single spasm of violence'. It is 'thin and fanatical in temper, mean in its categories and sourly lacking in ripeness and generosity in its grasp of life. It is the contemporary expression of the barbaric mind.'

There is only space here to give a brief idea of the general thrust of the arguments presented. One of the editors, A.E. Dyson, in 'The Sleep of Reason' (which 'brings forth Monsters'), sees the source of the student upsurge, leading to the search for 'frantic self-fulfilment divorced from reason and discipline', in a 'bankrupt and dangerous romanticism' having its roots in the work of Blake, Keats and Wordsworth. Here the essential notion is 'that men are born free and holy, but are crushed by false pressures from the social world'. Hence the domination of an 'optimistic romanticism' which becomes bankrupt at the very moment of its ascendency. Other writers attempt a more down to earth analysis. The fault has its origin in the tempestuous expansion of the early 1960s, an expansion 'wildly beyond the national capacity to pay for it' (D.C. Watt, on the LSE); this aspect is strongly argued by Kingsley Amis who, as far back as 1962, had argued 'more means worse'. Today's students demand participation simply because they want to negotiate less work, less studying. 'As a consequence of irresponsible expansionism, the universities today are full of students who do not understand what study is about, and who are painfully bewildered by the whole business and purpose of university life; more has meant worse,' he ends triumphantly. Student unrest is largely due to 'the presence in our universities of an academically unfit majority, or large minority'. This may be beyond cure, 'but that is no reason for allowing the symptoms to rage unchecked'.

The general tenor of these articles is clear enough. They set out to shock and they did shock, as we shall see. Brian Cox confined himself to a defence of examinations ('In a modern society, education can only thrive in a context of examinations,' are his opening words), but presumably he was also responsible for the editorial 'Letter to Members of Parliament' which centres on what is described as 'the progressive collapse of education' finding the roots of the trouble in the primary schools and utilising anecdotal evidence from 'a successful business man who left school at fourteen' and a correspondent to the *Daily Mail* (a Dolores Moore) who complained of 'illiterate school leavers'. In 'Comprehensive Disaster', R.R. Pedley, an independent school head, argued that the establishment of such schools was part of 'that sinister attack on excellence' evidenced in various ways by government and university committees, by 'hostility towards fee-paying schools', and by proposals for 'non-streaming from infant schools to universities'. So the way was prepared for a broader assault in the near future.

Seven months later, early in October 1969, Black Paper Two appeared. Entitled 'The Crisis in Education' and, at 160 pages, twice the length of the first, this was timed for publication just before the Conservative party conference, where a year earlier (readers may remember) Angus Maude had made a blistering attack on the swing to comprehensive education (see p.296). Black Paper Two also was designed to hit the headlines, and it did. In the lead article, Cyril Burt, whose fraudulent use of data had not yet been exposed, claimed that his 'researches' proved that 'today's standards in basic education are lower than they were 55 years ago, just before the 1914-1918 war' (as Cox and Dyson summarised it in their editorial). The data on which this surprising (and shocking) claim was made has since been shown to be equally fraudulent as other data used by Burt to shore up his theoretical standpoint concerning 'intelligence'.[19] Not known at the time, Burt's prestige ensured massive media coverage for these charges against the nation's schools, their teachers and administrators.

The first Black Paper, the editors now claimed, had broken the consensus on education. 'No longer can it be accepted that progressivism and comprehensive schemes are necessarily right, or that the future inevitably lies with them'. Perhaps that is why there was now a deliberate attempt to resuscitate the discredited ideology of intelligence testing, and to press its implications in terms of enhanced selective processes both within and between schools. Pride of place is given first to Cyril Burt, whose charges about standards were embodied in a characteristic, and lengthy article on 'The Mental Differences between Children'. This closes with an appeal for remedies in education to be 'guided, supervised and tested by scientific research'. In 'The Rise of the Mediocracy', H.J. Eysenck repeated, in a highly polemical (but again characteristic) article, the classic theories of psychometry; without the help of IQ tests a large number of people of '*mediocre* ability' will submerge 'many people of *superior* ability' (Eysenck's emphasis). This rise of a new mediocracy is, he concludes, 'socially unjust, nationally disastrous, and ethically unacceptable'. A third article, by Richard Lynn, also a Professor of Psychology, is perhaps the most provocative. Dealing also with the primacy of innate intelligence, Lynn claims as one of the most serious suppressions of truth by 'progressives' their assertion:

> that it is the fault of society that slum dwellers are impoverished and their children do badly at school. To the young red guards [the students, B.S.] it follows that society is unjust and must be overthrown. They do not realise that slum dwellers are caused principally by low innate intelligence and poor family upbringing, and that the real social challenge is posed by this

Analysis of the articles in Black Paper Two indicates the shift in the target for attack. Of 23 articles, six relate to universities and the student upsurge, but now there are eight focusing on comprehensive education – its disasters and difficulties (one, by Rhodes Boyson, then a comprehensive head, is concerned with the conditions for success). A group of four contributors (including G.H. Bantock) are concerned with the critique of primary (and 'progressive') education; three resuscitate intelligence test theory (as we have seen) while there is one generally declamatory article by a June Wedgwood Benn. This number also contains a combative riposte, by Amis and Conquest, to the reception of Black Paper One.

It is convenient, here, to jump ahead a little to the publication of Black Paper Three a year later, in November 1970 – some months after the June election which returned the Tories to power. For after this election (which, the Black Paperites hoped, would set everything right) there was a pause for some years before the Black Papers, now under a new joint editorship, took up the cudgels again. This third publication, triumphantly entitled *Goodbye Mr Short*, included only one article on universities (attacking the concept of the 'comprehensive university') out of a total of 21. The main thrust was, first, against comprehensive secondary education (five articles), as also against 'progressive' education (four articles, including two – again – by Boyson and Bantock), and very specifically against the move to non-streaming in both primary and secondary schools (in second articles by both Burt and Lynn). A strong defence was now mounted (by A.J.E. Doulton) of the direct grant schools (there had been one such article in the earlier Black Papers). But once again there was little on policy – what should actually be done to cure the nation's educational ills. The bulk of the articles in this, and indeed all three of the first set of publications, primarily reflected the disturbance, and indeed rage, of the authors at the new trends in education that characterised the 1960s. The attack was essentially destructive, reflecting also a nostalgia for the past – and past practices. Conscious of this criticism, Black Paper Three proposed, as a general policy, that selective education should be provided for between 5 and 8 per cent of pupils. But this was not worked out in any detail – nor seriously presented. It was later, in the 1970s, that the Black Papers began to articulate a specifically (Tory) educational policy.

A good deal of attention has been devoted to this first group of Black Papers – and deliberately, since this was the first serious assault mounted against the whole forward movement of the 1960s. Clearly sparked by the student revolt, the attack quickly spread right across the board, focusing finally on the key areas of advance – comprehensive education, the contemporary struggle to unify the single school as well as new developments in the primary schools. The main ideological focus was the defence of elitism (very overtly argued) against 'egalitarianism' – the attempt to provide equally for all. Exploiting an uneasiness about some of these developments, and the rate of change, the Black Paper editors and authors sought to whip up a strongly charged emotional barrier to prevent further advance and even turn back the clock. This initiative failed, at this moment, effectively to hit the target. 'The trouble', wrote the local authorities' journal *Education*, 'is that the Black Paper authors are so excessive in their "anti-egalitarian" zeal and are now emerging as so politically motivated that they lose all credibility and their targets go wholly unscathed.'[20] Nevertheless a constituency, of a sort, had been created – the editors claimed 80,000 copies of the first three Black Papers sold, largely to teachers, by 1971. The ideology there presented, modified of course by changing circumstances, was to re-emerge with greater force, and in new forms, as new crises developed within the economy and so within education a decade later. In the meantime, as we shall see in the next chapter, the Black Paper cry for a halt, in spite of the massive publicity it was accorded, hardly caused a ripple against the movement for change that now, some thought belatedly, was hitting the schools, in the form of a really powerful new swing towards comprehensive secondary education.

Notes and References

1. David McKie and Chris Cook (eds.), *The Decade of Disillusion: British Politics in the Sixties*, London 1972. See especially Chapter 8, 'The Quality of Life' by David McKie and Chapter 9, 'Politics Outside the System' by Hugo Young.

2. Brian MacArthur, 'The Education Debate' in ibid., Chapter 6, pp.167-80.

3. Surveys covering this period make it clear that the postwar expansion in student numbers at universities 'was not accompanied by increased participation from the lower socio-economic groups in society and all the evidence suggests that they continue to be under-represented amongst university students ... the continued under-representation from students with less socially and economically advantageous backgrounds cannot be denied'. Between 1961 and 1977 the age participation rate for the middle classes 'rose from 19.5 per cent to 26.6 per cent', but that for the working classes 'rose only from 3.2 per cent to 5.0 per cent'. Kenneth S. Davies, Paul Walker, David Tupman, 'Universities, Numbers, Money, Policies, 1945-85', Chapter 15 of W.A.C. Stewart, *Higher Education in Postwar Britain*, London 1989.

4. Educational expenditure, by both central and local government, exceeded defence expenditure for the first time in 1969-70, when it stood at £2,299 million compared with

£2,247 million spent on defence. See Appendix Tables 15 and 16, pp.601-2.

5. To give a single, but relevant example, in Japan the 'advancement' rate to upper secondary school level (fifteen to eighteen) where most pupils stay the full course, rose consistently from 57.7 per cent of the age group in 1960 to 81.2 per cent in 1970. In England and Wales, the percentage of each age group staying on in 1960 and 1970 were as follows:

	Aged 15	Aged 16	Aged 17
1960	31.0	15.4	7.6
1970	62.6	28.9	15.4

While all the percentages roughly doubled over this period, by 1970 these still lag very far behind the Japanese figures, especially for those aged 16 to 18. *Statistical Abstract of Education, Science and Culture*. Ministry of Education, Science and Culture, Japan, 1988 edn, p.24. *Education in 1961* and *Education and Science in 1970*. Ministry of Education and DES, pp.5 and 12.

6. For instance, on English developments specifically, Eric Ashby and Mary Anderson, *The Rise of the Student Estate in Britain*, London 1970; Colin Crouch, *The Student Revolt*, London 1970; Alexander Cockburn and Robin Blackburn (eds.), *Student Power*, Harmondsworth 1969; Harry Kidd, *The Trouble at the LSE, 1966-1967*, Oxford 1969; Tariq Ali (ed.), *New Revolutionaries; Left Opposition*, London 1969; E.P. Thompson (ed.), *Warwick University Ltd.*, Harmondsworth 1970; Students and Staff of Hornsey College of Art, *The Hornsey Affair*, Harmondsworth 1969.

7. This interpretation and that in the next paragraph, owes much to Eduard Goldstücker, 'Youth Separated by Thirty Years', an autobiographical account of the similarities and differences between the young people of the 1930s and those of the 1950s', *The Center Magazine*, Santa Barbara, California, Vol. VI, No. IV, July/August 1973, pp.37-46.

8. Campbell Stewart claims, on the basis of 'an authoritative, confidential and unpublished report ... by a disinterested observer' covering 1968-1973 that 'almost all 44 universities, a few art schools and polytechnics had several sit-ins lasting from a few hours to a few weeks', while some had meetings disrupted, break-ins to private rooms, etc. W.A.C. Stewart, *Higher Education in Post-war Britain*, London 1989, pp.121-2.

9. Jack Straw, 'Student Participation in Higher Education', Granada Guildhall Lecture, 6 October 1969 (mimeo).

10. Students and staff of Hornsey College of Art, *The Hornsey Affair*, Penguin Education Special, 1969, p.105 (chapter entitled 'The Educational Debate').

11. Ashby and Anderson, op.cit., pp.131-2.

12. Brian Simon, 'The Student Movement in England and Wales During the 1930s', *History of Education*, 1987, Vol.16, No.3, pp.189-203.

13. *Times*, 7 October 1969. Already at the Conservative Party conference the demand for effective representation and participation in university affairs was put with considerable force by student representatives. *Conservative Party Conference Report*, 1968.

14. Jack Straw, op. cit., p.1.

15. Select Committee on Education and Science, *Student Relations*, Vol.1, *Report*; Vols.II-VI, *Evidence and Appendices*; Vol.VII, *Documents*, 1969. For this committee, see Christopher Price MP, 'MPs and the Campus Revolt', *New Statesman*, 17 October 1969 – the committee, 'representing every sort of political opinion unanimously declined to take an anti-student backlash line' and 'backed the new move (initiated by the National Union of Students) for greater participation by students and staff in university affairs'.

16. Ashby and Anderson, op. cit., p.116.

17. This assessment is based on my own experience at Leicester University, together with discussions with other university teachers.

18. For a striking assessment of the Black Papers, see Frank Musgrove, 'The Black Paper Movement' in Roy Lowe (ed.), *The Changing Primary School*, London 1987.

Musgrove, Professor of Education at Manchester University, sees the Black Paper offensive as the expression of an elitist literary culture deriving from Matthew Arnold, and the work of the Cambridge critic, F.R. Leavis.

19. This specific article is discussed in some detail by Burt's official (and sympathetic) biographer, L.S. Hearnshaw, in *Cyril Burt, Psychologist*, London 1979. See especially pp.256-9, where the author reaches the conclusion that the data Burt utilised to support the thesis argued in this article were 'at least in part, fabricated'. A defence of Burt on this issue, mounted by Robert B. Joynson in *The Burt Affair*, London 1989, pp.205ff., is unconvincing.

20. *Education*, 27 November 1970. This journal's assessment is worth quoting. 'The first Black Paper, according to its editor, C.B. Cox, was "a forthright polemical onslaught on extremists", the second "substantiated the arguments" and the third ... "pleads for a settled policy of moderate reform". The reader would be hard put to discover just what these moderate reforms are. It is almost entirely the mixture as before, a somewhat petulant plea for a return to the *statu quo ante bellum* ... If there is any change it is towards an outright and enthusiastic political identity with what most of the contributors believe the policy of a Conservative Government ought to be. Whether many thinking Conservatives either at national or local level will embrace the black paper-weight message with the same enthusiasm is another matter.'

Part III

9 Downhill All the Way: The 1970s

1 Thatcher at the Helm

Although there had been moments of doubt, hesitation, signs of sharpening antagonisms and even confrontation (the 1968 cuts, the consequent postponement of raising the leaving age, the early Black Paper phenomenon), by 1970 educational advance was in full gear in every sector. In primary, secondary and across the board in further and higher education, expansion remained the order of the day. A whole new system of non-selective secondary education was now coming into being, opening new perspectives for the future. Educational expenditure now accounted for consistently higher proportions of gross domestic product and of public expenditure.

Morale was high among teachers,[1] local authorities and even at the DES. There was a general expectation of further growth, of exciting new innovations. To many, the traditional educational structure of the past seemed ripe for a new break-out where educational forms embodying new humanist perspectives might be made a reality. In view of the consensus achieved on many of these issues, the unexpected return of a Tory government in June 1970 seemed at that moment to present no immediate threat. Had not such a government a few years earlier fully accepted the Robbins committee's proposals and projections? The long-term significance of Edward Boyle's departure, and his replacement by Margaret Thatcher as shadow education minister in 1969 was not, then, generally understood.

The Heath government, however, ran into extreme

405

difficulties, both political and economic. During the four years it held power, five States of Emergency were declared, sharp industrial battles developed, particularly among the miners who, in 1972 and again in 1974, carried through a series of massive, highly organised, and finally successful strikes. It was as the outcome of the second of these that the government was defeated at the General Election of February 1974. Second, the oil price crisis of the late autumn of 1973, following the Arab-Israeli war, resulted in a massive quadrupling of the price of oil at a time when Britain was highly dependent on oil from the Middle East. The outcome was a series of panic measures climaxed by the three-day week and followed by radical cuts in public expenditure which particularly affected education (the 'Barber' cuts). 1973 also marked the beginning of the down-turn in pupil numbers in primary schools, heralding demographic contraction as a whole in place of the continuous expansion which had marked the post-war decades (see Appendix Table 2a, p.576). Although, in December 1972 Margaret Thatcher's White Paper entitled 'Framework for Expansion' announced a full further decade of educational growth, in fact the axe was already poised ominously overhead. That future was never to be realised. When the government fell only fourteen months later, it left behind a record rate of inflation, a record spending deficit and a record negative balance of payments.[2] By this time, also, the world of education, although cushioned from the immediate impact of both economic and political turbulence, was in disarray.

At the start of the Heath government's term of office, however, the main issue on which attention focussed was the future of comprehensive secondary education – now suddenly a contentious issue. To this we may now turn.

2 Spanners in the Works:
Thatcher and Comprehensive Education

Margaret Thatcher, shadow minister since October 1969, was, as expected, appointed Secretary of State for Education and Science in the new government.[3] She held this post uninterruptedly, remaining a loyal member of the government throughout its period of office. Her turn against Heath came later – in the leadership battles which followed his government's downfall.

Margaret Thatcher's rapid rise within the Tory Party had been carefully piloted by Edward Heath. She had been moved through various posts within the shadow government from the moment Heath gained the leadership in 1965. During this period, perhaps in an attempt to contain the growing rightist tendency within the party (sometimes virulently expressed, as we have seen, in the party conference education debates), Heath is assessed as giving 'full rein to the burgeoning radical wing of the party', so ensuring them 'a position they were never to lose'.[4] It was R.H.S. Crossman's perception that Thatcher was put into the shadow education post by, or as representing, Tory backlash groupings of the type that surfaced at the party conferences. Certainly it was in the field of education that what Cosgrave (Thatcher's sympathetic but perceptive biographer) defines as 'the sharper edge of the Heath counter-revolution' was seen in the first actions of the new minister as soon as the government took office.[5]

In the perception of a leading supporter, the Tories won the 1970 election 'against and not with the tide of opinion'.[6] This was certainly the case as far as the leading contemporary educational issue was concerned – comprehensive education. In their manifesto, the Tories had inserted a promise to withdraw circular 10/65.[7] Their determination to bring this into effect immediately caused an uproar. This was the issue that was to dominate the politics of education for the next three years, to climax in the late summer and early autumn of 1973.

Alongside action on comprehensive education, seen as retrogressive by almost the entire educational world, other measures early introduced hardly added to the new government's popularity. Museum charges were now imposed while, for a saving of £8 million agreed by Thatcher before the election, the provision of free school milk was curtailed – giving rise to the child's play-ground chant: 'Margaret Thatcher – milk snatcher'. These two measures, writes a historian of this government, 'produced small financial savings at an enormous political cost and gave the government the image of being hardhearted'.[8]

Withdrawal of 10/65

But the major immediate issue was certainly the impending withdrawal of circular 10/65. Immediately after the election of the new government the press and media generally were full of this proposed measure. Its significance was clear – it implied a specific threat to the further development of comprehensive education, now – in the words of a weighty analysis published, paradoxically, only one week before the election – 'Half Way there'.[9] 'Mrs Thatcher Will Withdraw Circular', reported the *Times Educational Supplement* a week after the election. Her first action, it is understood, 'will be to make this circular null and void either before or immediately after the Queen's speech on Thursday'.[10] 'A period of uncertainty now seems ahead for secondary schools', reported the *Guardian*, following this two days later with a report of plans for a national conference to mount a campaign 'to maintain the momentum of comprehensive advance'.[11] On 30 June circular 10/70 was published. This effectively implied the withdrawal of 10/65 under which the comprehensive transformation of secondary education had taken place over a period of precisely five years. It is wrong, the new circular argued, to impose a uniform pattern. Local authorities will now be 'freer' to determine secondary provision in their areas. Where a particular pattern is working well, the Secretary of State 'does not wish to cause further change without good reason'. If an authority has already had plans approved, they can go ahead, or notify the department of their wish to modify them. Those whose plans are now being considered by the department should say if they want them considered, or if they wish to withdraw them. The circular was not directly confrontational, in the sense that it neither demanded a return to selective systems nor prohibited the development of comprehensive schemes. It was, however, a clear indication to local authorities to retain existing selective systems and to draw back from comprehensive reorganisation – and was so recognised at the time.

This action triggered an immediate outcry. 'Fierce Reaction to Withdrawal of 10/65', reported the *Times Educational Supplement* three days later. On 8 July Edward Short initiated what turned out to be an extremely sharp debate in the Commons on the issue. This was accompanied by immediate criticism from a wide variety of organisations, local authorities and individuals. At the time circular 10/70 was issued, only fourteen of the then existing 163 local authorities in England and Wales had rejected circular 10/65's 'request' for the submission of plans. It was this action, writes Cosgrave, 'that marked her down as a target for many critics and enemies'. It is perhaps impossible, he continues, writing in the late 1970s,

> to recapture the full force of the passion of the moment, a passion so great that it was to lead later in the year to her husband suggesting that the pressure on her was so great, and her distress in its face so marked, that she should resign altogether from politics.[12]

However this may be, passions were certainly aroused (and within the Conservative Party as well as outside) by this action, which seemed to put at risk the major programme in education of the 1960s. This issue became the flashpoint of local politics throughout the election year (1970) and later, as we shall see.

The protests that poured in immediately after publication of the circular expressed shock and resentment. The Trades Union Congress complained that this action would prolong the effects of party political disputes upon the development of secondary education 'to the irreparable disadvantage of large numbers of children of all social classes'.[13] A delegation of protest from the NUT gained a promise that the minister would consult teachers and others before issuing another circular, 'but in most respects after an abrasive two hour meeting', runs the report, the NUT had 'little satisfaction in its complaints about the new policy'.[14] There are disturbing indications, reported the *Guardian*, 'that in some authorities mini-caucuses on the political right hope to use circular 10/70 for some angry hatchet work at the educational crossroads'. So the scene was set for sharp battles within Tory-controlled local authorities – marking a new phase in the long struggle for comprehensive education. This is where the major confrontations were to take place over succeeding months. Outcomes were unexpected.

Local Battles

'Tory Councils Storm over 10/70', reported the *Teacher* in September. 'Tory-controlled councils who dithered over secondary reorganisation when they received Mrs Thatcher's 10/70 Circular are now on the brink of decision.' By lobbing the ball back, Mrs Thatcher 'has started a resounding storm in local Tory parties'.[15] A crucial area was the Tory-controlled shire county of Bedfordshire, where the comprehensive plan was withdrawn by the council following 10/70. Divisions immediately appeared. 'It was a black day for the whole county when this decision was made,' said the chair of the education committee. 'Before the war we were among the backwoods in education. Our own special comprehensive system would have put us in the forefront. Now we are back to square one.'[16]

The county's teachers were reported as 'seething with discontent' with the county council's decision. At Dunstable Grammar School, 25 out of the total of 29 staff had come out in favour of the proposed comprehensive system earlier in the year. Now the county's education committee prepared to oppose its own council which had acted so precipitately. A 'battle royal' was expected at the October county council meeting. In Northumberland also, battles were predicted; a comprehensive scheme to complete reorganisation, which would almost certainly have been accepted before 10/70, was referred back by the DES, and the education committee was busy thrashing it out ('almost literally' according to reports).[17] In a survey article entitled 'Summer of the Backlash', the journal of the Confederation for the Advancement of State Education (CASE) dealt with the revolts in Bedfordshire and in particular in Surrey which was to be the focus of a classic struggle for comprehensive education. The Surrey STEP (Stop the Eleven Plus) was now established, sparked by CASE. A well organised campaign was already underway by September, involving a demonstration at the county hall attended, among others, by coachloads of students, a series of public meetings, a county wide petition, car stickers and deputations; Surrey teachers now 'formally threatened to boycott the 11-plus if the county does not go ahead with comprehensive plans'.[18] In Barnet, another Conservative authority, troubles were brewing and there again CASE helped establish another broadly based anti-selection group, 'The Association for the Abolition of Selection at Eleven' (AASE). The CASE article concluded, from survey material, that

> the anti-comprehensive backlash this summer has been real enough but it is possible to exaggerate the consequences. Most of the local authorities are conservative controlled and most are proceeding with comprehensive reorganisation.[19]

Through the autumn, action continued in defence of comprehensive education in these key areas. In Bedfordshire an 'action committee against selection', another mushrooming organisation, arranged a meeting attended by 500, addressed, among others, by the head of Dunstable Grammar School who expressed his support for the county's comprehensive scheme. Now Richmond (Surrey), one of the few authorities never to have responded to 10/65, decided, ironically in response to 10/70, to abolish selection (by a vote of 25 to six in the education committee), the council agreeing to the education committee's plans, but only insisting on more consultation as to the form of comprehensive schools to be established.[20] This decision was welcomed by the borough's 3,000-strong parents' association. The Richmond Association for State Education had brought out a plan for all-through comprehensives in May – just before the election. The education committee's plan, now presented, was for two sixth form colleges.

At this point a fierce attack was launched by the Bow Group of Tory moderates, both on the handling of the election, and on Thatcher's first act as Secretary of State. The *Guardian* reported that 'a special black mark' had been give to Mrs Thatcher by 'Mentor' in their publication. Withdrawal of 10/65 'has immensely strengthened reactionary forces within each education authority'. This is 'a classic case of an unnecessary decision being badly taken for reasons of political dogmatism'. Thatcher had done 'nothing to help progressive authorities and much to bolster reactionary ones'. This has been bad for education, 'and bad for the Conservative Party as well'.[21]

Now trouble surfaced in another Tory area. Early in October the Conservative-controlled Barnet council decided, by a vote of 40 to 20, to abolish selection by establishing fourteen all-through comprehensive schools. Questionnaires distributed to parents and teachers showed that 79.4 per cent favoured non-selective reorganisation. An amendment to retain five grammar schools was defeated by 42 to 21.[22] But further trouble was brewing over the Barnet issue.

At the Conservative Party conference which now took place (early October), Margaret Thatcher (who was loudly cheered) said there could only be one top priority, and theirs was primary schools (this had been emphasised in the Tory manifesto). An overwhelming majority was gained for a largely anodyne resolution which, however, welcomed the withdrawal of 10/65.[23] This was opposed by Clive Buckmaster, an early representative of the radical right, who attacked local authorities for going comprehensive and argued that grammar schools should be removed from the state system and allowed to become independent (as the means of their preservation).

Education, Thatcher replied to the debate, should give opportunities for people to use their talents. The government would continue to carry out its manifesto pledges 'and to increase the proud record of their party in education'. The opposition appeared half-hearted; no doubt the conference was pleased with Thatcher as minister, rather than Boyle.[24]

The party conference, however, proved no more than a 'hiccough in education' (see note 24). In practice, and in spite of 10/70, the comprehensive bandwagon rolled on – later described by Thatcher herself as a 'roller coaster' at this period. The new feature, of course, was the determination of new middle-class groupings, exemplified by CASE, to abolish selection and establish fully comprehensive systems. By the end of October the educational press was reporting, under the heading 'More Groups Fight Selection', that comprehensive pressure groups, 'their hopes heightened by recent successes in the London boroughs', were now campaigning vigorously in five of the nineteen places 'where the local authorities are bent on retaining selection'. In Bedfordshire an active campaign was underway, the local action committee organising rallies, lobbying councillors, now gaining support from teacher organisations and some clergy (including the Bishop of Bedford). Local campaigns organised by CASE or the Comprehensive Schools Committee (CSC) were underway in Birmingham, Buckinghamshire, Norfolk, Reading and Kingston on Thames – planning demonstrations and public meetings 'in an effort to get their authorities to abandon the 11-plus in any form'. In Birmingham 100,000 leaflets had been distributed. In Reading a local branch of CSC had been formed with backing from the NUT and other organisations – a broadly based campaign was being planned. A new group in Norfolk – the Campaign for the Advancement of Norfolk Education (CANE) had been formed, based on Surrey's STEP. At Kingston CASE and others were pressing for a referendum. Branches of CASE in South Buckinghamshire were meeting to co-ordinate activities. The effect of 10/70 was to trigger a powerful grass roots fightback, strengthening the movement, and the networks behind it, for comprehensive education.[25]

Public attention focused on Bedfordshire, a divided Tory council where the issue was very clear. Early in November the climax of the action committee's campaign came two days before the crucial council meeting, when the final decision would be taken. Here a traditional Conservative seat in North Bedford was won by a Liberal 'fighting on a comprehensive ticket'. This 'surprising victory' rattled the pro-grammar group, and was to prove decisive. The Bedfordshire vote was won, after a five-hour debate, by the casting vote of the chairman of the county council. 'The most dramatic victory to be won by comprehensive pressure groups so far,' reported the *Times Educational Supplement*. 'When Mr Leslie Bowles, the council chairman, cast his vote in favour of the comprehensive plan,' runs the report, 'there was a massive uplift of arms and hands and a prolonged burst of clapping from a packed audience gallery.'[26]

'Anti-comprehensive Bastions Topple', reported the *Times Educational Supplement*. Bedfordshire had voted to go comprehensive 'by a whisker'. The thin end of the wedge had been driven into Surrey. The grammar school fortresses of Barnet and Richmond had been toppled. 'The first round since Mrs Thatcher's circular 10/70 re-opened the selection controversy last June', concluded the journal, 'has ended with victories all the way for parents who have battled for the comprehensive cause.'[27]

The Secretary of State, however, had considerable powers to slow down the rate of change and this, as a lawyer, Margaret Thatcher fully understood. This provides the key to the next phase in this long drawn out battle to transform the divisive system of the past into something more generous and more resilient in the future. To this new phase we may now turn.

A Summer's Outrage

The withdrawal of Circular 10/65, and its replacement by 10/70 was more than a simple act of defiance. It meant an end to the 'request' that local authorities produce development plans relating to comprehensive education. Henceforward propositions to alter the status of a school had to be made for each specific school individually, to be considered according to procedures set out in Section 13 of the 1944 Act.[28] This required the issue of notices for each school, the decision to be made by the minister after consideration of objections. Taking the opportunity of a North of England education conference in January 1971, Thatcher stressed that development plans were now finished with.[29] Later in the House of Commons, answering a question on secondary reorganisation, she underlined the decision. 'Plans', she said, 'have no statutory significance, and there is now no obligation to submit them.'[30] From now on, then, an authority wishing to reorganise must submit every individual proposal for decision by the Secretary of State under Section 13 procedure.

But in spite of 10/70, and of the fact that the large majority of local authorities were now Conservative controlled, proposals continued to pour into the DES. The 11-plus issue, as the *Guardian* reported, 'has obstinately refused to go away'.[31] It should be remembered that at this time (1971), only 35 per cent of pupils of secondary school age were in 'comprehensive' schools (as defined by the DES) (see Appendix Table 7, p.589). Grammar and secondary modern schools, that is, the traditional divided system, with nearly two-thirds of all pupils, still largely dominated the maintained system. The future was by no means certain, though between January 1970 and January 1971 (which included six months of Labour government) 228 new comprehensive schools had been established.[32]

An attempt must be made to summarise the crowded and increasingly dramatic developments over the next three years – leading to the 'Summer's Outrage' of 1973.[33] This was a period of confrontational politics – between local authorities, parents and central government (in the person of Thatcher). As area after area (many of them Conservative-controlled) tried to realise their plans, Thatcher's resistance hardened, to reach a peak of conflict seldom experienced within the field of education – till then seen as an harmonious 'partnership' between the main protagonists.

The overall figures, covering the period as a whole, belie the intensity of the conflict; but they also reflect the growing determination to implement the comprehensive solution. The number of proposals relating to individual schools snowballed over these years. In April 1972 Thatcher reported a total of 1,400 proposals received by the DES. Seven months later (in October) the total reached 2,300. By December 1973, close to the government's demise, 3,612 proposals had been received.[34]

The great majority of these were accepted by Thatcher, as she pointed out, and, indeed, the actual number of comprehensive schools (again, as defined by the DES), increased from 1,250 in 1970 to 2,677 in 1974 – that is, more rapidly than at any time before or since,[35] and this indicates something of the power and force behind this movement (see Appendix Table 6a, p.586). But, given the politics of the time, and the fact that Conservative authorities often took the initiative, this drive could hardly be resisted. What could (might) be done was to render its full realisation nugatory by insisting on the preservation of specific grammar schools as independent entities; and, in general, this was the main direction of Thatcher's actions. Hence the title of this section.

The original flashpoints for action during 1971 were the Tory authorities of Barnet, Surrey, Lancashire and, to a certain extent, Bexley and Kingston. Parental protests at Barnet resulted in a deputation to the minister (Thatcher) in January. Two grammar school amalgamations were then refused by her under Section 13 procedure,[36] thus negating the implementation of the plan as a whole. Sharp criticisms were made at the council meeting in July where a resolution stressing 'grave concern' at Thatcher's decisions was carried. 'We are faced with a minister who is determined, come what may, that the spread of education shall be reserved for the privileged few,' the council's leader is reported as saying. Margaret Thatcher had taken on 'the role of Queen Canute' and had acted against the expressed wishes of the people of the borough.[37]

'One by one, watch them come home. Mrs Thatcher's pullets on their way to roost,' wrote the *Times Educational Supplement* in July.[38] 'Last week it was conservative Barnet, this time it is Tory Surrey.' In a comprehensive scheme for Walton-on-Thames, the authority intended to define the comprehensive catchment area strictly, and not to offer pupils within it any opportunity to go to grammar schools elsewhere in the county. 'Mrs Thatcher has rejected this and enforced her will within the thunderbolt of a formal direction under the rarely used Section 68 of the Education Act.' By this action, Mrs Thatcher appeared as 'the political champion of those Surrey voters who object to what their county council is doing'. The intention was clear, to deter other authorities and to encourage other objectors. 'But here, in its most emphatic form, is proof of the emptiness of the government's claim to support local decision making.'[39]

In April Lancashire disappointed some of its county Tories by reaffirming its policy of introducing comprehensive secondary education, so marking the failure of the 'keep-the grammar-schools' campaigns which had sprung up after 10/70. By September 1972, it was reported, seventeen of the 29 divisions and excepted boroughs would have completed or embarked on the change to comprehensive education.[40] But this scheme also ran into trouble a year later, when Thatcher vetoed (under Section 13) a plan to include Ormskirk Grammar School in the city's comprehensive plan. This was a typical example of the spanner wielded by the Secretary of State. The life and development of at least 21 local schools would be adversely affected by this decision, declared Jack Ashton, Chair of the Education Committee. 'It is to me quite incomprehensible and contrary to all natural justice and sound educational policy', he went on, 'that the protests of some people in relation to one school can so affect the lives of so many parents and children, whose views have not been consulted.'[41]

Actions of this kind seemed to have the effect of further consolidating support for comprehensive education. In April the annual conference of the National Union of Teachers carried overwhelmingly an amendment demanding a campaign to bring all selective schools within the comprehensive system.[42] Perhaps even more significant was the National Association of Head Teachers' vote for the implementation of a national policy of comprehensive education. Carried by 5,125 to 2,809 (almost 2:1) this was the association's strongest ever stand on this issue. In previous years it stood for cautious 'controlled experiments'.[43] Towards the end of the year, in an article entitled 'Ted's Slowest Learner', Richard Bourne of the *Guardian* referred to the 'new disenchantment with Mrs Thatcher'. Discussing the Surrey and Barnet decisions among others, he concluded that 'it is starting to look like a catalogue of decisions which show not only wrong-headedness, but a loss of credibility'.[44] But there was more to come.

The municipal elections of May 1971 had strengthened Labour's position in local government. Not only was the ILEA wrested from three years of Tory control (although the conservatives had continued labour's comprehensive policy), but in Birmingham the electorate had also returned a labour majority determined to implement a radical comprehensive plan. This was to prove a flash-point for the future. However the feelings aroused among teachers and others in areas frustrated by Thatcher's decisions powerfully surfaced early

the next year. A unanimous resolution by the 4,000 strong
Surrey Teachers' Association called on the Prime Minister, in
February, to dismiss Thatcher from office because she was
'proving to be an educational disaster' for the county and for
the country as a whole. The immediate issue was her refusal to
allow the closure of a particular grammar school (Whyteleafe).
The association pledged its support to the county council in
steps to go fully comprehensive. A spokesman for STEP was
reported as saying at this juncture that Mrs Thatcher was now
'thwarting every attempt by the local authority to implement
its comprehensive plans'.[45]

Particular concern was now expressed, by the local authority
journal *Education*, with Thatcher's recent decisions relating to
Worcestershire and the ILEA, as well as Surrey and Barnet.
All these gave serious cause for concern, pointing to 'a quite
negative attitude to the elementary necessities and to a reckless
application of indigestible doctrines'. 'Just what is DES policy
on secondary reorganisation?' asked the journal. In Worcestershire Mrs Thatcher had turned down three proposals in
one area relating to grammar schools, the result being that the
authority was placed in the impossible position of having to
retain selection at eleven within what it intended to be a
three-tier system. In addition the ILEA had been prevented
from carrying through important measures required to
complete comprehensivisation.[46]

A fortnight later the same journal reported Thatcher's
refusal to give the go-ahead for a comprehensive school at
Trowbridge (Wiltshire), requiring an amalgamation of a
grammar and secondary modern, even though no objections
had been made to her.[47] It was actions such as this that now led
the Association of Education Committees to carry a resolution
to the effect that each local authority had the right (within
certain conditions) to organise secondary education on
comprehensive lines and that such schemes 'should not be
modified by the Secretary of State so as to interfere with this
concept'. Later that year the AEC argued this issue in a
deputation to the minister.[48]

Far from holding back in the light of opposition, Margaret
Thatcher now deliberately raised the stakes. In a statement
reminiscent of Florence Horsbrugh's of 1953 (see pp.171-2), she
took the opportunity of the Conservative Party Conference in
October. The *Times* reported that, obviously struck by the

applause and support given to speeches in favour of retaining grammar schools, she said she hoped that those believing in the future of these schools 'would be as vocal in their own areas and outside the conference hall'. She was, she said, bound to take objections of local people into account. Where changes were proposed for famous grammar schools 'with supreme reputations', the objections came in 'thick and fast'. [49] Her object, of course, as in the case of Florence Horsbrugh twenty years earlier, was to ensure that these objections persisted. These gave her the necessary legal pretext for preserving grammar schools, and so resisting the establishment of genuinely comprehensive local systems.

What is Mrs Thatcher up to? was the title of a pamphlet published by the NUT in November 1972. This expressed growing concern within the teaching profession as to her objectives and the actual practical effect of what were increasingly seen as a series of arbitrary, indeed capricious decisions concerning school reorganisation. Through 1973 events moved to the climax of the late summer and early autumn. In May the NUT, certainly the leading teachers' organisation at this time, resolved at conference on a vigorous campaign for the withdrawal of 10/70, and asked the executive to support members refusing to take part in selective practices after September 1975, except in areas where reorganisation was accepted in principle and applied in practice.[50] In June the Association of Education Committees, then representing all such committees within local government, after a powerful debate including much criticism of Thatcher's decisions, declared in a resolution its strong support for the principle of comprehensive education as well as its concern that the continuance of selective systems in many areas of the country 'is resulting in inequality of opportunity, social divisiveness ... and wastage of resources'.[51] Other resolutions concerned Thatcher's use of Section 13 and the need to amend it so that opinions in favour of specific proposals, as well as objections, were taken into account.

But it was in July that matters reached a crisis as a result of decisions relating to both Birmingham and Liverpool – both by now Labour-controlled authorities. More than half the Birmingham proposals were rejected. This led to enormous resentment locally and nationally. 'The rejection by Mrs Margaret Thatcher of Birmingham's proposals for secondary reorganisation last week represents one of the biggest and most hostile confrontations between central and local government hitherto in Mr Heath's administration,' wrote the local authorities' official journal. This decision confirms that there is no national policy 'except to preserve the status quo'. The DES's reply to Birmingham not only reflects ideological prejudices, administratively it is 'grossly inept'. There is no pattern in the approach and rejections.[52] Teachers' leaders were 'bitterly resentful' of Thatcher's mutilation of the Birmingham plan.[53] With predictable determination, reported the *Times Educational Supplement*, Mrs Thatcher has cut Birmingham's reorganisation plan to pieces.[54] The situation at Liverpool was less dramatic, but similar. Two proud cities were thereby brought to their knees. They were not to forget it. These developments, incidentally, indicate that it was not only the 'new middle class' in the south of England that was now making the running, as is often suggested. The great industrial cities of the Midlands and the North, where the whole movement had originally been initiated nearly twenty years earlier, were now determined to carry through effectively their earlier policy decisions.

But this was not all. 'Outright Rejection for Burton-on-Trent', reported *Education* later in July. Here was Thatcher's 'latest victim'. Every one of the four propositions from this Labour authority was rejected.[55] In the autumn, due to questionable procedures under Section 13, the Surrey County Council as well as the NUT both officially sought counsel's opinion as to the legality of Thatcher's decisions. In September a long pamphlet, *Indictment of Margaret Thatcher* was published by the educational journal *Forum*. Based on a detailed analysis of the legal situation and DES and Thatcher actions, this concluded that the minister was clearly bending the law in the pursuit of her political objectives.[56]

Surrey's chief education officer had confirmed in August that the authority was seeking legal advice, and that Mrs Thatcher might face a high court action over her use of Section 13. Sheila Wright, Birmingham's education chair, confirmed the probability of similar action by the city. In a *Times Educational Supplement* leader that month, 'Rentacrowd for Section 13', Mrs Thatcher's 'spoiling tactics' came in for criticism. She all but destroyed secondary planning after taking office, it is argued, by abandoning development plan procedures used under the Labour government for school-by-school decision under Section 13. And when the main criteria for decisions have been objections and not the way the school might fit in with an authority's wider objectives, it has been easy enough to 'save our schools', or to save 'the loudest voiced grammar schools'.[57] The rate of rejection by Thatcher of proposals for change involving individual schools now mounted sharply. In April 1972, of 1,400 proposals, 46 were rejected. By October that year the *Times* reported 92 rejections from 2,300 proposals. But a year later, in November 1973, rejections reached 326 (from 3,612 proposals).[58] So confrontation was deliberately escalated.

The row over Surrey, Harrow and Barnet smouldered on through the autumn – 'One Accusation after Another' headlined the local authorities journal.[59] At Birmingham, Liverpool, Lancashire, Burton-on-Trent; in Buckinghamshire, Wiltshire, and now the North Riding and Sutton, the authorities, parental pressure groups, teachers, were licking their wounds – determining how best to achieve the local system desired by the elected representatives of the area. But now the issue was swamped by larger political considerations – the three-day week and the miners' strike. The whole sorry story of mindless resistance to a necessary change was lost in the chaos and confusion of the last months of the Heath government, of which Margaret Thatcher remained so loyal a member to the end.

3 Tory Policy, 1970-74

The withdrawal of circular 10/65 was not, of course, the only measure relating to education brought in by the Conservative government, though it was certainly the most important in terms of immediate contemporary politics, and the one that led to the sharpest controversy. But there were other measures – or priorities. One was, in many people's minds, closely connected with the 10/65 issue. This was the priority announced for primary- rather than secondary-school building. This had been included in the Tory election manifesto, and was in fact brought in as a clear and definite policy by the new government. The argument that primary building had been neglected historically compared to secondary was incontestible. But coming just at the point when a strong surge to comprehensive education was clearly evident, this policy appeared to many as, fundamentally, another means of ensuring the slowdown of this movement.

Under the heading 'Primary Plans Will Halt Other Building', Richard Bourne (of the *Guardian*) argued, in August 1970, that 'A complete halt in the improvement and replacement of secondary schools in 1973/4 will be the price of Mrs Thatcher's major renewal campaign for primary schools.' His source was a DES leaflet just issued on school building. During 1973-74 more than £48 million was earmarked for the improvement and replacement of old primary schools. This, he argued, will have 'a negative effect on comprehensive school planning'.[60]

Local authorities objected to this *dirigiste*, centralised direction as to how they should use resources allocated for capital projects. Up till now this had been a matter for local initiative, even if central authority agreement was required. Now the DES was arrogating to itself the right to determine the direction of all such expenditure. This resulted in one of the first serious local authority protests to central government on this issue.[61] How this policy affected one authority was made clear by an ILEA spokesman, Canon Harvey-Hinds. 'We are literally out of business for ten years as far as building or improving any secondary schools in London is concerned,' he said. An embargo had been placed on any secondary school building unless the need for 'roof over heads' could be proved. The ILEA was planning to spend some £40 million on improving 160 schools by 1980. These schools were decrepit; the resulting situation 'very serious'.[62]

The suspicions of those who felt that there was a hidden target within this general measure were clearly articulated by Edward Short, now shadow minister for education. The primary priority, he claimed, was wrong. It was aimed at stopping secondary reorganisation. Mrs Thatcher 'was making a mockery of secondary education for tens of thousands of children for ideological, elitist reasons'. The sharpness of this formulation well reflected the increasing polarisation within educational politics which marked this phase.[63]

The Heath government's image was early tarnished, as we have seen, by the withdrawal of school milk and the imposition of museum charges. Substantial reductions in public expenditure was a major platform of the party, though a U-turn later negated the policy (particularly through generous subsidisation of ailing industries – Rolls Royce, the Upper Clyde Shipbuilders, etc.). But at the start education participated in this smack of firm government. 'Tories may hit education to save £100 million', reported the *Guardian* in June 1970. Increases in the price of school meals, transport and library services were predicted. The Open University, about to recruit its first students, was to have its target reduced from 25,000 to 10,000. Building already projected for further and higher education was to be postponed, as well as putting the brake on secondary school building. All these, it was suggested, are being pressed for by the Treasury as part of the Tory review of public expenditure.[64]

If the government got off to a bad start as a result of these and other measures and statements, this was partially redeemed – in the eyes of the educational world at least – by the decision to implement the manifesto commitment to raise the school leaving age to sixteen; as, of course, provided for in the 1944 Act nearly three decades earlier. This measure, it will be remembered, had been due for implementation under the previous Labour administration, but was postponed in 1968 as part of Roy Jenkins' cuts of that year (see pp.297-8). On 3 March 1972 an Order in Council was made bringing the new leaving age into force that September – at the beginning of the school year. It had been preceded by circular 8/71 requiring local authorities to submit reports on their proposals in this regard. The first generation of secondary school pupils covered by this measure completed their compulsory school period (now five to sixteen) in 1974. The repercussions from this measure, therefore, form part of the next section of this chapter (as also those stemming from the local government reform act of 1972, which was implemented on 1 April 1974). It is, however, worth noting that, in 1972, well over 60 per cent of the relevant age group were already voluntarily staying on for a fifth year in maintained schools.[65] This was not, then, so major an undertaking as the rise from fourteen to fifteen in 1947, for which Ellen Wilkinson had had to fight within the Cabinet at that time.[66] It was, however, very widely welcomed, particularly by comprehensive school proponents, who saw new opportunities in the full five-year course now available for all.[67] It is from this time that the demand for a single examination for all at sixteen reached the point of potential realisation. As we shall see later, however, this road (unsurprisingly) became fraught with man- (and woman-) made obstacles.

The defence of selective education, particularly the grammar schools, and at almost any cost, was, as we have seen, the government's major aim in education. The 179 direct grant schools represented a cherished outpost of this system – since these received a direct subvention from the state (DES) and were not under local authority control. The Donnison Committee, proposing the integration of these schools into locally controlled comprehensive systems, had only reported, after detailed enquiry in 1970. This report was not only well researched, it was a closely argued, highly rational document, strongly supportive of comprehensive education (see pp.328-30). In a real sense it augured the death sentence on this particular category of schools, now seen as an historical anomaly.

In their manifesto, however, the Tories had promised to give encouragement to the direct grant schools. Critics recognised the importance of this at an early stage. In a main leader on education (the first of three) the *Guardian* predicted immediately after the election, that these schools, 'emerging from the shadow of Donnison', will be 'brandished as the standard bearers of conservative excellence'.[68] The journal of the local authorities, welcoming Thatcher's appointment (said to be 'right of centre in Tory terms') also predicted that she was planning action on direct grant schools, adding that 'it is easy to see that it could seriously damage the plans of any local authority bent on a genuine comprehensive scheme'.[69]

But it was not until over a year later that action was taken. In November 1971 the decision to increase subventions to the direct grant schools by £2 million was announced in the Queen's speech. This was roughly the amount that Edward Short had withheld in 1969 (in 1967 and 1968 he had refused to increase grants in line with the growth in teachers' salaries). This action was warmly welcomed, as might be expected, by the Headmasters' Conference, which went on to ask Thatcher to reopen the direct grant list. Perhaps it was a sign of things to come.[70]

This decision led to bitter exchanges in the House of Commons both then and later. Labour's opposition was unyielding.[71] The outcome, during the next Labour administration, was predictable.

What of more distant plans? The DES was, after all, responsible for the whole range of education, from nursery school to university. The Robbins committee had, a few years earlier (in 1963), sketched out a plan for higher education which reached to 1980; but circumstances had changed. The DES was not noted for its planning capability, but this also had changed, in intention at least. Early in 1971, a Planning and Research Branch (or unit) had been established. The outcome was the ill-fated White Paper, *Education: a Framework for Expansion* published in December 1972, and retailing at precisely 31½p.

It is here that we run into a paradox – or indeed a series of paradoxes. The Heath government was elected on a programme involving severe curtailment of public expenditure; yet here was a ten-year programme which claimed, at least, to be profoundly, indeed radically, expansionist. Certainly this is how Margaret Thatcher presented (or began to sell) the programme early in 1972 – several months before publication. Taking the opportunity of an invitation to speak to the annual conference of the NUT in April, she announced an increased school building programme now, she claimed, running at record levels, going on to underline the huge increase in public expenditure on education already taking place. In 1969-70 such expenditure totalled nearly £2 billion, but in the financial year just finishing (1971-72) the total would probably reach £2.5 billion (an increase of £500 million). Educational expenditure, she stated, now stood at 13 per cent of total public expenditure, but in 1975-76 (in three years' time) it was planned to reach 14 per cent. Her reasons for both present and future growth included as central the current and, more especially, the future planned expansion of nursery education. Having delivered this 'good news' (the 'bad news' was her remarks on secondary school reorganisation), Margaret Thatcher concluded with a resounding accolade to the NUT for its size, influence and professional expertise. It could contribute much to the debate about the future of education, she said.[72]

Further details of this great expansionist programme were presented, again by Margaret Thatcher, to the Tory Party conference early in October. Her speech on this occasion, according to the *Times Educational Supplement*, was far and away her most substantive speech to a Tory conference and indeed comprised an over-arching policy statement. 'A great expansion of nursery education and polytechnics in Mrs Thatcher's package', reported the *Times*. £41 million was to go on an increased building programme for polytechnics and other further education colleges. The committee on teacher training, chaired by Lord James and set up late in 1970, would shortly report and action would follow.[73] In her speech Thatcher stressed her new priority – systematic expansion of nursery education, the details of which were to be announced soon, including a measure of priority to areas of social handicap (i.e. positive discrimination, as suggested by Plowden, and now being researched by a team under Dr A.H. Halsey).[74] This, it seems likely, was Mrs Thatcher's high point as Secretary of State for Education (and Science).

The White Paper underwrote, and indeed extended, the expansionist theme of Margaret Thatcher's speeches. Government expenditure on education was set to rise over the next ten years (1971-72 to 1981-82) by £1,000 million – from £2,162 million to £3,120 million (at constant prices); a rise of 50 per cent in ten years. This covered (only) three-quarters of the Secretary of State's responsibilities. The government, it is argued, is, therefore, fully intending to continue the expansion in this field at an overall rate at least equal to, or greater than that achieved in the 1960s. That said, the bulk of the White Paper focused on higher (and further) education, the schools being very summarily dealt with in thirteen pages while over 30 are given to teacher training (a major concern following the James Report of 1972), to polytechnics and universities together with the proposed future pattern of higher education as a whole.

Certain points may be made. The White Paper certainly announced, as by now expected, a major advance in nursery education, where, as the paper pointed out, Britain lagged far behind most European countries.[75] The aim was to ensure that nursery education should be 'widely available' within ten years for children aged three and four, while priority would be given in the early stages 'to areas of disadvantage'. Staffing and the resources required are dealt with, while a research programme to monitor developments was announced. In terms of schooling, this was the major new proposal of the White Paper.[76] As regards schools generally, the White Paper set out capital and recurrent expenditure proposals for both primary and secondary schools. The main feature here is the discussion about, and proposals relating to, the increasing size of the teaching force required, based on a planned overall reduction of the staff-pupil ratio from 1:22.6 in 1971 to 1:18.5 in 1981. To achieve this, in a period, incidentally, when the primary school population would decline, would involve expanding the teaching force from 364,000 in 1971 to 510,000 in 1981 – an increase of 146,000.

As far as higher (and further) education is concerned, the White Paper also proposed, with one exception (teacher training), an expansionist programme. Its main significance, however, was the clear determination expressed to use this expansion to sharpen, and harden, the binary divide.

The paper proposed expansion of the number of students in full-time higher education from the 463,000 of 1971–72 to 750,000 ten years later. From 15 per cent of the age group in 1971, the stated aim was to reach 22 per cent in 1981. If this had in fact been achieved, Britain would have been on the edge of a break-through to mass higher education, as was already the case in the United States and the Soviet Union. This would involve a rapid and deliberate expansion of the polytechnics. The objective was that these (together with other 'non-university institutions') should recruit some 335,000 students (in England and Wales) by 1981. This would involve a net expansion in England and Wales of some 130,000 above the existing (1971–72) total of 204,000 in these institutions. The universities, with 236,000 full-time students, were also expected to expand to the same overall total, 335,000 in England and Wales – an increase of about 100,000, but, of course, from a larger base in buildings, staffing and equipment.[77]

Other features of the paper need not seriously concern us here. The main proposal, taken from the James Report, for the establishment of a two year 'Higher Education Diploma', was taken up and recommended to the polytechnics in particular. This report's recommendation to break the historic relation between colleges of education and universities through Area Training Organisations (set up as a result of the McNair Report of 1944 – see p.35) was warmly welcomed by the government which announced, in the White Paper, the proposed precipitous run-down of such colleges due to the now declining cohorts of pupils beginning to come through the system, and further proposed that many of these should, if not close, amalgamate with polytechnics or colleges of further education (the door was left open for a small minority to amalgamate with universities). Instead of the four-year degree course for teachers proposed by James, the government opted for a three-year course (for the BEd) which should *include* at least fifteen weeks' teaching practice. It was the priority given to polytechnic expansion, together with their fusion with the major part of the relatively substantial system of colleges of education, which reinforced the binary divide. No suggestion whatever was made as to the possible fusion of the two systems (universities and 'public sector institutions').[78]

Many of these plans were quickly shattered – or abandoned – particularly those relating to overall expansion of higher education. Between 1970 and 1973 the rate of growth at the universities in fact declined by more than 50 per cent.[79] The polytechnics were, however, built up more rapidly than the universities, while something of the nursery programme survived. There was also some decline in the pupil-teacher ratio. Though presented as a great programme of expansion, there were many who, after close examination, thought otherwise. Indeed the White Paper soon became known, at least as far as the schools were concerned, as a recipe for contraction, particularly in relation to the proposed cut-back in teacher supply. In June 1973 the Association of Education Committees came out firmly against these features of the White Paper.[80] The TUC also issued a statement on the same theme. This opposition was substantiated in July by a thoroughly researched report from Manchester University which, sharply critical of DES statistics, found that the 1981 target figures for teachers would in fact produce only a slight improvement on the 1971 position. To reduce all classes to 30, 59,000 more teachers would be needed than planned for.[81] But, in a sense, all such discussion proved academic. Educational planning was about to be overwhelmed by the economic crisis which hit the country in the autumn of 1973. From that point a wholly new perspective became dominant. Educational expansion, on the scale that had now persisted for two decades or more, was to become a memory.[82]

We now reach the point of the disintegration of the Heath government, under the combined impact of the oil crisis, massively rising inflation as well as the looming miners' strike leading to confrontation and finally to the dissolution of Parliament and the February election. Panic measures were the order of the day and these included a sudden massive blow at education which shook (or shocked) all concerned, and from which, in a sense, the system has never yet recovered. 'Britain's education system faces one of the grimmest years in living memory', wrote the *Times Educational Supplement*, on the announcement of the 'Barber cuts' of £200 million suddenly imposed in mid-December. These 'enormous cut backs' in public spending, to have immediate effect, meant that all new building must come to a complete halt until July 1974. All other spending was to be severely cut. These were 'far and away the worst cuts in my professional lifetime', said W.P. Alexander, Secretary of the Association of Education Committees. The only bright spot was that, though the government's White Paper *Framework for Expansion* was 'swept aside', the nursery programme would be protected.[83]

1973 began full of promise for education, wrote the local authorities' journal late in December, referring to the White Paper. In a speech to the Society of Education Officers in January Heath had gone out of his way to give a special assurance. 'The government are determined to do all in their power to give the education service the resources to achieve what the recent White Paper called your formidable task,' he was reported as saying. The Prime Minister gave the impression he meant what he said. It is now revealed, commented the journal, as an empty phrase. Almost all the material promises in the Thatcher White Paper will now come to nothing. Barber's Draconian measures are an even greater betrayal of political commitments than were Roy Jenkins's in 1968. The attack on public expenditure, the journal concludes, 'is simply a political ploy, a supposedly more popular measure than making inroads into private expenditure by way of taxation'.[84]

Higher and further education suffered particularly. On 21 December Margaret Thatcher gave details of 110 capital projects originally planned to start in 1973-74 which were now indefinitely postponed, following the issue of circular 15/73. These affected 30 universities and 80 non-university institutions (including polytechnics).[85] Late in January 1974 the *Times* reported that the universities would suffer most; the new cuts 'are far more brutal and debilitating than any previously experienced'. Cuts had also been made in health and welfare, the aim being to solve the present crisis by 'slashing demand'.[86] The *Guardian*, in a leader analysing the university cuts, focused on the freezing of higher education as opposed to the 'Frameworks' perspective'.[87] Cuts were also announced in the rate support grant.[88]

That the Heath government fell, is, of course, a matter of history (even though desperate attempts were made, immediately after the election, to patch up an alliance with the Liberals to keep Labour out). How, then, can we evaluate the four years of Tory rule, so far as education is concerned?

If, as is the thesis of this book, education is central to the mediation of the social order, then the verdict must be that much was achieved, often under difficulties, in terms of the maintenance of the status quo. Although Margaret Thatcher tried, and failed, to deflect local authorities from comprehensive reorganisation, she did succeed, through controversial use of her powers as secretary of state, in braking the rate of change, and above all in deliberately preventing many authorities from developing genuinely 'comprehensive' systems, by ensuring the survival of over 100 selective (grammar) schools within those systems. This had a two-fold effect. First, it ensured the continuance of selective processes, and second, it struck at the morale and élan of the movement as a whole, and therefore damaged it more or less severely. Further, the direct grant grammar schools were, as we have seen, brought in from the cold, even if the extension of the system, as demanded by right-wing groups, was not then considered a politically viable option. These schools, as outposts of the public (or independent) schools, had historically played an important part as a key feature of the hierarchic, selective (and therefore exclusive) system inherited from the past. The public schools themselves, of course, were under no kind of threat from this government.[89]

Finally, the decision was taken, as again we have seen, to build up and harden the binary divide within higher education – interestingly a 'consensus' policy inherited, of course, from Labour. In this area leading civil servants (especially Sir Toby Weaver, as he has claimed) played a distinctive role – this, in fact, was an important aspect of DES policy, but one deliberately espoused by the government.

The major strategy, or, better, tactic, of this government, it seems, was one of resistance to change, except in politically innocuous areas like nursery education. But the government, and Thatcher in particular, came under attack from educationists for in fact having no clear, distinctive policy, for instance, relating to secondary education where Margaret Thatcher's actions were widely seen as involving only a wilful, or increasingly capricious resistance.[90] This, of course, gave heart to right-wing groups which now began to burgeon and to attempt to exert increasing influence on the minister – the shape of things to come. The Black Paper grouping was quiescent during these four years, publishing Black Paper 2 just before the election in 1969, and another shortly after. But organisations such as the 'Council for the Preservation of Educational Standards' and the newly formed 'National Education Association' now surfaced, groupings that were to sprout 'like dragons' teeth' later in the decade, and to play a role in the return of the Thatcher government of 1979.[91]

The prolonged attempt to 'hold the line' led, as we have seen, to sharp confrontations between central and local government, confrontations that reflected increased polarisation within the world of education. The powerful movement of parents, teachers and local authorities determined on educational change gained, in spite of all the difficulties, considerable victories during these years. The percentage of pupils in 'comprehensive' schools in fact increased from 32 in 1970 to 62 in 1974 while the actual number of comprehensive schools more than doubled. The fact that at least half of these schools were in no sense 'genuinely' comprehensive, however, ensured difficulties in their functioning. This was Margaret Thatcher's legacy.

4 The Labour Governments

Against all expectations, once again, Labour won the election of February 1974, though gaining no overall Parliamentary majority. A second election was clearly necessary, if only to resolve the position, and this took place in October. Even then the government's overall majority was only three, to be eroded at subsequent by-elections. Harold Wilson's sudden, and totally unexpected, resignation took place in March 1976, James Callaghan succeeding him, leading a move to the right, upheld in office from 1977 by a pact with the Liberals who had thirteen MPs. Beset by economic, industrial and political problems and conflicts of all kinds, Callaghan held on, clinging to office through the famous 'winter of discontent' of 1978-79, finally resigning – the first government to be defeated on a no confidence motion for 50 years (by a majority of one). The second Labour administration held office for almost its full term – four and a half years. There is no doubt, however, that it paved the way, or provided the soil for the surge of the radical right – for the Thatcherite domination of the 1980s.

'A muted memory of mangled decline' is how Phillip Whitehead sums up the achievement of the two Labour administrations. Inheriting massive inflation from the Heath government, a trade union movement with its tail up following the miners' victory of 1974, a country engulfed in crisis, with the world on the brink of economic recession, Wilson set out to stabilise the situation through implementation of a policy very similar to Heath's – reductions in public expenditure and imposition of an incomes policy (to be realised in terms of the 'social contract'). Conflict naturally developed between the left in the party (and labour movement generally) which wanted radical ('socialist') measures and the 'moderate', or right wing of the party, epitomised in perennial conflict between the party's national executive committee and the government – a conflict that came to be personalised in Tony Benn on the one hand (though a member of the government) and Wilson, then Callaghan and Healey, on the other.[92] Shortly after Callaghan took over, in March 1976, the economic situation reached so critical a stage that recourse was had to the International Monetary Fund for substantial loans to bale the country out. Humiliating conditions were imposed, but this marked the ascendance of monetarism as determining fiscal policy – pursued with some energy by Dennis Healey as Chancellor. By 1977 the economic downturn had resulted in a decline of living standards by 7 per cent; to severe cuts in real wages and savage expenditure cuts in public services including education. Industrial conflict escalated through the winter of 1978-79, and, although inflation had now been brought under control, the government fell.[93]

Education, as a major function of government, was, of course, closely affected by all this – particularly in terms of resources, as we shall see. But of equal importance, if on another level, was increased polarisation. One issue on which the Labour administration appeared to be determined was the conclusion of secondary reorganisation. Not only within the Labour Party, but among the left generally, and, as we have seen, more widely still, this was a consensus policy, if only in the limited sense of a structural reform. It was pursued with a certain determination, though the government once again quailed before the prospect of legislation to ensure a national development (as it had attempted five years earlier, in 1969). In spite of this, opposition mounted, becoming more desperate than ever. Now the attack, by industrialists, politicians and above all through the media (press and television) turned on to comprehensive education with a bitter strength. A number of right-wing groupings now emerged, increasingly active. These became, during the late 1970s, crucial breeding grounds for Thatcherism, and for the electoral victory of 1979.

Labour was hardly well served by the three secretaries of state during this period. From March 1974 to June 1975 Reginald Prentice held the appointment, later actually (in October 1977) to cross the House and join the Tory Party. He was followed, for just over a year, by the 'forgotten' minister, Fred Mulley, chiefly memorable for his complaint that he had no powers to act. Finally Shirley Williams was appointed in September 1976, holding the job until the demise of the government two and a half years later, then leaving the Labour Party as one of the 'gang of four' who established the Social Democratic Party (SDP) in 1981. Good at talking, but indecisive and vacillating in action, her period of office is now generally evaluated as a disaster. Conflict sharpened; resources declined – by 1979 the system generally was in disarray.

5 The First Labour Government: Holding the Line

The Labour manifesto had highlighted intentions – a national system of nursery schools; big expansion of facilities for sixteen-to-nineteen-year-olds; the end of the 11-plus together with a pledge to speed the development of a national system of comprehensive education; tax relief for private schools to be withdrawn.[94] In the new parliament, Labour had 301 seats to the Tories' 297. Labour's victory, with only 37 per cent of the total vote, was due in part to the resurgence of the Liberals who polled their highest figure for forty years (over 6 million) – though winning only fourteen seats. With twelve Ulster

Unionists, seven Scottish Nationalists and four others, the position was unstable in the extreme.[95]

The new government inherited a chaotic financial position as well as industrial conflict. Some stability was gained, however, by rapid settlement of the miners' strike together with a number of fiscal measures that eased the immediate crisis. According to Whitehead there were no Cabinet discussions whatever on economic policy between the two elections – this was crisis management.[96] Nevertheless the Queen's government had to be carried on. The Education Secretary, Reginald Prentice, in fact issued a statement on comprehensive education only a few days after the government was formed. This stressed the government's determination to make progress as fast as possible towards ending selection. Circular 10/70 was to be replaced in its turn; consultations on this were already taking place. There was, however, to be no legislation. The new local authorities, which would be taking up their responsibilities under the 1972 Local Government Act on 1 April 1974, were to be invited to consider resubmitting proposals put forward by the old authorities and rejected by the last administration.[97]

This announcement 'has been given overwhelming support this week', reported the *Times Educational Supplement*. Many authorities, after years of frustration, were now 'overjoyed at the prospect'. Birmingham, whose ambitious consortium plan had been 'torn apart' by Margaret Thatcher, now announced its intention to re-submit. Other authorities took similar action.[98] Once more, in this sphere at least, things were on the move.

The new circular 4/74 was finally issued early in April. In announcing it, Prentice threatened legislation if it proved necessary. The circular itself he described as a 'tough document'. 'We shall be using our full powers under existing legislation', he said, 'to secure the co-operation of local authorities and voluntary bodies in making the fastest possible progress to a fully comprehensive system.'[99] Instead of 'requiring' authorities to go comprehensive, the circular 'looks to' authorities 'to secure the effective execution of this policy' under the secretary of state's 'control and direction'. Building allocations for secondary education would only be made where needed for comprehensive reorganisation.[100] It is worth recalling that, as a result of the surge forward in the last few years, 62 per cent of secondary school pupils (in maintained schools) were in comprehensive (and middle deemed secondary) schools at this point.[101] To complete this reform there was, therefore, still a long way to go. Right-wing Conservative resistance, powered by the grammar school lobby, now surfaced afresh. This is the era of the rise of Rhodes Boyson, ex-comprehensive school head and now a Tory MP. Maoist-Trotskyite cells were, he claimed, being formed in London's comprehensive schools; 'neighbourhood ghetto' schools were a disaster.[102] A sharp battle on the future of London's remaining 49 grammar schools (most of them 'voluntary aided') opened in June. Already a grammar school defence association, brought into being at a hastily organised meeting immediately after the election, promised 'the most mammoth-scale objection ever raised to any educational proposals'.[103] Undeterred, the ILEA, now controlled by Labour, decided to withdraw financial aid to these schools unless they co-operated. After a two-hour debate the education committee determined, by 46 votes to seven, to draw up plans for the final abolition of selection throughout inner London, in line with the Prentice circular. This decision was immediately welcomed by NUT members in London. It was bitterly contested by what was now a tiny Tory group on the ILEA.[104]

The whole issue was sharpened by the general awareness that a new election was imminent. Late in June Ted Heath, still the Tory leader, 'ditched' Van Straubenzee, the relatively moderate shadow minister (apparently 'without much ceremony'), replacing him with Norman St John Stevas who had earned a reputation as a 'shrill polemicist' as a junior minister under Thatcher. This was a clear reflection of the right-wing surge within the party, which was shortly (and improbably) to elect Thatcher as leader in place of Heath. Van Straubenzee, whose consensus 'Boyle-like' qualities were his undoing, was told by Heath he was 'too middle of the road'. Back-bench Tories exulted in the change, seen as a hardening of attitudes in advance of a general election. The message was that 'academic standards' and 'parental choice' were to be the battle cries. The pro-voucher lobby, aiming at a form of privatisation of the school system, was on the move.[105]

It may be that this is the point where the Tories finally turned their back on consensus policies in education. In a speech made shortly after his appointment St John Stevas stressed parental choice as the party's election platform, promising full support for those fighting reorganisation.[106] Early in July, arguing for 'parent power', St John Stevas launched a bitter attack on the government's policy. In reply, Prentice pointed to the schizophrenia in the Tory Party, the sharp difference between the middle-of-the-road view personified by Boyle and Van Straubenzee, and the backward view now presented by St John Stevas pandering to the most reactionary views of a minority.[107] At a Commons debate on comprehensives at this stage, the demand for the withdrawal of circular 4/74 was defeated (by 285 votes to 271).[108]

During this month (July), however, mass media coverage was given to a survey of examination results in Manchester which seemed to show that the unreorganised Roman Catholic sector was more successful (in terms of examination results) than Manchester's reorganised comprehensive schools.[109] Standards, however, were claimed as steadily improving by Lord Elwyn-Jones, Labour's Lord Chancellor, in a wide-ranging House of Lords debate at this time.[110] In August the local authorities' journal *Education* claimed that the Conservatives were aiming to get as much mileage as possible out of education, in terms of the coming election. The platform was primacy to parental choice, the rescinding of 4/74. This, the journal saw as 'a calculated risk', but Prentice had adopted a moderate line and tone and was not introducing legislation.[111] So the battle was carried on through the late summer months, the Tories finally coming out, late in August, with a six-point charter for parents, calling for variety and choice. It was, however, to receive a dusty answer.

If comprehensive education was the major issue on which battle lines were drawn, there was also the question of the management of the economy – and the related question of resources for education. In his April budget statement the Chancellor of the Exchequer (Dennis Healey) made it clear that there could be no question of restoring the 'Barber' cuts, hurriedly imposed in December, in education nor elsewhere. Targets for student numbers in higher education were also to come down – from the 700,000 of Thatcher's White Paper in 1980-81 perhaps to 600,000. 'Cynics will regard the speed with which the Labour government have adopted Mrs Thatcher's plan as more evidence of the phoney character of so much party disputation', – perhaps fair comment by the *Times Educational Supplement*.[112] Due to serious economic diffi-culties, Prentice announced, the government was not going to rescind the cuts, nor could he authorise a larger school building programme for the current year. The nation had lost £1,500 million as a result of the three-day week.[113]

Contraction had now become the norm, but at this stage few realised that this was now a long term situation. In August Anthony Crosland, now Secretary of State for the Environ-ment, publicly denied his 'revisionist' thesis of the 1950s (see p.321). He informed the new local authorities bluntly that the level of public expenditure could not continue to increase at the rate of the past few years. Something must be allowed for growth in real income. The government's priorities were higher pensions, subsidies for essential food and housing. Education was not mentioned by this former minister. 'The party's over.'[114]

It was at this point also that the Thatcher White Paper warnings about the reorganisation and contraction of teacher education, enhanced, as we have seen, by mismanagement by the DES, reached an early crisis. Plans for closures and mergers were rife – the whole system thrown into disarray. Articles appeared in the *Times Higher Educational Supplement* from college principals and their supporters denouncing these plans as outrageous and dictatorial. The DES was criticised for its 'strong-arm methods'; the whole exercise defined as 'a disastrous mistake'. This (DES policy) was now (characteris-tically) denounced by St John Stevas – a junior minister when the policy was announced (in the White Paper). There is no evidence whatever that either the Labour Party or government had any alternative policy to offer – or implement. In the general chaos of the time the decline of the colleges was accepted by both main parties as inevitable.[115]

So the government held on through the summer months of 1974 – gaining small majorities in the Commons for its essentially unadventurous, and certainly hardly socialist measures. In the country the new authorities were now settling down, the central positive feature being the planning and implementation of comprehensive reform. Rejecting plans (from Buckinghamshire) to enlarge grammar schools, Prentice gave the go-ahead to seven authorities for their comprehensive plans in his first month of office and more thereafter. In August

St John Stevas advised reluctant authorities to stall; to wait for the Tories to 'resume' office.[116] The economic outlook, however, remained sombre. Late in September Harold Wilson dissolved Parliament, clearly hoping for a success in a quick second election equivalent to that gained in 1966. In fact Labour gained eighteen MPs, largely at the expense of the Tories who lost twenty. This gave the government a majority of 42 over the Conservatives and, though 39 seats were held by minor parties (thirteen by the Liberals), the opportunity seemed to present itself of a longish period of stable government.[117]

6 The Second Labour Government, 1974-79

Years of Crisis: 1975-76

Labour's electoral victory in October meant that the Tories, under Heath's leadership, had lost two successive elections in a single year. The shock to the Conservative Party was intense – new fractures opened up; scapegoats must be found. Apocalyptic visions of disaster were now broadcast. Here was the soil promoting the growth of the radical right, now searching to jettison the past and strike out in new directions. Within a few months Margaret Thatcher had gained the leadership of the Tory Party, relegating Heath to the sidelines in what has been oddly described as a 'peasants' revolt' (of back-bench Tory MPs).[118]

The lead was taken by Keith Joseph in a dramatic speech immediately after the election which received enormous publicity. Now shadow Home Secretary, Joseph, speaking to the Birmingham Conservative Association, issued a strident call for a 'remoralisation' of national life. Labour had won the election, he claimed, simply because they were 'quite uninhibited in promising the earth'. Election auctioneering over the years had raised expectations which could not be satisfied, generating grievances and discontents. Values were being systematically undermined. Parents were being diverted from their duty as regards education, health, morality, advice and guidance. Delinquency, truancy, vandalism, hooliganism, illiteracy – all these accompanied the decline in educational standards; in the universities the 'bully boys of the left' were giving a foretaste of what a left-wing dictatorship would endeavour to achieve. The old values of patriotism and national pride had been denigrated in the name of internationalism. Particular venom was directed at 'left-wing intellectuals', motivated primarily 'by hatred of their own country'. In a powerful climax Joseph claimed that 'these well-orchestrated sneers' from their strongholds in the educational system and media 'have weakened the national will to transmit to future generations those values, standards and aspirations which have made England admired the world over'. They want the state 'to do more' to help the poor, so decrying self-discipline; the only real lasting help we can give to the poor, Joseph concluded, is to help them to help themselves.

After an encomium on Mary Whitehouse, an 'unknown woman' who dared speak up against the BBC, 'the educators and the false shepherds', Joseph continued with a call to arms. 'We must fight the battle of ideas', he said, 'in every school, university, publication, committee, TV studio, even if we have to struggle for a toehold there.' We, he claimed, 'have the truth'.

Joseph concluded with an old-fashioned eugenicist argument – that the lower classes (social classes 4 and 5) are producing a high and rising proportion of children, born to mothers 'least fitted to bring children into the world and bring them up'. The nation was, therefore, moving inexorably towards degeneration. The extension of birth control facilities to these potential mothers was, in fact, the only concrete proposal to come out of the speech, which concluded with a final attack on 'permissiveness' leading to disorder and anarchy.[119]

This speech was widely seen as a deliberate bid for the Tory Party leadership which, constitutionally, would have to be decided soon. If that was so, it misfired. Joseph's eugenicist solution was ridiculed in the popular press and elsewhere. It was this misjudgement that Joseph gave his close colleague, Margaret Thatcher, to understand as the reason he now decided not to go for the leadership. This left the way clear for Thatcher who had kept a low profile, and whose loyalty to Joseph is well known. A month later, towards the end of November, she had taken the decision to challenge Heath for the leadership.

These developments are referred to here because they epitomise the abrasive, aggressive, assertive outlook of the radical right within the Tory Party which, over the next decade, was to win hegemony. The rise of the right, reflected in education at this stage in a variety of ways as we shall see, was an important feature of the four years of the Labour administration – quick to grasp and exploit weaknesses, and searching always to seize the initiative. This needs to be borne in mind in any analysis of this period.

Comprehensive education, 1974-1976. With this tintabulation in the background, the new Labour government got on with its work, although rapidly running into a whole set of economic and political difficulties, including, as is now public knowledge, an organised attempt by a group in the secret service to destabilise Harold Wilson himself and the government as a whole.[120] Reginald Prentice continued to hold office as Secretary of State until succeeded by Fred Mulley eight months later. One aspect of 'unfinished business' from the 1960s was now given priority. Early in March 1975 the government announced its intention to withdraw financial support from direct grant schools, thus, in effect, abolishing this category in line with the recommendations of the Donnison Report (see pp.328-31). Of the 154 such schools then existing, 51 announced their intention of becoming comprehensive schools within the maintained system (these were mostly Roman Catholic schools serving their localities). The rest, including of course all the most prestigious, opted for independence. If this was scarcely a satisfactory solution, at least it put an end to this anomaly which had remained a contentious issue since the war. The Conservative Party, on the other hand, now bent its collective mind on how to siphon public money to support these schools while ensuring retention of their 'independence'.

The main issue, however, on which the new government appeared determined, was comprehensive reorganisation – though focusing very strictly on structural change rather than the concomitant educational and pedagogical issues involved, even if these were now becoming pressing.[121]

Circular 4/74, of course, still held sway. A survey undertaken in February 1975, ten months after its publication, indicated that progress had been slow. Of the 104 authorities now existing, only twenty were 'truly comprehensive', while a quarter of all pupils still sat the 11-plus. At least seven, and possibly as many as fourteen authorities had little or no intention of going fully comprehensive unless legislation was introduced. On the other hand the survey found that 70 per cent of children in maintained secondary schools now attended 'comprehensive' schools, only 9.5 per cent grammar schools (see Appendix Table 6a, p.586).[122]

One problem, of course, was that of finance – reorganisation cost money in terms of remodelling of schools. In August an extra £23 million was made available precisely for this purpose, even though overall public expenditure was being reduced.[123] Official information, following 4/74, showed that one-third of local authorities hoped to complete reorganisation by September 1976, another third by 1980, while the rest would take longer, a few refusing to submit any information whatever.[124]

To complete the reform, more drastic action seemed necessary, legitimised, it could be argued, by the election result. In December 1975 Mulley finally introduced an Education Bill to 'require' local authorities to go comprehensive – or rather, to empower the Secretary of State 'to call for proposals to complete reorganisation' where he felt further progress was necessary.[125] The Bill did not receive royal ascent until almost a full year later on 22 November 1976. Two days later the new Secretary of State (Shirley Williams) asked eight recalcitrant authorities to submit proposals within six months.[126] By January 1977 nearly 80 per cent of relevant pupils were in comprehensive schools. This was one reform that was still swinging – even if a critique now began to be mounted, of increasingly horrific proportions.

Comprehensive schools had, over the last few years, been established with considerable rapidity – nearly 400 in 1974-75 alone.[127] Certainly they opened new opportunities. But the schools also, of course, reflected the conflicts, antagonisms – in short the whole gamut of circumstances in which the mass of the people lived in the wider society. Inner-city schools in particular – now generally attended only by the most deprived and poverty-stricken section of the population – faced enormous social as well as educational problems in the attempt to realise the advantages of reorganisation. Suburban and rural areas generally did not face these problems, at least not to so exaggerated an extent.

On the whole the press and television had dealt fairly, even sympathetically (and sometimes enthusiastically) with the early comprehensive schools. Now there was one of those sudden changes, which sweep through the media from time to time. What can best be described as a demolition job suddenly got underway. Not only the popular press, but the (then) more respectable papers took the lead. In July 1974 Ronald Butt of the *Times* suddenly launched a ferocious assault on London's comprehensives as a whole, though space was given to Briault (Chief Education Officer) for a considered reply.[128] This was during the pre-election run-up and so understandable in this context; London's schools were certainly experiencing difficulties, due in particular to massive staff wastage at this time.[129]

But the new style of total, massive denigration was best epitomised in a full page feature article in the *Guardian* in December 1974.[130] Entitled 'What Century is This, Miss?' by Jill Tweedle (a *Guardian* occasional writer), this reported a visit to 'a large London comprehensive school'. The tone of this long article is effectively encapsulated in the subhead, printed in large bold type:

> Hulking boys with faint moustaches, hefty well developed girls charge like buffalo down the corridors designed for orderly queues and now bursting with a disorderly 1,135. The place smells of feet, oranges, sweat. Bodies pummel other bodies; no quarter is given to adults.

'My eyeballs are gritty and swollen. My head rings like a gong. I am jumpy and irritable, my stomach curdles with indigestible emotions. I have spent the day in a large London comprehensive school.' This is how the article starts, and how it proceeds throughout each of its six columns. Hardly a positive word is said – about the pupils at least, though the 'devotion of the teachers' earns a good word (this is 'absolute'). The impression is given that the whole school consists of 'ESN, maladjusted or anti-social children'. These, the author percipiently argues, should be segregated (at least for a time).

'What on earth are you doing?' wrote in Hunter Davies, then engaged on his own enquiry into life in a London comprehensive, three days later. 'How can a reputable paper let a reputable journalist like Jill Tweedie write a smearing, sneering, class-ridden, prejudiced, cliché-ridden article on a comprehensive – without even naming the school?'. Questioning her claim that 57 per cent of the school's pupils were

illiterate – Davies also challenged the school's anonymity as
'educationally criminal'. 'What borough is the school in? Is it
really comprehensive? In the ILEA there are no comprehensives since grammar schools exist.' Such an article, 'containing
sensational generalisations', ensures that 'everyone's prejudices against comprehensives will have been confirmed'.
Write about a sink school (Tweedie admits that the teachers
emphasised the school is '*not* typical') 'and you are bound to
sink the whole system'.[131]

Jill Tweedie's horrific account was countered a year later by
Hunter Davies's own in-depth study of another London
'comprehensive' – this time perhaps a more 'typical' one. This
was the Creighton School, in Haringey, North London – a
large comprehensive with 1,500 pupils. His account, which set
out candidly to explain 'just what it feels both to learn – and to
teach – there' (he was a qualified teacher himself) was
sympathetic and in many respects penetrating.[132] But the
damage was done – and worse was to come.

There is little doubt that the worst blow comprehensive
schools suffered at this time was a BBC 'fly on the wall'
Panorama programme (in March 1977) on what was officially
presented as 'a typical day in an average comprehensive'
(Faraday High School in Ealing – in fact a social priority
school). Here incompetent (actually probationary) teachers
were singled out for exposure, accompanied by the
disembodied 'talk over' directing the attention of viewers as
required. An image of chaos, crudities, incompetence, lack of
concern, confusion as to aims and purposes, squalor, dirt and
general failure was put across very forcefully.[133] So incensed
were the teachers of the authority and London teachers
generally that television cameras were kept out of London
schools for many years. The impact made was lasting – and
meant to be. For obvious reasons, the media, particularly
television, tended always to focus on London schools.
Comprehensive schools elsewhere were ignored – the
impression given that all comprehensive schools were similar
to those in the capital city.[134]

But of course it was not only the press and television that
now launched their slings and darts at the burgeoning
comprehensive system, just coming to fruition. In 1975 the
Black Paper movement re-emerged. *Fight for Education* was
introduced once again by a 'Letter to MPs and Parents' by

Brian Cox and Rhodes Boyson, now the joint editors. Presaging doom, havoc and general chaos if existing trends were not reversed, the editors proposed tests for all at seven, eleven and fourteen; those failing at fourteen should promptly leave ('the disappearance to apprenticeships and work of the fourteen-plus lesson-resisters would also be of considerable help'). The voucher system 'could be tried in Britain'; so far from there being a common curriculum within comprehensive schools (as the hated 'progressives' were then asking), each large comprehensive should offer 'at least four distinct courses'.

This Black Paper, which again received massive media exposure, attacked contemporary trends (as the authors perceived them) across the whole field of education, from primary school to university. Two articles focussed specifically on comprehensive education ('Comprehensive Mythology' by Fred Naylor, and 'Why Comprehensives Fail', by G. Kenneth Green). In 'Educational Consequences of Human Inequality', H.J. Eysenck once again presented the old fashioned psychometric theory in an article suffused by classic biological reductionism (e.g. 'the facts of human inequality demand different types of education for different children'; 80 per cent of total variance in intelligence is 'due to genetic causes' – most people, he says, interested in the field, 'will be now familiar with this'). Cyril Burt was also a contributor – before his exposure as fraudulent. The final item, 'Signs of the Times', is packed with newspaper articles depicting crises in comprehensive schools – obscenities, strains on the teachers, discipline, 'comprehensive disaster' and so on.

This Black Paper included a quotation from a *Daily Telegraph* article by St John Stevas, the Tory shadow minister. A quarter of a century's left-wing possession of the educational initiative, he argued, and 'the continuous advance of the comprehensive school', had left us with 'unprecedented worry and alarm among parents' about the quality of education. In particular they are concerned over 'standards of conduct, discipline and learning', and are 'horrified by the spread of truancy and violence'.[135] St John Stevas' own contribution was a short, highly legalistic, pamphlet written with Leon Brittan and published by the Conservative Political Centre (*How to Save your Schools*, July 1975). This was a handbook for local government activists, giving guidance on how to 'save the grammar schools' by utilising every possible legalistic procedure (or loophole) – Brittan is billed as Chairman of the Legal Sub-Committee of the Conservative Parliamentary Education Committee. Circular 4/74, it was argued (correctly) had no statutory validity, so no authority need comply. Proposals to alter the status of any grammar school should be met by mass objections under Section 13; petitions, meetings, marches should be organised. Now was the time for an all-out attack on comprehensive reorganisation.[136]

Criticism was not confined to politicians, Black Paperites and journalists. It was fed, especially during 1976, by weighty voices from industry – now experiencing increasingly difficult conditions due both to a world economic recession and the especially weak position of British industry. Some have held that the search was on for a scapegoat – it was not industry and its owners and managers that were failing the country, but the schools which were not producing sufficient recruits of the right standard. However that may be, a veritable avalanche of opinions, from an unexpected area, now hit the schools and their teachers. In an article entitled 'I Blame the Teachers', Sir Arnold Weinstock, managing director of GEC, led the attack early in 1976.[137] Sir Arthur Bryant (head of Wedgwood Pottery) and Sir John Methuen (director general of the CBI) also weighed in. 'Given prominence in the media in 1976,' as Clyde Chitty puts it, 'these painted a picture of unaccountable teachers, teaching an irrelevant curriculum to young workers who were poorly motivated, illiterate and innumerate.'[138]

The call for accountability – the Tyndale affair. But this was not the end. Yet other ingredients were now poured into what was becoming a veritable witches' brew, seized on by the media and given enormous exposure. First, the Tyndale affair, and second, a modest small scale research project that happened to fit the concerns of the times, the so called 'Bennett Report.' Both focused specifically on primary schools. Both achieved maximum media exposure in the summer and early autumn of this 'crisis' year of 1976.

It is impossible here to recapitulate the whole extraordinary story of the Tyndale saga – that of a small ILEA primary school whose teachers took the bit between their teeth and set out progressively to operate what some interpret as an extreme version of the Plowden Committee's philosophy of 'child-centred' education.[139] Though parents (the majority working-class) protested and voted with their feet, the teachers, who seemed to be possessed by an apocalytic vision as to the role of education in achieving social change, persisted. As controversy developed within the school and outside, rolls began to fall. From January 1974, when a new head and four new teachers were appointed (one of whom took the initiative), new pedagogical schemes, involving egalitarian structures in pupil-teacher relations, were introduced. Rolls fell further. In the autumn term 1975 the ILEA carried through an inspection. The staff thereupon went on strike. The number of pupils further declined. In desperation, and pressured through the media, after the inspector's report was submitted, the ILEA determined on a public enquiry. This opened on 27 October 1975. It lasted a full nine months, providing a great deal of sensational press copy. The Auld Report, as it was called after its chair, generally regarded as 'shrewd and fair minded'[140] was finally published in July 1976. The leading teachers were dismissed, and the school reorganised. The whole story is well documented, not only in the Auld Report itself, but also in a book by two journalists who covered the enquiry, and in a volume by the four teachers who were at the heart of the dispute.[141]

The Tyndale issue raised, in a very dramatic form, a number of issues of key importance. One of these, of course, was pedagogical – what was meant by 'progressive' education? What was the relation between freedom and authority in the classroom? Above all, what was the relation between learning and the deliberate structuring by the teacher of the child's activities? Tyndale procedures were identified with progressive 'child-centred' approaches – though taken here to extreme forms. The teachers themselves were identified with militant left-wing groupings. So a relationship was made, in the public eye, between 'progressivism' and the left – even though the clientele, in terms of the parents, who were clearly bewildered and out of sympathy with the teachers, were mainly working-class and Labour supporters.[142] Here the Tyndale affair links with the Bennett Report.

But, given that the teachers, claiming total autonomy (in terms of their 'professionalism') adopted and radically developed such approaches, and given that parents and others (ILEA inspectors) objected, this key issue was now clearly highlighted. To whom *were* the teachers responsible – or accountable? In theory the head had responsibility for the school and was accountable to the governors. These, in their turn, were, in theory, responsible to the local authority. That authority itself employed inspectors who were directly responsible to the Chief Education Officer, and so to the education committee – in this case the ILEA. And what about the DES? The role of HMI? And ultimately the Secretary of State?

All these issues were raised by the Tyndale affair, and in the Auld Report, which made a series of specific recommendations. But these are, perhaps, less important than the overall political and public impact of the affair as a whole. Teaching had been brought into disrepute. Generally speaking, immense damage had been done to the teaching profession as a whole. Teachers' (traditional) control of the curriculum – their autonomy – was now very sharply called into question. Teachers, schools, even local authorities as a whole, must be made 'accountable'. It was only after the Tyndale affair that the whole 'accountability' movement swept the schools, and their teachers.[143]

The Tyndale affair was complemented by the Bennett 'Report', unusually (for a small scale research project) given mass exposure in the media – and cleverly packaged, by an enterprising publisher, for just that purpose.[144] This was published in April 1976, that is, towards the close of the Tyndale enquiry. This 'process-product' research was presented as showing, to put it crudely, that 'formal' methods in the primary school were more 'effective' (in terms of learning) than 'informal' (Plowden type). Some years later Neville Bennett reworked his statistical data and came up with quite other conclusions.[145]. However the apparent message propagated at the time was precisely what fitted the requirements of the by now well orchestrated press and media propaganda drive that was then well underway.[146] All this formed the immediate background to James Callaghan's Ruskin Speech, to which we may now turn. Once again, progressive teaching approaches were under attack.

The Yellow Book and the Ruskin speech. Perhaps it was inevitable. Late in October 1976 the Prime Minister, now James Callaghan, intervened in his famous speech at Ruskin College, Oxford.

Concern about education, reflected in, or, better, promoted

by the mass media, appeared widespread. If the teachers, and the overwhelming majority of the schools themselves, including primary, were operating effectively, and remained highly valued by parents and local communities – that was not the point.[147] What seems best described as a propaganda crisis had reached alarming proportions. Now was the time to resolve that crisis – and set the scene for a new equilibrium. The lid was to come down; social order assured. From the start, as Phillip Whitehead has put it, Callaghan presented himself as a man who shared the general concern about disorder and falling standards. By a deliberate move to the right he attempted to meet what he perceived as current concerns. To the Labour Party conference of early October 1976 he gave a homily on public spending; at Ruskin, at the end of the month, on educational standards. Family values were stressed. By these means Callaghan sought to reassure audiences well beyond the Labour Party.[148]

Callaghan had asked Fred Mulley, soon after taking over as Prime Minister, to report to him on basic standards and teaching methods in primary schools, on curriculum choice and examinations in secondary schools, on career choice and ability and attitudes to work. He was prompted partly by his own policy unit (led by Bernard Donoghue, an ex-LSE don – now ennobled), and partly by the Cabinet office, where James Hamilton, shortly to be moved to the DES as permanent secretary, 'had a finger in the pie'.[149] Hamilton arrived at the DES when it had been about six weeks into what Stuart Maclure (then editor of the *Times Educational Supplement*) calls 'the feverish activity which produced the notorious Yellow Book'. This was a 60-page document passed to Callaghan's advisers in response to his request. It was just at the close of this period that Callaghan appointed Shirley Williams as Education Secretary in place of Mulley. 'Edited extracts' from the Yellow Book were published in the *Times Educational Supplement* on 15 October – clearly deliberately leaked to prepare the educational world for the shock of the Callaghan speech, to be made three days later, on 18 October.[150]

The Yellow Book must be seen for what it was – a briefing document for the Prime Minister – or rather, given its length and comprehensive coverage, for his advisers; that is, material that might be used for a Prime Ministerial pronouncement. It was, in fact, a policy document, concluding with sixteen specific recommendations. It is not known to what extent Fred Mulley had a hand in drawing it up, and if so, to what effect; the probability is that it was left to DES officials. But the new permanent secretary, Hamilton, certainly was involved. Already when appointed a confirmed centraliser, Hamilton was to use this opportunity to press hard for this approach. Shortly after his appointment he took the opportunity openly to stress this view. The DES, he said, must take 'a much closer interest' in the curriculum; indeed, 'the key to the secret garden of the curriculum must be found and turned.'[151]

The main points in the Yellow Book, as leaked, can be briefly summarised. Starting with an encomium on the 'magnificent job' done in the attempt to provide 'a genuinely universal free [system of] secondary education', to which end we have put in hand and largely carried out 'the greatest reorganisation of schools in our educational history', yet all is not well. The press and the media, 'reflecting a measure of genuine public concern' are full of complaints about the performance of the schools. Why? What has gone wrong? How can matters be set to rights?

The paper then dealt with primary and secondary schools in turn. In the former, while the 'child-centred' approach has been fully adopted only in a minority of schools, its influence on teaching methods is said to be widespread. In the right hands this approach can be admirable. But these 'newer and freer' methods can prove a trap to less able and inexperienced teachers who fail to recognise the careful planning and monitoring needed. Some teachers have allowed performance in formal skills to suffer as a result of 'uncritical application of informal methods'. The time is almost certainly right 'for a corrective shift of emphasis'. What is needed is more rigour, and HMI must stress the need for a systematic approach.

In the secondary schools the criticism is more diverse. This, the paper argues, partly follows criticism of primary schools, and is based on the 'feeling' that schools are becoming 'too easy going' demanding too little work and that inadequate standards of performance are reached in formal subjects. English and maths are the commonest targets. Some employers complain about the lack of basic mathematical skills as the necessary ground for technical training. Other criticisms relate to poor pupil choice systems for optional subjects, leading to insufficient opting for science and technical subjects in relation to the country's needs.

Some of these problems, it is argued, result from the existing transitional stage to comprehensive education, and are likely to be overcome. But the teaching force is inadequately equipped in terms of formal qualifications. In specialist subjects there are shortages (the Bullock committee found one third of teachers of English were not properly qualified).[152] Because of expansion, the teaching force contains 'a disproportionate number of young and inexperienced teachers'; these, coping with discipline problems, have been too ready to drop their sights in setting standards of performance. But generally and most important, teachers and schools may have over-emphasised the need to prepare boys and girls for their roles in society compared with the need to prepare them for the world of work. Not only teachers, but past governments can be blamed for this, but here, as in the primary schools, 'the time may now be ripe for a change'. Has the time not come for the establishment of a 'core curriculum' including vocational elements? Such a step would require 'extensive consideration and discussion'.

These are the main points in the leaked Yellow Book that directly concern us here. A number of other DES concerns were worked in – examinations, the neglected sixteen- to nineteen-year-olds, the Schools Council (whose performance has been 'mediocre'). The paper also contains an extravagant encomium on the work of HMI – 'without doubt the most powerful single agency to influence what goes on in schools', as well as a cry against further cuts in resources. Good ideas cannot be developed – necessary action could be totally frustrated by further cuts.[153] The paper concludes by stating frankly that it would be good to get on record from ministers, 'and in particular the Prime Minister', an authoritative announcement on the division of responsibility for what goes on in schools, suggesting that 'the Department should give a firmer lead'. This should firmly refute the argument that no one except teachers 'has any right to any say in what goes on in schools'. The climate for this, the paper concludes, may now be relatively favourable. Nor need there be any inhibitions for fear that the Department could not make use of enhanced opportunities 'to exercise influence over curriculum and teaching methods'. Here was a clear bid for greatly enhanced central control. To achieve this it was necessary to break the supposed power of the teachers in this area. How was the Prime Minister to react to this advice?

Callaghan adopted the bluff, common man approach at which he was past master (one does not become Prime Minister for nothing!). He was in a good position to launch a critique since, in common with the great majority of fellow citizens, he owed little to formal education himself. He launched quickly into a sharp, essentially populist attack on the 'educational establishment' (was this the first public use of this phrase, later to be exploited to the full by Kenneth Baker?). He had been inundated with advice as to what he should say – some helpful, others telling him 'to keep off the grass'. It was, he said, almost as though some people don't want public attention devoted to education – nor that profane hands should touch it. So, as a common man, he was going to have his say. 'I take it that no one claims exclusive rights in this field. Public interest is strong and legitimate and will be satisfied. We spend six billion a year on education, so there will be discussion.' All have a part to play.

Having opened things up in this way, Callaghan then focused on a number of specific issues. First, he was concerned at complaints from industry that new recruits 'sometimes do not have the basic tools to do the job that is required'; as also that industry is shunned by the fully educated, and that there appears to be a lack of relation between schools and industry. Moving on he reiterated Yellow Book advice about 'the new informal methods of teaching'. Parents were concerned. These can produce 'excellent results' in well qualified hands, but are much more dubious when they are not. Here he deliberately separated his critique from the Black Paperites: 'my remarks are not a clarion call to Black Paper prejudices,' adding 'we all know those who claim to defend standards but who are in reality simply seeking to defend old privileges and inequalities.' There is, he suggested, a good case for 'a basic curriculum' with 'universal standards'. This should be thoroughly aired. As far as educational aims are concerned there has been imbalance. Children should be fitted both for a lively constructive place in society *and* to do a job of work. The former has been stressed at the expense of the latter.

These were Callaghan's main points. He concluded by saying that he did not join those who painted a lurid picture of educational decline 'because I do not believe this is generally true'. But there were examples which gave cause for concern. The main issue was to achieve higher standards all round due to the complexity of the world we live in. He then rejected the DES plea for more resources. Much had been given. The need was to examine priorities, and to secure 'as high efficiency as possible by the skilful use of existing resources'. His object was to promote a wide-ranging public discussion. I have outlined concerns and asked questions, he concluded. 'The debate that I was seeking has got off to a flying start even before I was able to say anything at all' (a reference to press and other widespread comments on the leaked Yellow Book). 'I ask all ... to respond positively.'[154]

The intention was clear. On the political level, to steal the thunder of the Black Paperites and their colleagues (and these included St John Stevas and the radical right in the Tory Party), but, on a deeper level, to assert new forms of control over the social order – to issue a clear warning that educational developments should not get out of hand; in short to slam the lid and screw it securely down. This, of course, could hardly be overtly stated, but that it was the intention has been clearly shown in subsequent developments. To achieve this, a more direct central control by the DES was essential. This was asked for and, in essence, conceded. But existing resources were not to be extended. Concrete measures, for instance, relating to the crucial sixteen to nineteen age group, were not announced. No steps were suggested to prevent Great Britain from falling yet further behind comparable industrial countries in terms of access to tertiary and post-school education generally. Instead energies were funnelled into Shirley Williams' 'Great Debate', which marked the early months of the following year.

Last Gasps
1976 was a bleak year for the Labour government, as also for education. So critical had the economic situation now become that application was finally made to the International Monetary Fund for a massive loan to tide the country (over £9 billion). The IMF, in its turn, wanted 'humiliation' – the adoption of strict monetary policies involving severe cutbacks in public expenditure, so marking the end of any even marginally 'socialist' policies. The result, and the government's position, was now summarised by Anthony Crosland, then

Foreign Secretary, in his diary:

> Demoralisation of decent rank and file ... strain in trade union loyalty.
> Breeding of illiterate and reactionary attitude to public expenditure –
> horrible ... now no sense of direction and no priorities; only prag-
> matism, empiricism, safety first, pound supreme. Unemployment ...
> = grave loss of welfare, security, choice; very high price to be paid for
> deflation and negative growth.[155]

The battle in the Cabinet on the loan had been won. 'It was a
real battle, and it could have had a different result,' writes
Whitehead. 'The government was shaky ... its standing in the
polls and by-election results had never been worse.' In March
1977 it was brought to the brink of defeat by its own rebellious
back-benchers. On a no confidence vote it was saved by the
Liberals. This was the immediate background to the
Liberal-Labour pact, enabling the government to survive for
another 26 months. Now there were to be big expenditure cuts,
directed especially at local government, education and the
NHS. So resentment grew in Labour's own constituency.[156]

   The teachers, and the educational service as a whole, were
demoralised. Years of hammering by the media were having
their effect, but this had now been deliberately legitimised by
the Prime Minister himself, and by the DES, theoretically
responsible for the schools. Local government reform had not
helped. For one thing it led finally to the demise of the once
powerful, and influential, Association of Education Committees, which for decades had represented the local
authorities' views within the 'partnership'. The new bodies
formed never achieved that level of political 'clout', while the
DES, waiting in the wings, was very quick to seize the
opportunity to fill the resulting vacuum. In a powerful article
published in 1980 George Cooke, a Chief Education Officer
for fourteen years and past president of the Society of
Education Officers, sharply criticised the new set-up,
introduced by the Tories. Reorganisation brought no new and
improved system of finance. 'What we got was a nasty, shabby
political compromise, extravagant, ill-considered and ill-
timed.' The education service, being the biggest and most
expensive involved, 'inevitably suffered most as a result'.[157]

   Expenditure cuts (the Barber cuts of 1973-74) caused a
continuous state of anxiety. But this was compounded by the
new practice of 'corporate management' which 'inexorably' led

to a reduced status for education, and was brought in with reorganisation. This, together with the deterioration in the morale of the teachers has led, Cooke argues, to a situation where it is increasingly difficult for chief officers to find the new balance required between commitment (to the schools and the service) and survival. 'If you care too much', he concludes, 'you are likely to be deeply hurt.'[158]

It was not only in the schools that morale was low; the world of higher education was also in disarray. The most savage cuts were directed at the universities, where both capital and current expenditure were now suffering a precipitous decline.[159] The quinquennial financing system had now been abandoned and financing was based on a year-to-year system, usually without adequate compensation for inflation, still running at about 10 per cent per annum. This was also the period when massive cuts were made in initial teacher training (the total in public sector colleges in 1977-78 was down to 53,000 from the peak of 110,000 five years earlier),[160] leading to mergers and closures of many colleges, and to early retirement on an enormous scale by lecturers who would otherwise have contributed years of productive work (see Appendix Table 14a, p.597). Finally, 1977 was the year when the school population, after several years of continuous expansion, started its overall decline, though primary schools had already experienced this (see Appendix Tables 2a, 2b, 2c, pp.576-8). Contraction offered opportunities, as many pointed out; but in the economic, political and educational conditions now predominating, these were not to be exploited. Far from it. Contraction merely offered another excuse for yet further economies and worsening conditions. A downward spiral had set in.

The future of education was now (nominally at least) in the hands of Shirley Williams as Secretary of State. Following the Ruskin speech which set an agenda, it was her job to take things further. She came with a reputation in other departments and in Cabinet for presenting things well, but 'not really doing much'. In an interview in November 1976 she stressed her concern and her activity. 'This time', it was reported, 'there is a whirl of action which is quite disrupting the calm routines of the DES.'[161]

But ... was there? Or, to what effect? The 'Great Debate' set the scene – eight regional conferences (invitees only accepted) to be organised in January and February (1977) – though later there would be some action. But procrastination, indecision, delay at all costs – endless consultations now became the order of the day. With one exception, these marked Shirley Williams' term of office, while the ideals and objectives of teachers and local authorities were allowed to crumble and decay. The net effect of her term of office was to prepare the soil for a breakthrough by the radical right which now found renewed energy in the fight for its objectives.

The one exception was the actual *structural* change to comprehensive education. After all, the 1976 Act had just received royal assent (in November). It had to be implemented. On 25 November circular 11/76 was issued. This stated that

> at last the principle of fully comprehensive education is written into the law. It is a long time since the unfairness, the divisiveness and the wastefulness of selection for secondary education were first recognised, and over the last twenty years there has been accelerating progress towards a comprehensive system under Labour and Conservative governments alike.

75 per cent of pupils of secondary school age are now in comprehensive schools. The circular added that the Secretary of State had already asked eight local authorities to submit plans, and that she would be writing to others soon. By April 1978 Shirley Williams had required 38 local authorities to submit reorganisation plans – some of these were for a small group of schools, or even a single school. 33 of these had in fact submitted proposals by April. Two others intended to do so soon (Avon and Barnet). The three outstanding were Birmingham (now again a Tory authority), against whom legal proceedings had been started, Redbridge and Kirklees. As a result the secretary of state declared Redbridge and Sutton to be in default of statutory duty, directing them to submit proposals by 1 June. Kirklees was also warned. Williams regretted the drastic action needed, but announced her general satisfaction at the progress being made.[162] In the interview quoted earlier she had specifically underlined her support for comprehensive education.

But support stopped at structural change. If the transformation of the secondary system was to be made a reality, further steps were now urgently needed. In Chapter 6 we saw the strength of feeling expressed, by comprehensive teachers especially, on the need to introduce a *single* exam for all at sixteen in place of the three-fold division of the GCE, CSE and the rest that was imposed on comprehensive schools by procedures inherited from the past. Comprehensive education was intended, in the eyes of its supporters, to overcome precisely such divisions. Now that some 75 per cent of secondary pupils were in these schools, its introduction was urgent. Such an examination could also complement a revision of the curriculum to ensure it met the requirements of all pupils.

For several years (in fact since 1967) the Schools Council, responsible for examinations, had been working on this question. Working parties, consisting of experienced teachers and others, covered all the major subjects. Test papers were drawn up and tried out widely in the schools. The council came *unanimously* to the conclusion that such an exam was not only desirable, it was also entirely practical. As was their right and duty, in July 1976 it proposed adoption of this exam to the secretary of state.

What was the result? Procrastination and delay. Shirley Williams decided (officially) that further consultations were necessary, adopting the time-honoured device of setting up a committee to study the proposal and make recommendations (the Waddell committee, appointed in March 1977). The DES had, of course, made its distaste for the Schools Council very clear in the (leaked) Yellow Book. Examination policy, as we have seen (in Chapter 2) has always been a key weapon of social control – to be closely monitored. This was the position now. When the Waddell committee finally reported in July 1978, actually favouring the proposed examination, Williams took no decisive action. Yet further consultations were deemed necessary. Although accepting the proposal in principle in a White Paper (October 1978), the timetable proposed ensured that nothing effective could be done within the period of the existing Parliament. (In any case, by this time the government was on its last legs, and the proposition fell.[163])

This was by no means the only such case. In March 1978 the Warnock committee reported (on children with special educational needs). This report included many important recommendations. An authority in this area writes of the secretary of state's response:

Mrs Williams did what many an Education Secretary has done before her ... and in place of response embarked on rounds of extensive consultation with special interest groups, local education authorities, and in short virtually everyone who had given evidence to the Warnock Committee in the first place.[164]

Nothing whatever was done, or achieved. It was left to the next government to act on the committee's recommendations. The incoming administration's measure (1981) embodied only the barest minimum of these proposals. The opportunity for a generous adjustment had been lost.

There were other areas where positive decisions, followed by (the promised) action were badly needed – but were left in the air. Although a current issue on which (again) the Schools Council had been working, nothing was done to reform GCE A levels, which determined the narrow, academic speciali-sation symptomatic of grammar schools, but now imposed also on comprehensives. Nor was any support forthcoming to enable pupils to stay on in comprehensive (or other) sixth forms. No encouragement was given to the movement towards tertiary colleges, even though Ted Short, in the late 1960s, had encouraged this development while falling rolls were to demand it. No support was given to the Schools Council's initiative with the certificate of extended education (CEE), an exam for first-year sixth formers (the DES did not like it). No serious defence was made of the school meals service when this, in its turn, came under threat. 'She took water and washed her hands,' writes one embittered head, R.H. Spooner who accuses Shirley Williams, for all these and more, of 'irresolute behaviour', of pursuing a policy of 'masterly inactivity'. It is difficult not to agree with his overall assessment. Shirley Williams' 'disastrous tenure of office' was certainly one of the factors that ensured that comprehensive education at this crucial point in time could not, and did not, realise its potential.[165] 1977 was, in fact, the year when the students graduating from comprehensive schools were the first to experience the full, five-year course. The opportunity to ground a new drive forward on this base was lost in a welter of 'discussion'.

Nevertheless Shirley Williams had been appointed Education Secretary as a popular minister with public presentational skills to mastermind the 'Great Debate' sparked by Callaghan. The eight one-day regional conferences, each attended by a minister, and by about 250 people (both from within education and without) took place as planned.[166] It was never clear quite what was to be achieved, but, with hindsight, these further 'consultations' can be seen to have acted as a smoke screen covering the bid, by the DES and politicians, for more active central influence and control in key areas.

For one thing, as Denis Lawton had pointed out, the agenda was now deftly changed. Callaghan had defined four main areas of concern: teaching of the 'three Rs' in primary schools; the curriculum for older children in comprehensive schools; examination reform, sixteen-to nineteen-year-olds. The regional conferences, however, and the DES background paper now issued (see note 166) had a wider focus. The four issues singled out for discussion had become: the curriculum, as it affected children from the age of five to sixteen; the assessment of standards; the education and training of teachers; school and working life.

As Ted Wragg was to point out ten years later, 'one can begin to see how control in [the first] three of these areas has slipped firmly and irrevocably into the hands of the secretary of state'. The DES was on the march.[167]

One function of the 'Great Debate' was to act as a strong signal to teachers that the curriculum was not solely their concern; industrialists, parents and others were encouraged to intervene. Indeed to wrest control from the teachers was now clearly seen as politically necessary (hence the Yellow Book attack on the teacher-dominated Schools Council, as well as other indications).[168]

Each stage in this move, as was necessary if that shadowy entity 'public opinion' was to be brought along, was carefully prepared. As the 1977 DES *Annual Report* puts it, the 'Great Debate' agenda 'had been compiled in the light of a series of meetings ... with national organisations'. Following the regional conferences, 'ministers held a further round of meetings with the same organisations ... to consider further action'. The Green Paper *Education in Schools: A Consultative Document* was published in July. This outlined the government's views 'and set out proposals and recommendations'.[169] The Green Paper stressed accountability; the need for broad agreement on a frame-work for the curriculum (stressing gender and multi-racial issues); the need for 'coherent and soundly based means of assessment' for individual pupils, schools and for the educational system as a whole, including the use of new-type (APU) tests for monitoring pupils' performance; and the need for closer co-operation between local authorities, schools and industry.[170]

This was followed, after yet further consultations, by the issue of circular 14/77 in November. This asked local authorities to report on their curriculum arrangements by June 1978, their own procedures, balance and breadth of the curriculum, particular subject areas and related matters.[171] This might be regarded as a sharp reminder, to local authorities, to take curricular issues seriously and set their houses in order. It might also be seen as a sudden slap by the central authority in an area where it had not previously taken the initiative.

Just at this stage, with the local authorities in disarray, two books – or, perhaps, polemical pamphlets – were published, both, in essence, advocating a centralist solution: *Lessons from Europe*, by Max Wilkinson (a *Daily Telegraph* education correspondent) and *What Must We Teach?*, by Tim Devlin (former education correspondent of the *Times*) and Mary Warnock. Both begin by directing attention to Continental systems of administration – the French, German, Swedish, Dutch – in all of which the state has historically played a far greater role in the direct control of education than it had ever aspired to in Britain up to that time (1977).[172] In the countries studied, neither the teachers nor the local authorities could be said to have a recognised role in determining the curriculum. Neither book actually proposed that this country should slavishly follow Continental models, but the net outcome of what was proposed might have been very similar – and to assist this move seems to have been the underlying intention, as was suggested at the time.[173]

All this was not going on in a vacuum. The radical right and its allies were still on the warpath – and about to launch a particularly ferocious attack, this time in the field of higher education. Indeed the 'Gould' report, as it was called after its author, was published in September 1977, just a year after Callaghan's speech which had sought to calm things down.

'Several distinguished scholars have joined together to draw a map of hell', headlined the *Daily Telegraph* on publication of *The Attack on Higher Education, Marxist and Radical Penetration*. The *Times* simultaneously devoted many column inches on its front page to summarising its content, while treatment was widespread in other of the daily and weekend papers (*Guardian, Sunday Times, Observer*). The pamphlet presented a paranoic interpretation of what its author(s) perceived as a highly organised conspiracy to subvert higher education (and so society) as a whole. Its provenance, significantly, was the 'Institute for Conflict Studies' consisting of a group of right-wing academics and leading military and intelligence specialists (for instance, Vice Admiral Sir Louis le Bailly, Director General of Intelligence, Ministry of Defence 1972-75). The study group set up to promote this specific publication included, as well as Julius Gould (Professor of Sociology, Nottingham University) a number of increasingly well known Black Paper contributors (for instance Caroline Cox, Anthony Flew) while others were consulted as 'authorities' (Rhodes Boyson, C.B. Cox, Black Paper editors and others).

The *Times*, in particular, seemed reluctant to let the matter drop, printing through November (1977) a series of front-page articles in which members of the study group reiterated the views expressed in the report. Many individuals were 'named' in the report and in fact a widespread, sharp and immediate reaction, which took many forms, resulted in the pamphlet's general dismissal as a disreputable and shoddy piece of political pamphleteering, masquerading under the guise of the 'defence of standards'. Perhaps the last word fell to Peter Wilby, then educational correspondent of the *Sunday Times*. In a round-up of 'boobs of the year' by educational journalists, Wilby awarded his prize to Gould and his collaborators who, he said, alleged a Marxist conspiracy to undermine British higher education. 'They slung dirt in all directions,' he wrote. 'They produced not a shred of hard evidence to support their claims and they did more damage to their own cause than to anyone else's.'[174]

Given the enormous media coverage, especially in the 'quality press', the Gould report is likely to have had some effect – perhaps largely in heightening concern about political developments generally. This had been preceded, in March 1977, with yet another Black Paper, again edited by C.B. Cox and Rhodes Boyson, and contributed to by other 'Gould report' 'authorities' (Caroline Cox, Max Beloff). This packed number, with its by now inevitable apocalyptic 'Letter to Members of Parliament', contained a series of eleven articles attacking 'informal education', another seven on comprehensive schools and seven more on 'values' (one of the set of 'questions' here is: 'how much Marxist indoctrination is taking place in schools, colleges, polytechnics and universities?'). The Conservative Political Centre now also weighed in with a pamphlet by St John Stevas, *Better Schools For All: A Conservative Approach to the Problems of the Comprehensive School*. This defined Tory policy. Parental choice must be extended; specialised and selective schools preserved (alongside 'comprehensives'). Each school must develop separate curricula for each ability group. Proposals for a single exam at sixteen must be resisted. Direct grant schools should be resuscitated through the 'conservative' assisted places scheme.[175]

So battle lines were drawn. The National Council for Educational Standards (another 'front' for the Black Paper group), raised its activity. At a meeting in London in March 1978 Boyson presented his programme: more inspection by HMIs, national examinations at seven, eleven and fifteen, a check on school attendance figures, parental choice. Here Brian Cox inveighed against mixed ability teaching: traditional values were under attack from the left; here also Julius Gould poured scorn on 'wet liberals' who 'had not understood the seriousness of the Marxist infiltration of higher education'. Non-Marxists, he claimed, were being terrorised – many who had written in support of his pamphlet 'had felt too threatened to speak out in public'.[176] The impression given was that the country was on the edge of revolution.

Such was the situation when the Callaghan government plummeted to an ignoble defeat in March 1979, taking with it an abortive Education Bill (never enacted) which, in a belated but characteristic attempt to steal the Conservatives' clothes, made parental choice the only allocation factor in school entry – despite 'repeated requests from Labour party educators and others to balance it with the essential "nearest living" clause'.[177] Of course it was not only education that was now in disarray – during the 'winter of discontent' unresolved problems multiplied. But education was to be an important issue in the subsequent election. The Saatchi and Saatchi posters 'Educashun isnt Wurking' vulgarly popularised the Tory appeal. Rhodes Boyson was not boasting when he claimed he could fill any hall in the country with his diatribes. A great opportunity had been lost.

In the 1980s a new agenda was to be set for education. Its roots, however, had found fertile soil in the struggles, and especially the indecisions, of the 1970s – for education a truly wasted decade.

Notes and References

1. In spite of militant (including strike) action by teachers in 1969-70, which was, however, successful. See Vincent Burke, *Teachers in Turmoil*, Harmondsworth 1971, *passim*, and Roger V. Seifert, *Teacher Militancy*, Lewes 1987, pp.94-103.

2. Dennis Kavanagh, 'The Heath Government, 1970-1974' in Peter Hennessy and Anthony Seldon (eds.), *Ruling Performance, British Governments from Attlee to Thatcher*, Oxford 1987, p.232. The Heath government 'achieved higher average increases in annual rates of expenditure on education, the National Health Service and housing than the 1964-70 Labour government. Less surprisingly it also achieved faster rates of annual increases of spending on defence and law and order.' p.223.

3. The junior ministers appointed were William Van Straubenzee, Minister for Schools and Lord Belstead, Higher Education. Van Straubenzee had been brought in by Heath before 1970 as a junior education spokesman.

4. Patrick Cosgrave, *Margaret Thatcher, a Tory and her Party*, London 1978, p.147.

5. Ibid., p.154. For a recent analysis of Thatcher's period as Education Minister, Hugo Young, *One of Us*, London 1989, Chapter 6 (entitled 'Public Spender'). This focuses largely on her relations with Sir William Pile, Permanent Secretary at the DES, described as 'one of the abler officials of this neglected department', but includes speculation about Thatcher's level of involvement with the Heath's government's various policy U-turns, later widely condemned (especially by Thatcherites).

6. Douglas Hurd, *An End to Promises*, London 1979, p.149, quoted in Kavanagh, op. cit., p.234.

7. In a letter to the National Education Association in October 1969, Heath had stated that a conservative Secretary of State certainly 'would not continue to operate Circulars 10/65 and 10/66'. The *Times*, 21 October 1969; *Daily Mail*, 18 October 1969. It is worth noting that just at this moment Edward Boyle retired from politics, accepting the Vice-Chancellorship at Leeds University.

8. Kavanagh, op.cit., p.234. According to Cosgrave, Thatcher made this concession at the pre-election Selsdon Seminar while successfully preserving her primary school building programme. The measure, however, 'was not something forced on her' (Cosgrave, op.cit., pp.94-5). Her junior minister, now Sir William Van Straubenezee, has since retailed how he was left with the responsibility of carrying the school milk measure through the House of Commons, see 'My Mistress Margaret', *Times Educational Supplement*, 12 June 1987. On these and other measures relating to ancillary school social services, whereby £50 million were saved, Cosgrave concludes that 'the total cost to Margaret Thatcher's political reputation in the popular press and among those involved in educational work who stressed the social function of schools has never been recovered' (Cosgrave, op.cit., p.157). This was written in 1978.

9. Caroline Benn and Brian Simon, *Half Way There, A Report on the British Comprehensive School Reform*, was published (by McGraw Hill) on 10 June 1970. This book contained a full analysis of the development of this reform in terms of structural change, of the internal organisation, social and educational, of comprehensive schools, as well as a set of 31 recommendations for the reform's further development. It received considerable, largely sympathetic, press coverage. A second, revised and enlarged, edition was published by Penguin Education in 1972.

10. *Times Educational Supplement*, 26 June 1970.

11. *Guardian*, 24 and 26 June 1970. This conference was called by the Comprehensive Schools Committee.

12. Cosgrave, op.cit., p.154. Van Straubenzee has since claimed that he 'always regarded' the issue of this circular as 'a disastrous start' which largely contributed to 'Margaret's' personal unpopularity 'for the greater part of her time at the [Education] Department'. Its issue 'pre-emptorily and without any consultation' got her off to a 'thoroughly bad start'. The circular 'caused an absolute furore'. Indeed, he continues, 'I can recall one senior official of the department coming to see me one day to express the view that it was simply not possible to continue working in this atmosphere, and that the work of the department was really impossible.' *Times Educational Supplement*, 12 June 1987.

13. *Teacher*, 17 July 1970.

14. *Guardian*, 14 July 1970.

15. *Teacher*, 18 September 1970.

16. Ibid., 31 July 1970. Anthony Soskin, Tory MP for South Bedfordshire, made an impassioned plea at the Conservative Party conference in October for implementation of the original plan. While welcoming the Secretary of State's removal of compulsion to reorganise, 'I never envisaged, as I am sure neither did she, a situation where an accepted scheme for reorganisation of schools, worked out over a period of some six years, where millions of pounds have already been committed to school buildings, where children and teachers have geared their school lives to a carefully designed programme, should now find the whole of this threatened by a move to retain selection in secondary schools – a move based in this case on nothing but emotion and without a shred of educational or economic evidence to support it. It cannot have been the government's intention to suggest that local authorities, in the name of freedom, should commit themselves to misuse buildings and to incur heavy additional expenditure to retain a part of the educational system, which as each day passes is becoming more and more irrelevant and less and less acceptable to the public.' In her reply to this debate, Margaret Thatcher avoided this issue, making no comment. *Conservative Party Conference report, 1970*, pp.15-20.

17. *Teacher*, 18 September 1970.

18. *Times Educational Supplement*, 11 September 1970.

19. *Parents and Schools* (CASE), September/October 1970.

20. *Times Educational Supplement*, 2 October 1970. Richmond was one of the hardcore of six (out of twenty) London boroughs to retain the 11-plus during the Labour administration.

21. *Guardian*, 7 October 1970.

22. *Times Educational Supplement*, 9 October 1970.

23. Ibid.

24. Ibid., For Boyle, see note 7. Clive Buckmaster was the author of a pamphlet, published by the right-wing National Education Association on the eve of the conference. Entitled *Hiccoughs in Education*, this urged Thatcher to withdraw a 'substantial number' of grammar schools from the state system and turn them into direct grant schools. *Morning Star*, 9 October 1970; see also *Times Educational Supplement*, 9 October 1970. This journal also reported 'a suggestion very strongly going the rounds' at this conference, this 'was a school tax' of £5 per head per term per child. Ibid., 16 October 1970. The *Times* had recently suggested £2.

25. *Times Educational Supplement*, 30 October 1970.

26. Ibid., 6 November 1970.

27. Ibid., 6 November 1970. In a debate in the House of Lords, Lord Belstead, junior education minister, put his own gloss on these developments. Now that the 'sting of coercion' had been removed (10/65), it was no surprise that 'recalcitrant authorities' were moving.

28. This was, of course, the procedure obtaining before the issue of circular 10/65, though in certain circumstances it had been waived by the Secretary of State (e.g. by Hailsham in relation to the Leicestershire Plan). Section 13 had been amended by the 1968 Education Act, but procedures generally remained as before.

29. *Education* 15 January 1971.

30. Ibid., 14 May 1971.

31. *Guardian*, 11 May 1970.

32. *Education*, 4 August 1972.

33. The phrase is the heading of the editorial in the educational journal *Forum*, Autumn 1973 (Vol.16, No.1).

34. DES Press Notice, 4 April 1972; *Times*, 13 October 1972; *Times Educational Supplement*, 23 November 1973.

35. These totals include 'middle deemed secondary' schools. The proportion of all secondary schools, defined as comprehensive rose from 23.2 to 52.7 per cent between 1970 and 1974. The number of pupils in such schools increased in this period from under 1 million to well over 2 million (i.e. from 32 per cent of all pupils in maintained secondary and middle deemed secondary schools to 62 per cent). During these four years the number of grammar schools declined by 363 (from 1,038 to 675). *DES Report on Education*, No. 87, March 1977. (See Appendix Table 6a, p.586.)

36. *Times Educational Supplement*, 23 April 1971.

37. Ibid., 16 July 1971.

38. Ibid., 2 July 1971.

39. Section 68 of the 1944 Education Act is a 'longstop' section enabling the Minister 'on complaint by any person or otherwise' that an education authority 'have acted or are proposing to act unreasonably' to 'give such directions' as appear expedient. It was under this section that Thatcher acted in Surrey. This action appeared to contradict several definite statements by Thatcher in the House of Commons debate of 8 July 1970 (on the Queen's speech). 'The cardinal issue of secondary reorganisation', she then said, 'was whether the existing rights of local education authorities to decide what is best for their area should be upheld'. Earlier she referred to the Tory election manifesto in which 'we said clearly that we will maintain the existing rights of local education authorities to decide what is best for their areas'. *Hansard*, House of Commons, 8 July 1970, Cols.,677-9.

40. *Times Educational Supplement*, 23 April 1971.

41. *Teacher*, 1 September 1972. Ashton's statement went on 'except insofar as they have been expressed by the properly elected representatives who serve on the governing body of the Ormskirk Grammar School, on the divisional executive and on the county education committee'.

42. *Teacher*, 23 April 1971. The amendment was moved by Nan MacMillan, a highly respected London comprehensive head, once president of the NUWT.

43. *Guardian*, 2 June 1971.

44. Ibid., 7 October 1971.

45. *Times Educational Supplement*, 2 February 1972.

46. *Education*, 3 March 1972.

47. Ibid., 17 March 1972.

48. Ibid., 30 June 1972; 17 November 1972.

49. *Times*, 13 October 1972. It was, perhaps significantly, just at this point that Edward Boyle re-entered the fray. 'May I wish you the very best of good fortune in your STEP campaign in Buckinghamshire,' he wrote, supporting a local popular movement for comprehensive reorganisation. *Times Educational Supplement*, 17 November 1972.

50. *Teacher*, May 1973.

51. *Education*, 29 June 1973.

52. Ibid., 6 July 1973.

53. *Teacher*, 6 July 1973.

54. *Times Educational Supplement*, 6 July 1973. The chairman of the education committee stated 'Mrs Thatcher has left us with educational and administrative anarchy. If we were to accept her decision as it stands it would go against every principle that we have endeavoured to incorporate in our scheme including those set out in her own circular'. *Forum*, Vol.16, No.1, Autumn 1973.

55. *Education*, 20 July 1973.

56. *Indictment of Margaret Thatcher*, Leicester 1973. Described as 'one of the most

carefully documented attacks on Mrs Thatcher', in the *Times*, 12 October 1973, the pamphlet claimed that 'her procedure for dealing with reorganisation schemes undermines the statutory rights of democratically elected local authorities, and has aroused many protests to which no attention has been paid ... The [1944] Act has been contravened ... and there has been a complete confusion of law and policy'. See also the review by a legal commentator, Louis Blom-Cooper, *Times Educational Supplement*, 12 October 1973. The pamphlet's title derived from the contemporary arraignment of Richard Nixon for extra-legal activities as president of the United States. Though published anonymously, the author was Joan Simon.

57. *Times Educational Supplement*, 3 August 1973. In August Thatcher received the plaudits of the Tory Monday Club for saving at least 100 grammar schools. Clive Buckmaster, the club's spokesman, said that Thatcher had displayed 'exemplary qualities' in standing up to 'left-wing militants'. There was, he said, moral and physical subversion by ultra-left-wing activists determined to poison the minds and bodies of young people, firstly with permissiveness, pornography and sex and later with subversive propaganda, invitation to rebellion and addiction to drugs. These activists, he claimed, are most often to be found in 'mammoth comprehensives'. *Times*, 6 August 1973. A foretaste of what was to come!

58. *Times*, 13 October 1972; *Times Educational Supplement*, 23 November 1973. For a useful account, and interpretation, of these events and policies, see Roger Woods, 'Margaret Thatcher and Secondary Reorganisation, 1970-74', *Journal of Educational Administration and History*, Vol.XIII, No.2.

59. *Education*, 31 August 1973.

60. *Guardian*, 31 August 1970. Bourne also argued that the secondary school improvement drive of 1960-63, detailed in the leaflet, probably 'merely served to entrench the dogmas of the 11-plus, to be bought out with difficulty and expense over the years ahead'. This refers to the Eccles reorganisation drive.

61. A resolution passed by the Executive Committee of the Association of Education Committees in March 1971 protested against 'the increased practice of direction by government throughout the education service, and the consequent serious erosion of the essential function of the LEAs in the partnership between central and local government'. AEC minutes inserted in *Education*, 14 May 1971.

62. *Times Educational Supplement*, 15 October 1970.

63. *Education*, 12 November 1971. Report of Queen's speech debate.

64. *Guardian*, 27 June 1970, main front-page story by Richard Bourne, at this time the outstanding educational correspondent. The Open University had been lucky to survive. Ian Macleod, Chancellor of the Exchequer, had fought for its demise. Its survival, apparently, was one of Thatcher's victories. On 7 October 1970 the *Guardian* referred to Thatcher's successful defence of her budget from 'the Barber cuts' (Ian Macleod died after a month in office, being succeeded by Anthony Barber). Thatcher held later that her concessions were on peripheral matters – not educational, Cosgrave, op.cit., p.85. Later, Sir William Pile (then Permanent Secretary at the DES), claimed that Thatcher 'was all for killing the Open University, which I managed to argue her out of on the grounds that their degrees cost only half of Oxbridge's'. For Pile's reminiscences of this rather fraught period, see Peter Dunn, 'Insecurity at the Summit of Power', *Independent*, 29 April 1989. For the inception of the Open University, Walter Perry, *Open University*, Milton Keynes 1976, pp.10-30.

65. *DES Report 1972*. The actual figure given is 63.4 per cent.

66. See pp.97-100. In 1974 (January) the total number of pupils in maintained schools rose by 334,594 over the previous year, reflecting the new leaving age (see Appendix Table 2a, p.576). A proportion of these, however, represented increased numbers within the relevant age groups. See *DES Report*, 1974. (In the previous year the increase had been 138,885, *DES Report* 1973).

67. See especially, Caroline Benn, 'Making the Most of RSLA', *Secondary Education* (NUT), Vol.1, No.3, Summer 1971.

68. *Guardian*, 25 June 1970.

69. *Education*, 26 June 1970.

70. *Times Educational Supplement*, 12 November 1971.

71. See *Education*, 12 November 1971, which vividly reports Thatcher's fury at Labour gibes on this issue, and ibid., 20 October 1972.

72. DES Press Notice, 4 April 1972, 'Mrs Thatcher Addresses NUT'. The Surrey and Barnet NUT Associations, recently incensed by Mrs Thatcher's decisions on reorganisation, moved a motion to cancel her invitation to address the conference. This was lost, but a rival meeting in an adjoining room was held, attended by some 300 NUT delegates. This passed a motion supporting the two (Conservative) education committees. *Education*, 7 April 1972.

73. *Teacher Education and Training*, report of the Committee on Teacher Training, known as the James Report after its chair, Lord James of Rusholme (Eric James). This committee was set up by Margaret Thatcher as a result of growing concern about teacher education expressed by the Plowden Committee and others in the late 1960s. It reported, as requested, within twelve months, early in 1972. Several of its proposals underlay the white paper's proposals concerning the pattern of higher education.

74. *Times Educational Supplement*, 20 October 1972, *Times*, 13 October 1972.

75. In England and Wales only 5 per cent of the three year old age group were in (maintained) schools, less than 35 per cent of those in their fifth year. In France over 50 per cent of three-year-olds, and over 80 per cent of four-year-olds were provided with nursery places; in Belgium the equivalent figures were 80 per cent and over 90 per cent. *Education: A Framework for Expansion*, p.4.

76. Ibid., pp.4-9. The Plowden Report estimated that 700,000 'full time equivalent' places might be needed by 1981-82. 300,000 were at present available. The aim stated was to achieve the Plowden figure and timing.

77. A separate White Paper dealt with non-university higher education in Scotland, which was not a DES responsibility. The White Paper states that the government's overall objective is to increase students in higher education to 750,000 in 1981-82. This is broken down to 375,000 in universities (in England, Wales, Scotland and Northern Ireland), and 375,000 in non-university institutions (of which 335,000 would be in England and Wales).

78. The White Paper proposed the run down of students preparing to teach in colleges of education and polytechnics from 114,000 in 1971-72 to a total of between 60,000 and 70,000 by 1981. Output, it was calculated, would be sufficient to reach the 510,000 seen as necessary in 1981. Staff were warned that these amalgamation and closure proposals would involve major changes in the years ahead. The traumatic experiences that resulted are discussed in the next section of this chapter. It is worth noting that the White Paper said that the decline in teacher training places must be 'made up' elsewhere.

79. *Times Higher Educational Supplement*, 13 December 1974. Already in December 1972 the universities felt deeply threatened. Fraser Noble, Chair of the Vice Chancellors' Committee, in an unusually outspoken comment at this point, warned of 'an approaching period of unprecedented "contention"'. He drew attention to the increased dangers of direct interference, citing the government's 'time-wasting' proposals on student union finances, the Rothschild report on science research, and the prospect of a new squeeze on university finance over the coming years. *Guardian*, 21 December 1972.

80. *Education*, 29 June 1973. A successful amendment moved by David Blunkett (Sheffield) expressed 'complete opposition to the clear intention in the White Paper to slow down the rate of educational expenditure', as also to the run down in teacher training which 'will result in the perpetuation of over-size classes for years to come'.

81. *Forum*, Vol.16, No.1, Autumn 1973.

82. 'If higher education in Britain has ever enjoyed a golden age the summer of 1973 was it', writes Peter Scott, in an essay published fifteen years later. 'Self-confidence and success' were then 'the dominant characteristics'. The years immediately following, 1973-76, were years of 'planning blight', when 'chaotic conditions'

prevailed. Peter Scott, 'Higher Education' in Max Morris and Clive Griggs (eds.), *Education – The Wasted Years? 1973-1986*, London 1988, pp.127ff.

83. *Times Educational Supplement*, 21 December 1973.

84. *Education*, 28 December 1973. The Barber cuts totalled over £1,100 million. They were distributed as follows: education £182 million, defence £178 million, commerce and industry £290 million, roads, housing, etc. £392 million, health and social services £111 million. *Times Educational Supplement*, 21 December 1973.

85. *Education*, 4 January 1974.

86. *Times*, 23 January 1974.

87. *Guardian*, 23 January 1974.

88. In a powerful article analysing the chaotic cuts procedures in education, Tyrrell Burgess, then a member of the ILEA, concluded that 'the brutal incompetence of this government' meant the abandonment of any rational administration in education, and that this was likely to prove even more damaging than reductions in spending. 'The Death of the DES', *Times Educational Supplement*, 11 January 1974.

89. Indeed Van Straubenzee later proudly claimed that he and Thatcher together had taken secret legal steps to safeguard the charitable status of independent schools against a socialist attack. *Times Educational Supplement*, 13 September 1974. This appears to relate (perhaps among other things) to the repeal, in 1973, of the Endowed Schools Act of 1869, whereby jurisdiction over educational charities was transferred from the DES to the Charity Commissioners. The 1869 Act empowered Secretaries of State for Education 'to impose their will on virtually all public schools' (as the Donnison Commission realised, see p.324); transfer of responsibility to the Charity Commissioners removed them from control by accountable elected ministers to a body (the Commissioners) who 'in their quasi-judicial role are independent of the executive'. See Francis Gladstone, *Charity, Law and Social Justice*, London 1982, from which the first quotation above is taken (p.62), and Ian Williams, *The Alms Trade, Charities, Past, Present and Future*, London 1989, pp.72-3. The significance of this move was not, at the time, apparently recognised by the opposition in Parliament.

90. For instance, Stuart Maclure, 'An End to the Consensus?', *Times Educational Supplement*, 3 July 1970.

91. Black Paper Two was published in October 1969, Black Paper Three in November 1970. The 'Council for the Preservation of Educational Standards', which included several Black Paperites, was launched early in January 1971: leading members included Tom Howarth (High Master of St Paul's), Michael McCrum (Head of Eton), Angus Maude (Tory MP), A.E. Dyson (Black Paper editor), R.R. Pedley (public school head and well known controversialist), Rhodes Boyson (Tory MP), Max Beloff and others. See the *Teacher*, 7 January 1972, see also *Times Educational Supplement*, 7 January 1972. Journalist members included Ronald Butt (*Times*), and John Izbicki (*Daily Telegraph*). In addition, in 1970, the National Education Association had been formed 'to preserve grammar schools in secondary reorganisation areas', later sponsoring the 'National Campaign for the Advancement of Freedom in Education', *Times Educational Supplement*, 21 August 1973. The NEA pressurised Thatcher on parental choice. See *Education*, 18 February 1972; *Times Educational Supplement*, 29 September 1972.

92. This erupted into open conflict in the deputy leadership election in 1981.

93. Phillip Whitehead, 'The Labour Governments, 1974-1979' in Peter Hennessy and Anthony Seldon (eds.), *Ruling Performance*, pp.241-73.

94. *Education*, 15 February 1974. By this time the Liberal Party was also committed to comprehensive education. The Tory manifesto, which promised high priority for education, stressed regard for parents' wishes in secondary education, opposed the imposition of 'a universal system of comprehensive education', favoured direct grant schools and proposed a 'less rapid' development of further and higher education. Free nursery schooling, on the other hand, would be extended.

95. Whitehead, op.cit., p.242. The election took place on 28 February. MPs' numbers are from David Butler and Gareth Butler, *British Political Facts 1900-1985*, (6th edn.), London 1986.

96. Whitehead, op.cit., p.246.

97. *Education*, 15 March 1974.

98 *Times Educational Supplement*, 15 March 1974.

99. DES Press Statement, 16 April 1974. 'We are keeping open the option of seeking new legislative powers,' he said. 'I do not want to legislate at the moment ... but the circular represents a clear statement on national policy. I shall propose legislation if and when it becomes necessary to secure our objectives.'

100. *Times Educational Supplement*, 12 April 1974.

101. Of the 163 authorities at 31 March 1974 (before local government reorganisation), 72 had by now received approval to reorganise totally; 76 had reorganised in part only, and fifteen had received no approval to reorganise. DES Press Statement, 16 April 1974.

102. *Teacher*, 10 May 1974. Rhodes Boyson was a founder-member of the Comprehensive Schools Committee in 1965; later head of Highbury Grove School, ILEA, he had moved rapidly to the right, politically and educationally.

103. *Times Educational Supplement*, 5 April 1974.

104. *Teacher*, 7 June 1974. Circular 4/74 had specifically asked governors of voluntary (mainly church) schools (maintained by local authorities) to cooperate with comprehensive planning. London, although the pioneer comprehensive authority, had a disproportionate number of these (grammar) schools, and this had been a major brake on the secondary reorganisation from the start. The great bulk of these schools were, however, no longer viable, due to sharply falling rolls.

105. *Times Educational Supplement*, 28 June 1974. Van Straubenzee, appointed shadow minister for education immediately after the election, had been a junior minister (education) in the Heath government.

106. Ibid., 28 June 1974.

107. Ibid., 5 July 1974.

108. *Education*, 12 July 1974.

109. *Times Educational Supplement*, 19 July 1974.

110. Ibid.

111. *Education*, 2 August 1974.

112. *Times Educational Supplement*, 5 April 1974. Or, the leader added, as maintaining 'continuity' in policy and planning.

113. *Times*, 3 April 1974. However, in December, the government accepted the Houghton committee's recommendations for a substantial increase (of 29 per cent) in teachers' salaries.

114. *Education*, 2 August 1974; see also Susan Crosland, op.cit., pp.288-95.

115. *Times Educational Supplement*, 12 July 1974; *Times Higher Educational Supplement*, 12 July 1974; *Teacher*, 12 July 1974. For this entire episode, see David Hencke, *Colleges in Crisis*, Harmondsworth, 1978, *passim*. For the DES view (or that of the chief official concerned) Hugh Harding, *Education*, 5 January 1979, and Hencke's response in ibid., 19 January 1979.

116. *Teacher*, 2 August 1974.

117. The election took place on 10 October 1974. The results were Labour, 319; Tory, 277; Liberal, 13; Scottish National Party, 11; Plaid Cymru, 3; others (Northern Ireland), 12.

118. The phrase is Julian Critchley's, see Hugo Young, *One of Us*, London 1989, p.98.

119. *Sunday Times*, 20 October 1974. The speech was made three days before the new parliament met.

120. See David Leigh, *The Wilson Plot: The Intelligence Services and the Discrediting of a Prime Minister*, London 1988.

121. A major criticism of Labour policy covering the post-war period as a whole is made in *Unpopular Education, Schooling and social democracy in England since 1944* (Centre for Contemporary Cultural Studies, University of Birmingham), London 1981. This focuses on Labour's failure to transform the content of education and the schools' dominant ethos on a socialist basis. The analysis is unusual and certainly

stimulating, but the book suffers from a failure to recognise the (political) importance and social significance of the transition to comprehensive education.

122. *Times Educational Supplement*, 21 March 1975. The survey was undertaken by the journal itself.

123. Circular 8/75. The White Paper on public expenditure to 1979-80 now published (1975) reflected severe constraints due to the economic situation, but specifically gave priority to secondary school building to assist comprehensive reorganisation. *DES Report, 1975*, p.31-2.

124. *DES Report, 1975*, p.2.

125. The Bill also provided for a review of local authorities' arrangements for the take-up of places at non-maintained schools. Ibid., p.2.

126. *DES Report, 1976*, pp.2-3.

127. Official figures show the following percentage of secondary school pupils in maintained schools as at comprehensives: 1975, 68.6; 1976, 74.8; 1977, 79.3; 1978, 83.4; 1979, 85.9. DES, *Statistical Bulletin*, 13/79, November 1979.

128. *Times*, 18 July 1974; for Briault's reply, ibid., 27 July 1974. Van Straubenzee, among others, also published an indignant and challenging reply, 25 July 1974.

129. *Times Educational Supplement*, 3 May 1974. And perhaps also to a proportion at least of the newly recruited teachers, described at the time as imbued 'with newer notions about repressive middle class culture'. These 'came out of college with *Knowledge and Control* in the blood stream. They assume that to get on with working-class children you must pretend to be working-class. But children do not want you to play a patronising role.' David Felsenstein's critique of M.F.D. Young's thesis as set out in this book (London 1971) in a full-page discussion by several heads about their schools in *Times Educational Supplement*, 7 June 1974.

130. *Guardian*, 9 December 1974.

131. Ibid., 12 December 1974.

132. Hunter Davies's three articles titled 'The Truth about Comprehensives' were published in the *Sunday Times* 26 January, 2 February, 9 February 1976. They were later extended as a book, *The Creighton Story*, London 1976. In the conclusion to the third article, Davies wrote: 'There are bad comprehensives – but many of them are bad through never having been given a chance, by parents or the press, or because of local selection methods. Creighton is fortunate, but by no means unique, in having a truly comprehensive intake and it is making most of its ideals effective. It is a fine model for the future.'

133. See *Teacher*, 25 March 1977, for pupil, staff and NUT reaction to this film, which included contrived sequences, one of two girls smoking (invited by the production team to record the scene in a neighbouring block of flats). For the long term effect of this programme, see Maureen O'Connor, 'Old School Eyewash', *Guardian*, 3 May 1988.

134. The BBC made some restitution ten years later, with the series of programmes on Kingswood School at Corby which followed an adulatory series on a minor public school (Radley). The BBC, on this occasion, promised to be, and was, even-handed in its treatment. 'There was such a tremendous feeling of guilt at the BBC over the Ealing film,' said Tyler, the Kingswood head, 'that it has attempted since to be fair. O'Connor, ibid.

135. Quoted in C.B. Cox and Rhodes Boyson (eds.), *The Fight for Education*, Black Paper, London 1975, p. 64

136. This handbook seems to have had little effect; in practice the 1976 Education Act rendered it largely nugatory.

137. *Times Educational Supplement*, 23 January 1976. Ironically Sir Arnold Weinstock himself came under heavy criticism in 1988 in the financial columns of the quality press for financial and general mismanagement of GEC, which controls a vital sector of Britain's electrical engineering industry.

138. Clyde Chitty, 'Central Control of the School Curriculum, 1944-87', *History of Education*, Vol.17, No.4, December 1988.

139. This interpretation is open to question. The Tyndale teachers rejected all structures. Although Plowden was weak on articulating its approved pedagogy, the committee certainly did not recommend what can most accurately be described as anarchic procedures in the classroom.

140. *Times Educational Supplement*, 23 July 1976.

141. *William Tyndale Junior and Infant Schools Public Enquiry*, a report to the Inner London Education Authority by Robin Auld, QC, ILEA, July 1976. John Gretton and Mark Jackson, *William Tyndale: Collapse of a School or a System?*, London 1976. Terry Ellis, Jackie McWhirter, Dorothy McColgan, Brian Haddow, *William Tyndale, The Teachers' Story*, London 1976.

142. John P. White, in 'Tyndale and the Left', presented a penetrating critique of this situation; *Forum*, Vol. 19, No. 2, Spring 1977.

143. The new emphasis on accountability, which now took off, saw the publication of many books on this issue, for instance, Colin Lacey and Denis Lawton, *Issues in Evaluation and Accountability*, London 1981; Desmond L. Nuttall, *School Self-Evaluation, Accountability with a Human Face*, London 1981; Kathleen Ollerenshaw, *Accountability and the Curriculum*, London 1978; Maurice Kogan, *Education Accountability, an analytic overview*, London 1986; Clem Adelman and Robin J. Alexander, *The Self-Evaluating Institution, practice and principles in the management of educational change*, London 1982.

144. Neville Bennett, *Teaching Styles and Pupil Progress*, London 1976.

145. M. Aitkin, S.N. Bennett and J. Hesketh, 'Teaching Styles and Pupil Progress: A Reanalysis', *British Journal of Educational Psychology*, Vol.51, June 1981. In this article Bennett withdrew the original findings and offered others much more favourable to child-centred methods. On this occasion, the media (mass and otherwise) showed no interest whatsoever. For a discussion of this (complex) issue, see Maurice Galton, *Teaching in the Primary School*, London 1989, pp.25-8.

146. For an analysis, Centre for Contemporary Cultural Studies, *Unpopular Education*, pp.197ff.

147. In 1971, 83 per cent of a representative sample expressed themselves as satisfied or very satisfied with their child's primary schooling. By 1975 this had *risen* to 87 per cent expressing various degrees of satisfaction. A Gallup poll undertaken by the National Consumer Council in 1976 found a similarly high level of public support for schools. John Coe, 'Primary Schools' in Morris and Griggs, op.cit., pp.64-5.

148. Phillip Whitehead, op.cit., p.256.

149. This account is taken from an article about Sir James Hamilton by Stuart Maclure, *Times Educational Supplement*, April 1983.

150. The 'Yellow Book' has never been published in full. It was entitled 'School Education in England, Problems and Initiatives'. For a close analysis of the origins and background of this paper, and of James Callaghan's Ruskin speech, Clyde Chitty, *Towards a New Education System: The Victory of the New Right?*, London 1989, Chapter 3, 'The Yellow Book, the Ruskin speech and the Great Debate'.

151. Quoted by Keith Fenwick and Peter McBride, *The Government of Education*, London 1981, p.220. It is worth recalling here that in September 1976 the House of Commons expenditure committee produced its tenth report entitled 'Policy Making in the DES'. This all party group were severely critical of the DES as too secretive and too slow to give a lead. The committee argued that the education secretary should take more part in shaping the curriculum (but should not try to control it). The DES should make more documents open and encourage a wider debate about education, and the DES planners should spend more time considering broad educational objectives, and not confine themselves just to the allocation of resources. *Tenth Report of the Expenditure Committee: Policy Making in the DES.*

152. The Bullock committee had been established by Margaret Thatcher following suggestions that reading standards had declined. Its report, *A Language for Life*, was published in 1975 (HMSO).

153. Fifteen specific proposals were made for 'further action'. These include

exploration of the case and scope for a 'common core curriculum' involving 'greater vocational relevance for the 14 and 15s'; extending links between school and work; special attention to maths, science and modern languages; HMI involvement in initial teacher training; provision of adequate in-service training; priority for the 16-19 age group needs; a review of the functions and constitution of the Schools Council. Great emphasis is given to the need to strengthen HMI and for these to use 'a more direct style' – HMI should have a higher profile generally.

154. Callaghan summarised the main issues which 'cause concern' as follows:
(i)   methods and aims of informal instruction;
(ii)   the strong case for a 'core curriculum' of basic knowledge;
(iii) what is the proper way of monitoring the use of resources to maintain a proper national standard of performance;
(iv)   the role of HMI in relation to national standards;
(v)   the need to improve relations between industry and education.
He also referred to contemporary discussions on examinations and the Schools Council (referred to below), to sixteen to nineteen-year-olds, to recruitment of talented people into science and engineering, and to the forthcoming Taylor Report on School Governors. For a full report of this speech, *Education*, 22 October 1976.

155. Susan Crosland, *Tony Crosland*, London 1982, p.355.

156. Phillip Whitehead, op.cit., pp.258, 261. The Lib-Lab pact ended 'amicably' in the summer of 1978.

157. George Cooke, 'Too Tough at the Top', *Times Educational Supplement*, 1 February 1980.

158. Ibid., 'Corporate management', recommended by the Bains Report, was adopted throughout local government on reorganisation. Cooke's assessment of teacher morale in the period 1975-80 is worth quoting. This article was published early in 1980: 'During the last five years, I believe that the morale of the teachers has deteriorated markedly for reasons both external and internal to the profession. Among the external reasons were (obviously) the anxieties generated by retrenchment, reorganisation and contraction, the threat of unemployment or uncongenial employment and the constant stream of criticism. The politicians and the community at large turned on the education service and, skilfully confusing cause and effect in a grand bout of self-exculpation blamed it for virtually all the bad things in sight, from broken homes to declining industrial productivity.'

159. Capital expenditure on universities declined from £117 million to £70 million between 1976-77 and 1977-78; current expenditure from £708 million to £603 million – a decline of over £100 million in one year. *Education*, 19 January 1979.

160. Leonard Cantor, op.cit., p.302. The figures refer to England and Wales.

161. *Times Educational Supplement*, 19 November 1976. Interview by Auriol Stevens, headed 'No Time to Lose to Save the Nation'.

162. *DES Press Notice*, 28 April 1978.

163. Sir James Waddell chaired the 'Steering Committee' set up to consider the Schools Council's proposal. Its report was entitled 'School Examinations' (Cmnd. 7281). The White Paper was entitled 'Secondary School Examinations: a Single System at 16 Plus' (Cmnd. 7368).

164. Patricia Rowan, 'Special Schools' in Morris and Griggs, op.cit., p.98.

165. Robert Spooner, 'Secondary Schools' in Morris and Griggs, op.cit., pp.77-9.

166. There was an earlier stage, carried through in November and December, of consultations 'with a limited number of educational and industrial organisations', based on a DES paper 'outlining possible issues for consideration'. This was probably the process by which the agenda was changed (see next paragraph). See DES, *Educating our Children, Four Subjects for Debate* (background paper for the regional conferences February and March 1977, n.d., p.1).

167. Tedd Wragg, 'Sunny Jim's Storm Clouds Overhead', *Times Educational Supplement*, 17 October 1986. This (subtle?) deflection is discussed in Denis Lawton, *The Politics of the School Curriculum*, London 1980, p.39.

168. 'The "Great Debate" ' reflected a trend towards defining and limiting the boundaries of teacher autonomy. 'The very initiation of a public debate on education, involving the unprecedented consultation of industrial organisations and parents as well as educational organisations, served as an explicit reminder to the teaching profession ... that the curriculum was not solely their responsibility to determine ... thus the "great debate", irrespective of its content, simply as a *means* of intervening in education, helped to change the political context in which educational issues were discussed'. I. Bates, 'From Vocational Guidance to Life Skills; Historical Perspectives on Careers Education', in I. Bates *et al.* (eds.), *Schooling for the Dole? The New Vocationalism*, London 1984, p.199. Cited in Clyde Chitty, 'Central Control of the School Curriculum 1944-87', *History of Education*, Vol.17, No.4, December 1988.

169. *DES Report 1977*, p.41.

170. The Green Paper was seen as marking 'a new phase in its clear assertion of an active (leadership) role for the DES in relation to educational (as apart from administrative) matters'. It also opened the way for 'the imposition of mass testing of a limited and restrictive type covering the Three Rs by local authorities in the schools. *Forum*, Vol.20, No.1, Autumn 1978.

171. Circular 14/77, 'Local Education Authority arrangements for the School Curriculum', 29 November 1977.

172. Max Wilkinson, *Lessons from Europe. A Comparison of British and West European Schooling*, London 1977, and Tim Devlin and Mary Warnock, *What Must We Teach?* London 1977.

173. Brian Simon, 'To Whom do Schools Belong?', lecture organised by the Manchester Education Committee, 14 November 1978, reprinted in Brian Simon, *Does Education Matter?*, London 1985.

174. *Education*, December 1977. *The Attack on Higher Education* (the 'Gould' report) was answered in a pamphlet with the same title published by the Council for Academic Freedom and Democracy, n.d. 1977.

175. The construction of a specifically conservative education policy at this time (and earlier) is analysed in Christopher Knight, *The Making of Tory Education Policy in Post-war Britain*, London 1990.

176. *Times Educational Supplement*, 17 March 1978.

177. Caroline Benn, 'The Myth of Giftedness', *Forum*, Vol.24, No.2, Spring 1982. This Bill also attempted to deal with the sixteen to nineteen age-group and unemployment, and to give effect to some of the recommendations of the Taylor Report (*A New Partnership for our Schools*, 1977) concerning representation of parents and teachers on school governing bodies.

10   The Thatcher Governments, 1979–86

The last chapter focused attention at the close on the rise of the New Right – especially in the field of education, and there is little doubt that education was a leading issue on which the Tories gained votes in the General Election of May 1979. The 1980s saw two further Tory election victories under Margaret Thatcher's leadership, with the opposition split and generally in disarray. 'Thatcherism', which, by appealing to self-interest, individualism and the virtues of enterprise, sought to reverse the dominant ideas underlying the welfare state, began during this period to establish a certain hegemony, and this increasingly affected educational policy, particularly towards the close of the period.

Inflationary pressures were, however, paramount at the start, and it was in the economic and fiscal area that the first Thatcher government devoted its main efforts – at whatever cost to employment. A serious attempt was made to cut the supply of money while raising interest rates to such a level that the base of manufacturing industry was cut by 20 per cent. The huge loss in production that resulted rapidly pushed unemployment up from 1 to 2 million.[1] It was in this context of massive de-industrialisation, mounting unemployment (especially among youth) as well as savage cuts in public expenditure that the education service, now in any case facing contraction as a result of rapidly falling rolls, had to operate.

But education – the social services generally – were not a priority for the Thatcher government, initially at least. The immediate legislative measures of 1979–80, while imposing Tory manifesto policy, made no attempt at fundamentally changing the balance of forces, or traditional procedures within the field. Indeed, for several years, under Sir Keith Joseph as Secretary of State, no clear policy (except that of retrenchment) could be discerned. Partly as a result of this, together with the massive alienation of teachers which erupted in the so-called 'teachers' action' of 1985–87, education was suddenly caught in a situation of damaging crisis culminating in May 1986. At this stage, new policies emanating from the so-called Radical Right powerfully emerged and began clearly to influence government thinking.

A serious attempt was now made to turn the crisis into political advantage. In any case, something had to be done. The appointment of Kenneth Baker, a skilled communicator and politician, in place of the now discredited Keith Joseph, heralded a new phase. This culminated in the strangely ambiguous Education Act of 1988, which embodied several of the ideas propagated by the New Right. Described, by Peter Wilby, as a 'Gothic montrosity',[2] this Act was carried through parliament against the united opposition of all other political parties and of most of those directly concerned with education. As was the case with the Poll Tax, the government whips found it necessary to mobilise the most distant (and ancient) backwoods peers to get the crucial clauses through the Lords. So the situation was set for further struggles in the years ahead, if now in a new context.

This, and the following chapter, perhaps reflecting the importance of personalities in politics, are structured around the periods of office of the three succeeding secretaries of state. The first period, from May 1979 to September 1981, covers developments in the early months of the first Thatcher administration, with Mark (later Lord) Carlisle as Education Secretary. The second, from September 1981 to May 1986, is concerned with the four-and-a-half years of Sir Keith (later Lord) Joseph's hegemony. The third period is dealt with in Chapter 11 which starts with the appointment of Kenneth Baker and concludes with his demise as Education Secretary on 22 July 1989 – approximately a full year after the granting of royal assent to the Education 'Reform' Act in August 1988.

1 The First Period: May 1979 to September 1981

Parliamentary Action: The Two Bills
Education was given considerable priority by the new government at the start of its term of office in May 1979. With a comfortable majority (overall) of 43 in the Commons, little

difficulty was foreseen in carrying through measures relating to promises in the Tory manifesto.[3] In fact two Bills were presented in the first six months of office, the first, relating to comprehensive reorganisation, immediately after the re-assembly of parliament; the second, which covered a number of important issues, on 25 October. The first Bill received royal assent on 26 July 1979; the second on 3 April 1980.

Both Bills showed a clear continuity with traditional Tory policy, the first in terms of slowing, once again, the move to comprehensive secondary education; the second, in terms both of enhancing parental choice (which presented difficulties to comprehensive 'systems'), and of further subsidising private (and 'public') schools at the expense of the taxpayer. In addition, a number of administrative measures were included providing for the reduction of expenditure.

In the debate on the queen's speech the new Secretary of State, Mark Carlisle,[4] announced that the government 'will give the highest priority to a Bill to remove the compulsion on local education authorities to reorganise their schools on comprehensive lines'. The intention was, in effect, to revoke or repeal Labour's measure of 1976 (see p.440). As in 1970, the Tory government again stressed the importance of local authority autonomy in determining the pattern of their systems. This was, in effect, to declare that comprehensive education was no longer 'national policy', so giving the green light to authorities that wished not only *not* to reorganise their schools as comprehensive systems but to go further and split up existing schools to bring back the grammar/secondary modern division. Thus large authorities such as Essex and Kent now withdrew proposals to go comprehensive (submitted under the 1976 Act), and proposed to retain their existing divided systems in wide areas of the counties concerned, while urban authorities such as Bolton and Kingston-on-Thames took similar action. We will assess the general effect of this measure below.

Before passing to the, perhaps more important, 'number two Bill', it is worth noting further decisions aiming to negate measures taken by the Labour government. In July new regulations were issued relating to the powers of local authorities to finance pupils to attend independent schools. This was an area where the Labour government had been operating to some effect to put an end to a process which both underwrote selectivity and acted as a means of shoring up these schools. Efforts were to be made to extend this practice considerably – for instance the Greater Manchester Council (for a few years a Tory authority, but since abolished) set up a trust fund financed from the rates, using the income to subsidise pupils at independent schools. This ran into difficulties later, but the trend was clear.[5]

The major legislation of this period was, however, the second Education Bill introduced in the autumn (25 October). Two features deserve special attention – the introduction of the Assisted Places Scheme and the clauses relating to parental choice. We will take these in turn.

The Assisted Places Scheme (APS) was essentially a means of syphoning public money to independent schools without ensuring, at the same time, any return in public control. The technique used was the payment of fees of selected pupils directly to the schools concerned by the DES. It will be remembered that a similar solution to the financial crisis of the 'public' schools during the war was strongly advocated by these schools at the time (see pp.38-45). A scheme under the same title (APS) was certainly on the Ministry of Education's files during the 1950s when, for a time, it was seriously considered (p.196, n.88). Presented, in the press, as the brainchild of Stuart Sexton, now political adviser to Mark Carlisle,[6] the scheme was legitimated as a means whereby bright working-class children from inner cities might receive an education commensurate with their abilities. As many predicted at the time, it has not, in fact, worked out that way. The main beneficiaries have been relatively badly-off sections of the middle and particularly professional strata.[7]

The scheme was presented, by Mark Carlisle, as a means of restoring educational opportunities which were 'taken away by the destruction of the direct grant schools'.[8] By removing the direct grant these schools had enjoyed the previous government had not, of course, 'destroyed' the schools themselves. A few, as we have seen, had developed as comprehensive schools and now formed part of local systems. The bulk, however, had deliberately opted for independence. Some of these, as a result, were certainly in an unstable financial situation, so that extra financial help was to be welcomed. But involvement in the Assisted Places Scheme was offered, on certain specific conditions, much more widely, and there is little doubt that a number of independent schools were saved from bankruptcy by this measure.[9] Financial assistance was offered on a means test relating to parental income.

The cost of the scheme was estimated at £6 million in the first year, rising to around £70 million when fully established in seven years. But no, or 'very little' extra money was to be made available. Finance was to come from the education budget generally – that is, as critics were quick to point out, at a period of savage expenditure cuts – from resources that would otherwise have been available to local authorities for their systems.

As might be expected, the scheme was warmly welcomed by the 'public' and independent schools generally – consultations during the summer had made this clear. It was, however, very strongly contested, not only in parliament, but more widely. Generally it was seen as a divisive – even malevolent – action which not only underwrote, and extended, existing privileges, but also, by deliberately removing 'bright pupils', aimed a sharp blow at the burgeoning system of comprehensive education.

The 12,000 to 15,000 children to be selected each year for the scheme formed from between and 2 and 3 per cent of the age group, but Peter Newsam, then Chief Education Officer for the ILEA, calculated they formed some 20 per cent of the age group staying on at school to study in sixth forms or colleges for two or more A levels. In this sense alone the scheme comprised an extremely serious threat to the viability of advanced work in the publicly provided system – a point that has certainly been borne out in practice. But Newsam argued further that the additional transfers to independent schools at the age of sixteen then also suggested as part of the scheme, together with local schemes such as that at Manchester and the effect of tax rebates now given to high income groups, would result in increased demand for places in independent, as opposed to maintained schools. These factors, taken together, would be likely to have a profound effect on advanced work in maintained (and largely comprehensive) schools. Within a static or declining total of resources available to education, these measures reflected 'a shift in the balance of expenditure towards independent schools'.[10]

Such criticism was widely shared. The government's scheme, declared the *Times Educational Supplement*, 'has all the appearance of a thoroughly bad plan introduced at the wrong time'. The scheme is put forward as a rescue operation for bright children in urban schools. 'It offers to snatch a few brands from the burning fire while doing nothing for those same city comprehensives.'[11] The *Observer* was also sharply critical. The money (£70 million) would be desperately needed for books and equipment over the next few years for the schools attended by the vast majority of the nation's children.[12] Under the heading 'Mr Carlisle Legislates for Inequity' the *Guardian* devoted a main leader to a critique of this 'miserable measure'. There were many other issues that needed tackling; this was not the time to introduce new and even more socially divisive issues, particularly when coupled with the proposed abolition of free school meals and transport (as proposed in the second Bill).[13] Towards the end of the year, Neil Kinnock, then Labour's Shadow Minister for Education, gave a pledge on behalf of the party to scrap the scheme altogether, if returned to office.

But the second Education Bill went further than this. It also contained a group of clauses enhancing the scope of parental choice by placing a duty on local education authorities to comply with a school choice by a parent 'except where that would prejudice the provision of efficient education or the efficient use of resources'. Appeals committees were to be set up for dissatisfied parents; parents could also opt for a school outside their own LEA area.

While extending parental choice to some extent, these clauses were criticised as leading to a covert selectivity between comprehensive schools, so enhancing differentiation within comprehensive systems.[14] Further, these provisions enhanced the difficulties faced by local authorities in planning for contraction, necessary in view of falling rolls, with the objective of providing equally for all. 'Popular' schools would be likely to thrive. The so called 'unpopular' schools, largely those in disadvantaged areas in inner cities, would be likely to contract more rapidly than planned, so beginning a spiral of descent leading to closure. In the meantime the children in these schools would suffer. These clauses did contain a safeguard, however, in terms of the exception cited in the last paragraph. Authorities were able to use this formulation to cushion the schools against the worst effects of the Act, though, as we shall see, this safeguard was to be removed eight years later.

The Bill contained other features, mostly related to the

government's primary objective – cutting public expenditure. One set of clauses concerned a relaxation of central government control over local authorities; they 'freed' these from their statutory duty to provide school meals, milk and transport. During the second reading debate in the Commons, however, Carlisle admitted that the immediate aim of these clauses was to save money. The school meal service, he said, was currently subsidised to the tune of £400 million a year, and absorbed 7 per cent of total local authority expenditure.[15] The passage of the Bill in fact brought about the demise of the school meals service – at least in the form in which it had been established by the 1944 Education Act.

On transport, the Bill abolished the obligation on local authorities to pay the transport costs for children under eight living over two miles from the school, and for those over eight living more than three miles from school. On this specific issue, which was seen as a death-knell to village schools as well as discrimination against the poor, the government sustained a notable defeat in the House of Lords. This was administered by an alliance including the prestigious R.A. Butler, who made a rare appearance for this purpose, the Duke of Norfolk (secular leader of the Roman Catholics in the Lords), the Labour, Liberal and SDP opposition and many cross-bench peers.

That priority was given to two Education Bills so soon after the election indicated the importance attached by the new government to halting the move to comprehensive education and, at the same time, to shoring up and indeed strengthening the private sector (even if the latter objective was shrouded in a democratic rhetoric). The deliberate destruction of the school meals service – one of the very real achievements of the 1944 Act – was a clear blow at a key measure central to the war and post-war concept of the welfare state. Enhancement of parental choice had also the hidden but desired objective of increasing differentiation between schools in comprehensive systems. Populist policies such as this, to be exploited later in the decade, had now made their appearance in the form of legislation. Financial measures now followed suit.

Cuts in Expenditure and the Attack on Local Government
Several months before the second Education Bill was presented to parliament, Lady Young, Minister of State for

Education, announced at a Tory gathering that the Assisted Places Scheme, now being prepared for legislation, would survive the savage cuts in expenditure now being imposed on the education service.[16] The new government had been elected on a programme of reducing public expenditure and cutting taxes. The first budget, introduced in June, in fact cut the basic income tax rate to 30 per cent and lowered the top rate to 60 per cent – involving a major shift to indirect taxation. What appeared at the time to be swingeing cuts in educational expenditure were also announced – in the rate support grant (to local authorities), in direct government expenditure (£55 million), as well as in the Manpower Services Commission (£172 million).[17] So contraction, which had, of course, started earlier, now continued, setting the scene for the 1980s.

'Cuts, Cuts, Cuts' headlined the first issue of the *Times Educational Supplement* after the year-long closure of the Times group of newspapers in 1978–79. A detailed survey as to how these were hitting local authorities was presented. In practice, achieving the immediate savings called for (amounting to between £250 and £400 million) proved difficult if not impossible.[18] Plans were now made, however, to impose a reduction of 3.5 per cent on educational spending in the following year (1980–81). But it was during this year that long-term plans for contraction were announced, involving a reduction of public expenditure on education of as much as 9 per cent over three years.[19]

The policy of making reductions in public expenditure the 'first and over-riding priority' meant that the government could have 'no positive policies at all', argued Stuart Maclure in *Education*. Ministers were under the most solemn injunctions 'to do nothing and say nothing which could conceivably be interpreted as an invitation to spend'. The effect of this 'single-minded savagery' was spelt out in terms of unused swimming baths, trimmed capitation allowances, and 'all the other big and little badges of parsimony which will shame the local education authority scene'.[20] A year later, as further cuts in local authority expenditure were announced, protests mounted. 'By this time people in education are almost punch drunk by incessant announcements of further cuts in educational spending,' commented *Education* in August 1980. Riled over the defeat of the school transport proposals in the House of Lords (which the government did not think it wise to reverse in the Commons), the Treasury was said to be on the warpath, determined to claw back the £50 million expected saving. Mark Carlisle was now reported as resisting this further pressure – more cuts would threaten educational standards.[21] At the end of the year, however, the local authorities' journal was predicting that education would be one of the worst-hit services in 1981 as a result of the government's announcement of yet further cuts in local government expenditure. Would 1981 prove to be the worst year since the Geddes Axe?[22]

These fears were confirmed, in part at least, by the publication of a new White Paper on expenditure in March 1981. This made it clear that education was to be especially heavily hit. Both capital and current expenditure were targeted for continuous decline in the following three years – the total cut planned between 1980–81 and 1983–84 amounted to 7 per cent though for capital expenditure it reached over 30 per cent.[23]

Already a month earlier Her Majesty's Inspectors, in the first of their annual reports on the effects of local authority expenditure policies to be published, had given a clear warning as to the effect of the cuts on standards in schools and colleges. Nearly a third of the 980 schools visited were assessed as being in poor condition. Half of the local authorities had (radically) reduced repair and maintenance budgets; in one shire county no interior decoration had been undertaken in fifteen years. With the severe cut imposed on capital expenditure the basis was now laid for the continuous deterioration of the fabric of schools and colleges which characterised the 1980s.[24]

1981 is described, by a sympathetic commentator, John Vincent, as the 'pivotal year of Thatcherism', when after the 'heedless lavishness' involved in the tax cuts and pay increases of 1979–80, the government showed 'a new determination'.[25] In that year the public services borrowing requirement (PSBR) was slashed from £13.5 billion to £10.5 billion – the implications for education were spelt out in the White Paper. A central concern, to dominate throughout the 1980s, was to cut local government expenditure and, above all, to bring it under control. The ability of local government to fund developments relatively autonomously through raising the rates was the prime target. This is the era of rate-capping and the imposition of increasingly rigid controls, culminating in the poll tax of 1988. Between 1980–81 and 1985–86 educational expenditure, as a proportion of gross domestic product (GDP), declined drastically – from 5.5 to 4.8 per cent (see Appendix Table 15, p.599).

In May 1980 the Local Government, Planning and Land (No. 2) Bill, bringing with it new block grant arrangements for financing local government, was being debated to parliament. In effect the new grant involved an 'objective assessment' by the government), known as the 'grant-related expenditure' (GRE) assessment, of what a local authority would need to spend in order to provide a standard level of service. This was seen as a means of cutting expenditure by the back door, since, due to the complexity of the issue, few fully understood the proposals, nor the Bill's implications. This illustrates again, wrote W.H. Petty, then president of the Society of Education Officers, how 'action can be taken which could affect the education service drastically without the majority of the people engaged ... having any idea of what is taking place, or that the service could be affected at all'.[26] In an article entitled 'The Uncertainties and Iniquities of the New Block Grant', Jack Springett, Education Officer of the AMA, stressed that the new system 'places unlimited powers in the hands of ministers', and undermined local authorities' responsibilities for decision-making.[27] A devastating criticism was launched in a pamphlet entitled *Ten Billion Pounds: Whitehall's Takeover of the Town Hall*, by Tyrrell Burgess and Tony Travers. The Bill, which received royal assent late in 1980, was here characterised as heralding the demise of local government. The new block grant arrangements 'can surely be counted the most unpopular measure of the present government – and that is saying something', commented *Education* early in 1981. The AMA now decided to press for an early meeting with Mark Carlisle to tell him of 'the devastating effects of the block grant on urban schooling', a resolution at their conference expressing 'deep concern'.[28]

It was in 1981, then, that matters appeared to be building to a crisis. Where the government directly controlled expenditure, as, for instance, in the case of the universities, the cuts announced in July were horrific.[29] Resistance was building up, especially in areas sharply hit. Mass demonstrations, of teachers, students and others took place across the country – in London, Leicestershire and elsewhere. Local authority organisations, teachers' unions and others combined in a protest movement that was virtually unanimous.

Over the summer of 1981 unemployment reached the massive total of 2.6 million. While inflation had been brought down, Thatcher's deflationary measures were resulting in sharp social conflicts. Riots erupted in cities all over England – that at Toxteth in Liverpool being the most serious. The Cabinet, still mainly old-style Tories, revolted, leaving the Prime Minister virtually isolated.[30]

Her response was her 'most aggressive reshuffle'. Parkinson, Tebbit, 'Thatcherite stalwarts', now came in. The Cabinet was 'radicalised'. Mark Carlisle, who recently had stubbornly defended education in the Cabinet, protesting that further cuts must hit standards, was unceremoniously sacked. His place was taken by Thatcher's monetarist guru, Sir Keith Joseph. This reshuffle marked the beginning of Thatcher's real ascendancy within the Cabinet and party.[31]

Comprehensive Education and the Curriculum
In spite of the first Education Act, and the heavy emphasis on contraction, the transition to comprehensive education continued apace. Local authorities voted with their feet. In fact the momentum behind the movement probably slowed down in the new circumstances, but the trend was unmistakable. Further, moves to restore selection were strongly and successfully resisted by local populations.

Two controversial areas deserve a brief mention. By one vote the Tory-controlled Bolton council decided, after the passage of the 1979 Act, to scrap comprehensive plans due to come in in September. Nearly 3,000 children had suddenly to take the 11-plus, three-quarters of them being then relegated to the city's thirteen modern schools, the rest gaining places in the six grammars.[32] By 1983, however, no doubt aided by a swing to Labour, Bolton had a fully reorganised comprehensive system. Nearby, at Tameside, where Labour had just regained control, the council decided now to reverse Tory policy and implement its own, earlier comprehensive plan. Carlisle informed the council that this scheme was 'spent'. Once again there was legal action and the council was victorious.[33] By 1983, also, all Tameside's schools were comprehensive. In other areas also there was movement. In March 1980 Cornwall was able proudly to announce that the whole county had now gone comprehensive. A sixth form college had been opened in Penzance, fed by a number of reorganised eleven-to-sixteen comprehensive schools.

The strength of local feeling against the reintroduction of the 11-plus surfaced most dramatically at this time in distant Cumbria. Following the Tory return at the election, a scheme, drafted in secret, having this objective, ran into immense opposition. The Chief Education Officer (Peter Boulter) himself advised against it. Petitions were organised on a massive scale and thousands of signatures obtained. So many objections were made that the scheme was referred back for reconsideration. Parents at Cockermouth were reported as opposing the scheme by more than four to one.[34]

Generally, then, the swing to comprehensive education continued during the 'Carlisle' period. Inevitably, more grammar schools were merged into or developed as comprehensive. By January 1982, of the 315 remaining in May 1979, 130 had already been assimilated into comprehensive systems – the percentage of pupils in comprehensives had now risen (in England) to 89.3 (see Appendix Tables 5b and 6b, pp. 585 and 587). Possibly as a sign of a slight softening of attitudes, in August 1980 the DES agreed to contribute an annual grant (of £25,000) to the newly established Centre for the Study of Comprehensive Schools at the University of York.[35] It was becoming increasingly evident that the comprehensive school, in whatever form, was and must be the school of the future.

But, as Caroline Benn pointed out, in a characteristically well-informed and hard-hitting article, no more than 50 per cent of the existing schools were 'genuinely' comprehensive – that is, recruiting an intake that fully reflected the make-up of the local population, and so not subject to any kind of selective creaming.[36] Further, within both 'genuine' comprehensives and others, internal divisions were still imposed through the continued existence of the dual examination system (GCE and CSE) originally devised for the divided structure existing before comprehensive reorganisation. The previous Labour administration, as we have seen, had prevaricated on the issue of the substitution of a single examination (for all), though this had finally been proposed in a White Paper published in 1978 (Cmnd 7368), following the Waddell Committee's report (see p.455). This proposition, of course, fell with the government in 1979.

A single (reformed) examination at the age of sixteen

remained a primary objective for comprehensive school heads and teachers as more and more of these schools prepared to move into the 1980s. They were however, unsurprisingly, once more to be disappointed. In July 1979 Mark Carlisle announced in parliament that the plans for a single examination system had been temporarily shelved. The secretary of state was not happy that standards would be maintained if Labour's proposals were implemented. Yet further consultations were necessary.[37] The schools settled down once again to make the best of a bad job.

All was not lost, however – the pressure for this reform remained intense. After six months' further consultations, Carlisle finally announced the government's decision to reform the examinations at the age of sixteen in February 1980. The terms of the decision were, however, hardly those desired by comprehensive school teachers who saw the single exam at sixteen as a powerful means of unifying the school through a unification of the curriculum. What the government now decided was to create a single grading system, but, as Carlisle put it, one with 'heavy emphasis' on O levels. In each subject there were to be alternative papers at different levels of difficulty. The new 'single' examination was to be in operation in 1985 (that is, five years later). The examination boards were to produce national criteria defining the scope and character of the new examination in each subject. Only a limited role was to be allotted to the Schools Council – theoretically in charge of examinations. In practice, the DES would take control.[38]

At this stage, the government also turned down proposals from the Schools Council to broaden sixth form education by the introduction of a wider group of subjects in place of the traditional three A levels.[39] The long-standing practice of a highly specialised, academic sixth form education, characteristic of Britain alone among advanced industrial countries, was, therefore, allowed to continue. Responses, reported the DES, indicated that 'A levels were highly regarded' and that the proposals 'did not command general support'.[40] Traditional educational procedures were by these means reinforced. These decisions by government made it extremely difficult, if not impossible, for comprehensive schools to revise their curricula and procedures in terms of the needs of the great mass of the country's children, who now attended these schools.[41]

On a different level, however, these years saw a flurry of

activity on the curriculum – especially as secondary (comprehensive) schools were concerned. Two, or perhaps three, main strands were discernible. First, a growing insistence on the role of the secretary of state (or DES, rather) in determining procedures. In a review of the responses of local authorities to Circular 14/77, the secretaries of state (for England and Wales) said that they had 'an inescapable duty' to satisfy themselves that 'the work of the schools matched national needs'.[42] At the North of England Conference in January 1980 Mark Carlisle devoted his entire speech to the curriculum, taking his themes from two recent official publications: *A Framework for the School Curriculum* (a DES 'discussion' paper), and *A View of the Curriculum*, a contribution by HMI. Matters were taken a step further when Baroness Young made it clear that the government intended to introduce a core curriculum in October that year (1980), claiming that, of the 130 responses received to the first of these documents, most were favourable.[43]

This flurry of publications emanating from the DES presaged (or was seen to presage) an increasingly energetic bid for centralised control over the curriculum as argued for in the Yellow Book (and elsewhere). Control over the curriculum was, therefore, an area where conflicts were likely to develop, though the DES (which was primarily concerned – ministers come and go) was proceeding carefully and testing the ground with some caution. The models of the curriculum in these publications varied. Late in 1979 HMI had published a comprehensive survey of secondary schools in England.[44] This already suggested, in the words of the annual DES report, 'that it might be timely to seek a new rationale for the secondary school curriculum and a simpler structure with fewer options'.[45] The '*Framework ...*' discussion paper in fact proposed what Denis Lawton calls a 'bureaucratic' model, based on an objectives pattern. It was submitted to a devastating critique by the AMA who assessed the document as virtually of no value.[46] The HMI paper, *A View of the Curriculum*, was, however, widely welcomed in the educational world as a genuine attempt to apply new principles to the construction of the curriculum.[47]

In the following year further important papers were produced. *The School Curriculum*, published in March and derived from consultations on *A Framework ...*, appeared as a less aggressive document than its forebear and was given a cautious welcome by those representing local authorities[48] – partly, perhaps, because in this document the secretaries of state went out of their way to reaffirm their confidence in 'the statutory division of responsibility for the curriculum' among central government, LEAs, governing bodies and teachers. This was possibly a case of the government adopting the tactic *reculer pour mieux sauter*; in any case it temporarily allayed fears of centralised control which had come to the fore the previous year.

Finally, in April 1981, the Schools Council (well based in the schools themselves) entered the fray with *The Practical Curriculum*. Here were a number of radical proposals, based on actual innovations in the schools themselves, which had much to offer. But this was almost precisely the moment when the future of this organisation was overtly threatened. An enquiry into its future had been set up in March.[49] Its unpopularity in official circles (DES) was an open secret. It is difficult to estimate what effect these publications, and the activity relating to them, had on the schools themselves. As already indicated, actual government decisions on examinations were more likely to have determined procedures, fixing them in a traditional mould, than exhortations in any number of pamphlets, official or otherwise. It may be that this deluge of circulars, discussion papers, regional conferences,[50] etc., was not really directly concerned with the curriculum at all, but with the battle to alter power relations within the field of education.

Other Government Policies

Other aspects of the new Tory government's policies related to the twin drives – towards economies on the one hand, and towards more powerful centralised control on the other. Ironically, in view of her later persona as a minister at the time of the passage of the Baker Act, it was Angela Rumbold, former chair of CLEA (the local authorities' educational association) who most eloquently expressed the fear that control of education was being gradually prised loose from local government. Plans for setting up a national body for public sector higher education were, in her view, the first step along this road.[51] A leaked policy document to this effect motivated the local authorities to conduct an energetic fight to preserve control of what were, in fact, their own institutions, carefully nursed (in the case of the polytechnics) since their original designation in 1966 – and, of course, in their original form as local technical colleges for a long period before that.[52] Through the late spring and summer of 1981 local authority associations submerged political differences in a united stand in defence of their rights. This early, perhaps premature move was at that time defeated, the government shelving its 'nationalisation' plans for higher education.[53]

Other decisions related to retrenchment. That of raising overseas students' fees to cover the full economic cost aroused widespread opposition especially among students and university teachers who campaigned strenuously against the decision. At a full-scale debate in the House of Lords, Lord Boyle was among those who expressed total opposition to a policy which he saw as a damaging assault on cultural links – a view he also expressed in a strong statement to the Court at the University of Leeds.[54] But the measure which, perhaps, suffered most from the financial squeeze was the Education Act 1981 which gave effect to the recommendations of the Warnock Committee on children with special educational needs – now defined, by that committee, as comprising up to 20 per cent of all children. It will be remembered that the Labour administration failed to legislate on this issue, instead engaging on yet another round of consultations. The Tories, on their return, gave legislative priority to the two Bills discussed earlier – Warnock had to wait its turn until the following year.

When the Bill was eventually introduced, it did 'the bare minimum' to provide a legal framework for special education 'without spending any extra money at all'. Patricia Rowan, in a perceptive essay on this issue, concludes that the failure to deal effectively with Warnock's main priority areas was due to 'the government's implacable refusal' to allow that extra resources were necessary – not only to shift organisational structures but also attitudes in a new direction, involving the humanist perspective of bringing children with special educational needs together with all others.[55] The AMA, representing authorities which would be involved in implementing the proposals, stressed that extra resources would inevitably be needed to cover the equipment and spatial changes required.[56] Since the Bill provided no new resources, was it in fact seen by the government as a 'money-saving weapon', asked George

Cooke, ex-CEO and vice-chair of the Warnock Committee. By this time distrust of the government's intentions was becoming widespread.[57]

Finally, 1979–81 saw the start of the mass youth unemployment that characterised the 1980s, assisted both by the rapidity of scientific-technological change and by the government's deliberate policy of de-industrialisation. This took off with extraordinary rapidity in 1980–81, culminating in the inner-city rioting of the summer of 1981. Nearly 500,000 young people were expected to be out of work that summer when the Cabinet was asked to approve an emergency package of relief measures in a desperate attempt to cut youth unemployment. Employment Secretary, James Prior, now presented a scheme involving expenditure of £1000 million, and guaranteeing every sixteen-year-old leaver by 1983–84 access either to a job, to further education or to a place on the Youth Opportunity Programme (YOP).[58] In the meantime unemployed school-leavers returned to school in record numbers since jobs were not available.[59] Unsurprisingly no extra cash was allotted to cope with them. This unexpected task fell, of course, on the teachers.

This, then, was the immediate background when Keith Joseph took over as Secretary of State in September 1981.

2 The Hegemony of Keith Joseph, September 1981 to June 1986

Sir Keith Takes Over

Keith Joseph was to hold office for four-and-a-half years, the second longest continuous tenure of office in post-war history (see Appendix II, pp.569-70). It proved to be a disastrous period for education, culminating in a crisis almost reaching the proportions of a Greek tragedy – and having similar characteristics. How this came about forms the subject matter of this section.

Why was Joseph appointed – and Carlisle sacked? The simplest explanation is that Joseph specifically asked for the job, while Carlisle was an easily expendable 'wet'.[60] In spite of doctrinaire certainties expressed in his many speeches, Joseph's total conviction that he alone had access to 'the truth', that he understood the workings of the economy and was quite clear about the measures needed to put it right,[61] his tenure of the Department of Industry in the Tory administration had been notably unsuccessful. Though with a reputation for intellectual brilliance, sharp and incisive in the articulation of his views, Joseph's talents did not appear to include skills as a practical administrator in charge of an important government department, even though that department was specifically concerned with the wealth-producing sector (in Joseph's terms) – private industry. It was said that the appointment to education was made 'to break his fall'. Margaret Thatcher's loyalty to her mentor and friend is well known. Perhaps this provides a sufficient explanation.

The appointment was hardly regarded with enthusiasm by the education service. Joseph had, after all, made it very clear that he was no friend to the maintained system. 'Large, unstreamed comprehensive schools' could not be the way to educate Britain's youth; domination by left-wing or incompetent teachers was the rule. Mark Carlisle, 'an approachable and reasonably liberal minded "wet" ' was, according to Fred Jarvis (now Secretary of the NUT) to be replaced by 'the high priest of monetarism ... who will apply spending cuts with relish and doubtless ask for more'.[62] In fact Keith Joseph was said to be the only 'spending minister' who never went into the so-called Star Chamber (a Cabinet committee) to argue the case for more resources for education. As a confirmed monetarist he could not bring himself to take such action.

Some light on Keith Joseph's personal views on education as social policy may be culled from a book he co-authored, published in the year of the Tories' return. Appropriating the title of R.H. Tawney's famous book, *Equality*, Joseph set out an opposite thesis. It is widely accepted, he wrote, 'that it is a proper, indeed a major, function of the state to shift incomes and savings from the richer to the poorer members of society'. Such redistribution is unwise. But, more important, 'it is also morally indefensible, misconceived in theory and repellant in practice'. The use of the word 'repellant' is symptomatic.[63]

A main thesis in Joseph's 1970s' speeches is that money spent on public services deprives private industry – the wealth-producing sector – of resources, and is, therefore, generally to be deplored, especially if the services so provided are not up to scratch. Finding himself in charge of a department of state which had crucial responsibilities for just such a service appears to have subjected Keith Joseph to severe and continuous strain. How could *he* be held responsible for such a service? Clearly he could not – history (or Margaret Thatcher) had somehow wished on him a situation that was profoundly contradictory. A prescient comment made at the close of his first year of office sums up the situation very precisely:

> Sir Keith Joseph has not tried to give the lead that belongs to his office because he is determined to stand back and maintained a pained detachment, lest anybody should suppose him to be, in some small way, responsible for the shortcomings which he observes within the education system.[64]

It is not surprising, then, that on taking office, Keith Joseph focused immediately on two specific issues – the need for retrenchment, and the equally pressing need (in his view) to get rid of bad, ineffective or weak teachers. At the Tory Party Conference in October 1981, less than a month after taking office, Joseph took the opportunity to confirm (in his new post) his unswerving attachment to diminishing commitment in government expenditure. 'More money does not necessarily mean higher standards,' he intoned, a truism having a certain overtone which he was to repeat, with only minor variations, over the years. The fall in resources, he added, 'has been substantially less than the fall in pupil numbers'. So there were no real grounds of complaint. It was 'a deeply depressing message', commented *Education*. The star (at fringe meetings) was Rhodes Boyson, now Minister for Schools, who called for the introduction of vouchers and a return to selection.[65] Perhaps oddly, this conference carried a resolution 'reaffirming' the party's commitment to comprehensive education. Moved by Demetri Argyropulo (chair of the Conservative National Advisory Committee on Education), he argued 'to a manifestly resistant audience' that the party had to support comprehensives because 90 per cent of secondary children went to them. The motion was supported by Van Straubenzee who also protested very strongly against educational retrenchment. 'Don't push us too far,' he said. The cuts were beginning to enter the bone. In his reply, Joseph said that, although comprehensives had come to stay (significantly adding 'for the time being at least'), he wished 'we had gone less fast'.[66]

Next it was the turn of the teachers. At the annual North of England Conference in January 1982 – a major platform for ministerial policy pronouncements – Joseph went out of his way to remind local education authorities of what he described as their duty to the 'trading base' of the nation. He then turned to attack bad teachers and ineffective curricula in 'some' schools. If the curriculum is to be protected, he said, 'there will have to be compulsory redundancies', going on to make it clear that the education service was suffering self-inflicted damage from incompetent teachers.[67]

The educational world, then, received nothing but a sharply aggressive message from the new minister (and his senior under secretary) during the first months of office – and this was to continue. Some months later (September 1982) a Central Policy Review staff ('think tank') paper on cutting public expenditure, being considered by the Cabinet, was leaked to the press (apparently by a 'wet'). This proposed huge cuts in health and education, together with a policy of deliberate erosion of benefits through inflation. This leaked paper sent shock waves through the Cabinet and, of course, far beyond.[68] Although denials followed, this report was in the background when Joseph addressed the Tory conference early in October. Here he declared the main planks of his 'policy' to be the introduction of a voucher scheme (or a pilot) and the substitution of student loans for grants. Both these are, in fact, peripheral issues, commented the educational press. Both are intensely controversial. Neither could have any impact on schools for years to come. While the minister 'has flown his colours proudly by reminding the party faithful of the purity of his devotion to a free market in education, he has depressingly little else to show for his labours'.[69]

At this time, Keith Joseph took a decision which deeply shocked the educational (and local government) world, relating to reorganisation due to falling rolls. Manchester finally decided on a tertiary college scheme, involving the transformation of their all-through eleven-to-eighteen schools to a system of eleven-to-sixteen schools feeding sixth form colleges. Decision rested with the secretary of state under Section 13 procedure. Joseph responded by refusing to allow three 'prestigious' comprehensives (in surburban areas) to be so transformed.[70] The rest of the scheme (involving inner-city schools) could go ahead. The three schools excepted by Joseph, were, he said, 'of proven quality', and should not be disturbed. This, of course, made something of a nonsense of the scheme as a whole.

Gone is the policy of ensuring, with falling rolls, the maintenance of 'a system of good schools' as advocated by the first serious study of this issue in the recently published Briault Report, commented *Education*. 'From now on Sir Keith's policy appears to be one of survival of the fittest with the less fit losing their sixth forms.'[71] 'In my experience', reported Dudley Fiske, Manchester's CEO, to his education committee, 'there is no precedent for such action by a secretary of state'; the decision was an 'outrage'. The 'mushroom system' of seven or eight eleven-to-eighteen schools providing sixth forms for a larger number of eleven-to-sixteen proposed by Joseph, found little favour. 'Confusion and uncertainty' were now prevalent in the schools; 'there is a real prospect now of the loss of experienced staff of good quality and of a total loss of confidence on the part of the parents'.[72] Conservative local government leaders also protested; at the North of England Conference in January 1982, held at Leeds, Councillor Patrick Crotty, the ebullient Tory lord mayor of Leeds and former education committee chair (and strongly pro-comprehensive) was the first off the mark, roundly attacking Sir Keith Joseph (a Leeds MP) for his treatment of Manchester's reorganisation plan. This was the business of the local authority, he said, and the authority should be left to get on with it.[73]

Keith Joseph's idiosyncratic – and ideologically motivated – pronouncements on the curriculum were also now becoming an increasingly worrying cause for concern, particularly among secondary school teachers. In March 1982 he was reported as drawing applause from the Institute of Directors in a speech in which he exhorted schools to 'preach [*sic*] the moral virtue of free enterprise and the pursuit of profit'. Entrepreneurs should go into the schools and put this message across rather than leave it to the teachers.[74]

A year later Joseph startled the educational world by rejecting a proposal that science (physics) syllabuses, being prepared for the new examination at the age of sixteen should contain aims relating to the social, economic and technical applications of science. Proposed examinations, in Joseph's view, should not involve the wider social and economic applications of science. This decision, which lay with the secretary of state, appeared as a ban on syllabuses carefully worked out by representative committees of science teachers.[75] Considerable anger was expressed by the Association for

Science Education (ASE), a prestigious and long established association uniting science teachers, at its conference in the summer. The decision was there characterised as a political ban. Government fears of the growing popularity of the peace movement probably triggered the controversial decision to outlaw questions of a social and economic nature, said the ASE.[76]

The reason for the growing concern among teachers was that it was now becoming apparent that the secretary of state had powers to determine important aspects of the curriculum personally by utilising his powers to accept, or reject, proposals relating to the criteria to be used in setting the new examination, if and when this was to be brought in. Any statement by Joseph as to what should, or should not, be taught naturally now assumed significance. At about this time, Keith Joseph, for instance, took the opportunity of a conference of American historians to call for the teaching of 'national values' in the study of history. 'History teaching should foster pride in Britain,' he was reported as saying. 'Pride in British culture and past national achievements should be the central aim.'[77] In a powerful main leader the following week, the *Times Educational Supplement* took Joseph to task for his comments. Headed 'Wrong Tone of Voice – Wrong Voice', the journal commented on the storm raised by Joseph on physics teaching; now historians were told they should teach shared values which are a distinctive feature of British society. This renewed doubts about the whole criteria exercise. The degree of political interference – as in the case of the physics criteria – was obvious.[78]

There was at this stage growing confusion about the new examination among those most closely concerned. Work on this had been going on for years – to little outward effect. Carlisle, as we have seen, after initial prevarication, had accepted its inevitability, but in terms of a very conservative model. Now there was new uncertainty. ' "Canute" Joseph Told not to Resist the 16-plus Tide', headlined the report of a speech by the chair of the joint council for 16-plus national criteria. The new exam was 'an absolute necessity'. An enormous amount of work had been done – much of it wasted due to the prevarications of successive governments. Keith Joseph, who by now had been in office a full year, had contributed uncertainty.

> Sir Keith has taken us further down the road of doubt by implying that his whole judgement on 16-plus will be whether he likes the criteria or not ... the irony is we are working in the dark – we have no idea on what criteria the criteria will be judged.[79]

A full year later things were much the same. Was there to be a show-down over the new exam, the *Times Educational Supplement* asked. Keith Joseph regards himself (and his Welsh counterpart) 'as the final arbiter of what should or should not be examined in all the new exams'. Parts of a recent letter from the secretaries of state to the bodies concerned 'makes chilling reading'.[80]

Another idiosyncratic action of Keith Joseph's initiated soon after taking office, was his treatment of the Social Science Research Council.[81] Joseph, whose eugenicist views mentioned earlier had been severely criticised by social scientists, conceived a distrust for such research. Only three months after taking office he commissioned Victor (Lord) Rothschild, head of Heath's think tank, a hard-headed natural scientist, to review the work of the council. It was generally thought that he wanted a negative report.

In fact he was in for a surprise. Rothschild went into the issue very thoroughly and made up his own mind about the nature and value of research in the social sciences, whose record he found highly impressive. To close the council, Rothschild reported, would be totally irresponsible – an act of 'intellectual vandalism'. In October 1982 an announcement was made. The SSRC was saved, but, in what seemed to many as an act of spite, its budget was severely cut (again). The *THES* wrote:

> It is clear that the climate of opinion engendered by Lord Rothschild, a natural scientist, by members of the ABRC (Advisory Board for Research Councils), and by the majority of academics, made it impossible for Sir Keith to close the council.[82]

Not content with simply cutting the budget, Joseph reacted petulantly to this forcing of his hand. There is no such field as 'social science', as he let it be known. The council must change its name. Joseph, of course, held the purse strings and so the future of the council was in his hands (he was Secretary of State for Education *and Science*). It is sad to recall that the council supinely agreed to this, renaming itself the 'Economic and

Social Research Council' by which name it is still known. A clear case, some argued, of *le trahison des clercs*.[83]

If the SSRC decision – or non-decision – largely affected the universities, already reeling under the most severe cuts imposed on any part of the system, two curricula initiatives were directed at the schools early in Keith Joseph's second year of office. These were the Technical and Vocational Educational Initiative (TVEI), suddenly announced to an astounded educational world in November 1982, and the Lower Achieving Pupils Project (LAPP), of January 1983. TVEI was apparently concocted by David (later Lord) Young, then director of the MSC, and Margaret Thatcher herself, together with Keith Joseph. Enormously generously funded, and controlled by the MSC (and not the DES), this was announced as a pilot scheme to provide equipment, teachers and other support to local authorities willing to co-operate. These were asked to submit proposals relating to individual participant schools. The scheme got off the ground in September 1983 with fourteen co-operating authorities. It was clearly a bid to shake up the schools, and to develop new forms of vocationally and technically orientated curricula for the fourteen-to-eighteen age group. Introduced from above with no consultation whatever with those directly concerned (teachers and local authorities) the scheme, although provided with resources on an extraordinarily generous scale and so naturally attractive at a time of more general penny-pinching economies, met with a good deal of suspicion and hostility at the start. The scheme was boycotted by most Labour authorities, but sufficient co-operated to meet the government's target.[84]

The Lower Achieving Pupil Project, on the other hand, was a DES initiative, and was directed at those pupils in secondary schools Keith Joseph had designated as the 'bottom 40 per cent' in his Sheffield speech. The financial resources made available for this project were a great deal less than the MSC provided for TVEI. Here also thirteen local authorities were finally selected for the pilot projects. At this stage Keith Joseph stressed that he hoped the project would encourage a shift away from narrowly academic teaching towards approaches better suited to the needs of the 'less able'.[85]

Both schemes caused concern, especially among those working to develop a unified curriculum for all aged eleven to sixteen in comprehensive schools, including science and technology as vital components, but for *all*. TVEI, according to MSC guidelines, must only be made available to named pupils. LAPP was for 'the bottom 40 per cent' however these were defined. The move towards a single examination for all was now, at least, on the agenda. Was this, then, simply a new attempt to impose a tripartite division within comprehensive schools – the academic (working for GCE O and A levels), the technical (TVEI pupils) and the rest (the 'low achievers')? In the atmosphere of the time, given the distrust by now engendered as to government intentions, it seemed very like it. The initial objectives of comprehensive education seemed to be receding out of reach; distanced by distortions inflicted on the inner organisation of the schools by external forces, too powerful to resist.[86]

Yet more shocks were in store, however, in what may fittingly be described as Keith Joseph's first term. In April 1982 Joseph suddenly announced the actual abolition of the Schools Council and its replacement by two quangos, one to cover the curriculum, the other examinations, to be chosen and appointed directly by himself as secretary of state. The Trenaman Report, commissioned by Carlisle, had been highly critical. The council was dominated by power politics, was anti-intellectual, too complicated and overstretched. It did, however, important work, and could do more. Nancy Trenaman, Principal of St Anne's College, Oxford, in fact recommended that the council should continue in being, though with drastic reductions in size and in the number of its committees. The DES, in its (leaked) 'confidential' evidence, claiming that the council was too pro-teacher and 'plainly hostile to the department', had proposed its replacement by a single body of nominees. This was specifically rejected by Nancy Trenaman. Plans were then re-worked for two bodies to take its place. 'The government's approval of that scheme was announced to a startled educational world last Thursday,' reported the *Times Educational Supplement*.[87] The DES, it will be remembered (see pp.449, 455) had been gunning for the Schools Council at least since 1976 (and probably earlier) – even if it was originally its own brainchild (see pp.312-4).

The secretary, John Mann (a highly respected ex-CEO) responded immediately. By strengthening central control of the examination system and the curriculum (both Schools

Council responsibilities) Sir Keith Joseph was opening the door to abuse by a future 'unscrupulous secretary of state'. Criticising the separation of examinations from the curriculum in the new dispensation, John Mann charged that this action could only be interpreted 'as a move to greater central control of what happened in schools'.[88]

The Schools Council fought back with wide support especially from local authorities and teacher organisations.[89] But there was nothing it could do. The decision was taken – and clearly a crucial one. From now on there was to be no semi-official but independent body offering advice to the government, or for that matter to the schools. The Central Advisory Councils for England and Wales were no longer in being, even though these were strictly enjoined by act of parliament. The DES was out on its own – no doubt rankled by the plundering of its traditional territory by the upstart MSC, it could now assert its control over examinations and the curriculum. As a final twist of the knife, Joseph announced that next year's funds to the beleaguered Schools Council were to be cut by £1 million, one third of the total (the council was given two years to wind up its affairs).[90] DES officials axed 33 of their curriculum projects in a final act of vindictiveness.

'The English education system is in a mess', commented the *Times Educational Supplement* at the end of 1982, offering its readers a Happy New Year. 'Morale is low' – partly for unavoidable reasons like falling numbers and reduced expectations, but 'partly because education is in the dog-house, the butt of indiscriminate criticism, much of it prompted by the need to find a scapegoat for larger ills like unemployment'. And indeed unemployment had escalated with extraordinary rapidity over the last two years. The whole enterprise, however, suffered from lack of leadership. Not only was Sir Keith standing back and maintaining his stance of 'pained detachment', but the actual commitment of the whole group of ministers at the DES to the maintained system 'is now suspect'. First, the Assisted Places Scheme; now advocation of vouchers and other forms of privatisation indicated a clear lack of support for the service for which they were responsible. The secretary of state needed to act as a catalyctic agent within what was a complex system. 'So long as he stands aloof and seeks to hector and preach, he is more or less impotent'.[91]

By this time the government had held office for three and a

half years; Joseph a little over one year. The Falklands War, of course, had taken place during the early summer of 1982. Asked at a press conference in February 1983 what she was going to do about education, the Prime Minister replied bluntly, 'It's a disaster.' Then she added, 'Is there anyone here from education?'. Fortunately there wasn't. This aside, according to the *Guardian*, 'can have offered little comfort to Sir Keith Joseph, the Education Secretary or any of his departmental colleagues'.[92]

As we have seen, by the early summer of 1983 things had not changed. But more generally Thatcherism (or the Thatcher government) retained its popularity, gaining votes among skilled trade unionists and the working class, especially in the South-East, to add to its traditional constituency. Though the overall Tory vote at the general election in June 1983 was slightly down, the opposition on this occasion (the first since the formation of the SDP) was almost equally divided, and this allowed a large influx of Tory (not necessarily Thatcherite) members.[93] The Conservative administration now took over for its second term with a largely increased overall majority (of 144) in the Commons. How would education fare during Margaret Thatcher's second term?

Years of Crisis, 1983 to 1986

The election result naturally enhanced Margaret Thatcher's authority in the government, and among the country at large. However, as Vincent puts it, 1983 was 'a lost year'; the government visibly lacking an agenda.[94] Nowhere was this more apparent than in education, where Keith Joseph retained his post as Secretary of State – although with a new team of ministers.[95] Policy making continued to be pragmatic – buffeted by events as we shall see, though underlying tendencies, particularly towards enhanced central control, continued to operate. Vouchers, and the total privatisation of the system that they implied, were early rejected, a matter to which we shall return. Within this vacuum, a major event took place which, while at the time appearing peripheral, was to have a long term influence on future developments – the confrontation on the issue of comprehensive education in the Tory-controlled borough of Solihull.

The Solihull adventure. The Solihull affair was sparked by a public opinion poll, reported towards the close of 1983, which seemed to indicate that a majority of those questioned supported the selective grammar/secondary modern school set-up in preference to comprehensives. This was given wide media coverage, as was normal for any news critical of comprehensive education. The outcome was predictable. Some 60 Tory MPs, perhaps sensing electoral advantage, signed a parliamentary motion favouring return to selective education. In addition, one of the new junior ministers at the DES, Robert Dunn, now made a series of weekend speeches advocating a return to grammar schools.

Solihull was among a number of Tory-controlled local authorities which leapt on the bandwagon, proposing the transformation of two successful comprehensives as grammar schools. The fact that all the other schools in the authority's area would, in effect, be downgraded as secondary moderns was not mentioned. It immediately became clear, however, that those in control had totally failed to evaluate the feeling among the local population in support of their schools. There was a massive outcry – large meetings took place at which enormous majorities voted clearly against the council's proposals; in particular, very effective joint activity by parents (who set up a defence association) and teachers' associations, especially the NUT, was a feature of the campaign.

In the face of this opposition, the original scheme was withdrawn, but, in an attempt to save face, a second scheme was then officially presented, now proposing that one school only should be transformed. But this again met with a further massive outcry, together with another energetic campaign launched by the local NUT Association in co-operation with parents and the local communities. So this scheme also had to be abandoned.[96]

Solihull had opted, and in a very clear manner, to retain its comprehensives, and no more was heard of the original project. Just after the return of a Tory government, and in the area of a well established Tory authority, a clear and precise public test brought out very dramatically the degree of support existing for local comprehensive systems. Whatever people may have said at this time to public opinion pollsters, whose questions relate to abstract issues and are carefully worded, when the issue was brought down to earth in an attempt to destroy local systems, comprehensive education, it seemed, could call on a really massive degree of support. This was the lesson from the Solihull adventure.

This lesson was driven home by concurrent developments in other areas. Attempts in Berkshire and Wiltshire to extend existing selective procedures now met with an equally unyielding opposition from local populations, again involving mass meetings and consistent pressure on local Tory councillors. In both cases local populations opted to retain non-selective procedures and, in effect, to defend existing comprehensive schools and systems. At Redbridge also an overt attempt to turn back the clock and reintroduce (or extend) selective schooling was again met with a public outcry, and a clear rejection by the majority of the people living in the area.

It was at this point, and clearly as a result of these developments, that Keith Joseph hauled down the flag emblazoning the reintroduction of grammar schools, now neatly substituting a different, yet similar perspective. Queried on television about these events, Joseph made a remark which quickly became notorious:

> If it be so, as it is, that selection between schools is largely out, then I emphasise that there must be differentiation within schools.[97]

Indeed differentiation *within* schools (an academic track via GCE, a technical-vocational track via TVEI, a 'bottom 40' track via LAPP) now appeared as long-term policy. Other pressures, for instance more open enrolment since the 1980 Act, were now leading to enhanced differentiation between schools within comprehensive systems, such a tendency being promoted by resource starvation. This now increasingly motivated greater reliance on parental financial support which varied, of course, according to levels of affluence or poverty in local communities. Both these tactics, or strategies, negated the realisation of objectives endorsed by comprehensive supporters – the provision of systems of schools of equal excellence. There remained, however, in reserve, another strategy – the *circumvention* of comprehensive systems by new types of school, ideas beginning now to germinate in the minds of the Radical Right.

Tory policies. As mentioned earlier, two tendencies in Tory policy-making, which appeared as mutually contradictory, had by now emerged: that focusing on privatisation, using the rhetoric of power to the parents, parental choice, etc, and that focusing on the drive to strengthen central control, using the rhetoric of enhancing 'quality'. The power-base of the former lay in the Conservative Party conference, fuelled by the pamphlets and thinking of such organisations as the Institute for Economic Affairs (with its 'Hobart papers') which united a small group of right-wing economists. The power-base of the centralising tendency clearly lay in the DES itself (as in the MSC) and to that extent was a bureaucratic response to social, economic and political pressures which transcended party, expressing deeper underlying concerns and solutions. Conservative politicians, not wishing at this time to face the probable anarchy of radical privatisation proposals, tended now to give their support to enhanced central control over the maintained system, while seeking to allay the demands of the parental choice and influence lobby by such measures as more open enrolment (the 1980 Act), enhancing the parental role on governing bodies (the White Paper *Parental Influence at School, May 1984*, the 1986 Education Act, and like measures).[98] Keith Joseph, as the responsible minister, was caught in the crossfire between both tendencies.

The Tories had gone to the polls, once again, on the slogan of parental choice. In a 'letter to voucher supporters' soon after taking office, Joseph had already half committed himself to the voucher solution. 'I am intellectually attracted to the idea of education vouchers as a means of eventually extending parental choice and influence yet further and improving educational standards,' he had assured them.[99] At the Tory Party conference a year later (1982) his speech had mainly focused on this issue. '[We] are concerned not only with the rich and the clever', he said. 'We want to extend choice to every person. That is what a properly constructed voucher system could do.'[100] During the succeeding year, however, whether as a result of DES opposition or for other reasons is not clear, Joseph announced very precisely that 'the voucher, at least in the foreseeable future, is dead'. This announcement was made after the June election (1983). He reiterated this standpoint, equally firmly, in the House of Commons the following June (1984), saying that '... the idea of vouchers is no longer on the agenda'.[101]

The voucher scheme, as propagated by the Institute of Economic Affairs, was certainly radical. In essence the idea was to issue a voucher covering the cost of education in maintained schools to all parents, who could then use it to purchase an education for their child at the school of their choice, maintained or private. So education would become consumer rather than 'producer' oriented. This method of financing, if we assume its practicability, would have meant (and was designed to mean) taking education completely out of the control of local authorities. It was seen as having the additional advantage of breaking the power of the teachers' unions. The control of education would be directly handed to the parents on whose financial power (through vouchers) the schools depended. These would now become more responsive to parental wishes. The local government 'monopoly' would be broken. Education would now be subjected to the free play of the market.

The proposal to introduce such a scheme, involving immensely complex changes in public finance, the immediate and large scale disruption of local authorities, likely massive teacher antagonism as well as complex legal problems, would hardly be likely to appeal to practising politicians, except perhaps as an experiment on a modest, local scale.[102] No other country had moved in this direction. The scheme was, in fact, the brainchild of a group of academics who were, themselves, certainly convinced of its practicability and its effectiveness – based on abstract reasoning utilising economic concepts of the classical era. These were impatient of criticism, brushing aside objections as the expected reactions of bureaucrats (in the case of the DES) concerned only to further their own personal interests.[103] Their pressure on succeeding secretaries of state (Prentice, Mulley) and on James Callaghan during the Labour administration increased after 1979 with the return of the Tories. But it was at this stage – in 1983 – that the scheme had its (perhaps temporary?) quietus, and, paradoxically, at the hands of a secretary of state who was a leading representative of the New Right – indeed, largely, its guru.

Direct, immediate, massive privatisation, then, was out as government policy. What took its place, if gradually, as the main thrust was centralisation, the strengthening of DES and government control at the expense of the other 'partners' – particularly local authorities and teachers. The time was ripe for such a move – in the tactical sense. The political clout carried by the local authorities had been greatly weakened as a result of local government reorganisation in 1974, as we have already seen. The once powerful Association of Education Committees was wound up and there was now no effective body that could speak for education on behalf of the local authorities as a whole.[104] The teacher unions were, as always, split, but more important, the NUT had been losing its hegemonic status over the years and might now be effectively marginalised.[105] The central authority, the DES, MSC, or whatever, was poised to occupy the resulting vacuum. The DES had made an overt bid to do just this in the Yellow Book (see pp. 446-51). It had since then received a green light. DES officials, at least, were clear as to objectives.

Light has been thrown on the thinking of top officials in the DES precisely at this time by the publication of unusually frank interview material derived from a research study on central-local relations. The determination to achieve fully centralised power and control is made very clear indeed, and relates here to new policies seeking to impose sharp forms of differentiation on students at and before the age of 16, both within comprehensive schools and the system of further education.[106]

A senior DES official is, for instance, quoted as insisting that

> There is a need especially in the sixteen-to-nineteen areas, for a centrally formulated approach to education: we need what the Germans call 'instrumenterium' through which ministers can implement and operate policy.[107]

Again, on the curriculum and assessment procedures for this grouping:

> I see a return to centralisation of a different kind with the centre seeking to determine what goes on in institutions: this is a more fundamental centralisation than we have seen before.[108]

Further statements by DES officials at this time related to the current attempt to restructure the curriculum within the school system as a whole, on lines which will be referred to below. As one official was quoted as saying:

> Our focus must be on the strategic questions of the content, shape and purpose of the whole educational system and absolutely central to that is the curriculum. We would like legislative powers over the curriculum and the power to control the exam system by ending all those independent charters of the examination bodies.[109]

The argument for centralising powers is based on the need for explicit social engineering to cope with the dangers arising from over-education in a contracting labour market. 'There has to be selection', the 'anonymous' official is quoted as saying, 'because we are beginning to create aspirations which society cannot match'. There followed an interesting admission:

> *In some ways this points to the success of education in contrast to the public mythology which has been created.* When young people drop off the education production line and cannot find work at all, or work which meets their abilities and expectations, then we are only creating frustration with perhaps disturbing social consequences. We have to select: to ration the educational opportunities so that society can cope with the output of education [my emphasis, B.S.].[110]

The arrogation of centralised powers, in defiance of traditional 'partnership' systems, was seen as having a clear social purpose:

> We are in a period of considerable social change. There may be social unrest, but we can cope with the Toxteths, but if we have a highly educated and idle population we may possibly anticipate more serious social conflict. *People must be educated once more to know their place* [my emphasis, B.S.].[111]

The conclusion the study's author (Stewart Ranson) derived from this (and other) evidence was that 'the state is developing modes of control in education which permit closer scrutiny and direction of the social order'.[112]

This, of course, is no new thing in the history of education; indeed involvement by the state in the restructuring and control of education for social/political purposes has been apparent from the middle of the last century and earlier. What was new in the early-mid 1980s were the modes of control now being developed and brought into play. Significantly, the state, instead of working through and with other social organisations (specifically local authorities and teachers' organisations), was now very clearly seeking a more direct and unitary system of control than had ever been thought politic – or even politically possible – in the past. It is this that requires attention.

The centralising thrust. The anonymous DES high official(s), just quoted, focused attention particularly on the need for 'full central control over the school curriculum and examinations'.

If publicly uttered, this would have created a sensation at that time (1983–84). DES documents and official speeches still accepted the responsibilities of local authorities (and to some extent of heads and governing bodies) for the curriculum and these, indeed, were to be written into the 1986 Education Act. Explicit disclaimers were still being made relating to central control. However, the new managerial, top down approach was made abundantly clear, perhaps deliberately, by Keith Joseph early in 1985. In interpreting this move, at this particular time, reference should be made to the humiliating U-turn Joseph was forced to make by the massed ranks of Tory MPs only a month earlier. This relates to the intention to find resources for scientific research by cutting student grants and enhancing contributions towards university tuition fees in higher education from better-off parents. A near unanimous revolt at a meeting of Tory MPs (250, said mostly to be 'baying for blood') led to the immediate reversal of this policy announced by a bewildered (or crest-fallen) Secretary of State in the House of Commons the following day. This episode, which has clear implications relating to the sociology and class position of the Conservative Party, raised the issue of Joseph's competence as a minister. Whatever his great merits in the past, writes Joseph's biographer, colleagues 'frankly considered that ... Keith was now expendable'.[113]

It was, then, soon after this traumatic experience with his own party that Joseph now took up the cudgels in relation to the state of the schools. It was now clearly necessary that he should re-establish himself as a strong minister. 'Today I shall speak mostly about teachers, the main agents for the delivery of the curriculum.' Beginning his speech with these words to the North of England conference in January, Joseph went on to outline a programme of action relating to appraisal, teacher management and training, again emphasising his view that teachers' pay should be linked to performance and subject to assessment.[114] This quickly became a main cause of dispute between the teaching profession and the secretary of state.

But it was the concept of teachers as 'agents' whose job was the 'delivery' of the curriculum (rather than, for instance, the nurturing of specific abilities and skills) which marked, or acted as a signal of, a new stage in teacher-state relations. Teachers, and their organisations, were by this language no longer seen as partners in the control of education, but as 'agents' subject, presumably, to a higher body, the state, whose curricula definitions were now seen to prevail, and which therefore required 'delivery' to pupils. The downgrading of the teachers' professional role implied by such language, undoubtedly contributed to the growing alienation of teachers over this period.[115]

But it was not only teachers who were no longer seen as, or treated as, partners, but others as well, in particular local government. Thus George Cooke, President of the Society of Education Officers in 1975 and at this time its general secretary (1978–84), explained that the block grant arrangements, already referred to, meant that, through central government assessment of the amount of 'grant related expenditure' (GRE) which each authority should spend in its services, how much could be raised from rates and therefore what difference should be payable as grant, authorities were now being put 'under much greater pressure to spend as the government intended they should'. Subsequent rate-capping legislation imposed restrictions on the right of authorities to determine the level of their own rates. Further, the money for the new, centrally administered, 'Education Support Grants' from 1985–86 was simply deducted directly from the block grant. 'Thus, in every possible way financially, the LEAs were tied down and cut back,' Cooke wrote in his analysis of 'the march of centralism' in 1986.[116]

Local authorities, or rather their responsibilities, were also very substantially eroded, as we have seen, by the MSC – the government's preferred organisation for dealing with youth unemployment. By 1983 the MSC was offering some 350,000 one-year training places to unemployed school leavers at a cost of £1,000 million. This was later expanded covering a two-year course costing a further £1,000 million. Local authorities, according to George Cooke, were marginalised by these developments – signifying

> a clear rejection of the former 'partnership' and a massive vote of no confidence in the ability of local government (and equally of the DES) to tackle the problems of youth unemployment and training swiftly and decisively'.[117]

Nor, writes Cooke, was this all. Through the TVEI initiative a new arm of central government reached directly into the schools, funding *and monitoring* educational programmes for school pupils aged between fourteen and eighteen. The MSC's takeover of work-related Non Advanced Further Education (NAFE) in local authority colleges, again involving deductions from the grant settlement, was only another arm of this policy.[118]

For a government elected on the promise to 'roll back the frontiers of the state', this was not a bad record. But there were other indications of a determined centralist drive. These included the inauguration of a system of centrally prescribed specific grants to support government initiatives in the schools, such as TVEI. The 'TRIST' (TVEI-related in-service training) initiative of 1985 had this objective, requiring a sudden, immediate response in the early summer of that year.[119] This was followed by 'GRIST' (grant related in-service training), after the passage of the 1986 Act which legitimated this form of direct funding. Joseph's announcement of the TRIST special grants was immediately denounced by the AMA which held that his determination to control from the centre the in-service training of teachers employed by local authorities could 'only end in state domination of what is taught in our schools'.[120]

Other actions during this period underlined the determination of the central authority increasingly to go it alone, if only (sometimes) symbolically. The abolition of the Schools Council has already been referred to: through the 1986 Education Act the Central Advisory Councils, both that for England and that for Wales, established in 1944, were abolished, and this without any suggestion for the establishment of any organisation which could draw both on expert and public opinion and act in an advisory capacity to the politicians and civil servants. In fact one of the last remaining representative advisory bodies, the Advisory Committee on the Supply and Education of Teachers (ACSET), was also abolished in 1985. This advised the secretary of state on teacher supply. Advice given, which related to the need both to increase the number of new teachers and to increase resources for in-service training was reported as having been 'unpalatable' to Sir Keith. The result was summary extinction.[121]

Finally, on the crucial issue of the curriculum, and in spite of official disclaimers, the Joseph period saw continuous and increasing pressure from the centre towards a nationally prescribed curriculum even if, at this stage, this was seen as differentiated into three main streams (academic, vocational and the rest). Circulars 6/81 and 8/83 both required action by LEAs in their areas, and these were accompanied with and followed by a veritable spate of guidance and discussion documents and reports both from the DES and HMI. Tim Brighouse, then Oxfordshire's CEO, commented that, from 1977 to 1985, 'the HMI and DES between them published twice as much on the curriculum as they published previously in the years since the 1870 Education Act'.[122] While the White Paper *Better Schools* (1985) made it clear that the aim was national agreement on the objectives and content of the school curriculum, it was there specifically stated that local authorities and schools should both have specific responsibilities in defining the curriculum.

A major step towards central control in this area, however, came with the long-delayed announcement by Joseph in June 1984 of his acceptance of the new examination at the age of sixteen. This did not embody the aspirations of the comprehensive movement which had fought so long for a single, unifying examination for all. The new general certificate of secondary education (GCSE), Joseph announced, 'will be a system of examinations, not a single examination'. There will be 'differentiated papers and questions in every subject'. Seven grades would be established, the top three A-C being the responsibility of the (university dominated) GCE boards, the rest D-G of the CSE boards.[123] Thus a clear and sharp differentiation between those candidates entering for higher grades and those entering for the lower was built into the system as a whole from the start. A new, more precisely rationalised system of differentiation now covering *all* students took the place of the old.[124]

The measures relating to GCSE embodied a clear bid for centralised control not only over the secondary curriculum as a whole but over each of its differentiated levels. This was achieved by the definition of 'national criteria' covering examinations at every level. These 'criteria' acted as 'instruments' by which control was shifted to the centre, in this case to the secretary of state who alone had the power to approve them.[125] It was now becoming abundantly clear that the stage was being set for a government (or central) take over both of examinations (and assessment) and of the curriculum.

The reaction to centralisation. What was perceived as an increasingly ruthless drive towards central control of all aspects of education (including the universities) began now to elicit an impassioned response from those who put their faith in local initiatives and in the professional responsibilities and expertise of teachers. This was well articulated in a powerful article by Harry Judge, ex-head of Banbury School and now director of the Education Department of Oxford University. 'The morale and confidence of the education service', he wrote in October 1985, 'is now at a desperately low point.' The present mood (and it must be remembered that he wrote during the teachers' action, to be discussed shortly) 'is without precedent, certainly within the working lifetime of the older among us and, arguably, at any time over the past century'. Why? We know the orthodox answer; falling rolls, political intransigence, teacher militancy, and etc. But what gives them unmanageable form is something much simpler, and more fundamental.

'At the root of the trouble', Judge went on, there lies a conscious effort to subvert the institutional basis of our educational system. This involves 'an assault upon autonomy, and an attempt to accumulate all effective power in the hands of an aggressive central government'. This began before the election of a Conservative government (i.e. with Callaghan's Ruskin speech of 1976). Moreover, unless this centralising tendency can be challenged and checked, the habits and assumptions of the past decade will automatically be projected into the gloomy future.

Judge argued that:

> The root error is that government (any government) should be in charge of education. And it is a monstrous error, poisoning the whole system with the noxious juices of impotence, frustration, servility and patronage. It is this error which is the cause and magnifier of all our ills.

Now, he added, instructions, requests, initiatives and press releases (by the score), exhortations and rebukes 'pour in a cataract from Elizabeth House [DES] and the weasel bodies which now depend on it'. Money is manipulated, through education support grants, the MSC, etc. 'There is only one orthoxody, and teachers may exercise a proper initiative only inside the boringly precise fence of currently defined objectives.'

Schools are not outposts of the state, Judge concluded. They are rooted in local communities, of which they are part, and serve their needs. Teachers work for their pupils and not for the secretary of state. Local authorities should provide the framework for that work. Can we, he asked, build a coalition along these lines?[126]

It is impossible here to give more than one or two examples of the strength of feeling now expressed within the educational world. We may focus on a representative figure, the President of the Society of Education Officers for 1985–86, Jackson Hall, Chief Education Officer for Sunderland. His presidential address (in January 1985) focussed very precisely on 'the centralist tendency', giving a close analysis of developments and issuing a clear warning. Jackson Hall conceded that important features of the education service should be uniform; nobody supports localism 'to the extent of leaving the wheel to be invented in every school and classroom'. Equally it would be ludicrous to argue for 25,000 autonomous schools or 400,000 autonomous teachers. But the present push to centralised power and decision-making carried clear dangers.[127]

'I cannot believe', he said, 'that the DES has a grand design to centralise the service'. What it demonstrably does have, however, 'is a predisposition towards a managerial and market model and, increasingly, a chilling philistinism which it reveals in public comment and criticism'. It is not surprising, he went on, 'that the centralist tendency has forfeited the co-operation and goodwill of the service on which everything depends'. It is to be hoped that this is temporary – 'otherwise the next ten years will see a recession in quality comparable with the failure in British industry'.

There are two issues that the secretary of state should attend to, Hall argued.

The first is to restore the morale of the service. The sustained public criticism over the last decade, the inadequate funding of the service (and not only salaries), the erosion of its status and the general uncertainty about the future, have reduced morale to a disabling level and the relationships of the historic partners – DES, LEAs and teachers – are at an all-time low. Disillusion and pessimism are rampant throughout the service. If this threat is not tackled urgently and successfully the prognosis for the service must be profoundly and frighteningly pessimistic. [Secondly,] we must reconstruct a contemporary version of the post-war partnership, [with] scope for real debate, real learning and real negotiation in the kind of collective leadership education requires.

The secretary of state, Hall concluded, referring to Joseph's Sheffield speech, 'should seek to have 500,000 allies, not 500,000 agents'.

It was at this point that Oxford University took the unprecedented step of rejecting the proposition to confer an honorary degree on Margaret Thatcher – normally conferred on Prime Ministers within a year of their taking office. As Hugo Young writes, 'the announcement [to confer the degree] produced an immediate eruption of feeling at Oxford'. Objectors mobilised and organised – the matter became a national issue. By 738 votes to 319 the degree was refused. The statement by the 275 leading objectors referred to Mrs Thatcher's record as it pertained both to the universities and to education in general. Her government, they wrote, had 'done deep and systematic damage to the whole public education system in Britain, from the provision for the youngest child up to the most advanced research programmes'. This damage, they held (continues Young) 'might be irreparable'. Because Oxford was 'widely perceived to stand at the pinnacle of British education', it would be specially inappropriate for Oxford 'to accord such a wrecker its highest token of approval'. By withholding it, 'Oxford would be acting for the entire academic world.'[128]

The universities had certainly been hit particularly hard by the Thatcher governments. In 1981 they had been given one month to plan an 18 per cent cut in budgets over three years, involving the loss of 3,000 posts. After the 1983 election yet further cuts had been imposed. The whole atmosphere and ethos of the universities were being changed; but those objecting were also well aware of the severe damage being inflicted on the school system as a whole. By this stage (early 1985) almost the entire educational world was very gravely concerned about existing tendencies, and what the future might hold.

Accelerating chaos: January to December 1985. Jackson Hall's presidential address to the Society of Education Offices, referred to above, was given early in January 1985. It contained a clear warning concerning the effect of government measures on the morale of the eduction service as a whole, including teachers. What he was unable to foresee, or predict, was that the next two years would see the longest and most damaging confrontation between teachers and the state ever yet experienced – to culminate almost in the total breakdown of the education service. It is these events, and the succeeding confrontations they led to, that give credibility to the parallel of a Greek tragedy. The secretary of state, by his implacable actions, almost brought the entire edifice crashing around him. In the end, the issue could only be solved by his fall.

The 'teachers' action', as their forms of combat came to be called, was sparked not only by pay demands and their rejection, but also by a deep concern about conditions of work. In his Sheffield speech, as we have seen, Joseph already overtly linked appraisal with pay. This deeply antagonised teachers before the start of salary negotiations. Joseph had made no secret of his belief in market forces and ex- penditure cuts. Appraisal, with its overtones of control, appeared at this point as a weapon not only to weed out incompetent teachers and disrupt the existing career structure, but also as a means of getting rid of those who were considered politically, or otherwise undesirable.[129] Further, as the pay dispute got under way, Joseph started by suggesting a new list of teacher duties, at the same time castigating teachers as 'mad' to propose a 7 per cent increase. Sufficient numbers of intending teachers were coming forward, Joseph argued, so what's wrong with pay levels? It was this simplistic market-place reasoning, publicly expressed, that fuelled teacher alienation.[130] Teachers had, in fact, shown considera- ble restraint in their salary claims over a number of years, and by now had fallen far behind comparable professions – as survey analyses showed.[131] As the 'action' hotted up, relations were increasingly soured.

Towards the end of the year the political editor of the *Sunday Times*, Michael Jones, summed up the situation as he saw it.[132] The dispute had become a national scandal. It had begun in February (1985) when the NUT started its 'withdrawal of goodwill' actions in support of a claim for a £1,200 pay rise for all teachers, costed at 12.4 per cent of the national salary bill. The employers (local authorities) offered 4 per cent (under government guidance); this was rejected. There now took place an escalating campaign by the teachers. In February the NUT told its members not to supervise at lunchtime breaks, nor to attend staff-parent meetings outside school hours. Selective strike action for up to three days a week began later that month. In May the employers increased their offer to 5 per cent. By the end of the summer term in July NUT members had taken part in 200,000 days of strike action. A new offer was now made of just over 6 per cent (informally), tied to the condition that teachers agreed to a new salary structure and a new conditions of service contract (including appraisal) by October. To this the NUT replied with a counter-claim of over 7.5 per cent and a commitment to restore the 1974 (Houghton) levels over a phased period.[133]

Since then, the report continued, the government attitude to comparability exercises turned sour (except for top people – civil servants, judges, generals, who all received massive increases at this time based on this principle). Now things were dragging on into a second year. Joseph had recently said that it was not for the government to produce a new initiative. The NUT was equally determined (a huge ballot majority for a series of half-day strikes had just been recorded); the NAS/UWT also had now announced a 35 per cent claim for next year.[134] One shudders to think what will happen, concluded Michael Jones. There is a strong suspicion that the old-style relations between the state and teachers are irreparable, and that a new contract will have to be negotiated. Joseph has now said he is ready to put an extra £1,250 million on the table (over four years, and with conditions attached). But he has set his face against an independent peer review. Meanwhile the children suffer. This assessment was made towards the end of November, 1985.

This summary description, of course, ignores the incredible complexity of the negotiating procedures involving local authorities and the government, as well as the divisions among the several teacher unions, their alliances and solidarities.[135] It also ignores any evaluation of the actual experience of the teachers (by and large a conservative and 'respectable' profession, in spite of its public image, fostered by the media), and of the real agonising involved in the various forms of action. What was remarkable, and ultimately of profound significance politically, was the very wide degree of public support given to the teachers by parents whose children, of course, suffered but who increasingly saw, as the action dragged on, the government as the leading culprit. Basically it was this which, in the last resort, forced a solution – however unsatisfactory.[136]

Götterdämmerung: January to May 1986. The North of England

Education Conference in January 1986 was a sombre occasion. In his presidential address John Tomlinson sharply expressed the feelings of the educational world.[137] The public education system was now at a turning point. Control was being wrested from the schools and local authorities by central government. Teachers and local authorities had responded positively to the great debate (in ways which had been 'constructive and full of imagination'). The schools had now been through ten years of contraction. But while that had been managed, teachers and their collaborators 'have been subjected to both accusations of having failed the nation, and that, as part of the public service, they are non-productive and parasitic' (Keith Joseph's line). The discretion of local authorities over finance and policy had been largely removed. The government, with its Assisted Places Scheme, flirtation with vouchers, talk of direct grant schools, credit and distinction grades in GCSE, together with its resistance to an opening of opportunities in higher education, appeared as ambivalent. Amid so much that was new, 'there has been no single, comprehensive statement by the government of a unifying vision of the direction of change and the goals now being set for education and training for a new society'. Indeed, the years were slipping by, while lack of direction, confusion and open confrontation were the order of the day.

Shortly after, on 1 February 1986, Keith Joseph was reported as telling his constituents that he would be retiring from parliament at the next election.[138] This announcement ushered in a new period of instability. From the moment Joseph made this statement, reported the *Daily Telegraph* shortly after, 'it was inevitable that calls would come for his resignation as education secretary. It is now clear that the question is no longer if, but when.'[139] In fact Joseph was to cling on for another three months. But from this moment speculation was rife as to who would succeed, sharp divisions appearing within the Tory Party itself, the various contenders jockeying for position, while the teachers' action escalated.

Now the Tory Radical Right re-emerged. Joseph had been a disappointment – vouchers had been rejected. The Institute of Economic Affairs now published *The Riddle of the Voucher*, expertly timed, suggesting the moment had come. Oliver Letwin, Joseph's 'political adviser', argued for more assisted places in a 'greatly expanded private sector'. This would be the solution to the 'educational crisis'.[140] In March the government was reported as considering the return of separate grammar and technical schools, the pressure coming from some 60 back-bench MPs including the right wing '92 group' which regularly met the Prime Minister.[141] Popular schools, with grant support from central government would, it was being argued, find it comparatively easy to go independent. 'Unpopular' schools would be forced to close; schools could be prised loose from local authorities.[142] The same report highlighted a plan to set up a string of technical schools for bright eleven-to-eighteen-year-olds – a feasibility report was being prepared by Robert Dunn (junior minister) relating to opening twenty such schools in urban areas, with 1,000 pupils each selected for their scientific and technological potential – the government to pay grants for each pupil with an appeal to industry for help. These and similar proposals were being pressed for inclusion in the Tory Party manifesto for the probable coming election by, for instance, the 'No Turning Back' group of Tory MPs. At this point (March) the Prime Minister was reported as wanting a radical manifesto which would defy growing cabinet and party demands for a retreat from vintage Thatcherism. A 'credit' system (similar to vouchers) was being considered which would enable parents to choose between the state and private schools. Direct grant primary schools were being considered for inner cities. This report (in the *Times*) concluded by saying that the 'great beauty' of the Tory party was that the reins of power are held by the party leader and close colleagues. The next manifesto was in the charge of Norman Tebbit (then chair of the party).[143]

'Suddenly education is somewhere near the central area of the political stage,' wrote John Fairhall of the *Guardian* at this time. Thatcher had, until now, left things to Keith Joseph, but now things have changed. The Prime Minister had let it be known she is 'worried' about education and wants to do something about it. New educational kites are flying in all directions, the '92 group' suddenly emerges, Rhodes Boyson at their head. What is being brewed up is a double diversion. First, the electorate must be diverted from the country's economic and employment crisis on to law, order and education. Then, in education, attention has to be focused on 'new' initiatives such as vouchers and industrialists funding a handful of experimental schools. This 'audacious attempt' to switch public awareness from potential vote losers to hopeful vote winners 'is a mark of her confidence in her own omnipotence'. For the Prime Minister to succeed, Fairhall concludes, 'would be very sad'.[144]

It was at this point that the pressure was on, from across the political spectrum, for Sir Keith to go and go quickly. The campaign started in the *Times* with an article by Ronald Butt entitled 'Why Sir Keith Should Go Now' – this was from the right-wing angle. What matters is 'to get the local education barons and their nominees out of the schools, which should control their own budgets and preferably fix their own teachers' pay'. There was no time to lose. Keith Joseph was going anyway, so why not now? This would give time to his successor to get things going.[145] A week later the *Daily Telegraph*, concerned about Tory Party unity, called on Joseph to retire immediately – 'What will have to be done in the end would be better done quickly' (influenced by a leader writer's trace memory of the murder scene in Macbeth?).[146] In the *Guardian* Hugo Young pointed out that all the talk was about finding a policy to put into the manifesto. Joseph was billed to depart in the autumn. In the meantime 'classrooms sink into inanition'. What use is a minister whose demise comes closer every day? 'What use a third term promise when past and present are catastrophe?' This article was headed 'Snapping the Threads of the Social Fabric'.[147]

Keith Joseph, however, held on – lecturing teachers, announcing new centralising policies and perspectives, as if totally unconscious of the cauldron bubbling at his feet. The perceptive might have gleaned a warning from a Mori poll of mid-April. Answering the question 'which party has the best policies to deal with education and schools?' only 16 per cent chose the Conservatives, 46 per cent Labour. This was the lowest point reached in support for the Tories in education in a steady decline over the previous two years.[148] A fortnight later disaster struck.

On 8 May most of the country went to the polls for widespread municipal elections. On the same day three parliamentary by-elections were scheduled. The results, for the government, were shattering. Great cities and shire counties swung to Labour and the Alliance. The parliamentary by-elections confirmed this tendency – recording a national surge against the government. All commentators were agreed that the perceived decay in public services, and in particular in education, was central.[149] The effects had seeped through 'and a very high electoral price is being paid for it'. Thatcher's response was characteristic. 'We must now keep up with our politics and redouble our efforts to win the next election,' she told party workers after this 'crushing defeat at the polls'. But, she added, 'We've got to do something about education.'[150] In spite of positive achievements by Keith Joseph, wrote Demetri Argyropulo of the party's National Advisory Committee on Education, 'the Conservatives have managed to alienate almost every group of people involved in education'.[151]

It was at this point that Joseph finally resigned (16 May). In the inner-party battle the Radical Right had apparently not won out. In choosing Kenneth Baker – earlier closely associated with Edward Heath and so for some years in the doghouse – Margaret Thatcher put her money on someone proved to have been an able minister who, in contrast to Joseph, had a developing reputation as a good communicator. 'He has been chosen for his political skills and his gift for communication,' wrote Julian Critchley. 'He has arrived on the stroke of the eleventh hour.'[152]

Notes and References

1. Victor Keegan, *Guardian*, 18 July 1988.

2. *Independent*, 28 July 1988.

3. The Conservatives won 339 seats; Labour, 269; the Liberals, 11; others, 16. The Conservatives gained 37.9 per cent of the total vote to Labour's 37.1. Butler and Butler, op.cit., p.228.

4. Mark Carlisle had been the Tory front-bench spokesman on home affairs, 1969–70; parliamentary under secretary of state, Home Office, 1970–72, and minister of state, Home Office in 1972–74. A lawyer, educated at Radley (a minor public school) and Manchester University, he was one of the few Cabinet members not educated at Oxford or Cambridge. Only two of the new cabinet (one being Mrs Thatcher, the other John Biffen) did not attend a public school, the Cabinet containing six old Etonians, three Wykehamists, one Harrovian (Joseph) and one from Rugby. This was largely the shadow Cabinet Thatcher had inherited from the years of opposition.

5. Manchester District Council challenged this initiative in the courts, winning the case. This judgement was then overturned (by Lord Denning) in the Appeal Court. The scheme went ahead for a few years, ending with the loss of Tory control and the abolition of the metropolitan counties in 1985.

6. *Observer*, 15 July 1979. Stuart Sexton was bequeathed to Carlisle by his shadow predecessor, St John Stevas.

7. An SSRC-ESRC research project found that 'many assisted-place holders come from "submerged" middle-class backgrounds already well endowed with cultural capital', and that 'relatively few assisted place holders come from "unambiguously working class backgrounds" ', Geoff Whitty, John Fitz and Tony Edwards, 'Assisting Whom? Benefits and Costs of the Assisted Places Scheme' in Andy Hargreaves and

David Reynolds (eds.), *Education Policies: Controversies and Critiques*, London 1989. For the full report on this research project, Tony Edwards, John Fitz and Geoff Whitty, *The State and Private Education: an evaluation of the Assisted Places Scheme*, London 1989.

8. *Teacher*, 2 November 1979.

9. Conditions included (i) schools applying to participate to be inspected; if accepted, accounts and planned fee increases to be submitted annually to the education department; (ii) schools applying to negotiate a 'contract' with the education department determining the percentage of places (up to 100 per cent) to be 'assisted'; (iii) a single entrance test for all pupils to be administered (constructed by each school individually); places to be offered strictly on academic results; (iv) parents' incomes to be assessed on national scales, grants to relate to these. *Observer*, 15 July 1979.

10. *Education*, 24 August 1979.

11. *Times Educational Supplement*, 30 November 1979. Ministers, the critique continues, know the scheme to be bad (the Cabinet was said to have been split on the issue). 'They are saddled with the scheme as a legacy from the Blessed Norman [St John Stevas, B.S.], endorsed by the ever-watchful denizen of No. 10. Its only enthusiastic supporter in Elizabeth House is Mr. Stuart Sexton.'

12. *Observer*, 13 October 1979. Provision for expenditure on the Assisted Places Scheme in 1989–90 was in fact just over £59 million. *Education*, 17 November 1989.

13. *Guardian*, 5 November 1979. In an unusually outspoken comment submitted to the secretary of state the Society of Education Officers said that 'The picture of LEAs running establishments little better than good secondary modern schools, while their able children go to independent schools, is unacceptable.' *Education*, 2 November 1979.

14. Caroline Benn, *Forum*, Vol.22, No.2, Spring 1980. Under the banner of slogans like 'choice', Benn argued, new, socially based, differentiating structures are being built into the publicly provided school system.

15. *Teacher*, 2 November 1979.

16. *Education*, 29 June 1979.

17. *Education*, 15 June 1979; *Teacher*, 29 June 1979.

18. *Times Educational Supplement*, 16 November 1979. The journal concluded that the actual cuts achieved at that time amounted to about £100 million in England and Wales.

19. *Education*, 28 March 1980, reporting the White Paper, *The Government's Expenditure Plans 1980–81 to 1983–84*, Cmnd 7841, 26 March 1980.

20. *Education*, 29 June 1979. In the year the *Times Educational Supplement* did not appear, *Education* offered its editor (Maclure) a guest column to express his views.

21. *Education*, 29 August 1980.

22. *Education*, 19/26 December, 1980, 2 January 1981. In April 1980 rectification of teachers' salaries which had again fallen far behind comparable professions, was made when the government reluctantly accepted the Clegg award, giving increases of from 17 to 25 per cent.

23. White Paper, *The Government's Expenditure Plans 1981–82 to 1983–84*, Cmnd 8175, 10 March 1981. The proposed expenditure on education was as follows:

Expenditure on Education and Science
(England and Wales) (£ million)

Year	Capital	Current	Total
1980–81	462	7,719	8,528
1981–82	400	7,440	8,186
1982–83	350	7,300	8,000
1983–84	320	7,170	7,840

Source: *Education*, 13 March 1981

24. *Education*, 20 February 1981.

25. John Vincent, 'The Thatcher Governments, 1979–87' in Peter Hennessy and

Anthony Seldon (eds.), *Ruling Performance, British Governments from Attlee to Thatcher*, Oxford 1987, pp.283–5.

26. *Education*, 16 May 1980.

27. *Education*, 1 August 1980.

28. In an assessment of the significance of this measure, Dudley Fiske (CEO Manchester) wrote: 'We now seem to have reached a most peculiar position where the LEAs have a responsibility to their electorates for the condition of the education service in their areas, but are effectively denied the powers necessary to deal with these responsibilities.' *Education*, 7 November 1980.

29. *Education*, 10 July 1981. Recurrent grant to universities (GB) was planned to drop from £879.82 million in 1981–82 to £808.07 million in 1983–84. The total number of university students was projected to decline from 260,970 in 1979–80 to 248,720 in 1983–84. Parkes, Chair of the UGC, estimated that this would mean the reduction of academic staff at universities by 3,000 and of 4,000 non-academic staff. These cuts were characterised by Merrison (Vice-Chancellor, Bristol) as 'a kind of madness'. *Education*, 20 March 1980.

30. Vincent, op.cit., pp.286–7. In the opinion polls the SDP-Liberal Alliance now had 45 per cent of the vote (November 1981). See also Hugo Young, op.cit., Chapter 11 'The Capture of the Cabinet', pp.192–222,and, for Toxteth, pp.238–9.

31. *Education*, 18 September 1981. For the September reshuffle, Vincent, op.cit., pp.286–7; Hugo Young, op.cit., pp.216–22.

32. Auriol Stevens, 'The Grammar Schools' Last Stand', *Observer*, 13 May 1979.

33. See *Education*, 13 June 1980.

34. *Guardian*, 21 October 1979.

35. This grant was unilaterally withdrawn, significantly, in 1988.

36. Caroline Benn, 'The New 11-plus for the Old Divided System', *Forum*, Vol.22, No.2, Spring 1980. This article is highly critical of government policy – especially Education Bill No.2.

37. *Daily Telegraph*, 24 July 1979.

38. *Education*, 22 February 1980. The 1985 objective was, of course, never achieved. During the reign of Sir Keith Joseph a further three years were lost. See pp.493–4.

39. Schools Council, *Examinations at 18-plus: the N and F Studies*. The Schools Council had done an enormous amount of consultation on this question and given the issue, generally regarded as highly important, a great deal of attention.

40. *DES Report 1979*, p.xi.

41. In December 1979 the Schools Council again proposed a new examination for first year sixth form pupils (aged seventeen). The objective was to provide an exam for students aged sixteen having no clear career intention but wishing to remain in full time education for another year. See *Proposals for a Certificate of Extended Education* (Cmnd. 7755), known as the Keohane Report. This examination was later officially rejected in favour of a pre-vocational examination at seventeen.

42. *DES Report 1980*, p.3.

43. *Education*, 24 October 1980.

44. *Aspects of Secondary Education in England* (HMSO), 1979.

45. *DES Report 1979*, p.x.

46. *Education*, 18 July 1980; see also ibid., 11 July 1980. The AMA, now under Labour control, saw *A Framework ...* as a clear move towards government imposition of a core curriculum. For Denis Lawton's critique, *The Tightening Grip, Growth of Central Control of the School Curriculum*, London 1984.

47. HMI proposed a curriculum based on 'areas of experience', so specifically rejecting a simple subject-based curriculum.

48. *Education*, 27 March 1981.

49. Nancy Trenaman, Principal of St Anne's College, Oxford, was deputed by the Secretary of State to enquire into the council's function, constitution and methods of work in March 1981. Her report, *Review of the Schools Council* (DES), published later that year, is discussed in the next section. See *DES Report 1981*, p.9. Later that year

John Tomlinson made a powerful defence of the Schools Council in his presidential address to the education section of the British Association (*Education*, 4 September 1981).

50. In May 1980 the DES announced a series of ten one day regional meetings, each chaired by a DES minister, to be held between October 1980 and June 1981. The aim was reported to be 'to promote a wider understanding of DES work', to encourage cooperation between employers, local education authorities and schools, and 'to stimulate further development of school and industry links'. *DES Report 1980*, p.7.

51. *Education*, 30 January 1981.

52. Ibid., 15 February 1981.

53. Ibid., 12 June 1981; 17 July 1981; 24 July 1981. This was the origin of the National Advisory Board for Public Sector Higher Education, established in 1984.

54. *Hansard*, House of Lords, 13 December 1979, Vol.403, No.60, col. 1332–5; see also *Guardian*, 23 November 1979. Overseas students fees had initially been raised by Anthony Crosland in 1967.

55. Patricia Rowan, 'Special Schools' in Max Morris and Clive Griggs (eds.), *Education – the Wasted Years? 1973–1986*.

56. *Education*, 24 July 1981.

57. *Education*, 24 April 1981. The Bill received royal assent on 30 October 1981. It was implemented on 1 April 1983. A well informed statement on the problems involved and developments since is Patricia Rowan, op.cit.

58. *Education*, 10 July 1981. Clare Short, Director of Youth-aid, predicted that unemployment would continue to rise and that there would be an outcry for law and order policies. Ibid.

59. Ibid., 14 August 1981.

60. Morrison Halcrow, *Keith Joseph, A Single Mind*, London 1989, p.164.

61. Sir Keith Joseph, *Stranded on the Middle Ground*, Centre for Policy Studies, 1976. This slim publication contains several of his speeches delivered between 1974 and 1976. In the introduction (p.8) Joseph says that the pamphlet includes speeches 'I have given on the moral case for capitalism to about 25,000 students at some 60 public meetings at universities and polytechnics during the past two years.'

62. *Education*, 18 September 1981.

63. Keith Joseph and Jonathan Sumption, *Equality*, London 1979, pp.18–9. Here is another characteristic phrase: 'Archbishop Temple said that "the Christian conception of men as members of the family of God forbids the notion that freedom may be used for self-interest". This is quite simply wrong.' Ibid., p.120.

64. *Times Educational Supplement*, 31 December 1982. For an acute assessment of Keith Joseph's outlook at this point in time, Joan Simon, 'Education, Morality and the Market', *Forum*, Vol.25, No.3, Summer 1983.

65. *Education*, 16 October 1981.

66. Ibid.

67. Ibid., 8 January 1982. Joseph's speech is reported in full in ibid., 15 January 1982.

68. *Times Educational Supplement*, 24 September 1982. For this paper, its provenance and effect, Hugo Young, op.cit., pp.298ff.

69. Ibid., 8 October 1982. A week earlier the same journal had announced that the government was considering a trial run with vouchers in Kent. Joseph had made no secret of the fact that he was 'intellectually attracted' to vouchers, and that he hoped to announce the names of local authorities chosen for the trial at the conference. His speech would show his 'firm resolve' to try the experiment. Over the last year, DES officials had written thousands of words on the topic. Oliver Letwin, 26-year-old Old Etonian and Cambridge graduate, just appointed 'adviser' to Joseph, had a special interest in vouchers. Ibid., 1 October 1982.

70. The three schools were Parrs Wood (in Didsbury), Burnage and Whalley Range High Schools.

71. *Education*, 20 November 1981.

72. *Education*, 4 December 1981. Keith Joseph's 'decision in respect of Manchester's

sixth forms must be one of the worst decisions ever made. A whole city is to be denied the right to manage its own education service, something it is charged with by law, simply to satisfy the wishes of some parents at 3 out of 24 schools in the city. The decision was made against all professional advice, overturning one of the most carefully prepared schemes that can ever have been submitted to the education department and jeopardising the education of the majority of the city's children'. Auriol Stevens, *Observer* education correspondent, in *Education*, 18/25 December 1981.

73. *Education*, 8 January 1982. A year later Joseph approved a reorganisation plan for York involving eleven-to-sixteen schools and a sixth form college. This involved the merging of three grammar schools and the closure of one. Joseph regretted the loss of the grammar schools but accepted that falling rolls compelled it. There was a low level of objections while the majority of governing bodies supported it. DES Press Release, April 1983. In May 1983, however, Joseph rejected Cumbria's plan to close two grammar schools. The aim was to establish eleven-to-sixteen schools and a sixth form college. Joseph said this reorganisation was not in the interests of the children. *DES press release*, 11 May 1983. In March 1983 it was reported that the grammar school total had dropped to less than 200. *Times Educational Supplement*, 25 March 1983. For a perceptive case study of the Manchester decision, see Stewart Ranson, *The Politics of Reorganising Schools*, London 1990, pp.48-86.

74. *Times Educational Supplement*, 26 March 1982.

75. Ibid., 18 March 1983. See also Angela Dixon, 'Keith Joseph and the science criteria', *Forum*, Vol.26, No.3, Summer 1984.

76. Ibid., 19 August 1983.

77. Ibid., 15 April 1983.

78. Ibid.

79. Ibid., 15 October 1982.

80. Ibid., 16 September 1983.

81. One of the five research councils (e.g. Medical Research Council, Science and Engineering Research Council, etc.), this was established in 1967, following the Clapham Report. The 1960s, of course, saw a big expansion of the social sciences, assisted by the work of this council, which covered economic history, psychology, sociology, anthropology, education and similar areas. In 1981 its grant was £20.7 million (compared with £216.8 million for science and engineering and £101.7 million for medicine). *DES Report 1981*, p.54.

82. *Times Higher Educational Supplement*, 15 October 1982; see also ibid., 22 October 1982, 'A Victory for the Academic Community'.

83. Lord Rothschild's reaction to this change of name was withering. 'Sociologists all over the country', he was reported as saying, '... will welcome the originality and intellectual penetration of the Secretary of State's proposal to substitute the old English word *Wissenschaft*, for Science in the name of the SSRC ... Sir Keith's proposal is timely, creative, logical, apposite, epistemologically unassailable and psychologically desirable. The changes affecting the names of the other research councils are equally desirable and imaginative. Only fools could deny that PERCS, BURPS, and TWERPS, are more indicative of the work of these three research councils than their present misnomers'. *Times Higher Educational Supplement*, 22 October 1982.

84. According to Gosden, the MSC was chosen as the leading instrument for TVEI since at this time, due to 'the atmosphere of negative restraint it was impossible for the secretary of state to take even a minor educational initiative with any success if finance were involved'; even if the money could have been made available via the DES there was no way, under the prevailing grants system, by which it could have been earmarked specifically for this (or any other costly) state determined initiative. Hence recourse to the MSC. Peter Gosden, 'Education Policy 1979–84' in David S. Bell (ed.), *The Conservative Government 1979–84*, London 1985, pp.118-9. TVEI was later generalised, though on the basis of greatly reduced funding per school.

85. *Times Educational Supplement*, 21 January 1983. In 1989 HMI issued 'a highly critical report' on DES involvement in LAPP, claiming that the DES failed to set proper objectives and that the whole scheme was introduced without adequate preparation. The scheme was administered by never more, and often less than, the equivalent of 1.2 'hard-pressed civil servants'. The only guidance made available to LEAs had to be derived from a press release on the Secretary of State's original speech. *Guardian*, 26 September 1989. With hindsight, this scheme appears as window-dressing, though HMI say that 'the commitment, enthusiasm and imagination of teachers stands out'. Ibid.

86. Professor Malcolm Skilbeck, Schools Council Research Director and a strong proponent of comprehensive education condemned those introducing TVEI as 'educational antediluvians'. TVEI was a direct attack on the principles underlying comprehensive education. Crash courses in vocational preparation and the division into academic and vocational cannot be accepted 'whatever the power of its proponents or the resources at their disposal'. Lecture at UEA in memory of Lawrence Stenhouse, *Times Educational Supplement*, 15 July 1983. A different criticism was made by Sheila Browne, the prestigious but departing senior chief HMI. Academic education, especially at sixth form level was threatened by TVEI. The scheme required careful monitoring. Ibid., 23 September 1983.

87. *Times Educational Supplement*, 30 April 1982. The two committees established were the secondary Schools Council and the School Curriculum Development Committee.

88. Ibid., 30 April 1982. In October 1978 Professor Max Beloff had brought the Tory party conference to its feet with a plea to abolish the Schools Council 'within one week of returning to power'. In the last period of Tory Party opposition the Schools Council constantly featured on the 'hit list' of bodies to be abolished (apparently under the influence of Mrs Thatcher). Ibid. No doubt the SSRC was another, a plan very clearly thwarted by Lord Rothschild. Mrs Trenaman, Principal of St. Anne's College, Oxford, carried rather less clout. This 'independent' enquiry also came up with the wrong answer – probably inconveniently. Political imperatives took precedence.

89. The *Times Educational Supplement* published a full page article by the Schools Council in July; this was highly critical of the proposal to appointment the two quangos which the council believed would do great harm. Ibid., 2 July 1982. In October the two local authority organisations, the AMA and ACC, expressed strong opposition to this plan, but demanded representation on the two committees. An impressive, and dignified protest was made by the Schools Council chair, Sir Alex Smith, Director of Manchester Polytechnic. The whole issue is discussed in Maurice Plaskow (ed.), *The Life and Death of the Schools Council*, London 1985.

90. *Times Educational Supplement*, 22 October 1982.

91. Ibid., 12 November 1982, 31 December 1982.

92. *Guardian*, 23 February 1983.

93. Conservatives won 397 seats (42.4 per cent of the total vote), Labour 209 (27.6 per cent), Liberals 17 (13.7 per cent), Social Democrat 6 (11.6 per cent), others 21 (4.6 per cent). Labour polled 3 million fewer votes than in 1979. Michael Foot was leader of the opposition between 1980 and 1983, being now succeeded by Neil Kinnock (opposition spokesman on education, 1979–1983).

94. Vincent, op.cit., p.288.

95. After the election, Rhodes Boyson moved to Social Security and William Shelton, William Waldegrave and Paul Channon (Arts) all moved to other appointments. Joseph's ministerial team now consisted of two new parliamentary under secretaries of state, Peter Brooke and Robert Dunn. Lord Gowrie was appointed Minister for the Arts, now redefined as a free-standing office under the Lord President of the Council. *DES Report 1983*, p.111.

96. For the Solihull affair see Michael Richer, 'Parent Power and Selection in Solihull', *Forum*, Vol.27, No.1 Autumn 1984. Of some significance, perhaps, was the defeat of Peter Tebbit (brother of Norman Tebbit, then a Cabinet minister) by a local residents'

association candidate representing the opposition movement. 'And perhaps', writes Richer, 'he has passed back to the government, the message that selection is a non-starter in Solihull; which probably means it is unacceptable anywhere.' Ibid. The author (Richer) was an industrialist, actively involved in the parental organisation – Solihull Parents for Educational Equality (SPEE). This article vividly reconstructs these events.

97. *Times Educational Supplement*, 17 February 1984.

98. The tendency towards enhanced central control was also reflected in the Labour Party.

99. Joseph's letter is reproduced in Arthur Seldon, *The Riddle of the Voucher*, London 1986, p.36. The letter was addressed to the Friends of the Education Voucher Experiment in Representative Regions (FEVER).

100. Ibid., p.xii.

101. Ibid.

102. A pilot scheme was proposed for Kent in 1982, based partly on a feasibility study of 1978, *Times Educational Supplement*, 1 October, 1982. It would, however, have required legislation which was not forthcoming. Seldon, op.cit., pp.46–7. A number of further schemes were proposed at this time. Ibid., pp.47ff.

103. The most cogent statement is probably Seldon, op.cit. This includes a brief history of the idea and includes much criticism of 'an ambitious bureaucracy' – the DES, pp.75ff.

104. Both the AMA and ACC had education committees; these associated together in the Council of Local Education Authorities (CLEA); but the latter never acquired the authority and prestige of the Association of Education Committees.

105. NUT (in-service) membership, which had reached 240,399 in 1980, had dropped, by 1985, to 213,514 (information from NUT).

106. Stuart Ranson, 'Towards a Tertiary Tripartism: New Codes of Social Control and the 17-plus' in Patricia Broadfoot (ed.), *Selection, Certification and Control*, London 1984.

107. Ibid., p.238.

108. Ibid.

109. Ibid., p.224.

110. Ibid., p.241.

111. Ibid.

112. Ibid.

113. Halcrow, op.cit., pp.180–3.

114. *DES Press Notice*, 11 January 1985.

115. During his speech, Joseph said that he was told that, in his words, 'morale is low', that teachers feel 'under-valued and under paid', and that some of his own remarks 'may have contributed to such feelings'. 'If that is true,' he went on, 'it must be because I am constantly seeking ways to bring about improvements, rather than rest on statements about the much that is already good.' His overt linking of appraisal with pay, however, led to a deep suspicion of his approach, and was assessed as an important stage in the further alienation of the teaching profession. See *Guardian*, 15 January 1985.

116. He added 'in virtually every respect, except the scheme for assisted places in independent schools, the government's education policy at this time was "conditioned by its overall desire to cut public spending" '. George Cooke, 'Increasing Problems' in George Cooke and Peter Gosden, *Education Committees*, London 1986, pp. 131–2.

117. Ibid., p.133.

118. Ibid., p.134. This takeover resulted finally in a compromise which allowed for plans for each LEA to be drawn up in consultation with the MSC, employers and unions, and the setting up of a national advisory group concerned with the whole area. So the local authorities 'were allowed to retain some shreds of their dignity'. Ibid.

119. For a contemporary evaluation of TRIST, foreshadowed in the White Paper *Better Schools*, see Norman Barlow, 'TRIST and the Future of In-Service Training',

Forum, Vol.29, No.1, Autumn 1986.

120. *Guardian*, 20 March 1985. Local authorities, until then, had full control over in-service provision for their own teachers. The new procedures appeared to arrogate this right to the centre.

121. *Times Higher Educational Supplement*, 6 February 1985. See also *Times Educational Supplement*, 15 February 1985.

122. Cooke, op. cit., p.135, quoting Brighouse in *Education*, February 1985.

123. *Times*, 21 June 1984. The first students to sit this examination did so in 1988.

124. For an acute analysis of this, see Caroline Gipps, 'Differentiation in the GCSE'. *Forum*, Vol.29, No.3.

125. *Sunday Times*, 17 March 1985. In 'Tighter Reins in Schools', Peter Wilby commented on the move to central control over the school curriculum emerging clearly after the publication of outline syllabuses for the new examination. In the past, examination boards had freedom to produce these; now all must be submitted to the secretary of state and conform to defined criteria. Some of the proposed syllabuses, he said, were highly controversial.

It is ironic to note that the Waddell Report on the 16-plus stated categorically that control of the new examination 'should not rest finally with central government', a judgement reiterated in the subsequent White Paper (Jackson Hall, *Forum*, Vol.28, No.1).

126. *Times Educational Supplement*, 11 October 1985.

127. Jackson Hall, 'The Centralist Tendency', *Forum*, Vol.28, No.1 – a shortened version of his SEO presidential address, delivered in January 1985.

128. Hugo Young, *One of Us*, London 1989, pp. 401–4.

129. 'Militant' action, claimed the *Times* characteristically at this point, is often led locally by political militants 'who would be the first to be exposed by a better system of teacher appraisal'. 8 January 1985.

130. *Guardian*, 15 January 1985; see also article by John Fairhall, ibid., 4 June 1985.

131. Roger Seifert, *Teacher Militancy, A History of Teacher Strikes 1896–1987*, London 1987, pp.205–6.

132. *Sunday Times*, 24 November 1985.

133. It is worth noting that the teachers' action, which won widespread popular support, was undertaken immediately after the defeat of the miners' strike by the government (or Coal Board). It embodied different forms of industrial conflict.

134. At about this time, Mark Carlisle came out publicly in favour of the teachers, arguing that their pay should be comparable to that of professionals in the private sector. 'The desire to achieve reduction in public expenditure,' he said, 'important though it is, cannot be achieved at the cost of those employed in the public service.' Carlisle directly challenged Joseph as to any inflationary tendency – the public sector, he argued, does not lead in pay increases (Joseph had dismissed the teachers' call for restoration to Houghton levels (a rise of 34 per cent) as a return to inflationary pay settlements of the past). *Guardian*, 18 October 1985.

135. Parallel action by Scottish teachers was largely successful, partly because in Scotland the EIS (Educational Institute of Scotland) unites the great majority of teachers at all levels.

136. The *Times Educational Supplement* commented, late in October 1985, that 'it has been remarkable how long parental support for the justness of the teachers' pay claim has lasted in the face of persistent disruption of their children's schooling and often of their own lives and careers' (25 October 1985). A full, blow-by-blow account of the teachers' action during 1985 and into 1986 is given in Seifert, op. cit.

137. *Guardian*, 3 January 1986. Tomlinson, later a professor at Warwick University, had been secretary of the doomed Schools Council, and earlier CEO for Cheshire.

138. *Guardian*, 1 February 1986.

139. *Daily Telegraph*, 25 February 1986.

140. *Independent*, 6 February 1986. 'There is a real chance now', concluded Letwin, 'of turning our maintained schools gradually into independent, professional institutions

whose clients' fees are fully paid by the state, instead of fragments of a vast nationalised industry, woefully mismanaged, strike bound and desolate.' (Letwin had until recently been a member of the Prime Minister's policy unit.)

141. *Daily Telegraph*, 10 March 1986. The '92 group' of MPs took its name from the number of the house where they met – there were not 92 members.

142. Ibid.

143. *Times*, 10 March 1986.

144. *Guardian*, 11 March 1986. It should be remembered that the government sustained a serious crisis in the Westland affair which climaxed in January, leading to the resignation of Michael Heseltine and Leon Brittan, two leading members of the Thatcher Cabinet. A public opinion poll in early February had indicated that Conservative support had slumped so badly that, if an election had been held then, 247 Tory MPs would have faced defeat. Voters were dissatisfied with government policies on defence, education, the health service and employment – the last three by overwhelming majorities. Andrew Gamble, 'Westland Fallout', *Marxism Today*, March 1986.

145. *Times*, 27 March 1986.

146. *Daily Telegraph*, 8 April 1986.

147. *Guardian*, 8 April 1986.

148. *Times Educational Supplement*, 20 March 1987.

149. *Sunday Telegraph*, 11 May 1986, Edward Pearce, 'A Vote of No Confidence'.

150. *Times Educational Supplement*, 16 May 1986.

151. *Education*, 16 May 1986.

152. *Daily Telegraph*, 22 May 1986. In the same issue, the paper's educational correspondent (Izbicki) wrote 'Education will never be the same again after Keith Joseph. Morale among school teachers and academics is at rock bottom – and that must count as the most important failure of Sir Keith Joseph's reign. No amount of agonising on his part could correct that.'

11 The Rise of the Right: Kenneth Baker and the 1988 Education Act

1 Kenneth Baker's First Year

Kenneth Baker, appointed, as we have seen, on 16 May 1986, was to have one year to turn things around before the general election which took place on 11 June 1987. During this year, particularly towards its end, the outlines of a specifically Tory policy on all the major issues were to be articulated. But at the start – immediately after the May elections of 1986 – no clear policy yet existed. In default of this, conservative politicians and industrialists now suddenly turned on the schools in a series of vicious attacks. At this point also HMI documented the profoundly negative impact on standards of the now rapidly deteriorating state of the schools. Throughout the year the teachers' dispute rumbled on – a continuous background of discontent and alienation among the classroom practitioners. A particular feature was the increasingly active intervention of a number of right-wing pressure groups which clearly had the ear of the Prime Minister. A major change, however, which clearly helped the government image, was, in contrast to the Joseph years, the ready syphoning of enhanced resources towards education, allowing some relaxation and a hope for the future.

'Tories Schools Onslaught Opens Election Battle', reported the *Times Educational Supplement* on 16 May 1986. 'A spate of attacks on the schools by government ministers and senior business men has angered educationists this week.' This onslaught, the journal reported, came as leading Conservatives were predicting that education would be a central issue at the next general election. The most extravagant of this criticism was expressed in a Channel 4 television debate on education and training, in which Lord Young agreed enthusiastically that the schools were failing industry – a proposition put by business men in the debate and reported to be the response of an overwhelming majority of employers whose opinions were surveyed for the programme. The specific charges made were later fully rebutted, but the strategy was now becoming clear – to shift the blame for what government policy had done to the schools onto the schools themselves – the teachers, administrators, even local government as a whole. This became increasingly apparent as the year proceeded.[1]

The deteriorating state of the schools was now highlighted in the 1985 (annual) HMI report on the effect of local authority expenditure on educational provision. This presented 'a grim picture', as the *Guardian* put it, serving further to embarrass a government already on the defensive on education. The greatest concern was shown on the quality of teaching, but even here the problems highlighted were blamed largely on inadequate resources. Poor accommodation, the lack of books and other essential equipment were the main cause of deterioration. The report painted a picture of a service 'in desperate need of more funds'. Many parents were paying for extra facilities while many students were struggling to cope. The previous year's report had warned that, without urgent attention the cost of putting things right would become prohibitive, but there had been no such improvements. The situation was likely to continue to worsen.[2]

It is hardly surprising, then, that Kenneth Baker, on taking office (and surely with the agreement of the Prime Minister) immediately made a bid 'to get more cash for schools', as the *Daily Telegraph* put it. This paper announced that Baker already had such an assurance from Mrs Thatcher (though Nigel Lawson wanted tax cuts), and that DES officials were preparing just such a bid at the annual spending review, including sufficient resources to put in hand a crash programme for school maintenance.[3] We will see, shortly, that Baker's efforts in this direction certainly had some success.

A Radical Solution?

The search was now on, within a tightly limited time schedule, for a set of viable educational policies which would both appeal to the Conservative Party and to the popular vote. Such a policy had to address the perceived weaknesses of the educational system, as now propagated for some years, and propose a set of measures that would carry conviction – among politicians, industrialists, and, if possible, even among educationists. The search for such a policy took place in a context of conflict – even crisis. Supporters of 'the new realism' now saw their chance, and looked for a radical solution. The growing hegemony of Thatcherite solutions, involving competition, individualism, with a focus on 'enterprise' formed the context of the battleground where new approaches vied for victory.

In July (1986) the right wing (as the educational press put it) unveiled its reform package in a pamphlet dramatically entitled *SOS: Save our Schools*. This was published by the 'No Turning Back Group' of Tory MPs. Three specific reforms were proposed: the creation of independent school boards (governing bodies), dominated by parents; direct funding of schools by the DES on the basis of pupil numbers, the boards having powers to fix salaries, and to determine all expenditure; the right for parents to send their children to any school prepared to accept them.[4] Generally the group argued that schools should be run on more competitive lines, that grants should follow pupils so that the more successful schools would expand and so be allocated more finance; that head teachers should have the power to hire and fire teachers and would, in effect, become managing directors answerable to a board of governors.[5]

The group were reported as believing that its ideas were in tune with those of Margaret Thatcher. However Kenneth Baker was also reported to have been very angry about a draft he saw before publication, insisting on changes. At this point ministers felt such a publication would be unhelpful, since at this time they were focusing on restoring confidence in the government among teachers and others. On the other hand Mrs Thatcher had promised a member of the group that the pamphlet would be required reading for the education secretary and herself during the summer holidays.[6] And apparently it was, since the pamphlet's proposals were in fact largely embodied in the Conservative Party manifesto for the election next year.

There were several other similar initiatives by right wing groups and individuals during the year. In July Sir John

Hoskins, Director General of the Institute of Directors (and head of Thatcher's policy unit from 1979 to 1982), urging a radical Tory manifesto, proposed abolition of the rate support grant by transferring educational spending to central government. In the meantime schools should be forced to operate an 'open school policy', successful schools should be allowed to expand to meet demand and all first choices honoured. In the longer term education credits should be introduced, for use both in state and private schools. Generally, spending on welfare should be drastically overhauled to ensure it went only to those 'in greatest need'.[7] At this point (July 1986) Robert Dunn, the School Minister, issued a call to 'privatise education'. The role of state intervention should be confined to helping those who are not properly catered for in a free market system ('there will always be someone'). The need was to move to a more responsive market system – of separate independent schools directly accountable to parents and children.[8]

Throughout the year the pressure continued. In January 1987 the Hillgate Group, described as 'an influential right-wing group of politicians and industrialists', published *Whose Schools?* which demanded the removal of schools from local authority control as well as an independent enquiry into HMIs.[9] Many authorities, it was argued, taking advantage of their wide-ranging statutory powers, 'had acted in ways detrimental to the education of children entrusted to their care'. Schools should, therefore, be removed from their control, be owned by individual trusts and funded directly by the government.[10] As the election approached the pressure increased, even reaching a level of hysteria at a meeting of the Freedom Association in London in May, at which the focus was on the curriculum. By this time it was evident that the Tory right had in fact gained most of what it wanted in terms of proposals for structural reform.[11]

Policy Making
Reference has already been made to Kenneth Baker's immediate bid for more cash for education – in sharp contradiction to Keith Joseph's policy of continuously enhanced retrenchment. From the moment of taking office, Baker made a series of announcements relating to increased resources covering almost every area of education. His first act was to

provide another £20 million for books and equipment for GCSE (powerfully demanded by the teachers); an extra £30 million was then found for in-service teacher training in other fields. When local authorities threatened to cut 9,400 places in polytechnics (due to lack of funds), Baker gave them an extra £54 million. When the UGC said that there would have to be university closures (for the same reason), Baker asked the Cabinet for another £114 million for the current year – substantially more for the next two years. In October Baker told primary teachers that he had got more cash. He also announced his preparedness to settle the teachers' pay issue (if on his terms) – likely to be a costly operation.[12]

Some of this extra finance was already gained in July, when Nicholas Ridley announced a further £2.9 billion for all public services, of which education was expected to get about half. Planned educational spending (by the government) in 1986–87 was £10.49 billion, but the budget estimate showed likely actual spending to reach £11.57 billion. Early in October (1986) provisional figures were announced which showed a further increase in the following year – to £11.94 billion. Such targets, as the *Guardian* commented, were 'unprecedented after recent years' – would this policy of increased spending, they asked, outlast the election?[13]

There was, then, partially at least, a deliberate attempt by the government to buy itself out of the crisis – to show some concern about conditions in the schools and the health of the system as a whole. This covered the early phase of Baker's stewardship. From October (1986) onwards, however, in a series of carefully planned announcements to particular audiences, the new secretary of state began progressively to reveal the main strands of policy which were to be fully articulated in time for their incorporation in the Tory manifesto in the run-up to the general election. We may consider these in turn.

The first of these proposed initiatives was announced by Kenneth Baker at the Conservative Party conference in October 1986. This was his announcement of a new network of state-funded and business-sponsored city technology colleges. Twenty 'pilot' colleges were to be established in inner-city areas, a move, said Baker, 'to increase the range and quality of education in areas where it is most needed'. Cheers greeted Baker's pledge that the colleges would be government-funded independent schools run by educational trusts and not part of the local education authority ... They will [he continued] be financed by my department with private sector sponsors making a substantial contribution towards the costs.

The proposed curriculum would have a strong emphasis on technological, scientific and practical work, business studies and design. The first of these would open in 1988. While Labour saw education as 'a means of social engineering', he concluded, Tories saw it as 'a springboard for individualism, opportunity and liberty'.[14]

Baker's speech at this conference also contained populist statements concerning the curriculum. 'I want to see', he said, 'the basic elements of education, the three Rs, restored to their central place in the curriculum.' 'I want to see', he went on, 'children taught to respect authority in a moral and disciplined framework'.[15] It was by such measures, and such sentiments, that a serious attempt was now being made to win back the initiative. If this was the first major policy statement to be made by Baker, just five months after taking office, others were now to follow with ascending frequency.

Three months later, in January 1987, Baker took the opportunity of the minister's annual speech to the North of England Conference to announce his intention of introducing a national curriculum laid down by statute for children aged between five and sixteen. No mention was made at this stage of testing or assessment; the speech focused on the curriculum and the introduction of 'national criteria' for each subject.

In this speech, Baker took the attack on the existing system one stage further. This – the present 'national system, locally administered' – was derided as 'maverick, eccentric and muddled'. 'In my view,' he said, 'the country is entitled to an education system which not only works well but is also intelligible and shows where responsibility and accountability lie.' Local authorities, unsurprisingly, came under attack – some carried their ideology to the point of irresponsibility where pupils were getting a 'raw deal'. Such practices were spreading, he claimed, and this justified treatment of the educational system as a whole.[16]

The secretary of state argued that the British system should be brought much closer to 'the rest of Europe', with schools following 'more or less standard national syllabuses' – a phrase used twice in this speech. He expressed his own conviction that

Britain must move nearer to the kind of curricular structure which obtains elsewhere in Western Europe. He stressed, however, his own pledge that national curriculum criteria would be arrived at through a national process in which local education authorities, teachers, parents and industry all played their part. He did not outline, however, how this was to be done, and concluded:

> We cannot continue with a system under which teachers decide what pupils should learn without reference to clear nationally agreed objectives and without having to expose, or if necessary justify, their decisions to parents, employers and the public.[17]

The idea of a statutorily determined 'national curriculum', including definition of precise 'syllabuses' for each subject, as proposed by Baker, was greeted, as we shall see, with profound concern by many teachers and educators. On the other hand, a consensus on the need for a common curriculum had been developing now for some years, though hardly as something to be imposed by statute. Nevertheless this was the route chosen by this government and from now on adhered to with a steely purpose. But all this was to be taken further a few months later.

Early in April 1987 Kenneth Baker surprised a meeting of the House of Commons Select Committee on Education by a series of announcements. These concerned his intention to legislate in the next parliament to ensure that all children received a grounding in mathematics and English, science, a foreign language, history, geography and technology. This, he said, could be guaranteed only if 'required and enforceable by law'. But now he added his rider. The efficiency of the national curriculum he said would be measured by tests for pupils aged seven, eleven and fourteen – these tests to be based on attainment targets that 'would allow for differences in ability'. Baker stressed again that he did not intend to impose a national curriculum – its content must be largely determined by professional educators, primarily teachers.[18]

A few days later, Baker announced yet another initiative. On 17 April he was reported as 'stealing the limelight' at the Secondary Heads Association Conference with his plans to devolve financial control of schools to heads and governors. All secondary schools and all primary schools with over 200 pupils will have control of their own finances by the early 1990s if the government returns to office, he told the conference.[19] The aim will be 'to delegate everything that can be delegated to the schools for management by the governors and heads'. Within four years we will want to see all secondary schools and the bigger primaries in charge of their own budgets. 'So ... schools should be able to determine how many staff and of what kind they should have.' They would also be free to decide how much to spend on lighting, heating, micro-computers. There would be full freedom of virement; surpluses could be carried forward. The local authority would act as paymaster and employer.[20]

Finally, at the end of April – just three weeks before the dissolution of parliament, 'the clearest hint' was given that a re-elected Conservative government would 'allow schools to opt out of the local education authority system'. The city technology colleges (CTCs), Baker told the House of Commons, would 'point the way ahead for many other types of school after the election'.[21] The reference was, of course, to direct funding and independence from the local authority. Although little noticed at the time, this presaged what was to be a central feature of the manifesto, now clearly already in draft for the election. This announcement provoked a furious response from, amongst others, Dr Leonard, Bishop of London; but this will be referred to later.

The general election date was sealed by the outcome of the local government elections which took place on 6 May. Labour lost control of three metropolitan districts (though no other single party gained control), while winning back Liverpool from the Liberals. But the results gave heart to the Conservatives, and the Prime Minister now announced the dissolution of parliament (18 May). The election date was announced for 8 June. The tone of the struggle on education was set by Bob Dunn (junior education minister). A re-elected Conservative government would, he said, massively expand the number of city technology colleges and embark on the course that would eventually lead to 'the denationalisation of education'. Right-wing supporters within the Conservative Party were told that they must be patient and wait 'just a little bit longer' for local authority control of education to be 'finally broken'. The CTC pilot programme of 'only' twenty CTCs would certainly be expanded after the election – there could be as many as '220, maybe 420 colleges'. The Tory proposal to allow schools to take as many pupils as they could physically cope with, in tandem with the plan to give heads control of school budgets and the right to opt out of council control, was the first step in the campaign to break the LEA monopoly.[22]

The main objective, or target, of Tory policy in education was now quite clear – to break the power and control of local authorities as the condition for developing a variety of competing types of secondary school. All the measures already discussed were included in their manifesto: local financial management – devolution of budgetary control to the schools; open enrolment; opting out; city technology colleges. The statutory imposition of a national curriculum together with assessment (testing) at the ages of seven, eleven, fourteen and sixteen was also included. It was on this education policy that Tories entered the election.[23] The whole campaign, which had been built up over the previous year, was based on the stringent critique of the 'failure' of the existing system – a point stressed at this point in a main editorial in the *Times Educational Supplement*. The TES argued that:

> After eight years of Conservative rule Mrs Thatcher's ministers might reasonably be cast in the role of defenders of the present education system. Not a bit of it. Mr Kenneth Baker's stance is that of a radical iconoclast ... he admits no responsibility for the present state of education. [The Conservatives] have succeeded in repudiating and blaming [faults] on the 'system'. So we have the strange phenomenon of the government attacking the education system and decrying its faults, while the teachers and administrators defend it ... The kind of destructive criticism which has characterised the government's dealings with the schools over the past six years has been profoundly damaging to the long-term health of the education service.[24]

Alternative Policies

A good deal of attention has been paid to the formulation of Conservative policies since they in fact won the election and quickly proceeded to implement them. However, at the time, this outcome seemed by no means certain. Opinion polls through the preceding year had given ambivalent pointers although as the election approached the Conservatives gained a clear lead over a divided opposition. The Alliance (SDP and Liberals) fought and hoped (at least, in public) for a hung parliament right up to polling day. Labour prospects were enhanced by a highly professional television campaign. Only attentive observers of educational affairs, and not many of these, fully grasped the emergence of Tory policy and its implications: for these there was always the possibility that it might never be implemented. That is why, when very shortly after their election victory, the new government announced its education policy in a series of seemingly hurriedly concocted 'consultation papers', they were generally received with shocked amazement by the educational – and wider world. But this is to trespass on the next section.

Opposition to different aspects of government policy built up during the year as it was progressively revealed. In the summer of 1986, under the umbrella of CLEA (Council of Local Education Authorities) the two main local authority organisations (AMA and ACC) began to develop a broad campaign involving parents, teachers and many other social organisations in defence of the role of local authorities and their control of local school systems.[25] The TUC also developed its own campaign under the slogan 'Education under Threat'.[26] Tory moderates now also leapt to the defence of the local authorities.[27] In October the Labour Party conference came out for a policy of tertiary education for all young people aged between sixteen and nineteen,[28] combining education with training. In November the Secondary Heads Association came out in 'unequivocal opposition' to city technology colleges.[29] Local authorities and teachers' organi- sations totally opposed the teachers' pay Bill introduced in November, which abolished the Burnham Committee and all teachers' negotiation rights – throughout the year the teachers' action was continued and this (objectively) had the effect of syphoning the energy of teachers' organisations away from long-term policy issues.[30] Very strong opposition – indeed shock – was manifested in widespread responses to the threat of the legal imposition of a national curriculum, and later, of mass testing. Tim Brighouse, Oxford's Chief Education Officer, now emerged as a leading proponent of this opposition. In an article entitled 'A Dangerous Totali- tarianism' he argued that the announcement of legislation was 'as dangerous as it is breathtaking'.[31] The proposals were 'narrowly prescriptive', said Michael Duffy, President of SHA at their annual conference in April – 'an exercise in prescribing content and exercising quality control'. It is the duty of government 'to care for the public education service in its charge; not just to drip-feed it, bribe it for acceptable behaviour, and frequently bawl it out in public'. He told Kenneth Baker that his support for his schools 'is at best equivocal. Your call for a return to professionalism rings hollow to teachers who have been deprived of the most basic of professional rights.'[32] Stuart Maclure, in a signed article in the *Times Educational Supplement*, now took Baker to task for his 'centralising tendencies', putting Baker's initiative down to the coincidence of hard-left LEAs and the emergence of a regime at the centre which had decided to raise the Conservative political profile in education.[33] Much hostility was immediately engendered to the testing proposals when these first surfaced as firm government policy in April, both among teachers' organisations generally and among assessment experts.[34] As the weeks went by, opposition appeared to harden across the board. A highly outspoken intervention was now made by Dr Leonard, Chairman of the Church of England Board of Education, speaking at the launch of a petition organised by the local authority Campaign for Local Education (which aimed for 1 million signatures by the end of June). Any attempt to undermine the principles of the 1902 Act – which replaced School Boards with LEAs – would be 'both foolish and dangerous', he said.

> If any political party is contemplating an education system in which individual school governing bodies are responsible only to themselves and the secretary of state, then they must realise they would be destroying an essential layer of professional support within the structure.[35]

This critique was to be followed up later.

The Labour Party's election manifesto contained no surprises in the field of education: nursery education for all three-and four-year-olds whose parents wish it; smaller classes and the provision of books and equipment (without voluntary fund raising); free school meals; 'a flexible but clear core curriculum'; a comprehensive tertiary system of post-school education; end of the 11-plus everywhere; two years' education and training for all sixteen-year-olds; and other related measures. The policy was essentially evolutionary. In this, of course, it contrasted sharply with that of the Tories.[36]

The Election Campaign and its Outcome

The general election would, of course, be determined on a wide range of issues and attitudes of which educational measures and policies were only one, if perhaps of greater importance than usual. Baker had certainly succeeded in raising the level of support for Conservative policy in education since the all-time low of April 1986, when it gained only 16 per cent support. By the end of that year Tory support had nearly doubled to 30 per cent (February 1987), but this declined in March and April to 25 and 28 per cent respectively. Support for Labour's educational policies had, however, shown a continuous decline from 40 per cent in January to 32 per cent in April – the gainers had been the Alliance, up from 13 to 19 per cent over the same period ('don't knows' remained steady at about 20 per cent).[37] A possible explanation for the decline in Labour's support early in 1987 lay in the probability that many linked Labour with the continuing teachers' action – selective strike action continued right up to the election, though the Labour Party attempted to have this called off.[38]

The election campaign reached its high point in the early days of June. It was marked by what appeared as a clear rift between the Prime Minister and the education secretary on a crucial issue – would 'opted out' (grant maintained) schools be able to introduce selective procedures and would they charge fees? Kenneth Baker refuted both propositions on a BBC programme, but only the next day Margaret Thatcher appeared to say the precise opposite. The press picked this up as a major issue – or blunder, though Baker glossed it over a few days later. This is what comes, remarked the *Times Educational Supplement*, of 'Making it up as They Go Along ...', the title of a major leader. Tory policies had been 'dreamt up by back-room advisers' whose only contacts in education 'are with a coterie of far-right academics and publicists ...'. None of the detail, this journal claimed, has been worked out. All there is are 'a few manifesto slogans' on the basis of which the Prime Minister and the secretary of state for education 'have to make up policy as they go along'. This is 'palpable nonsense', and the result of this illusion 'has been plain for us all to see' in the bungled electioneering that took place over this issue.[39] Frustration and clear anger – even contempt were now apparent.

The outcome, however, is part of history. The general election took place on 11 June. It resulted in an unexpectedly large parliamentary majority for the Conservatives. Once again, the opposition was divided. Winning 43 per cent of the vote, the Tories gained 60 per cent of the seats in the Commons so obtaining a majority of over 100. The Prime Minister's eyes were already fixed on achieving her long-desired fourth term, and with it the final eradication of socialism.[40]

2 Bill into Act

The 'Great Education Reform Bill', as it was originally described, was first officially announced in parliament in the Queen's Speech at the end of June 1987 – just three weeks after the election. This measure, and that concerning the poll tax, were described by the Prime Minister as 'flagship' legislation by the new government. Both had the objective of diminishing the role of local government seen, in the field of education, as the means of liberating the schools from what was perceived as an ossifying, and in some cases malign control. The ideology powering the proposed measure was overtly that of the market place; schools, as semi-independent corporations, would be put in a position where they would have to compete for customers, or go under. Parents would be free to opt for the school of their choice. New types of schools would be established alongside local 'comprehensive' systems. Competition and choice were to be the watchwords. The outcome must be a general improvement in quality – the raising of standards. A subsidiary, but desired outcome, would be a victory in the next election.[41]

The Consultation Papers

The priority to be given to education was underlined by the issue (in inadequate numbers) of a series of 'consultation papers' already towards the end of July (though promised earlier). Clearly there would be no time, given the government's determination, to publish the normal white paper outlining proposals for discussion, which usually precedes major legislation. The four papers now issued covered the central measures of the proposed Bill so far as these concerned the schools: Financial delegation (or local financial management); open entry; 'opting out'; the curriculum and assessment (testing) – known as 'the Red Book' after its cover. A consultation paper was also issued on the ILEA (proposing powers to opt out by its constituent London boroughs). Other papers related to 'maintained further education' and to the universities and higher education generally with which the Bill was also concerned.[42]

The main series of consultation papers, affecting schools, were, as already mentioned, made available at the end of July. Responses were asked for in all cases within two months – by the end of September. This narrowed time-scale led to an almost unanimous cry of protest by those most directly involved. How could parents (with children at home), governors, teachers' organisations and others meet effectively during the summer months to consider and articulate their responses? Consultations, it was recalled, relating to the two great earlier Education Acts – those of 1918 and 1944 – had been carefully conducted by government over a period of two or even three years (for the 1944 Act, see pp.45-54). All organisations had had the opportunity to express their views, to publish them, to meet with and negotiate directly with the ministers concerned (H.A.L. Fisher and R.A. Butler). But no such procedures were to be followed in this case. The issue was urgent, and should therefore be dealt with quickly.[43]

But it was only with the actual publication of the consultation papers that many individuals and organisations first grasped the full scope and direction of the government's intention. The result was shock on a wide scale – particularly among those directly involved, but also among labour and social organisations generally, including both the Anglican and Catholic churches. The outcome was that, in spite of the difficulties of the summer months, hundreds and even thousands of responses reached the DES by early October, and these covered the entire spectrum of organisations concerned directly with the schools. On 'opting out', for instance, these, according to press reports, expressed unanimous hostility. 'Overwhelming condemnation of the government proposals to allow schools to opt out of local authority control has come from education officers, teachers, local government and all the larger organisations of parents,' reported the *Times Educational Supplement* on 2 October 1987. 'It is now clear that Mr Kenneth Baker will face unprecedented hostility from educational professionals if he presses ahead without significant amendments to his opting out legislation.'[44]

The 20,000-odd responses to the consultation paper, comprising some 25 million words, were in fact pigeon-holed by the government. No summary nor any analysis was ever issued. Copies were made available to MPs in the House of Commons library. Otherwise they were ignored. Attempted negotiations with the Education Secretary, for instance by the local authorities, were short, bitter and achieved nothing.[45] Experience later showed that only those with organised political clout – and representation in the Lords – would make some impact – specifically the churches and the universities. Otherwise opposition was dismissed as the self-interested standpoint of educationists. Early in October, when the strength of this initial reaction became apparent, Kenneth Baker set the tone in his speech to the Conservative Party conference. His attack then focused on 'the educational establishment' who 'simply refused to believe that the pursuit of egalitarianism is over'.

> I have to say that we will not tolerate a moment longer the smug complacency of too many educationists, which has left our national educationl performance limping along behind that of our industrial competitiors.[46]

Here there was no recognition that a Conservative government had been responsible for education since 1979 (and, since 1951, for 25 years out of a total of 36).

The full extent, and unity, of the opposition to the government's main proposals, as outlined in the consultation papers, was made abundantly clear at a meeting convened by the Council of Local Education Authorities which, sinking some political differences, took the initiative in setting up a standing conference on education, together with representatives of teachers' and parents' organisations, the Institute of Directors, the Trades Union Congress and the Anglican, Roman Catholic and Methodist churches. The aim was to 'attempt to find a broad based collective voice' in response to the government's projects 'in a climate of growing opposition to the proposals'.[47] The initial conference of this organisation –

attended by 180 representatives from 60 organisations – took place in Birmingham on 26 October. Described as 'historic' in the educational press, the conference expressed virtual unanimity on all the main issues.[48] One outcome of the consultation process had been to encourage every organisation to define its standpoint on each item. This meeting, at which representatives summarised their organisations' views, enabled each to realise how far their own assessments were widely shared. At this stage, then, it seemed to many that some modifications of the initial proposals might be won. Others, however, tended to stress the inflexible determination of the government to carry through the original (manifesto) proposals intact.[49]

The Education Bill

In the meantime, the government pressed on with its plans. A central feature of the proposed legislation, as we have seen, was the statutory imposition of a 'national curriculum' involving, as set out in the consultation paper, the definition of attainment targets, programmes of study and related assessment procedures which must include 'nationally pre-scribed tests'. These were to be defined for each of the eight 'foundation subjects' listed in the paper, though 'guidelines' only were to be acceptable in the case of two of the 'subjects', art/music/drama/design (defined as a single subject) and physical education. Kenneth Baker stressed in the run-up to the election that teachers would determine the curriculum.

Already in July the Education Secretary appointed three Working Parties to prepare proposals in these areas. Two, science and mathematics, were concerned with subject areas, both aspects of the 'core curriculum', as defined, which included English on which a committee was already sitting (the Kingman Committee). A third Working Party, the so-called 'Task Group on Assessment and Testing' (TGAT) was also now appointed. All three groups were asked to provide interim reports within six months (by January 1988), and final reports within a year.

This is how matters stood when the Bill was finally published on Friday 20 November 1987.[50] It was immediately apparent that, in spite of an overwhelmingly critical response, embodied in what the *Guardian* called 'an unprecedented 16,500 replies' to the consultation papers, the clauses of the Bill precisely

reflected the proposals as originally outlined. The one concession that had been made, although this was not reflected on 'the
face of the Bill', concerned the time to be devoted to the
compulsory element of the 'national curriculum' – instead of the
75–85 per cent proposed in the 'Red Book' (and this excluded
religious education), verbal assurances were now given reducing this to 70 per cent.[51] There were one or two other minor
concessions. But the main thrust of the Bill, concerning structural change in particular, remained unchanged. In particular, no
concessions had been made on the two central features of the
policy in so far as they concern the schools – open enrolment and
opting out.

The Bill, as first presented to parliament, contained a total of
137 clauses. These covered the national curriculum; testing and
assessment; open enrolment; financial delegation to schools;
opting out (of grant maintained schools); the break-up of the
ILEA. One clause related to city technology colleges. In addition, three sets of clauses covered further and higher education;
financial delegation to colleges, independence of polytechnics
and new funding arrangements for polytechnics and universities; the ending of tenure in universities (and elsewhere). The
main proposals in these latter cases also followed very precisely
the suggestions in the relevant consultation papers. One feature
of the Bill which now came to the fore concerned the enormous
number of new powers to be taken by the secretary of state.
From the 30 or so foreshadowed in the consultation papers,
these were now calculated as varying between 175 and 200.[52]

The first major debate in the House of Commons (on the
second reading) took place on 1 December 1987. In presenting
the Bill, Kenneth Baker stressed that its major aim was to raise
'the quality of education' by injecting 'a new vitality' into the
system. This, he claimed, had 'become producer-dominated'.
'This Bill will create a new framework, which will raise standards, extend choice, and produced a better-educated Britain.'

A reasoned response was made by Labour's new shadow
education minister, Jack Straw, who argued that the Bill would
'severely damage' education.

> Under the disguise of fine phrases like 'parental choice' and
> 'decentralisation' the Bill will deny choice and instead centralise power
> and control over schools, colleges and universities in the hands of the
> secretary of state in a manner without parallel in the western world.

Instead of being titled the 'Education Reform Bill' it should be called the 'Education (State Control) Bill'.

The subsequent debate followed normal parliamentary procedures, the only unusual feature being a 'blistering attack' by Edward Heath, from the Conservative benches, on the Bill as a whole. Its espousal of parental choice was, according to Heath, 'largely a confidence trick', while opting out was part of a policy which would inevitably lead to selection and fee-paying. Heath also attacked the proposal (as he saw it) to 'dictate' to universities what they should do and how they were going to do it, while the Secretary of State for Education and Science was accused of taking more power than any other member of the Cabinet – 'more power than the Chancellor, more power than the Secretary of State for Defence. More power than the Secretary of State for Social Services – and direct power too'. The proposals generally were 'divisive' and 'would be fatal to a large number of children'. The Bill was contrary to the 'one nation' Tory tradition; it would 'undermine and destroy the educational system'.[53]

The government carried the second reading debate by 348 votes to 241, a majority of 107. Ted Heath was the only Conservative to abstain 'as Tory colleagues bayed and barracked on the back benches'.[54] The Bill now passed to the Commons committee for detailed consideration of its clauses; this was expected to take at least two months, so the Bill was not expected to return for the report stage debate until mid-March. It would then go to the Lords when the Bill's opponents hoped that important modifications might be secured – perhaps particularly to the opting-out clauses and those relating to the break-up of the ILEA.

At this stage (January 1988) the interim reports of the Mathematics and the Science Working Groups, and that concerning assessment (TGAT) were published. The maths report, an intelligent discussion of the nature of mathematics, learning problems involved, pupil attitudes and like matters did not meet the Education Secretary's requirements. Mr Baker responded with a sharp letter to the group's chair (who resigned pleading pressure of other responsibilities). The report certainly lent no support to the type of 'bench mark' mass testing in mathematics at that time apparently desired. A new chair and several new members were now appointed and a more acceptable final response expected. The science group's interim report, while perhaps more acceptable to the government, also warned against mass, prescriptive testing at seven, eleven, fourteen and sixteen. It was the TGAT report, however, whose proposals appeared novel, and more closely related to 'formative' assessment than to the simple 'nationally prescribed tests' originally proposed (in the consultation paper), though the report proposed the final categorisation of all children by sixteen on a ten-point scale, and supported the publication of (unadjusted) test results of children aged seven and above.[55]. At this stage (or shortly after) a leaked letter from 10 Downing Street seemed to indicate a strong difference of view between the Prime Minister (who was chair of the Cabinet committee overseeing the bill) and the Education Secretary; the former stressing the need for mass prescriptive testing as in the original consultation document.[56]

So things moved on and, to some extent, the nature of the discussion changed. From January to March, as we have seen, the Bill was in committee where it ceased to make headline news. In spite of weeks of intensive meetings, often into the small hours of the morning, when almost every clause was challenged by the opposition parties, not a single concession of any importance was made by the government – or, to put the matter obversely, not a single gain, in the form of a successful amendment, was achieved by the opposition, of course greatly outnumbered in terms of voting power. The only possibility of any serious change in the Bill's contents depended entirely on dissident votes by some of the committee's Tory members. Press reports indicated that two or three possible revolts, in this sense, were effectively contained by the government. The Labour opposition's declared aim was to win the argument, if it could not win majorities for amendments. On some issues this objective was achieved.

Late in March the Bill was returned to the full house virtually unchanged. It was in the final debate on the report stage that the government suddenly accepted a proposition by two ex-ministers, which resulted in writing into the Bill a series of clauses involving the actual *abolition* of the Inner London Education Authority, in place of its death by a thousand cuts as proposed initially. The initiative for this action was taken by Michael Heseltine and Norman Tebbit – for primarily political reasons as was argued at length in the press. In response, London parents immediately organised an intensive ballot of those involved – Londoners with children in ILEA schools – supervised by the Electoral Reform Society. This returned a massive vote against the decision which, it was hoped, would influence proceedings in parliament. 94 per cent of those voting (137,000 parents) overtly rejected the proposition, only 8,000 accepting it, or 5.5 per cent – a majority 19:1. The vote drew 57 per cent of those eligible to vote – a much higher proportion than normally achieved in local elections.

This, then, was the only major change when the Bill passed the Commons. It now moved to the Lords, expanded now from 137 to 198 clauses. The extra clauses were largely government amendments required to fill out the detail of the original Bill, which had clearly been hurriedly drafted. Though now one-third heavier in weight, its content remained precisely as originally conceived in the July consultation papers.

Outside Parliament
In the spring of 1988 growing hostility to the Bill, or to different aspects of it, expressed itself in the form of parliamentary lobbies, mass rallies, meetings and conferences, organised on both a local and national scale. The London parents' ballot has already been referred to. At the annual conference of the National Confederation of Parent Teachers Associations, which united over 4 million parents in affiliated organisations, a continuing national campaign was decided on to fight, in particular, the government's opting out proposals. In March a number of events took place, timed to influence proceedings in the Lords. The National Union of Teachers organised a rally at the Albert Hall with national speakers representing a broad spectrum, including bishops from both the Anglican and Roman Catholic churches (both made powerful speeches against the Bill in general). In the same month the Trades Union Congress organised a parliamentary lobby and mass rally at Westminster Hall. The National Union of Students was also active, organising demonstrations and meetings both locally and nationally. Typical of the growing awareness of the need for united action was the 'demonstrative conference', attended by over 500, organised by the independent educational journal *Forum* also in March, with the co-operation and support of 25 national organisations representing parents, teachers, students, voluntary organisations or many kinds, local authorities and the labour

movement. Here a 'statement of intent' was carried by acclamation. Identifying the major areas requiring amendment, the conference members pledged themselves, if the bill passed 'virtually unamended', 'to carry through a powerful campaign in the country to protect schools and colleges from the bill's worst effects, and to preserve and develop the publicly provided system at all levels'. In particular, the statement ended, 'conference pledges itself to fight to strengthen the existing system of comprehensive primary and secondary education under popular, democratic control'.[57]

At this stage also a number of publications, including critical analyses of the Bill, made their appearance. The speed at which the government had operated made it difficult for such analyses to be compiled in time to influence events. The main publication here was certainly a *tour de force*; Julian Haviland, an experienced political journalist, produced *Take Care, Mr Baker!*, described as 'a selection from the advice on the government's Education Reform Bill which the Secretary of State invited but decided not to publish'. Believing himself that the Bill had great potential 'both for good and for harm', the editor wrote that the publication was intended to assist parliament to do its work. 'If the burden of this book seems overwhelmingly critical,' Julian Haviland wrote, 'it is because it accurately reflects the weight of the advice offered.' Haviland concludes his preface in the following terms:

> I believe that readers will find the weight of the testimony here very persuasive. It is hard to read what follows without believing that parliament will still have much to do to make the Bill, with all the regulations and circulars that will follow from it, a respectable piece of work.[59]

Other publications in the spring included a pungent theoretical critique, *Education in the Market Place*, sub-headed *The Ideology Behind the 1988 Education Act*, by Professor Ted Wragg, published by the NUT, and *Bending the Rules. The Baker 'Reform' of Education*, by the present author. The Education Reform Group published two pamphlets, *Opting out of the Baker Proposals*, by Philippa Cordingley and Peter Wilby (education editor of the *Independent*), and *ILEA: Unsuitable Case for Treatment?* by Martin Lightfoot and Patricia Rowan. All these were fairly 'instant' responses; but the situation made this necessary. Such publications contributed to the discussion and debate on the Bill which continued both in the educational and the national press and on television.

The Bill in the Lords

Early in April the Bill passed to the Lords. It was here that opponents of the Bill, or of different aspects of it, hoped to achieve some successes with a series of amendments which could draw the teeth of the Bill itself, particularly as regards its structural aspects. Lord Whitelaw had himself earlier suggested that two aspects of the Bill might well face defeat in the Lords – the (original) proposals relating to the ILEA, and the opting out clauses. The possibility of substantial amendment arose from the knowledge that, as well as the labour peers (about 120), Liberal and SDP peers (over 50) opposed aspects of the Bill, while the bishops (26) were also known to be antagonistic to certain aspects (e.g. opting out); further, about 250 peers sit on the cross-benches and owe allegiance to no political party. Finally the Lords had a record of rejecting aspects of government measures over recent years. There was certainly an overall majority of hereditary peers normally supportive of the government (about 600); but the great bulk of these seldom attended.

A full-scale debate took place on the Bill's second reading in April. This lasted two days and covered the main measures in the bill as a whole. Conflicts of views on the ILEA (which found many supporters, including some on the government benches), on opting out, religious education and certain aspects of the clauses relating to universities were here presaged. The Bill moved to the committee of the house early in May. Unlike procedure in the Commons, the committee of the Lords consists of the full house. There followed several weeks of intensive debate on every aspect of the Bill, now much extended, as we have seen.

There is not space here to deal in any detail with the debates in the Lords which were lengthy and, in general, well and seriously argued. Although a strong fight was put up, particularly by the Labour, Liberal and SDP opposition, but by others also on certain issues, as far as the main thrust of the Bill embodied in the schools clauses is concerned, only one major victory was achieved. This was on procedures relating to opting out, the successful amendment laying it down that the ballot of parents relating to this issue would only have validity if more than 50 per cent of all parents registered voted in the ballot (in place of the Bill's proposal that a simple majority of those actually voting was all that was necessary to spark an application by the governors for grant maintained status). To move ahead for a moment, this was not accepted by the government, the final clause, however, did include a concession – if less than 50 per cent voted in the first ballot, then a second ballot had to be held within fourteen days.

As far as the main measures affecting schools are concerned, then, the Bill was successfully piloted through a (clearly troubled) House of Lords in the early summer, all these gaining assent. Lord Joseph's personal (but interesting and tenacious) battle against the imposition of the full 'national curriculum' failed (though gaining support) as did all other attempts at modification of the Bill's school proposals. An amendment on the ILEA, asking only that there should be a pause for consideration before abolition, which gained widespread cross-bench and even Conservative support, was in fact voted down. This, recognised as being a vulnerable area, was achieved by the mobilisation of a large number of the usually non-attending 'backwoods' peers on the night of the vote (equivalent or nearly so, to the massive mobilisation of such peers a week later to vote down Lord Chelwood's motion, again asking for a pause and rethink on the poll tax). In this connection Lord Hailsham's characterisation of a previous government as an 'elective dictatorship' was widely cited. The government legitimately (but perhaps not altogether democratically) relied on its majority of more than 100 in the Commons to ensure its passage there. In the Lords it relied on the in-built majority of hereditary peers, only a proportion of whom normally attend, to force through aspects, or measures, seen generally as highly controversial.[60]

The government did, however, accept certain amendments in the Lords pressed very strongly by the universities, which are well represented there. These concerned writing a definition of academic freedom on to 'the face of the Bill' (as the phrase goes) – this relates to the Bill's abolition of tenure at universities. Other minor concessions concerned clauses relating to funding. Further, as concerns the schools, much time was spent in the Lords on the issue of religious education (almost totally ignored, interestingly, in the original Bill); and particularly on the inclusion of collective worship 'wholly or mainly of a Christian character' – the result of amendments pressed by the Tory right and supported by a group of elder statesman (Lords Home, Eccles, Boyd Carpenter, Hailsham) which draws attention to the social purposes embodied in the Bill as a whole. Here a compromise solution was found largely through the diplomatic skills of the Bishop of London, who had behind-the-scenes discussions both with representatives of the various religious faiths and with the government as the Bill moved through the Lord. Such discussions were described, by the Bishop of Rochester, as negotiations on a moving staircase. A few minor amendments were also made (by the government, but resulting from representations) aiming to improve the position of children with special educational needs. Those specifically concerned and knowledgeable about the problems the 'national curriculum' and assessment proposals seemed likely to give these children had made energetic attempts to achieve amendments they held were necessary. They were, it seems, only partially successful.[61]

As must be clear from this analysis, necessarily brief, in spite of the opposition in the country described earlier, and of the efforts of the opposition parties and others in parliament, the Bill in fact passed successfully through all its stages by mid-summer. The final debates in the House of Commons took place in July. At this stage, once again, a large number of government amendments were rushed through in minimum time, in spite of opposition protests. The Bill gained royal assent on 29 July. Although now an enormous measure, comprising 238 clauses (101 *more* than when originally published) and 13 schedules, it had been pushed through parliament at great speed, retaining throughout its original pattern as set out in the consultation papers a year earlier. It now took its place on the statute book.

3 Implementing the Act, 1988–89

Structural Changes
With the passage of the Act on schedule, as it were, the

government now held the initiative, immediately showing a certain steely purpose in its implementation. Here the main focus at the start was, as far as the schools were concerned, the construction of a third tier as Margaret Thatcher had promised as a main objective – the grant maintained schools (opting out) and city technology colleges.[62] Both these were to be funded directly by the state through the DES (though industry was to provide the bulk of the capital funds for CTCs while the finance for grant maintained schools was to be clawed back from local authorities). These new types of school were to be established outside, and independent of local authority systems. It was clearly of the utmost importance for the government to make a success of both these initiatives. Political futures depended on it. The Prime Minister herself had made it clear (in a television broadcast) that she hoped that most schools would opt out.

One day before the Bill received royal assent the 'grant maintained schools trust' was launched 'to help parents who want their schools to opt for grant maintained status'. Financed (apparently) by industry, the trust describes itself as 'an entirely independent, non-profit making body' but 'fully briefed by the Department of Education and Science'.[63] Its first chair, Steven Norris, was an ex-Tory MP, its director (Andrew Turner) a previous education adviser to the Conservative Research Department, the bulk of the trustees being industrialists.[64] This body immediately circulated all chairs of school governing bodies and heads with well designed publicity urging opting out (the leaflet's heading was 'The New Choice in Education' with a large red tick). This literature descended on the schools early in August – just a few days after the passage of the Act.

At the same time, a further important (and unusual) step was taken by the Secretary of State. A ban was imposed on the consideration by the DES of all plans for reorganisation of local authority systems. Such plans were largely concerned with the reorganisation of local systems in the face of rapidly falling secondary rolls, as until now insisted on by the government acting on the advice of the Audit Commission. Plans of this kind involved amalgamations, closures, the construction of tertiary systems (including loss of sixth forms by some schools), and so on. Such reorganisation was seen as essential in terms of the rational use of resources, and the construction of viable and effective local systems in circumstances of demographic change.

Nevertheless the ban was imposed, leading to what Gordon Cunningham, Secretary of the ACC, described as a 'planning blight' on reorganisation.[65] The objective appears to have been to allow schools, threatened with closure or amalgamation, to apply for grant maintained status (or to opt out) to remain as they were. Indeed this was explicitly confirmed by Kenneth Baker in answer to a challenge from Jack Straw.[66] The matter was complicated by the fact that new governing bodies, with broader parental representation as laid down in the 1986 Education Act, had to be reconstituted by the end of September. The pressure to hasten these procedures from the centre resulted in threatened legal action by some authorities.[67]

Enough has been said to make it clear that considerable pressure was rapidly exerted on the schools (or, rather, governing bodies) to consider the grant maintained option from the moment the Bill became law. On the other hand, local authorities, proud of their systems and wishing to keep them as viable entities under local control, fought against the grant maintained option with considerable energy (even Solihull, perhaps the leading Tory authority, opposed opting out). The result was that, nearly one year after the passage of the Act (July 1989), far from there having been a scramble to opt out, as predicted by some, only some twenty schools had been given the go-ahead to become grant maintained (of over, 3,000 secondary schools in England and Wales), though a few others had so voted, having still to submit an application. Further the bulk of both categories of schools were those faced with amalgamation, closure or some other change in status as part of a reorganisation scheme – these schools wished to remain unchanged in their existing position. Very few schools had voted to opt out simply to free themselves from local authority control.[68] It was noticeable that comprehensive schools in affluent areas, which were thought likely to head the rush to opt out, were conspicuous by their absence.

Generally, then, it seems, that, approximately one year after the passage of the Act, honours were about even. Since the great bulk of the schools opting out were in fact what have been described as 'lame ducks', the government could hardly claim the exercise as a success. On the other hand, this legislation remains on the statute book.[69] How things develop in the future clearly depends on the balance of forces in succeeding years.

If the grant maintained schools initiative got off to a sticky start, the same is true of that concerning city technology colleges which, of course, had been underway since October 1986, well before the Education Bill was first presented. A single section in the Act relating to CTCs legitimised this initiative in the sense of providing a legal basis for public money to be spent both on capital and on recurrent expenditure. Here again, immediately the bill received royal assent, a trust was set up at the DES, this time funded with public money with a staff of sixteen. Its objective was to propagate this initiative, its chair being Cyril Taylor, a Conservative MP, knighted in 1989 'for services to education'. The trust pursued an aggressive policy in the attempt to realise Kenneth Baker's assurance to the Conservative Party conference in October 1986 that twenty of these 'colleges' would open in inner cities by September 1990.

As is well known, this initiative received a dusty answer from most of the leading industrialists in the country who preferred to use such (limited) resources as they were prepared to make available for education to support the publicly provided system of secondary schools.[70] In addition, attempts made to transform existing comprehensive schools to CTCs ran into immense local and parental opposition in some cases.[71] Difficulties also arose in the attempt to obtain sites. By the summer of 1989, in fact, only one CTC had been opened – that at Kingshurst in Solihull – at a cost to public funds of £6.5 million (with £2.5 million raised by private sponsors). In September 1989 two further CTCs opened, that at Nottingham (costing £7.2 million from public funds, with £1.7 million coming from private sponsorship), and that in Middlesbrough (£6 million and £1.5 million respectively). Eight more were scheduled for September 1990, and two or three others may be on their way.[72] Total public funds committed to cover these developments by June 1989 amounted to just under £60 million, with £17.25 million raised from private sponsors.[73] The DES's latest estimate of total capital costs to 1989, and over the succeeding three years, is £126.3 million.

It became clear in October 1989 that the mounting cost to the taxpayer, together with widespread criticism of this initiative, caused the government to draw in its horns. It was then announced that the number of City Technology Colleges projected was to be limited to the original twenty, first announced by Kenneth Baker at the Conservative Party conference of 1985 – the triumphalist proposals by Robert Dunn in 1987 (see p.533) having been put aside.

Although proponents of CTCs claimed that they were likely to be locally popular (over-subscription, of course, involves utilisation of selection procedures at ten or eleven), local authorities generally were opposed, regarding them as divisive as well as possibly severely destructive of local systems and planning. However that may be, it is clear that there are real problems in developing this system of schools which will be under no form of public, or democratically accountable control (governors are to be appointed largely by sponsors). While, therefore, it is clear that a statutory and financial basis had been laid for a new, third tier of schooling, as was the original intention, its basis remains tenuous, and, of course, subject to decisions in the future resulting from changed political circumstances. In the meantime, in the defence of their own systems, local authorities have been adapting their own approaches and mounting successful operations strengthening their own base.[74]

But, of course, the main thrust of the Act was towards the introduction of market forces in determining the pattern of educational developments generally. Here the key measures relate to the new conditions determining 'open entry', and those relating to local management of schools (LMS) with its introduction of 'formula funding' (funding based on numbers of pupils, or 'bums on seats'). Open entry allows popular schools to expand almost without limit, and, of course, conversely, 'unpopular' schools, mostly in inner cities, to contract and finally face closure. Formula funding, together with governor control of schools (and funds) is the condition for the success of this strategy.

At the time of writing (summer 1989) it is too early to assess the overall effect of these policies. While the conditions relating to open entry came into force immediately on the passage of the Act, and the new governing bodies, (as reconsituted under the 1986 Act, though now with greatly increased powers), are already in place, local authority proposals relating to formula funding had to be submitted to the DES by September 1989 and this system is due to be operative in all areas by April 1993. The probable social effect of these measures will be to reinforce existing local hierarchies of schools and intensify their differentiated structure. The net result, if these measures are implemented unchanged, may be to develop a school system in the image of the French sociologist Bourdieu's critique of existing systems – that is, systems precisely reflecting existing social gradations and patterned to ensure their reproduction (and so, perpetuation).[75] But, as with all such plans, outcomes may, in practice, prove unexpected.

Curriculum and Assessment

A central feature of the Act was, of course, measures relating to the imposition of a national curriculum with its attendant definitions of attainment targets, programmes of study and assessment procedures. Here again implementation, if in a formal sense, followed quickly on the Bill's receiving royal assent, though some preparatory work had taken place while the Bill was still in parliament, as we have seen earlier in this chapter. The final reports, for instance, of two working parties – mathematics and science – were already to hand when the Act was passed, while 'shadow' committees covering examination and assessment and the curriculum had been appointed by the Secretary of State during the early summer of 1988.

With the passage of the act these two committees were effectively established (the Schools Examinations and Assessment Council and the National Curriculum Council), each member of both, and their chairs, being personally appointed by the Secretary of State. So the local authorities now finally lost the right to appoint representatives on the curriculum committee. Over succeeding months the timetable for the introduction of the national curriculum was clarified, while further working parties were established covering English and technology (both reported in the early summer of 1989), history and geography. At the same time various consortia started work on designing the assessment process, based on the TGAT proposals, generally accepted by the Secretary of State.[76]

The timetable for implementation can be briefly summarised. First, in September 1989, all primary pupils aged between five and seven and all secondary school pupils aged from eleven to fourteen began to be taught the new programmes in maths and science (and, in the case of primary pupils, English) 'for a reasonable time'. Also from this date all primary schools were expected to adopt for five-year-olds the attainment targets, programmes of study and assessment arrangements for the core subjects of maths, science and English, while at the same time eleven- and twelve-year-olds (in middle and secondary schools) followed the same procedure relating to the third 'key' stage for maths and science. In September 1990 technology for five-year-olds and English and technology for eleven- to twelve-year-olds commences while the second key stage (seven- to eight-year-olds) maths and science, and probably English and technology is also brought in. Thereafter implementation will take place year by year as the first cohorts move through the first three stages. In the autumn of 1992 the fourth key stage commences in certain subjects. Assessment procedures are planned to become operative alongside the introduction of attainment targets and programmes of study. These will function on a trial basis during the first year so that the second cohort will be the first to be reported on – those starting key phases 1 and 3 in the autumn of 1989 who will all be finally assessed and reported on in 1992–93. The full implementation of these complex procedures will, therefore, take several years (the first reported assessment in modern languages is provisionally planned for 1997).[77]

Much concern was expressed during the passage of the Bill about the greatly enhanced powers accorded to the Secretary of State over very many matters, including the curriculum and assessment. While the Act does define precise consultation procedures, clarifying in particular the role of the curriculum and assessment councils, the Secretary of State is accorded the power, under the Act, of finally rejecting or modifying any advice or proposals evolving through this procedure, and substituting his (or her) own decisions: provided only that the reasons for taking such action are explained to parliament. In fact full use has already been made of the threat of these powers in relation to post-consultation proposals concerning each of the three core subjects – science (where the proposals for study for 25 per cent of the time available has been reduced to 12.5 per cent for 'some' pupils), mathematics and English.

In history also the Secretary of State has intervened in a very specific manner. Such actions to date appear to have had as their objective simplification and reduction of programmes of study to allow more mechanical forms of assessment, and all have been strongly contested by those directly concerned.[78] The outcome of some of these differences of view remains to be seen.

As preparation were made to impose the national curriculum and assessment procedures from above, the situation on the ground, relating to resource and particularly teacher supply, was less than happy. The government had, for instance, siphoned more money as capital for twenty (or less) CTCs than it had earmarked for the introduction of the national curriculum in all the schools of England and Wales (some 30,000). The curriculum naturally has immense resource implications, perhaps particularly in the areas of science and technology, but it seems unlikely that these will be forthcoming on the scale required. Equally, or perhaps more critical, is the problem of the fully qualified teachers who will be needed in the immediate future, since both core and foundation subjects are to be taught to all pupils up to the age of sixteen. Assessment of the shortfalls in science, maths, modern languages and CDT (craft, design, technology) are immense. Proposals by the Secretary of State for new teacher categories requiring less training (articled and 'licensed' teachers, etc.), for the importation of thousands from the Continent and even from Hong Kong are at best short-term crisis measures. At this stage the government showed no intention of solving the problem of teacher supply by radical improvement in salaries and conditions of work, the restoration of negotiating procedures and the like (this was, in the summer of 1989, postponed for a further two years). In the meantime, in certain areas in London, local authorities lacked the resources enabling them to deliver any education at all, let alone the national curriculum. Such conditions cast doubt, in the minds of many, on the extent of the government's commitment to deliver what, in effect, is increasingly seen as an entitlement curriculum for all whatever disagreements there may be on procedures, and the actual programmes of study. The continued alienation of the teaching profession is another very serious factor militating against success.[79]

The Future

This analysis has focussed on the sections of the act relating to schools. There were other important measures relating to the abolition of the ILEA where, from 1 April 1990, education became the responsibility of the twelve boroughs (and the City of London) which previously comprised this body, and to the field of further and higher education. These latter changes are of profound significance. 'One set of long-standing conventions has been swept away,' writes Stuart Maclure in an assessment of the Act. 'The foundations have shifted.' The idea of universities 'as independent centres of learning and research, capable of standing out against government and society, and offering critical judgements of varying objectivity, informed by learning and protected by the autonomy of historic institutions, is discarded'. Instead the universities 'are made the servants of the state and its priorities'. They, like the rest of the education system, 'are to be used in the attempt to create a nation of enterprise and to discredit the "dependency culture" associated with the forty years after World War Two'.[80] The polytechnics and advanced further education generally, as well as the 400-odd local colleges of further education, are also brought into the new dispensation partly as corporations with new, industrially dominated governing bodies responsible, like the schools, for their own finances.

The 1988 Education Act, driven through parliament by a Conservative majority, certainly created a new situation. It altered the context in which the struggles of the future will take place, as well as creating new systems, through education, of social control. Unlike any other country in Europe, the entire child population (always excepting those in independent schools) is to be subject to assessment at the ages of seven, eleven, fourteen and sixteen – as first proposed by Rhodes Boyson and the Black Paper of 1975, following the student upsurge of the late 1960s. All are to be assessed on a ten-point scale. Each, in future, is 'to know their place' (see p.504). Such, at least, is the present intention.

But no Act of Parliament can legislate human aspirations. Struggles on education have taken place unceasingly for over 200 years. One thing is certain – these will continue into the future. A specific phase, however, is now over. On 22 July 1989 Kenneth Baker was appointed chair of the Conservative Party – his well-known presentational skills now seen as of more value to an ailing party than to the country's educational system. Though, through the Education Reform Act, he had in fact re-established his party's reputation in education, opinions on his departure were various. 'He leaves Britain's schools in a worse state than he found them', was the view of the *Independent*; British education, at the end of the 1980s, was 'in disarray'.[81] His successor, John MacGregor, previously Minister of Agriculture, soon made it clear, however, that policy was unchanged.

The last half century, as the reader who has stayed with me will surely agree, has been a period of struggle, of rebuffs, but sometimes of victories in the continuing endeavour to ensure access for all to a full, all-round education embodying humanist objectives and including science and technology – and conceived, one might add, in a generous spirit involving recognition of the full mystery of human potential. That struggle will continue – for such must surely remain the perspective for the future.

Notes and References

1. *Times Educational Supplement*, 16 May 1986. John Egan (Jaguar Cars) said that a third of the applicants for apprenticeships were 'barely literate'. The Coventry deputy chief education officer later challenged him to produce his evidence. APU surveys showed that 94 per cent of those tested could do the tasks Egan said they couldn't. The same issue reports Geoffrey Pattie, Minister of Information Technology, who asserted that 'schools are turning out dangerously high quotas of illiterate, innumerate, delinquent unemployables'.

2. Report by Her Majesty's Inspectors on the effects of local government expenditure on education provision in England and Wales, 1985; *Guardian*, 22 May 1986.

3. *Daily Telegraph*, 23 May 1986. It is of some interest that, at this point, Labour had surged to a 9 per cent lead in the opinion polls (Labour 39 per cent, Alliance 30 per cent, Tories 28 per cent), *Guardian*, 22 May 1986.

4. *Times Educational Supplement*, 25 July 1986.

5. *Sunday Times*, 20 July 1986. The ideas in this pamphlet were essentially the same as in the group's pamphlet, *No Turning Back*, published in November 1985, when Margaret Thatcher met the group and asked it to flesh out its proposals. *Times Educational Supplement*, 25 July 1986.

6. *Sunday Times*, 20 July 1986.

7. *Sunday Telegraph*, 27 July 1986.

8. *Guardian*, 29 July 1986.

9. *Education*, 2 January 1987. HMI were described as 'as likely as any other section of the educational establishment to be subverted by bureaucratic self-interest and fashionable ideology'.

10. *Education*, 2 January 1987. The pamphlet's authors included Professor Scruton, Baroness Cox, Lawrence Norcross and John Marks.

11. This meeting demanded a total ban on teaching about homosexuality in schools, peace studies to be outlawed, the retention of GCE O level, the eradication of 'pseudo-subjects' and their replacement by 'the basics', the scrapping of the Race

Relations Act and the Commission for Racial Equality. It was at this meeting that Robert Dunn, Schools Minister, declared 'the battle has just begun'. *Times Educational Supplement*, 15 May 1987, article by Brian Hugill. For a thorough analysis of the influence and character of the New Right on education, see Clive Griggs, 'The New Right and English Secondary Education' in Roy Lowe (ed.), *The Changing Secondary School*, London 1989.

12. *Guardian*, 9 October 1986, article by Sarah Boseley. She starts by saying '20 new CTCs are the latest and most dramatic manifestation of a new big spending policy by Kenneth Baker'.

13. Ibid. Commenting on the public expenditure White Paper, published early in November, *Education* quoted Baker as claiming that 'Education has been given the highest priority for public spending next year of every government department'. The White Paper indicated (he said) an increase in public expenditure on education of 18.8 per cent above the previous White Paper of a year ago. In fact, *Education* calculated, the increase was only 1.5 per cent in real terms, while much of this was being held back to encourage greater efficiency. *Education*, 14 November 1986.

14. John Pienaar's report, *Independent*, 7 October 1986. Replying to a parliamentary question three months later (in January 1987), Angela Rumbold (junior minister) stated that as regards CTCs, the DES had contacted 1,800 companies, all English local authorities, 200 charitable organisations and a wide variety of other organisations since the October announcement. *Education*, 30 January 1987. As is well known, they received a fairly dusty answer.

15. Ibid.

16. *Education*, 16 January 1987. The speech also stressed the role of the parent as 'customer'.

17. Ibid.

18. *Times Educational Supplement*, 10 April 1987. Baker told the committee that he was convinced that there was a national consensus on the need for a 'core curriculum' – it was not a party matter.

19. Ibid., 17 April 1987.

20. Ibid.

21. Ibid., 1 May 1987.

22. Ibid., 15 May 1987.

23. The Tories also promised to expand the Assisted Places Scheme from 25,000 pupils to 35,000; to 'continue to defend the right to independent education'; to permit inner London boroughs to submit proposals relating to opting out from the ILEA; to replace the UGC with the UFC; to remove polytechnics and other higher education colleges from local authority control and convert them into 'free standing corporate bodies' under boards of governors; to set up the PCFC; to review the student grant system and to issue a green paper on teachers pay machinery. Ibid., 22 May 1987.

24. Ibid., 15 May 1987.

25. Ibid., 25 July 1986.

26. *Guardian*, 30 June 1986.

27. *Times Educational Supplement*, 1 August 1986.

28. *Times Higher Educational Supplement*, 3 October 1986. The conference also, against the platform, demanded radical measures to bring independent schools into public ownership.

29. *Education*, 7 November 1986.

30. *Education*, 12 December 1986. The Teachers' Pay and Conditions Act was rushed through Parliament and received Royal Assent on 2 March 1987. On the same day Kenneth Baker imposed a settlement of 16.4 per cent with five allowances above the professional grade, and contractual duties which included 195 days per year and 1,265 hours per year. Both the teachers' unions and the local authorities condemned the Act, which led to further strikes over the following months. Seifert, op.cit., pp.250ff.

31. *Times Educational Supplement*, 24 April 1987. In this article, Brighouse said that the government's latest educational initiatives 'will be good for canine obedience, but

will be bad for developing adults who are confident, unafraid and autonomous'. Let us hope it is what it appears, 'mainly a populist election gimmick, designed to distract attention from the starvation of the state education system over the last few years'.

32. Ibid., 17 April 1987. Baker's performance at this conference, reported the *Times Educational Supplement*, 'had been as smooth as ever'.

33. Ibid.

34. Ibid., 1 May 1987; 22 May 1987.

35. Ibid., 1 May 1987.

36. Ibid., 27 May 1987. The main feature of the Alliance programme, set out in a very lengthy manifesto, was a promise to increase investment in education and training by an additional £2 billion per annum beyond that planned by the Conservatives by the fifth year. The Alliance also proposed to create a united Department of Education, Training and Science, and to restore negotiating rights to teachers.

37. Ibid., 15 May 1987, article by Demetri Argyropulo.

38. Ibid., 15 May 1987; 22 May 1987.

39. Ibid., 29 May 1987.

40. See Brian Simon, *Bending the Rules, The Baker 'Reform' of Education*, London 1987, pp. 11–2.

41. As Margaret Thatcher, in an interview shortly after the election, put it: 'Just as we gained political support in the last election from people who had acquired their own homes and shares, so we shall secure still further our political base in 1991–92 – by giving people a real say in education and housing.' The proposed Education Bill 'is the key to the future: the biggest and most important legislation in the forthcoming parliamentary session'. *Independent*, 17 July 1987.

42. Several consultation papers, elaborating proposals made in a White Paper, *Higher Education: Meeting the Challenge* (1 April 1987) were issued over the next two or three months. These related to 'nationalisation' of polytechnics and other institutions of further education; the establishment of the Polytechnics and Colleges Funding Council (PCFC) and the Universities Funding Council (UFC); proposals for 'contract' funding.

43. Both the 1918 and the 1944 Act were consensus measures, supported by *all* parties represented in parliament. The 1902 Education Act, on the other hand, was forced through by an overwhelming Tory majority; see Brian Simon, *Education and the Labour Movement*, London 1965, pp. 165–246.

44. *Times Educational Supplement*, 2 October 1987.

45. *Guardian*, 1 October 1987; 22 October 1987. See *Bending the Rules*, pp.58–8.

46. *Independent*, 8 October 1987.

47. *Times Educational Supplement*, 25 September 1987.

48. See *Standing Conference on Education, SCE, report on the first Standing Conference on Education, Monday 26 October 1987*, Council of Local Education Authorities, December 1987; see also *Summaries of Responses to the Government's Consultation Papers on Education*, prepared by CLEA for the October conference (Mimeo).

49. 'We are a very strong government', Thatcher had insisted to Peter Jenkins of the *Independent* in an interview on education in September 1987.

50. For the launch of the Bill and the press reactions, *Bending the Rules*, 3rd edn., pp. 158–9.

51. The Bill (and subsequent Act) defines the subjects to be taught, but not the amount of time to be devoted to the 'national curriculum' as a whole, nor to individual subjects specifically. Such definitions were to be included in later 'orders' ('for a reasonable time' seems the likely condition in most, but not all cases).

52. Sir Peter Newsam argued, in October 1987, that the 'constitutional questions' so raised might prove ultimately to be even more important than all the practical aspects with which the bill was overtly concerned, since powers were now 'contained within one individual'. The constitutional issue now emerging is discussed in 'The Constitutional Dimension', Chapter 10 of Julian Havilland (ed.), *Take Care, Mr. Baker!*, London 1988, and in 'Constitutional Issues', Chapter 5 of Brian Simon, *Bending the Rules*, London 1988, where Newsam's criticisms are reported.

53. *Hansard*, House of Commons, Vol.123, No.55, 1 December 1987, Cols.771ff.

54. *Times Educational Supplement*, 4 December 1987.

55. A perceptive contemporary critique is Caroline Gipps, 'The TGAT Report: Trick or Treat?', *Forum*, Vol.31, No.1., Autumn 1988; see also Harry Torrance (ed.), *National Assessment and Testing: A Research Response*, British Educational Research Association, April 1988.

56. *Times Educational Supplement*, 18 March 1988.

57. For a full report of this conference (by Edward Blishen) together with the 'statement of intent', *Forum*, Vol.30, No.3, Summer 1988.

58. Political Editor of Independent Television News, 1968–81 and of the *Times*, 1981–85.

59. Julian Havilland, op.cit., p.viii.

60. On this issue Baroness Warnock wrote shortly after the Bill's passage that many of the opposition and cross-bench peers had been 'outraged ... by the power of the government, in the end, to win a vote by whipping in those hereditary peers who seldom or never appear except when so instructed, and who know nothing whatever about the subject of the debate'. There were several such occasions, she adds, 'in the troubled passage of the recent education bill through the house. It is hard at such times not to despair of the system.' *New Statesman and Society*, 16 September 1988, pp.40–2.

61. See Klaus Weddel 'Special Educational Needs and the Education Reform Act', *Forum*, Vol.31, No.1, Autumn 1988, for a critical evaluation. Klaus Weddel is Professor of Educational Psychology at the University of London Institute of Education.

62. 'You are going to have *three* systems. First there will be those who wish to stay with the local authority', then 'you are going to have direct grant schools' (funded directly by the state, BS), 'and then you are going to have a private sector with assisted places'. Margaret Thatcher interview, *Independent*, 14 September 1987.

63. The Grant Maintained Schools Trust, press release 28 July 1988. The DES is, however, now funding part of the work of the GMS Trust, a grant of £150,000 having been made in 1989, *Times Educational Supplement*, 8 September 1989.

64. For instance, Ron Baird, group director of Saatchi and Saatchi; Tony Berry, chairman of Blue Arrow plc; John Ashcroft, chairman and chief executive of the Coloroll Group; Kent Price, director of Chloride Group plc.

65. 'The charge towards opting out puts a total planning blight on the whole of school reorganisation in the country,' *Education*, 12 August 1988.

66. Current school closure and reorganisation proposals have been suspended until 30 November 'to allow newly-constituted governing bodies time to consider whether the new opportunity offered by grant maintained status is one they wish to pursue'. DES press release, October 1988.

67. See *Education*, 26 August 1988, 2 September 1988, 9 September 1988.

68. A survey on opting out by the *Times Educational Supplement* in June 1989 indicated that, of the nineteen schools given the go-ahead to become grant maintained, thirteen were escaping amalgamation, closure, or evolution as comprehensive schools (from grammar); three wished to avoid changes in selection procedures. A further seven schools had submitted opting-out proposals and were awaiting a decision – all these without exception wished to avoid amalgamation, closure etc. Of sixteen further schools which had voted to opt out but had not yet submitted proposals for grant maintained status, ten were doing so to avoid amalgamation, reorganisation or closure, etc. Three schools had their opting-out proposals rejected, while fifteen, after balloting, had voted against opting out. *Times Educational Supplement* 16 June 1989. By mid-January 1990 the total of schools whose applications had been accepted reached 32.

69. Though the Labour Party has announced its intention of repealing this section of the Education Act.

70. 'All major firms (apart from British American Tobacco) have boycotted the scheme anxious, in many cases, not to harm their good relations with schools in the

state sector ... Of 1,800 firms approached, only 17 have responded positively.' Clyde Chitty, 'City Technology Colleges, A Strategy for Elitism', *Forum*, Vol.31, No.2. For a later assessment of the situation relating to CTCs and GMSs, see Brian Simon, 'Thatcher's Third Tier: Bribery and Corruption', *Forum*, Vol. 32, No.3, Summer 1990.

71. A tough battle was, for instance, fought by the governors, parents and others in 1989 to prevent the transformation of Riverside, a popular community comprehensive in Thamesmead, into a CTC. This was finally successful, and the proposal dropped.

72. Rosie Waterhouse, 'Mounting Costs of Baker's Beacons', *Independent*, 29 June 1989.

73. Cyril Taylor claimed at this time that private sponsors had in fact contributed £40 million 'to date', though some of this was for CTCs 'that have not yet been announced'. *Independent*, 7 July 1979.

74. The AMA, for instance, published in November 1988 a reasoned and detailed handbook of guidance for parents and governors on opting out, *Grant Maintained Schools, Independence or Isolation?* In the summer of 1989 local authorities and trade unions established 'Local Schools Information' (LSI) to provide a source of independent information and advice for schools considering opting out, and 'to explain the arguments for local control of education by democratically elected and accountable representatives'.

75. Pierre Bourdieu and Jean-Claude Passeron, *Reproduction in Education, Society and Culture* (trans. Richard Nice), London 1977.

76. But with some significant differences. Whereas TGAT recommended that assessment results should only be published within the context of a report on the work of the school as a whole, this provision was ignored in the ministerial pronouncement. This also strongly recommended that results at age 7 should be published, over-riding serious doubts on this by TGAT. Stuart Maclure, *Education Re-formed, A Guide to the Education Reform Act 1988*, London 1989, pp.13-4.

77. Ibid., pp.22–23. For a useful analytical critique of the curriculum proposals, Geoff Whitty, 'The New Right and the national curriculum: State Control or Market Forces?', *Journal of Education Policy*, 1989, Vol.4, No.4.

78. For a summary of these actions, *Independent*, 4 September 1989, article by Peter Wilby.

79. 'A recent Gallup poll of teachers found one in three actively considering leaving the profession. Nine out of ten believe they are "seriously undervalued and misjudged".' *Guardian*, 12 July 1989.

80. Maclure, op.cit., p.88.

81. *Independent*, 25 July 1989; 17 July 1989.

Appendix I

General Election Results, 1935–1987

	Total Votes	MPs Elected	Percentage Share of Total Vote
1935, November			
Conservative	11,810,158	432	53.7
Liberal	1,422,116	20	6.4
Labour	8,325,491	154	37.9
Independent Labour Party	139,577	4	0.7
Communist	27,117	1	0.1
Others	272,595	4	1.2
Turnout 71.2 per cent			
1945, July			
Conservative	9,988,306	213	39.8
Liberal	2,248,226	12	9.0
Labour	11,995,152	393	47.8
Communist	102,780	2	0.4
Common Wealth	110,634	1	0.4
Others	640,880	19	2.0
Turnout 72.7 per cent			

	Total Votes	MPs Elected	Percentage Share of Total Vote
1950, February			
Conservative	12,502,567	298	43.5
Liberal	2,621,548	9	9.1
Labour	13,266,592	315	46.1
Communist	91,746		0.3
Others	290,218	3	1.0
Turnout 84.0 per cent			
1951, October			
Conservative	13,717,538	321	48.0
Liberal	730,556	6	2.5
Labour	13,948,605	277	48.4
Communist	21,640		0.1
Others	177,329	3	0.6
Turnout 76.7 per cent			
1955, May			
Conservative	13,286,569	344	49.7
Liberal	722,405	6	2.7
Labour	12,404,970	277	46.4
Communist	33,144		0.1
Others	313,410	3	1.1

	Total Votes	MPs Elected	Percentage Share of Total Vote
1959, October			
Conservative	13,749,830	365	49.4
Liberal	1,638,571	6	5.9
Labour	12,215,538	258	43.8
Communist	30,897		0.1
Plaid Cymru	77,571		0.3
Scottish National Party	21,738		0.1
Others	12,464	1	0.4

Turnout 78.8 per cent

	Total Votes	MPs Elected	Percentage Share of Total Vote
1964, October			
Conservative	12,001,396	304	43.4
Liberal	3,092,878	9	11.2
Labour	12,205,814	317	44.1
Communist	45,932		0.2
Plaid Cymru	69,507		0.3
Scottish National Party	64,044		0.2
Others	168,422		0.6

Turnout 77.1 per cent

	Total Votes	MPs Elected	Percentage Share of Total Vote
1966, March			
Conservative	11,418,433	253	41.9
Liberal	2,237,533	12	8.5
Labour	13,064,951	363	47.9
Communist	62,112		0.2
Plaid Cymru	61,071		0.2
Scottish National Party	128,474		0.2
Others	170,569	2	0.6

Turnout 75.8 per cent

	Total Votes	MPs Elected	Percentage Share of Total Vote
1970, June			
Conservative	13,145,123	330	46.4
Liberal	2,117,035	6	7.5
Labour	112,179,341	287	43.0
Communist	37,970		0.1
Plaid Cymru	175,016		0.6
Scottish National Party	306,802	1	1.1
Others	383,511	6	1.4
Turnout 72.0 per cent			
1974, February			
Conservative	11,868,906	297	37.9
Liberal	6,063,470	14	19.3
Labour	11,639,243	301	37.1
Communist	32,741		0.1
Plaid Cymru	171,364	2	0.6
Scottish National Party	632,032	7	2.0
National Front	76,865		0.3
Others (GB)	131,059	2	0.4
Others (NI)	717,986	12	2.3
Turnout 78.7 per cent			
1974, October			
Conservative	10,464,817	277	35.8
Liberal	5,346,754	13	18.3
Labour	11,457,079	319	39.2
Communist	17,426		0.1
Plaid Cymru	166,321	3	0.6
Scottish National Party	839,617	11	2.9
National Front	113,843		0.4
Others (GB)	81,227		0.3
Others (NI)	702,094	12	2.4
Turnout 72.8 per cent			

	Total Votes	MPs Elected	Percentage Share of Total Vote
1979, May			
Conservative	13,697,690	339	43.9
Liberal	4,313,811	11	13.8
Labour	11,532,148	269	36.9
Communist	15,938		0.1
Plaid Cymru	132,544	2	0.4
Scottish National Party	504,259	2	1.6
National Front	190,747		0.6
Ecology	38,116		0.1
Workers Rev. P.	13,535		0.1
Others (GB)	85,338		0.3
Others (NI)	695,889	12	2.2
Turnout 76.0 per cent			
1983, June			
Conservative	13,012,315	397	42.4
Liberal	4,210,115	17	13.7
Social Democrat	3,570,834	6	11.6
(Alliance)	(7,780,949)	(23)	(25.4)
Labour	8,456,934	209	27.6
Communist	11,606		0.04
Plaid Cymru	125,309	2	0.4
Scottish National Party	331,975	2	1.1
National Front	27,065		0.1
Others (GB)	193,383		0.6
Others (NI)	764,925	17	3.1
Turnout 72.7 per cent			

From 1974 onwards, no candidates in Northern Ireland are included in the major party totals although it might be argued that some independent Unionists should be classed with the Conservatives and that Northern Ireland Labour candidates should be classed with Labour.

	Total Votes	MPs Elected	Percentage Share of Total Vote
1987, June			
Conservative	13,736,337	375	42.2
Alliance (Liberal/SDP)	7,341,152	22	22.6
Labour	10.029,944	229	30.8
Plaid Cymru	123,589	3	0.4
Scottish National Party	416,873	3	1.3
Others (GB)	151,517	1	0.5
Others (NI)	730,152	17	2.2

Turnout 75.4 per cent

Source: 1935 to 1983 inclusive, D. Butler and G. Butler, *British Political Facts*, 6th edn, London 1986; 1987, House of Commons Information Office.

Appendix II

Presidents of the Board of Education (October 1938 to August 1944) Ministers of Education (to April 1964) and Secretaries of State for Education and Science (thereafter)

Date	Presidents of the Board of Education
27 October 1938-3 April 1940	Earl De La Warr (Nat Lab)
3 April 1940-20 July 1941	Herbert Ramsbotham (Con)
20 July 1941-3 August 1944	R.A. Butler (Con)

Ministry of Education created 3 August 1944	*Ministers of Education*
3 August 1944-25 May 1945	R.A. Butler (Con)
25 May 1945-9 August 1945	Richard Law (Con) (Minister not in Cabinet)
3 August 1945-10 February 1947	Ellen Wilkinson (Lab)
10 February 1947-2 November 1951	George Tomlinson (Lab)
2 November 1951-18 October 1954	Florence Horsbrugh (Con) (Minister not in Cabinet until 3 September 1953)
18 October 1954-13 January 1957	Sir David Eccles (Con)
13 January 1957-17 September 1957	Viscount Hailsham (Con)
17 September 1957-15 October 1959	Geoffrey Lloyd (Con)
14 October 1959-13 July 1962	Sir David Eccles (Con)
13 July 1962-1 April 1964	Sir Edward Boyle (Con)

Department of Education and Science created 1 April 1964	*Secretaries of State for Education and Science*
1 April 1964-18 October 1964	Quintin Hogg (formerly Vt Hailsham) (Con)
1 April 1964-18 October 1964	Sir Edward Boyle (Con) Minister of State Education (Both Ministers in Cabinet)
18 October 1964-22 January 1965	Michael Stewart (Lab)
22 January 1965/29 August 1967	Anthony Crosland (Lab)
29 August 1967-6 April 1968	Patrick Gordon Walker (Lab)

6 April 1968-20 June 1970	Edward Short (Lab)
20 June 1970-3 March 1974	Margaret Thatcher (Con)
5 March 1974-10 June 1975	Reginald Prentice (Lab)
10 June 1975-10 September 1976	Fred Mulley (Lab)
10 September 1976-5 May 1979	Shirley Williams (Lab)
5 May 1979-14 September 1981	Mark Carlisle (Con)
14 September 1981-16 May 1986	Sir Keith Joseph (Con)
16 May 1986-22 July 1989	Kenneth Baker (Con)
22 July 1989	John MacGregor (Con)

Appendix III

Permanent Secretaries, Education (and Science) 1937 to 1989

1937	(Sir) Maurice Holmes
1945	Sir John Maud
1952	(Sir) Gilbert Flemming
1959	Dame Mary Smieton
1967	Sir Herbert Andrew
1970	(Sir) William Pile
1976	(Sir) James Hamilton
1983	(Sir) David Hancock
1989	John Caines

(Titles acquired while in office are given in parenthesis.)

Appendix IV

Statistical Tables

The bulk of the statistical tables which follow relate specifically to England and Wales. However, from 1978, the Department of Education and Science publications covered England only, the Welsh Office publishing (from 1976) *Statistics of Education in Wales*. For this reason, while a number of tables cover both England and Wales up to 1977 (inclusive), from that date (1978) it has been necessary to include tables covering England and Wales separately. For instance, Table 2a covers full-time pupils in maintained schools in England and Wales together for the period 1946 to 1977, while Table 2b covers full-time pupils in England only from 1978 to 1988 and Table 2c gives the same information for Wales only for these years.

Statistics covering universities, however, are provided for Great Britain as a whole (England, Wales and Scotland), while the Robbins Committee, of course, was also concerned with Great Britain. Tables 14a and b, therefore, which cover full-time students within higher education as a whole, present data for Great Britain.

Finally, statistical data concerned with calculations relating to Gross Domestic Product (GDP), from which the proportion devoted to educational (and defence) expenditure may be derived, relate to the United Kingdom (England, Wales, Scotland and Northern Ireland). Tables 15, 16 and 17, which relate to these issues, are, therefore, concerned with the United Kingdom as a whole.

These matters should be borne in mind when consulting the tables in this Appendix.

1   Live births, England and Wales, 1938-1987.
2a   Total number of full-time pupils in maintained all-age, primary and secondary schools in England and Wales, 1946-1977.
2b   Total number of full-time pupils in maintained primary and secondary schools in England, 1978-1988.
2c   Total number of full-time pupils in maintained primary and secondary schools in Wales, 1978-1988.

Table 1
Live Births, England and Wales, 1938-1987

1938	621,204	1963	854,055
1939	614,479	1964	875,972
1940	590,120	1965	862,725
1941	579,091	1966	849,823
1942	651,503	1967	832,164
1943	684,334	1968	819,272
1944	751,478	1969	797,538
1945	679,937	1970	784,486
1946	820,719	1971	783,155
1947	881,026	1972	725,440
1948	775,306	1973	675,953
1949	730,518	1974	639,885
1950	697,097	1975	603,445
1951	677,529	1976	584,270
1952	673,735	1977	569,259
1953	684,372	1978	596,418
1954	673,651	1979	638,028
1955	667,811	1980	656,234
1956	700,335	1981	634,492
1957	723,381	1982	625,931
1958	740,715	1983	629,134
1959	748,501	1984	636,818
1960	785,005	1985	656,417
1961	811,281	1986	661,018
1962	838,736	1987	681,511

Sources: Office of Population Censuses and Surveys, *Birth Statistics, England and Wales, 1979*, Series FMI No.6, Table 1.1 (to 1979), and Series FMI No.16, 1987, Table 3.1 (for 1980-87).

Table 2a
Total Number of Full-time Pupils in Maintained All-age, Primary and Secondary Schools in England and Wales, 1946-1977

	Total pupils in all-age schools, aged two to seventeen	Total pupils in primary schools	Total pupils in secondary schools	Total pupils in primary and secondary schools (excluding all-age schools)
1946	1,099,091	3,735,680	1,268,531	5,004,211
1947	1,091,861	3,699,503	1,334,772	5,034,275
1948	1,021,107	3,812,193	1,544,158	5,356,351
1949	945,902	3,874,463	1,654,313	5,528,776
1950	871,930	3,955,472	1,695,683	5,651,155
1951	823,875	4,004,701	1,732,997	5,737,698
1952	770,082	4,213,756	1,756,256	5,970,012
1953	693,626	4,436,140	1,769,848	6,205,988
1954	636,246	4,553,953	1,821,862	6,375,815
1955	582,388	4,600,862	1,914,814	6,515,676
1956	530,126	4,592,216	2,056,870	6,649,086
1957	437,083	4,590,052	2,186,497	6,776,549
1958	338,875	4,508,415	2,331,063	6,839,478
1959	267,350	4,308,194	2,592,993	6,901,187
1960	220,198	4,201,123	2,723,158	6,924,281
1961	170,465	4,132,542	2,828,975	6,961,517
1962	130,077	4,129,578	2,835,712	6,695,290
1963	92,617	4,144,546	2,780,782	6,925,328
1964	50,557	4,203,949	2,829,747	7,033,696
1965	30,100	4,273,101	2,819,054	7,192,155
1966	16,142	4,366,372	2,816,793	7,183,165
1967	7,288	4,502,197	2,832,851	7,335,048
1968	5,547	4,655,010	2,895,387	7,550,397
1969	3,213	4,788,591	2,959,661	7,753,002
1970	681	4,912,874	3,045,974	8,054,576
1971		5,021,593	3,143,879	8,264,338
1972		5,112,920	3,251,426	8,366,333
1973		5,148,965	3,362,554	8,513,728
1974		5,146,546	3,723,743	8,870,289
1975		5,097,329	3,826,646	8,923,975
1976		5,048,370	3,935,500	8,983,870
1977		4,943,142	4,038,763	8,981,905

Notes

1. Up to 1977, DES (and earlier Ministry and Board of Education) annual reports and statistics of education covered both England and Wales. The figures given in this table are compiled from these annual *Reports* and *Statistics of Education*. From 1978 these publications cover England only, while the annual *Statistics of Education in Wales* (No. 1, 1976) covers Wales.

2. Primary School totals include pupils at immigrant centres from 1970.

3. Pupils in Special schools are not included. In 1972 these amounted to about 113,000 pupils.

4. Middle schools, which may be deemed either primary (pupils aged eight to twelve) or secondary (pupils aged nine to thirteen), were first established in September 1968 and are included under the heading 'primary' or 'secondary' as appropriate.

5. The figures in this Table coincide with those given in *Statistics of Education*, 1978, Vol.1, *Schools*, Historical Table A, for 1947 to 1966. Those for primary pupils for the years 1967 to 1975 sometimes differ by a few hundreds. Secondary totals coincide throughout (to 1975) except for 1969, when there is a difference of about 5,000.

Table 2b
Total Number of Full-time Pupils in Maintained Primary and Secondary Schools in England, 1978-1988

	Primary	Secondary	Total
1978	4,499,633	3,851,271	8,350,904
1979	4,370,801	3,872,036	8,242,837
1980	4,210,328	3,866,102	8,076,430
1981	4,020,964	3,839,858	7,994,078
1982	3,838,907	3,798,000	7,768,318
1983	3,660,634	3,740,944	7,530,462
1984	3,571,376	3,645,586	7,340,758
1985	3,542,076	3,525,771	7,067,847
1986	3,388,517	3,548,313	6,936,830
1987	3,575,935	3,239,512	6,815,447
1988	3,618,300	3,070,172	6,688,472

Source: DES, *Statistics of Education, Schools*, 1978-1988.

Table 2c
Total Number of Full-time Pupils in Maintained Primary and Secondary Schools in Wales, 1978-1988

	Primary	Secondary	Total
1978	300,153	241,661	541,814
1979	292,996	241,662	534,658
1980	283,940	240,771	524,711
1981	271,976	239,641	511,617
1982	260,732	237,156	497,888
1983	248,564	235,625	484,189
1984	243,588	231,512	474,100
1985	241,934	226,446	468,380
1986	241,339	218,378	459,717
1987	241,985	209,909	451,894
1988	245,300	199,279	444,579

Source: *Statistics of Education in Wales*, Nos.3-13, 1978-1988.

Table 3a
Total Number of Teachers in Maintained Primary and Secondary Schools in England and Wales, 1946-1977

	Primary	Secondary	Total
1946	116,820	58,455	175,275
1947	123,316	65,476	188,792
1948	126,323	71,112	197,435
1949	127,766	76,999	204,765
1950	130,046	80,545	210,591
1951	133,567	84,015	217,582
1952	137,260	86,290	223,550
1953	141,200	88,001	229,201
1953	144,825	90,543	235,368
1955	148,739	94,390	243,129
1956	150,513	99,412	249,925
1957	151,538	105,671	257,209
1958	149,798	112,606	262,464
1959	146,473	123,255	269,728
1960	144,693	131,591	276,284
1961	144,247	138,728	282,975
1962	144,952	148,843	293,795
1963	144,267	144,483	288,750
1964	146,530	147,615	294,145
1965	151,084	150,736	301,822
1966	155,944	153,318	309,262
1967	161,523	155,984	317,507
1968	166,883	159,964	326,847
1969	173,485	165,184	338,669
1970	180,008	171,343	351,351
1971	187,581	175,222	362,803
1972	196,920	184,985	381,905
1973	203,604	196,666	400,270
1974	208,813	213,127	421,940
1975	213,055	222,591	435,646
1976	213,738	231,076	444,814
1977	210,729	237,305	448,034

Note: 'Teachers' include full-time teachers and the full-time equivalent of part-time teachers. From 1971 onwards the teacher numbers relate to qualified teachers only.
Source: *Statistics of Education*, 1978, Vol.1, *Schools* Table A, p.3.

Table 3b
Total Number of Teachers in Maintained Primary and Secondary Schools in England, 1978-1988

	Primary	Secondary	Total
1978	193,521	227,379	420,900
1979	192,462	231,404	423,866
1980	188,603	232,457	421,060
1981	181,310	230,928	412,238
1982	174,240	228,397	402,637
1983	168,514	227,084	395,598
1984	165,637	224,648	390,285
1985	164,429	218,605	385,034
1986	165,318	212,641	377,959
1987	168,385	207,180	375,565
1988	169,700	199,584	369,284

Source: *Statistics of Education, 1988. Schools,* Table A30/38, p.167.

Table 3c
Total Number of Teachers in Maintained Primary and Secondary Schools in Wales, 1978-1988

	Primary	Secondary	Total
1978	13,197	14,070	28,507
1979	13,251	14,256	27,507
1980	12,955	14,334	27,289
1981	12,481	14,259	26,740
1982	11,870	14,084	25,954
1983	11,434	14,119	25,553
1984	11,264	14,123	25,387
1985	11,054	13,815	24,859
1986	10,942	13,429	24,191
1987	10,953	13,002	23,955
1988	11,078	12,639	23,717

Source: *Statistics of Education in Wales*, Nos.3-13, 1978-88.

Table 4a
Pupil-teacher Ratios in Maintained Primary and Secondary Schools in England and Wales, 1946-1977

Number of Pupils per Teacher

	Primary	Secondary	Primary and Secondary
1946	32.0	21.7	28.6
1947	30.0	20.4	26.7
1948	30.2	21.7	27.1
1949	30.3	21.5	27.0
1950	30.4	21.1	26.8
1951	30.0	20.6	26.4
1952	30.7	20.4	26.7
1953	31.4	20.1	27.1
1954	31.4	20.1	27.1
1955	30.9	20.3	26.8
1956	30.5	20.7	26.6
1957	30.3	20.7	26.3
1958	30.1	20.7	26.1
1959	29.4	21.0	25.6
1960	29.0	20.7	25.1
1961	28.6	20.4	24.6
1962	28.5	19.7	24.1
1963	28.7	19.2	24.0
1964	28.7	19.2	23.9
1965	28.3	18.7	23.5
1966	28.0	18.4	23.2
1967	27.9	18.2	23.1
1968	27.9	18.1	23.1
1969	27.7	17.9	22.9
1970	27.4	17.8	22.7
1971	26.9	17.9	22.6
1972	26.1	17.6	22.0
1973	25.4	17.1	21.3
1974	24.8	17.5	21.1
1975	24.2	17.2	20.6
1976	23.9	17.0	20.3
1977	23.8	17.0	20.2

Source: *Statistics of Education, 1978*, Vol.1, *Schools*, Table A, p.3.

Table 4b
Pupil-teacher Ratios in Maintained Primary and Secondary Schools in England, 1978-1988
Number of Pupils per Teacher

	Primary	Secondary	Primary and secondary
1978	23.6	16.9	20.0
1979	23.1	16.7	19.6
1980	22.7	16.6	19.4
1981	22.6	16.6	19.3
1982	22.5	16.6	19.2
1983	22.3	16.5	18.9
1984	22.1	16.2	18.7
1985	22.2	16.1	18.7
1986	22.1	15.9	18.6
1987	21.9	15.6	18.4
1988	22.0	15.4	18.4

Source: *Statistics of Education*, 1988, Table A30/88, p.167.

Table 4c
Pupil-teacher Ratios in Maintained Primary and Secondary Schools in Wales, 1978-1988
Number of Pupils per Teacher

	Primary	Secondary
1978	22.6	17.0
1979	22.0	16.8
1980	21.9	16.6
1981	21.7	16.6
1982	21.9	16.7
1983	21.8	16.5
1984	21.6	16.2
1985	21.9	16.2
1986	22.1	16.1
1987	22.1	15.9
1988	22.1	15.5

Source: *Statistics of Education in Wales*, Nos.3-13, 1978-1988.

Table 5a
Total Number of Pupils in Different Types of Maintained Secondary Schools in England and Wales, 1946-1977

	Modern	Grammar	Technical	Bilateral & Multilateral	Compre-hensive	Other Secondary
1946	719,682	488,931	59,918			
1947	763,719	504,599	66,454			
1948	960,500	511,960	71,698			
1949	1,058,127	523,904	72,282			
1950	1,095,247	503,008	72,449	16,991	7,988	
1951	1,135,253	510,987	74,927		11,830	
1952	1,150,840	518,570	78,310		8,536	
1953	1,150,213	525,447	83,684		10,504	
1954	1,185,360	534,064	90,132		12,306	
1955	1,234,174	528,455	87,366	48,928	15,891	
1956	1,340,591	544,119	90,746	54,099	27,315	
1957	1,424,041	558,645	94,469	66,926	42,416	
1958	1,456,960	608,034	97,485	32,759	75,081	93,503
1959	1,595,559	641,044	99,224	37,319	107,186	112,661
1960	1,637,879	672,881	101,913	38,359	128,835	143,291
1961	1,698,379	696,677	97,039	44,166	141,899	150,815
1962	1,675,957	708,343	97,411	45,258	157,477	151,266
1963	1,609,307	722,492	92,504	47,274	179,013	130,192
1964	1,640,549	726,075	88,501	47,903	199,245	124,474
1965	1,555,132	718,705	84,587		239,619	221,011
1966	1,524,832	712,968	73,644		312,281	193,518
1967	1,459,377	694,898	69,704	Middle	407,475	201,397
1968	1,367,367	655,702	62,021	deemed	604,428	205,869
1969	1,303,751	631,948	56,627	secondary	772,612	194,723
1970	1,226,619	604,916	43,700	36,549	937,152	197,038
1971	1,163,442	573,646	37,525	55,286	1,128,417	185,563
1972	1,085,850	540,049	33,271	74,932	1,337,242	180,082
1973	965,753	496,766	25,321	123,265	1,580,406	171,043
1974	856,749	411,195	21,144	173,145	2,136,958	124,552
1975	697,850	343,658	18,049	207,344	2,459,648	100,097
1976	589,286	295,162	15,002	223,081	2,753,327	59,642
1977	493,158	256,040	13,673	245,446	2,982,441	48,005

Source: DES Annual *Reports* and *Statistics of Education*, 1946-1977.

Note: The development of bilateral schools led to a new classification in the statistics of secondary schools. Up to 1950 these were classified as modern, grammar and technical. The 1950 report introduced a new classification.

From this point the categories became (i) modern, and modern streams in bilateral and multilateral schools, (ii) grammar and grammar streams in bilateral and multilateral schools, and (iii) technical and technical streams in bilateral and multilateral schools. The 'comprehensive' category was also introduced in 1950 for the first time. Further changes were made in 1958. In the *Report* for that year it is stated that, when the 1950 changes were introduced, 'it was still ... assumed that in all schools except comprehensive schools separate grammar, technical and modern elements could be distinguished, and multilateral and bilateral schools were broken down into "streams" under these headings'. The recent tendency towards increased flexibility of organisation, the *Report* continues, 'has made this assumption less and less realistic and it has been found impossible to discover a clear-cut category for every secondary school. A new category of "other secondary schools" has therefore been introduced for the purposes of the statistical tables and at the same time the attempt to distinguish the grammar and technical "streams" in grammar-technical bilateral schools has been abandoned'. The *Report* then details how certain marginal schools are classified as grammar or modern, but then adds: 'Where there is an intermediate range of schools, broadly of the "selective central" type and previously classified as modern schools, these are included among the wide variety of schools grouped together as "other secondary schools". Schools are classed as bilateral or multilateral schools where they consist of two or three separate grammar, technical and modern elements recruited on the same basis as grammar, technical and modern schools elsewhere in the same local authority's area. Other schools for pupils of all levels of ability are classified as comprehensive schools.' *Education in 1958*, pp.29-30.

Later, in 1982, it is stated: 'Secondary education is provided mainly in three types of schools, the *secondary modern*, the *secondary grammar* and the *comprehensive school* (sixth form colleges are included). A school is classified *comprehensive* when its admission arrangements are without reference to ability and aptitude ... Schools which do not fall into any of the categories mentioned are classified as *other secondary schools*'. *Statistics of Education*, 1982, *Schools*, p.2.

Table 5b
Total Number of Pupils in Different Types of Maintained Secondary Schools in England, 1978-1988

	Modern	Grammar	Technical	Middle deemed secondary	Compre-hensive	Other secondary
1978	385,672	195,526	12,369	257,766	2,955,788	44,150
1979	328,090	162,993	12,394	266,102	3,061,587	40,870
1980	261,524	142,588	11,327	266,634	3,147,246	36,783
1981	228,648	130,849	10,158	268,296	3,168,337	43,728
1982	211,367	123,944	8,701	271,322	3,150,313	41,054
1983	192,351	117,147	8,673	262,975	3,128,793	39,678
1984	171,473	117,187	1,828	253,182	3,075,523	28,221
1985	164,650	113,264	2,502	238,660	2,891,943	27,254
1986	143,208	102,792	2,451	223,960	2,893,644	22,462
1987	133,835	99,636	2,326	210,143	2,780,611	12,943
1988	124,296	98,912	2,303	200,010	2,631,618	13,033

Source: Statistics of Education, Schools, 1978-1988.

Table 5c
Total Number of Pupils in Different Types of Maintained Secondary Schools in Wales, 1978-1988

	Modern	Grammar	Compre-hensive	Other
1978	10,900	7,807	223,073	671
1979	5,431	3,596	231,922	713
1980	6,484	3,585	229,966	736
1981	4,245	3,184	231,435	777
1982	4,056	3,155	229,209	736
1983	3,049	2,278	229,548	750
1984	2,125	1,661	227,927	783
1985	1,528	1,174	222,957	787
1986	1,359	1,111	215,066	822
1987	1,189	1,062	206,860	798
1988	1,075	971	195,882	1,351

Note: Over this period, there were no pupils in Wales listed as attending 'Technical' and 'Middle deemed secondary' schools.

Source: Statistics of Education in Wales, 1978-1988.

Table 6a
Comprehensive (Including Middle Deemed Secondary) Schools and Pupils in England and Wales, 1950-1976 Numbers of Schools and Pupils and Percentages of Each

	Number of compre-hensive schools	Percentage of all maintained secondary schools	Number of pupils in compre-hensive schools	Percentage of all secondary pupils in maintained schools
1950	10		7,988	0.3
1951	13		11,830	
1952	9		8,536	
1953	11		10,536	
1954	13		12,306	
1955	16		15,891	0.6
1956	31		27,315	
1957	43		42,416	
1958	86		75,081	
1959	111		107,186	
1960	130		128,835	4.7
1961	138		141,899	
1962	152		157,477	
1963	175		179,013	
1964	195		199,245	
1965	262	4.5	239,619	8.5
1966	387	6.7	312,281	11.1
1967	508	8.9	408,056	14.4
1968	748	13.4	606,362	20.9
1969	976	17.8	777,082	26.2
1970	1,250	23.2	973,701	32.0
1971	1,520	28.7	1,183,703	37.7
1972	1,777	34.1	1,412,174	43.4
1973	2,137	41.4	1,703,671	50.7
1974	2,677	52.7	2,310,103	62.0
1975	3,069	61.0	2,666,992	69.7
1976	3,387	68.0	2.976.408	75.6

Note: Middle deemed secondary schools (and pupils in such schools) are included from their inception in 1965 to 1976.
Source: DES *Report on Education*, No.87, March 1977, for 1965 to 1976 inclusive. Earlier data derived from, or given in DES *Statistics*, Vol.1, p.viii, 1968 and Vol.1, 1970.

Table 6b
Comprehensive Schools in England (Excluding Middle Deemed Secondary), 1977-1988
Numbers and Percentages of Schools and Pupils

	Number of compre-hensive schools	Percentage of all maintained secondary schools	Number of pupils in comprehensive schools	Percentage of all secondary pupils in maintained schools
1977	2,875	68.9	2,766,616	77.9
1978	3,077	74.8	2,955,788	82.2
1979	3,203	79.3	3,061,587	84.9
1980	3,318	82.1	3,147,246	87.4
1981	3,361	83.8	3,168,337	88.7
1982	3,358	84.7	3,130,313	89.3
1983	3,340	85.5	3,128,793	90.0
1984	3,291	86.7	3,075,523	90.7
1985	3,249	86.7	2,981,943	90.7
1986	3,226	88.1	2,893,644	91.4
1987	3,206	88.8	2,780,611	91.8
1988	3,153	88.9	2,631,618	91.7

Source: *Statistics of Education, Schools*, 1980, Table A3/80, for 1977-80; ibid., 1988, Table A3/88, p.114, for 1981-88. Percentages calculated from data given in these Tables.
Note: Table 6b *excludes* middle schools deemed secondary. For overall percentages of pupils in comprehensive schools (including those in middle schools deemed secondary), see Table 7.

Table 6c
Comprehensive Schools in Wales, 1977-1988. Numbers and Percentages of Schools and Pupils

	Number of comprehensive schools	Percentage of all maintained secondary schools	Number of pupils in comprehensive schools	Percentage of all secondary pupils in maintained schools
1977	206	84	215,036	90
1978	214	84	223,071	92
1979	224	88	231,922	96
1980	220	91	229,966	96
1981	222	92	231,435	97
1982	224	93	229,209	97
1983	226	95	229,548	97
1984	227	95	227,927	98
1985	230	95	222,957	98
1986	230	95	215,066	98
1987	228	96	206,860	99
1988	226	97	195,882	99

Source: *Statistics of Education in Wales*, 1977-1988.

Table 7
Number (and Percentage) of Pupils in Comprehensive Secondary Schools (Including Middle Deemed Secondary) in Great Britain, 1965-66 to 1986-87, by Country

| | ENGLAND | | | | | | WALES | | SCOTLAND | |
| | (a) Comprehensive | | (b) Middle deemed secondary | | (c) Cols a + b | | | | | |
	Pupils	%	Pupils	%	Pupils	%	Pupils	%	Pupils	%
1965-66	262,000	9.9	–	–	262,00	9.9	50,000	28.3	–	–
1970-71	1,017,000	34.4	55,000	1.9	1,072,000	36.3	112,000	58.5	184,000	58.7
1975-76	2,544,000	68.8	233,000	6.0	2,767,000	74.8	208,000	88.5	349,000	87.6
1980-81	3,168,000	82.5	268,000	7.0	3,436,000	89.5	231,000	96.6	392,000	96.0
1982-83	3,129,000	83.6	263,000	7.0	3,392,000	90.6	230,000	97.4	385,000	96.5
1983-84	3,076,000	84.4	263,000	6.9	3,329,000	91.3	227,000	98.0	377,000	96.7
1984-85	2,982,000	84.5	239,000	6.8	3,221,000	91.3	223,000	98.4	363,000	96.4
1985-86	2,894,000	85.4	224,000	6.6	3,118,000	92.0	215,000	98.5	361,000	100
1986-87	2,781,000	85.8	210,000	6.5	2,991,000	92.3	207,000	98.5	344,000	100

Sources: *Education Statistics for the United Kingdom*, 1986, Table 17, p.22, and ibid., 1988, Table 18, p.22. Column (c) is calculated from the data given.

Table 8
Pupils in Different Types of Maintained Secondary Schools
(Including Middle Deemed Secondary) in England, 1978-1987
(Percentages in Each Type of School)

	Pupils (to nearest hundred)	Middle deemed secondary	Compre-hensive	Modern	Grammar	Technical and other
1978	3,851,300	6.7	76.1	10.0	5.1	1.5
1979	3,872,000	6.9	79.1	8.5	4.2	1.4
1980	3,866,100	6.9	81.4	6.8	3.7	1.2
1981	3,839,900	7.0	82.5	6.0	3.4	1.1
1982	3,780,000	7.1	82.9	5.6	3.3	1.1
1983	3,740,900	7.0	83.9	5.1	3.1	1.1
1984	3,645,600	6.9	84.4	4.7	3.2	0.8
1985	3,525,800	6.8	84.6	4.7	3.2	0.7
1986	3,388,500	6.6	85.4	4.2	3.0	0.7
1987	3,239,500	6.5	85.8	4.1	3.1	0.5

Source: DES *Statistical Bulletin* 6/88, May 1988.

Table 9
Number of Pupils in Direct Grant, Independent ('Recognised as Efficient'), and Independent ('Other') in England and Wales (1950-1977), and in England Only (1978-1988)

England and Wales	Direct Grant Schools	Independent ('recognised as efficient) schools		'Other' independent schools
1950	84,891	203,843		305,591
1955	91,186	258,619		251,705
1957	94,203	278,691		233,610
1960	110,272	293,954		198,146
1961	121,663	300,569		194,872
1962	123,310	304,227		190,732
1963	128,873	305,430		180,028
1964	124,627	307,674		162,710
1965	125,202	306,638		151,569
1966	125,966	308,898		140,878
1967	127,212	306,772		136,911
1968	128,555	301,700		127,738
1969	128,451	301,166		116,083
1970	129,096	303,977		109,811
1971	128,111	305,533		102,861
1972	128,108	311,116		97,959
1973	130,090	315,391		96,273
1974	130,880	324,326		94,821
1975	130,818	328,521		93,137
1976	130,558	324,011		90,597
1977	127,976	322,851		89,038
England only				
1978	115,476	312,748		90,081
1979	107,665		413,102	
1980	102,175		423,020	
1981	NIL		515,742	
1982			510,074	
1983			503,156	
1984			500,845	
1985			501,422	
1986			504,235	
1987			514,855	
1988			522,949	

Sources: The data for 1950 to 1960 inclusive are from *Statistics of Education*,

1967, Vol.1, *Schools*; thereafter they are from the annual *Statistics of Education*. The Direct Grant category included 'Special' schools which received a direct grant. There were about 8,000 pupils in such schools during this period. For this reason the figures given for direct grant pupils are larger than those given in the 1978 edition of *Statistics of Education*, Vol.1, *Schools*, Table B.

Notes
1. The Direct Grant category of schools ceased to exist in 1981, consequent on the Labour government's legislation of 1978 (see p.439). Hence the rise in that year in the number of pupils in independent schools.
2. Arrangements for 'recognition as efficient' were terminated in April 1978. From January 1979 independent schools have been classified as a single group. From January 1980 figures for independent schools include direct grant schools which are registered as independent schools in receipt of direct grant (see *Statistics of Education*, 1988, Vol.1, *Schools*, p.iii).
3. From 1977 Welsh statistics have been presented separately. In 1977 there were 3 Direct Grant schools in Wales with 1,667 pupils. In that year there were also 8,740 pupils in independent schools ('recognised as efficient'), and 1,678 in independent schools ('other'). *Statistics of Education in Wales, No.3, 1978, Table 1.01*.

Table 10a
Percentage of Pupils in Maintained Secondary Schools in England Staying on at School over the School Leaving Age, 1978-1987

	Percentage remaining at school aged sixteen	Percentage remaining at school aged seventeen
1978	24.3	16.1
1979	24.4	15.7
1980	25.0	15.6
1981	25.9	16.2
1982	28.8	17.1
1983	28.9	17.9
1984	27.4	17.3
1985	26.7	16.6
1986	26.9	16.3
1987	26.3	16.3
1988	26.6	16.0

Note: the percentage expresses the number of pupils aged sixteen and seventeen in January expressed as a percentage of the fifteen-year-olds one and two years earlier)

Table 10b
Regional and Gender Differences in Staying on at School in England, 1988

1988	Percentage remaining at school aged sixteen	Percentage remaining at school aged seventeen	
Greater London	33.8	16.1	Maximum
South West	23.3	14.5	regional differences
Boys	25.4	15.7	Gender
Girls	27.9	16.4	differences

Note: The percentages are calculated on the same basis as for Table 10a.
Sources: 1978-1987, DES *Statistical Bulletin*, 6/88, May 1988; 1988, *Statistics of Education*, 1988, Vol.1, *Schools*, Table A14/88 (B), p.133.

Table 11a
Post-compulsory Participation Rates (Great Britain), 1975-1987. Educational and Economic Activities of Sixteen-to-Eighteen Year-olds at January Each Year (Percentage of Age Group)

	School	NAFE*	Higher Education	In employment (outside YTS)	On YTS	Unemployed
1975	16	8	3	65	0	8
1981	16	11	3	53	5	13
1982	18	11	3	42	9	17
1983	17	10	3	43	10	17
1984	17	10	3	42	10	16
1985	17	10	3	42	10	16
1986	17	11	3	43	10	15
1987	17	11	3	43	12	14

Sources: *Educational Statistics in the United Kingdom*, 1986 edn., Table 19; ibid., 1987 edn., Table 19; ibid., 1988 edn., Table 21.

Table 11b
Post-compulsory Participation Rates (Great Britain) Educational and Economic Activities of Sixteen-to-Eighteen Year-olds, 1987 (Percentage of Age Group)

In full-time education			In employment (outside YTS)	On YTS†	Unemployed
	School	NAFE*	Higher Education			
16-year-olds						
1987	31	15	–	17	27	11
17-year-olds						
1987	19	12	1	44	10	14

Source: *Educational Statistics for the United Kingdom*, 1988 edn., Table 21.

* Non Advanced Further Education
† Youth Training Scheme

Table 12a
Participation in Full-time Education and Training of Sixteen-to-Eighteen Year-olds, 1981 (Percentage of Age Groups)

Country	School	Other	Total
USA	65	14	79
Netherlands	50	21	71
Japan	58	11	69
France	33	25	58
Italy	16	31	47
Germany	31	14	45
United Kingdom	18	14	32

Source: DES *Statistical Bulletin*, 10/85, Table 2.

Table 12b
Enrolment in Full-time and Part-time Education (General and Vocational) at Eighteen, 1985-86

Country	Percentage of age group
Germany	84
Switzerland	73
Belgium	69
Denmark	67
Finland	65
Norway	63
Netherlands	59
United States	59
France	56
Canada	53
Austria	48
Greece	43
Ireland	40
New Zealand	22
United Kingdom	21
Turkey	15

Source: OECD, *Education in OECD Countries*, 1988, p.71.

Table 13

GCE and CSE Examination Data for England, 1973-74 to 1985-86 (Leavers from Maintained Secondary Schools, as Percentage of all Leavers)

	(a) Leavers with 1 or more A Level passes	(b) Leavers with no A Level passes but with 5 or more higher grade 0 Level or CSE results	Cols (a) + (b)	(c) Leavers with no A Level passes but with 1 to 4 higher grade 0 Level or CSE passes	Cols (a) + (b) + (c)	(d) Leavers with no higher grade 0 Level or CSE results: 1 or more other grades	No GCE or CSE qualifications
1973-74	12.5	8.2	20.7	24.9	45.6	32.8	21.6
1974-75	12.4	7.8	20.2	26.0	46.2	33.9	19.8
1975-76	12.8	8.0	20.8	26.4	47.2	35.3	17.5
1976-77	12.7	8.8	21.5	27.3	48.8	35.5	15.7
1977-78	12.7	8.8	21.5	27.2	48.7	36.2	15.0
1978-79	12.6	9.1	21.7	27.8	49.5	37.0	13.6
1979-80	12.6	9.1	21.7	27.7	49.4	37.8	12.8
1980-81	13.5	9.2	22.7	27.3	50.0	38.0	12.0
1981-82	14.1	9.9	24.0	27.3	51.3	37.5	11.2
1982-83	14.4	10.0	24.4	28.0	52.4	37.5	10.1
1983-84	14.3	10.5	24.8	27.5	52.3	37.7	9.9
1984-85	13.9	10.8	24.7	27.6	52.3	37.7	9.9
1985-86	13.6	11.0	24.6	27.5	52.1	37.8	10.1
1986-87	13.9	10.6	24.5	27.9	52.4	37.7	9.9
1987-88	15.2	12.6	27.8	27.6	55.4	34.5	10.1

Sources: Given in, or derived from, *Statistics of Education, School Leavers, GCE and CSE*, 1983, for 1973-74 to 1975-76; ibid., Table C3, 1986, for 1976-77 to 1985-86; ibid., Table C3, 1987, for 1986-87; ibid., Table C3, 1988, for 1987-88.

Table 14a
Higher Education: Full-Time Students in Universities, Teacher Training and Further Education (Following Advanced Courses) in Great Britain, 1944-1978

	Universities	Teacher Training			Further Education			Total
	University students (thousands)	Students in initial teacher training courses in public sector higher education (thousands)			Students in advanced courses (full-time and sandwich) leading to recognised qualifications at grant-aided establishments of further education (thousands)			Number (thousands)
1944	38							
1945	52							
1946	69							
1947	79							
1948	84							
1949	85							
1950	85	Bracketed = England and Wales						
1951	84							
1952	82				Bracketed = England and Wales			
1953	81	(24)						
1954	82	(25)			(10)			
1955	85	(25)			(11)			
1956	90	(26)			(13)			
1957	95	(27)			(16)			
1958	100	(29)			(21)			
1959	104	(31)			(24)			
1960	108	(34)			(27)			
1961	113	(34)			(24)			
1962	119	(47)			(28)			
1963	126	(54)			(33)			
1964	139	(62)			(40)			
		England and Wales	Scotland	Total (GB)				
1965	169	(71)	9	80	(50)			
					England and Wales	Scotland	Total (GB)	
1966	184	(83)	10	93	(54)	5	59	336
1967	200	(94)	11	105	(66)	6	72	377
1968	211	(102)	12	114	(76)	6	82	407
1969	219	(105)	13	118	(83)	7	90	427
1970	228	(106)	13	119	(88)	8	96	443
1971	235	(108)	14	122	(84)	9	93	450
1972	230	(110)	14	124	(96)	11	107	470
1973	224	(108)	13	121	(100)	12	112	447
1974	251	(101)	12	113	(106)	na		470
1975	261	(87)	11	98	(127)	na		486
1976	272	(65)	9	74	(141)	na		487
1977	281	(53)	7	60	(150)	na		491
1978	288	(44)	5	49	(150)	na		487

Table 14b
Full-time Students in Universities, Polytechnics and Colleges (Following Advanced Courses), Great Britain 1979-1987

	Students in universities	Students in polytechnics and colleges (including initial teacher training in public sector institutions)	Total
1979	293,000	217,000	510,000
1980	299,000	222,000	521,000
1982	295,000	258,000	553,000
1983	292,000	273,000	565,000
1984	291,000	283,000	573,000
1985	296,000	288,000	594,000
1986	301,000	295,000	596,000
1987	305,000	303,000	609,000

Notes
1. These tables give data for full-time students only, not part-time students. In 1986 there were about 350,000 part-time students following advanced courses in Great Britain.
2. Scottish data for full-time students in advanced courses in further education was not made available. The Scottish Education Department ceased publication of the annual *Statistics of Education* in 1977. The SED did, however, supply data for Scottish students in initial teacher training.
3. A new method of presenting data for Great Britain was introduced in 1979, hence the division of these data into two separate tables.
4. The figures for the total number of students (right hand column) between 1974 and 1978 (inclusive) do not include students on advanced courses in further education in Scotland. There were probably about 12,000 of these (perhaps more).

Sources: Universities: 1944 to 1978, W.A.C. Stewart, *Higher Education in Postwar Britain*, Table 15.1, p.268 (from annual UGC returns). Thereafter from DES *Statistical Bulletin* 4/89, March 1989. Teacher training: 1958 to 1978 (England and Wales). W.A.C. Stewart, op.cit., Table 16.3, p.302 (from *Education Statistics for the UK*). Further Education: 1954 to 1978 (England and Wales), W.A.C. Stewart, op.cit., Table 16.1 p.300. Scottish data, 1966 to 1973, *Statistics of Education* (annually). 1979 to 1988 from DES *Statistical Bulletin* 4/89, March 1989.

Expenditure on Education, United Kingdom, 1953-54 to 1986-87

	Central government £ millions	Local authorities £ millions	Total £ millions	GDP at market prices £ millions	Educational expenditure as percentage of GDP
1953-54	46.9	460.3	507.2	16,905	3.0
1954-55	50.4	503.5	553.9	17,852	3.1
1955-56	54.6	552.4	607.0	19,306	3.1
1956-57	61.4	663.8	725.2	20,561	3.5
1957-58	72.7	666.9	739.6	21,785	3.4
1958-59	83.9	708.0	791.9	22,628	3.5
1959-60	94.3	765.7	860.0	23,992	3.6
1960-61	109.3	819.4	928.7	25,872	3.6
1961-62	138.4	918.6	1,057.0	27,341	3.9
1962-63	165.7	1,022.71	1,188.4	28,632	4.1
1963-64	198	1,129	1,327	30,473	4.3
1964-65	239	1,213	1,452	33,686	4.3
1965-66	278	1,358	1,636	35,886	4.5
1966-67	308	1,446	1,754	38,026	4.6
1967-68	341	1,626	1,967	40,121	4.9
1968-69	357	1,762	2,119	43,573	4.9
1969-70	372	1,927	2,299	46,573	4.9
1970-71	422	2,318	2,740	52,407	5.2
1971-72	509	2,631	3,140	59,265	5.3
1972-73	605	3,103	3,708	66,620	5.6
1973-74	670	3,566	4,236	74,597	5.7
1974-75	781	4,752	5,533	89,186	6.2
1975-76	980	6,043	7,023	112,030	6.3
1976-77	1,099	6,760	7,859	130,596	6.0
1977-78	1,058	7,247	8,305	151,457	5.5
1978-79	1,161	8,008	9,169	172,769	5.3
1979-80	1,394	9,223	10,617	206,743	5.1
1980-81	1,779	11,270	13,049	236,400	5.5
1981-82	1,797	12,291	14,088	259,696	5.4
1982-83	2,022	13,136	15,158	283,078	5.4
1983-84	2,222	13,862	16,084	305,153	5.3
1984-85	2,289	14,392	16,681	329,300	5.1
1985-86	2,398	15,041	17,439	361,300	4.8
1986-87	2,652	16,390	19,042	386,200	4.9

Notes

1. The breaks in the four series in the Table arise from both changes in the methods of calculation and the way government data has been published.

2. Expenditure under the heading 'Central government' covers direct expenditure by central government to specific institutions; e.g., from 1971, to the Open University.

Expenditure under the heading 'Local Authorities' includes moneys both raised from the rates and received as grants from central government. The proportion contributed by each source has varied over time. Between 1975-76 and 1982-83 the contribution from central government fell from 66.0 per cent to 57.1 per cent; that from rates increased from 34.0 per cent to 42.9 per cent, *Education*, 12 February 1982. Between 1982-83 and 1986-87 the proportion borne by central government consistently declined. See Brian Simon, *Bending the Rules*, first edn., 1988, pp.179-80.

3. Figures for expenditure by central government and local authorities are the sum of both current and capital expenditure.

Source: CSO, *National Income and Expenditure*; CSO, *Annual Abstract of Statistics*.

Table 16
Educational and Defence Expenditure, United Kingdom, 1966 to 1986-87

	Defence Expenditure £ millions	GDP £ millions	Defence Expenditure as percentage of GDP	Educational Expenditure as percentage of GDP
1966	2,145	38,026	5.6	4.6
1967	2,329	40,121	5.8	4.9
1968	2,363	43,468	5.4	4.9
1969	2,247	46,573	4.8	4.9
1970-71	2,503	52,407	4.8	5.2
1971-72	2,828	59,265	4.8	5.3
1972-73	3,092	66,620	4.6	5.6
1973-74	3,484	74,597	4.7	5.7
1974-75	4,164	89,186	4.7	6.2
1975-76	5,346	112,030	4.8	6.3
1976-77	6,158	130,586	4.7	6.0
1977-78	6,787	151,457	4.5	5.5
1978-79	7,455	172,769	4.3	5.3
1979-80	9,178	206,743	4.4	5.1
1980-81	11,182	236,400	4.7	5.5
1981-82	12,607	259,696	4.8	5.4
1982-83	14,412	283,078	5.1	5.4
1983-84	15,487	305,153	5.1	5.3
1984-85	17,122	329,300	5.1	5.1
1985-86	17,943	361,300	4.9	4.8
1986-87	18,163	386,200	4.7	4.9

Note: The figures in the right-hand column are taken from Table 15.

Source: CSO, *National Income and Expenditure*; CSO, *Annual Abstract of Statistics*.

Table 17
Education Expenditure per Pupil/Student, United Kingdom, 1970-1986

	Total number of pupils	Total number of students	Total number of pupils and students	Educational expenditure in 1985 prices £ millions	Educational expenditure per pupil/student £s (constant prices)
1970	9,327,100	207,100	11,398,100	13,908	1,220
1971	9,566,700	206,000	11,626,700	14,672	1,260
1972	9,829,600	208,300	11,912,600	15,982	1,340
1973	10,006,700	209,700	12,103,700	16,292	1,340
1974	10,422,700	214,700	12,569,700	17,565	1,390
1975	10,501,800	223,700	12,738,800	18,265	1,430
1976	10,575,900	221,600	12,701,900	17,780	1,390
1977	10,586,200	208,700	12,673,200	16,710	1,320
1978	10,490,200	218,400	12,674,200	16,625	1,310
1979	10,353,900	209,400	12,447,900	16,719	1,340
1980	10,770,900	209,200	12,862,900	17,657	1,370
1981	10,525,300	213,600	12,661,300	17,285	1,360
1982	10,234,700	219,300	12,427,700	17,383	1,390
1983	9,949,700	230,200	12,251,700	17,558	1,430
1984	9,724,700	235,400	12,078,700	17,330	1,430
1985	9,544,300	241,900	11,963,300	17,232	1,440
1986	9,384,800	248,200	11,866,800	17,981	1,510

Notes
1. Pupil totals (columns 2 and 4) comprise full-time and part-time equivalent of full-time pupils. Students (Columns 3 and 4) defined as students in further education at major establishments (full-time and sandwich, part-time day and evening, autumn term). Students attending adult education centres are excluded.
2. Deflator = Implicit Deflator arising from total domestic expenditure.

Source: CSO, *National Income and Expenditure*; CSO, *Annual Abstract of Statistics*.

Bibliography

1 Books and Pamphlets

Addison, Paul, *The Road to 1945*, 1975.

Aldridge, Richard, and Leighton, Margaret, *Education: Time for a New Act?*, 1985.

Alexander, Sir William, *Towards a New Education Act*, 1969.

Armstrong, Michael, and Young, Michael, *The Flexible School*, 1966.

Ashby, Eric, and Anderson, Mary, *The Rise of the Student Estate in Britain*, 1970

Assistant Masters, Incorporated Association of, *Teaching in Comprehensive Schools, a second report*, 1967.

Association of Directors and Secretaries of Education, *A Plan for Education*, 1942.

Association of University Teachers, *Submissions to the Committee on Higher Education*, 1961.

Auld, Robin, *William Tyndale Junior and Infant Schools Public Enquiry*, 1976.

Bantock, G.H., *Education in an Industrial Society*, 1963.

Bantock, G.H., *Education and Values: Essays in the Theory of Education*, 1965.

Barker, Rodney, *Education and Politics 1900–1951, a Study of the Labour Party*, 1972.

Barnett, Corelli, *The Audit of War*, 1986.

Bates, I. *et al.* (eds.), *Schooling on the Dole? The New Vocationalism*, 1984.

Beales, A.C.F. *et al.*, *Education. A Framework for Choice*, 1967.

Bell, David, S., *The Conservative Government 1979–84*, 1985.

Bell, Robert and Prescott, William (eds.), *The Schools Council: A Second Look*, 1975.

Benn, Caroline and Simon, Brian, *Half Way There*, 2nd edn., 1972.

Benn, Tony, *Office Without Power, Diaries 1968–72*, 1988.

Bennett, Neville, *Teaching Styles and Pupil Progress*, 1976.

Best, Geoffrey, *Mid-Victorian Britain, 1851–1875*, 1973.

Blackburn, Fred, *George Tomlinson*, 1954.

Blackie, John, *Good Enough for the Children?*, 1963.

Blackie, John, *Inside the Primary School*, 1967.

Blackie, John, *Changing the Primary School: an integrated approach*, 1974.

Blaug, Mark, Peston, Maurice and Ziderman, Adrian, *The Utilisation of Educational Manpower in Industry, A Preliminary Report*, 1967.

Bourdieu, Pierre and Passeron, Jean-Claude, *Reproduction in Education, Society and Culture* (trans. Richard Nice), 1977.

Brown, Mary and Precious, Norman, *The Integrated Day in the Primary School*, 1975.

Browne, Joan, 'The Transformation of the Education of Teachers in the 1960s' in Fearn, Edward and Simon, Brian (eds.), *Education in the Sixties*, 1980.

Buckmaster, Clive, *Hiccoughs in Education*, 1970.

Bullock, Sir Alan, *The Life and Times of Ernest Bevin*, Vol.1, *Trade Union Leader*, 1960.

Burke, Vincent, *Teachers in Turmoil*, 1971.

Burt, Cyril (ed.), *How the Mind Works*, 1933.

Butler, David and Butler, Gareth, *British Political Facts, 1900–1985*, 6th ed., 1986.

Butler, Lord, *The Art of the Possible*, 1971.

Butler, Lord, *The Art of Memory*, 1982.

Cairncross, Alec, *Years of Recovery, 1945–51*, 1984.

Calder, Angus, *The People's War, Britain 1939–45*, 1969.

Cantor, Leonard, 'Public Sector Higher Education: 1945–85' in Stewart, W.A.C., *Higher Education in Postwar Britain*, 1989.

Carswell, John, *Government and the Universities in Britain*, 1985.

Castle, Barbara, *The Castle Diaries, 1964–70*, 1984.

Centre for Conflict Studies, *The Attack on Higher Education*, 1987.

Centre for Contemporary Cultural Studies, *Unpopular Education, Schooling and Social Democracy in England since 1944*, 1981.

Chitty, Clyde, *Towards a New Educational System: A Victory for the New Right?*, 1989.

Clarke, Fred, *Education and Social Change*, 1940.

Clegg, A.B., *The Excitement of Writing*, 1966.

Cockburn, Alexander and Blackburn, Robin (eds.), *Student Power*, 1969.

Cole, Margaret, *What is a Comprehensive School? The London Plan in Practice*, n.d.(1955?).

Communist Party of Great Britain, *Britain's Schools*, n.d.(1943).

Communist Party, *Higher Education in the Nuclear Age, A Communist Plan*, n.d.(1958).

Communist Party, *The Development of Higher Education in Britain*, 1961.

Conservative Party Sub-Committee on Education,
Looking Ahead (first interim report), September 1942.
A Plan for Youth (second interim report), September 1942.
The Statutory Education System (third report), January 1944.

Cooke, George and Gosden, Peter, *Education Committees*, 1986.

Co-operative Union, war-time booklets No.1, John Thomas, *Plans for an Educated Democracy*, 1942.

Corbett, Anne, 'Teachers and the Schools Council' in Bell and Prescott (eds.), op.cit.

Cosgrave, Patrick, *Margaret Thatcher, a Tory and her Party*, 1978.

Council for the Democratic Reconstruction of Education, *A Democratic Reconstruction of Education*, 1942.

Cox, Brian and Dyson, A.E. (eds.),
Black Paper 1, *Fight for Education*, March 1969.
Black Paper 2, *The Crisis in Education*, October 1969.
Black Paper 3, *Goodbye Mr. Short*, November 1970.

Cox, C.B. and Boyson, Rhodes (eds.),
Black Paper 4, *The Fight for Education*, 1975.
Black Paper 5, *Black Paper 1977*, March 1977.

Crosby, Travis L., *The Impact of Civilian Evacuation in the Second World War*, 1986.

Crosland, C.A.R., *The Future of Socialism*, 1956.

Crosland, C.A.R., *The Conservative Enemy*, 1962.

Crosland, Susan, *Tony Crosland*, 1982.

Crossman, Richard, *The Diaries of a Cabinet Minister*,
Vol.I, *Minister of Housing, 1964–66*, 1975.
Vol.II, *Lord President of the Council and Leader of the House of Commons, 1966–68*, 1976.
Vol.III, *Secretary of State for Social Services, 1968–70*, 1977.

Cruickshank, Marjorie, *Church and State in English Education*, 1963.

Cunningham, Peter, *Curriculum Change in the Primary School since 1945*, 1988.

Curtis, S.J., *Education in Britain Since 1900*, 1952.

Dancy, J.C., *The Public Schools and the Future*, 1963.

Davies, Hunter, *The Creighton Story*, 1976.

Dennison, W.F., *Education in Jeopardy, Problems and Possibilities of Contraction*, 1981.

Dent, H.C., *A New Order in English Education*, 1942.

Dent, H.C., *The New Education Bill, what it contains, what it means, and why it should be supported*, 1944.

Dent, H.C., *Education in Transition*, 1944.

Dent, H.C., *Secondary Education for All*, 1949.

Devlin, Tim and Warnock, Mary, *What Must we Teach?*, 1977.

Dienes, Z.P., *Mathematics in Primary Education*, 1966.

Douglas, J.W.B., *The Home and the School*, 1964.

Edwards, E.G., *Higher Education for Everyone*, 1982.

Edwards, Tony, Fitz, John and Whitty, Geoff, *The State and Private Education: An Evaluation for the Assisted Places Scheme*, 1989.

Eliot, T.S., *Notes Towards a Definition of Culture*, 1949.

Ellis, Terry, McWhirter, Jackie, McColgan, Dorothy and Haddow, Brian, *William Tyndale, The Teachers' Story*, 1976.

Eyken, William Van Der and Turner, Barry, *Adventures in Education*, 1969.

Fenwick, I.G.K., *The Comprehensive School 1944–1970*, 1976.

Fenwick, Keith and McBride, Peter, *The Government of Education*, 1981.

Fieldhouse, Roger T., *Adult Education and the Cold War*, 1985.

Fisher, Peter, *External Examinations in Secondary Schools in England and Wales, 1944–1964*, 1982.

Flew, Anthony, *Power to the Parents: reversing educational decline*, 1987.

Floud, Jean, 'Karl Mannheim' in Raison, Timothy (ed.), *The Founding Fathers of Social Science*, 1969.

Floud, J., Halsey, A.H. and Martin, F.M., *Social Class and Educational Opportunity*, 1956.

Ford, Julienne, *Social Class and the Comprehensive School*, 1969.

Freeland, George, 'Purpose and Method in the Unstreamed Junior School', in Simon, Brian (ed.), *Non-Streaming in the Junior School*, 1964.

Furneaux, W.D., *The Chosen Few. An Examination of Some Aspects of University Selection in Britain*, 1961.

Galton, Maurice, *Teaching in the Primary School*, 1989

Galton, Maurice, Simon, Brian and Croll, Paul, *Inside the Primary Classroom*, 1980.

Gamble, Andrew, *The Free Economy and the Strong State: the Politics of Thatcherism*, 1988.

Gardner, D.E.M., *Susan Isaacs, the First Biography*, 1969.

Giles, G.C.T., *The New School Tie*, 1946.

Gipps, Caroline and Goldstein, Harvey, *Monitoring Children: an evaluation of the Assessment of Performance Unit*, 1983.

Gladstone, Francis, *Charity, Law and Social Justice*, 1982.

Gordon, Peter, Aldrich, Richard and Dean, Dennis, *Education and Policy in the Twentieth Century*, forthcoming.

Gosden, P.H.J.H., *The Evolution of a Profession*, 1972.

Gosden, P.H.J.H., *Education in the Second World War*, 1976.

Gosden, P.H.J.H., and Sharp, P.R., *The Development of an Education Service, the West Riding, 1889-1974*, 1978

Gosden, Peter, *The Education System Since 1944*, 1983.

Gosden, Peter, 'Education Policy, 1979-84' in Bell, David S. (ed.), *The Conservative Government, 1979-84*, 1985.

Gould, Ronald, *Chalk Up the Memory; the autobiography of Sir Ronald Gould*, 1976.

Grace, Gerald, *Teachers, Ideology and Control*, 1978.

Grant, Neil, 'Citizen Soldiers: Army Education in World War II' in Formation Editorial Collective, *Formation of Nation and People*, 1984.

Green, Andrew, *Education and State Formation*, 1990.

Greenough, A. and Crofts, F.A., *Theory and Practice in the New Secondary Schools*, 1949.

Gretton, John and Jackson, Mark, *William Tyndale: Collapse of a School or System*, 1976.

Griffin-Beale, Christopher (ed.), *Christian Schiller in His Own Words*, 1979.

Hailsham, Lord, *The Door Wherein I Went*, 1975.

Halcrow, Morrison, *Keith Joseph: a Single Mind*, 1989.

Halsey, A.H. (ed.), *Ability and Educational Opportunity*, 1961.
Halsey, A.H. *Educational Priority, EPA Problems and Policies*, Vol.I, 1972.

Halsey, A.H., Floud, J., and Anderson, C. Arnold (eds.), *Education, Economy and Society*, 1961.

Hargreaves, Andy and Reynolds, David (eds.), *Education Policies: Controversies and Critiques*, 1989.

Hargreaves, David H., *Social Relations in a Secondary School*, 1967.

Hargreaves, David H., *The Challenge for the Comprehensive School; Culture, Curriculum and Community*, 1982.

Harris, Jose, 'Political Ideas and Social Change' in Smith, Harold L. (ed.), *War and Social Change*, 1986.

Haviland, Julian (ed.), *Take Care, Mr. Baker!*, 1988.

Hearnshaw, L.S., *Cyril Burt, Psychologist*, 1979.

Hencke, David, *Colleges in Crisis*, 1978.

Hennessy, Peter and Seldon, Anthony (eds.), *Ruling Performance, British Governments from Attlee to Thatcher*, 1987.

Hewton, Eric, *Education in Recession, Crisis in County Hall and*

Classroom, 1986.

Hillgate Group, *No Turning Back*, 1985.

Hillgate Group, *Whose Schools?*, 1986.

Hoffman, J.D., *Tories in Opposition, 1945–51*, 1964.

Holly, Douglas, *Society, Schools and Humanity*, 1971.

Holly, Douglas, *Beyond Curriculum*, 1973.

Horne, Alistair, *Macmillan, 1957–1986*, Vol.II, 1989.

Hough, J.R., *Education and the National Economy*, 1987.

Howard, Anthony, *RAB, the Life of R.A. Butler*, 1987.

Hurd Douglas, *An End to Promises*, 1979.

Incorporated Association of Assistant Masters, *Memorandum on the Education Bill*, n.d. (1943?).

Inglis, Ruth, *The Children's War*, 1989.

Jackson, Brian and Marsden, Dennis, *Education and the Working Class*, 1962.

Jackson, Brian, *Streaming: an Education System in Miniature*, 1964.

Jackson, Brian and McAhone, Beryl, *Verdict on the Facts*, 1969.

James, Eric, *The Content of Education*, 1949.

James, Eric, *Education for Leadership*, 1951.

James, H. Philip, *The Reorganisation of Secondary Education*, 1980.

James, Robert Rhodes, *Anthony Eden*, 1986.

Jenkins, Peter, *Mrs Thatcher's Revolution*, 1987.

Jones, Donald K., 'Planning for Progressivism: the Changing Primary School in the Leicestershire Authority during the Mason Era' in Lowe, R. (ed.), *The Changing Primary School*, 1987.

Jones, Donald K., *Stewart Mason, the Art of Education*, 1988.

Jones, Ken, *Right Turn: The Conservative Revolution in Education*, 1989

Joseph, Sir Keith, *Reversing the Trend: a Critical Re-Appraisal of Conservative Economic and Social Policies*, 1975.

Joseph, Sir Keith, *Stranded on the Middle Ground? Reflections on Circumstances and Policies*, 1976.

Joseph, Keith and Sumption, J., *Equality*, 1979.

Joynson, Robert B., *The Burt Affair*, 1989.

Judge, Harry, *A Generation of Schooling*, 1984.

Kavanagh, Dennis, 'The Heath Government, 1970–1974' in Hennessy and Seldon (eds.), op.cit.

Kettler, David, Meja, Volker and Stehr, Nico, *Karl Mannheim*, 1984.

Kogan, Maurice, *The Politics of Education*, 1971.

Kogan, Maurice, *Educational Policy-Making: a study of interest groups and Parliament*, 1975.

Kogan, Maurice, *The Politics of Educational Change*, 1978.
Kogan, Maurice, *Education Accountability, an analytic overview*, 1986.
Knight, Christopher, *The Making of Tory Education Policy in Post-War Britain*, 1990.

Laban, Rudolf, *Modern Educational Dance*, 1948.
Labour Party, *Learning to Live*, 1958.
Labour Party, *The Years of Crisis, Report of the Labour Party's Study Group on Higher Education*, n.d.(1963).
Lacey, Colin, *High Town Grammar: the school as a social system*, 1970.
Lamb, Richard, *The Eden Government*.
Lawton, Denis, *The Politics of the School Curriculum*, 1980.
Lawton, Denis, *The Tightening Grip, growth of central control of the school curriculum*, 1984.
Layard, Richard, King, John and Moser, Claus, *The Impact of Robbins*, 1969.
Loader, Colin, *The Intellectual Development of Karl Mannheim*, 1985.
London County Council, *London Comprehensive Schools: a survey of sixteen schools*, 1961.
Lowe, Roy (ed.), *The Changing Primary School*, 1987.
Lowe, Roy, *Education in the Post-War Years: a social history*, 1988.
Lowe, Roy (ed.), *The Changing Secondary School*, 1989.
Lowndes, G.A.N., *The Silent Social Revolution, an account of the expansion of public education in England and Wales 1895–1965*, 2nd edition 1969.
Lunn, Joan C. Barker, *Streaming in the Primary School*, 1970.
Luria, A.R. and Yudovich, F. Ia., *Speech and the Development of the Mental Processes in the Child* (ed. and trans. by Joan Simon), 1959.

MacArthur, Brian, 'The Education Debate' in McKie, David and Cook, Chris (eds.), *The Decade of Disillusion: British Politics in the Sixties*, 1972.
Macdonald, Iverach, *History of The Times*, Vol. V., 1984.
Mack, E.C., *Public Schools and British Opinion Since 1860*, 1941.
Maclure, Stuart, *One Hundred Years of London Education 1870–1970*, 1970.
Maclure, J. Stuart, *Education Documents*, 4th edn., 1979.
Maclure, Stuart, *Educational Development and School Building: Aspects of Public Policy, 1945–73*, 1984.
Maclure, Stuart, *Education Re-formed, a Guide to the Education Reform Act 1988*, 1989.
MacNicol, John, 'The Effect of Evacuation of Schoolchildren on

Official Attitudes to State Intervention' in Smith, Harold L. (ed.), *War and Social Change*, 1986.

Manzer, Ronald, 'The Secret Garden of the Curriculum' in Bell and Prescott (eds.), op.cit.

Marsden, Dennis, *Politics, Equality and Comprehensives*, 1971.

Marshall, Sybil, *An Experiment in Education*, 1963.

Martin, F.M., 'An Enquiry into Parents' Preferences in Secondary Education' in Glass, D.V. (ed.), *Social Mobility in Britain*, 1954.

Mason, S.C., *The Leicestershire Experiment and Plan*, 1960.

Mason, S.C. (ed.), *In Our Experience*, 1970.

McCallum, R.B. and Readman, A., *The British General Election of 1945*, 1947.

McKie, David and Cook, Chris (eds.), *The Decade of Disillusion: British Politics in the Sixties*, 1972.

McLachlan, Donald, *In the Chair. Barrington-Ward of The Times, 1927–1948*, 1971.

McPherson, Andrew and Raab, Charles, *Governing Education: a Sociology of Policy Since 1945*, 1989.

Middleton, Nigel and Weitzman, Sophia, *A Place for Everyone*, 1976.

Minney, R.J., *The Private Papers of Hore-Belisha*, 1960.

Mitchell, F.W., *Sir Fred Clarke, Master-Teacher 1880–1952*, 1957.

Monks, T.G. (ed.), *Comprehensive Education in England and Wales*, 1969.

Monks, T.G. (ed.), *Comprehensive Education in Action*, 1970.

Moodie, Graeme C., *The Universities: a Royal Commission?* 1959.

Moon, Bob, *The 'New Maths' Curriculum Controversy, an International Story*, 1987.

Moorhouse, Edith, *A Personal Story of Oxfordshire Primary Schools*, 1985.

Morgan, Kenneth, *Labour in Power 1945–51*, 1984.

Morris, M. and Griggs, C. (eds.), *Education – The Wasted Years? 1973–1986*, 1988.

Mountford, Sir James, *Keele, an Historical Critique*, 1972.

Müller, D.K., Ringer, Fritz and Simon, Brian (eds.), *The Rise of the Modern Educational System*, 1987.

Murphy, James, *Church, State and Schools in Britain, 1800–1970*, 1971.

Musgrove, Frank, 'The Black Paper Movement' in Lowe, R., (ed.), *The Changing Primary School*, 1987.

National Association of Labour Teachers, *The Post-War Reconstruction of Education*, 1941.

National Association of Schoolmasters, 'The Postwar Reconstruction of Education', n.d. (1942) (Mimeo, DES library).

National Union of Students, *Memorandum to the Committee on Higher Education*, 1961.

National Union of Teachers, *Inside the Comprehensive School*, n.d. (1958).

No Turning Back Group, *SOS: Save Our Schools*, 1986.

O'Connor, Neil, *Speech and Thought in Severe Subnormality, an experimental study*, 1963.

Parker, H.M.D., *A Study of Wartime Policy and Administration*, 1957.

Parkinson, Michael, *The Labour Party and the Organisation of Secondary Education, 1918–1965*, 1965.

Pedley, Robin, *Comprehensive Schools Today*, n.d.(1955)?

Pedley, Robin, *Comprehensive Education, a new approach*, 1956.

Pedley, Robin, *The Comprehensive School*, 1963.

Perry, Walter, *Open University, a personal account by the first Vice Chancellor*, 1976.

Peston, Maurice and Corry, Bernard (eds.), *Essays in Honour of Lord Robbins*, 1972.

Peston, Maurice, *Public Goods and the Public Sector*, 1972.

Petch, J.A., *Fifty Years of Examining: the Joint Matriculation Board, 1903–1953*, 1953.

Peters, R.S. (ed.), *Perspectives on Plowden*, 1969.

Pile, W., *The Department of Education and Science*, 1979.

Plaskow, Maurice (ed.), *Life and Death of the Schools Council*, 1985.

Pollard, Sidney, *The Development of the British Economy, 1914–67*, 2nd edn., 1969.

Potter, F.F., *Educational Journey, Memories of Fifty Years in Public Education*, 1949.

PSW (Educational) Publications, *Indictment of Margaret Thatcher*, 1973.

Ranson, Stewart, 'Towards a Tertiary Tripartism: new codes of social control and the 17-plus' in Broadfoot, Patricia (ed.), *Selection, Certification and Control*, 1984.

Ranson, Stewart, *The Politics of Reorganising Schools*, 1990.

Redcliffe-Maud, Lord, *Experiences of an Optimist, the memoirs of John Redcliffe-Maud*, 1981.

Rée, Harry, *The Essential Grammar School*, 1956.

Reynolds, David and Sullivan, Michael, *The Comprehensive Experiment, a comparison of the selective and non-selective system of school organisation*, 1987.

Richmond, W. Kenneth, *The Literature of Education: a critical bibliography 1945–1970*, 1972.

Richmond, W. Kenneth, *Education in Britain since 1944: a personal retrospect*, 1978.

Ridgeway, Lorna and Lawton, Irene, *Family Grouping in the Infants' School*, 1965.

Robbins, Lord, *The University in the Modern World*, 1966.

Rogers, Vincent (ed.), *Teaching in the British Primary School*, 1970.

Rowan, P., 'Special Schools', in Morris and Griggs (eds.), op.cit.

Rubinstein, David, and Simon, Brian, *The Evolution of the Comprehensive School, 1926–72*, 2nd edn., 1973.

Saint, Andrew, *Towards a Social Architecture, the Role of School Building in Post-War England*, 1987.

Salter, Brian and Tapper, Ted, *Education and the Political Order*, 1978.

Salter, Brian and Tapper, Ted, *Education, Politics and the State*, 1981.

Saran, Rene, *Policy Making in Secondary Education: a case study*, 1973.

Scott, Peter, *The Crisis of the Universities*, 1984.

Scott, Peter, 'Higher Education' in Morris and Griggs, op.cit.

Seaborne, Malcolm and Lowe, Roy, *The English School, its architecture and organisation*, Vol.II, *1870–1970*, 1977.

Seifert, Roger V., *Teacher Militancy, a history of teacher strikes 1896–1987*, 1987.

Seldon, Anthony, *Churchill's Indian Summer, The Conservative Government 1951-55*, 1981.

Seldon, Arthur, *The Riddle of the Voucher*, 1986.

Selleck, R.J.W., *English Primary Education and the Progressives 1914–1939*, 1972.

Semmel, B., *Imperialism and Social Reform*, 1960.

Silberman, Charles E., *Crisis in the Classroom*, 1970.

Silver, Harold, *A Higher Education: the Council for National Academic Awards*, 1990.

Simon, Brian, *A Student's View of the University*, 1943.

Simon, Brian, *Intelligence Testing and the Comprehensive School*, 1953.

Simon, Brian, *The Common Secondary School*, 1955.

Simon, Brian (ed.), *New Trends in English Education*, 1957.

Simon, Brian, *The Two Nations and the Educational Structure, 1780–1870*, (first published as *Studies in the History of Education, 1780–1870*, 1960).

Simon, Brian and Simon, Joan (eds.), *Educational Psychology in the USSR*, 1963.

Simon, Brian, *Intelligence, Psychology and Education, a Marxist critique*, 1971.

Simon, Brian, 'Education in Leicestershire', in Pye, N. (ed.), *Leicester and its Region*, 1972.

Simon, Brian, *The Politics of Educational Reform, 1920–1940*, 1974.

Simon, Brian (ed.), *Margaret Gracie, a teacher for our time*, 1983.

Simon, Brian, 'The Primary School Revolution: Myth or Reality?', in Simon, Brian and Willcocks, John (eds.), *Research and Practice in the Primary Classroom*, 1981.

Simon, Brian, *Does Education Matter?*, 1985.

Simon, Brian, *Bending the Rules, the Baker 'Reform' of Education*, 1988.

Simon, of Wythenshawe, Lady, *Three Schools or One?*, 1948.

Spender, Dale, *Learning to Lose*, 1980.

Spooner, Robert, 'Secondary Schools', in Morris and Griggs, op.cit.

Stewart, Michael, *Life and Labour*, 1980.

Stewart, W.A.C., *Higher Education in Postwar Britain*, 1989.

Stocks, Mary, *Ernest Simon of Wythenshawe*, 1963.

Students and staff of the Hornsey College of Art, *The Hornsey Affair*, 1969.

Tanner, Robin, *Double Harness, An Autobiography by Robin Tanner, Teacher and Etcher*, 1987.

Taylor, L.C., *Resources for Learning*, 1971.

Taylor, William, *The Secondary Modern School*, 1963.

Thompson, Joan, *Secondary Education for All*, 1947.

Thornbury, R.E., *Teachers' Centres*, 1973.

Tibble, J.W. (ed.), *The Study of Education*, 1966.

Titmuss, Richard, *Problems of Social Policy*, 1950.

Torrance, Harry (ed.), *National Assessment and Testing: a Research Response*, 1988.

Trades Union Congress, *Memorandum on Education After the War*, 1942.

Travers, Tony, *The Politics of Local Government Finance*, 1986.

Vaizey, John, *The Costs of Education*, 1958.

Vaizey, John, *Education for Tomorrow*, 1962.

Vaizey, John, *Education in the Modern World*, 1967.

Vaizey, J. and Sheehan, J., *Resources for Education*, 1968.

Vaizey, John, *In Breach of Promise*, 1983.

Vernon, Betty D., *Ellen Wilkinson*, 1982.

Vernon, P.E. (ed.), *Secondary School Selection*, 1957.

Vigotski, L.S., *Thought and Language*, 1962.

Vincent, John, 'The Thatcher Governments' in Hennessy and Seldon (eds.), op.cit.

Walford, Geoffrey (ed.), *British Public Schools: policy and practice*, 1984.

Watts, John (ed.), *The Countesthorpe Experience*, 1977.

Weber, Lillian, *The English Infant School and Informal Education*, 1971.

White, John, 'The End of the Compulsory Curriculum' in *The Curriculum: The Doris Lee Lectures*, 1975.

White, John, 'Instruction or Obedience' in Bell and Prescott (eds.), op.cit.

Whitehead, Phillip, *The Writing on the Wall: Britain in the 70s*, 1985.

Whitehead, Phillip, 'The Labour Governments, 1974–1979', in Hennesy and Seldon (eds.), op.cit.

Whitty, Geoff, Fitz, John and Edwards, Tony, 'Assisting Whom? Benefits and Costs of the Assisted Places Scheme', in Hargreaves and Reynolds (eds.), op.cit.

Williams, Ian, *The Alms Trade. Charities, Past, Present and Future*, 1989.

Willis, P., *Learning to Labour: How Working Class Kids Get Working Class Jobs*, 1977.

Wilkinson, Max, *Lessons from Europe. A Comparison of British and West European Schooling*, 1977.

Wilson, Martin, *Epoch in English Education, Administrator's Challenge*, 1984.

Wilson, N. Scarlyn, *Education in the Forces, 1936–46. The Civilian Contribution*, n.d. (1948–49?).

Wilson, Percy, *Views and Prospects from Curzon Street*, 1961.

Wolpe, Ann Marie and Donald, James (eds.), *Is There Anyone Here From Education?*, 1983.

Woods, D., *The Divided School*, 1979.

Woolnough, Peter E., *Physics Teaching in Schools, 1960–85*, 1988.

Workers' Educational Association, *Plan for Education*, 1942.

Worsley, T.C., *Barbarians and Philistines: Democracy and the Public Schools*, 1940.

Worsley, T.C., *The End of the 'Old School Tie'*, 1941.

Worsley, T.C., *Flanelled Fools*, 1967.

Wrigley, Jack, 'Confessions of a Curriculum Man' in Plaskow, M. (ed.), op.cit.

Yates, Alfred and Pidgeon, D.A., *Admission to Grammar Schools*, 1957.

Young, Hugo, *One of Us*, 1989.

Young, Michael, *The Rise of the Meritocracy*, 1961.

Young, Michael F.D., 'On the Politics of Educational Knowledge: some preliminary considerations with particular reference to the

Schools Council' in Bell and Prescott (eds.), op.cit.
Young, Michael F.D. (ed.), *Knowledge and Control*, 1971.

2 *Articles*

Aitken, M., Bennett, S.N., and Hesketh, J., 'Teaching Styles and Pupil Progress: a reanalysis', *British Journal of Educational Psychology*, Vol.51, 1981.

Bailey, Bill, 'The Development of Technical Education, 1934–39', *History of Education*, Vol.16, No.1, 1987.
Barlow, Norman, 'TRIST and the Future of In-Service Training', *Forum*, Vol.22, No.2, 1980.
Bealing, Deanne, 'The Organisation of Junior School Classrooms', *Educational Research*, Vol.14, 1972.
Benn, Caroline, 'Reorganisations: the State of Play', *Comprehensive Education*, No.3, 1966.
Benn, Caroline, 'A New Education Act?', *Forum*, Vol.11, No.3, 1969.
Benn, Caroline, 'Making the Most of RSLA', *Secondary Education*, Vol.1, No.3, 1971.
Benn, Caroline, 'The New 11-plus for the Old Divided System', *Forum*, Vol.22, No.2, 1980.
Benn, Caroline, 'Comprehensive School Reform and the 1945 Labour Government', *History Workshop Journal*, No.10, 1980.
Benn, Caroline, 'The Myth of Giftedness', *Forum*, Vol.24, No.2, 1982.
Blishen, Edward, 'Conference on Non-Streaming', *Forum*, Vol.5, No.2, 1963.
Blishen, Edward, 'What Happened to Reality? Forum's demonstrative conference in opposition to the Education "Reform Bill" ', *Forum*, Vol.30, No.3.
Boyle, Edward, 'The Politics of Secondary Schools Reorganisation: some reflections', *Journal of Educational Administration and History*, Vol.4, No.2, 1982.
Burt, Cyril, 'The Education of the Young Adolescent: The Psychological Implications of the Norwood Report', *British Journal of Educational Psychology*, Vol.13, Part 3, November 1943.
Burt, Cyril, 'An Enquiry into Public Opinion Regarding Educational Reform', *Occupational Psychology*, Part 1, Vol.17, 1943; Part 2, Vol.18, 1943.

Chitty, Clyde, 'Central Control of the School Curriculum', *History of*

Education, Vol.17, No.4, 1988.

Chitty, Clyde, 'City Technology Colleges, a strategy for elitism', *Forum*, Vol.31, No.2, 1989.

Clarke, Fred, 'Educational Research in the New Setting' *British Journal of Educational Psychology*, Vol.XIV, Part 1, 1944.

Clegg, Alec, 'Teamwork and Beauty', *Times Educational Supplement*, 20 September 1974.

Clegg, Alec, 'A Subtler and More Telling Power', *Times Educational Supplement*, 27 September 1974.

Clegg, A.B., 'Some Problems of Administration in West Riding Grammar Schools', *Researches and Studies*, No.7, January 1953.

Cooke, George, 'Too Tough at the Top', *Times Educational Supplement*, 1 February 1980.

Corbett, Anne, 'Education, How Balanced?', *New Society*, 25 July 1968.

Dean, D.W., 'Problems of the Conservative Sub-Committee on Education, 1941–45', *Journal of Educational Administration and History*, Vol.III, No.1, December 1970.

Dean, D.W., 'Planning for a Postwar Generation: Ellen Wilkinson and George Tomlinson at the Ministry of Education, 1945–51', *History of Education*, Vol.15, No.2, 1986.

Dixon, Angela, 'Keith Joseph and the Science Criteria', *Forum*, Vol.26, No.3, 1984.

Donnison, David, 'A Comprehensive Role for the Independent Schools', *Times*, 23 July 1970.

Dyhouse, Carol, 'Towards a "Feminine" Curriculum for English Schoolgirls: the Demands of Ideology, 1870–1963,' *Women's Studies International Quarterly*, Vol.1.

Floud, Jean, 'Further Memorandum', *Higher Education* (the Robbins Report), *Evidence*, Part Two.

Gamble, Andrew, 'Westland Fallout', *Marxism Today*, March 1986.

Gipps, Caroline, 'Differentiation in the GCSE', *Forum*, Vol.29, No.3, 1987.

Gipps, Caroline, 'The TGAT Report: Trick or Treat?', *Forum*, Vol.31, No.1, 1988.

Goldstücker, Eduard, 'Youth Separated by Thirty Years, an autobiographical account of the similarities and differences between the young people of the 1930s and those of the 1960s', *The Center Magazine*, Santa Barbara, California Vol.VI, July/August 1973.

Gosden, P.H.J.H., 'From Board to Ministry: The impact of the war on the Education Department', *History of Education*, Vol.18, No.3.

Hall, Jackson, 'The Centralist Tendency', *Forum*, Vol.28, No.1, 1985.

Halsey, A.H., and Gardner, L., 'Selection for Secondary Education', *British Journal of Sociology*, March 1953.

Halsey, A.H., 'The Public Schools Debacle', *New Society*, 25 July 1968.

Haywood, Roy, and Wootten, Mary, 'The Gateshead LAPP: Pre-vocational Education in a Cold Climate, *Forum*, Vol.29, No.3, 1987.

Heaton, Neville, 'Forty Years On', *Times Educational Supplement*, 28 August 1984.

Hobby, B.F., 'Report from the West Midlands', *Forum*, Vol.1, No.3, 1959.

Hughes, H.D., 'In Defence of Ellen Wilkinson', *History Workshop Journal*, No.7, 1979.

Huxley, Julian, 'Philosophy of the Norwood Report', *Times Educational Supplement*, 28 August 1943.

Jefferys, Kevin, 'R.A. Butler, the Board of Education and the 1944 Education Act, *History*, 69 (227), 1984.

Johnson, R., 'Thatcherism and English Education: Breaking the Mould, or Confirming the Pattern?', *History of Education*, Vol.18, No.2, 1989.

Kerr, John F., 'Introducing the Schools Council', *Forum*, Vol.9, No.1, 1966.

King Raymond, 'The London School Plan: The Present Stage', *Forum*, Vol.1, No.1, 1958.

Knowlson, H., 'Report from Bristol and the West', *Forum*, Vol.2, No.3, 1960.

Kogan, Maurice, 'The Plowden Report Twenty Years on', *Oxford Review of Education*, Vol.13, No.1, 1987.

Lovett, T., 'Comprehensive Years – Progressive Differentiation', *Times Educational Supplement*, 27 January 1956.

Marsden, Dennis, 'Which Comprehensive Principle?', *Comprehensive Education*, No.13, 1969.

Marshall, T.H., 'Up and Down the Social Scale', *Times Educational Supplement*, 20 August 1954.

McMullen, I., 'Flexibility for a Comprehensive School', *Forum*, Vol.10, No.2, 1968.

McMullen, I., 'Countesthorpe College, Leicestershire', *Forum*, Vol.14, No.2, 1972.

Moran, P.R., 'The Integrated Day', *Educational Research*, Vol.14, 1971.

O'Connor, Maureen, 'Old School Eyewash', *Guardian*, 3 May 1988.

Pedley, Robin, 'Report from Yorkshire', *Forum*, Vol.2, No.1, 1959.

Pinder, Ray, 'Non-Streaming in Comprehensive Schools', *Forum*, Vol.9, No.1, 1966.

Plowden, Bridget, ' "Plowden" Twenty Years On', *Oxford Review of Education*, Vol.13, No.1, 1987.

Price, Christopher, 'MPs and the Campus Revolt', *New Statesman*, 17 October 1969.

Price, Paul, 'Comprehensive reorganisation and the direct grant grammar schools', *Aspects of Education*, 1986.

Raven, James, 'British History and the Enterprise Culture', *Past and Present*, No.123, 1989.

Richer, Michael, 'Parent Power and Selection at Solihull', *Forum*, Vol.27, No.1, 1984.

Rogers, Rick, 'CASE for Revival', *Times Educational Supplement*, 13 January 1980.

Rowan, Patricia, 'Out of the Shade', 75th Anniversary number of the *Times Educational Supplement*, 1985.

Rubinstein, David, 'Ellen Wilkinson Reconsidered', *History Workshop Journal*, No.7, 1979.

Scott, Peter, 'The prophet who had his way', *Times Higher Educational Supplement*, 10 February 1978.

Simon, Brian, 'The Study of Education as a University Subject', *Studies in Higher Education*, Vol.8, No.1, 1983.

Simon, Brian, 'The Student Movement in England and Wales during the 1930s', *History of Education*, Vol.16, No.3, 1987.

Simon, Joan, 'Report from South Wales', *Forum*, Vol.1, No.2, 1959.

Simon, Joan, 'The Swing Towards Comprehensive Education: Sheffield and Bradford', *Forum*, Vol.6, No.3, 1964.

Simon, Joan, 'The Swing Towards Comprehensive Education, 2, Lancashire', *Forum*, Vol.7, No.2, 1965.

Simon, Joan, 'Education, Morality and the Market', *Forum*, Vol.25, No.3, 1983.

Simon, Joan, 'Promoting Educational Reform on the Home Front: *The TES* and *The Times*, 1940–44', *History of Education*, Vol.18, No.3, 1989.

Simon, Lord, 'A Royal Commission for the Universities?', *Universities Quarterly*, Vol.XIII, No.1, 1958.

Smith, George, 'Whatever Happened to Educational Priority Areas?', *Oxford Review of Education*, Vol.13, No.1, 1987.

Straubenzee, Sir William Van, 'My Mistress Margaret', *Times Educational Supplement*, 12 June 1987.

Straw, Jack, 'Student Participation in Higher Education', Granada Guildhall Lecture, 6 October 1969 (mimeo).

Summerfield, Penelope, 'Education and Politics in the British Armed Forces in the Second World War', *International Review of Social History*, XXVI, 1981, Part 2.

Thompson, D., 'Towards an Unstreamed Comprehensive School', *Forum*, Vol.7, No.3, 1965.

Vernon, P.E., 'Memorandum', *Higher Education*, (the Robbins Report), *Evidence*, Part Two.

Wallace, R.G., 'The man Behind Butler', *Times Educational Supplement*, 27 March 1981.

Wallace, R.G., 'The Origins and Authorship of the 1944 Education Act', *History of Education*, Vol.10, No.4, 1981.

Wann, Peter, 'The Collapse of Parliamentary Bipartisanship in Education, 1945–53', *Journal of Educational Administration and History*, Vol.III, No.2, 1971.

Waterhouse, Rosie, 'Mounting Cost of Baker's Beacons', *The Independent*, 29 June 1989.

Weaver, Toby, 'Policy Options for Post-tertiary Education', *Higher Education Review*, Vol.14, No.2, 1982.

Weddel, Klaus, 'Special Educational Needs and the Education Reform Act', *Forum*, Vol.31, No.1, 1988.

Weston, Penelope, 'If Success had Many Faces', *Forum*, Vol.28, No.3, 1986.

White, John P., 'Tyndale and the Left', *Forum*, Vol.19, No.2, 1977.

Whitty, Geoff, 'The New Right and the National Curriculum: State Control or Market Forces?', *Journal of Education Policy*, 1989, Vol.4, No.4.

Wiseman, Stephen, 'Higher Degrees in Education in British Universities', *British Journal of Educational Studies*, Vol.II, No.1, 1953.

Woods, Roger, 'Margaret Thatcher and Secondary Reorganisation, 1970–74', *Journal of Educational Administration and History*, Vol.XIII, No.2.

3 Official Publications

Reports of official committees, etc. (selected)

1868 Report of the Royal Commission known as the Schools Inquiry Commission (the Taunton Report), Vol.1.

1938 *Secondary Education with Special Reference to Grammar Schools and Technical High Schools*, Report of the Consultative Committee of the Board of Education (the Spens report).

1941 *Education After the War* (the 'Green Book'), reprinted in Middleton and Weitzman, op.cit.

1943 *Curriculum and Examinations in Secondary Schools* (the Norwood report).

1943 *Abolition of Tuition Fees in Grant-Aided Secondary Schools* (Fleming Committee, interim report).

1944 *The Public Schools and the General Educational System*, Report of the Committee on Public Schools (the Fleming report).

1944 *Teachers and Youth Leaders*, (the McNair report).

1945 *Higher Technological Education*, (the Percy report).

1946 *Scientific Manpower* (the Barlow report). Cmd 6824.

1948 *Secondary Education*, Report of the Central Advisory Council for Education (Scotland).

1949 *The Future of Secondary Education in Wales*, Report of the Central Advisory Council for Education (Wales).

1954 *Early Leaving*, Report of the Central Advisory Council for Education (England).

1959 *15 to 18*, Report of the Central Advisory Council for Education (England) (the Crowther report).

1960 *Secondary School Examinations other than GCE* (the Beloe report).

1960 *Grants to Students* (the Anderson report).

1963 *Half our Future*, Report of the Central Advisory Council for Education (England) (the Newsom report).

1963 *Higher Education*, Report of the Committee on Higher Education (the Robbins report). Cmnd 2165.

1964 *Report of the Working Party on the Schools Curricula and Examinations* (the Lockwood report).

1966 *Report of the Study Group on the Government of Colleges* (the Weaver report).

1967 *Children and Their Primary Schools*, Report of the Central Advisory Council for Education (England), (the Plowden report).

1968 *Primary Education in Wales*, Report of the Central Advisory Council for Education (Wales), (the Gittins report).

1968 *Enquiry into the Flow of Candidates in Science and Technology into Higher Education*, Report of the Council for Scientific Policy (the Dainton report), Cmnd 3541.

1968 *The Flow into Employment of Scientists, Engineers and Technologists*, report of the Working Group on Manpower for Scientific Growth (the Swann report), Cmnd 3760.

1968 Public School Commission, *First Report*, (the Newsom report).

1970 Public School Commission, *Second Report, Report on independent day schools and direct grant grammar schools* (the Donnison report).

1972 *Teacher Education and Training*, report of the Committee on Teacher Training (the James report).

1977 *A New Partnership for our Schools*, (the Taylor report), Cmnd 7841.

1978 *Examination at 18-plus: the N and F Studies* (Schools Council. Working Paper No.60).

1978 *Report of the Committee of Enquiry into the Education of Handicapped Children and Young People* (the Warnock report).

1978 *School Examinations*, (the Waddell report), Cmnd 7281.

1978 *Secondary School Examinations: a Single System at 16 Plus*, Cmnd 7368.

1979 *Proposals for a Certificate of Extended Education* (the Keohane report), Cmnd 7755.

1981 *Education for 16–19 year olds*. A review undertaken for the Government and the Local Authority Associations (the Macfarlane report).

1981 *A New Training Initiative*, Cmnd 8458.

1983 *Teaching Quality*, Cmnd 8836.

1984 *Parental Influence at School: a New Framework for School Government in England and Wales*, Green Paper, Cmnd 9242.

1985 *Education for All*. The report of the Committee of Enquiry into the Education of Children from Ethnic Minority Groups (the Swann report) Cmnd 9453.

1985 *Better Schools*, Cmnd 9469.

4 University Theses

Kopsch, Hartmut, 'The Approach of the Conservative Party to Social Policy during World War Two', unpublished PhD thesis, University of London, 1970.

Marsh, Leonard, 'Case Study of the Process of Change in Primary Education, Oxfordshire and the West Riding, 1944–72', unpublished PhD thesis, University of York, 1987.

Morris, Robert, 'Education Policy and Legislation: a Critical

Examination of the Arguments for a New Major Education Act to Replace that of 1944', unpublished PhD thesis, University of Leeds, 1988.

Richardson, M.D., 'The Politics of Educational Reform: a study of the London Labour Party and the reform of secondary schooling, 1918–1950', unpublished PhD thesis, University of London, 1989.

Thompson, D., 'Organisation in the Comprehensive School: an investigation into the effects on certain educational results of the transition from streamed to unstreamed forms of organisation in a large comprehensive school', unpublished PhD thesis, University of Leicester, 1973.

Wallace, R.G., 'Labour, the Board of Education and the Preparation of the 1944 Act', unpublished PhD thesis, University of London, 1980.

5 Journals

Comprehensive Education (Bulletin of the CSC), 1965–89.
Education, 1939–89.
Forum for the discussion of new trends in education, 1958–1989.
Journal of Education, 1939–44.
Oxford Review of Education, 1987.
Political Quarterly, 1951–52.
Spectator, 1939–41.
Times Educational Supplement, 1939–89.
Times Higher Educational Supplement, 1971–89.
The Teacher (formerly *The Schoolmaster*), 1939–89.

6 Conference Reports

Conservative Party Conference Reports, 1950–1988.
Labour Party Conference Reports, 1941–1988.
Trades Union Congress Reports, 1941–1988.

7 Manuscript Sources

British Museum: Chuter Ede Diaries (12 Vols.), British Museum Additional MSS 59690–59702
Public Record Office: Specific references to (i) Cabinet papers and minutes, (ii) Ministry and Department of Education (and Science) archives are provided in the notes.

Name Index

Subject Index

Subject Index